Handbook of Local Government Fiscal Health

Edited by

Helisse Levine, PhD
Long Island University

Jonathan B. Justice, PhD
University of Delaware

Eric A. Scorsone, PhD
Michigan State University

World Headquarters
Jones & Bartlett Learning
5 Wall Street
Burlington, MA 01803
978-443-5000
info@jblearning.com
www.jblearning.com

Jones & Bartlett Learning books and products are available through most bookstores and online booksellers. To contact Jones & Bartlett Learning directly, call 800-832-0034, fax 978-443-8000, or visit our website, www.jblearning.com.

Substantial discounts on bulk quantities of Jones & Bartlett Learning publications are available to corporations, professional associations, and other qualified organizations. For details and specific discount information, contact the special sales department at Jones & Bartlett Learning via the above contact information or send an email to specialsales@jblearning.com.

Production Credits
Publisher: Michael Brown
Managing Editor: Maro Gartside
Editorial Assistant: Chloe Falivene
Editorial Assistant: Kayla Dos Santos
Associate Production Editor: Rebekah Linga
Senior Marketing Manager: Sophie Fleck Teague
Manufacturing and Inventory Control Supervisor: Amy Bacus
Composition: Cenveo Publisher Services
Cover Design: Scott Moden
Cover Image: © Unscrew/ShutterStock, Inc.
Printing and Binding: Edwards Brothers Malloy
Cover Printing: Edwards Brothers Malloy

Library of Congress Cataloging-in-Publication Data
Levine, Helisse.

Handbook of local government fiscal health / Helisse Levine, Jonathan B. Justice, and Eric Scorsone.—1st ed.

p. cm.

Includes bibliographical references and index.

ISBN 978-0-7637-9230-5 (pbk.)—ISBN 0-7637-9230-6 (pbk.) 1. Local finance—United States. 2. Local government—United States. I. Justice, Jonathan B. II. Scorsone, Eric A. (Eric Anthony) III. Title.

HJ9145.L485 2012

336'.01473—dc23

2011044781

6048

Printed in the United States of America
16 15 14 13 12 10 9 8 7 6 5 4 3 2 1

Contents

Foreword

The time is right for this book. We have been experiencing a deep recession, the national government's programs to help the local governments through the recession have been terminated, teachers throughout the country are receiving pink slips, public pension benefits are being cut back, and some cities and counties have declared bankruptcy or come very close to it. Vallejo, California, declared bankruptcy in May 2008, a victim of the burst housing bubble in California. In November 2011, Jefferson County, Alabama, entered bankruptcy, caused by a combination of a sewer bond gone wrong, corruption, overspending, a devastating tornado, and a drop in revenues. By the end of 2011, public safety retirees had agreed to accept pension cuts in negotiations with bankrupt Central Falls, Rhode Island. Detroit, Michigan and Harrisburg, Pennsylvania were engaged in contentious wrangles over possibilities for retrenchment, state takeovers, or Chapter 9 filings. Michigan had appointed emergency managers to run the cities of Benton Harbor, Flint, and Ecorse, as well as the Detroit School District. Of course, not all cities are quite this seriously in trouble, and few observers lend credence to predictions of a massive wave of municipal bond defaults, but the loss of property tax revenues from the housing market collapse combined with state reductions in aid because of their own problems, and the failure of many pension funds because of stock market drops has affected many if not most U.S. cities, counties, and school districts. This book will not solve all these problems, but it should make many of them seem more manageable.

This book is impressive, first, because of its scope. I think it is fair to say that local government fiscal health has never before been addressed simultaneously from so many different vantage points. The topic coverage is nothing short of stunning, from tax and expenditure limitations to the intergovernmental revenue system, from postemployment benefits to slack and rainy-day funds, from definitions and problem identification to causes, solutions, and impacts over the short and long haul. Second, this book is impressive for its depth, covering in detail the literature on each topic, offering case studies, recent cross-sectional data, and original analysis, and for putting issues into historical context. The essays, each written by known scholars in their fields, fit together, overlapping and providing context and support for each other. In my experience such thoughtful combinations of essays are rare. Third, this book is impressive because it moves beyond the literature: it links a thoughtful sifting of the literature with current research to formulate practical advice for public officials struggling with fiscal stress.

The aim of the book is not, however, to formulate a set of rules that can be used without much thought. The unstated premise of the book is that public managers don't need a how-to manual, but rather a deeper understanding of what is going on. They need to be able to identify problems down the road, not just current budgetary imbalances, and they need to be able to link the problems they see with a specific set of solutions.

Revenue mixes are changing, with what effect? To what extent are local fiscal problems brought about by overly elastic revenue bases that grow with good economic times but fall too quickly, too far when the economy falters? What should you do if your revenue mix is likely to generate too much volatility? What do you need to project, in the way of revenues, or expenditures, or the effects of tax increases, or declines in the selling prices of housing? How do you make such projections and how much trust should you put in short-term versus long-term models? How good a basis are such projections for policymaking? Many financial advice givers, including bond-rating agencies, have insisted that contingency funds of various sorts should be squirreled away during the boom years to smooth revenue declines during periods of recession if revenues are overly elastic—but does this work? Does it matter what form the savings take or how they are actually used? What about tax and expenditure limitations (TELs): are they a major contributor to fiscal stress, or would revenue increases have been off the table for political reasons regardless of the so-called TELs? No matter what the question, these authors take the reader a little deeper into the subject. Even those readers who know a lot about finance, and have a good grasp of how local officials deal with fiscal stress, will find something new in these chapters, something that will deepen their understanding or change the way they think about a given problem.

Academics and their students as well as practitioners will find this book satisfying, though they may focus on different aspects of the presentations. The manner in which fiscal stress is portrayed results in a good understanding of local public finance more generally, the constraints on revenue and spending, the intergovernmental system, the tax mix, and revenue projections. The authors are thoughtful in their reviews of the literature, generally showing the weaknesses as well as the conclusions, pointing out where better reporting, more consistent time series data, or more sophisticated analysis is needed. They also point to avenues for future research, the logically important topics that have not yet been discussed in the academic literature. Equally important, the book represents a kind of model of how intellectual discussion should proceed, from thoughtful analysis of what is to be measured, to how various measures work and their shortcomings, to a careful look at the problems from nearly all possible angles. The authors home in on specifics and back off to show the forest as well as the trees.

The chapters are generally well written and free of most academic jargon, and where technical terms are used, they are defined and explained. It is easy and rewarding to dip into individual chapters without necessarily committing oneself to reading the whole book. This book is welcome, not only for its timeliness and practical usefulness but also for revivifying a literature that had begun to stultify. It is difficult to know what one can say that is new or useful about municipal fiscal stress, but this book points the way.

Irene Rubin, Professor Emerita
Northern Illinois University

Contributors

William G. Albrecht, PhD
Associate Professor
Department of Public Administration
University of North Carolina at Pembroke

Deborah A. Carroll, PhD
Associate Professor
Department of Public Administration and Policy
University of Georgia

Steven C. Deller, PhD
Professor
Agricultural and Applied Economics
University of Wisconsin-Madison

Jacob Fowles, PhD
Assistant Professor
School of Public Affairs and Administration
University of Kansas

Christopher B. Goodman, MPA
Doctoral Candidate
Department of Public Administration and Policy
University of Georgia

Cleopatra Grizzle, PhD
Assistant Professor
School of Public Affairs and Administration
Rutgers University-Newark

Rebecca Hendrick, PhD
Associate Professor
Department of Public Administration
University of Illinois at Chicago

Beth Walter Honadle, PhD
Professor of Planning
College of Design, Architecture, Art, and Planning
University of Cincinnati

Benoy Jacob, PhD
Assistant Professor
School of Public Affairs
University of Colorado-Denver

Robert S. Kravchuk, PhD
Professor
Department of Political Science and Public Administration
University of North Carolina at Charlotte

Kenneth A. Kriz, PhD
Associate Professor
School of Public Administration
University of Nebraska-Omaha

Josephine M. LaPlante, PhD
Associate Professor
Muskie School of Public Service
University of Southern Maine

Gao Liu, PhD
Assistant Professor
School of Public Administration
University of New Mexico

Craig S. Maher, PhD
Associate Professor
Department of Public Administration
University of Wisconsin-Oshkosh

Justin Marlowe, PhD
Assistant Professor
Daniel J. Evans School of Public Affairs
University of Washington

Dean Michael Mead
Research Manager
Governmental Accounting Standards Board
Lecturer
Rutgers Business School
Rutgers University

Jun Peng, PhD
Associate Professor
School of Government and Public Policy
University of Arizona

Christina Plerhoples, MA
Doctoral Candidate
Department of Agricultural, Food, and Resource Economics
Michigan State University

Gary R. Rassel, PhD
Associate Professor
Department of Political Science and Public Administration
University of North Carolina at Charlotte

Donijo Robbins, PhD
Professor
School of Public, Nonprofit, and Health Administration
Grand Valley State University

Qiushi Wang, PhD
Assistant Professor
School of Public Affairs and Administration
Rutgers University-Newark

Lynne A. Weikart, PhD
Practitioner-in-Residence
Political Science Department
James Madison University

Juita-Elena (Wie) Yusuf, PhD
Assistant Professor
Department of Urban Studies and Public Administration
Old Dominion University

Chapter 1

Introduction

by Eric A. Scorsone, Helisse Levine, and Jonathan B. Justice

Since the Great Recession of 2008–2009, the fiscal health of local governments in the United States has become a frequent topic of discussion. This interest demonstrates the adage "all that was old is new again" as concerns over local governments' fiscal health rise to the fore on a regular, cyclical basis. The 19th century and the first half of the 20th century saw recurrent local-government fiscal and debt crises in the United States associated with recessions, financial panics, and occasional governmental fecklessness. After the post-World War II decades of steady, incremental growth in government budgets, older local governments in particular returned to ground in the face of recessions, tax revolts, and suburbanization in the mid- to late-1970s. Although the economic bubbles of the late 1990s and mid 2000s offered temporary respite, the current fiscal climate is very challenging, and it seems unlikely that local governments will experience sustained relief from fiscal constraints in the foreseeable future. Undoubtedly, the fiscal health of local governments, both in periods of strength and periods of economic weakness, will remain a concern of policymakers at all levels of government.

Local governments themselves face the challenges of managing citizens' undiminished service expectations, the cost of postemployment benefits for past as well as present employees, and the withdrawal of recurring federal and state assistance associated with what Chris Hoene and Michael Pagano have termed, "fend-for-yourself federalism" (Hoene and Pagano, 2003). As they exhaust the less politically fraught, short-term responses to recession and fiscal shocks, local governments increasingly are confronting the financial and political challenges of reconciling constituents' desires for services with their willingness to pay taxes (and fees for service).

For state policymakers, the fiscal health of local government is important given the fiduciary responsibilities and partnership between the two levels of government. Local governments carry out many functions on behalf of state government, such as sewer and water services, police and fire protection, parks and recreation, land use planning and zoning, tax collection, and many others. These vital public services may be threatened if a local government is not fiscally sustainable. Thus, over decades, state policymakers have enacted laws to monitor, track, and address fiscal problems among local governments.

For federal policymakers, although one step removed from local government, the fiscal stability of these entities matters as well. Billions of dollars of spending flow through local governments to provide services such as community development block grants, homeland security, and many other programs. As one example, the New York City Police department plays a vital role in protecting dignitaries during large United Nations meetings. Thus, the fiscal health of New York City may matter greatly to the federal government. Again, local officials often are the ones carrying out functions the federal government deems necessary.

The fiscal bottom line ultimately comes back to local elected officials. In 2007, according to the Census of Governments, there were 89,476 local governments in the United States. This figure includes 3,033 counties, 19,492 cities, 16,519 towns, 37,381 special districts, and 13,051 school districts. Among these government entities, there were more than 500,000 elected officials. These responsible parties must bear the burden of ensuring that their local government entity remains fiscally solvent and healthy to carry out important public functions.

A variety of factors affect the fiscal health of local governments. Revenues, or the incoming sources of funds that include taxes and fees, are the backbone upon which government spending and service provision rests. Revenue forecasting must be done with care and attention to ensure that appropriate budget plans can be made. Further, the structure and adequacy of local revenue systems determine the ability of government to keep up with spending pressures and avoid the buildup of fiscal stress.

A second factor is the spending side of the equation. Local governments face many stakeholders in building their spending plans. Local citizens may demand certain services, the federal government may have many strings attached to funding sources, and state governments may mandate a variety of functions. Furthermore, local governments must purchase labor and materials in national and even global marketplaces, where cost pressures and inflation are out of their hands. Fiscal health is ultimately driven by how governments manage revenue and spending decisions in an economic and social environment that is largely out of their control. Thus, fiscal health is an adaptive process of strategic decision making requiring knowledge of a variety of functions, services, and tools. The chapters in this handbook have been written with this framework in mind.

This handbook provides an accessible compilation of the traditional literature and the most current thinking about the range of topics concerned with understanding and maintaining local governments' fiscal health and serves as a useful desk reference for students, practitioners, and academics. Each chapter is written both to complement the other contributions in the volume and to stand alone as a conceptual and practical guide to its topic. Toward that end, our contributors have provided glossaries of key terms, questions for review and discussion, and recommendations of resources for further reading and applications of the material. Although the volume's focus is on the U.S. setting, and the details of some aspects of accounting standards and intergovernmental relations in particular are quite specific to the United States, most if not all of the chapters address broadly applicable questions of local public finance and financial management and will have applications beyond the United States.

The organization of the book centers around seven parts. Following the editors' Introduction, the chapters in Fiscal Health and Sustainability Concepts and Measures,

(Part I) define and assess the overall context of the fiscal health/stress literature from a conceptual perspective. In Assessing the Financial Condition of Local Governments: What Is Financial Condition and How Is It Measured? (Chapter 2), Benoy Jacob and Rebecca Hendrick explore a broad conceptual framework for understanding local government fiscal health. They first review some of the challenges in defining the scale and scope of the term *fiscal health*. This review leads the authors to conclude that each conceptual strategy has strengths and weaknesses. The specific purpose of the term "fiscal health" may determine the type of system that should be used. In a review of Measuring and Predicting Local Government Fiscal Stress: Theory and Practice (Chapter 3), Jonathan Justice and Eric Scorsone suggest some strategies for measuring and predicting fiscal health and stress. Building on Jacob and Hendrick's chapter, they begin with the premise that fiscal health is to some extent in the eyes of the beholder, that it is shaped by a complex web of interdependent factors over time so that measurement is difficult and prediction even more so, and that different stakeholders may have different definitions of fiscal health as well as different analytic resources and access to information. They go on to offer a framework of considerations for stakeholders to use in designing measurement and prediction systems appropriate to their own specific needs, together with bibliographic references to a range of examples of indicators and measurement systems developed for a range of uses and users.

There has been a long history of attempts since the 1970s to assess and predict fiscal stress among local entities. Contributors to Financial Reporting and Modeling (Part II) focus on the measurement of fiscal stress in local governments. The chapters in this section review past attempts to measure stress as well as propose new measurement strategies. In The Development of External Financial Reporting and Its Relationship to the Assessment of Fiscal Health and Stress (Chapter 4), Dean Mead discusses the specific notion of financial condition and how it has evolved over time. From representative tax systems, accounting standards, and municipal credit analysis to the most recent updates to generally accepted accounting principles (GAAP) for U.S. state and local governments, this chapter identifies key milestones and how they have affected and been affected by attempts to understand and predict fiscal health and stress. Finally, the state of fiscal health analysis is discussed in light of the most recent government accounting standards. Kenneth Kriz explores the venue of revenue forecasting in, Long-Term Forecasting (Chapter 5). Part of the fiscal health story is ensuring that adequate revenues are available as a spending plan moves forward. As the complexity and speed at which the economy changes increase, local officials face ever increasing demands to improve their assessment of future revenue streams. Inaccurate revenue forecasts can seriously hamper fiscal health. Dr. Kriz provides an extensive overview of forecasting approaches including qualitative and quantitative strategies. These are critical tools in the fiscal health of local governments.

The book turns to issues surrounding pensions and other postemployment benefits (OPEB) that represent a crucial and newly salient arena of fiscal health and stress (Part III). Many state and federal laws constrain and shape the type of obligations in which local governments engage. Previous fiscal stress measurement systems have not always accounted for these obligations. Chapters in this section assess the potential influence of pension and OPEB obligations on fiscal stress and their implications for fiscal stress measurement systems. In Postemployment Benefits and Fiscal Analysis (Chapter 6), Dean Mead provides an excellent overview of the postemployment benefits offered through local governments. The first section describes these postemployment benefits, and the next section describes how the short- and long-term costs of benefits are calculated and reported. Recent years have seen dramatic improvements in the calculation and disclosure of liabilities for postemployment benefits by U.S. state and local governments that follow GAAP. Mead offers suggestions on the role of postemployment benefits in measuring and maintaining overall local government fiscal health. Sustainable Approaches to Retiree Benefits: Options and Implementation for Program Design and Financing (Chapter 7), written by Jun Peng, describes the types of approaches needed to address the costs associated with these postemployment benefits. It describes different approaches in how these benefits are offered and the potential costs and benefits of such approaches. This discussion includes the differentiation between defined contribution and defined benefit plans. Finally, reference is made to how postemployment benefit changes influence local government fiscal health.

Revenue Elasticity and Adequacy (Part IV) focuses on revenue systems as a crucial part of the fiscal health equation. Given the wide degree of variance in property tax limitations and the variety of local option taxes, these considerations should be part of any fiscal stress measurement and management approach. During an analysis of Public-Finance and Fiscal-Federalism Perspectives on Local Government Revenue Bases and Fiscal Sustainability (Chapter 8), Donijo Robbins provides a broad overview of the role of government in our society and communities. Local governments have long played an important role in shaping and reshaping communities and providing basic services that citizens experience on a daily basis. This discussion provides some perspective on how we understand the role of government and what questions should be asked regarding the appropriate role of government in the 21st century. These questions are particularly relevant as the United States faces the long-term fiscal dilemma of an aging population and large scale government debt. In Understanding and Measuring Elasticity, Volatility, and Implications for Local Government Fiscal Health (Chapter 9), Deborah Carroll and Christopher Goodman look at the stability and change of various tax revenues that local governments rely on. Given that revenue stability is a critical element in determining when a local fiscal crisis may occur, these are important issues. A review of the existing empirical literature of revenue elasticities is provided and how to calculate revenue responsiveness or elasticity is illustrated. These are important points of analysis in assessing potential and actual local fiscal health.

Alternative strategies used to address business cycles, especially as governments enter into periods of fiscal stress, are explored in Business Cycles, Bubbles, and Reserve Funds: Cutback Management for the 21st Century (Part V). The four chapters in this section discuss the use of alternatives such as the use of reserve funds and the overall management of funds across time. In Fiscal Stress and Cutback Management Among State and Local

Governments: What Have We Learned and What Remains to Be Learned? (Chapter 10), Christina Plerhoples and Eric Scorsone offer an assessment of the use of cutback management strategies in state and local government since the 1970s. This discussion contributes to our understanding, via the many empirical analyses done since 1970, about which approaches governments are likely to use, including budget cutting and revenue raising, in times of fiscal stress. This information can assist policymakers and practitioners in assessing past performance of various strategies and build awareness of alternative approaches. While this literature has grown over the past 30 years, many avenues of research remain open to researchers, particularly in the area of the long-term implications of cutback management strategies. The next topic, A Framework for Deciphering and Managing the Fiscal Environment by Josephine LaPlante, offers a new and striking visual approach to understanding local finances. First, Dr. LaPlante reviews some of the previous contributions to understanding local fiscal health. The visual figure she provides in Chapter 11 gives us a glimpse of the complex web within which fiscal health is structured. On one hand, we must understand the revenue dynamics that allow local governments to raise funds. The other side of the equation is spending needs and mandates, some of which can be controlled and some of which cannot. She also highlights that capital investment both drives and is a consumer of funds. Another key element is the service environment within which a government must operate. Some environments may be harsher (e.g., older housing and higher poverty levels) and require a greater level of spending than others that lack these issues. The final section, using this visual framework, allows us to understand how careful comparative analysis of fiscal health should proceed.

During a review of Fiscal Slack, Reserves, and Rainy Day Funds (Chapter 12), Justin Marlowe makes it clear that beyond basic rules of thumb such as the "five percent rule," there is at present little real knowledge of how slack financial resources do or should affect fiscal health. His review of the literature suggests that no consistent approach exists even for determining what level of slack or reserves exists for any local government, which may account for the dearth of clear empirical conclusions to date. However, it is clear that accounting standards are moving toward improving and standardizing the measurement of slack, and this in turn may lead to more conclusive research. The section concludes with the topic of Managing Investments and Investment Risks (Chapter 13), by William Albrecht. Dr. Albrecht helps us understand investments and their relationship to local government fiscal health. The analysis focuses on the nature of investment risk from the perspective of local government management and shows that adequate cash flow and liquidity must be ensured while still gaining some return on investment from idle cash. Foregoing any return on investment may also be problematic as it helps in some small manner to balance overall government spending needs. Specific risk management tools are explored.

Whether a fiscal early warning system is deployed or not, there are cases where states have been forced to takeover or intervene in local units of government. Four chapters on Intergovernmental Considerations (Part VI) examine the roles of state governments in regulating, constraining, overseeing, and intervening in local governments' fiscal affairs; assess the effectiveness of these strategies and policies; and offer recommendations for future interventions. In Local Government Fiscal Health: An Intergovernmental Perspective (Chapter 14), Beth Walter Honadle addresses the issue of understanding local governments within the overall framework of the federal system. Dr. Honadle describes the various intergovernmental relationships between both state and local government and federal and local government. This intergovernmental framework provides an important perspective on the implications of intergovernmental structures for fiscal health. The clear implication is that fiscal health is strongly tied to intergovernmental arrangements. In Monitoring the Fiscal Health of America's Cities (Chapter 15), Lynne Weikart focuses on a different aspect of intergovernmental arrangements. Dr. Weikart discusses the federal and state role in monitoring and if necessary intervening in local fiscal affairs. There is a specific section that discusses various state approaches to monitoring fiscal health. Finally, the roles of not-for-profit organizations and bond rating agencies in monitoring local governments' fiscal health are examined.

In Measuring the Impacts of TELs on Municipal Financial Conditions (Chapter 16), Craig Maher and Steven Deller present information regarding the role of tax and expenditure limitations on the fiscal health of government. Increasingly, questions have been asked about the dozens of tax and expenditure limitations (TELs) imposed on local governments in the wake of Proposition 13 in California in 1978. For some observers, these limitations have restrained government appropriately while for others they have led to chronic fiscal stress and the inability to finance basic public services. Maher and Deller's findings tentatively support the notion that TEL's may actually force governments to better manage resources rather than create chronic fiscal stress. Using a sample of more than 1,000 municipalities in 47 states, they find that the severity of state-imposed TELs is associated with statistically significant but small differences not always in the hypothesized directions. Given the relative weakness of the statistical findings however, the more important lessons from this chapter may be that further research is needed and that past findings exhibited considerable analytical problems in attempting to model causal relationships of environmental and organizational characteristics with fiscal health. Next, in The Defragmentation of Authority: A Consolidation Approach to Public Service Delivery (Chapter 17), Helisse Levine suggests that despite the "one shot" infusion of Recovery Act funding for education programs, currently, the sustained, statewide economic decline is directly linked to financial challenges being felt by local school districts across the state. Dr. Levine presents a simulation model to ascertain whether the consolidation of Nassau County's 56 school districts will reduce administrative costs. Although cost savings, as a result of economies of scale, may result from consolidation across smaller sized districts, local control in the form of school board composition must be weighed against the economic differences in citizen demand for and value placed on those "public" goods.

We conclude with Debt Capacity, Management, and Policy (Part VII), which addresses debt obligations given their key role leading to the potential insolvency of a local government. This section covers current debt obligations, state policies to address local government debt commitments, and the influence of debt on fiscal health in general.

Kenneth Kriz and Qiushi Wang present Measuring and Monitoring Debt Capacity and Affordability: Market- and Nonmarket-based Models in Chapter 18, which draws our attention to the variety of approaches that have been used to assess the potential burden of debt on overall local government fiscal health. They discuss some of the traditional models for assessing debt capacity, including the bond rating agencies' approaches. The quality and effectiveness of these traditional debt scoring models is assessed and a very concise yet broad overview of debt modeling approaches is provided. In their review of State Fiscal Constraints on Local Government Borrowing: Effects on Scale and Cost (Chapter 19), Juita-Elena (Wie) Yusuf, Jacob Fowles, Cleopatra Grizzle, and Gao Liu turn their attention to the state's role in regulating municipal debt. Debt plays an important role in understanding local fiscal health. The authors take care to detail the different approaches states have used to limit municipal debt, including debt limits, TELs, and referendum requirements. Their review of the research to date finds that despite state attempts to limit debt, local governments have been able to circumvent these limits. This explains at least in part why overly burdensome debt still plays an important role in local government fiscal health. Good Debt Gone Bad: The 2008–2009 Crisis in Municipal Debt Markets (Chapter 20), by Gary Rassel and Robert Kravchuk, rounds out this section, with a specific focus on the most recent "Great Recession" and its implications for local fiscal health. They suggest that the municipal debt market remains solid following the Great Recession but will require new analytical tools with the decline of bond insurers. The suggestion is that variable rate debt will retain an important role in the market despite some recent problems. The final suggestion is that new risk assessment tools will be required.

Reference

Hoene, C. W., & Pagano, M. A. (2003, October). Fend-for-yourself federalism: The impact of federal and state deficits on America's cities. *Government Finance Review, 19,* 36–42.

Part I

Fiscal Health and Sustainability Concepts and Measures

Chapter 2

Assessing the Financial Condition of Local Governments

What Is Financial Condition and How Is It Measured?

by Benoy Jacob and Rebecca Hendrick

Introduction

Clearly assessing the financial condition of local governments is fundamental for the effective administration of the American federal system. Federal and state governments are interested in assessing local financial condition for purposes of distributing grants and aid as well as monitoring local fiscal distress. Similarly, local governments monitor many aspects of their own fiscal health as part of their financial management and fiscal policymaking activities. A host of factors affect local government finances, and no single metric is able to fully account for the various components of financial condition. Thus, scholars and practitioners employ a variety of measures, each offering partial insights into a locality's fiscal state of affairs.[1] Additionally, financial condition is sensitive to the particular features of the locality under consideration. Thus, it is not clear that a partial measure used to describe the financial condition of one city can be effectively employed in another city, particularly when the context differs (e.g., a small rural city being compared to a central city or comparing two similar cities in different states). Such partial measures, however, may not be a bad thing. Given the heterogeneity of local government, one size cannot, and should not, fit all. Nevertheless, the wide range and uses of financial condition measurements makes it difficult for the scholar and practitioner to determine how best to approach the problem of assessing financial condition. That is, it is difficult to answer the simple question of: *What is a government's financial condition and how do you assess it?*

In its simplest terms, a local government's financial condition represents its ability to meet financial and service obligations. Unfortunately, this concise definition leads to a host of additional questions. First, at what level must obligations be met? Is a local government in better financial condition if it can meet its obligations at a higher level, or is there a threshold at which its fiscal condition is considered sound? Second, over what period of time should the obligations be met? Should good financial condition be a function of meeting long-run obligations only, near-term obligations, or both?

Third, does financial condition depend on meeting all obligations or only the primary ones? And fourth, to what extent is financial condition in a current time period dependent on financial condition in a prior time period.

For instance, is a government that is in good financial condition, in that it can meet its financial and service obligations in the immediate term but is experiencing a decline in ability to meet future obligations better or worse off than a government in poor but improving condition? In other words, is financial condition a static or dynamic concept? In listing these questions, our goal is not to be comprehensive but rather to emphasize that the simple question of financial condition is unlikely to yield to a simple answer. Thus, to understand the broader issue of: "what is financial condition?" one needs a conceptual framework that addresses these issues. Such is the task undertaken in this chapter.

Rather than present the reader with one "correct" definition and method of measuring local financial condition, this chapter provides a comprehensive overview of the concept and discusses how financial condition develops over time. It also identifies different dimensions and properties of component indicators that are used in constructing composite measures of financial condition and explains how these indicators can be measured. The moral of the story is that there is no one best way to measure or assess financial condition, and no single composite measure exists that recognizes all its features.

The chapter proceeds by describing financial condition as the result of a process characterized by the strategic choices of local officials with respect to goals regarding different forms of solvency. The targets of these strategic choices are the factors that shape the local/internal fiscal structure of the locality. However, the choices themselves are shaped by the limitations, advantages, and other features of localities' fiscal environment over which local officials have less control, and are often motivated by changes to that environment. This framework helps specify the concept of financial condition more completely and helps the reader organize, apply, and interpret the many component measures of financial condition used in the profession.

The Concept of Financial Condition

The fiscal pressures that central cities faced in the late 1970s and early 1980s spawned numerous efforts across disciplines and organizations to assess local government fiscal health and financial performance and, in some cases, develop indices of these conditions. The varied uses and foci of these types of measures indicate the difficulty of defining financial condition in a way that fully recognizes its diversity. Financial condition must be conceptualized in a manner that acknowledges its multiple time frames and the complexity of government fiscal action, which suggests that financial condition is not static. Along this vein, one of the more useful specifications of financial condition is put forward by Groves, Valente, and Nollenberger (2003) who propose four different types of solvency—long-run, service level, budgetary, and cash. Defined in this manner, solvency distinguishes among different stages of fiscal condition and levels of financial and service obligations.

The solvencies also take into account different characteristics of government's internal fiscal structure and external fiscal and political environment (Groves et al., 2003). Although these solvencies are related in the sense that a government with poor solvency in one area is likely to have poor solvency in other areas and vice versa, this is not always the case. First, *long-run solvency* refers to the long-run balance between government revenues and spending needs and implies that government has the ability to adapt to uncertain future fiscal conditions, some of which may be severe shocks. Second, *service-level solvency* refers to the ability of government to provide adequate services to meet the health, safety, and welfare needs of its citizens given its revenue resources. Third, *budgetary solvency* is defined as the ability to balance the budget or generate enough resources to cover expenditures in the current fiscal year. Finally, *cash solvency* is the government's ability to generate enough cash over 30 or 60 days to pay its bills.

Although recognizing different solvencies is a key step in conceptualizing financial condition, this framework is not sufficient. By itself, it says little about which structural or environmental factors should be examined in different time periods. In our conceptualization of financial condition, "time" is a critical variable. Time, particularly with respect to financial conditions, means different things to different people. Accountants think about time in terms of cash or accrual reporting. Social scientists, more generally, think about it in terms of proximate versus remote causes. Our approach is somewhat different. We conceptualize time in terms of the way events within the same "system" (or dimension of financial condition) affect each other more directly and rapidly than events across system. Further defining solvencies and identifying relevant factors to examine in the context of these different time frames will offer more clarity.

Financial condition applied to long-run and service-level solvency is a function of both current and future fiscal obligations and resources. Because current financial and service obligations often stretch into the future (e.g., debt and pension obligations), assessments of current financial condition also must recognize current and likely future fiscal states. However, the future is unknown, making assessing long-run and service-level solvency imprecise. That is, conditions that affect a government's ability to meet its obligations, which include features of its fiscal structure (e.g., tax rate, types of revenues collected, debt levels) and environment (e.g., costs, service needs, political demands), can change dramatically over time. Thus, our assessment of financial condition in either time frame can be, at best, only a good estimate.

From examining fiscal trends, we know that current states (fiscal structure and environment) are the best predictor of future fiscal states, but current states become less useful predictors in more volatile environments. We also know that many aspects of a government's current financial condition are a direct function of past states and that change in fiscal structure and environment is often incremental (Wildavsky and Caiden, 2000). Ultimately a government's current financial condition is the result of many decisions made by public officials over time regarding its fiscal structure. These decisions also are made in the context of state *institutions* and other internal and external conditions that constrain choices, provide opportunities, and establish fiscal goals that are particular to the government.

The next section presents a model of financial condition that is process based. This model focuses on the strategic decision making of public actors who must navigate changing fiscal and political environments.

The Financial Condition Process

Figure 2.1 presents a dynamic model of financial condition that is presented by Hendrick (2011, p. 25). The model demonstrates that financial condition is a process shaped by the external fiscal environment as well as local decisions or choices. It suggests that: (1) there is a relationship between current choices and future opportunities (and vice versa), (2) there are factors that are less controllable by local decision makers (e.g., the environment), and (3) the relationship between the environment and the decision maker is mediated by risk and slack. At the core of the model are the strategic choices public officials make with respect to current needs. These choices are made either in response to changes in the environment or in the hope of changing the external environment. This in turn, has an effect on the opportunities and constraints that the agency will face in the future. Thus, when making current strategic choices, decision makers must be cognizant of future implications.

The center box of our model represents the local government and identifies various features of its internal fiscal structure that directly affect financial condition. Financial

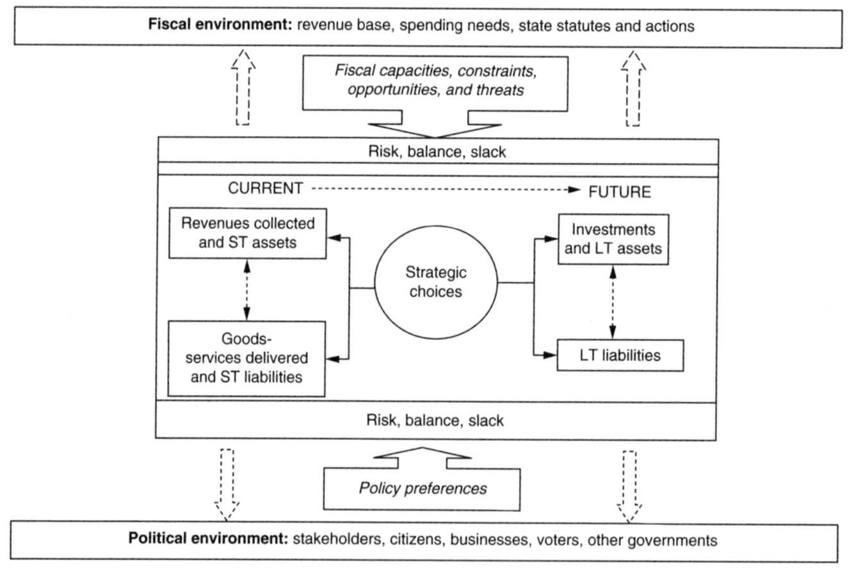

Figure 2.1 The Financial Condition Process

From *Managing the fiscal metropolis: the financial policies, practices, and health of suburban municipalities* by Rebecca Hendrick.

condition and fiscal structure are a function of two types of choices public officials make over time:

1. The types and levels of:
   a. **Current** revenues to collect (and other short-term assets), and
   b. **Current** services/goods to deliver (and other short-term liabilities).
2. The types and levels of:
   a. **Future** or long-term assets to invest in (e.g., capital infrastructure and investments in the form of cash or economic development. Their fiscal value is in the potential payoffs or increase in revenue streams that result from investments and leverage of current assets) and
   b. **Future** liabilities to incur (e.g., current spending claims made on future revenue streams including repayment of debt, pension payouts, deferred equipment maintenance, and capital improvements).

The dotted lines between current revenues and spending and future assets and liabilities signify that the two components of each pair are interdependent. Due to balanced budget requirements that legally constrain the spending habits of cities, local governments cannot spend more than they collect in revenues, although certain features of their fiscal structure, as discussed later, provide some short-term flexibility in this matter. Similarly, short-term assets, those required to fund government during the fiscal year, must be matched with short-term liabilities. Thus, choices concerning current revenues and spending are often made in conjunction with each other, and the outcomes are highly correlated. Choices regarding future assets and liabilities are also interdependent, albeit less so than current revenues and liabilities. Although fiscal choices about future liabilities often take investments and long-term assets into account, many times they do not. Additionally, the uncertainty of future states makes the correlation between long-term investment and liability choices less than the correlation between short-term revenues and expenditures.

The heavy dotted line between current and future states show that strategic choices about current states can have an effect on future states independent of the conscious decisions officials make about future states. For instance, the decision to lower sales taxes can, over time, create an imbalance of revenues to spending that was unintended, especially if spending is not reduced or other revenues increased. On the other hand, officials often make conscious choices to increase or reduce future liabilities by issuing more debt or refinancing existing debt at a more favorable interest rate.

The strategic choices, at the core of the model, are made in a context of the fiscal and political environments. Both environments affect a government's financial condition and structure via the opportunities they present and the constraints they impose, but are less "controllable" by officials than the targets of strategic choices. That is, although some environments are more constraining or demanding than others, governments have a broad range of choices they can make about current and future assets and liabilities.

The local fiscal environment includes state statutes that directly determine many features of their fiscal structure and financial management practices, such as which local taxes can be levied, the size of the fund balance, the level of pension fund contributions, the amount of state and federal aid or shared revenues received, and even types and levels of service to provide. These statutes constrain the actions of local governments and, therefore, affect their financial condition. Local governments in states that withdraw state aid because of their own fiscal problems will have to adjust spending and revenues in a similar fashion. In this case, governments with a wealthy revenue environment and many revenue opportunities will be better able to cope with fiscal shocks or to take advantage of fiscal opportunities.

The political environment, which includes voters, citizens, businesses, taxpayers, and other governments and financial stakeholders, defines the policy and fiscal preferences within which local government officials operate. For example, although voters generally dislike property taxes, they may still pressure officials to spend more on public services, which often lead public officials to defer maintenance, increase liabilities, or raise fees and other taxes to balance their budget during difficult financial periods. As indicated by the thick dotted arrows between fiscal/political environment and the center box in Figure 2.1, public officials have less control over the external environment (e.g., property values, crime rates, and economic growth) than their internal fiscal structure (e.g., property tax rate, police spending, and debt levels). Two examples will help clarify the relationship between the internal and external dimensions.

First, the government of a municipality with high crime has higher spending obligations and is likely to spend more for police services than a government of a low-crime municipality. However, the level of actual spending on police services is constrained by their revenue capabilities (i.e., fiscal capacity) and the level at which they choose to meet this obligation (i.e., policy preference). Given the same revenue potential, some governments may spend more than they need for police service, and others may spend less. Likewise, the government of a municipality with high property values requires proportionally less of that revenue base and a lower tax rate to fund the same level of services as a government of a municipality with low property values.

Second, although most features of the environment do not change rapidly, some can change dramatically in a short period and have a more immediate and direct effect on fiscal choices. For example, a municipality experiencing a natural disaster, such as a flood, will be forced to drastically increase its spending for policy and public services. This change will undoubtedly constrain future fiscal choices and fiscal structure. Similarly, an income-tax dependent municipality facing a severe recession that lays off many of its citizens must quickly adjust its spending downward or other revenues upward to compensate.

Adaptation of fiscal structure to the environment.

Over time, fiscal and political environments change, thereby altering a government's external constraints and opportunities. Such changes require that a city adjust its fiscal structure accordingly (i.e., revise or rethink their strategic choices). Thus, understanding the government's exposure to change and subsequent ability to adapt are important for evaluating its financial condition (i.e., determining whether the measure of financial condition reflects fiscal health or fiscal stress). This section discusses three features of the relationship between government fiscal structure and environment that are useful for assessing the different types of solvency. These features are *risk, slack,* and *balance.* Later sections discuss how to measure these features.

Fiscal *risk* refers to a government's exposure or vulnerability to detrimental future fiscal shocks and changes in the environment. All things being equal, a government that faces more risk is less able to adapt to environmental changes and, therefore, is in worse financial condition than a government facing less risk. For example, a government that relies heavily on sales taxes, which are highly elastic, is more vulnerable to declines in the economy than one that relies heavily on property taxes, which are more stable and less affected by the economy.[2] Thus, a significant downturn in retail sales may reduce sales taxes dramatically in the "sales tax reliant" locality, which worsens its financial condition, but will have little effect on the public officials in the "property tax reliant" locality. On the other hand, the "sales tax reliant" locality is likely to accumulate surplus revenues during good economic periods by comparison to the second in which property values and taxes increase more slowly.

The second concept—fiscal *slack*—refers to the pool of resources available to a government in excess of what is necessary to produce a minimum level of services. Fiscal slack can be surplus monetary resources, such as the fund balance or rainy day fund, or nonmonetary resources such as excess employees. Fiscal slack can also be uncollected revenue from that portion of the revenue base available to the government through higher taxation. On the expenditure side, fiscal slack can be discretionary spending such as capital maintenance and travel that can be easily reduced during difficult financial periods (Hendrick, 2004). In general, larger governments tend to have more slack in nonmonetary areas than smaller ones due to their greater number of activities and opportunities to generate surplus resources, and governments with a wealthier revenue base have more slack than governments with poorer revenue base (higher revenue reserves). However, smaller governments tend to maintain higher cash resources (*fund balances*).

Slack is also an important counterweight to risk because, all other things being equal, governments with more slack have greater flexibility and capacity to absorb environmental changes—either positive or negative—and, therefore, less overall risk. The sales tax dependent government in the previous example could significantly reduce its risk by keeping excess sales taxes collected during good fiscal periods in a surplus fund to compensate for sales tax shortages during bad fiscal downturns. Governments with slack also have greater capacity to take advantage of opportunities to improve their financial condition, such as grants or economic development proposals that are expected to reduce expenditures or increase revenues in the future.

The third concept—*balance*—reflects the extent to which a government has adapted its *current* fiscal structure to the demands, pressures, opportunities, constraints, and likely *future* changes in the environment (Clark and Ferguson, 1983). Financial condition, according to this perspective, depends on the appropriateness or fit of the fiscal structure to the environment and other features of the government's fiscal structure. This concept emphasizes that financial condition cannot be assessed independently of the context. In other words, financial condition and solvency are contingent upon other environmental and structural factors.

For example, we can examine whether revenues collected are balanced with or appropriate for the government's revenue base, whether actual spending is balanced with current and future obligations, and whether slack is balanced with risk. The fiscal structure of a government that relies heavily on property taxes but has significant retail sales and the opportunity to levy a sales tax is not balanced with its revenue environment, especially if voters are highly opposed to raising property taxes. Although the government may perceive it has lower financial risk because property taxes are more stable than sales taxes, it may be unable to raise enough property taxes to cover current or future spending needs. In this case, spending is not balanced with obligations, and the government should consider collecting more sales taxes to generate additional revenue. The government also should increase its surplus funds to mitigate the increased financial risk associated with being more dependent on sales taxes, which then brings its slack into balance with its risk.

The Components of Financial Condition

Table 2.1 presents a two-dimensional scheme for organizing the components and measures of financial condition that is also presented by Hendrick (2011, p. 32). Each of these components is an important factor that needs to be measured as part of any evaluation of financial condition. The vertical dimension reflects capacities, constraints, or net financial

TABLE 2.1 Classification of Financial Condition Measures and Areas of Measurement

Revenues, Assets, and Other Resources (capacities)		
Economic & Revenue Base (& Elasticity)	Dependence on Intergovernmental Revenues	Revenues Collected & Outstanding
State Economy	Tax Rates, Fees, & Charges	Accounts Receivable
Revenue Capacity	Budgeted Revenues (& Diversification)	Fund Balance
Residents & Businesses (Growth)	Revenue Reserves	Cash & ST Investments
Physical Assets & LT Investments	Surplus Resources	Revenues Collected & Outstanding
Recurring Intergovernmental Revenues		Accounts Receivable

(*continued*)

TABLE 2.1 Classification of Financial Condition Measures and Areas of Measurement (cont.)

Expenditures and Liabilities (constraints)		
Spending Needs & Demands, Costs	Budgeted Expenditures (& Fixity)	Accounts Payable (terms, fixity)
Residents & Businesses (Growth)	Spending Priorities	Short-Term Debt
State & Federal Mandates		
Long-Term Debt		
Unfunded Pension Liabilities		
Deferred Maintenance		
Net Financial Condition: Balance and Solvency		
Long-Term Solvency	Service Level Solvency	Cash Solvency, Budgetary Solvency
Spending Needs Relative to Revenue Wealth	Revenue Burden	Operating Position
Long-Term Liabilities / Long-Term Wealth	Spending Relative to Needs	Liquidity
	Slack Relative to Risk	Expenditures Relative to Revenues
		ST Slack Relative to ST Risk

ATTRIBUTES
Over Time/Future ◄——► Current
Less Controllable ◄——► More Controllable
External /Environment ◄——► Internal/Fiscal Structure
Stable ◄——► Volatile

From *Managing the fiscal metropolis: the financial policies, practices, and health of suburban municipalities* by Rebecca Hendrick.

condition (moving from top to bottom). Capacities include government revenue, credits, assets, and other resources. Constraints include expenditures, debits and liabilities, and net financial condition that focuses on balance measures that correspond to the different types of solvency. The horizontal dimension (moving from right to left), classifies the components according to the attributes or properties at the bottom of the table.

Although the measures are presented in three groups, the attributes range along a continuum. Measures on the left-hand side of the table represent aspects of financial condition that are less controllable, more stable, more long term or future focused, and they tend to be part of the government's environment. Measures on the right-hand side of the table represent aspects that are more controllable, more volatile, more short term or focused on current events, and they are part of the government entity itself. We must also note that the fiscal features listed in each cell of the table are not exhaustive and represent, in most cases, general types of indicators or areas of measurement rather than specific measures. The next three subsections of this chapter describe some of the measures or areas of measurement within each row category in more detail.

Revenues, Assets, and Other Resources

From an accounting perspective, an *asset* is anything the government owns that can produce an economic benefit. From a more general economic perspective, an asset is simply any form of wealth. Thus, it encompasses external resources that the government has access to or which give it the capacity to meet obligations and improve financial condition. Assets can be short-term investments and cash balances that are used to manage cash flow during the fiscal year, slack resources that help manage budgetary risk, long-term physical assets such as buildings, and excess revenue capacity. Because revenues are a government's most important asset, we review these first.

Local governments have two basic types of revenue—intergovernmental and own-source. *Intergovernmental revenues* are funds received from the state or federal governments for specific functions (grants) or for general financial assistance (aid). *Own-source revenues* are generated from resources within the local government's jurisdiction, although other governments can collect them and distribute them to the owner government at regular intervals. Local own-source revenues include property taxes, user fees, and other charges and, in some states, may include other taxes such as sales and income. Local governments meet most of their service and financial obligations with own-source revenue, but much of their revenue is intergovernmental in the form of general assistance from state government based on a share of state taxes.

To understand the role of own-source revenues in financial condition, it is useful to consider its different features relevant to long-term and service-level solvency. Berne and Schramm's Revenue-Economy Relationships Model (1986, p. 99) is very useful in this regard.

According to **Figure 2.2**, the local *economic base* is the total amount of economic resources within a jurisdiction, regardless of whether a government has access to them. It is a function of the fiscal environment's *economic performance* and *economic structure*. Economic performance represents the jurisdiction's level of economic activity and is measured by one or more indicators such as percentage unemployment, resident income, and poverty level. *Economic structure* is the composition of economic activity in the jurisdiction such as land use (residential, commercial, industrial), type of jobs and commerce, transportation facilities, and the regional or state economy.

The *revenue base* refers to that portion of the economic base that the jurisdiction has access to through specific revenue-raising mechanisms according to state statute and

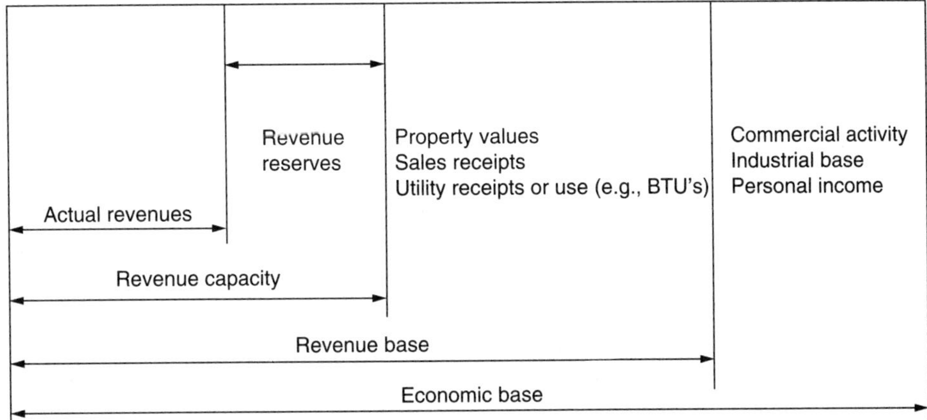

Figure 2.2 Revenue Economy Relationships

Modified from Berne, R., and Schramm, R. (1986). Pp. 99, Figure 4-1. *The financial analysis of governments*. New Jersey: Prentice-Hall.

other legal and institutional constraints. For example, if a local government has access to sales taxes, then sales receipts are one part of its revenue base. The more sales receipts generated by businesses within its jurisdiction, the wealthier its sales tax base. For governments that cannot levy a sales tax, sales receipts are simply part of its economic base. Most local governments have access to property values (property tax), and some have access to sales receipts, resident and nonresident income (payroll tax), and other sectors of the economy (e.g., utility usage and development). Income per capita is also considered to be a good measure of total revenue base wealth in governments with few revenues generated from businesses or nonresidents (Berne and Schramm, 1986). The value of the revenue base also is greatly affected by population growth and economic development, which, over time, may increase property values and the revenue generated from fees (e.g., building permits).

Revenue capacity reflects that portion of the revenue base the government can actually tax, which also is established in most cases by state statute. For instance, all state governments grant local governments access to property values, but many state governments limit the maximum property tax rates local governments can levy, which establishes local governments' revenue capacity on the property tax revenue base. A local government's revenue-raising capacity is thus the maximum level of revenue it could raise from the taxes and fees that comprise this portion of the revenue base.

Actual revenue is the amount of revenues the government chooses to collect via its tax rates, fee rates, and charges. *Revenue reserves* are excess or slack revenue capacity that the government has access to but has not used (reserves = capacity - actual). If a locality tapped its revenue base to the full potential, actual revenues would equal revenue capacity and revenue reserves would equal zero. Both actual revenues and revenue reserves are not really features of government environment because, to a great degree, elected officials who determine tax rates, fees, and specific charges for services control them. As discussed previously, governments with more revenue reserves have greater capacity to meet their fiscal and service obligations during fiscal shocks and downward fiscal trends. They also have more capacity for investments that take advantage of economic development opportunities to improve service-level solvency in the long run.

Because a significant portion of most local governments' total revenue is from state government, it is an important factor in their financial condition. State revenue in the form of grants tends to be one-time or nonrecurring revenues that have specific obligations attached to them, and recurring state aid is usually distributed by formula (e.g., based on population or need) and has few obligations. Thus, the state economy, which determines the pool of state revenue available to distribute to local government, is an important factor in local financial condition.

The problem with this arrangement for local governments is that they do not control how much state revenue is distributed to them, and history tells us that intergovernmental state and federal funds are not guaranteed. They can, and have been, withdrawn almost at will. However, to some extent, local governments do control the degree to which they rely on state-shared revenue (grants and recurring aid) to meet service and financial obligations. Local governments that rely more on intergovernmental revenue have a more uncertain and precarious future and, therefore, face more risk than those relying on intergovernmental revenues to a lesser degree.[3]

In general, reliance on intergovernmental revenue is a function of both state statutes that limit local government autonomy over the own-source revenues it can collect and the wealth of its revenue base. Governments with low fiscal autonomy or a poor revenue base will depend more on intergovernmental revenue out of necessity. However, some governments with high autonomy and adequate revenue bases may choose to rely on intergovernmental revenue to satisfy taxpayer's demands for low taxes or to increase expenditures beyond what they would be otherwise.

Governments also can rely to a greater or lesser extent on different sources of own-source revenue. Governments that rely equally on many revenue sources have a diversified revenue structure. The elasticity or volatility of the different revenues will determine whether or not a diversified revenue structure is better than relying on one or two revenue sources. The concept of *revenue elasticity* indicates the responsiveness of a particular revenue base or revenue source to changes in the overall economic base, national economy, or personal income; the more elastic a revenue base, the more variability in the revenues collected given the same tax rate. In most cases, income taxes have the highest elasticity and property taxes have the lowest. The elasticity of sales taxes also is relatively high (Mikesell, 2011, 350).

Governments that rely on elastic revenue sources face more financial risk from fiscal downturns but may take in more revenue than they need during good economic periods due to the greater wealth of these revenue bases. However, reliance on elastic revenue sources still presents uncertainty and a lack of stability that makes maintaining financial condition more difficult. Generally speaking, governments with more diversified revenue are likely to be in better financial shape than governments that rely more heavily on one revenue source. Additionally, governments that rely on property taxes may be better off than those relying on sales taxes or even a diversified set of elastic revenues unless the latter has balanced its risk with adequate slack (e.g., surplus resources or revenue reserves).

On the right-hand side of Table 2.1 in the capacities row, assets consist primarily of cash, short-term investments, and surplus resources (fund balances). These assets are features of the government's fiscal structure over which they have a lot of control and which may change often during the fiscal year. **Table 2.2** (Berne and Schramm, 1986, p. 316) presents a more detailed view of the time frames associated with the revenue-based financial condition measures in Table 2.2. Specifically, Table 2.2 distinguishes the short-term sources of cash and revenue from the long-term sources of cash revenue, both of which are assets.

On the balance sheet, fund balances (and retained earnings) are the residual equity or net assets in each account. More generally, residual equity is the difference between all assets and liabilities. Fund balances, however, are more specific and represent the accumulation of monetary surpluses (revenues minus expenditures) and are easily accessible

TABLE 2.2 Sources and Uses of Cash and Revenue in Governments

Time Horizon	Sources of Cash and Revenues	Uses of Cash and Revenues
Short Term ↑	Draw down cash balances	Build up cash balances
	Convert short-term assets into cash (e.g., sell securities, speed up collections, reduce inventories)	Convert cash into other short-term assets (e.g., buy securities, build up inventories)
	Incur short-term liabilities to gain cash (e.g., borrow short term, slow down payments of accounts payable)	Use cash to lower short-term liabilities (e.g., retire short term debt, speed up payment of accounts payable)
	Increase operating revenues or decrease operating expenditures	Increase operating expenditures or decrease operating revenues
	Increase long-term borrowing or cut back capital expenditures	Increase capital expenditures or repay long-term borrowing
↓ Long Term	Secure new revenue sources or raise fees and taxes	Expend funds on new projects and programs or increase funding for existing projects and programs

Reproduced from Berne, R., and Schramm, R. (1986). Pp. 316, Figure 8-1. *The financial analysis of governments*. New Jersey: Prentice-Hall.

to meet obligations during the fiscal year.[4] Governments also have more than one fund balance, which offers opportunities to borrow across accounts (called *interfund transfers*). Other types of short-term assets and resources that affect cash and budgetary solvency are the ability to speed up revenue collections (e.g., accounts receivable), short-term investments, and saleable physical assets.

Another consideration in assessing financial condition on the "current end" of the continuum is the extent to which revenues and fund balances within different accounts are reserved for specific purposes according to state or local statute. For instance, state governments may require that the gasoline taxes they share with local governments be reserved for road maintenance and construction, or local governments themselves may earmark particular revenues for specific purposes. It is especially common for governments to manage the risk of elastic revenues by earmarking these revenues for nonrecurring expenditures (e.g., capital spending). Therefore, although fund balance, as a percentage of total expenditures or revenues, is a good general measure of short-term financial condition, percentage *unreserved fund balance* might be more appropriate. Another useful measure is the ratio of restricted operating revenues to total operating revenues, which indicates the government's level of flexibility in meeting short-term liabilities.

Expenditures and liabilities. As reflected by the second row in Table 2.1, a liability is anything that is owed by the government to another party, and, hence, represents a constraint on governments' fiscal activities. More specifically, a liability is the sacrifice of current or future economic benefits that the government must make to satisfy current and past obligations. Liabilities on the left-hand side of the table represent fiscal obligations covering an extended period of time, such as the obligation to deliver services in the long-run and meet future obligations including pensions, repayment of debt, and capital replacement. Similar to the left-hand side of the assets row, most of these liabilities represent environmental conditions over which government has less control and which tend to remain stable over time.

Spending *needs* are determined by features of the environment that dictate the level of expenditures the government requires to adequately provide for the health, safety, and welfare of its residents and visitors. For instance, crime levels affect spending needs for police services. The age of infrastructure influences spending for fire services, public works, building inspection, and capital spending. The income level of residents, their job rate, and the threat of health problems (e.g., mosquito-borne diseases) shapes spending for health and welfare services. Population growth and economic development also greatly increase government spending needs, especially for the construction of infrastructure, and create obligations for more services in the future.

Another source of spending needs is the costs of personnel, materials, supplies, equipment, and other items used in service delivery, especially labor and transportation costs. Costs are also a significant factor in capital outlays for construction and land acquisition. Other spending needs may be dictated by federal or state mandates that specify the types or levels of services local governments must provide. Spending mandates exist in a variety of areas, but are especially prevalent for pensions, health care, and water and sewerage services. To some extent, the institutional environment, including overlapping governments, also determines a government's spending needs. Many types of local governments exist in one area such as counties, townships, municipalities and special districts. Which services local governments distribute depends on state statute and how the roles of local governments have evolved over time. Spending *demands*, in contrast, reflect the spending priorities of its residents, clients, and other stakeholders who influence government expenditures through the political process.

Long-term borrowing, underfunded pension obligations, and deferred infrastructure maintenance and replacement also create long-term or future obligations for most governments. Although current decisions to create these obligations are controllable, their effect on future fiscal states is not. In this case, governments faced with obligations to repay past debt or make up for past underfunding of pensions and infrastructure repair cannot control the pressures this places on current spending. In contrast, the level of expenditures governments make to meet current service obligations is more controllable.

Not all cities facing similar spending needs are going to fund current service obligations at the same level due to variations in spending demands, which are filtered through the political process and transformed into expenditure priorities.[5] To some extent, expenditure priorities can be observed from the percentage of total expenditures budgeted for different services, programs, or areas of expenditure, once a government's service needs and other fixed liabilities are taken into account. Spending for services is also affected by how fixed current expenditure obligations are relative to each other. Personnel expenditures and repayment of debt, for instance, are relatively fixed by comparison to maintenance and equipment expenditures that can be deferred more readily. The level of fixed liabilities relative to other liabilities represent the ease with which portions of governments current expenditures can be altered in the near term to react to fiscal shocks and take advantage of fiscal opportunities. Thus, *expenditure fixity* is a form of slack (i.e., the less fixity, the more slack).

Liabilities on the right-hand side of Table 2.1 represent obligations that must be met within a time frame that is shorter than the fiscal year, such as accounts payable or short-term debt, to deliver the services and meet the obligations specified in the budget. As with expenditure categories, accounts payable also have different levels of fixity. For instance, some bills or amounts owed during the fiscal year must be paid immediately or regularly (e.g., wages); other payments can be delayed to improve cash flow in the short run.

Net financial condition. The last row in Table 2.1 represents measures that can be used to reflect whether a government's fiscal structure is balanced with its environment or other conditions relevant to the different types of solvency.[6] On the left-hand side of the table, long-term solvency could be assessed by measures that examine aggregate spending needs relative to total revenue wealth. For instance, measures such as the age of infrastructure and crime per capita could be used as indicators of overall spending needs. These measures then could be compared to total assessed value or income in a municipality to determine a government's long-term solvency. Alternatively, one could develop composite measures of spending needs and wealth that combine individual indicators such as those just listed (Aaronson, 1984; Hendrick, 2004; Ladd and Yinger, 1989). Looking at future obligations, one can compare long-term liabilities (e.g., debt), to long-term relevant assets (e.g., value of infrastructure minus depreciation) to determine the long-term solvency of physical assets. More generally, one might even attempt to forecast future service needs and revenue wealth based upon demographic trends.

With respect to service-level solvency, *revenue burden*—the ratio of actual revenues to revenue base or revenue capacity—is one of the most important measures of financial condition. Revenue or tax burden for individual revenue bases is the same thing as the tax or charge rate. Total revenue burden would be the sum of all tax rates or the sum of all revenues relative to the sum of all revenue capacities. This measure is presented in the center of this row because its numerator, actual revenues, is relatively controllable and a feature of the government's fiscal structure, but its denominator, revenue base, is part of the less controllable environment. On the spending side, comparing actual spending to spending needs would indicate the extent to which the government's service obligations are being met.

One might also use measures of slack relative to risk to assess service-level solvency. For instance, surplus funds, such as rainy day funds and fund balances, could be compared to dependence on elastic or uncertain revenue sources (e.g., percent of total revenue that are intergovernmental). Theoretically, slack could be measured with a composite indicator that incorporates different sources of slack including the fund balance, capital spending, and discretionary spending (Hendrick, 2006). A similar composite indicator could be constructed for risk, but it would have to recognize uncertainty about future events, which is entirely overlooked by most assessments of government financial condition.

Cash and budgetary solvency are assessed primarily by examining features of the government's fiscal structure that affect its ability to balance its budget and pay bills during the fiscal year. Also called the operating position, measures of short-term solvency include liquidity, fund balances, operating deficits or surpluses, short-term borrowing, fixity of accounts payable, and dependability of accounts receivable. Liquidity is the ratio or balance of cash and current assets to current liabilities. Operating deficits and surpluses measure whether revenues are balanced with expenditures, however, they are more meaningful if they are considered in conjunction with the fund balance.

For instance, some governments may run deficits to reduce fund balances that are too high for their environment or relative to other features of their fiscal structure. In this case, operating deficits do not mean that revenues are out of balance with expenditures but that the fund balance is out of balance with other conditions. We have emphasized in other places that fund balances must be compared to other features of the government's fiscal structure and environment to assess short-term and even mid-term financial condition. Similarly, high levels of liquidity may not be necessary in governments with stable revenue streams and fixed expenditures.

One final consideration in assessing financial condition is that all the measures represented in Table 2.1 can be examined over time, and, to some extent, these trends can be used to predict future fiscal states. However, as discussed previously, incorporating dynamic states into an assessment of financial condition is not straightforward. Are current fiscal states more relevant to financial condition than the degree of change in past fiscal states? Similarly, how important is long-term fiscal solvency relative to budgetary and cash solvency? Are local governments with long-term solvency likely to remain that way regardless of fiscal shocks and poor cash or budgetary solvency? To what extent does poor cash or budgetary solvency threaten a government's service-level solvency? How should we integrate the time dimension (past, current, and future) and the different types of solvency into our assessment of local financial condition? How should our choice of measures and methods of integration change for different applications or purposes of assessing financial condition? Unfortunately, the profession does not have clear answers to these questions. However, the distinct nature of the features and attributes of financial condition measures and their contingent relationships make a case for assessing financial condition within each area of solvency separately rather than trying to measure across the continuums and collapsing them into one single composite measure. This includes the time dimension and indicators of change.

A related unanswered question is how do we know whether fiscal features associated with the different solvencies are balanced or appropriate for other features associated with that solvency or other types of solvency? For instance, how do we know whether revenue burden is appropriate to spending needs and demands? Likewise, how do we determine whether fund balances or liquidity match other features of the government's fiscal structure or environment? Here too, further study will help establish objective standards regarding what types of fiscal structures are successful in what types of environments. Ultimately, we still have to make a judgment about what constitutes success and good fiscal performance. Four approaches to making such judgments are described in the next section.

Strategic Decision Making

Thus far, we have focused our discussion of financial condition on the issue of balance—the extent to which a government has adapted its current fiscal structure to the demands, pressures, opportunities, constraints, and likely future changes in the environment. Implicit in this discussion is the strategic decision-making of public officials. This section describes the underlying logic of some of these strategic decision processes. In doing so, it links the ideas of solvency, balance, risk, and slack with the components/measures that compose financial condition.

Long-run solvency, as defined previously, emphasizes long-run balance between available revenues and spending needs. The revenue base and capacity, which is the pool of resources from which revenues are generated, is part of the government's environment. The value and size of the pool are affected by general economic conditions and institutional constraints, such as state statutes, that limit its access to this base. Most factors that generate spending needs in a locality and the value and size of the revenue pool are fairly stable over time and so are critical to long-term solvency. A government whose revenue base/capacity is balanced with its spending needs will have more long-run solvency than one whose spending needs are higher than what the revenue base/capacity can support. A local government has less direct control over these features than the revenues it actually collects or the money it spends to deliver services, but financial decisions also affect long-term solvency. If a government has maximized its collection of available revenue from the revenue base, then it has no revenue reserves or slack to accommodate increases in spending needs or opportunities (e.g., matching grants) that require additional funds. In this case, its long-run solvency is lower because its risk to future changes in the fiscal environment is higher, and its investment potential is lower.

Long-run solvency also encompasses future assets and liabilities and unknown future states of the environment and fiscal structure. According to Figure 2.1, a government that is balanced in the long run has an appropriate level of future liabilities given its likely future resources. Long-run solvency is harder to determine than other aspects of financial condition given the uncertainties of future states, but if a government has had low resources historically due to a poor revenue base and high spending needs, chances are its future environment will be similar. Unless there is evidence of positive future changes, such as an influx of development that raises property values, this government should limit future liabilities to better insure a good financial condition in the future and improve long-run solvency.

Compared to long-run solvency, service-level solvency focuses on the extent to which governments are balancing near-term spending obligations, actual spending, available revenues, and revenues collected. Although a government with poor long-term solvency is less likely to provide adequate services and, therefore, have poor service-level solvency (and vice versa), the two concepts are different. For instance, a government with good long-term solvency may not tax or spend enough due to political constraints to adequately meet the health and safety needs of its citizens. Alternatively, a government with a poor or constrained revenue base can improve its service-level solvency by spending only what it needs to deliver a basic level of services, reducing liabilities, and increasing surplus internal resources to handle emergencies. One might describe this government as having adapted its fiscal structure to its environment as evidenced by the balance between revenues collected and revenue base, expenditures and spending needs, and structural features such as surplus resources.

A wealthy government's fiscal structure also may be poorly adapted to its environment by spending more than it needs, not collecting enough revenue to cover spending, and then trying to make up the shortfall with risky high-paying investments and increases in future liabilities (e.g., reduced pension funding). Such poor service-level solvency is, in many cases due to political pressure. Although its revenue base and spending needs indicate good long-term solvency, its service-level imbalances due to fiscal choices over time will have made it quite vulnerable to events in the near term. One significant fiscal shock, such as a recession, large number of retirements or lawsuits, could dramatically reduce funding for basic services and the level and quality of services it provides for an extended period of time.

Strictly speaking, budgetary solvency is the level of balance between revenues, expenditures and surpluses at the end or the beginning of the fiscal year. Normally, governments project at the beginning of the fiscal year that revenues will equal expenditures at the end of the fiscal year. But if economic (or political) conditions worsen unexpectedly or if officials' estimates of revenues and expenditures are simply inaccurate, then the budget will not be balanced at the end of the fiscal year unless there is enough slack in the fiscal structure to lower spending or enough slack in the fiscal environment to raise revenues. In most cases, raising tax rates during the fiscal year (if state statutes or political pressure allow for this) will not generate enough revenues to solve mid-year fiscal problems due to the cycles of collection. Thus, governments rely primarily on slack in their fiscal structure to reduce risk and achieve budgetary solvency. However, governments with more stable revenues and better service-level solvency face less risk and, therefore, will need less slack to be solvent and balanced at this level.

At the most immediate level, problems with cash solvency and cash flow emanate from two sources—(1) fiscal shocks that unexpectedly speed up or add payments, or slow down or diminish revenues; and (2) not functioning with enough slack to cover expected timing differences between revenues coming in and payments going out. Generally, governments with poor service-level and budgetary solvency tend to have poor cash solvency; they operate with less slack and a narrower margin of error. That said, wealthy governments and those with good budgetary solvency can also have cash flow problems if risks and cash trends are not recognized and planned for. As with the other solvency levels, good cash solvency means having an appropriate fiscal structure and maintaining a balance between short-term assets and short-term liabilities.

Recognizing that financial condition is dynamic suggests two additional factors that should be taken into account. These factors, which are not easily reflected in a two-dimensional diagram such as Figure 2.1, are uncertainty about future fiscal states and the role of past fiscal trends. We have already discussed how current decisions impact future financial condition when, for instance, officials are able to push spending obligations forward in time. This strategy does not eliminate government obligations making them a factor in its current financial condition and a feature of its fiscal structure. But future obligations are different from current fiscal states because of the uncertainty surrounding their impact. Thus, uncertainty is an important consideration in financial condition.

The second factor deals with the problem of incorporating changes in past fiscal states relative to current fiscal states in measures of financial condition. Obviously, a government undergoing declines in any level of solvency or deterioration of conditions that affect solvency will be worse off than one experiencing stability or improvements. It is much more difficult, however, to assess the financial condition of a government that has a wealthy yet declining revenue base compared to one with a poor but stable revenue base. Which government has lower long-term or service-level solvency? The answer is not intuitive and demonstrates that financial condition is not just an objective state to be measured, but is also a qualitative judgment.[7]

This discussion of financial condition and its time frames, levels, and characteristics reveals a complex phenomenon that is not easy to measure. However, several themes have emerged that will guide the next sections that focus on judging and measuring financial condition. First, properties of the environment, fiscal structure, and levels of solvency are related. Financial condition in the longer-term (e.g., long-term and service-level solvency) tends to be a function of future events and features of the system that are less controllable and more external or environmental. By comparison, financial condition in the shorter term (e.g., budgetary and cash solvency) is more a function of immediate events and relatively controllable features of the system that are part of the government's internal fiscal structure. For instance, a government's financial condition in the long run will depend greatly on the wealth of its revenue base, which is part of its environment and not likely to change or be affected by officials' fiscal choices in the immediate future. In contrast, officials have much greater control over how to manage cash flow through manipulation of the government's fiscal structure.

The caveat to these relationships is that features affecting government financial condition in the longer term provide the context for altering or maintaining financial condition in the shorter term. Ultimately, governments with a poor long-term solvency will have more difficulty maintaining good financial condition in the short run due to external and uncontrollable characteristics that have established its fiscal structure over time. In other words, a government with poor long-term and service-level solvency is more likely to have poor budgetary and cash solvency. It is also more likely to have higher future liabilities, greater risk, less slack, and a fiscal structure that is more unbalanced and inappropriate for its environment. Similarly, a government with good long-term and service-level solvency is more likely to have good budgetary, cash solvency, and so on. However, these outcomes are not certain.

A government with a poor revenue base and sound financial decisions may find it difficult, but not impossible, to maintain budgetary and cash solvency. Alternatively, a government with a strong revenue base may have low short-term solvency due to unsound fiscal practices. Over time, sound fiscal practices and productive choices could, conceivably, improve the poor government's service-level solvency, and unsound fiscal practices could threaten the wealthy government's service-level solvency. These examples suggest that interpreting financial condition requires understanding not only fiscal issues at a particular point in time, but also how it relates to the past and anticipated future. Such considerations require the analyst to interpret financial condition in normative terms in order to designate fiscal health and fiscal stress.

The second theme from this section is that features relevant to different time frames and levels of financial condition often vary and affect overall financial condition in convoluted ways that make the effects of some factors conditional on the effect of others.

For instance, the level of surplus resources that is appropriate and necessary to maintain budgetary solvency depends on risks inherent in the fiscal structure (e.g., high dependence on sales tax), the volatility of the environment (where sales receipts come from), and opportunities for obtaining additional revenues. The complexity and contingent nature of the relationships between these features, thus, makes it difficult to construct a single comprehensive indicator of fiscal health or financial condition that spans all areas of solvency. Rather, it suggests that key dimensions of financial condition be identified, measured separately, and assessed in relation to one another to produce a complete and more accurate picture of fiscal conditions. The next section presents a brief description of different popular methods for measuring financial condition.

Strategies for Measuring Financial Condition

While scholars and practitioners have developed a host of measures of financial condition, the underlying logic of these measures is much less varied. In this section, we describe and assess four broad approaches that have been used to evaluate and interpret financial condition. In particular, we consider the use of: trend analysis, group norms, benchmarking, and multiple indices.

The first approach is to simply consider the trends of different fiscal indicators. One example of this approach is the Financial Trend Monitoring System (FTMS) developed by the International City/County Managers Association (Groves et al., 2003). It is a comprehensive measurement system for assessing the four areas of solvency (described in the previous section) using 36 different financial indicators in 11 different categories. The strength of this particular system is that it examines the indicators over time (at least five years) to identify financial trends affecting the different areas of financial condition before they become a significant problem and threaten the government's solvency. The weakness of this system is that it requires a great deal of data to measure all the indicators. Thus, while it is a very useful, proactive tool for local officials to determine sources of fiscal imbalances within their own governments, it is not very useful for assessing financial condition across many governments.

More generally, describing the trends of a particular government's (or agency's) finances is a useful first step. A trend analysis, such as the FTMS, offers the analyst an opportunity to describe "what is going on." However, this approach offers few insights with respect to "where one should be." For example, a government that is in a poor state of affairs but where trends are improving would look the same as another government with improving trends but in better financial shape. The FTMS does not evaluate the *initial* financial condition of either government so both would be assessed as headed in the same 'positive' direction, even though the first municipality is in poorer fiscal health. To avoid this problem many analysts employ group comparisons or some form of benchmarking.

The group comparison approach measures a small number of fiscal factors and then considers these measured against some group norm. For example, Terry Clark and Lorna Ferguson (1983), directly incorporate the concept of balance into their analyses of financial condition. They define financial condition, or fiscal stress, as the extent to which a government (a complex system) has adapted its fiscal structure (fiscal policy outputs) with the risks, demands, and pressures of the environment (private sector) to reduce the incidence of short-run budgetary and fiscal deficits (pp. 44–45). Using ratios and two indices, their approach assesses *city wealth* and *functional performance* for each city relative to the others in "the group." More precisely, the City Wealth Index combines measures of different components of the revenue base (environment) with measures of dependence on revenues from each base component (fiscal structure). The Functional Performance Index assesses total expenditures for each municipality that are considered to be "normal" for its reference group. In this case, the reference group may be all governments in a state or region, and normal can be defined as the median or mean of that group.

Another oft-used group comparison is the Representative Tax System (RTS) and Representative Revenue System (RRS) (ACIR, 1962). Similar to Clark and Ferguson, the RTS and RRS assess a government's fiscal position by comparing its features to a group norm rather than an absolute standard of fiscal health. Specifically, the RRS and RTS use the normal (median or average) tax and revenue rates of an area to determine the amount of total revenue a government in that area could obtain if it taxed at these "normal," baseline rates. Although the RTS focuses on taxes, its method has been adapted to other revenues and expenditures (Kincaid, 1989) and expanded upon by others in the academy and policy arenas (Ladd and Yinger, 1989).

Both systems provide a detailed picture of the revenue side of service-level solvency, and they can be easily adapted to measure the expenditure side. However, neither the RRS nor the RTS recognize the time dimension of fiscal condition that was discussed previously. Specifically, changes in features relevant to long-term and service-level solvency mean something very different than the relative long-term and service-level solvency of a municipality at one time period. A more general critique of the group comparison approach is based on whether or not the group mean is a reasonable barometer for evaluating financial condition? What if the entire region is fiscally distressed? In such a situation, one's finances could look very good, relative to the group mean, but still be poor in absolute terms.

This last issue has been picked up in recent efforts to assess financial condition against an "industry benchmark" (Sohl et al., 2009). There have not been many attempts to assess financial condition against an industry benchmark; however, in a recent piece, Sohl et al. (2009) provide some guidance as to how to undertake such an approach. They argue that to properly assess financial condition (without falling into the problem of a poor comparison group) is to consider some measure of financial condition and then benchmarking the municipality's position over time against an industrywide standard. They suggest a two-phased approach. The first phase combines both trend analysis and group comparisons to provide some important insights into the overall fiscal environment in which the city is operating. The second phase considers the particular city under investigation against some industry standard (the authors suggest using the Government Finance

Officers Association's [GFOA's] recommended standards). The primary weakness with this approach is that an 'industry standard' does not really exist. Thus, the choice of a benchmark is somewhat arbitrary.

Like the group norm and benchmarking approach to measuring financial condition, the final approach—the use of multiple indices—is an explicit effort to incorporate some normative component into the assessment. These approaches allow the analyst to develop specific scores on different dimensions of fiscal condition. As a result, these analytical approaches are useful tools for practitioners looking for simple assessments that can be easily interpreted by citizens and politicians.

For example, the Brown 10-point test—developed in conjunction with the GFOA—provides a means for smaller municipalities to quickly and easily assess their overall financial condition. The test instructs governments to compare their government's scores on ten ratios to those calculated for all cities in their population range that received GFOA's Certificate of Achievement for Excellence in Financial Reporting at a particular date (Brown, 1993). The test consists of four steps: (1) calculate ten ratios that assess balance in fiscal structure and environment using data from the annual financial report, (2) compare each ratio to those reported for similar sized cities in the Brown article and assign a score based on the quartile in which the ratio is located, (3) sum the scores for all ratios, (4) assess the summary grade according to the following scheme:

Scores of 10 or more	Among the *best*
Scores from 5 to 9	*Better* than most
Scores from 1 to 4	About *average*
Scores from -4 to 0	*Worse* than most
Scores of -5 or less	Among the *worst*

The key to constructing this comprehensive measure of financial condition is comparing the ratios calculated for an individual government to those calculated, grouped by quartiles and population, and reported by Brown and GFOA.[8] This method provides a comparative perspective on the fiscal features in the government that is not provided by the FTMS. However, the quartiles reported by Brown apply only to larger (e.g., populations > 50,000) municipalities and may not be appropriate for very small municipalities (e.g., populations < 5,000).

Another scoring system was developed by Kloha, Weissert, and Kleine (2005). They developed their scoring system in response to particular failures they identified with the existing systems, especially as the 10-point system. In particular, they sought to eliminate the excessive number of variables used in many measures while incorporating more relevant ones, such as socio-economic characteristics, take into account differing demands, and moving away from relative group comparisons. This last characteristic is important. In the 10-point system, someone in the group will always be in the bottom quartile and someone will always be in the top quartile. The 10-point system developed by Kloha, Weissert, and Kleine, however, offers a more "absolute" measure.

Their approach involves four steps. First, a specific variable is created to measure an important component of local public finance, for example, real taxable value growth. Second, a standard is set for each variable to distinguish better or worse performance. Third, if the local government scored "good" on the variable it received 0 points. Finally, the points are summed for each municipality. The more points a locality received the worse it was doing. The result of this approach is the following "early warning system":

0–4 points Fiscally Healthy
5 points Fiscal Watch
6–7 points Fiscal Warning
8–10 points Fiscal Emergency

Similar scoring systems have been developed by specific agencies to evaluate their own fiscal health (see, e.g., Illinois State Board of Education). The problem with these measures has to do with the difficulty of combining component indictors across financial condition measurement dimensions and solvency areas in a linear way. First, this method obscures the contextual meaning of indicators in each dimension. We have shown through examples that how one indicator, such as fund balance level, is interpreted often depends on another indicator, such as dependence on elastic revenues. Second, combining fiscal indicators from different dimensions using equal weights, as do the two 10-points systems, assumes that all components contribute equally to overall financial condition, which may not be appropriate. For instance, high revenue and debt burden may contribute more to overall financial condition than budgetary surpluses and deficits and, therefore, should not be weighted more in the combined measure.

Given the host of scoring systems available to analysts to measure financial condition, the decision of which one to use should focus on which system incorporates the variables most relevant to their needs. Analysts also can choose different approaches based on trends, group norms, benchmarks or indices, and within those approaches one can choose different methods. Their choices should be based on a deep understanding of the particular city or region to be studied. Thus, the notion of financial analysis being based on an objective quantification of financial condition conducted at arms length should be avoided. Regardless of the approach and method chosen, the analyst should also employ some qualitative data collection. This could be done *before* the analysis to guide one with respect to the best approach and method, as well as *after* the study to help in the final interpretation of the results.

As we portrayed at the outset of the chapter, the moral of the story, is that there is no single best strategy for assessing financial condition. Rather, analysts and scholars, need to understand the different dimensions of financial condition, how they relate to each other and determine their meaning based on an honest assessment of current and future fiscal risks. This assessment could take the form of a comparison to a group norm or to some industry benchmark. The analyst, however, needs to acknowledge that the different strategies have both strengths and weaknesses and understanding these is critical to an accurate assessment of local financial condition.

Conclusion

This chapter has sought to answer the question: *what is a government's financial condition and how do you assess it?* To that end, we have argued that financial condition is less a state of being as much as a dynamic and fluid process. Accordingly, we present financial condition as a multi-dimensional phenomenon that is shaped by external factors (i.e., fiscal structure and political) and subsequent internal policy choices. Further, we have argued that it is particularly useful to consider financial condition in terms of four different forms of solvency: long run, service level, budgetary, and cash. This approach allows one to consider the dimensions of revenue (e.g., economic base, intergovernmental revenues, and accounts receivable) and expenditure (e.g., debt and accounts payable) both as individual components and as composite parts that come together in the current and future time periods. However, a key lesson in this chapter is that any consideration of future "states" will be imprecise at best as longer-term dimensions tend to be less controllable (though often stable) and generally external to the municipal agency. Consequently, all descriptions of financial condition should take account of the *uncertainty* of the future state. More precisely, measures of financial conditions should evaluate the features that are in place to address an uncertain future, namely, *risk* and *slack*.

It has been shown in this chapter that fiscal slack can take various forms, such as a rainy day fund or extensive expenditures that can be cut in times of need and the amount of slack within a system is related to the amount of fiscal risk a municipality has undertaken or is willing to undertake. Our model, then, also implies that a sound fiscal environment will be characterized by a *balance* among slack, risk, and fiscal structure.

The presentation of these strategies demonstrates that no single measure is likely to provide a complete picture of financial condition. Both policy analysts and academics should be cautioned that a more appropriate approach would be to employ multiple measures across various dimensions and time frames for revenue, expenditures, and net financial condition before coming to any conclusion. For the practitioner, questions remain as these recommendations may not be satisfying. Which measure is best? Under what circumstances should I employ one measure over the other? If I employ several measures, how do I know which measure provides the most accurate information? What is an appropriate balance among slack, risk, and fiscal structure?

Unfortunately, these questions do not have answers, but we offer some practical direction with respect to the appropriate use of the measures themselves, as well as the concepts of slack and risk. First, we have demonstrated that analysts should not rely on any single measure of financial condition, but we also suggest that one use caution in selecting the measures to be employed. Simply put, no measure is perfect and they cannot be selected arbitrarily. Rather, analysts should be cognizant of the limitations and data requirements of each measure as well as the audience for which the analysis is being prepared. For example, one might want to employ the FTMS because it is comprehensive and recognizes conditions over time, however its data requirements (and subsequent time requirements) might make this approach impractical. Further, public officials may or may not be as interested in the financial trends of their particular municipality as much as they are in understanding how their jurisdiction compares with others that have similar characteristics. Although the analyst may prefer the power of the FTMS, he or she would be better served by using the Clark and Ferguson measure or the RTS. In short, analysts will do well to err on the side of pragmatism when determining which measure of financial condition to employ.

Second, we have argued in this chapter that financial condition is a complex phenomenon that is shaped by the political and fiscal environment, which varies drastically from one jurisdiction to the next. In this case, the balance between risk and slack is inherently contingent on the locality in which the analysis is being conducted. Thus, there is no absolute threshold number that one can point to and say: "that is a perfect amount of slack" or "here is the perfect balance." In the absence of such numbers, we suggest that analysts move beyond a purely technical approach to these concepts and consider how they might change given different political landscapes. Such an approach would require analysts to interpret both risk and slack within the local context. To that end, an analysis of financial condition should engage elected officials in an active dialogue to make clear the degree to which they and their constituents are more or less risk averse. The idea is to balance technical analysis with a broader understanding of the unique fiscal features of a particular jurisdiction.

The lesson to be gained from this chapter is simply that financial condition is not easy to grasp. It is multidimensional, often context specific, and its causal factors often operate in nonlinear ways. However, a sound approach to understanding financial condition is to embrace this complexity as opposed to trying to simplify it into a few core components. To this end, the model and measures described should provide the reader with the tools to confidently assess and interpret the financial condition of municipal agencies.

Endnotes

1. For example, economists working in this area developed composite measures of financial condition that focused primarily on environmental factors, such as poverty and property values, that determine spending needs and available revenue (Ladd and Yinger 1989; Bahl 1984; ACIR 1971, 1979, 1988). See Burchell et al. 1981; Aaronson 1984; and Ross and Greenfield 1980 for comprehensive summaries and critiques of the many composite measures developed during this period. Other composite measures or systems are intended to be used internally by local officials for financial management and developing fiscal policy (Aaronson and King 1978; Groves et al, 2003; Brown 1993; Honadle and Lloyd-Jones 1998). External agents, such as investors and lenders, also use these types of measures for assessing bond purchases and determining interest rates (Moody's Investor Services, 2000; Standard & Poor's, 2002).
2. Elasticity is an economic concept that refers to rate of change and is described in greater detail in the section entitled Net Financial Condition.
3. Chapman (1988) refers to this type of risk as local fiscal immunity autonomy.
4. Mathematically, fund balances are assets minus liabilities.
5. A well articulated example of this is developed in Stonecash and McAfee (1981).
6. Also notice the extent to which ratios play a role in measuring the state of balance.

7. Indices developed and analyses of financial condition performed by the U.S. Advisory Commission on Intergovernmental Relations, the U.S. Department of Treasury, and The Urban Institute incorporate past changes in fiscal features using different methods. Also, the ICMA Financial Trend Monitoring System (Groves et al., 2003) uses five-year trends to assess financial condition.
8. The study does not indicate if the figures reported in the quartiles are corrected for inflation, which is necessary to compare ratios calculated in other years to those in the report.

Glossary

Asset: From an accounting perspective, an asset is anything that the government owns that can produce an economic benefit. From a more general economic perspective, an asset is simply any form of wealth. Cities have long-term assets such as capital infrastructure, as well as short-term assets such as current revenues.

Balance: reflects the extent to which a government has adapted its *current* fiscal structure to the demands, pressures, opportunities, constraints, and likely *future* changes in the environment (Clark and Ferguson, 1983).

Budgetary Solvency: the ability to balance the budget or generate enough resources to cover expenditures in the current fiscal year.

Cash Solvency: the government's ability to generate enough cash over 30 or 60 days to pay its bills. Also called the operating position.

Economic Base: is the total amount of economic resources within a jurisdiction, regardless of whether a government to access them. It is a function of the fiscal environment's *economic performance* and *economic structure.*

Economic Performance: represents the jurisdiction's level of economic activity and is measured by one or more indicators such as percentage unemployment, resident income, and poverty level.

Economic Structure: is the composition of economic activity in the jurisdiction such as land use (residential, commercial, industrial), type of jobs and commerce, transportation facilities, and the regional or state economy.

Elasticity: *See* Revenue Elasticity.

Expenditure fixity: the degree to which expenditures can be altered or deferred. Personnel expenditures and repayment of debt, for instance, are relatively fixed by comparison to maintenance and equipment expenditures that can be deferred more readily. The level of fixed liabilities relative to other liabilities represent the ease with which portions of governments current expenditures can be altered in the near term to react to fiscal shocks and take advantage of fiscal opportunities.

Fund Balance: On the balance sheet, fund balances (and retained earnings) are the residual equity or net assets in each account. More generally, residual equity is the difference between all assets and liabilities. Fund balances, however, are more specific and represent the accumulation of monetary surpluses (revenues minus expenditures) and are easily accessible to meet obligations during the fiscal year. Governments also have more than one fund balance, which offers opportunities to borrow across accounts (called *interfund transfers*). *See also* Unreserved Fund Balance.

Institutions (or environment): refer to the rules, both formal and informal, that constrain decision making. (In this chapter, we focus on the fiscal and political institutions that constrain the strategic fiscal decisions of local governments.)

Intergovernmental Revenue: funds received from the state or federal governments for specific functions (grants) or for general financial assistance (aid).

Liability: anything that is owed by the government to another party, and, hence, represents a constraint on governments' fiscal activities. More specifically, a liability is the sacrifice of current or future economic benefits that the government must make to satisfy current and past obligations.

Long-run Solvency: refers to the long-run balance between government revenues and spending needs and implies that government has the ability to adapt to uncertain future fiscal conditions, some of which may be severe shocks.

Own-source Revenue: are generated from resources within the local government's jurisdiction, although they can be collected by other governments and distributed to the owner government at regular intervals. Local own-source revenues include property taxes, user fees, and other charges and, in some states, may include other taxes such as sales and income.

Revenue Actual: is the amount of revenues the government chooses to collect via its tax rates, fee rates, and charges.

Revenue Base: that portion of the economic base that the jurisdiction has access to through specific revenue-raising mechanisms according to state statute and other legal and institutional constraints.

Revenue Capacity: reflects that portion of the revenue base the government can actually tax, which also is established in most cases by state statute.

Revenue Elasticity: indicates the responsiveness of a particular revenue base or revenue source to changes in the overall economic base, national economy, or personal income; the more elastic a revenue base, the more variability in the revenues collected given the same tax rate. In most cases, income taxes have the highest elasticity and property taxes have the lowest. The elasticity of sales taxes also is relatively high.

Revenue Reserves: are excess or slack revenue capacity that the government has access to but has not used (reserves = capacity – actual). If a locality tapped its revenue base to the full potential, actual revenues would equal revenue capacity and revenue reserves would equal zero.

Risk (fiscal): a government's exposure or vulnerability to detrimental future fiscal shocks and faster changes in the environment.

Slack (fiscal): the pool of resources available to a government in excess of what is necessary to produce a minimum level of services. Fiscal slack can be surplus monetary resources such as the fund balance or rainy day fund or nonmonetary resources such as excess employees. Fiscal slack can also be uncollected revenue from that portion of the revenue base that is available to the government through higher taxation. On the expenditure side, fiscal slack can be discretionary spending such as capital maintenance and travel that can be easily reduced during times difficult financial periods.

Service-level Solvency: the ability of government to provide adequate services to meet the health, safety, and welfare needs of its citizens given its revenue resources.

Unreserved Fund Balance: Fund balances within different accounts are reserved for specific purposes according to state or local statute. Therefore, although fund balance, as a percentage of total expenditures or revenues, is a good general measure of short-term financial condition, percentage unreserved fund balance might be more appropriate.

Discussion Questions

1. Think about the state and local governments in which you work. What are particularly important aspects of their financial condition?
2. Using Figure 2.1, identify important aspects of your governments' fiscal and political environments.
3. Using Figure 2.2, identify the components of your governments' economic bases, revenue bases, and revenue capacities.
4. What do you think are particularly important criteria or methodologies for assessing your governments' financial condition? For instance, is it more important to measure changes in components of financial condition or compare components of financial condition to other governments?
5. What types of criteria or methods are most likely to be valued and used by officials at the local level, policymakers at the state level, students studying financial management and public finance at the state and local level, scholars, and citizens?

Recommended Resources

Carr, J. (1984). Crisis and constraint in municipal finance: Local fiscal prospects in a period of uncertainty. New Brunswick, NJ: Center for Urban Policy Research.

City/County Managers Association at www.icma.org North Carolina

Department of State Treasurer (Municipal Fiscal Analysis Dashboard) at http://www.nctreasurer.com/dsthome/StateAndLocalGov/lgcreport

Government Finance Officers Association at www.gfoa.org International

Ladd, H. F., and Yinger, J. M. (1989). America's ailing cities: Fiscal health and the design of urban policy. Baltimore: Johns Hopkins University Press.

Standard & Poor's. (2002). Public finance. New York: McGraw Hill.

Nollenberger, K., Groves, S. M., and Valente, M. G.. (2003). Evaluating financial condition: A handbook for local government, 4th ed. Washington, DC: ICMA.

References

Aaronson, J. R. (1984). Municipal fiscal indicators. In J. Carr, *Crisis and constraint in municipal finance: Local fiscal prospects in a period of uncertainty* (pp. 3–53). New Brunswick, NJ: Center for Urban Policy Research.

Aaronson, J. R., and King, A. E. (1978). Is there a fiscal crisis outside of New York? *National Tax Journal, 31*(2), 135–155.

Advisory Commission on Intergovernmental Relations. (1962). *Measures of state and local fiscal capacity and effort.* M-16. Washington, DC: ACIR.

Advisory Commission on Intergovernmental Relations. (1971). *Measuring the fiscal capacity and effort of state and local areas.* Washington, DC: ACIR.

Advisory Commission on Intergovernmental Relations. (1979). *Measuring the fiscal blood pressure of the states: 1964–1975.* Washington, DC: ACIR.

Advisory Commission on Intergovernmental Relations. (1988). *State fiscal capacity and effort.* M165. Washington, DC: ACIR.

Bahl, R. (1984). The Fiscal Health of the State and Local Government Sector. In *Financing State and Local Government in the 1980's* (pp. 33–51). New York: Oxford University Press.

Berne, R., and Schramm, R. (1986). *The financial analysis of governments.* New Jersey: Prentice-Hall.

Brown, K. W. (1993). The 10-point test of financial condition: Toward an easy-to-use assessment tool for smaller governments. *Government Finance Review, 9*(1), 21–25.

Burchell, R. W., Listokin, D., Sternlieb, G., Hughs, J. W., and Casey, S. C. (1981). Measuring urban distress: A summary of the major urban hardship indices and resource allocation systems. In R. Burchell and D. Listokin (Eds.), *Cities Under Stress.* Piscataway, NJ: Center for Urban Policy Research.

Chapman, J. I. (1988). Land use planning and the local budget: A model of their interrelationships. *Public Administration Review, 4*(4), 800–806.

Clark, T. N., and Ferguson, L. C. (1983). *City money: Political processes, fiscal strain and retrenchment.* New York: Columbia University Press.

Groves, S. M., Godsey, M. W., and Nollenberger, R. K. (2003). *Evaluating financial condition: A handbook for local government* (4th ed.). Washington, D.C.: ICMA.

Hendrick, R. (2004). Assessing and measuring the fiscal health of local governments: Focus on Chicago suburban municipalities. *Urban Affairs Review, 40,* 78–114.

Hendrick, R. (2006). Role of slack in managing local government fiscal conditions. *Public Budgeting and Finance,* 26(1): 14–46.

Hendrick, R. (2011). *Managing the fiscal metropolis: the financial policies, practices, and health of suburban municipalities.* Washington, DC: Georgetown University Press.

Honadle, B. W., and Lloyd-Jones, M. (1998). Analyzing rural local governments' financial condition: An exploratory application of three tools. *Public Budgeting and Finance,* 18(2), 69.

Kincaid, J. (1989). Fiscal capacity and tax effort of the American states: Trends and issues. *Public Budgeting and Finance,* 9(3), 4–26.

Kloha, P., Weissert, C. S., and Kleine, R. (2005). Developing and testing a composite model to predict local fiscal distress, *Public Administration Review*, 65(3), 313–323

Ladd, Helen, F., and Yinger, M. J. (1989). *America's ailing cities: Fiscal health and the design of urban policy.* Baltimore: Johns Hopkins University.

Mikesell, John, L. (2011) *Fiscal administration* (8th ed.). Belmont, CA: Wadsworth.

Moody's Investor Services. (2000). *Moody's rating methodology handbook.* New York: Moodys.

Ross, J. P., and J. Greenfield. 1980. Measuring the health of cities. In *Fiscal stress and public policy*, edited by C. Levine and I. Rubin, 89–110. Beverly Hills, CA: Sage.

Sohl, S., Peddle, M. T., Thurmaier, K., Wood, C. H., and Gregory, K. (2009). Measuring the financial position of municipalities: Numbers do not speak for themselves. *Public Budgeting and Finance*, 29(3), 74–86.

Standard & Poor's. (2002). *Public finance.* New York: McGraw Hill.

Stonecash, J., and McAfee, P. (1981). Ambiguities and limits of fiscal strain indicators. *Policy Studies Journal*, *10*(December), 379–395.

Wildavsky, A., and Caiden, N. (2000). *The new politics of the budgetary process* (4th ed.). New York: Addison-Wesley Pub Co.

Chapter 3

Measuring and Predicting Local Government Fiscal Stress

Theory and Practice

by Jonathan B. Justice and Eric A. Scorsone

Introduction

This chapter explores the matter of how to choose or design systems of measures and indicators used to assess, and ideally to predict, local governments' fiscal health and fiscal stress. Suitable systems can help provide local-government managers, elected officials, state governments, residents, creditors, vendors, and other stakeholders with efficient and effective ways to know whether, when, and how to respond to local fiscal condition administration. Although the central focus is on fiscal measures and indicators, it is important to note that financial measurement and prediction are only part of what generally is, or in many instances ought to be, a larger system of information, procedures, and people concerned with detecting, predicting, preventing, and when necessary, reacting to serious local fiscal problems. In addition to identifying local governments that are already insolvent or imminently likely to default on financial obligations, appropriately designed and implemented fiscal reporting and measurement can serve as diagnostic and predictive tools within larger systems that use an attention-conserving, mixed-scanning (Etzioni, 1967) approach to identify and analyze cases that merit a more in-depth investigation or intervention regarding their fiscal health with the goal of determining whether, when, and how to respond (Clark and Chan, 1990; Coe, 2008).

The major sections of this chapter present in turn a review of some key underlying concepts of fiscal health and stress, a very brief context-setting review of some salient episodes in U.S. history, an open-systems view of local-government finance and the determinants of fiscal health and stress, a discussion of some of the practical challenges and tradeoffs involved in selecting and using fiscal indicators, an overview of selected measurement approaches and indicator systems, and finally some concluding observations.

Fiscal health is a complex normative concept, and its definition is to some degree audience specific. For example, a municipal bondholder might judge as acceptably healthy a government making timely payments of principal and interest, even at the expense of drastic cuts in its parks and recreation budget, while a parks-using citizen of the same jurisdiction might be less impressed. Fiscal stress is in some ways easier to identify, but (like fiscal health) it is shaped by a complex and often unpredictable interaction of environmental and organizational factors. The measurement and especially prediction of fiscal health and stress are therefore complicated by both descriptive uncertainty and normative ambiguity (see March, 1978, 1994). Further challenges arise because of practical constraints on analysts' attention and access to data; tradeoffs of data availability, relevance, timeliness, and comprehensiveness; and trade-offs of indicators' and measurements' accuracy and predictive power against ease of computation and interpretation. Many different indicators and indicator systems are available, each of which has specific strengths and weaknesses, and therefore advantages and disadvantages for specific audiences.

A large number of indicator and fiscal health-monitoring systems have been devised over the past half-century, meant for use by local-government managers (e.g., Brown, 1993, 1996; Groves, Godsey, and Shulman, 1981; Groves, Nollenberger, and Valente, 2003) or by external monitors such as state governments, citizens, creditors, or credit-rating agencies (e.g., Clark and Chan, 1990; Coe, 2007, 2008; Kloha, Weissert, and Kleine, 2005b; Moody's Investors Service, 2010; Wang, Dennis, and Tu, 2007). Each has its own explicit or implicit operational definition of fiscal health, its own approach to identifying and measuring the most relevant dimensions of health (or disease) and aggregating them into an overall diagnosis, and its own requirements both in terms of the quantity and quality of data required and in terms of how easily the data can be acquired, analyzed, and interpreted.

For example, monitoring systems designed to be used primarily by a local government's own managers, such as the International City/County Management Association's (ICMA) Financial Trend Monitoring System (FTMS) (Groves et al., 2003), may adopt a comprehensive approach that requires assembling large quantities of organizational and environmental data to construct a continuously maintained series of dozens of indicators over several years. The FTMS provides no specific benchmarks or simple yes/no decision rules for taking action. Systems aimed at attention-constrained external monitors such as state governments may use only a handful of individual indicators, constructed annually from data routinely reported to them by the subject local governments, and may further condense those few indicators into a single index value (e.g., Brown, 1993; Kleine, Kloha, and Weissert, 2002; Maher and Nollenberger, 2009). By contrast with the FTMS, at least some of the systems designed for external monitoring do offer at least relative rankings, rules of thumb, or benchmarks to characterize local governments' fiscal health and in some cases to trigger actions of varying kinds.

One clear lesson from reviewing the literature is that no one system can be expected to serve all audiences and needs. Another is that it is possible, given an understanding of a specific stakeholder's needs and ability to acquire and interpret information, to make a reasonably appropriate choice or adaptation of measurement approaches and specific indicators, starting from a large and still growing body of published research and recommendations. Finally, it is important to keep in mind that measures of fiscal health and systems of indicators serve only a diagnostic function: actually preventing or ameliorating local government fiscal emergencies and defaults requires the effective implementation of a larger system of institutions and procedures for maintaining local governments' fiscal health.

Concepts of Fiscal Health and Stress

As with human health and sickness, fiscal health and stress are defined in a variety of ways, with differences attributable to the definer's particular concerns as well as to situational factors.[1] Participants in the municipal bond market, for instance, are likely to be most concerned with a jurisdiction's ability (and willingness) to make timely payments of principal and interest due over the lifetime of a bond issue. Local governments' managers, elected officials, appointed board members, and residents might be additionally concerned with the ability to sustain a desired level of services and activities over both short and long periods of time. Vendors might be concerned primarily with a government's ability to pay their invoices over a standard 30- or 60-day billing period or over the duration of a contract. Because local governments in the United States are legally creatures of the states, state governments might be concerned with all of these abilities, particularly to the extent that local governments' ill health might require politically and/or financially costly intervention on the state's part.

Following Jacob and Hendrick in this volume (and Groves et al., 1981), we approach *fiscal health* broadly in terms of four organizational fiscal abilities or "solvencies": (1) the ability to meet immediate financial obligations such as paying vendor invoices and salaries (*cash solvency*), (2) the ability to meet all the organization's financial obligations over the course of a given budget year (*budgetary solvency*), (3) the ability to meet all financial obligations in future periods (*long-run solvency*), and (4) the ability to finance the provision of a quantity and quality of services adequate for "the general health and welfare of a community" (Groves et al., 1981, p. 6) (*service-level solvency*).[2] Within this framework, fiscal health can further be understood as encompassing the *resiliency* that enables government organizations to withstand external economic disruptions such as financial crises and recessions and to cope with population growth and decline and other demographic changes (Groves et al., 2003, p. 2).

A complementary framework developed by the Public Sector Accounting Board (PSAB, 2007, pp. 6–7) of the Canadian Institute of Chartered Accountants (CICA) identifies three "elements of financial condition": (1) sustainability, (2) flexibility, and (3) vulnerability. *Sustainability* encompasses the abilities required by all four of the preceding solvencies, with the additional criterion that a government is able to meet its financial and service commitments "without increasing the relative debt or tax burden on the economy within which it operates." *Flexibility* "is the degree to which a government can change its debt or tax burden on the economy within which it operates" to meet its financial and service obligations. *Vulnerability* "is the degree to which a government is dependent on sources of funding outside its control or influence or is exposed to risks that could impair" its ability to meet its obligations. As the PSAB noted, these elements are interdependent. For example, an increase in intergovernmental funding for some services may increase sustainability at the same time as it decreases flexibility.

Fiscal stress in general terms can be understood as a government's actual or potential failure to satisfy one or more of the solvency, sustainability, flexibility, and vulnerability conditions of fiscal health. According to Danziger (1991, p. 169), "Fiscal stress is typically defined as a (usually growing) imbalance between the demands for a government's resources and its access to the private or public financial resources to meet those demands." Clark and Ferguson's *fiscal strain* construct (Clark, 1994; Clark and Ferguson, 1983; Pammer, 1990) focuses on the ways in which persistent maladaptation of an organization's financial structure and choices to the availability of private-sector resources in its fiscal environment contributes to fiscal stress. This is closely related to the PSAB's sustainability element: fiscal strain occurs when a government enters into commitments that are not fiscally sustainable over time in its relevant political economy. A concern with adaptation also raises the matter of not just ability, but also *willingness* to pay: a government's ability to extract resources from its environment depends not just on the availability of private-sector wealth and income but also on the willingness of residents and elected officials to appropriate enough of that wealth and income to meet a given level of governmental obligations.

In the short-term time frames related to cash and budgetary solvency, the U.S. Advisory Commission on Intergovernmental Relations (ACIR 1973, p. 3) defined a city financial *emergency* as the inability to maintain services because a lack of cash or appropriations authority prevents the city from paying obligations due. Municipal *defaults* are actual failures to meet financial obligations and can range from purely technical violations of debt covenants to slightly late payments to complete failures to make payments of principal or interest due.

In short, various constructs of fiscal health incorporate one or more of at least three time horizons—the very short term, the budget year, and periods longer than a year—and three kinds of fitness—paying financial obligations, supporting a desired level of service delivery, and doing so within the constraints of a given political economy. They also incorporate judgments about whether a government will be able to resist unwanted decreases in each kind of fitness over time—resiliency or sustainability—and whether it can make appropriate changes in resource acquisition and allocation in response to internal or external stimuli—flexibility. These individual normative concerns will vary in their precise meaning and relative importance according to any given stakeholder's role or relationship with a government and will be situated within a specific historical and spatial context. Thus a given fiscal characteristic may seem healthier at one time, or in one state or region, or in relation to the concerns of one stakeholder, than at another time or place or in the eye of a different beholder. This by no means implies that fiscal health is a meaningless notion—and the centrality of being able to pay for obligations from legally available resources is the stable core of every aspect of fiscal health in any event—only that its precise meaning, and therefore its operational definition and measurement, will not be exactly the same for every organization and stakeholder or even for the same organization at different times.

U.S. Historical Context: Salient Episodes and Responses

History does in fact appear to repeat itself, at least to some degree. The history of local-government finance in the United States includes several episodes of fiscal problems of varying causes and severity but with a number of recurring themes. These historical episodes have shaped the legal institutions, politics, and managerial practices of public budgeting and finance. Of particular interest for present purposes, historical events have also shaped practitioners' and academics' understandings of how to define, predict, and deal with fiscal health and stress. This section provides a very brief review of four salient episodes—bond defaults during the 19th century, the Great Depression, widespread fiscal distress of large cities in the 1970s and 1980s, and the most recent recession—as background for the following section's review of the literature on the causes of fiscal stress.

Nineteenth-Century Bond Defaults and Responses

Alberta Sbragia's *Debt Wish* (1996) provides a capsule history of some key events in 19th century municipal finance. State government bond defaults following the 1839 depression in the United States, which resulted from failures of both ability and willingness to repay, and the 1870s railroad bond defaults and repudiations by Southern states led to a consensus favoring the states' imposing borrowing restrictions on themselves in the forms of state constitutional limits on the issuance of state debt on behalf of private corporations as well as requirements for electoral approval of individual issues. The late 19th century also saw a trend toward the provision of more capital-intensive services by city governments, both for their own sake and as instruments of economic development, especially in the form of railroad-aid bonds. The resultant explosion of local-government debt and two waves of local-government defaults in the economic downturns that began in 1873 and 1893 (see ACIR, 1973, pp. 9–11) led states to adopt limits on local governments' borrowing ability.

Sbragia's account reveals that those limits on local borrowing—including referendum requirements, limits on permissible annual debt-service expenditures, and/or limits on aggregate outstanding bonded debt—worked both to control municipal indebtedness and to stimulate the design of inventive ways to circumvent the limits. For present purposes, one such technique of particular interest is the creation and use of public authorities and other off-balance-sheet entities. Together with local-government fragmentation (whether or not strategically motivated), this can foster the accumulation of very significant burdens of *overlapping debt*, which although not directly visible in total on the balance sheet of any individual entity, can represent a serious burden on the willingness and ability of taxpayers to support the operations and debt service of any or all of the overlapping entities. Thus actual as well as potential fiscal stress and emergencies precipitated by heavy debt burdens prompted both institutional controls to limit the risk of excessive debt and strategies to circumvent those safeguards. Circumvention strategies typically involve forms of public debt that draw on the same underlying private sector resources and willingness to pay as general-purpose local governments' general funds and other operating and investment funds but aren't reported in those funds' financial statements.

The Great Depression

During the Great Depression of the 1930s, U.S. cities' vulnerability to defaults resulted from rapid growth in service demands, heavy debt burdens, persistent structural budget deficits, slowness in reducing controllable costs, and reliance on short-term debt to finance deficits (ACIR, 1973). The ACIR concluded that a number of organizational policies and practices combined with the effects of the economic depression to bring about financial emergencies and to exacerbate them (p. 28). Factors leading to emergencies included revenue-expenditure imbalances in nondepression fiscal periods, poor budgeting and financial reporting, and high fixed debt-service expenditures relative to total expenditures. Once governments got into trouble, some exacerbated their difficulties by being slow to reduce controllable expenditures and by financing operating deficits with short-term debt.

Examining the fiscal landscape of the early 1970s, the ACIR noted that state governments tended to restrict the ability of local governments to raise tax revenues in response to economic downturns, forcing governments without very large reserves to rely on draconian expenditure cuts (or, as would become clear in the 1975 crisis of New York City, short-term borrowing). Perhaps unsurprisingly given the source, the ACIR argued strongly for the virtues of well-designed systems of state and federal intervention as both preventive measures and remedies for local financial emergencies.

Fiscal Stress and Cutback Management in the 1970s and 1980s

The late 1970s and early 1980s brought a wave of fiscal stress among large central cities, arguably driven by population migration, land-development trends, and recessions and stagflation as well as by urban political realities and political/managerial errors,[3] but compounded in at least some cases by taxpayer revolts that resulted in a variety of legal tax and expenditure limitations (TELs—see Maher and Deller in this volume). This period generated a large and largely insightful body of literature using a variety of research methodologies to understand, predict, explain, and recommend responses to urban fiscal (dis) stress (including but by no means limited to ACIR, 1985; Burchell and Listokin, 1981; Carr, 1984; Clark and Ferguson, 1983; Groves et al., 1981; Ladd and Yinger, 1989; Levine, 1978, 1979; Rubin, 1982).

One review of this literature (Pammer, 1990, Ch. 1) organized the explanations offered for fiscal strain into four categories. One group of explanations posited external factors such as economic decline and migration as the underlying causes of fiscal strain: the loss of businesses and higher-income households left cities with diminished revenue bases and at the same time populations in need of proportionately higher levels of public services (e.g., Howell, Stamm, and First National Bank of Boston. Economics Dept., 1979).[4] A second group blamed urban political culture, coalition politics, and the powerful political influence of public-employee unions for bloated city payrolls and low productivity. A related group of explanations in the public choice literature attributed fiscal trouble to bureaucratic expansion and clientelism in monopolistic bureaucracies and the self-interest of budget-maximizing bureaucrats (e.g., Borcherding, 1977; Downs, 1967). A fourth set of explanations focused on management problems including the short-term perspective of annual budgeting (Stanley, 1976), simple bad management (Martin, 1982), and vicious circles of decline (Rubin, 1987).

Although New York City is probably not typical of U.S. local governments, its experience over this period is instructive and even in some ways representative, and demonstrates the recurrence to some degree of history (for one concise account with a distinct point of view, see Weikart, 2009). In the years leading up to its 1975 default, the City, already burdened by significant fixed expenses and debt, and losing population and industry, expanded its scope of service provision, financed a structural deficit with short-term notes that it rolled over at year-end, and concealed much of this unsustainable behavior with poor financial reporting. A strict recovery regime was put in place and administered by the state, which resulted in significant short-term retrenchment. Even as the City's finances grew stronger and services and infrastructure spending were restored in the late 1980s and 1990s, structural deficits and heavy reliance on debt to support the city's capital program persisted.

From 1990 to the Present

U.S. local governments did fare better in the upturns of the 1990s, before the bursting of the dot-com bubble, and in the early 2000s before the bursting real estate bubble and subsequent financial crisis of 2008. Still, even before the 2007–2009 recession, we nonetheless seem to have become accustomed to the existence of seemingly permanent structural budget deficits and significant debt burdens in good times and in bad, often in the form of unfunded postemployment benefit obligations (see Dean Mead's and Jun Peng's chapters in this volume) as well as bonded debt (see chapters in this volume by Kriz and Wang, Yusuf et al., and Rassel and Kravchuk).

Great Recession

The 2007–2009 "Great Recession" and its aftermath have brought a handful of highly visible actual and potential defaults and bankruptcies attributable to debt in various forms, such as unfunded postemployment benefits (e.g., Vallejo, California), infrastructure-related debt (e.g., Harrisburg, Pennsylvania's incinerator project and a sewer system in Jefferson County, Alabama) and overly optimistic economic development projects (e.g., Alabama's VisionLand theme park). Significant concentrations of local government financial distress have occurred in states where real estate bubbles grew the most and fastest, such as Nevada and Florida, as well as in areas already burdened by economic malaise and population loss even during the 2002–2007 economic expansion, such as Michigan, where several cities had come under state control as of early 2011. In other words, all that was old is new again: the current round of fiscal problems (and the associated cutback management strategies—see Scorsone and Plerhoples in this volume) are varied but familiar in their mix of forms and causes. Heavy debt accumulations, fallout from the exuberance of rapid growth and economic boosterism, persistent fiscal strain resulting from more rapid growth (or less rapid decline) of spending demands than available willingness and ability to pay, external shocks or cycles (intergovernmental as well as economic), and political and managerial behaviors all appear still to be important shapers of fiscal health.

Modeling the Causes and Characteristics of Fiscal Stress

Conditions of fiscal health, stress, and strain generally result from a variety of environmental, political, and managerial factors, and from the interactions among those factors. Poor fiscal health may be attributed to environmental decline, environmental shocks, and/or to political and managerial failings that may include poor judgment, mal- or misfeasance, or failure by managers and elected officials to adapt the organization's patterns of resource acquisition and use to environmental conditions. It may also be in part or in whole a consequence of decisions made by current officials' and voters' predecessors, as in the 2009 bankruptcy of Vallejo, California, or New York City's famous 1975 fiscal crisis. Thus efforts to anticipate rather than simply react to fiscal stress must attempt to identify appropriate indicators of a government's relevant environmental and organizational as well as purely financial conditions. This complexity and interaction are compounded by the normative ambiguity of how to define fiscal health in the first place and by the descriptive and explanatory uncertainty associated with any effort to predict the future. Even authors who explicitly simplified their analysis by excluding political variables such as residents' willingness to pay taxes and fees, and the behavior of elected officials, observed, "Financial condition is a complex concept, reflecting a myriad of factors and requiring analysis and measurement along many dimensions. No single measure, formula, or rule of thumb is adequate to evaluate the financial complexities of governments. A multifaceted approach is needed" (Berne and Schramm, 1986, p. 373).

Any system for measuring and predicting fiscal health and stress therefore will build on an implicit or explicit model of fiscal health and its observable causes and effects. Following Jacob and Hendrick in the preceding chapter, we rely explicitly upon the premise that local-government organizations are *open systems*: entities that are influenced by, and in turn influence, their environments (also see Berne and Schramm, 1986; Clark, 1994; Clark and Ferguson, 1983; Groves et al., 2003; Hendrick, 2004). A local government's fiscal condition is determined by controllable and uncontrollable features of its environment, its elected officials' and employees' own behaviors and adaptation to that environment, and over time the changes in and continuous interactions among environmental and organizational characteristics and behaviors. Fiscal health and fiscal stress in any specific instance, then, may be attributable to any or all of: political, legal, social, economic, and natural environmental conditions; previous, current, and future organizational resources; previous, current, and future decisions by a jurisdiction's elected officials, managers, and citizens; the resulting obligations and expenditure requirements; and the complex interactions between a government organization's behavior and its environment over time. In short, elements found in any or all the four categories of explanation presented by Pammer (1990) are relevant influences on local government fiscal health, at least to some extent in some circumstances.

Given the complexity and multidimensionality of fiscal health, stress, and their causes, models of fiscal health can vary significantly in the degree and manner of representing and measuring the relevant constructs and their relationships. In this section, we provide a very brief overview of some of the types of variables and measures identified in the literature as relevant. The point is not to provide an exhaustive treatment, but to highlight that any type of indicator or measure is meaningful only in the context of some explanatory, or at least predictive, model that relates the measured variable to the aspects and determinants of organizational solvency or resiliency that are of greatest interest to the analyst.

One attractively intuitive and straightforward exposition of an open-systems model tied explicitly to a system of indicators of fiscal health is provided by the ICMA's FTMS (Groves et al., 1981; Groves et al., 2003). The current edition of the FTMS identifies 42 indicators in three categories of "factors affecting financial condition"—environmental, organizational, and financial—and three corresponding general analytic concerns (Groves et al., 2003, p. 6):

- "Does the external environment provide enough resources to pay for the demands it makes?"
- "Do management practices and legislative policies enable your government to respond appropriately to changes in the environment?"
- "Is your government paying the full cost of operating, or is it postponing costs to a future period when revenues may not be available to pay these costs?"

This three-part structure will serve as an organizing framework for our analysis.

Organizational Environments: Resources and Demands

A local government's environment generates both demands for spending and the wealth from which resources are drawn to satisfy those demands. Relevant aspects of a local government's environment include socioeconomic and demographic characteristics and their changes and trends over time; legal, political, and institutional (including intergovernmental) conditions, changes, and trends; and physical and natural conditions. Examples of socioeconomic and demographic conditions would include aggregate and per capita local wealth, generally measured for local-government purposes as the market value or assessed valuation of taxable property, income, and other measures of private-sector economic resources and "tax capacity" or "fiscal capacity" (e.g., ACIR 1990; Berry and Fording, 1997); conditions and trends in the larger economy; and demographic characteristics such as total population, average age and age distribution, education and poverty rates, homogeneity or heterogeneity of tastes and service needs, and migration patterns.

One interesting question raised by Wang, Dennis, and Tu (2007) is the role of socioeconomic factors in defining fiscal health or financial condition. Some authors have attempted to build fiscal stress measures by including socioeconomic adjustments (e.g., Ladd and Yinger, 1989). On the one hand, fiscal health may very well be related to conditions such as poverty, unemployment, housing conditions, age profile, and other factors. For example, an older population may require more transit oriented services or more frequent use of emergency medical services. On the revenue side, depending on the nature of the state's statutory framework, a community with a heavy presence of industrial and commercial property may generate more revenues than one that is without such facilities or more residential in nature. Although there is some research on these relationships, it is far from entirely clear the nature of the appropriate set of cause and effect pathways between socioeconomic variables and financial condition.

Wang, Dennis, and Tu (2007) assert that they are attempting to measure the financial condition of a government and that this differs from an analysis of factors that drive or determine financial condition. This is an important distinction, however, as to whether socioeconomic adjustments are in essence driving factors that explain financial condition but do not define financial condition or whether they should be used in effect to define the very essence of financial condition or fiscal health. Ladd (1989) uses socioeconomic factors such as the age of housing to make adjustments to expenditures. Her final measure of fiscal health uses socioeconomic variables to adjust both revenues and expenditures to compute an adjusted fiscal health index for American cities. This is a case where socioeconomic variables are used in the definition of fiscal health as opposed to being used as factors that explain fiscal health or financial condition.

Besides socioeconomic factors, political, legal and institutional elements would include local political culture(s) and tastes as well as those of the enclosing state government; the nature of and relationships among local and enclosing interest groups and political leadership (see Clark and Ferguson, 1983; Levine, Rubin, and Wolohojian, 1981; Rubin, 1982, and other examples of the large literature on fiscal stress of the 1970s and 1980s); specific intergovernmental policies adopted by other levels of government, such as mandates, grants-in-aid, or restrictions on local governments' powers of annexation (see Rusk, 1999); tax and expenditure limitations (see Maher and Deller, and Yusuf, Fowles, Grizzle, and Liu in this volume); laws stipulating local governments' freedom of action in other ways (e.g., Chapman, 2003); and the existence of overlapping jurisdictions that draw on the same tax bases or local economy, including the special districts sometimes created to circumvent debt or spending limits on general-purpose jurisdictions.

For example, Minge (1977) summarized some of the ways in which a local government's political and institutional environment, as expressed through law, can influence its fiscal health. Mandates unaccompanied by full funding constitute a kind of negative slack by requiring some portion of a jurisdiction's (necessarily finite) available resources to be allocated to the mandated purposes. Laws may also require certain minimum levels of spending for some of the discretionary activities local governments engage in. Local governments typically have access to only specified revenue bases, with that access often constrained through state-imposed limits on rates or revenues, and diluted through earmarking of specific revenues for specific purposes. The creation of overlapping jurisdictions constrains the local private sector's ability and willingness to pay for any one of the jurisdictions. And if Minge had been writing just a few years later, he might also have noted that limits on expenditures as well as on revenues can reduce a government's ability to maintain a constant level of services in the face of price or cost increases.

Finally, the physical environment—both built and natural, as well as the interactions between them—has implications for fiscal health and stress, both through risks of disasters and catastrophic losses and through longer term needs to build or restore infrastructure. In the United States, disasters in the first half of 2011 alone included levy-destroying floods and city-demolishing tornadoes, which imposed costs for disaster response in the short term and will require extended periods of expensive rebuilding at the same time as revenues are depressed in the wake of the devastation. The complex challenges to organizational risk preparedness and management in New Orleans during and after Hurricane Katrina in 2005, for example, illustrated some of the potential in any jurisdiction for interactions among risks associated with the natural environment, infrastructure, intergovernmental factors, demographic and socio-economic characteristics, and political cultures and institutions.

The FTMS groups environmental factors into five categories: community needs and resources, which help to determine the demand for and availability of resources to pay for local infrastructure and services (12 indicators are used to characterize this category); intergovernmental constraints such as mandates and TELs (two indicators); disaster risk (one indicator); political culture (no specific indicator is provided); and external *economic conditions* (no specific indicator).

Organizational Characteristics and Behavior

Stonecash and McAfee (1981) criticized some of the 1970s literature on urban fiscal stress as presuming the inevitability of a vicious circle of poverty → welfare spending → burdensome taxes → outmigration of the rich and middle class → worsening poverty operating on powerless local governments. As a corrective, they documented the differing fiscal responses of city governments to similar environmental conditions. Although their choice of illustrative cities—Newark, New Jersey, as the exemplar and New York City as the laggard—may seem ironic with 30 years' hindsight, the point remains valid: in spite of external constraints, local governments' managers and political leaders usually have at least some discretion and autonomy of action, and their choices will at least mediate even if they cannot obviate the effect of environmental conditions on fiscal performance.

Given the potential ability of innovative managers and political leaders to act to avoid or mitigate fiscal stress or crisis despite a tough socioeconomic environment, several relevant characteristics might provide guidance in understanding these situations. These conditions might include the organizational form of a local government and the quality of its management and leadership. Aspects of organizational performance relevant to fiscal health would include productivity and efficiency measures, the scope and variety of responsibilities and services provided, and the intensity of services, as well as any number of more specifically financial practices and policies. The FTMS focuses explicitly on financial "management practices and legislative [reflecting the ICMA's emphasis on council-manager forms of local government] policies."

Of course, even in the absence of economic strain or stress, poor management can undermine fiscal health. Troublesome financial management practices highlighted by the FTMS include a variety of behaviors that perpetuate structural deficits (such as using reserves or one-time accounting changes to balance annual operating budgets), defer current costs to future periods (such as underfunding maintenance or postemployment obligations), or ignore future costs associated with current decisions. Here the FTMS provides not indicators but a checklist for identifying whether, when, and with what consequences such practices have occurred (Groves et al., 2003, p. 149). These practices may be among the most important factors that lead to fiscal stress and even crisis in rich as well as poor jurisdictions and good times as well as bad.

Managerial decisions and practices are likely to be shaped in very large part by the policies and policy preferences expressed or implied by the elected officials governing an organization (and certainly this seems appropriate if we adhere to a norm of democratic administration). Policy preferences and policy guidance may be mutually contradictory, starkly unrealistic, oriented to short-term expediency at the expense of sustainability, or even entirely absent in ways that can have material influences on managerial choices and fiscal health, particularly as they sometimes interact with similarly incompatible or contingently unhelpful professional norms (e.g., Miller and Justice, 2011). At the same time, local managers and elected officials may undertake actions that prevent fiscal crisis even in the face of economic stress and collapse such as happened during the Great Recession of 2008–2009. Thus a complete model of fiscal health would incorporate financial management practices and the policy leadership and preferences of the elected officials or their appointees at the head of an organization.

Organization–Environment Fit and Financial Measures

Most frameworks for conceptualizing and measuring fiscal health are at root concerned with the current and future adaptation of a local government's organizational structure, policies, and practices to the demands and resources presented by its environment. The question of adaptation also introduces the matter of time (also see Jacob and Hendrick in this volume), as organizations over short or long periods of time reveal how well adapted they are by their continuing success or by their decline or demise. In the FTMS framework, cash solvency—the ability to pay financial obligations today—can be independent of budgetary or long-term solvency, as is implied for example by the focus on deficit-perpetuating financial practices. The notion of service-level solvency implies a qualitatively different kind of adaptation: not just the ability to meet financial obligations but also to accomplish the governments' mission at least to some minimally acceptable degree. Although the specific language and nuances of concepts vary among the various frameworks—the FTMS's four solvencies plus resiliency, PSAB's sustainability-flexibility-vulnerability, Hendrick's risk-balance-slack, Clark's fiscal strain, GASB's financial position-fiscal capacity-service capacity, and so on—the basic analytic problems are the same: whether a local government can pay its obligations, the costs of accomplishing its mission now, and how likely it is to continue doing so into the future.

Thus, for example, accumulations of slack in the form of financial reserves or untapped fiscal capacity may help a government cope with one-time natural and manmade disasters and shocks or maintain a fairly constant level of activity across seasonal and cyclical fluctuations in the environment, if its officials adopt appropriate policies and practices. An analyst might use measures of fund balance, unrestricted net assets, or even untapped debt or tax capacity to indicate this accumulation of slack (see Marlowe in this volume for an extended treatment of financial slack). Adapting to recurring cycles or shocks or to more monotonic long-term trends might require substantive structural change in policies and practices, including choices about the scope and level of services in the government's mission as well as more narrowly financial choices such as whether and how to institutionalize countercyclical financial policies. The FTMS measures adaptation using the multiyear trends of six categories of financial indicators: revenues and revenue characteristics (nine indicators, including a measure of reliance on intergovernmental aid), expenditures (five indicators), operating position (four indicators), debt (four indicators), unfunded postemployment liabilities (three indicators), and capital plant (two indicators). Other approaches have attempted to measure organizational fitness for purpose (e.g., Ladd and Yinger, 1989), tax effort, or the ratios of spending and revenue to local economic resources (e.g., Clark, 1994; Clark and Ferguson, 1983).

Practicalities of Diagnosis and Prediction

In measuring and predicting fiscal health and stress, as in other efforts to measure and predict complex phenomena, measurement and predictive validity, reliability, and timeliness are constrained by factors including the appropriateness of the measurement model and selected indicators; the scarcity of attention and analytic resources; data quality, relevance, timeliness, and availability; comparability across jurisdictions and time; uncertainty (of estimates, forecasts, and to some degree causality); and the normative ambiguity of the fiscal health construct itself. The accuracy and usefulness of indicators will also depend upon the timeliness and quality of the calculations used to convert those data into indicators and to compile those indicators into indexes or other summary judgments of fiscal health and stress. And however good the measurements may be in their own terms, their usefulness will ultimately be determined by the people and procedures in place for making use of them.

This section begins by discussing these considerations of measurement-system and individual-indicator quality and feasibility, including tradeoffs among them, with an eye to helping analysts and stakeholders select indicators and design systems of indicators appropriate to their particular needs and resources. We then provide a brief discussion—illustrative rather than exhaustive—of some additional practicalities of fiscal-health measurement, which together with the measurement systems and other resources cited in this chapter and the in-depth treatments of specific aspects of fiscal health and its measurement in subsequent chapters of this book, can help analysts to design (or select) appropriate measurement systems for their own needs. Given the complexity, ambiguity, and uncertainty involved, treating the evaluation of fiscal health from the perspective of a stakeholder-specific research-design problem is, we argue, a more broadly useful approach than any attempt to stipulate "one best way" would be.

Design Goals/Criteria

Two overarching design goals for a measurement approach are quality and feasibility. Quality in this instance means that a system of measures provides meaningful, valid, and reliable information to support decisions by a given stakeholder or category of stakeholders concerned with evaluating a single organization, multiple organizations, or an entire class of governments. Feasibility means that information of sufficiently high quality can be generated (and acted upon) using an acceptable level of data-gathering and analytic resources, attention, expertise, time, and money. Two helpful and complementary discussions of criteria-based approaches for choosing indicators and integrating them into systems for assessing fiscal health are those provided by Clark and Chan (1990), who focus on using a quantitative scoring system to evaluate individual indicators for possible inclusion in a measurement system, and Kloha, Weissert, and Kleine (2005a, p. 317), who use a more qualitative method to design an index of fiscal health based on several contributing indicators and intended to support state-government oversight. (We should note as well that the question of whether to combine multiple indicators into a composite index or category of health is another matter for the designer or chooser of a system to consider explicitly.) Honadle and Lloyd-Jones (1998) provide a useful case-based treatment of the process of selecting an indicator system for a client.

Quality can be divided into three subdimensions: usefulness, validity, and reliability. Usefulness to support decisions is a primary criterion of quality for any form of financial information (Finkler, 2009), including indicators and measures of fiscal health. Clark and Chan (1990) suggest that relevance is the most important of their seven criteria for choosing individual indicators and weight it to account for nearly a third of the total score for an indicator. They also include timeliness of the indicator's availability as a criterion but weight it lightly (at 2/33 of the total weight), at least for their specific example of designing a measurement system to assess aspects of fiscal health relevant to the municipal bond market with its focus on the long term. Kloha, Weissert, and Kleine (2005a) also place relevance as well as frequent availability of the data used to construct indicators among their nine index-design criteria. They additionally call out the need for the final measure of health to be available and comprehensible to relevant stakeholders—for their purposes this includes elected officials and the public in addition to technical specialists—and the importance of being able to predict fiscal stress before it occurs.

Validity refers to whether an indicator or composite evaluation is actually correct. Kloha, Weissert, and Kleine (2005a) emphasize three criteria related to validity: "theoretical validity"—whether a measure corresponds to some variable that is meaningful in the context of an established causal theory of fiscal stress—the ability to distinguish between fiscally healthy and unhealthy governments, and the ability of a measurement system to provide a "historical sense of the progression of difficulty." Clark and Chan (1990) identify freedom from bias (5/33 weight) and comparability (1/33 weight) as two criteria in this subcategory. (See the following discussion of comparison as the basic method of financial analysis, which clarifies why we treat comparability as a criterion of validity and why we would weight it more heavily than Clark and Chan do.)

Reliability refers to whether a measurement can be reproduced. The use of disclosed and widely available data and methods of calculation promotes reliability by permitting other analysts to reproduce measurements and analyses. We place Clark and Chan's (1990) verifiability (5/33 weight) and quantifiability (5/33) criteria in this subcategory, since both qualities facilitate the confirmation by repetition or by other analysts of indicator calculations and values (and in so doing, also promote comparability). Kloha, Weissert, and Kleine (2005a) call out resistance to manipulation and gaming as a distinct criterion here, and their emphasis on uniformity and public availability of data is also relevant to reliability.

Feasibility is the ability of an interested party actually to carry out and act upon the fiscal health or stress analysis. Clark and Chan (1990) identify the accessibility of data as a moderately important criterion (5/33). Kloha, Weissert, and Kleine (2005a) call for the use of "publicly available, uniform, and frequently available data" as a single criterion, which implicates feasibility (all three characteristics) as well as usefulness (frequent availability) and reliability (uniformity and public availability). One additional criterion of feasibility, not explicitly identified by either of our sources but implied at least to some degree by Kloha, Weissert, and Kleine's criterion of availability and comprehensibility, is that the computation and use of an indicator or composite measure not require greater investment of analytic resources—including money, time, expertise, and decision makers' attention—than justified by the quality and importance of the information generated. That is, it must be feasible to generate the information desired, and we do not want to devote resources to making information "better" than it needs to be for our purposes. (e.g., Mead's discussion of "fiscal" versus "financial" measures in Chapter 4 of this volume: the measurement needs of academic analysts trying to verify theories of fiscal stress across a multistate sample of local governments may justify the expenditure of more analytic and interpretive effort than would be required to suit the mixed-scanning needs of an oversight body interested in identifying the handful of local governments in their state that require further investigation.)

Design Considerations/Applications

Practical considerations for assessing fiscal health will probably include, although they will not be limited to, the types of decision rules to use, the information required by those decision rules, appropriate comparisons to make, and the data and computation requirements.

Decision rules, indicators, and indexes.

The choice of decision rule(s) associated with a measurement system is driven fundamentally by the intended use of those measurements. Indicators may be considered individually or they may be aggregated into a single composite index value, trading descriptive richness against parsimonious presentation. Decision rules may trigger a specific action, with or without allowing discretion on the decision maker's part, or they may simply provide advisory categorizations. Consider the examples of the systems used by two states—Michigan and North Carolina—to assess the fiscal health of their local governments.

Michigan's fiscal health index (Kleine, Kloha, and Weissert, 2003; Kloha et al., 2005a) combines 9 separate indicators into a composite index score of up to 10 points. The resulting point scores are used to categorize local governments as "fiscally healthy," "fiscal watch," "fiscal warning," or "fiscal emergency." In the Michigan example, these scores and the resulting categorizations are calculated annually by the state Treasury Department and made available on its website. The information does not trigger any mandatory action, but is used as one piece of a broader set of tools in assessing the existence of fiscal stress. An analogous kind of decision rule is bond ratings: they aggregate numerous items of analytic information in order to assign each rated entity to a published credit-quality category in a way that does not directly require specific responses[5] but might be used by a variety of stakeholders to make decisions about whether to buy bonds, what interest rate to demand, and so forth. Alternatively, a Michigan-type system could conceivably be used to mandate a specific response to a local government that appears in the fiscal warning or emergency category.

One advantage of compiling a single composite index number and set of categories, not limited to this example, is that it makes possible a simple decision rule that can be employed (once the index is designed and calculated, at any rate) by a nonspecialist. Disadvantages include the difficulties of combining multiple dimensions of a phenomenon into a single number both in terms of adequately weighting the relative importance of the various dimensions and in terms of identifying appropriate benchmark scores to trigger particular actions. Although the Michigan index was quite carefully designed to be an improvement on previously used indexes (see Kloha et al., 2005a), it has also been subject to considerable criticism regarding its validity (see Crosby and Robbins, 2010; Plerhoples and Scorsone, 2010).

These criticisms may have as much to do with the inherent difficulty of reducing a construct as contingent and multidimensional as fiscal health to a single index value as with any particular deficiencies of the Michigan index specifically. Hendrick noted that the multidimensionality of fiscal health and stress make it very difficult, if not impossible, to devise a single index for assessing them. The three dimensions she identified—environment, fiscal structure, and adaptation of structure to environment—and their several subdimensions all "may vary independently or in nonlinear ways" (2004, p. 85). Her solution was to develop four separate indices, each combining several indicator measures, encompassing local private-sector wealth, local service needs, fiscal balance, and fiscal slack. Computation of index values for a sample of Chicago suburbs demonstrated that the relationships among the dimensions and subdimensions were sufficiently complex to frustrate efforts to compile a unidimensional index.

North Carolina's system of overseeing local governments' fiscal health (Coe, 2007) by contrast emphasizes individual scrutiny of local governments by an office of professional experts. A variety of individual indicators—of both *financial condition* as revealed by financial reports and the quality of financial reporting itself—are used by staff of the state's Local Government Commission to identify cases requiring intervention. Types of intervention include sending "white letters" to call local governments' attention to reporting deficiencies, sending "unit letters" requiring local governments to identify and take action to correct material financial problems, providing direct technical assistance, issuing warnings of possible takeovers, and actual state interventions when necessary. This system relies on multiple individual indicators, professional judgment, and a more complex and qualitative decision rule, rather than a single composite index and categorizations based on a single point score. Advantages of this kind of measurement system include its flexibility and direct linkage to a variety of proactive responses. Possible concerns include the need for expert staffing and the importance of uniformly well qualified staff and well documented procedures to ensure and demonstrate reliability and validity in assessments of fiscal health and the appropriateness of the responses to assessments.

Making comparisons.

"Almost all of financial analysis involves comparisons of one sort or another. Measures of a government's financial condition are compared with experts' standards, legal ceilings or floors, measures for the same organization at different points in time, and measures for a set of similar organizations" (Berne and Schramm, 1986, p. 85). Measures by and large are meaningless out of context: Is a given value cause for concern or congratulations? What response is appropriate, if any? Any useful interpretation of measures or indicators takes place in the context of specific legal or financial benchmarks, somewhat less precise rules of thumb, changes or stability over time, and/or relative positions and rankings among peer organizations.

For example, one commonly used balance-sheet indicator of cash solvency is the quick ratio—highly liquid assets such as cash, marketable securities, and receivables, divided by current liabilities. Let us say we calculate the quick ratio for a government to be 1.2. Knowing that a common generic rule of thumb is that the quick ratio should be at least 1.0 lets us interpret the value 1.2 as probably being acceptable. Comparing this year's 1.2 to last year's 1.3 and the 1.4 of two years ago, on the other hand, might lead us to conclude that the trend is unfavorable. Knowing that peer jurisdictions were generally similar in both their present ratios and recent trends, however, might alleviate somewhat our concern about the negative trend. On the other hand, if our quick ratio is 0.8, and that puts us squarely in the center of our peer group, we might worry about the entire category of organizations, including our own. Alternatively, we might shrug it off, if we have reason to think that values as low as 0.8 are in fact acceptable for governments of our type, size, environment, scope of responsibilities, and/or even particular timings of fiscal year-end and property tax due dates (since balance sheets may be compiled at an extreme point in the annual cycle of cash disbursements and revenue collections).

This simple example illustrates the principle and at the same time raises the question of competing bases of comparison. Can one form of comparison suffice? What are the best peer organizations, rules of thumb, or benchmarks to use as references for cross-sectional or longitudinal comparisons? What are the appropriate intervals or points in time for longitudinal comparisons, taking into account seasonal and cyclical patterns of variation as well as long-term trends? Are multiple types of comparison required? How can we choose among different approaches to comparison or between comparisons of the same indicator that point to different interpretations? All of these questions must be addressed, implicitly or explicitly, by the designer of a fiscal stress or health measurement system.

For example, Kleine, Kloha, and Weissert (2003) criticized Brown's (1993; 1996) 10-point test for providing only a relative ranking for each of its measures—comparison to a peer group. Their solution, a mix of absolute indicators (e.g., whether population has decreased from the previous year) and comparisons to means and standard deviations for peers, has in turn been criticized for failing to compare indicator values to specific normative benchmarks (see Crosby and Robbins, 2010). In part, this reflects the concern that a government that is doing well by the standards of a peer group on the verge of collective bankruptcy might well itself be in serious trouble. It also reflects the difficulty of identifying appropriate peers, in light of local governments' widely varying historical and environmental contexts and service mixes (Chaney, Mead, and Schermann, 2002, illustrate this effectively), differing legal requirements and scope of government from state to state (see Minge, 1977), and different political and managerial responses to environmental conditions (see Stonecash and McAfee, 1981).

Further, both the Brown and the Kloha et al. systems were developed before the full implementation of the Governmental Accounting Standards Board's Statement 34 (GASB 34), and therefore rely on financial measures based on governments' general funds, which typically account for the single largest share, but not necessarily a large majority, of a government's operating activities. As Chaney, Mead, and Schermann note, "[T]he inherent flexibility of fund accounting often results in governments reporting similar programs in different fund types or spread across multiple funds. This can seriously threaten an analyst's ability to make comparisons" (2002, p. 26). One solution is to use as data sources financial statements that comply with generally accepted accounting principles (GAAP), which now that GASB 34 is fully effective include accrual-basis statements of government-wide net assets and activities (revenues and expenses). This solves the problem that different local governments will have different fund structures, but introduces some challenges of its own.

First, even under current GAAP, "governments of similar size and geographic location may not be comparable if they have drastically different revenue sources or operating issues or have chosen different accounting options (such as the modified approach to depreciating infrastructure assets)" (Chaney et al., 2002, p. 30). Second, not all local governments produce GAAP-compliant financial reports: some states require their local governments to do so, and governments active in the bond market are likely to do so, but GASB research suggests that half or more of U.S. local governments do not (Mead, 2008). Third, governmentwide indicators can obscure troubled funds (Crosby and Robbins, 2010). Finally, challenges to the comparability as well as entity-specific validity of GAAP and non-GAAP data sources alike include the question of how to factor in overlapping debt, certificates of participation (COPs), and other forms of debt that affect local governments or their taxpayers but do not appear on their financial statements.

Additional complications arise in the form of variations among local governments in their revenue capacity and effort, service quality and scope of services, and their interactions with environmental demands and political expectations. A number of approaches are possible for calculating standardized benchmarks, such as the representative tax system, representative revenue system, total taxable resources measure, representative expenditure indexes, and inventories of common municipal functions. Challenges to be taken into account in employing such standardized models include complexities in calculating and using them, and the need to factor in inter- and intrastate idiosyncrasies of history, political culture, and preferences. These complications have generally prevented any of these approaches from being placed into widespread use. They generally run afoul of the feasibility criterion for system designers (see Mead, Chapter 4 in this volume, on "fiscal" versus "financial" approaches to analysis).

One further problem with cross-sectional comparisons is the inherent ambiguity of some indicators. For example, are high revenues per capita a healthy sign, indicating good resource availability in the environment (Petro, 1998), or a worrisome indication that a local government has reached the limits of its citizens' willingness to pay taxes? Indeed, a case can be made that virtually all purely cross-sectional measures are inadequate as the sole means for assessing fiscal health beyond the current fiscal period (cash and budgetary solvency) and that only longitudinal measures can support confident inferences about fiscal health and stress in the long term (Stonecash and McAfee, 1981, pp. 390–391). For example, the FTMS by design avoids cross-sectional comparisons almost entirely, focusing instead on identifying multiyear trends in a variety of financial, environmental, and adaptation dimensions. Here, "The emphasis is put on the analyst's professional experience, knowledge of the city, and judgment. With the exception of credit industry benchmarks for six of the indicators, [the FTMS offers] no standards by which a city could measure the existence or magnitude of a problem" (Groves, Godsey, and Shulman, 1981, p. 18). But this potentially significant reduction in ambiguity of measurement and the attendant gains in validity come at the price of potentially greater ambiguity of interpretation, since it is up to the individual analyst or local government to supply interpretive guidelines for evaluating the significance of the trends and judging when their current values are such that a particular evaluation and response is appropriate.

Less open-ended forms of longitudinal indicator include measures of the changes from one period to another of some cross-sectional indicator. These might be changes in financial or fiscal strain ratios, in common-size or per capita ratios, or in relative rankings within a comparison group. They might indicate simply whether a value or ranking increased or decreased over the period, what the magnitude or rate of change was over the period, or whether the change was significantly more or less than some benchmark or group average.

Challenges for using longitudinal measures, especially in forms less open ended than the FTMS, include the challenges of gathering consistent and comparable data for multiple periods of time, and accounting for inflation and seasonal and cyclical patterns. Failure to take inflation into account can result in misinterpretation of trends. For example, a nominal (unadjusted for inflation) increase of 3% in total revenues or expenditures from one year to the next is actually a decrease in real (adjusted for inflation) terms if inflation exceeded three percent. Adjustments for inflation can make indicator values more comparable over time. Cyclical variations due to the ordinary business cycle are perhaps the most troublesome if unacknowledged but also perhaps the easiest to be prepared for. For example, knowing that the United States experienced a severe recession from late 2007 to early 2009 would help the analyst put into context a decrease in real income-tax revenues from 2007 to 2010: worrisome, perhaps, but probably attributable to economic conditions rather than financial mismanagement. Typical advice here is to compare values at similar points in the business cycle—such as peak to peak or trough to trough—whenever possible.

Data and calculations: Sources, and quality.

The problem of gaining access to appropriate and timely data on local finances should not be underestimated in designing a fiscal stress or health system. Some states have provided this data on a timely and electronic basis (e.g., Pennsylvania, Colorado, and Michigan), while others have not. GAAP-compliant reporting is available for up to half of local governments in the United States (Mead, 2008), mostly the larger ones and those in states with legal requirements for GAAP compliance, and usually within six months of year-end (Mead, 2011). Thus, data availability remains a major challenge to local government fiscal stress analysis systems, especially those meant to assess large numbers of smaller governments.

For example, the FTMS is plainly designed for use within a local government and not with an eye to supporting external oversight. It requires access to and analysis of an enormous amount of information, much of which is not contained in annual financial reports or other publicly available sources, as well as significant time and attention on the part of analysts and decision makers. This simply raises the question of how and where data are obtained for such analysis. In some states, this type of analysis may require extremely time consuming data entry from individual reports.

Revenue and spending data are not the only potential problem. Measurement of debt and other noncurrent liabilities can be a challenge as well. Crosby and Robbins (2010, p. 15) found inconsistent reporting by Michigan local governments of debt service payments and of what kinds of future obligation were reported as noncurrent liabilities. There is also the question of whether to measure debt service as an accrual-type interest expense or as a budgetary cash-flow measure of principal and interest combined. Crosby and Robbins also found inconsistencies in whether various types of accrued obligations to employees for unused compensated absences were reported as liabilities. In states with highly specific legal requirements for reporting, this may be less an issue if the analyst uses the state-required reports, although possibly with the tradeoff that such information may not conform to GAAP.

There is also the question of how to treat off-balance sheet debt such as bonds issued by special districts associated with a general-purpose government, other overlapping debt, and various "nondebt" forms of long-term liabilities such as certificates of participation (COPs) and postemployment obligations (see Mead, Chapter 6 in this volume, for some indicators that could be used for postemployment obligations). All of these challenges mean that the problem of data availability should not be overlooked. The best conceptual fiscal stress or health system cannot function without appropriate access to data.

Indicator and index validation.

As Hendrick (2004, pp. 105–107) noted, research and indicator systems to date have not conclusively resolved the question of how to map short-term measures of fiscal health to longer term fiscal sustainability and resilience, particularly in light of the uncertainties associated with predicting the size and timing of the business cycle as well as one-time natural, political, and economic events with implications for governments' solvency. In part this is due to the relative rarity since the 1930s of observations of the dependent variable of interest: municipal defaults and other fiscal emergencies (Clark, 1977). Over the period 2007–2009, however, the United States has experienced the most severe recession since the 1930s. The current combination of financial turmoil, economic downturn, and accumulated postemployment liabilities may produce large enough numbers of fiscal emergencies and defaults to test the predictive and corrective abilities of the systems for identifying and predicting fiscal stress currently in use.

There are also a number of precedents for testing the validity of measurement approaches without waiting for new problems to emerge. Validation approaches include retrospective case studies, correlation analyses, and regression and other statistical models testing the ability of indicators to predict defaults or other fiscal emergencies (e.g., ACIR, 1973; Kloha et al., 2005a; or the prediction models of nonprofits' demise cited by Greenlee and Tuckman, 2007); simulation testing of local governments' ability to withstand cyclical and other environmental challenges and financial risks (e.g., Snow, Gianakis, and Fortess, 2008); comparison of indicator and index values or interpretations to those of other accepted indicators and indices (e.g., Hendrick, 2004; Honadle and Lloyd-Jones, 1998); and judgmental assessments of face, construct, and predictive validity by practitioners and academics (e.g., Kloha et al., 2005a, 2005b).

Some Construction Notes

Given the foregoing discussion, we have no intention of recommending a specific system of measurement or even a particular approach to measuring fiscal health or fiscal stress. What we can offer is a rudimentary framework of considerations as a starting point to structure the choice or design of a measurement system, including some brief notes on some data sources and several practitioner-oriented systems and techniques that can be approached both as potential systems and as sources of raw materials—concepts, models, measures, and methods—that might serve as inspiration and building blocks for one's own design.

The starting point for design will generally be to define the system's purpose and audience(s) as well as its core concept(s) of fiscal health, which generally will be both audience- and purpose-specific, and to place those considerations in the context of available data and analytic resources. Then individual indicators, indexes, interpretive benchmarks, and procedures for acting upon them can be developed. A first concern of course is to identify the core concept(s) of health at issue: does it include maintaining service levels as well as meeting financial commitments? And does it include doing so without increasing the governments' demands on total local economic resources and/or without requiring assistance from higher levels of government? Or is the primary focus simply to avoid defaults or severe financial emergencies? How far forward in time should fiscal health be predicted (and how feasible is it to make valid projections over the desired period)?

Second, what types of decisions, decision makers, and interventions does the system need to support? For instance, is the system intended for use by an oversight body or other external entity concerned with large numbers of governments, such as a state or independent fiscal office or a citizen organization? Or, at the other extreme, is it aimed at analyzing a single local government? Is there a preference for leaning toward pessimism or optimism about governments' fiscal health in the absence of perfect certainty? Is the apparent precision of an index with categories such as fiscal watch and fiscal emergency necessary for use by decision makers or to justify their actions, or is a more openly judgment-based approach such as that of the FTMS satisfactory? How much information and what presentations of information are appropriate to the relevant decision makers, given their technical backgrounds and available time and attention? Is the analysis a one-time project, or is the intention to implement an ongoing system of analysis?

Finally, given the basic goals of measurement, system design also has to take into account basic considerations of resource availability and feasibility. What levels of expertise and staffing are available to support the system? What kinds of budgetary and financial reporting and databases are routinely available to the relevant analysts and decision makers concerning the subject local government(s)? Data will also usually be required on aspects of the organizational environment: economic and demographic conditions; legal, institutional and political variables; and other conditions relevant to the analyst's particular concerns and conception of fiscal health.

The PSAB (2007, para. 32) and CICA (1997, p. 12) distinguish three types of indicators. "Government specific" indicators are those that require only data on government finances, such as those available from government financial reports. Financial ratios (quick, current, debt-to-assets, times-interest-earned, and so on) are one common type of government specific indicator. "Government related" indicators combine government financial data with information about the government's environment (here we have broadened slightly the CICA/PSAB language, expanding from "economy" to include other aspects of a government's environment, and we include examples CICA might not consider relevant to their concept of financial condition). Examples might include ratios such as debt per capita or as a share of taxable assessed valuation, measures of specific local vulnerability to environmental or man-made disasters (such as the availability of cash reserves and debt capacity to respond to and reconstruct after hurricanes in Florida or tornadoes in Oklahoma), or Clark's measures of fiscal strain. Finally, "economywide" indicators use data about aspects of the government's environment that directly affect financial condition, such as demographics, income and gross product, inflation, or tax and expenditure limitations.

Aimed at analysts and decision makers within local governments themselves, the FTMS (Groves et al., 1981, 2003) is one valuable resource, both for its 42 trend indicators and several additional measures and criteria, and for its helpful discussions of data sources, inflation adjustments, and other basic considerations of analysis. Challenges to implementation of the full FTMS include the lack of exact interpretive guidance previously noted, the need to calculate large numbers of indicators for several years, and its reliance on internal sources of data. The available edition of the FTMS at this writing also does not make use of the governmentwide statements now included in GAAP-compliant financial reports. External as well as internal analysts will nevertheless find the FTMS useful as a source of ideas and techniques. For one case study of adapting the FTMS to suit a specific organization's needs, see Genito (2005). Another venerable system oriented to internal analysts and trend-based measures was developed in the late 1970s by the Small Cities Financial Management Project and includes detailed guidance for calculating 28 different indicators (Rosenberg and Stallings, 1978).

Useful resources for analysts willing and able to devote significant resources to each local government and interested in making use of the information provided in GAAP-compliant financial reports include the generic approaches and numerous indicator and ratio calculations offered by Ives (2006) and Mead (2001a), as well as Mead's (2001b) school district-specific system of 33 ratios and interpretive guidance. As with the FTMS, these systems may be adopted in whole or in part or used as sources of raw material for the development of an original measurement system.

Several systems have been designed to calculate overall indexes or relative rankings of fiscal health using a dozen or fewer individual indicators. Brown's (1993; 1996) original 10-point test was designed to allow internal analysts to compare their own jurisdictions to peer governments, taking advantage of the databases of local-government financial indicators compiled and made available for purchase each year by the Government Finance Officers Association. Subsequent work has criticized this system for being purely relative (Kloha et al., 2005a) and defended and updated it (Maher and Nollenberger, 2009). Mead (2006) proposed an alternative set of indicators that rely on governmentwide data from GAAP-compliant financial reports, rather than the fund-based indicators in the original 10-point test.

For external oversight, several recent articles propose and critique indexes and systems of indicators and oversight for state governments (Coe, 2007, 2008; Crosby and Robbins, 2010; Kleine et al., 2002, 2003; Kloha et al., 2005a, 2005b; Plerhoples and Scorsone, 2010). Although it is focused on state governments and the details of its construction and data sources are not specified, Moody's (2010) U.S. states credit scorecard illustrates one potentially useful approach to choosing and integrating 14 indicators of political economy and environment as well as financial variables into an overall index value and ranking.

Other systems developed for external analysis include the elaborate, pre-GASB 34 system developed by Terry Clark and colleagues to assess fiscal strain and its determinants (e.g., Clark, 1977, 1994; Clark and Ferguson, 1983) and several simpler, pre-GASB 34 (e.g., Hughes and Laverdiere, 1986) and post-GASB 34 systems (e.g., Wang et al., 2007).

English-language accounts of systems or lists of indicators and concepts with international applications are also readily available for countries including Australia (Local Government Association of South Australia, 2006), Canada (CICA, 1997; PSAB, 2007), Spain (Zafra-Gomez, Lopez-Hernandez, and Hernandez-Bastida, 2009a, 2009b), and Thailand (Krueathep, 2007).

Conclusion

We may find ourselves slightly disappointed, even if not at all surprised, to acknowledge that there is unlikely to be a magic solution to the problem of measuring and predicting fiscal stress. It seems possible that cash and budgetary solvencies can in many cases be adequately evaluated by well designed and well implemented cross-sectional financial indicators, such as ratio measures of financial position, financial performance, and liquidity, particularly in cases where GAAP-compliant financial statements are available for local governments (for more on this point, see Chapter 4, "The Development of External Financial Reporting and Its Relationship to the Assessment of Fiscal Health and Stress" in this volume). Except in instances where catastrophic political dysfunction prevents officials from conducting the normal business of adopting and executing budgets (see Stonecash and McAfee, 1981, p. 392), cross-sectional measures of this type can tell us with reasonable confidence whether a government can pay its bills in the current period. Long-term and service-level solvency, however, are harder to evaluate, even with the use of well designed longitudinal measures, given the very large array of environmental and organizational uncertainties and contingencies that can influence local governments' fiscal health and adaptation over time. That said, evolving accounting standards continue to improve the quality and availability of decision-relevant information under GAAP (see Chapters 4 and 6 in this volume, "The Development of External Financial Reporting and Its Relationship to the Assessment of Fiscal Health and Stress" and "Postemployment Benefits and Fiscal Analysis").

Although it seems reasonable therefore to employ indicators, either individually or aggregated into indexes, as a way to identify cases that require either further investigation or immediate takeover, it is unlikely that any system of indicators can substitute for case-specific analysis in efforts to identify threats to fiscal health in future periods. In efforts to evaluate long-term or service-level solvency, indicators will in most cases best serve to alert the analyst to governments—or even to specific aspects of a specific government's finances and environmental (mal)adaptation—that merit more extensive scrutiny and, if appropriate, fiscal intervention or another response. In other words, a mixed-scanning approach seems to be called for in most cases, for internal as well as external analysts.

In fact, as Coe (2007, 2008) has observed in extolling the virtues of the North Carolina state government's system of municipal financial oversight, it is not the specific financial indicators used or even the precise system within which those indicators are employed that makes North Carolina a model. Rather it is that North Carolina's system employs a mixed-scanning model that uses locally meaningful measures constructed from readily available data as one component of an integrated system of people, information, and procedures. The "best practices" here are the systematic tailoring of indicators and their use to the stakeholder's specific needs and information-gathering and -analysis resources (and vice versa), and the incorporation of those indicators into a larger system of adaptive and case-specific investigation, judgment, and response. Accordingly, although we cannot stipulate one best way for all readers, we hope that this chapter, together with the in-depth treatment of the various dimensions and determinants in subsequent chapters of this volume, can serve as a resource for concerned oversight officials, citizens, local-government officials, and others who wish to understand, improve, or design situationally appropriate systems for evaluating and responding to fiscal health.

Recommended Resources

Selected sources of general guidance for public-sector fiscal/financial literacy and analysis

Old and out of print, Berne and Schramm's (1986) *The Financial Analysis of Governments* is nevertheless still an enormously useful and widely cited textbook/guide for understanding and assessing fiscal health. Currently available textbooks include Finkler's (2009) financial management-focused text, which includes good chapters on reading government financial reports for U.S. state and local governments and analyzing governments' financial condition, and Mikesell's (2010) public finance-oriented text, which provides good and relatively nontechnical discussions of taxes and U.S. fiscal institutions.

GASB's User Guides series of books are inexpensive and accessible guides to interpreting and analyzing U.S. GAAP-compliant state and local government financial reports. The *Analyst's Guide* (Mead, 2001a) and the guide to notes and supplemental information (Mead, 2005) will be of greatest interest for the analyst. The series also includes full length and condensed volumes oriented to general, nonspecialist audiences. See www.gasb.org.

Selected sources of guidance and data for fiscal health specifically

In addition to this volume and the sources cited in the Some Construction Notes section of this chapter, Hendrick (2004) provides a systematic review of many academic as well as practitioner-oriented systems of fiscal health measurement, keyed to a conceptual framework very similar to the one laid out by Jacob and Hendrick in Chapter 2 of this volume. Honadle, Cigler, and Costa's (2004) *Fiscal Health for Local Governments* provides a comprehensive and accessible overview of the topic. The PSAB's (2009) completed project web page at http://www.psab-ccsp.ca/projects/completed-projects/pf_item14561.aspx provides an overview of PSAB's indicators project, a clearly written and very useful statement of principles (PSAB, 2007), and a link to the executive summary of the original CICA (1997) research report.

Endnotes

1. In fact, one author contributing to this volume has suggested, and we are inclined to agree, that fiscal health is so complex and contingent that it is as much a normative construct as a descriptive one (B. Jacob, personal communication, July 29, 2010). As with human health, the fiscal health of a given local government at any one time can be assessed in any number of ways, at least up until the point of actual default, insolvency, or massive service cuts and layoffs such as those in Camden, New Jersey (Katz, 2011), or some other type of fiscal crisis.
2. While the four solvencies form a roughly ascending hierarchy of degrees of health, they can also be somewhat independent of each other. It may be that our government can easily pay its bills this week (healthy in terms of cash solvency) but will have to reduce service levels below the locally preferred level in order to continue doing so over time (stressed in terms of service-level solvency). Also possible is the case of an organization with reasonable long-term and service-level solvencies that faces a short-term cash-flow mismatch that results in cash insolvency.
3. New York City's 1975 default, for example, came about in large part as the result of a heavy debt burden, major expansion in service expenditure commitments, persistent structural deficits, poor cost control, and politically expedient but fiscally unsustainable reliance on short-term debt to finance recurring operating deficits.
4. A contemporary extension of this might be the recent attention to the "shrinking cities" phenomenon as cities such as Detroit and St. Louis find themselves with populations (and so revenue bases) much smaller than in their heydays, but spread over the same land area, so that they still have to maintain the same extent of infrastructure and serve the same land area as when their populations were two or three times as great.

5. It is true, however, that bond ratings can indirectly dictate action to the extent that some investors are required either by federal or state regulatory requirements or by their own policies not to hold bonds rated below the BBB threshold that defines "investment grade" instruments.

Glossary

Default: failure by a creditor, such as a government bond issuer, to meet one or more of its obligations under the terms of credit. Defaults can range from fairly minor technical violations of promises made to lender and bondholders, such as maintaining a certain financial practice or ratio, to failures to pay principal or interest due.

Economic condition: According to GASB (n.d.), "Economic condition is a composite of a government's financial health and its ability and willingness to meet its financial obligations and commitments to provide services. Economic condition includes three components: financial position [assets, liabilities, and net assets], fiscal capacity [ability and willingness to meet financial obligations], and service capacity [ability and willingness to meet service obligations]." Note that this definition explicitly incorporates willingness as well as ability to meet obligations. For purposes of this chapter, economic condition is broadly synonymous with fiscal health or financial condition.

Financial condition: defined by Berne (1992, p. 17) as "the probability that a government will meet both its financial obligations to creditors, consumers, employees, taxpayers, suppliers, constituents, and others as they become due and its service obligations to constituents, both currently and in the future." Note that this definition implicitly incorporates willingness as well as ability to meet obligations. Elements of financial condition include sustainability, flexibility, and vulnerability (see CICA, 1997; PSAB, 2007). For purposes of this chapter, financial condition is treated as broadly synonymous with fiscal health or economic condition although the elements and indicators identified by the PSAB do emphasize long-term and service-level solvencies somewhat more than cash or budgetary solvencies.

Financial emergency: a government's inability to maintain services because a lack of cash or appropriations authority prevents it from paying obligations due.

Fiscal health: subject to a given stakeholder's specific interests and concerns, fiscal health is defined by a government's ability to meet its financial and/or service-provision commitments over a variety of time periods. One widely employed framework articulates fiscal health in terms of four organizational fiscal abilities, or "solvencies": (1) the ability to meet immediate financial obligations such as paying vendor invoices and salaries (*cash solvency*); (2) the ability to meet all the organization's financial obligations over the course of a given budget year (*budgetary solvency*); (3) the ability to meet all financial obligations in future periods (*long-run solvency*); and (4) the ability to finance the provision of a quantity and quality of services adequate for "the general health and welfare of a community"(Groves et al., 1981, p. 6) (*service-level solvency*). For purposes of this chapter, fiscal health, financial condition, and economic condition are all treated as broadly synonymous.

Fiscal stress: a government's actual or potential failure to satisfy one or more of the conditions of fiscal health that define fiscal health for a given government and stakeholder(s).

Fiscal strain: a maladaptation of an organization's financial structure and choices to the availability of private-sector resources in its fiscal environment (see Clark, 1994). Fiscal strain occurs when a government has entered into commitments that are not fiscally sustainable over time in its relevant political economy (private sector wealth, intergovernmental resources, and political culture and institutions).

Overlapping debt: debt held or incurred by government organizations other than the immediate subject of analysis, but which will draw on the same underlying base of private-sector resources for payment of principal and interest. For example, if we are concerned with a specific municipal government, we may also be concerned with debt issued by the enclosing county government as well as the three independent school districts and four special-district governments that cover some or all of the municipality's geographic jurisdiction, since they will draw on the same base of private sector wealth.

Solvency: *See* "Fiscal Health."

Discussion Questions

1. What are the critical trade-offs facing a designer of a fiscal stress system? What factors would shape a designer's decision to go in one direction or another? (These questions might be best answered in a specific decision-making context.)
2. What is and what should be the role of external socioeconomic forces in shaping a fiscal stress analysis system? What are the problems of building a fiscal stress system that ignores socioeconomic factors?
3. What are the advantage and disadvantages of a cross-sectional versus a longitudinal analysis of fiscal stress? Is one approach inherently better than another? Can they be combined?

References

Advisory Commission on Intergovernmental Relations. (1973). *City financial emergencies: The intergovernmental dimension*. Washington, DC: U.S. Government Printing Office.

Advisory Commission on Intergovernmental Relations. (1985). *Bankruptcies, defaults, and other local government financial emergencies* (No. A-99). Washington, DC: U.S. Government Printing Office.

Advisory Commission on Intergovernmental Relations. (1990). State fiscal capacity and effort 1990. Retrieved June 27, 2011, from http://purl.access.gpo.gov/GPO/LPS28323

Berne, R. (1992). *The relationships between financial reporting and the measurement of financial condition*. Norwalk, CT.: Governmental Accounting Standards Board of the Financial Accounting Foundation.

Berne, R., and Schramm, R. (1986). *The financial analysis of governments*. Englewood Cliffs, NJ: Prentice-Hall.

Berry, W. D., and Fording, R. C. (1997). Measuring state tax capacity and effort. *Social Science Quarterly, 78*(1), 158–166.

Borcherding, T. E. (Ed.). (1977). *Budgets and bureaucrats: The sources of government growth*. Durham, NC: Duke University Press.

Brown, K. W. (1993). The 10-point test of financial condition: Toward an easy-to-use assessment tool for smaller cities. *Government Finance Review, 9*(6), 21–27.

Brown, K. W. (1996). Trends in key ratios using the GFOA Financial Indicators Databases 1989–1993. *Government Finance Review, 12*(6), 30–34.

Burchell, R. W., and Listokin, D. (1981). *Cities under stress: The fiscal crises of urban America*. Piscataway: Center for Urban Policy Research, Rutgers, the State University of New Jersey.

Canadian Institute of Chartered Accountants. (1997). Indicators of government financial condition. Retrieved July 7, 2011, from http://www.cica.ca/research-and-guidance/research-activities/other-publications/archives—studies/item13035.pdf

Carr, J. H. (Ed.). (1984). *Crisis and constraint in municipal finance: Local fiscal prospects in a period of uncertainty*. New Brunswick, NJ: Center for Urban Policy Research.

Chaney, B. A., Mead, D. M., and Schermann, K. R. (2002). The new governmental financial reporting model: What it means for analyzing government financial condition. *The Journal of Government Financial Management, 51*(1), 26–31.

Chapman, J. I. (2003). Local government autonomy and fiscal stress: The case of California counties. *State and Local Government Review, 35*(1), 15–25.

Clark, T. N. (1977). Fiscal management of American cities: Funds flow indicators. *Journal of Accounting Research, 15*, 54–94.

Clark, T. N. (1994, June). Municipal fiscal strain: Indicators and causes. *Government Finance Review, 10*, 27–30.

Clark, T. N., and Chan, J. L. (1990). Monitoring cities: Building an indicator system for municipal analysis. In T. N. Clark (Ed.), *Monitoring local governments: How personal computers can help systematize municipal fiscal analysis* (pp. 63–161). Dubuque, IA: Kendall/Hunt Publishing Company.

Clark, T. N., and Ferguson, L. C. (1983). *City money: Political processes, fiscal strain, and retrenchment*. New York: Columbia University Press.

Coe, C. K. (2007). Preventing local government fiscal crises: The North Carolina approach. *Public Budgeting & Finance, 27*(3), 39–49.

Coe, C. K. (2008). Preventing local government fiscal crises: Emerging best practices. *Public Administration Review, 68*(4), 759-767.

Crosby, A., and Robbins, D. (2010, April). *An evaluation of Michigan's fiscal indicator scores*. Paper presented at the Midwest Political Science Association Annual Conference, Chicago.

Danziger, J. N. (1991). Intergovernmental structure and fiscal management strategies: A crossnational analysis. *Governance, 4*(2), 168–183.

Downs, A. (1967). *Inside bureaucracy*. Boston: Little, Brown.

Etzioni, A. (1967). Mixed-scanning: A 3rd approach to decision-making. *Public Administration Review, 27*(5), 385-392.

Finkler, S. A. (2009). *Financial management for public, health, and not-for-profit organizations*. Upper Saddle River, NJ: Prentice Hall.

Genito, M. A. (2005, April). Developing a financial trends report. *Government Finance Review, 21*, 42–45.

Governmental Accounting Standards Board. (n.d.). Economic condition assessment. Retrieved July 8, 2011, from http://www.gasb.org/jsp/GASB/Page/GASBSectionPage&cid=1176156742174

Greenlee, J. S., and Tuckman, H. (2007). Financial health. In D. R. Young (Ed.), *Financing nonprofits: Putting theory into practice* (pp. 315–335). Lanham, MD: AltaMira Press.

Groves, S. M., Godsey, W. M., and Shulman, M. A. (1981). Financial indicators for local government. *Public Budgeting & Finance, 1*(2), 5–19.

Groves, S. M., Nollenberger, K., and Valente, M. G. (2003). *Evaluating financial condition: A handbook for local government* (4th ed.). Washington, DC: International City/County Management Association.

Hendrick, R. (2004). Assessing and measuring the fiscal heath of local governments: Focus on Chicago suburban municipalities. *Urban Affairs Review, 40*(1), 78–114.

Honadle, B. W., Cigler, B. A., and Costa, J. M. (2004). *Fiscal health for local governments: An introduction to concepts, practical analysis and strategies*. Boston: Elsevier Academic Press.

Honadle, B. W., and Lloyd-Jones, M. (1998). Analyzing rural local governments. financial condition: An exploratory application of three tools. *Public Budgeting & Finance, 18*(2), 69–86.

Howell, J. M., Stamm, C. F., and First National Bank of Boston Economics Dept. (1979). *Urban fiscal stress: A comparative analysis of 66 U.S. cities*. Lexington, MA: Lexington Books.

Hughes, J. W., and Laverdiere, R. (1986). Comparative local government financial analysis. *Public Budgeting & Finance, 6*(4), 23–33.

Ives, M. (2006). *Assessing municipal financial condition*. Croton-on-Hudson, NY: Martin Ives and David R. Hancox.

Kleine, R., Kloha, P., and Weissert, C. S. (2002). *Fiscal stress indicators: An assessment of current Michigan law and development of a new "early-warning" scale for Michigan localities*. East Lansing: Institute for Public Policy and Social Research at Michigan State University.

Kleine, R., Kloha, P., and Weissert, C. S. (2003, June). Monitoring local government fiscal health: Michigan's new 10 point scale of fiscal distress. *Government Finance Review, 19,* 18–23.

Kloha, P., Weissert, C. S., and Kleine, R. (2005a). Developing and testing a composite model to predict local fiscal distress. *Public Administration Review, 65*(3), 313–323.

Kloha, P., Weissert, C. S., and Kleine, R. (2005b). Someone to watch over me: State monitoring of local fiscal conditions. *The American Review of Public Administration, 35*(3), 236–255.

Krueathep, W. (2010). Measuring municipal fiscal condition: The application of U.S.-based measures to the context of Thailand. *International Journal of Public Administration, 33*(5), 223–239.

Ladd, H. F., and Yinger, J. (1989). *America's ailing cities: Fiscal health and the design of urban policy.* Baltimore: Johns Hopkins University Press.

Levine, C. H. (1978). Organizational Decline and Cutback Management. *Public Administration Review, 38*(4), 316–325.

Levine, C. H. (1979). More on cutback management: Hard questions for hard times. *Public Administration Review, 39*(2), 179–183.

Levine, C. H., Rubin, I. S., and Wolohojian, G. G. (1981). *The politics of retrenchment: How local governments manage fiscal stress*. Beverly Hills, CA: Sage Publications.

Local Government Association of South Australia. (2006). *Local government financial indicators* (Information Paper No. 9). Adelaide, SA: Local Government Association of South Australia.

Maher, C. S., and Nollenberger, K. (2009, October). Revisiting Kenneth Brown's "10-point test." *Government Finance Review, 25,* 61–66.

March, J. G. (1978). Bounded rationality, ambiguity, and the engineering of choice. *Bell Journal of Economics, 9*(2), 587–608.

March, J. G., with the assistance of C. Heath (1994). *A primer on decision making*. New York: Free Press.

Martin, J. K. (1982). *Urban financial stress: Why cities go broke*. Boston: Auburn House.

Mead, D. M. (2001a). *An analyst's guide to government financial statements*. Norwalk, CT: Governmental Accounting Standards Board.

Mead, D. M. (2001b). Assessing the financial condition of public school districts: Some tools of the trade. In W. J. Fowler, Jr. (Ed.), *Selected papers in school finance* (pp. 59–76). Washington, DC: U.S. Department of Education, National Center for Educational Statistics.

Mead, D. M. (2005). *What else you should know about your local government's finances*. Norwalk, CT: Governmental Accounting Standards Board.

Mead, D. M. (2006). A manageable system of economic condition analysis for governments. In H. A. Frank (Ed.), *Public financial management* (pp. 383–419). Boca Raton, FL: CRC.

Mead, D. M. (2008). *State and local government use of generally accepted accounting principles for general purpose external financial reporting* (Research brief). Norwalk, CT: Governmental Accounting Standards Board.

Mead, D. M. (2011). *The timeliness of financial reporting by state and local governments compared with the needs of users* (Research brief). Norwalk, CT: Governmental Accounting Standards Board.

Mikesell, J. L. (2010). *Fiscal administration: Analysis and applications for the public sector* (8th ed.). Boston: Wadsworth.

Miller, G. J., and Justice, J. B. (2011). Debt management networks and the proverbs of financial management. *Municipal Finance Journal, 31*(4), 19–40.

Minge, D. (1977). Law as determinant of resource allocation by local government. *National Tax Journal, 30*(4), 399–410.

Moody's Investor Service. (2010). *Special comment: U.S. states credit scorecard*. New York: Moody's Investor Service.

Pammer, W. J., Jr. (1990). *Managing fiscal strain in major American Cities: Understanding retrenchment in the public sector*. New York: Greenwood Press.

Petro, J. (1998). Fiscal indicator reports and ratio analysis: Benchmarking Ohio municipalities and school districts. *Government Finance Review, 14*(5), 17–21.

Plerhoples, T., and Scorsone, E. (2010). *An assessment of Michigan's local government fiscal indicator system* (Issue paper). Lansing, MI: Michigan Senate Fiscal Agency.

Public Sector Accounting Board. (2007, September). Statement of principles: Indicators of government financial condition. Retrieved September 28, 2010, from http://www.psab-ccsp.ca/projects/current-projects/item14558.pdf

Public Sector Accounting Board. (2009, March). Indicators of government financial condition. Retrieved June 24, 2011, from http://www.psab-ccsp.ca/projects/completed-projects/pf_item14561.aspx

Rosenberg, P., and Stallings, C. W. (1978). *Is your city heading for financial difficulty?: A guidebook for small cities and other governmental units*. Chicago: Municipal Finance Officers Association.

Rubin, I. S. (1982). *Running in the red: The political dynamics of urban fiscal stress*. Albany: State University of New York Press.

Rubin, I. S. (1987). Estimated and actual urban revenues: Exploring the gap. *Public Budgeting and Finance, 7*(4), 83–94.

Rusk, D. (1999). *Inside game/outside game: Winning strategies for saving urban America*. Washington, DC: Brookings Institution Press.

Sbragia, A. M. (1996). *Debt wish: Entrepreneurial cities, U.S. federalism, and economic development*. Pittsburgh, PA: University of Pittsburgh Press.

Snow, D., Gianakis, G., and Fortess, E. (2008). Simulating Massachusetts municipalities' recession readiness: Early warning of a perfect storm? *Public Budgeting & Finance, 28*(1), 1–21.

Stanley, D. T. (1976). *Cities in trouble*. Columbus, OH: Academy for Contemporary Problems.

Stonecash, J., and McAfee, P. (1981). The ambiguities and limits of fiscal strain indicators. *Policy Studies Journal, 10*(2), 379–395.

Wang, X., Dennis, L. M., and Tu, Y. S. (2007). Measuring financial condition: A study of U.S. states. *Public Budgeting & Finance, 27*(2), 1–21.

Weikart, L. A. (2009). *Follow the money: Who controls New York City mayors?* Albany, NY: State University of New York Press.

Zafra-Gomez, J. L., Lopez-Hernandez, A. M., and Hernandez-Bastida, A. (2009). Developing an alert system for local governments in financial crisis. *Public Money & Management*, 29(3), 175–181.

Zafra-Gomez, J. L., Lopez-Hernandez, A. M., and Hernandez-Bastida, A. (2009). Developing a model to measure financial condition in local government: Evaluating service quality and minimizing the effects of the socioeconomic environment: An application to Spanish municipalities. *The American Review of Public Administration*, 39(4), 425–449.

Part II

Financial Reporting and Modeling

Chapter 4

The Development of External Financial Reporting and Its Relationship to the Assessment of Fiscal Health and Stress[1]

by Dean Michael Mead

Introduction

The purpose of this chapter is to follow the development of external financial reporting by state and local governments in the United States, specifically in terms of how it has been prompted by the need to assess the fiscal health of governments or the presence of fiscal stress and, in turn, influenced how those assessments are performed. Beginning with the nascent attempts to standardize financial reporting in the early 20th century and reaching the relatively recent transition to accrual-based, consolidated reporting, this chapter identifies key milestones and how they have affected and been affected by attempts to understand and predict fiscal health and stress.

This chapter is divided into six sections. The first two sections provide historical context regarding the early efforts to professionalize governmental financial management (including financial reporting) and the evolution of standards of accounting and financial reporting, respectively. The next section discusses the most widely used systems of fiscal health and stress analysis among state and local governments. The following section covers perhaps the most momentous change in governmental accounting, the advent of accrual-based, consolidated financial reporting. The penultimate section considers the influence of that change thus far on fiscal health and stress assessments. The chapter rounds out with a section of concluding remarks.

Professionalizing State and Local Government Financial Management in Response to Fiscal Stress

As the 20th century was dawning, the population of U.S. cities was increasing rapidly, and the governments of those cities were expanding as quickly. Massive public works projects were undertaken, and sprawling public agencies were developing to serve the burgeoning citizenry. Governments were financed almost entirely by taxes on real and personal property at that time, so as governments grew by leaps and bounds, property tax bills did as well. One thing not increasing, though, was the transparency of government—its activities largely took place beyond the public purview, and little daylight was shed on its operations. These were ideal conditions for corruption.

Although there is no shortage of examples of public officials of that time lining their own pockets and those of their friends in the private sector with taxpayer money, the public's desire to prevent thievery was not the sole—and perhaps not even the major—driving force behind the accountability measures that developed in the first quarter of the 20th century. Corruption scandals provided the impetus for reform, but reformers had a broader agenda in mind than simply bringing malefactors to justice. Those within government were equally eager to identify better means by which to demonstrate government's accountability to the public. As Kahn (1997) relates, cities seeking greater autonomy or "home rule" from their state governments were instrumental in fostering the creation of new methods for proving their financial prudence and fidelity. Two organizations built the foundation of public oversight of governments—the National Municipal League (the League) and the New York Bureau of Municipal Research (the Bureau).

The League and the Bureau

The League, an umbrella organization of good government groups from around the country, published in 1900 *A Municipal Program,* which proposed model state constitution amendments and laws for incorporating municipalities, and included essays on issues related to municipal reform. One of those essays described several aspects to the accountability of governments: In addition to keeping government efficient and economical, there is a "political" accountability by which the public should be able to hold government officials accountable for their actions and decisions. Publicity—in the form of widespread reporting of information and analyses of that information—was seen as central to successful accountability efforts.[2]

The League's publication ushered in the modern era of municipal accounting reform. Kahn (1997) described the League's rationale for improved accounting and the public dissemination of accounting information as five-fold:

1. The public could make informed decisions about whom to elect
2. Greater control could be exerted over the nongovernmental entities operating public service franchises under contract with government
3. Financial stability, and thereby a government's credit, would improve
4. Comparisons could be made among cities
5. States would be better able to oversee municipal affairs.

Rationales three through five are directly related to the assessment of fiscal health and stress.

Distinct from improvements in accounting and financial reporting, the budget reform movement was initiated by the New York Bureau of Municipal Research. The founders of the Bureau, which was created in 1907, saw the budget as not only a means of holding government accountable, but more importantly as a method by which citizens could exercise responsible participation in democratic government. Unlike the accounting reforms, which were premised on a detached and objective rendering of information, the budgetary process was an opportunity for citizens to express their preferences and take a direct hand in guiding a government's policies. The Bureau's research and advocacy, at first focused on New York City government, soon spread throughout the country.

The Bureau mustered a staff of experts dedicated to pursuing better governmental practices on behalf of the citizenry. The leading lights of the Bureau were William Allen, Frederick Cleveland, and Henry Bruere. Allen viewed the Bureau's role as educating and empowering the citizenry by publicizing and disseminating information about government. Cleveland was a technician devoted to the objective, thorough, and scientific exploration of issues of municipal reform. Whereas Cleveland spoke the language of the expert, Allen was deft at translating the work of Cleveland and others on the staff into text and graphical representations that could resonate with the common person. Bruere was a facilitator, championing efforts to work cooperatively with government officials to win them over to the Bureau's way of seeing things.

Citizen Research Organizations

The Bureau was likely an early model for many of the citizen research organizations (CROs) that would be created in the next quarter century. Kahn's (1997) description of the triumvirate's disparate, yet complementary personalities and points of view could form a template for the mission of a CRO. Together, these three reformers embodied the activities of the typical modern CRO—education of the public through the dissemination of information, based on objective research and analysis, in conjunction with efforts to influence government officials and work in concert with them to improve government. CROs continue to function importantly today in every state and most major cities and counties.

CROs study and monitor the raising and stewardship of public resources and the efficiency and effectiveness with which governments use those resources. They typically focus on a particular state or local government, rather than studying public policy or finance in general. Many CROs are run on a shoestring with few full-time staff; this is typical of taxpayer organizations, which tend to concentrate on advocating lower taxes, often through lobbying. Other CROs are nonpartisan applied policy research shops, some with staffs of 10 to 15 persons, with interests in a broad range of policy and finance issues. Most CROs fall somewhere in between, varying in the size of their budget and staff and in their particular research interests. One thing they share in common is a membership comprising local individuals and businesses, from which much of the CROs' financing is derived.

CROs bring expertise and experience to the table that few individual citizens have. Furthermore, those with the requisite knowledge usually do not have the time necessary to devote to the process of collecting and analyzing financial information and drawing conclusions about fiscal health and stress. Instead, CROs collect government information, analyze it, and educate the public about what they have found. The staff at CROs were among the first to assess the financial health of state and local governments. Created or expanded in the wake of the Great Depression, as many of them were, the CROs kept a weather eye open for signs of returning fiscal stress.

The impact of these CROs, spread across the country, cannot be understated. Although the Bureau had national influence, it was nevertheless centered in New York. The CROs, on the other hand, were on the front lines, working with public officials to improve financial management practices, to communicate the demands of the populace, and to assist government in meeting those demands. CROs help citizens hold their governments accountable and act on the public's behalf to hold governments accountable directly. The information demands of the citizenry and businesses, communicated by CROs, had an immediate impact on the development of external financial reporting by state and local governments.

Over the years, the number of CROs has decreased as their primary funders, businesses, have merged or been acquired or have shifted their attention from an altruistic interest in the greater good to lobbying for policy that benefits their profitability and self-interest. Nevertheless, there are still many CROs that act as watchdogs over government finances, assess government fiscal health, and alert the public about fiscal stress. Among the more influential groups are the Boston Municipal Research Bureau, Bureau of Governmental Research (New Orleans), Citizens Budget Commission (New York), Citizens Research Commission of Michigan, Civic Federation (Chicago), Florida TaxWatch, Howard Jarvis Taxpayers Association (California), Massachusetts Taxpayers Foundation, Public Affairs Research Council (Louisiana), and Texas Taxpayers and Research League.

The Foundations of Governmental Accounting and Fund Accounting in Particular

The development of a common framework and language of accounting for governments took the form of a series of influential texts published in the early 1900s. First among these, at least chronologically—Cleveland's *Chapters on Municipal Administration and Accounting* (1909)—begins like a treatise on the ills of municipal graft, reflecting the original impetus for the Bureau, before laying out an approach to proper financial management. A subsequent tome, *Handbook of Municipal Accounting*, coauthored in 1913 with Herman Metz, former comptroller of the City of New York, was a more straightforward manual for financial management, accounting, and financial reporting (Bureau of Municipal Research, 1913). Thirty-five years later, Lloyd Morey identified the *Handbook* as the most significant contribution of the 1910–1919 period to governmental accounting (quoted in Potts, 1976).

Governmental accounting's most unique feature, what distinguishes it from the way businesses track their finances, is fund accounting. Fund accounting involves the allocation of financial information into separate groupings—*funds*—organized around similar activities. Each fund has its own set of *assets* and *liabilities*, inflows and outflows, separate from those of other funds.

Both of the aforementioned texts espoused fund accounting. Cleveland favored fund accounting for comparability purposes (Potts, 1976), with a mind toward standardizing the accounts and funds governments used. Others, including the League, viewed fund accounting as a means of fiscal control. The League also differed in its emphasis on cash-basis receipts and disbursements, whereas Cleveland was a proponent of a commercial-type accrual basis that, for example, excluded bond proceeds and inflows related to future periods from revenue.

Ultimately, recognition of the differences between governments and businesses and the needs of their constituents proved the enduring influence on governmental accounting and financial reporting and its embrace of funds. The period leading up to the 1930s saw the publication of a series of accounting textbooks specifically oriented to governments, further developing the state of the art. The most enduring of these texts included Eggleston (1914), Oakey (1921), and Morey (1927) (Hebert, 1986). Most, if not all, of the major features of annual government financial statements through the end of the century can be traced back to these seminal volumes.

The Standardization of Governmental Accounting

Although the foundations of governmental accounting were put in place in the first three decades of the 1900s, there still was no authoritative, widely accepted set of rules that applied to all governments and against which financial reporting could be audited. That began to change in 1935 with the creation of the National Committee on Municipal Accounting.

Ad Hoc Standards Setting

Founded by the Municipal Finance Officers Association (MFOA, now called the Government Finance Officers Association, GFOA), the Committee issued 13 pronouncements on state and local governmental accounting during its 6 years of operation. Those pronouncements were recognized by the American Institute of Accountants as authoritative for the purpose of conducting audits (Hebert, 1986). The blueprint for the government financial report was fully set forth in Bulletin No. 6, *Municipal Accounting Statements,* and the methods of auditing these reports were detailed in Bulletin No. 8, *Municipal Audit Procedure.* The Committee's work solidified the principles that the objectives of governmental accounting were different from those of businesses (Morey, 1934) and, therefore, a different approach to accounting was needed (namely, fund accounting).

The Committee was reconstituted in 1948 after a seven-year hiatus as the National Committee on Governmental Accounting. The new Committee's chief work was Bulletin No. 14, *Municipal Accounting and Auditing,* issued in 1951, which reviewed and updated the earlier Committee's pronouncements and remained the primary source of accounting guidance for governments for almost two decades (Hebert, 1986). Two years later, the Committee shut down until 1967, at which time it produced a consolidated volume of the prior pronouncements in the form of *Governmental Accounting, Auditing, and Financial Reporting* (GAAFR) (Freeman and Allison, 2006). This landmark publication, known popularly as the Blue Book, was given authoritative status by the American Institute of Certified Public Accountants (AICPA).

Standards setting remained a more or less periodic activity until the Committee was renamed the National Council on Governmental Accounting (NCGA) and began to operate as a continuous board of 21 volunteers (Hebert, 1986). The NCGA laid out in 1979 the financial reporting model as it would exist until 1999 in Statement 1, *Governmental Accounting and Financial Reporting Principles.* This, too, would be recognized as authoritative by the AICPA.

NCGA Statement 1 envisioned a comprehensive annual financial report (CAFR) comprising three parts—an introductory section, financial section, and statistical section. The introductory section would contain prefatory information, such as a letter from the government executive or finance officer and an organizational chart of government officials. The statistical section would present schedules containing financial, economic, demographic, and operating information for the past ten years. The heart of the CAFR, the financial section, would include the audited financial statements and notes, as well as supporting schedules with more detailed information.

Those financial statements, notes, and supporting information continued to be based on a fund presentation, aggregating funds by type in single columns (see a review on "The Financial Condition Process" within **Figure 2.1** and a review on "Revenue Economy Relationships" within **Figure 2.2**). The combined balance sheet presented assets, liabilities, and fund balance (the difference between assets and liabilities) for all of the funds. Separate statements of inflows and outflows were prepared for the *governmental funds* (general fund, special revenue funds, debt service funds, and capital projects funds) and expendable trust funds on the one hand, and *proprietary funds* (enterprise funds and internal service funds) and nonexpendable trust funds on the other hand.

The information for the governmental funds and expendable trusts was presented on a *modified accrual basis of accounting* and current financial resources measurement focus. That meant that, in general, only current assets and current liabilities of the government's basic services (police, fire, sanitation, and so on) were included in the governmental fund type columns of the balance sheet, and not *capital assets* or bonds and other long-term liabilities. The balance sheet did include two columns, *account groups,* which listed general fixed assets (usually not including bridges, water mains, roads and other *infrastructure* assets) and long-term debt. Account groups were not funds and were not netted to calculate a longer-term financial position measure.

By contrast, the funds other than the governmental funds used an accrual basis of accounting and economic resources measurement focus. All assets and liabilities, both current and noncurrent were presented, as well as all inflows and outflows of resources regardless of whether cash was received during or soon after the fiscal year (as is the case with current financial resources and modified accrual).

The financial report also included a statement comparing the government's budget with its actual results. The budget information represented the final modified budget, rather than the original budget. The information was presented on the government's budgetary basis of accounting, rather than on the modified accrual basis required for governmental funds. Lastly, a proprietary funds cash flow statement also was presented.

Formal Standards Setting: The Creation of the GASB

The NCGA represented the first ongoing body setting accounting and financial reporting standards for state and local governments. However, it comprised volunteer members and its staff actually were employees of the MFOA. Consequently, the NCGA was not perceived to have the independent status of the Financial Accounting Standards Board (FASB), which had full-time members, its own research and technical staff, and operated under the oversight of the private Financial Accounting Foundation (FAF). When the FASB began in 1980 to publicly express its belief that its standards were applicable to nonbusiness entities, including governments,[3] discussions about establishing a government-oriented equivalent to the FASB began in earnest.

The Governmental Accounting Standards Board (GASB) was created in 1984 as the result of an agreement between the FAF and major professional associations in the government arena. The agreement effectively delegated to the GASB the authority of the state governments to establish accounting rules for their local governments. The AICPA recognized the GASB as the setter of *generally accepted accounting principles* (GAAP) under Rule 203 of its Code of Professional Conduct, just as it had done for the FASB with respect to business and nongovernmental not-for-profits. As of the end of 2011, the GASB had issued 64 statements of governmental accounting standards, six interpretations of standards, five statements of governmental accounting concepts, and numerous technical bulletins, implementation guides, and other forms of guidance. Perhaps the most important of all of these is Statement No. 34, *Basic Financial Statements—and Management's Discussion and Analysis—for State and Local Governments* (discussed later in this chapter), which replaced the state and local government financial report required by NCGA Statement 1.

The GASB was modeled after the FASB's structure and processes, though the GASB would have four part-time members and a full-time chairman. This would change in 1997, when the Board was expanded to seven members, though still part-time except for the chairman (Bean, 2009). One of the new members was an experienced analyst of government financial health and stress from a CRO.

Regulatory and Statutory Reporting

Most of the nearly 90,000 state and local governmental entities in the Unites States do not prepare GAAP-based financial reports. Just 36 states require some or all of their local jurisdictions to do so (Mead, 2008). However, virtually all prepare and report financial information due to regulatory or statutory requirements.

The Governments Division of the U.S. Bureau of the Census administers a survey of state and local governments every five years that requires detailed financial information. This information is published in the Census of Governments. States and large cities and counties are surveyed annually, and the resulting information is published in annual updates. The Census data are widely used by economists analyzing fiscal health and stress in the aggregate among states and regions (discussed further later in this chapter), by CROs comparing state and city government finances, and many others. This data is, in fact, more often used than financial report information because it is available for all governments in a comparable form.

Many governments also are subject to oversight reporting requirements imposed by the federal and state governments. School districts are required to submit detailed reports to state departments of education, which in turn report to the federal Department of Education. Counties and other localities are often required to report to their state governments their fund balance, *revenues* and *expenditures*, outstanding debt, and other information. This information may be used by oversight bodies to monitor financial health and predict stress, and may be available for use by legislators, CROs, and others.

Traditional Approaches to Assessing Fiscal Health and Stress Based on Financial Reporting

During the last half of the 20th century, academics and practitioners developed two parallel but distinct approaches—let's call them the *fiscal* and *financial* approaches, respectively—to assessing fiscal health and stress. The centerpiece of the fiscal approach was the long-running effort of the Advisory Commission on Intergovernmental Relations (ACIR) to assess *fiscal capacity* with the use of the "representative tax system" (RTS) and other measures. In this arena, fiscal capacity is a jurisdiction's ability to raise its own revenues to finance public services, without respect to the level of taxes it actually imposes (Ferguson and Ladd, 1986). The debate over the best way to measure fiscal capacity, specifically the fiscal capacity of states, is rancorous and deeply political, because measures of fiscal capacity are employed to determine how to allocate billions of dollars of annual federal aid to states and their localities. The choice of measure is particularly crucial for redistributive programs—a state may come out a big winner using one measure, and a loser using another.

Selma Mushkin and Alice Rivlin initially devised the RTS in 1962 for ACIR as an alternative to the use of population or per capita income as a deciding rule for distributing aid. The RTS measures the total and per capita revenue that each state would raise if a set of national average tax rates were applied to a common set of 26 tax bases (Cohen and Lucke, 1985). In so doing, the RTS measures the potential revenue each state could raise if they all used the same tax system. A similar measure, the "representative revenue system" or RRS, adds user charges and other nontax revenues to the RTS (Cohen, 1989). Both measures can be used to determine a state's *fiscal effort*, the relative burden it places on each tax base, by comparing the amount of revenue actually raised from a particular tax with the amount that potentially *could be* raised based on the RTS or RRS. The ACIR also developed a representative expenditure system that essentially divides actual outlays for a particular service by a representative measure calculated by multiplying an actual workload measure for the service in a given state by a representative expenditure per unit of workload (Rafuse, 1990).

Under the RTS, the relative fiscal capacity of states was in some cases markedly different than when measured using per capita income. Consequently, ACIR's work in this area was highly controversial. A sizable literature has been built on the criticism and defense of the ACIR's methods, as well as on attempts to refine its measures or replace them. Akin (1973) and Gold (1986) describe well the debate that ensued.

Another relevant strain of the fiscal approach developed in the wake of the fiscal crises in New York City and elsewhere in the mid-1970s, with the aim of finding measures that would allow an analyst to anticipate financial difficulties. The "fiscal stress" literature subsequently picked up steam as many governments encountered budget deficits in the recession of the early 1980s. (See, for example, Bradbury, 1983; Benson et al., 1988; Clark and Ferguson, 1983; Clark, 1994.)

Although the fiscal approach to assessing fiscal health and stress is informative, particularly from an academic perspective, for at least four reasons it is less useful to practitioners—governmental financial managers seeking to steer their governments on a healthy path and external persons in need of financial information on which to base decisions such as whether to buy a government's bonds. First, the fiscal approach tends to employ one or a few measures that are the product of sometimes complicated equations. Second, the literature tends to be national in scope, being more concerned with developing relative measures among the states rather than examining the circumstances of a particular jurisdiction. Third, the fiscal approach often combines jurisdictions in its analysis, such as a state and its localities or a locality and the surrounding economic area. Fourth, this approach often uses federal economic data, rather than information derived from individual government financial reports, producing a homogenized data set that may not be useful for making decisions relative to an individual government. The financial approach to fiscal health and stress developed in part because of these shortcomings.

Financial Condition Guides and Comprehensive Systems

Perhaps the best known comprehensive model for assessing financial health based on extensive set of indicators is the International City/County Management Association's (ICMA) *Evaluating Financial Condition: A Handbook for Local Government* (Groves and Valente, 1994). The three editions of the ICMA Handbook published between 1980 and 1994 were intended to be a management tool, rather than an academic inquiry, for assessing a government's *financial condition.*

The ICMA Handbook identifies four potential meanings to financial condition—cash solvency, budgetary solvency, long-run solvency, and service level solvency (Groves, Godsey, and Shulman, 1981). Cash solvency is a government's capacity to generate enough cash or liquidity to pay its bills. Budgetary solvency is a government's ability to generate sufficient revenues over the normal budgetary period to meet expenditure obligations and not incur deficits. Long-run solvency refers to a government's long-run ability to pay all the costs of doing business, including expenditure obligations that normally appear in each annual budget, as well as those that show up only in the years in which they must be paid. Finally, service level solvency relates to whether a government can provide the level and quality of services required for the general health and welfare of a community.

Twelve factors affect this conception of financial condition. There are six financial factors (revenues, expenditures, operating position, debt structure, unfunded liabilities, and condition of capital plant) that are the results of how five environmental factors (community needs and resources, external economic conditions, intergovernmental constraints, natural disasters and emergencies, and political culture) are responded to by organizational factors (management practices and legislative policies). ICMA suggests three dozen indicators for evaluating the financial factors and community needs and resources, which it calls "quantifiable indicators of financial condition." However, such an evaluation must take place in light of the other five factors—the "environmental and organizational aspects of financial condition."

Believing the ICMA's system might be too cumbersome, especially for smaller cities, Brown (1993) developed a simpler assessment tool for monitoring financial progress. Brown's "10-point test" involves three steps. First, 10 fairly common ratios are calculated for the particular city of interest. These include three ratios each reflecting on operating position, debt structure, and revenues, and an expenditure ratio. Second, the calculated ratios are compared with the ratios of similarly sized cities; the comparison group is built from the GFOA's Financial Indicators Database. The Database contains information drawn from the financial reports submitted by governments to the GFOA's Certificate of Achievement for Excellence in Financial Reporting program.

Third, the city is graded based on where its ratios fall within the distribution of the comparison group. A ratio within the fourth or highest quartile is graded +2; in the third quartile, +1; in the second, zero; and in the lowest, -1. These grades are summed to provide a total score, which can be compared with other governments and monitored over time.

Berne's Approach.

Perhaps the only textbook in recent memory entirely devoted to the topic of governmental financial analysis is Berne and Schramm's *The Financial Analysis of Governments* (1986), though it is long out of print. As a textbook, it takes a more theoretical approach to developing a framework and methods for analyzing government finances. Consequently, it is less practical as a ready assessment tool than the documents already discussed. Nonetheless, it has been influential among practitioners analyzing fiscal health and stress and their conceptions of the factors that are important to understanding the financial health of a government and how to examine those factors.

Berne and Schramm define financial condition simply as "the probability that a government will meet its financial obligations." Financial condition is the product of available resources, on the one hand, and expenditure pressures, on the other. In addition to current expenditure pressures from constituent demands for certain quantities and qualities of service and intergovernmental mandates, governments are subject to expenditure pressures from past decisions and commitments. The resources available to a government are a combination of internal resources that can be converted into cash with varying degrees of difficulty and external resources that can be tapped.

The availability of external resources is ascertained through revenue analysis, which entails an examination of the community's economic base, the government's revenue base, actual revenues, and revenue capacity and reserves. Current expenditure pressures are considered via expenditure analysis, which includes a review of actual expenditures by purpose over time, assessment of the effects of input prices, exploration of the relationship between inputs and service outputs, and comparisons of the foregoing information with community needs in light of production and service conditions. Analyses of outstanding debt and pensions provide information about the expenditure pressures of past commitments, and generally involve looking at debt structures, burdens, and affordability, as well as the funding status of pensions. Lastly, internal resource analysis involves examinations of liquidity and cash flows, and fund balances and other balance sheet accounts.

Practical applications of Berne and Schramm's paradigm may be found in the financial condition analyses performed for AMBAC by Berne and Drennan (1985, 1987a, and 1987b). Their analyses of the fiscal and economic condition of the states of New York, California, and Texas are substantially based on the approach outlined in the textbook. Together, these documents foreshadow Berne's conclusions in a GASB Research Report (Berne, 1992).

Berne expanded on his textbook definition of financial condition in the Research Report, stating that governmental financial condition:

- includes a time dimension
- is rooted in the government's economic environment
- is a multidimensional or multiconstituency concept with complex interdependencies
- involves implicit as well as explicit obligations.

Relative to the needs of persons assessing governmental financial condition, Berne cited ten specific weakness in the then-current reporting practices of governments.

1. There was no single place where users could turn with regularity to obtain information for assessing financial condition.
2. Despite the improvements in governmental accounting principles and the increased compliance with GAAP, there still were governments where GAAP compliance is far from complete.
3. From a financial condition perspective, there was the need for a more detailed disclosure of the measurement focus and basis of accounting (MFBA).
4. With a typical governmental fund structure it was sometimes very difficult to separate capital from operating transactions.

5. When budgetary and actual information were compared in the CAFR, the detailed and precise explanations required to accurately understand the relationships between the budgetary and accounting formats often were not presented.
6. Interfund transfers, which contribute to the difficulty of separating operating from capital transactions, often were not disclosed in sufficient detail for financial condition analysis.
7. The absence in most accounting reports of a statement of cash receipts and disbursements was a shortcoming for financial condition analysis.
8. The reporting of long-term liabilities and assets was also an area where current accounting practices fall short for financial condition analysis.
9. Although the reporting of information on pensions had improved with GASB Statement No. 5, the reporting of the funding status of other postemployment benefits, for example medical plans, was not up to the same standards.
10. On the long-term assets side, financial reporting was not very helpful for financial condition analysis. The current reporting of long-term assets and capital improvements did not permit an assessment of the government's condition of capital stock.

Many of these weaknesses were addressed in subsequent GASB pronouncements, most notably: Statement 34; Statement No. 38, *Certain Financial Statement Note Disclosures*; Statement No. 27, *Accounting for Pensions by State and Local Government Employers*; and Statement No. 45, *Accounting and Financial Reporting by Employers for Postemployment Benefits Other Than Pensions*.

Berne provided a short list of "key aspects of financial condition" that he concluded were not addressed in the NCGA Statement 1 model at the time of his study. The status of each of the key aspects remains the same under the Statement 34 model discussed later.

1. Economic and demographic information was reported only sporadically.
2. Most financial reporting did not even attempt to make interjurisdictional comparisons, and even the reporting of time series information was limited.
3. The political dimensions of financial condition were difficult to capture in financial reports.
4. A complete assessment of financial condition requires knowledge of how effectively and efficiently the resources raised are being used to deliver services. Within the current financial reporting framework, there was no requirement to report on "service efforts and accomplishments," which would assist in assessing the government's operations.

Municipal Credit Analysis

Another category of the financial approach to fiscal health and stress relates to the credit rating process. Municipal bond analysts at the credit rating agencies and in buy-side shops at mutual funds and casualty insurance companies are essentially judging a government's ability to repay its debts on time. The process by which this is done is proprietary, and its specifics—in terms of the information used, the ratios calculated, the relative weight given to individual components, and so on—vary from company to company. In truth, credit rating is a qualitative activity that weighs many factors without a specific or easily understood formula. (Loviscek and Crowley, 1996) To those on the outside, the process is essentially a black box.

For many years, the three dominant rating agencies produced books and pamphlets describing how they rate debt. However, these documents tended to describe the rating process in broad terms, identifying categories of important factors, but not specifically laying out the rating equation.[4] External pressure to be more transparent has led to somewhat more disclosure from the rating agencies regarding the factors they consider important and the types of information they utilize, but the underlying calculus that results in a particular rating remains proprietary and beyond public scrutiny.[5]

The credit analysis of general obligation debt depends on four groups of information (Feldstein and Goode, 2008):

1. The government's debt structure and security for the bonds
2. The government's budgetary operations
3. The government's revenue streams
4. The economy

The first group encompasses a review of the various types and amounts of debt a government has, including overlapping and underlying debt borne by its taxpayers, as well as non-debt liabilities such as unfunded retirement benefits. Budgetary information includes past results and future plans, budgetary powers and procedures, and history of taxpayer participation via budget and debt referenda. Revenue analysis focuses on available revenue streams over time. The final group looks at a variety of indicators, including property values, building permits, principal employers and taxpayers, unemployment rates, and so on.

Credit analysis of revenue bonds focuses on a different set of information, because repayment of the debt depends on the viability of the pledged revenue stream, rather than on the overall financial viability of the governmental entity.[6] As such, revenue bond analysis is less informative for understanding how the assessment of financial health and stress has developed.

State Systems of Measuring Financial Health and Stress

During the early part of the 2000s, the State of Michigan began to reconsider its local government fiscal monitoring program. Required to take fiscally distressed cities into essentially a "receivership," the Department of the Treasury, which was responsible for operating the program, sought to shift the program's focus from identification of dire fiscal problems and assumption of financial management to early detection of stress and preventive action. The "Local Government Fiscal Responsibility Act" provided that the Department of the Treasury conduct a preliminary review of a local government's financial status if one or more of 14 potentially problematic conditions exist. These conditions include: a claim from a creditor that a government is more than six months in arrears for an amount exceeding the greater of $10 million or 1 percent of the annual general fund budget, bond payment default or violation of bond covenants, failure to comply with the state law requiring that local governments provide an audited annual financial report to the state, and delinquency in distributing tax revenues collected on behalf of another jurisdiction.

If the Department of the Treasury's review concludes that a serious financial problem may exist (or if the governing body of the government requests assistance), the governor appoints a review team that conducts a more thorough financial review. If the review team concludes that a financial emergency exists and no consent agreement can be reached with the government setting forth a plan to resolve the emergency, a verification process begins in which the governor holds public hearings and provides the opportunity for appeal by the local government. Ultimately, if the financial emergency is confirmed, the state's Local Emergency Financial Assistance Loan Board appoints an emergency financial manager, who takes over responsibility for the financial management of the local government under the direction of the Board. Throughout the process, the emphasis is on trying to agree with the government on an acceptable recovery plan that the government itself would implement, under the guidance of the state, in order to avoid taking responsibility away from the government.

Crucial to the success of this new system was the development of a financial assessment methodology that would accurately predict impending fiscal distress. The Department of the Treasury enlisted the aid of local academics to construct and test the assessment tool. The academics reviewed the 30 indicators that the state's previous financial monitoring program employed and found that they were susceptible not only to missing true financial emergencies, but also to concluding that a financial emergency exists where it truly does not (Kleine, Kloha, and Weissert, 2003). To develop a new assessment tool, the academics were attracted to Brown's 10-point test because it appeared appropriate to Michigan's needs and had influenced the development of monitoring systems in other states. However, they concluded that some of its measures were not good predictors of distress (or, at a minimum, were ambivalent predictors) and that the state would not be able to access some of the information required.

The academic team came up with a 10-point scale of their own, in which a government is penalized points for poor performance on each of 9 indicators:

- Change in population
- Change in real taxable value of property
- Large decrease in real taxable value
- General fund expenditures as a percentage of taxable value
- General fund operating deficit

- Prior general fund operating deficits
- General fund balance as a percentage of general fund revenues
- Current or previous year deficit in a major fund
- General long-term debt as a percentage of real taxable value.

A score of 0-4 is interpreted as fiscally healthy and no action is taken. A score of 5 is categorized as "fiscal watch," and the local government is notified of its score. A score of 6-7 results in a "fiscal warning"—the government is placed on a published list for the current and following year. Finally, a score of 8-10 is deemed a "fiscal emergency," and the government is not only placed on the published list but also receives automatic consideration for the gubernatorially appointed fiscal review team just described. The academic team used this system to analyze 150 Michigan cities for 1991-2001 and found that it performed fairly well in identifying the governments that had had financial emergencies that led to a state takeover (Kloha, Weissert, and Kleine, 2005).

In Florida, auditors are required under the Local Government Financial Emergencies Act to inform local governments if their financial condition is deteriorating such that a financial emergency may occur. The Auditor General (2001) developed procedures and a set of financial indicators for auditors to use in making this determination. The Auditor General's procedural guide defines financial condition as "a local governmental entity's ability to provide services at the level and quality that are required for the health, safety, and welfare of the community, and that its citizens desire."

The Auditor General's methodology employs 14 recognizable indicators, including typical measures of financial position (such as unreserved fund balance compared to expenditures and revenues) and financial condition (a quick ratio, for instance, and the difference between revenues and expenditures). The methodology also uses a measure of flexibility (intergovernmental revenues divided by total revenues), an indicator of debt affordability (debt service divided by expenditures), and revenue-raising capacity (millage rates compare to legal limits).

The Shortcomings of the Traditional Approaches

The traditional approaches to assessing financial health and stress detailed thus far have been used meaningfully and successfully for many years. They are, however, inherently flawed in several ways due to problems with the financial statement information they utilize, though the progenitors of these approaches can hardly be blamed for using what was available to them.

First, the focus of these approaches is almost exclusively on budgetary and short-term information. This is because governmental accounting standards did not require reporting of long-term debts and capital assets related to general governmental activities, information crucial to getting a picture of a government's long-term financial prospects. Second, analysis generally was limited to certain segments of a government (most often, the governmental funds or just the general fund and some special revenue funds) and did not contemplate the overall financial health of the government.

Consequently, to the extent that analysts performed assessments of comprehensive, long-term financial health, they were based on incomplete or second-best information. Comprehensive analysis often involved combining information from the various funds a government reports; however, this information is incompatible, as the basis of accounting and measurement focus used in the governmental funds was different from that used in other funds. The fact that the financial statements included total columns misled some to believe that such a consolidation was feasible (though the total columns were labeled "memorandum only"). (See **Figures 4.1** and **4.2**)

Third, assertions of being able to compare governments were undermined by flexibility in the accounting standards and resulting variation in financial reporting across governments. Governments have considerable flexibility in choosing which funds they want to report and even in which funds they want to report certain activities. For example, elementary and secondary education may be in the general fund of some governments or in a special revenue fund of other governments. Tax-supported garbage collection would be reported in the general fund, whereas garbage collection financed with user fees would be reported outside of the governmental funds entirely. Within the funds, the labels applied to revenue and expenditures can vary significantly: Similar activities may be labeled differently, and two different revenue streams may be reported with the same label. Focusing analysis on the general fund (or governmental funds as a whole), as many analysts of financial health and stress have done, risks comparing apples and oranges and drawing incorrect conclusions about a government's condition relative to its peers.

The Advent of Consolidated Full Accrual Accounting

When the GASB was created in 1984, the key project on the agenda it inherited was the development of a new blueprint for state and local government financial reports, one that addressed the shortcomings inherent in the existing fund-based reporting model. In June 1999, the GASB released Statement 34, the culmination of that project. The new annual financial report required by Statement 34 may be described as having three parts:

1. *Management's discussion and analysis*—a form of *required supplementary information (RSI)* that appears at the front of the financial report
2. Basic financial statements—a government's financial statements and note disclosures
3. Required supplementary information—additional disclosures that follow the basic financial statements

This portion of the chapter considers in turn the notable aspects of each of these three major parts.

Management's Discussion and Analysis

As envisioned by the GASB, MD&A was intended to be a concise, objective introduction to a government's financial report and a summary analysis of the information contained in the statements. In addition to providing a guide to the organization of the financial report, MD&A offers condensed financial information derived from the financial statements. This information is accompanied by explanations from a government's finance officers, focusing on how the government's finances changed during the year. Specifically, the analysis by the finance officers should explain:

- The government's overall financial position and results of operations, and the changes in them, as well as the governmental and business-type activities separately (business-type activities are those that operate like businesses, charging a fee for services, such as an electric utility)
- Balances and transactions of individual funds, significant changes, and any limitations on the availability of fund resources for future use
- Significant budget variations
- Significant capital asset and long-term debt activity
- Facts or issues of which a government is aware as of the date of the auditor's report that are expected to significantly affect the government's finances.

MD&A essentially incorporates the initial steps of fiscal health or stress analysis into the financial report, highlighting key changes over time and during the fiscal year. Its explanations help to answer the questions that arise when a financial statement user performs initial analysis, such as percentage change and percentage distribution calculations.

Basic Financial Statements

The centerpiece of Statement 34 was the revision and expansion of the "general purpose financial statements" governments were previously required to prepare. Statement 34 applied the term "basic financial statements" to this part of the new financial report and added two new accrual-based statements for the government as a whole, improved the existing fund-based financial statements, and added several new disclosures to the financial statement notes.

Government-wide financial statements.

Perhaps the most significant change introduced by Statement 34 was the requirement that governments for the first time prepare financial statements that provide comprehensive information for the entirety of a government's operations. The *statement of net position* and *statement of activities*, as they are called, are prepared using the accrual basis of accounting and the economic resources measurement focus.[7] These statements display separately the information for a government's "governmental activities" and "business-type activities," as well as its "component units." The government-wide statements do not report information regarding a government's fiduciary activities, such as public employee pensions or trusts. The GASB's reasoning for reporting this information distinctly in separate *fiduciary funds statements* was that the resources related to fiduciary activities belong to others and are not available to support the government's programs.[8] Including these resources in the government-wide statements might mislead a user's conclusions about the financial position and condition of a government.

A significant feature of the statement of net position is the presentation of capital assets at historical cost less accumulated depreciation and the inclusion of long-term debts (see **Figure 4.3**). Previously, capital assets and long-term liabilities were only reported in "account groups" in the fund-based statements (refer to **Figure 4.1**). In some cases, this was the first time that governments had reported infrastructure assets such as roads, bridges, and water mains.[9] Capital assets are valued initially on the statement of net position at their historical cost.

Net position—essentially the difference between assets and liabilities—is divided into three categories. The portion of net position invested in capital assets is shown separately, minus outstanding debt related to those assets. The remaining net position is then divided between that restricted to specific purposes and the remainder that is unrestricted. Net position is considered restricted when constraints are externally imposed, or internally through constitutional provisions or enabling legislation. The restricted net position further is divided by major category of restriction.

The second government-wide statement, the statement of activities, is designed to focus not only on the bottom-line change in net position but also to provide useful information about the cost of public services and how they are financed (see **Figure 4.4**). The upper half of the statement flows from left to right (expenses, program revenues, then net [expense] revenue), and then continues downward (general revenues such as taxes, other changes in net position, leading to total change in net position).

The left-hand column of the statement presents expenses by functional or program category. A functional classification is the minimum requirement of Statement 34, but governments are encouraged to provide more detailed programmatic and service-level information if it is useful to the users of their financial statements.[10] If a government wishes to allocate indirect expenses, such as general government, to the direct expense categories, it must include an additional column, to the right of the expenses column, displaying the allocation amounts.[11]

The program revenues are presented in columns to the right of the expenses. Program revenues are those proceeding from the activities themselves, such as greens fees at a municipal golf course or license fees and fines, as well as grants and contributions that are restricted to specific programs. The latter group is divided between those grants and contributions for operating purposes and those for capital purposes.

Subtracting expenses from program revenues produces the "net (expense) revenue" amounts in the right-hand columns. These amounts represent the "net cost" to the public: The portion of program costs that is not self-financed but rather requires financing from

Combined Balance Sheet: All Fund Types, Account Groups, and Discretely Presented Component Units
June 30, 1995
(dollars in thousands)

	Governmental Fund Types				Proprietary Fund Types		Fiduciary Fund Type	Account Groups		Totals Primary Government (Memorandum Only)	Component Unit	Totals Reporting Entity (Memorandum Only)
	General	Special Revenue	Debt Service	Capital Projects	Enterprise	Internal Service	Trust and Agency	General Fixed Assets	General Long-Term Debt		School District	
Assets and other debits												
Assets												
Cash and cash equivalents	$x,xxx	$x,xxx	$x,xxx	$x,xxx	$x,xxx	$x,xxx	$x,xxx	—	—	$xx,xxx	$xxx	$xx,xxx
Cash and cash equivalents–nonexpendable trust	—	—	—	—	—	—	x,xxx	—	—	x,xxx	—	x,xxx
Investments	x,xxx	x,xxx	x,xxx	x,xxx	xx,xxx	xx	xx,xxx	—	—	xx,xxx	xxx	xx,xxx
Receivables (net of allowances)	xxx	x,xxx	xx	xxx	xxx	xxx	xxx	—	—	x,xxx	—	x,xxx
Due from other funds	xx	—	—	xx	xx	xx	—	—	—	xxx	—	xxx
Due from component unit	xx	—	—	—	—	—	—	—	—	xx	—	xx
Inventories	xx	—	—	—	xxx	xx	—	—	—	xxx	—	xxx
Prepaid items	xx	—	—	—	—	xx	—	—	—	xxx	xxx	xxx
Advances to other funds	xx	—	—	—	—	—	—	—	—	xx	—	xx
Restricted assets	—	xx	—	—	xx,xxx	—	—	—	—	xx,xxx	—	xx,xxx
Deferred charges	—	—	—	—	xxx	—	—	—	—	xxx	—	xxx
Fixed assets	—	—	—	—	xxx,xxx	x,xxx	—	$xx,xxx	—	xxx,xxx	xx,xxx	xxx,xxx
Other debits												

Figure 4.1 Illustrative Pre-Statement 34 Combined Balance Sheet (*continued*)

Combined Balance Sheet: All Fund Types, Account Groups, and Discretely Presented Component Units
June 30, 1995
(dollars in thousands)

	Governmental Fund Types				Proprietary Fund Types		Fiduciary Fund Type	Account Groups		Totals Primary Government (Memorandum Only)	Component Unit	Totals Reporting Entity (Memorandum Only)
	General	Special Revenue	Debt Service	Capital Projects	Enterprise	Internal Service	Trust and Agency	General Fixed Assets	General Long-Term Debt		School District	
Amount available in debt service fund	—	—	—	—	—	—	—	—	$x,xxx	x,xxx	—	x,xxx
Amount to be provided for retirement of long-term debt	—	—	—	—	—	—	—	—	xx,xxx	xx,xxx	—	xx,xxx
Total assets and other debits	$x,xxx	$x,xxx	$x,xxx	$x,xxx	$xxx,xxx	$x,xxx	$xx,xxx	$xx,xxx	$xx,xxx	$xxx,xxx	$xx,xxx	$xxx,xxx
Liabilities, equity and other credits Liabilities												
Accounts payable	$xxx	$xxx	—	$xxx	$x,xxx	$xxx	$xxx	—	—	$x,xxx	$xx	$x,xxx
Compensated absences payable	xxx	—	—	—	xxx	xx	—	—	$x,xxx	x,xxx	x	x,xxx
Claims and judgments payable	—	—	—	—	—	—	—	—	xxx	xxx	—	xxx
Due to other funds	xx	—	—	—	xx	xx	—	—	—	xxx	—	xxx
Due to primary government	—	—	—	—	—	—	—	—	—	—	xx	xx
Matured bonds payable	—	—	$xx	—	xx	—	—	—	—	xx	—	xx
Interest payable	—	—	x	—	xx	—	—	—	—	xx	—	xx
Deferred revenue	xxx	—	xxx	—	xxx	—	—	—	—	x,xxx	—	x,xxx
General obligation bonds payable	—	—	—	—	x,xxx	—	—	—	xx,xxx	xx,xxx	—	xx,xxx

Revenue bonds payable	—	—	—	—	xx,xxx	—	—	—	—	xx,xxx	—	xx,xxx
Capital leases payable	—	—	—	—	xx	—	—	—	xxx	xxx	—	xxx
Total liabilities	x,xxx	xxx	xxx	xxx	xx,xxx	xxx	xxx	—	xx,xxx	xxx,xxx	xx	xxx,xxx
Equity and other credits												
Investment in general fixed assets	—	—	—	—	—	—	—	$xx,xxx	—	xx,xxx	xx,xxx	xx,xxx
Contributed capital	—	—	—	—	xx,xxx	x,xxx	—	—	—	xx,xxx	—	xx,xxx
Retained earnings												
Reserved	—	—	—	—	x,xxx	—	—	—	—	x,xxx	—	x,xxx
Unreserved	—	—	—	—	xx,xxx	xxx	—	—	—	xx,xxx	—	xx,xxx
Fund balances												
Reserved for encumbrances	xxx	xxx	—	x,xxx	—	—	—	—	—	x,xxx	xxx	x,xxx
Reserved for recreation	xxx	—	—	—	—	—	—	—	—	xxx	—	xxx
Reserved for public safety	xx	—	—	—	—	—	—	—	—	xx	—	xx
Reserved for debt service	xx	—	x,xxx	—	—	—	—	—	—	x,xxx	—	x,xxx
Reserved for employee retirement system	—	—	—	—	—	—	xx,xxx	—	—	xx,xxx	—	xx,xxx
Unreserved	x,xxx	—	—	—	—	—	xxx	—	—	x,xxx	x,xxx	x,xxx
Total equity and other credits	x,xxx	x,xxx	x,xxx	x,xxx	xxx,xxx	x,xxx	xx,xxx	xx,xxx	—	xxx,xxx	xx,xxx	xxx,xxx
Total liabilities, equity, and other credits	$x,xxx	$x,xxx	$x,xxx	$x,xxx	$xxx,xxx	$x,xxx	$xx,xxx	$xx,xxx	$xx,xxx	$xxx,xxx	$xx,xxx	$xxx,xxx

Figure 4.1 Illustrative Pre-Statement 34 Combined Balance Sheet (cont.)

Combined Statement of Revenues, Expenditures, and Changes in Fund Balances/Equity
Governmental Fund Types and Discretely Presented Component Units
June 30, 1995
(dollars in thousands)

	Governmental Fund Types				Totals Primary Government (Memorandum Only)	Component Unit	Totals Reporting Entity (Memorandum Only)
	General	Special Revenue	Debt Service	Capital Projects		School District	
Revenues							
Taxes	$xx,xxx	$x,xxx	$x,xxx	—	$xx,xxx	$xx,xxx	$xx,xxx
Licenses and permits	x,xxx	—	—	—	x,xxx	—	x,xxx
Intergovernmental	x,xxx	xxx	—	$xxx	x,xxx	xx,xxx	xx,xxx
Charges for services	x,xxx				x,xxx	—	x,xxx
Fines	xxx	—	—	xx	xxx	—	xxx
Interest	xxx	xxx	xxx	xxx	x,xxx	—	x,xxx
Miscellaneous	xxx	xxx	—	—	xxx	—	xxx
Total revenues	xx,xxx	x,xxx	x,xxx	xxx	xx,xxx	xx,xxx	xx,xxx
Expenditures							
Current							
General government	x,xxx	—	—	—	x,xxx	—	x,xxx
Public safety	xx,xxx	—	—	—	xx,xxx	—	xx,xxx
Highways and streets	x,xxx	xxx	—	—	x,xxx	—	x,xxx
Sanitation	x,xxx	—	—	—	x,xxx	—	x,xxx
Economic development	—	xxx	—	—	xxx	—	xxx
Culture and recreation	x,xxx	xxx	—	—	x,xxx	—	x,xxx

Education	—	—	—	—	—	xx,xxx	xx,xxx
Capital outlay	—	—	—	x,xxx	x,xxx	x,xxx	x,xxx
Debt service							
Principal	—	—	x,xxx	—	x,xxx	—	x,xxx
Interest	—	—	x,xxx	—	x,xxx	—	x,xxx
Total expenditures	xx,xxx	x,xxx	x,xxx	x,xxx	xx,xxx	xx,xxx	xx,xxx
Excess (deficiency) of revenues over (under) expenditures	x,xxx	xx	(x,xxx)	(x,xxx)	xxx	(x,xxx)	(x,xxx)
Other financing sources (uses)							
Operating transfers in	x,xxx	xx	x,xxx	x,xxx	x,xxx	—	x,xxx
Operating transfers in–primary government	—	—	—	—	—	xx	—
Operating transfers out	(x,xxx)	—	—	(xxx)	(x,xxx)	—	(x,xxx)
Operating transfers out–component unit	(xx)	—	—	—	(xx)	—	(xx)
Proceeds of refunding bonds	—	—	x,xxx	—	x,xxx	—	x,xxx
Payment to refunded bond escrow agent	—	—	(x,xxx)	—	(x,xxx)	—	(x,xxx)
Capital leases	xxx	—	—	—	xxx	—	xxx
Total other financing sources (uses)	(x,xxx)	xx	x,xxx	x,xxx	x,xxx	xx	x,xxx
Excess of revenues and other financing sources over (under) expenditures and other financing uses	x,xxx	xxx	x,xxx	x,xxx	x,xxx	(x,xxx)	x,xxx
Fund balances/equity–beginning	x,xxx	x,xxx	xx	xxx	x,xxx	x,xxx	x,xxx
Fund balances/equity–beginning	$x,xxx	$x,xxx	$x,xxx	$x,xxx	$x,xxx	$x,xxx	$xx,xxx

Figure 4.2 Illustrative Pre-Statement 34 Combined Income Statement

Government-Wide Statement of Net Position
As of December 31, 2011

	Primary Government			
	Governmental Activities	Business-type Activities	Total	Component Units
ASSETS				
Cash and cash equivalents	$ 13,597,899	$ 8,785,821	$ 22,383,720	$ 303,935
Investments	27,365,221	—	27,365,221	7,428,952
Receivables (net)	12,833,132	3,609,615	16,442,747	4,042,290
Internal balances	175,000	(175,000)	—	—
Inventories	322,149	126,674	448,823	83,697
Total current assets	54,293,401	12,347,110	66,640,511	11,858,874
Noncurrent assets:				
Restricted cash and cash equivalents	—	1,493,322	1,493,322	—
Capital assets:				
Land and nondepreciable infrastructure	88,253,120	3,836,119	92,089,239	—
Depreciable infrastructure, net	30,367,241	30,952,214	61,319,455	751,239
Depreciable buildings, property, and equipment, net	51,402,399	116,600,418	168,002,817	36,993,547
Total noncurrent assets	170,022,760	152,882,073	322,904,833	37,744,786
Total assets	224,316,161	165,229,183	389,545,344	49,603,660
DEFERRED OUTFLOWS OF RESOURCES				
Accumulated decrease in fair value of hedging derivatives	1,754,896	—	1,754,896	2,987,635
Total deferred outflows of resources	1,754,896	—	1,754,896	2,987,635

LIABILITIES				
Current liabilities:				
Accounts payable	8,538,206	751,430	9,289,636	4,790,967
Current portion of long-term obligations	9,236,000	4,426,286	13,662,286	1,426,639
Total current liabilities	17,774,206	5,177,716	22,951,922	6,217,606
Noncurrent liabilities:				
Noncurrent portion of long-term obligations	83,302,378	74,482,273	157,784,651	27,106,151
Total liabilities	101,076,584	79,659,989	180,736,573	33,323,757
DEFERRED INFLOWS OF RESOURCES				
Service concession arrangement payment	1,435,599	—	1,435,599	
Total deferred inflows of resources	1,435,599	—	1,435,599	—
NET POSITION				
Net investment in capital assets	103,711,386	73,088,574	176,799,960	15,906,392
Restricted for:				
Capital projects	11,705,864	—	11,705,864	492,445
Debt service	3,020,708	1,451,996	4,472,704	—
Community development projects	4,811,043	—	4,811,043	—
Other purposes	3,214,302	—	3,214,302	—
Unrestricted (deficit)	(2,904,429)	11,028,624	8,124,195	2,829,790
Total net position	$ 123,558,874	$ 85,569,194	$ 209,128,068	$ 19 228,627

Figure 4.3 Illustrative Government-wide Statement of Net Position

Government-Wide Statement of Activities
for the Year Ending December 31, 2011

Functions/Programs	Expenses	Indirect Expenses Allocation	Program Revenues: Charges for Services	Program Revenues: Operating Grants and Contributions	Program Revenues: Capital Grants and Contributions	Net (Expense) Revenue and Changes in Net Position — Primary Government: Governmental Activities	Primary Government: Business-type Activities	Primary Government: Total	Component Units
Primary government:									
Governmental activities:									
General government	$ 9,571,410	$ (5,580,878)	$ 3,146,915	$ 843,617	$ —	$ —	$ —	$ —	$ —
Public safety	34,844,749	4,059,873	1,198,855	1,307,693	62,300	(36,335,774)	—	(36,335,774)	—
Public works	10,128,538	3,264,380	850,000	—	2,252,615	(10,290,303)	—	(10,290,303)	—
Engineering services	1,299,645	111,618	704,793	—	—	(706,470)	—	(706,470)	—
Health and sanitation	6,738,672	558,088	5,612,267	575,000	—	(1,109,493)	—	(1,109,493)	—
Cemetery	735,866	55,809	212,496	—	—	(579,179)	—	(579,179)	—
Culture and recreation	11,532,350	1,858,966	3,995,199	2,450,000	—	(6,946,117)	—	(6,946,117)	—
Community development	2,994,389	1,740,265	—	—	2,580,000	(2,154,654)	—	(2,154,654)	—
Education (payment to school district)	21,893,273	—	—	—	—	(21,893,273)		(21,893,273)	—
Interest on long-term debt	6,068,121	(6,068,121)	—	—	—	—	—	—	—
Total governmental activities	105,807,013	$ 0	15,720,525	5,176,310	4,894,915	(80,015,263)	—	(80,015,263)	—
Business-type activities:									
Water	3,595,733		4,159,350	—	1,159,909	—	1,723,526	1,723,526	—
Sewer	4,912,853		7,170,533	—	486,010	—	2,743,690	2,743,690	—
Parking facilities	2,796,283		1,344,087	—	—	—	(1,452,196)	(1,452,196)	—
Total business-type activities	11,304,869		12,673,970	—	1,645,919	—	3,015,020	3,015,020	—
Total primary government	$ 117,111,882		$ 28,394,495	$ 5,176,310	$ 6,540,834	(80,015,263)	3,015,020	(77,000,243)	—

Component units:								
Landfill	$ 3,382,157	$ 3,857,858	$ —	$ 11,397	—	—	—	487,098
Public school system	31,186,498	705,765	3,937,083	—	—	—	—	(26,543,650)
Total component units	$ 34,568,655	$ 4,563,623	$ 3,937,083	$ 11,397	—	—	—	(26,056,552)
General revenues:								
Taxes:								
Property taxes, levied for general purposes					51,693,573	—	51,593,573	—
Property taxes, levied for debt service					4,726,244	—	4,726,244	—
Franchise taxes					4,055,505	—	4 055,505	—
Public service taxes					8,969,887	—	8,969,887	—
Payment from Sample City					—	—	—	21,893,273
Grants and contributions not restricted to specific programs					1,457,820	—	1,457,820	6,461,708
Investment earnings					1,958,144	601,349	2,559,493	881,763
Miscellaneous					884,907	104,925	989,832	22,464
Subtotal, excess (deficiency) of revenues over expenses					(6,269,183)	3,721,294	(2,547,889)	3,202,656
Special item—gain on sale of park land					2,653,488	—	2,653,488	—
Transfers					501,409	(501,409)	—	—
Total general revenues, special item, and transfers					76,900,977	204,865	77,105,842	29,259,208
Change in net position					(3,114,286)	3,219,885	105,599	3,202,656
Net position—beginning					126,673,160	82,349,309	209,022,469	16,025,971
Net position—ending					$ 123,558,874	$ 85,569,194	$ 209,128,068	$ 19,228,627

Figure 4.4 Illustrative Government-wide Statement of Activities

general revenues—principally taxes—and other sources. In this sense, program revenues are those that reduce the net cost of programs to the public. The lower portion of the statement describes how the net cost of public services was financed. All taxes are included in general revenues, even those that are dedicated to specific purposes.[12] The statement concludes with the overall change in net position.

Another new feature introduced by Statement 34 was the separation of "special and extraordinary items" from other revenues and expenses.[13] Extraordinary items are transactions or other events that are both unusual in nature and infrequent in occurrence. An example might be the cost of cleaning up after a tornado in a northeast state (where tornadoes hardly ever occur), as well as any federal disaster aid that is received. A special item is a transaction or other event that is within the control of management and *either* unusual in nature or infrequent in occurrence. An example might be a government selling a substantial piece of property. By showing these items separately, the statement allows users to determine if a government faced out-of-the-ordinary costs or if it resorted to atypical sources of financing in order to make ends meet.

Fund financial statements.

The advent of the new government-wide statements did not mark the demise of fund accounting and reporting in the United States.[14] There was considerable sentiment among the GASB's constituency—not only the community of financial statement users, but also preparers and auditors—that fund financial information would continue to be essential to understanding a government's finances and should be retained. The GASB's research further suggested that the usefulness of fund financial information, as then presented, could be significantly improved. Specifically, the GASB discovered intense interest among users in detailed fund financial information related primarily to individual funds rather than aggregated fund types.[15] As a result, Statement 34 replaced fund-type reporting with "major fund" reporting for the governmental and enterprise funds.[16]

Major fund reporting results in the most significant funds being displayed individually in the statements. Specifically, Statement 34 requires that the following funds be shown in their own columns:

- A government's main operating fund (usually its general fund)
- Any governmental or enterprise fund that fits both of these criteria:
  - Total assets (plus deferred outflows), liabilities (plus deferred inflows), revenues, or expenditures/expenses (not including extraordinary items) of the fund are at least 10% of the corresponding total for all funds (either all governmental or all enterprise, whichever is appropriate) *and*
  - Total assets (plus deferred outflows), liabilities (plus deferred inflows), revenues, or expenditures/expenses (not including extraordinary items) of the fund are at least 5% of the corresponding total for all governmental and enterprise funds combined
- Any other governmental or enterprise fund that a government believes is particularly important to the users of its financial statements.

The remaining "nonmajor" funds are combined and shown in single columns for the governmental funds and for the proprietary funds. Governments that prepare a comprehensive annual financial report (CAFR) also provide supplementary "combining" financial statements that display the nonmajor funds individually.

The move to major fund reporting is far and away the most substantial change in fund reporting. Otherwise, the fund financial statements continue to provide much the same information. The governmental funds financial statements—the balance sheet (**Figure 4.5**) and the statement of revenues, expenditures, and changes in fund balances (**Figure 4.6**)—are still prepared using the modified accrual basis of accounting and current financial resources measurement focus.

Statement 34 added a set of reconciling adjustments that explain how fund balance and change in fund balance differ from governmental activities net assets and change in net assets in the government-wide financial statements. These reconciliations will often appear at the bottom of the statement (such as in **Figure 4.5**) but may also appear on a succeeding page. Some governments will also provide additional explanatory details of the reconciliation in the notes to their financial statements.

Three financial statements are required to be presented for the proprietary funds—a statement of net position, statement of revenues, expenses, and changes in fund net position, and statement of cash flows. Major fund reporting applies to the enterprise funds (essentially the business-type activities), but the internal service funds (which provide services to other parts of the government) are aggregated in a single column. The statement of cash flows uses the direct method of presentation, dividing inflows and outflows among four categories—cash flows from operating activities, capital and related financing activities, noncapital financing activities, and investing activities. The statement then presents a reconciliation explaining the difference between the cash flow results for operations and the accrual-basis results in the statement of revenues, expenses, and changes in fund net position.

The last two required financial statements cover the fiduciary funds—those that report on a government's activities as a fiduciary or agent over resources that belong to others and are not available to the government. The most common form of fiduciary activity is sponsorship of a pension plan, but other activities include investment pools, private-purpose trusts, and agency funds (in which a government holds resources temporarily before passing them along, as a county might do when collecting property taxes on behalf of smaller governments and school districts). The two statements are the statement of fiduciary net position and the statement of changes in fiduciary net position. Unlike the activities reported in the other funds, the activities in the fiduciary funds are not included in the government-wide financial statements.

Notes to the financial statements.

In general, the note disclosures already required by prior GASB pronouncements were left as is.[17] The most significant new disclosures required by Statement 34 were those relating to capital assets and long-term debts. The purpose of these notes was twofold:

Balance Sheet
Governmental Funds
As of December 31, 2011

	General	Housing Programs	Community Redevelopment	Road Construction	Other Governmental Funds	Total Governmental Funds
ASSETS						
Cash and cash equivalents	$ 3,418,485	$ 1,236,523	$ —	$ —	$ 5,606,792	$ 10,261,800
Investments	—	—	13,262,695	10,467,037	3,485,252	27,214,984
Receivables, net	3,644,561	2,953,438	353,340	11,000	10,221	6,972,560
Due from other funds	1,370,757	—	—	—	—	1,370,757
Receivables from other governments	—	119,059	—	—	1,596,038	1,715,097
Liens receivable	791,926	3,195,745	—	—	—	3,987,671
Inventories	182,821	—	—	—	—	182,821
Total assets	$ 9,408,550	$ 7,504,765	$ 13,616,035	$ 10,478,037	$ 10,698,303	$ 51,705,690
LIABILITIES AND FUND BALANCES						
Liabilities:						
Accounts payable	$ 3,408,680	$ 129,975	$ 190,548	$ 1,104,632	$ 1,074,831	$ 5,908,666
Due to other funds	—	25,369	—	—	—	25,369
Payable to other governments	94,074	—	—	—	—	94,074
Deferred revenue	4,250,430	6,273,045	250,000	11,000	—	10,784,475
Total liabilities	7,753,184	6,428,389	440,548	1,115,632	1,074,831	16,812,584
Fund balances:						
Nonspendable						
Inventories	182,821	—	—	—	—	182,821
Liens receivable	791,926	—	—	—	—	791,926

Restricted for:						
Community development	—	576,376	2,119,314	—	—	2,695,690
Debt service	—	—	—	—	3,832,062	3,832,062
Capital projects	—	—	—	5,792,587	1,814,122	7,606,709
Other purposes	310,027	—	—	—	1,405,300	1,715,327
Committed to:						
Community development	—	500,000	11,056,173	—	—	11,556,173
Capital projects	—	—	—	2,569,818	—	2,569,818
Public safety	40,292	—	—	—	—	40,292
Other purposes	—	—	—	—	1,330,718	1,330,718
Assigned to:						
Parks and recreation	100,000	—	—	—	—	100,000
Capital projects	—	—	—	1,000,000	1,241,270	2,241,270
Unassigned	230,300	—	—	—	—	230,300
Total fund balances	1,655,366	1,076,376	13,175,487	9,362,405	9,623,472	34,893,106
Total liabilities and fund balances	$ 9,408,550	$ 7,504,765	$ 13,616,035	$ 10,478,037	$ 10,698,303	

Amounts reported for *governmental activities* in the statement of net position are different because:	
Capital assets used in governmental activities are not financial resources and therefore are not reported in the funds.	161,082,708
Other long-term assets are not available to pay for current-period expenditures and therefore are deferred in the funds.	9,348,876
Internal service funds are used by management to charge the costs of certain activities, such as insurance and telecommunications, to individual funds. The assets and liabilities of the internal service funds are included in governmental activities in the statement of net position.	2,994,691
Long-term liabilities, including bonds payable, are not due and payable in the current period and therefore are not reported in the funds.	(84,760,507)
Net position of governmental activities	$ 123,558,874

Figure 4.5 Illustrative Governmental Funds Balance Sheet

Statement of Revenues, Expenditures, and Changes in Fund Balances
Governmental Funds
For the Year Ended December 31, 2011

	General	Housing Programs	Community Redevelopment	Road Construction	Other Governmental Funds	Total Governmental Funds
REVENUES						
Property taxes	$ 51,173,436	$ —	$ —	$ —	$ 4,680,192	$ 55,853,628
Franchise taxes	4,055,505	—	—	—	—	4,055,505
Public service taxes	8,969,887	—	—	—	—	8,969,887
Fees and fines	606,946	—	—	—	—	606,946
Licenses and permits	2,287,794	—	—	—	—	2,287,794
Intergovernmental	6,119,938	2,578,191	—	—	2,830,916	11,529,045
Charges for services	11,374,460	—	—	—	30,708	11,405,168
Investment earnings	552,325	87,106	549,489	270,161	364,330	1,823,411
Miscellaneous	881,874	66,176	—	2,939	94	951,083
Total revenues	86,022,165	2,731,473	549,489	273,100	7,906,240	97,482,467
EXPENDITURES						
Current:						
General government	8,630,835	—	417,814	16,700	121,052	9,186,401
Public safety	33,729,623	—	—	—	—	33,729,623
Public works	4,975,775	—	—	—	3,721,542	8,697,317
Engineering services	1,299,645	—	—	—	—	1,299,645
Health and sanitation	6,070,032	—	—	—	—	6,070,032
Cemetery	706,305	—	—	—	—	706,305

Culture and recreation	11,411,685	—	—	—	—	11,411,685
Community development	—	2,954,389	—	—	—	2,954,389
Education—payment to school district	21,893,273	—	—	—	—	21,893,273
Debt service:						
Principal	—	—	—	—	3,450,000	3,450,000
Interest and other charges	—	—	—	—	5,215,151	5,215,151
Capital outlay	—	—	2,246,671	11,281,769	3,190,209	16,718,649
Total expenditures	88,717,173	2,954,389	2,664,485	11,298,469	15,697,954	121,332,470
Excess (deficiency) of revenues over expenditures	(2,695,008)	(222,916)	(2,114,996)	(11,025,369)	(7,791,714)	(23,850,003)
OTHER FINANCING SOURCES (USES)						
Proceeds of refunding bonds	—	—	—	—	38,045,000	38,045,000
Proceeds of long-term capital-related debt	—	—	17,529,560	—	1,300,000	18,829,560
Payment to bond refunding escrow agent	—	—	—	—	(37,284,144)	(37,284,144)
Transfers in	129,323	—	—	—	5,551,187	5,680,510
Transfers out	(2,163,759)	(348,046)	(2,273,187)	—	(219,076)	(5,004,068)
Total other financing sources and uses	(2,034,436)	(348,046)	15,256,373	—	7,392,967	20,266,858
SPECIAL ITEM						
Proceeds from sale of park land	3,476,488	—	—	—	—	3,476,488
Net change in fund balances	(1,252,956)	(570,962)	13,141,377	(11,025,369)	(398,747)	(106,657)
Fund balances—beginning	2,908,322	1,647,338	34,110	20,387,774	10,022,219	34,999,763
Fund balances—ending	$ 1,655,366	$1,076,376	$13,175,487	$9,362,405	$9,623,472	$34,893,106

Figure 4.6 Illustrative Governmental Funds Statement of Revenues, Expenditures, and Changes in Fund Balances

(1) to provide additional detail beyond the information shown on the face of the financial statement and (2) to show how capital assets and long-term liabilities changed over the course of the year. The capital assets note shows major classes of capital assets—such as land, buildings, and equipment—individually. For each class of capital assets, the note shows both the total original purchase price or construction cost (historical cost) and the total depreciation that has accumulated over time, as well as how these amounts changed during the year.

The long-term liabilities note is arranged similarly to the capital assets note: governmental and business-type activities are shown separately, and major categories of long-term liabilities are listed for each. The columns show (1) the beginning-of-the-year balances for each type of liability, (2) new liabilities incurred during the year (additions), (3) amounts of liabilities paid during the year (reductions), and (4) the amounts still outstanding at the end of the year.

Required Supplementary Information

In addition to introducing MD&A, Statement 34 also requires and improves upon another piece of RSI, the budgetary comparison. Statement 34 requires governments to prepare budgetary comparisons for the general fund and any special revenue fund that has a legally adopted annual budget.[18] Statement 34 substantially improved the usefulness of the budgetary comparison (**Figure 4.7**) by requiring the presentation of information from the originally adopted budget, in addition to the final modified budget and the actual results for the year. All governments must present a reconciliation that describes the differences, if any, between the budgetary-basis information in the actual results column with the modified accrual information in the governmental funds statement of revenues, expenditures, and changes in fund balances.

Economic Condition and the Revamping of the Statistical Section

The movement toward government-wide reporting of economic resource flows presaged a shift in the GASB's thinking about fiscal health and stress. To recognize financial reporting's emphasis on more comprehensive measurement of a government's financial status and to avoid the confusion attendant with the varied definitions then in use of the terms financial position and financial condition,[19] the GASB developed the term *economic condition:*

<u>Economic Condition</u>—Economic condition is a composite of a government's financial position and its ability and willingness to meet its financial obligations and service commitments on an ongoing basis. Economic condition includes three components: financial position, fiscal capacity, and service capacity.

<u>Financial Position</u>—Financial position is the status of a government's assets, deferred outflows, liabilities, deferred inflows, and net position, as displayed in the basic financial statements.

Budgetary Comparison Schedule for the General Fund
For the Year Ended December 31, 2002

	Budgeted Amounts		Actual Amounts	Variances—Positive (Negative)		Budget to GAAP	Actual Amounts
	Original	Final	Budgetary Basis	Original to Final	Final to Actual	Reconciliation	GAAP Basis
REVENUES							
Property taxes	$ 52,017,833	$ 51,853,018	$ 51,173,436	$ (164,815)	$ (679,582)	—	$ 51,173,436
Other taxes—franchise and public service	12,841,209	12,836,024	13,025,392	(5,185)	189,368	—	13,025,392
Fees and fines	718,800	718,800	606,946	—	(111,854)	—	606,946
Licenses and permits	2,126,600	2,126,600	2,287,794	—	161,194	—	2,287,794
Intergovernmental	6,905,898	6,571,360	6,119,938	(334,538)	(451,422)	—	6,119,938
Charges for services	12,392,972	11,202,150	11,374,460	(1,190,822)	172,310	—	11,374,460
Interest	1,015,945	550,000	552,325	(465,945)	2,325	—	552,325
Miscellaneous	3,024,292	1,220,991	881,874	(1,803,301)	(339,117)	—	881,874
Total revenues	91,043,549	87,078,943	86,022,165	(3,964,606)	(1,056,778)	—	86,022,165
EXPENDITURES							
Current:							
General government	11,837,534	9,468,155	8,621,500	2,369,379	846,655	9,335	8,630,835
Public safety	33,050,966	33,983,706	33,799,709	(932,740)	183,997	(70,086)	33,729,623
Public works	5,215,630	5,025,848	4,993,187	189,782	32,661	(17,412)	4,975,775

(continued)

Figure 4.7 Illustrative Budgetary Comparison

Budgetary Comparison Schedule for the General Fund
For the Year Ended December 31, 2002

	Budgeted Amounts		Actual Amounts	Variances—Positive (Negative)		Budget to GAAP	Actual Amounts
	Original	Final	Budgetary Basis	Original to Final	Final to Actual	Reconciliation	GAAP Basis
Engineering services	1,296,275	1,296,990	1,296,990	(715)	—	2,655	1,299,645
Health and sanitation	5,756,250	6,174,653	6,174,653	(418,403)	—	(104,621)	6,070,032
Cemetery	724,500	724,500	706,305	—	18,195	—	706,305
Culture and recreation	11,059,140	11,368,070	11,289,146	(308,930)	78,924	122,539	11,411,685
Education—payment to school district	22,000,000	22,000,000	21,893,273	—	106,727	—	21,893,273
Total expenditures	90,940,295	90,041,922	88,774,763	898,373	1,267,159	(57,590)	88,717,173
Excess (deficiency) of revenues over expenditures	103,254	(2,962,979)	(2,752,598)	(3,066,233)	210,381	57,590	(2,695,008)
OTHER FINANCING SOURCES (USES)							
Transfers in	939,525	130,000	129,323	(809,525)	(677)	—	129,323
Transfers out	(2,970,256)	(2,163,759)	(2,163,759)	806,497	—	—	(2,163,759)
Total other financing sources and uses	(2,030,731)	(2,033,759)	(2,034,436)	(3,028)	(677)	—	(2,034,436)
SPECIAL ITEMS							
Proceeds from sale of park land	1,355,250	3,500,000	3,476,488	2,144,750	(23,512)	—	3,476,488
Total other financing sources (uses) and special items							

Net change in fund balance	(572,227)	(1,496,738)	(1,310,546)	(924,511)	186,192	57,590	(1,252,956)
Fund balances—beginning	3,528,750	2,742,799	2,742,799	(785,951)	—	165,523	2,908,322
Fund balances—ending	$ 2,956,523	$ 1,246,061	$ 1,432,253	$ (1,710,462)	$ 186,192	$ 223,113	$ 1,655,366

Explanation of differences:

(1) The City budgets for claims and compensated absences only to the extent expected to be paid, rather than on the modified accrual basis.	$ (129,100)
Encumbrances for goods and services ordered but not received are reported as expenditures in the year *the orders are placed* for budgetary purposes, but are reported in the year the goods and services *are received* for GAAP purposes.	186,690
Net increase in fund balance—budget to GAAP	$ 57,590

(2) The amount reported as "fund balance" on the budgetary basis of accounting derives from the basis of accounting used in preparing the City's budget. (See the notes for a description of the City's budgetary accounting method.) This amount differs from the fund balance reported in the statement of revenues, expenditures, and changes in fund balances because of the cumulative effect of transactions such as those just described.

Figure 4.7 Illustrative Budgetary Comparison (cont.)

Fiscal Capacity—Fiscal capacity is the government's ability and willingness to meet its financial obligations as they come due on an ongoing basis.

Service Capacity—Service capacity is the government's ability and willingness to meet its commitments to provide services on an ongoing basis.

These definitions derived from the GASB's review of its own concepts statements, the Berne study, a 1981 NCGA Research Report, *Objectives of Accounting and Financial Reporting for Governmental Units: A Research Study,* and other relevant literature. Research conducted by the GASB, asking panels of persons experienced in assessing financial health to compare the existing financial reporting model with these definitions, concluded that a CAFR "contains most, if not all, of the information needed to assess financial position; some but not enough information about fiscal capacity; and little information about service capacity."[20] The panelists identified the statistical section of a CAFR as a particularly valuable source of relevant information, a point also made in the Berne study. The GASB decided to turn its attention to the statistical section, which had not been revisited since the issuance of NCGA Statement 1.

The statistical section project culminated in Statement No. 44, *Economic Condition Reporting: The Statistical Section—an amendment of NCGA Statement 1,* issued in 2004. Statement 44 incorporated the government-wide information required by Statement 34, organized the statistical section along categories of information, updated the requirements to reflect changes in the governmental environment (such as the increasing issuance of long-term debt other than general obligation bonds), and aligned the schedules more closely with the needs of users of financial reports.

Statement 44 requires 17 schedules, most covering the past 10 fiscal years, presenting five types of information: financial trends, revenue capacity, debt capacity, demographic and economic information, and operating information. The financial trends schedules present net position and fund balance and both government-wide and governmental funds inflows and outflows, essentially like 10 years' worth of financial statements lined up side-by-side. Revenue capacity schedules present information about a government's most significant own-source revenue—sources like taxes and fees, which are imposed by a government itself, as opposed to sources like intergovernmental aid. These schedules present detail about the two factors that directly influence the amount of revenue that will be received—the rate that the government levies (or charges, in the case of fees) and the rates of overlapping governments, and the base that the rates are applied to. A third schedule lists a government's largest tax (revenue) payers. A fourth schedule of property tax levies and collections is presented only if a government's most significant own-source revenue is a property tax.

Four schedules address a government's debt burden and ability to issue additional debt. The first two debt schedules present all of a government's outstanding long-term debt and just the debt repaid with general resources, respectively. A third schedule adds overlapping debt into the mix—the proportionate share of the debt of overlapping governments that is applicable to the taxpayers of a government. The last debt schedule shows how the legal limit on how much debt a government can have outstanding is calculated.

The statistical section includes at least two schedules that contain demographic and economic information about the government's geographic area. One schedule should include, at a minimum, population, total personal income, per capita personal income, and the unemployment rate. A government may also present other indicators, such as median age of the population, average educational attainment, employment, school enrollment, and so on. Governments also present a schedule of their ten largest employers, including the number of persons each employs and the number of employees divided by total employment.

The last three schedules provide information about a government's operations and resources—numbers of government employees by function, operating indicators (demand or level of service for each of the functions), and capital assets (volume, usage, or nature of the capital assets related to the functions).

Fiscal Health and Stress Analysis after Statements 34 and 44

In the year that followed the issuance of Statement 34, the GASB began publishing a series of guides to using the new, Statement 34-based financial reports. The guides were written primarily for laypersons and presumed no prior knowledge of accounting. Their purpose was to help interested nonaccountants understand what information the reports contained and what that information could be used for. One volume was directed at persons with prior experience analyzing governmental financial health and stress and some rudimentary understanding of governmental accounting (Mead, 2001a). This guide and a subsequent paper (Mead, 2001b) laid out an approach to financial analysis built on 37 ratios in seven categories:

1. Common size ratios—percentage distribution and change
2. Financial position ratios, such as net position divided by total expenses and change in net position divided by total expenses
3. Liquidity ratios, including current and quick ratios
4. Solvency ratios, including leverage ratios (such as debt-to-assets) and coverage ratios
5. Fiscal capacity ratios, such as debt or taxes divided by property value, personal income, and population
6. Risk and exposure ratios, such as expenditures divided by property tax revenues
7. Miscellaneous other ratios, including the pension funding ratio, unfunded pension liability divided by property value, employees per pupil, maintenance and repair expenses divided by capital assets, and accumulated depreciation divided by capital assets.

The key feature of this approach was its primary focus on the government as a whole and its comprehensive, economic condition, which incorporated both government-wide and fund-based financial information and both a long-term and short-term view.

The ICMA Handbook

In 2003, ICMA published a fourth edition of its Handbook (Nollenberger, Groves, and Valente, 2003) The ICMA's basic approach to analyzing the financial health of a government remained essentially unchanged. It continued to focus on 12 factors–six *financial* factors that are the results of how five *environmental* factors are responded to by *organizational* factors (in other words, management practices and legislative policies). In addition, few changes were made to the ratios and other information required for the ICMA's methodology; they were not revised to incorporate the new information resulting from Statement 34.

One notable change anticipated the issuance by the GASB of standards for measuring and reporting the obligations and costs related to other postemployment benefits (OPEB) such as retiree health insurance (see Chapter 6, Postemployment Benefits and Fiscal Analysis). The prior "accumulated employee leave" indicator was revised to a "post employment (sic) benefits" indicator that includes the unfunded actuarial accrued liability for retiree health insurance, though not for other forms of OPEB.

Other changes were more noticeable in the indicators for the environmental and organizational factors. Population density, population under 18 and over 64, top taxpayers, home ownership rate, and crime rates were added as community needs and resources indicators. The Handbook also expanded on the analysis of more qualitative factors, such as intergovernmental constraints, political culture, and risk of disaster.

Smaller-Scale Approaches

The GASB and ICMA approaches have the same key shortcoming as the earlier editions of the Handbook; namely, three dozen indicators could prove too unwieldy for use by taxpayers, legislators, and many finance officers. Chaney, Mead, and Schermann (2002) proposed a smaller set of potential new ratios with the intention to spur the discussion of how to use Statement 34 information to assess financial condition. The article suggested six ratios and calculated them using two early implementers of Statement 34. Each of the ratios was calculated separately for governmental activities and business-type activities, as well as for the total primary government:

- Financial position–unrestricted net assets divided by expenses
- Financial performance–change in net assets divided by total net assets
- Financial performance–general revenues plus transfers divided by expenses
- Liquidity–cash, current investments, and receivables divided by current liabilities
- Solvency–long-term debt divided by assets
- Solvency–change in net assets plus interest expense divided by interest expense.

The accounting firm of Crawford & Associates, P.C., developed an indicator system that is founded on post-Statement 34 financial reporting. The Crawford Government Finance Performeter™ is an overall "reading" or number on a scale of 1–10 (10 being "excellent financial health"). The overall reading is based on the calculation and evaluation of performance measures in the following categories—change in overall financial condition, intergenerational equity, level of reserves or deficit, revenue dispersion, self-sufficiency, capital asset condition, financing margin, debt load, solvency, and liquidity.

Many of these measures use government-wide and full accrual information. For example, change in overall financial condition is the percentage change in primary government net assets. Debt load is calculated as debt service as a percentage of expenditures for both governmental and business-type activities. Level of reserves employs unrestricted net assets in its calculation. Capital asset condition, which measures the extent to which capital assets are reaching the end of their useful lives, divides accumulated depreciation by historical cost. One of the solvency ratios is net assets as a percentage of total assets.

The new 10-point test developed in Michigan borrowed the framework of Brown's test, but comprises a different set of indicators. Further, it took little notice of Statement 34, with the exception of its reference to major funds. The simplicity of Brown's 10-point test makes it a useful tool for local governments, especially smaller ones with few financial or accounting staff. Unfortunately, Brown either used proxies or included no indicators at all to address long-run financial issues; as a result, the test is skewed toward the short run and largely ignores long-run concerns that have a significant impact on financial health and stress.

Mead (2006) attempted to update the 10-point test to encompass a long-run, government-wide perspective while maintaining the basic 10-point structure. Two of Brown's "operating position" ratios were retained—unreserved general fund balance divided by general fund revenues, and general fund cash and investments divided by general fund liabilities (though the latter was revised to remove deferred revenues). However, his ratio of modified accrual revenues to expenditures was replaced with an accrual-based ratio of change in governmental activities net assets divided by total governmental activities net assets. Brown's three "revenues" ratios—per capita revenues, general fund revenues from own sources as a percentage of total general fund sources, and general fund sources from other funds as a percentage of total general fund sources—were replaced with a ratio of intergovernmental aid divided by total revenues for the primary government and a ratio of self-sufficiency: net (expense) revenue for governmental activities divided by total governmental activities expenses.

Brown's ratio of per capita direct long-term debt was replaced with a more comprehensive measure of *total outstanding debt* per capita for the primary government. His other "debt structure" ratios—debt service divided by total revenues and total general fund liabilities divided by total general fund revenues—were kept but revised. In the former, noncapital governmental funds expenditures were used in the denominator instead of revenues; the latter became a government-wide ratio of primary government liabilities (less deferred revenue) divided by primary government revenues. A fourth ratio was added to capture the ability to repay enterprise fund-related debt—enterprise funds operating revenue plus interest expense, divided by interest expense. Finally, Brown's "expenditures" measure of operating expenditures divided by total expenditures, which purported to indicate whether infrastructure was being properly maintained, was highly problematic and certainly less useful than some of the new capital asset information resulting from Statement 34. Consequently, it was replaced with a ratio of percentage change in net value of capital assets.

The first scholarly article to apply Statement 34-based ratios to assessments of financial health was likely Wang, Dennis, and Tu (2007). Using a framework similar to the ICMA's four types of solvency, the authors collected information from state financial reports to calculate 11 financial ratios.

Conclusion

The interconnectedness between accounting and financial reporting standards and the assessment of fiscal health and stress dates back nearly a century. The assessment of government finances has been influenced by the information that is readily available, as determined by the standards, and the standards in turn have been updated and improved to better meet the needs of individual and organizations concerned with fiscal stress and health.

This relationship continues to function to this day. Standards setting continues to occur in a charged environment of competing needs among varied stakeholders. At least twice in the past 15 years the GASB's independence has been seriously challenged by constituent groups unhappy with the areas for which it has considered establishing standards. The creation of Statement 34 was dogged by the opposition of the Government Finance Officers Association (GFOA) to the reporting of infrastructure assets. Subsequently, the GFOA called for the dissolution of the GASB in response to the GASB's work on service efforts and accomplishments reporting. In both instances, the GASB issued its pronouncements despite the threats to its independence.

A key message to be taken from these episodes is that the needs of the user of governmental financial information are preeminent in the setting of accounting and financial reporting standards. Satisfying the information needs of persons assessing governmental fiscal health and fiscal stress and governmental accountability is the main purpose of accounting standards setting. The needs and concerns of the preparers and auditors of governmental financial reports are closely considered and taken very seriously by the GASB, which seeks to strike a balance between the competing needs of its constituents. But ultimately, the provision of information for making decisions and assessing accountability remains the GASB's *raison d'être.* A provision in the 2010 Dodd-Frank Act establishing an independent funding source for the GASB, replacing the voluntary governmental support that has historically left the GASB with sizable annual deficits, holds the promise of shielding the GASB from further undue influence.

This intervention is timely, as the need for scrutiny of government finances continues to grow, leading the GASB to explore financial reporting in forms that diverge from traditional historical financial statements, forms likely to raise the ire of some constituent organizations. The national recession beginning in 2008 and the subsequent wave of fiscal stress in state and local governments, for example, has placed greater emphasis on understanding whether governments have the financial wherewithal to continue operating in the future as they have in the past. Under the general rubric of *fiscal sustainability,* public sector standards setters at the international, national, and subnational levels have been considering *forward-looking information* that would be valuable to determining if governments are on a fiscally sustainable path.

Federal Accounting Standards Advisory Board (FASAB) Statement 36, *Comprehensive Long-Term Projections for the U.S. Government,* requires the federal government and its agencies to present a basic financial statement that contains the present value of projected receipts and noninterest spending under current policy without change for the next 75 years, the relationship of these amounts to projected gross domestic product (GDP), and the change from the previous year. RSI would contain projected trends in receipts and spending, deficits, and Treasury debt held by the public as a percentage of GDP, as well as results under alternative scenarios.

As of this writing, the GASB has proposed a requirement that state and local governments report projected inflows and outflows of resources for each of the next five years, at a minimum, as RSI, as well as projected financial obligations and service interdependencies (GASB, 2011). The International Public Sector Accounting Standards Board also is working in this area and issued a consultation paper, *Reporting on the Long-Term Sustainability of Public Finances,* in November 2009.

The effect of the national recession and the stock market tumble on the funded status of public employee pension plans has brought to bear unprecedented scrutiny of retirement benefits, including retiree health insurance. Coincidental with this heightened attention, the GASB has reviewed and proposed significant revisions to its standards for pension reporting. The proposals would result in the unfunded pension liability being reported for the first time as a liability of the government promising the benefits. They would also result in the cost of pension benefits being recognized immediately in some cases, and in general more quickly than under the existing approach of amortizing costs over a period of up to 30 years.

Considerable interest in *popular reporting* has been spurred by greater awareness in the general public of the financial challenges of their governments. Reporting in a manner that is more broadly accessible than the audited annual financial report has been discussed and experimented with for several decades. This area, too, has been a past topic of exploration by the GASB, though not one in which it has established any standards or suggested guidelines. Carried for many years on the GASB's technical agenda as a potential project, the combination of new efforts to encourage popular reporting by governments and greater demand for generally digestible information may lead the GASB to shift from passive to active exploration of a standardized approach to reporting to the average citizen.

In sum, the outlook for the provision of decision-useful and analysis-ready governmental financial information is for greater and more transparent disclosure. As financial issues proliferate and exacerbate, and as media attention to these issues intensifies, the demand for understandable and meaningful information is likely to grow concomitantly. This scenario bodes well for the person seeking new and more informative information with which to assess the fiscal health of governments and to evaluate and anticipate fiscal stress.

Endnotes

1. The opinions expressed in this chapter are those of the author. Official positions of the Governmental Accounting Standards Board are established only after extensive public due process and deliberation.
2. This section on the National Municipal League and the New York Bureau of Municipal Research draws heavily on Kahn (1997).
3. For example, see FASB Statement No. 35, *Accounting and Reporting by Defined Benefit Pension Plans.*
4. See, for example, Moody's (1989), Standard & Poor's (1993), and Fitch IBCA (now FitchRatings) (2000).
5. See, for example, Standard & Poor's (2005).
6. Feldstein (2008) specifically identifies these areas of concern: limits of the basic security; flow-of-funds structure; rate, user charge, or dedicated revenue and tax covenants; priority of the pledged revenue claims; and additional bonds test.
7. For fiscal years beginning prior to January 1, 2012, the statement of net position was called the "statement of net assets." Statement No. 63, *Financial Reporting of Deferred Outflows of Resources, Deferred Inflows of Resources, and Net Position,* changed the name to reflect that the financial statement included not only assets and liabilities, but also deferred outflows of resources and deferred inflows of resources. Net assets is the difference between assets and liabilities, whereas net position equals assets and deferred outflows minus liabilities and deferred inflows. See GASB Concepts Statement No. 4, *Elements of Financial Statements.*
8. See GASB Statement 34, paragraphs 298–299.
9. Reporting infrastructure assets was previously optional. See NCGA Statement 1, paragraph 40.
10. GASB Statement 34, paragraph 355.
11. GASB Statement 34, paragraphs 42 and 357.
12. Although dedicated taxes may be restricted by a government to financing a particular program or function, they do not derive from the activities of the program or function, as do user charges. See Statement 34, paragraphs 373–375.
13. The following changes in net position are also shown separately at the bottom of the statement as a source of financing the net cost of services: contributions to term and permanent endowments; contributions to permanent fund principal; and transfers between governmental and business-type activities.
14. Under Statement 34 fund statements are conceptually on an equal footing with the government-wide statements.
15. GASB Statement 34, paragraphs 380–381.
16. Internal service funds and fiduciary funds still employ fund-type reporting.
17. The GASB reviewed the body of existing note disclosures in a separate project that resulted in Statement 38, issued in June 2001. The GASB subsequently made extensive changes to the note disclosures and RSI for pensions and other postemployment benefits; see Chapter 6, Postemployment Benefits and Fiscal Analysis.
18. Although the GASB favors presenting the budgetary comparison as an RSI *schedule,* governments have the option to present the comparison as one of the basic financial statements.

19. See Mead, 2002.
20. Statement 44, paragraph 53.

Glossary

Accrual basis of accounting: the basis of accounting used in all financial statements except governmental funds financial statements and the proprietary funds statement of cash flows.

Assets: resources a government owns or controls that can be used in the provision of services or the generation of other resources to support service provision.

Capital assets: assets with useful lives extending beyond one year, such as buildings, equipment, and infrastructure.

Expenditures: outflows of resources, under modified accrual, that occur when resources are consumed or goods and services are purchased and received.

Expenses: outflows of resources, under full accrual, that occur when assets are consumed or costs are incurred.

Fiduciary fund: a fund that accounts for resources belonging to others that a government holds in a fiduciary or agency capacity; fiduciary fund types include pension and other postemployment benefit, private-purpose trust, investment trust, and agency funds.

Fund: an accounting construct that is allocated its own set of assets and liabilities associated with a particular function, program, or activities; the financial transactions of a fund represent just a portion of the government's overall financial activity.

Generally accepted accounting principles (GAAP): the body of standards that explain how finances should be accounted for and reported.

Governmental fund: a fund that accounts for the basic, typically tax-supported activities of a government; governmental fund types include general, special revenue, debt service, capital projects, and permanent funds.

Infrastructure: especially long-lived capital assets, such as roads, bridges, and sewers.

Liabilities: amounts a government owes to others.

Management's discussion and analysis (MD&A): a narrative section preceding the financial statements that summarizes the financial activity covered by the financial statements and provides explanations for the financial results of the period.

Modified accrual basis of accounting: the basis of accounting used in the government funds financial statements.

Proprietary fund: a fund that accounts for activities that charge a fee for services, such as water and sewer; proprietary fund types include enterprise and internal service funds.

Required supplementary information (RSI): unaudited information that governments are required to present with financial statements and notes, such as management's discussion and analysis.

Revenues: inflows of resources that are measurable and collectible; under modified accrual, they are also available to finance current-period expenditures.

Discussion Questions

1. In what ways did GASB Statement 34 improve the usefulness of state and local government financial reports for assessing fiscal health and stress? In what ways, if any, was the pre-Statement 34 financial report more useful for assessing fiscal health and stress?
2. What issues do the various approaches to assessing fiscal health and stress share in common?
3. "The approaches to assessing fiscal health and stress have changed dramatically since the issuance of GASB Statement 34." Do you agree with this statement? Why or why not?
4. Who has historically had the greatest impact on the determination of what information state and local governments are required to report about fiscal health and stress–financial reformers, citizen research organizations, municipal bond analysts, professional associations, or others? Support your conclusion.

Recommended Resources

Gauthier, S. (2012). *Governmental Accounting, Auditing, and Financial Reporting.* Chicago: Government Finance Officers Association.

Governmental Accounting Standards Board, www.gasb.org

Governmental Accounting Standards Board. (2011). *Codification of Governmental Accounting Standards, 2011–2012.* Norwalk, CT: Financial Accounting Foundation.

Mead, D. M. (2012) *An Analyst's Guide to State and Local Government Financial Statements* (2nd ed.). Norwalk, CT: Financial Accounting Foundation.

References

Akin, J. S. (1973). Fiscal capacity and the estimation method of the Advisory Commission on Intergovernmental Relations. *National Tax Journal, 26*(2), 275–291.

Auditor General, State of Florida. (2001). *Local governmental entity financial condition assessment procedures* (draft). Tallahassee: Auditor General, October.

Bean, D. R. (2009). A look back at 25 years of high-quality standards-setting. *Journal of Government Financial Management,* Fall, 26–39.

Benson, E. D., Marks, B. R., and Raman, K. K. (1988). Tax effort as an indicator of fiscal stress. *Public Finance Quarterly, 16*(2), 203–218.

Berne, R. (1992). *The relationship between financial reporting and the measurement of financial condition.* Norwalk, CT: Governmental Accounting Standards Board.

Berne, R., and Drennan, M. (1985). *The fiscal and economic condition of New York.* NY: AMBAC.

Berne, R., and Drennan, M. (1987a). *The fiscal and economic condition of Texas.* NY: AMBAC.

Berne, R., and Drennan, M. (1987b). *The fiscal and economic condition of California.* NY: AMBAC.

Berne, R., and Schramm, R. (1986). *The financial analysis of governments.* Englewood Cliffs, NJ: Prentice-Hall.

Bradbury, K. L. (1983). Structural fiscal distress in cities—causes and consequences. *New England Economic Review,* January/February, 32–43.

Brown, K. W. (1993). The 10-point test of financial condition: Toward an easy-to-use assessment tool for smaller cities. *Government Finance Review, 9*(6), 21–26.

Bureau of Municipal Research. (1913). *Handbook of municipal accounting.* New York: D. Appleton and Company.

Chaney, B. A., Mead, D. M., and Schermann, K. R. (2002). The new governmental financial reporting model: What it means for analyzing government financial condition. *Journal of Government Financial Management, 51*(1), 26–31.

Clark, T. N. (1994). Municipal fiscal strain: Indicators and causes. *Government Finance Review,* June, 27–29.

Clark, T. N., and Ferguson, L. C. (1983). *City money: Political processes, fiscal strain, and retrenchment.* New York: Columbia University Press.

Cleveland, F. A. (1909). *Chapters on municipal administration and accounting.* New York: Longmans, Green, and Co.

Cohen, C. E. (1989). State fiscal capacity and effort: An update. *Intergovernmental Perspective,* Spring, 15–20.

Cohen, C. E., and Lucke, R. B. (1985). The measurement of state-local fiscal capacity and the 1983 representative tax system estimates. *Intergovernmental Perspective,* Fall, 22–28.

Crawford & Associates, P. C. (n.d.). The Crawford government finance Performeter: A financial statement analysis using indicators of the financial health and success of the City of Guymon, Oklahoma as of and for the year ended June 30, 2001. Oklahoma City, OK.

Crawford & Associates, P. C. (n.d.). The Performeter: A financial statement analysis using indicators of the financial health and success of the State of Michigan as of and for the year ended September 30, 2001. Oklahoma City, OK.

Eggleston, D. C. (1914). *Municipal accounting.* New York: The Ronald Press Company.

Feldstein, S. G. (2008). General analytical framework for assessing the credit worthiness of revenue bonds. In S. G. Feldstein and F. J. Fabozzi, Jr. (Eds.), *The handbook of municipal bonds* (Chapter 49, pp. 809–812). Hoboken, NJ: John Wiley & Sons, Inc.

Feldstein, S. G., and Goode, T. J. (2008). How to Analyze General Obligation Bonds. In S. G. Feldstein and F. J. Fabozzi, Jr. (Eds.), *The handbook of municipal bonds* (Chapter 48, pp. 789–808). Hoboken, NJ: John Wiley & Sons, Inc.

Ferguson, R. F., and Ladd, H. F. (1986). Measuring the fiscal capacity of U.S. cities. In H. C. Reeves (Ed.), *Measuring fiscal capacity* (Chapter 5, pp. 141–168). Boston: Oelgeschlager, Gunn & Hain, in association with the Lincoln Institute of Land Policy.

Fitch IBCA. (2000). *Local government general obligation rating guidelines.* New York: Fitch IBCA, May 23.

Freeman, R. J., and Allison, G. S. (2006). A century of governmental accounting and financial reporting leadership. *Government Finance Review,* April, 40–47.

Gold, S. D. (1986). Measuring fiscal effort and fiscal capacity: Sorting out some of the controversies. In H. C. Reeves (Ed.), *Measuring Fiscal Capacity* (Chapter 2, pp. 29–50). Boston: Oelgeschlager, Gunn & Hain, in association with the Lincoln Institute of Land Policy.

Governmental Accounting Standards Board (GASB) (2011). Preliminary views, *Economic condition reporting: Financial projections.* Norwalk, CT: GASB.

Groves, S. M., and Valente, M. G. (1994). *Evaluating financial condition: A handbook for local government.* Washington, DC: International City/County Management Association.
Groves, S. M., Godsey, M., and Shulman, M. A. (1981). Financial indicators for local government. *Public Budgeting & Finance, 1*(2), , 5–19.
Hebert, M. (1986). *An investigation of the effect of alternative presentation formats on preparers and users of city financial reports.* Doctoral dissertation, Texas Tech University.
Kahn, J. (1997). *Budgeting democracy: State building and citizenship in America, 1890–1928.* Ithaca, NY: Cornell University Press.
Kleine, R., Kloha, P., and Weissert, C. S. (2003). Monitoring local government fiscal health: Michigan's new 10 point scale of fiscal distress. *Government Finance Review, 19*(3), 18–23.
Kloha, P., Weissert, C. S., and Klein, R. (2005). Developing and testing a composite model to predict local fiscal distress. *Public Administration Review, 65*(3), pp. 313–323.
Loviscek, A. L., and Crowley, F. D. (1996). Municipal bond ratings and municipal debt management. In G. J. Miller (Ed.), *Handbook of Debt Management* (Chapter 24, pp. 475–514). New York: Marcel Dekker, Inc.
Mead, D. M. (2001a). *An analyst's guide to government financial statements.* Norwalk, CT: GASB.
Mead, D. M. (2001b). Assessing the financial condition of public school districts: Some tools of the trade. In W. Fowler (Ed.), *Selected Papers in School Finance, 2000–01* (pp. 55–76). Washington, DC: US Government Printing Office.
Mead, D. M. (2002). *Economic condition reporting literature review.* Paper presented at the February 2002 public meeting of the Governmental Accounting Standards Board, February 4, 2002.
Mead, D. M. (2006). A manageable system of economic condition analysis for governments. In H.A. Frank (Ed.), *Handbook of public financial management* (pp. 383–417). New York: Taylor & Francis.
Mead, D. M. (2008). *State and local government use of generally accepted accounting principles for general purpose external financial reporting.* Norwalk, CT: GASB.
Moody's Investors Service, Public Finance Department. (1989). *Moody's on municipals: An introduction to issuing debt.* New York: Moody's.
Morey, L. (1927). *Introduction to governmental accounting.* New York: John Wiley & Sons, Inc.
Morey, L. (1934). Principles of municipal accounting. *The Accounting Review, 9*, 319–325.
Nollenberger, K., Groves, S. M., and Valente, M. G. (2003). *Evaluating financial condition: A handbook for local government.* Washington, DC: ICMA.
Oakey, F. (1921). *Principles of government accounting and reporting.* New York: D. Appleton and Co.
Potts, J. H. (1976). *An analysis of the evolution of municipal accounting to 1935 with primary emphasis on developments in the United States.* Doctoral dissertation, Graduate School of Business, University of Alabama.
Rafuse, R. W., Jr. (1990). A walk on the expenditure side: "Needs" and fiscal capacity. *Intergovernmental Perspective,* Fall, 25–30.
Standard and Poor's Corporation. (1993). *Municipal finance criteria.* New York: S&P.
Standard and Poor's Corporation. (2005). *Standard & Poor's public finance criteria 2005.* New York: The McGraw-Hill Companies, Inc.
Wang, X., Dennis, L., and Tu, Y. S. (2007). Measuring financial condition: A study of U.S. states. *Public Budgeting & Finance, 27*(2), pp. 1–21.

Chapter 5

Long-Term Forecasting

by Kenneth A. Kriz

Introduction

On many occasions, decision makers need forecasts of important variables to inform them of the best decision. Consider a state legislator who is considering a policy to offer tax incentives to businesses that relocate to the state. She would need an accurate forecast of future business generation to form a "baseline" against which the marginal effects of the policy could be calculated and against which the success of the policy could be evaluated. Also, there are many occasions when public administrators who inform decision makers need good forecasts to frame the decision. Consider a city Finance Director who is asked to evaluate the revenue effects of exempting food purchases from sales tax. To begin to evaluate the marginal effects, the Finance Director would need to be able to forecast the dollar volume of grocery purchases many periods into the future.

The consequences of inaccurate (bad) or biased (even worse) forecasts can hardly be overstated. During the first year of the presidential administration of Ronald Reagan, officials at the Office of Tax Analysis in the Department of the Treasury were asked to produce a forecast model of revenues and spending the administration proposed. When the results of the forecast model showed large deficits being created by revenue lost through proposed tax cuts and increases in spending in many areas (especially national defense), these results were brought to the attention of top administration officials. The response, according to then Director of the Office of Management and Budget David Stockman, was to reprogram the models (Greider, 1982). These more forgiving forecasts gave the administration political space to pass the Economic Recovery and Reinvestment Act of 1981 (ERRA 81). The consequences were devastating for federal government finances. The revenue forecasts far exceeded actual revenues. Spending forecasts fell far short of actual spending. The result was a then record budget deficit for fiscal year 1983, causing a loss of confidence in the new administration (and leading to the passage of the Tax Equity and Fiscal Responsibility Act of 1983, which partially undid the major changes in budget direction realized in ERRA 81).

Definitions and Principles

Before we discuss different forecast models, some preliminaries are in order. We first must define what we mean by forecasting as well as define some concepts of forecasts, what the results of forecasting are, and some other terms that help evaluate competing forecast models and put the forecast models in context.

Forecasting Defined

To start, one might reasonably ask what constitutes a forecast. When looking at various forecast models, this only becomes more of a relevant issue. Some forecast models are extremely detailed, with many mathematical equations, graphs, and much discussion of the development of the model. Others are sparser, consisting only of an estimate and perhaps some graphs. A logical question is whether the two are both forecasts, only the more detailed one, or if the detailed one is something more than a forecast. The answer is that both can be forecasts, as long as they share the element that they make a prediction about the future value of some variable. We define *forecasting* broadly as the process of making statements about the value of variables whose values have not yet been realized. This mirrors the definition in several textbooks (Diebold, 2007), but often these other definitions replace the term "the value of variables" with "events." We place the focus on forecasting the value of variables because ultimately these variables tell us more about the event than a simple definition of an event. To illustrate, consider the statement "it will rain tomorrow." This is considered a forecast under previous definitions of forecasting. However, to us this is such a spectacularly incomplete statement as to render the "forecast" worthless. Neither the amount of rain nor the timing is specified. Proper forecast models delineate important variables in terms that decision makers need. If we define the decision maker as a person deciding whether to take an umbrella to work or an event planner trying to decide whether to hold an event outside, we need to produce a forecast that includes the time and intensity concepts of rain. So to us, a forecast would be: "it will rain approximately one inch from 11 AM to 3 PM tomorrow." An even more detailed forecast would be as shown in **Figure 5.1**.

Components of Time-Series Data: Trends and Patterns

Before we can start discussing various terms in forecasting, we have to understand the basic terms in looking at data that moves over time. Most often in forecasting, we are looking for trends and patterns in data. The easiest way to introduce the various terms is through an example. Consider a set of time-series data on monthly cash receipts of the US Federal Government (**Figure 5.2**). The raw data is shown in light gray. It seems to exhibit periods of jagged up and down movements, but does show a positive slope over time.

The positive, upward slope in receipts over time is highlighted in black. This is the *trend* of the data. The trend indicates that over the entire time frame of the data, the mean of the data is increasing. Underlying growth dynamics usually cause trends in data. In this case,

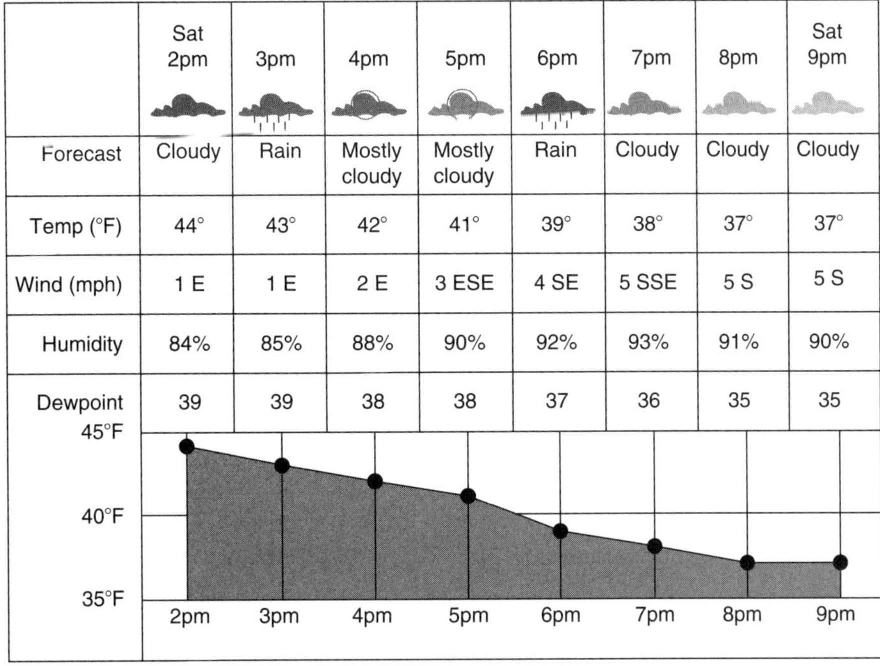

	Sat 2pm	3pm	4pm	5pm	6pm	7pm	8pm	Sat 9pm
Forecast	Cloudy	Rain	Mostly cloudy	Mostly cloudy	Rain	Cloudy	Cloudy	Cloudy
Temp (°F)	44°	43°	42°	41°	39°	38°	37°	37°
Wind (mph)	1 E	1 E	2 E	3 ESE	4 SE	5 SSE	5 S	5 S
Humidity	84%	85%	88%	90%	92%	93%	91%	90%
Dewpoint	39	39	38	38	37	36	35	35

Figure 5.1 Hourly Detailed Weather Forecast for Portland, OR, November 27, 2010.

Source: http://www.accuweather.com/us/or/portland/97200/forecast-hourly.asp (Accessed November 27, 2010).

as the population and economy grow, the economic activity that forms the base of revenues for the federal government also increases systematically. Another distinct pattern in the data is that during somewhat shorter periods of time (lasting two to four years), the data moves up and down in a somewhat smooth pattern around the trend. This shorter-term *cycle* around the trend is shown in dark gray. This reflects short-term business cycles indicating economic recessions and expansions. A third distinct pattern in the data is a regular pattern each year of locally high and low points of revenues. One such short-term high is labeled in the figure. Each April the U.S. Federal Government receives the greatest influx of receipts when individual income tax returns are filed. Though not labeled, there are also local "peaks" in June, September, and December; presumably these are from quarterly estimated tax payments and corporate income tax filings. There are also local "troughs" of receipts in February, May, July, and November. This regular annual pattern is called a *seasonal cycle* or *seasonal* for short and typically represents regular operating patterns or some sort of recurring annual pattern (in retail sales data there is a marked seasonal occurring in November and December as holiday shopping takes place).

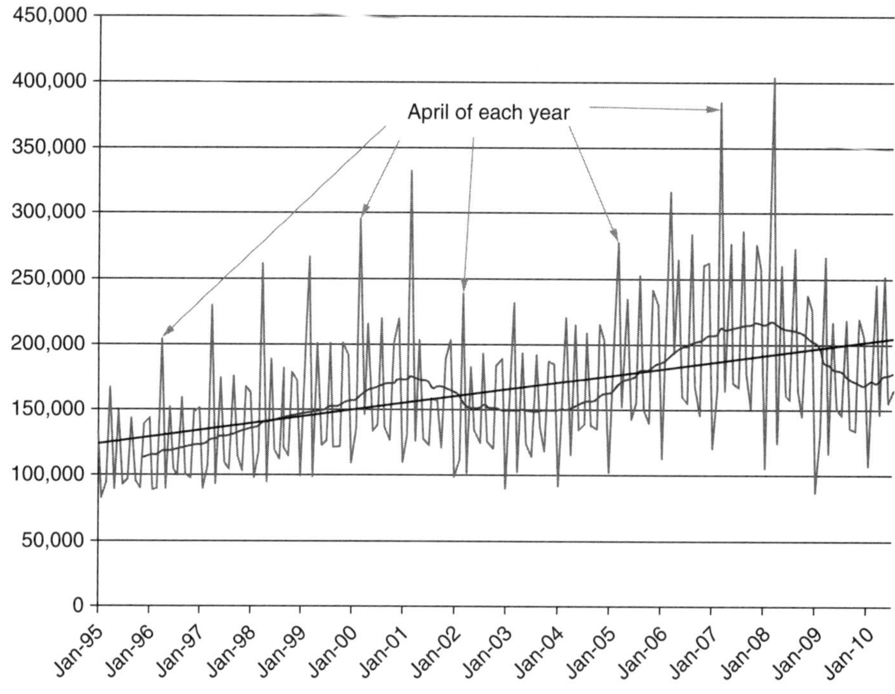

Figure 5.2 Monthly U.S. Federal Government Receipts (000s $), January 1995–August 2010.

Source: U.S. Department of the Treasury, Monthly Treasury Statements.

The final component of time-series data that must be taken into account is the *error* in the data. This is difficult to picture in a theoretical sense, but it represents irregularities in the pattern of data. Assume for a second that you have developed a good model of the time-series data. It would be based on the major three time-series properties of the data that we just discussed: trend, cycle, and seasonal. However, there would still be a component that would be difficult to explain because of its irregularity. Perhaps in some years the April high points of receipts are less peaked as compared to the rest of the year (in Figure 5.2, this occurs in 2002, 2003, and 2004, likely as a result of the tax cuts passed during the 107th and 108th Congresses and signed into law by the Bush Administration in 2001 and 2003). And because models frequently involve the use of historical patterns (either explicitly or implicitly), if the pattern changes unexpectedly, the model will consistently have errors until the new pattern becomes apparent. Both types of errors are shown in **Figure 5.3**, which is the same monthly data on U.S. Treasury receipts, except "zoomed in" to the 2007–2010 period and with a quantitative forecast model included in the graph.[1]

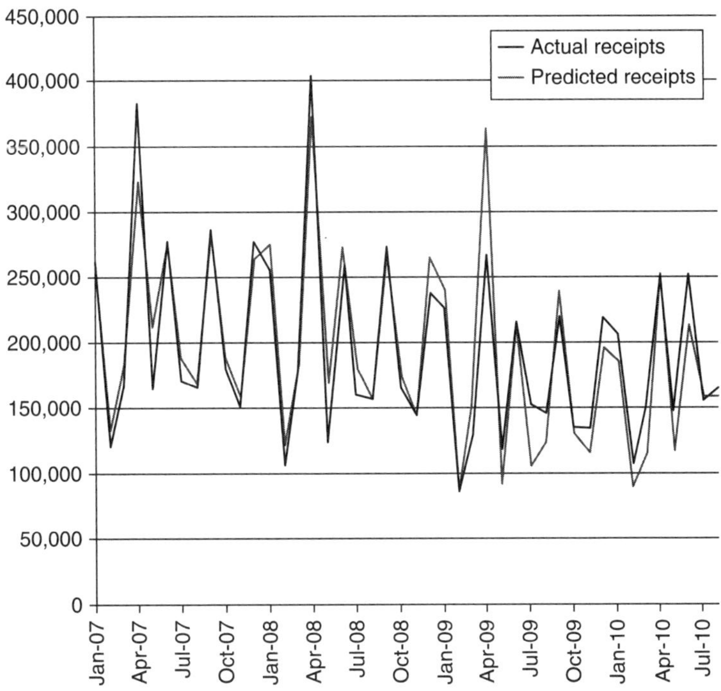

Figure 5.3 Actual and Predicted Monthly U.S. Federal Government Receipts (000s $), January 2007–August 2010.

First, with respect to the seasonal error, in both April 2007 and April 2008, the forecast model underestimated the actual receipts by a relatively large amount (more than 15% in 2007 and 7.3% in 2008). This was due to the fact that revenue peaks were much smaller in 2006 and 2005 compared to those years. So the model "expected" revenue peaks to be of a similar magnitude. Then, after 2008, the model "learned" the pattern and forecast a very strong April 2009 peak. However, the United States had entered a strong recession during 2008, and the expected peak did not materialize. Therefore the April 2009 forecast was more than 36% **greater** than the actual value. An example of the second type of error (one that comes from changes in underlying relationship between variables) is seen in the data when the recession developed during late 2007 and into 2008. As U.S. economic conditions deteriorated, the model consistently overestimated receipts (from October 2007 to September 2008, only **3** months were underestimated and then only by small amounts). Then when the economy turned around in the middle of 2009, the model began to consistently underestimate revenue (from July 2009 to June 2010, only September and April were overestimated, also by relatively small amounts). There are various ways to measure the errors of forecasts; we consider them in later sections.

The Time Dimension of Forecasts

One of the most important dimensions of forecasts is the time dimension when the values of the variables are needed. *Short-term* forecasts are typically prepared when managers need to make an important operational decision, such as the staffing for a public golf course over a summer season or the planning of a treasurer for in-year cash flow and investment planning. These forecasts are typically made for periods of less than one year. Short-term forecasts tend to emphasize recent deviations from long-term trends, with the cyclical nature of data series as well as idiosyncratic errors being the predominant factors in determining short-term forecasts. *Medium-term* forecasts of one to three years are used most often to develop programs. Once strategic plans have been made for organizations and policies have been created to set the organization's direction, accurate forecasts are needed to set the parameters of programs. For example, once general transportation strategy and approaches have been established, forecasts of the medium-term usage of transportation systems will be necessary to guide infrastructure investment and planning, decide on system operations parameters (such as hours of operation, routing of busses, and many other operating characteristics). Medium-term models inform more strategic organizational decisions, such as the need for certain services and the adjustment of policies to meet budgetary imperatives. Medium-term forecasts strike a balance between long-term trends and shorter-term cycles. Errors in medium-term models tend to come from misunderstanding where the data is in cyclical terms.

Once the time frame for forecasts gets past three years, we enter the world of *long-term* forecasting. Long-term forecasts inform strategic planning processes. They help set the overall direction for the organization and (most relevant for this volume) facilitate the assessment of long-term fiscal health and changes needed to maintain or enhance that health. Long-term forecasts necessarily emphasize trends because in the long-term, the cyclical nature of series is relatively less important than in medium or short terms. Errors in long-term forecasts tend to arise from misunderstanding shifts in trends or changes in longer-term cycles. Because this chapter of the book deals with long-term forecasting, we will be concentrating on models that include some specific notion of trends in forecasts.

Principles of Forecasting

There are some basic principles of which all forecasters must be cognizant. These are:

1. Forecasting is never perfect; there is always error, and the predicted error should be included in forecasts to give the consumers of the forecast a sense for how reliable the forecasts may be;
2. The errors of forecasts get larger over time; long-term forecasts should be taken with a substantial "grain of salt";
3. All forecast techniques assume either explicitly or implicitly that we can learn from the past; if the future patterns are significantly different from the past, our errors will be larger than estimated; and if we ignore some past history either intentionally or inadvertently, we are putting the consumers of forecasts at risk; and

4. Forecasting tends to be more accurate at higher levels of aggregation; in the long-term we should forecast only highly aggregated values.

We next consider each principle in turn. The first principle should be obvious but oftentimes is either ignored or minimized. Error is a necessary part of forecasting. If we knew what the future held without error, we would simply put together decisions using the known future values of variables. In this perfect world, all of our models would be deterministic with no uncertainty. Though such forecast accuracy is a theoretical possibility, in practice even the best forecasters have made errors, sometimes very substantial ones. However, often this tenet is not recognized or followed well, especially in cases of public policy forecasting. Consider as an example the forecasts associated with the balances of the Social Security Trust Fund. As part of the exercise in forecasting future payroll tax revenues and payouts from the fund to retired and disabled workers, the trustees of the fund develop a set of economic forecasts. Using the forecasts in the 1994 report of the Chief Actuary,[2] gross domestic product (GDP) was forecast over the next 75 years. In **Figure 5.4** we show their three projections for GDP, the Low Cost, Intermediate Cost, and High Cost projections in light gray, gray, and dark gray, respectively (Board of Trustees, 1994).

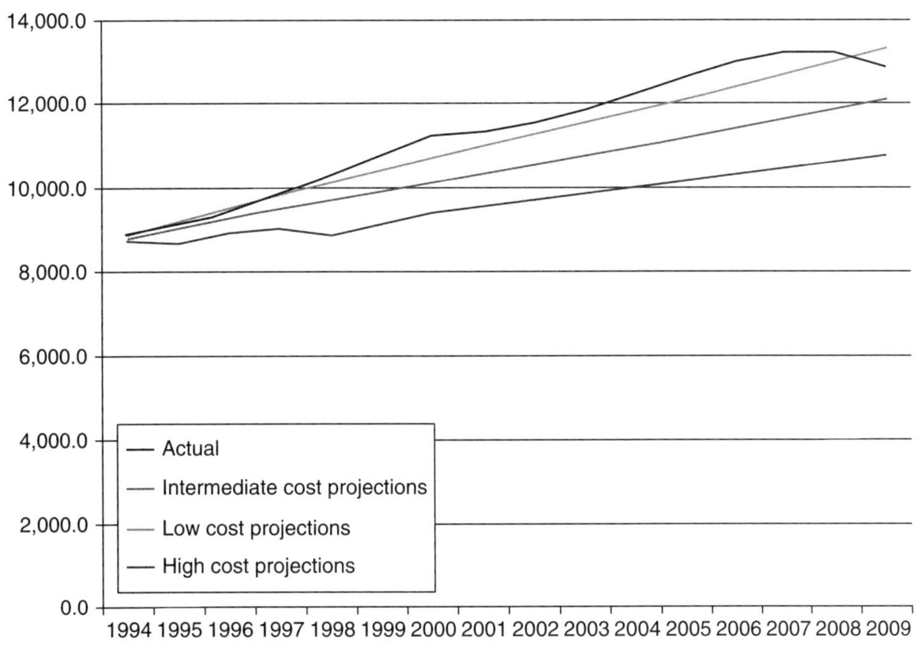

Figure 5.4 Actual and Predicted Gross Domestic Product, 1994–2009.

Source: Author's calculations from (The Board of Trustees, Federal Old-Age and Survivors Insurance and Disability Insurance Trust Funds, 1994; U.S. Bureau of Economic Analysis, 2011).

The names of the projections correspond to the long term cost of maintaining Social Security benefits; hence the Low Cost projection is the highest projection for GDP as this will minimize the cost to the system.

Though there is quite a large difference between the growth rates in the various scenarios, only the Intermediate Cost projections were published in the public press release. The Low Cost and High Cost estimates were buried in the technical report. Part of the problem with not acknowledging errors can be seen in a perpetuation of poor forecasting results. On Figure 5.4, we've also included the actual growth path of real GDP over the forecast period (U.S. Bureau of Economic Analysis, 2011). Until the last year of data available (2009), all of the projections of the Chief Actuary were below the actual values. Only then in the midst of what has been called by many the worst recession since the Great Depression did the actual value of GDP come down to the Low Cost projection. However, despite the readily apparent errors in the projections (and because the errors were all in the same direction we can use the term bias), the Office of the Chief Actuary actually lowered their long-term growth projections. Though only in the long-run can we see whether these lower estimates are accurate, certainly we can call into question the lack of both disclosure of forecast errors and the use of forecasting errors to improve forecast models.

The second forecasting principle is that forecast errors get larger over time. This can be thought of in the following way. Consider if we were forecasting the standings of our favorite sport. If we had to forecast the standings one game into the future, we would probably get very close to an accurate forecast. But if we were to forecast 20 games into the future, the uncertainties about factors that might affect the results of any given game or set of games would mount. Therefore, we can be less certain about forecast values the more distant the results. An example of this is shown in **Figure 5.5**. This figure

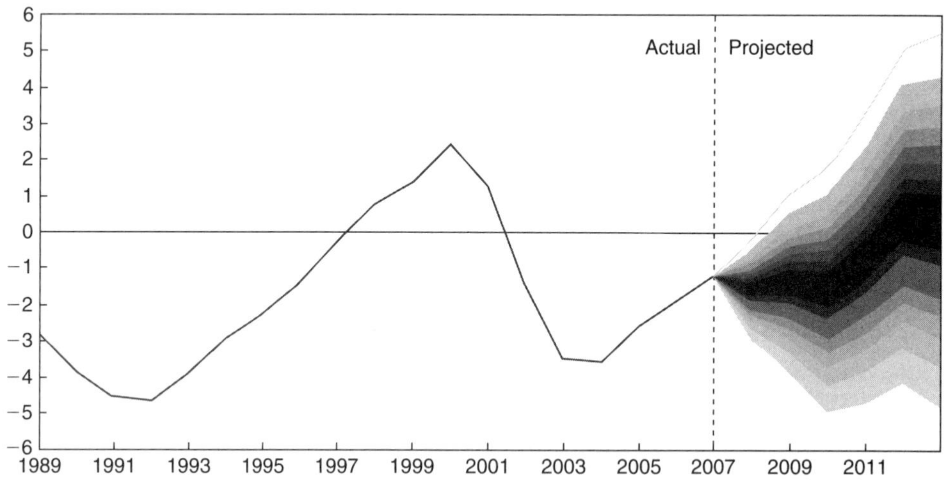

Figure 5.5 Actual and Projected Budget Position as Percentage of Gross Domestic Product, 1989–2018.

was once included in each year's Budget and Economic Outlook, published by the U.S. Congressional Budget Office (for an unknown reason, the figure was last included in the January 2008 Outlook). The baseline budget projection is in the center of the black area of the projection region. As the shades of the regions of the projections get lighter, they show lower probabilities of the outcomes indicated. From this type of "fanchart," we can ascertain a confidence level. According to the CBO, there is a 90% chance that the surplus/deficit budget outcome for a forecast year will fall within the entire area of the fan. So for 2009, there was a 90% chance that the government will have between a 1% of GDP surplus and a deficit of approximately 4% of GDP. Notice how the error term grows over time. By the end of the forecast period, there is an equal probability of having a 5% surplus or 5% deficit. Such uncertainties should be made explicit in forecasts.

The third principle of forecasting states that all models of what will happen in the future are more or less informed by what has happened in the past. The amount of past information that is incorporated into forecast models determines their relative level of naiveté. *Naïve models* are ones that incorporate very little information from past patterns or relationships. More sophisticated models incorporate much information about patterns of growth, change, and fluctuations in data as well as relationships between and among the variables that forecasters are trying to model and other variables whose values might affect the value of the forecasted variable.

When forecasting short-term models, all of the data components just discussed (trend, cycle, and seasonal) are valuable in predictions. For medium- and especially long-term forecasts, the trend component tends to be overwhelmingly the most important piece of information. Typically longer-term forecasts are at a level of time aggregation such that seasonal cycles are not necessary. And over longer time frames, the trend dominates the cycle, making it less important. Further, cycles are notoriously difficult to forecast in that their timing tends to be irregular. Because of these factors, the most important piece of past information to incorporate into a long-term forecast is the past trend in the data.

Capturing the true trend and incorporating it into the forecast is oftentimes easier spoken than accomplished. Several observations are necessary to detect long-term trends, and often there is simply not the history of continuous and consistent recordkeeping required to generate clean long-term data. Sometimes it is necessary to use shorter periods of data to estimate longer-term trends. This can be a very hazardous enterprise when attempting to make long-term predictions. A prime example of this can be found in the forecasts of default rates used in pricing models for collateralized mortgage obligations (CMOs) and collateralized debt obligations (CDOs) during the housing market boom of the 2000s. According to some insiders, default rate forecasts were based on only the most recent several years of data (Gerardi et. al, 2008), a period that had seen mostly benign economic conditions and consistently increasing housing prices. Therefore, owner-occupied home loans had a relatively low default rate, and there were few or no instances of mass defaults spread over disparate geographic regions as one might see during a general slump in housing. Because of this, CDOs and CMOs were overpriced relative to their intrinsic risk, and this amplified the flow of funds into the housing sector.

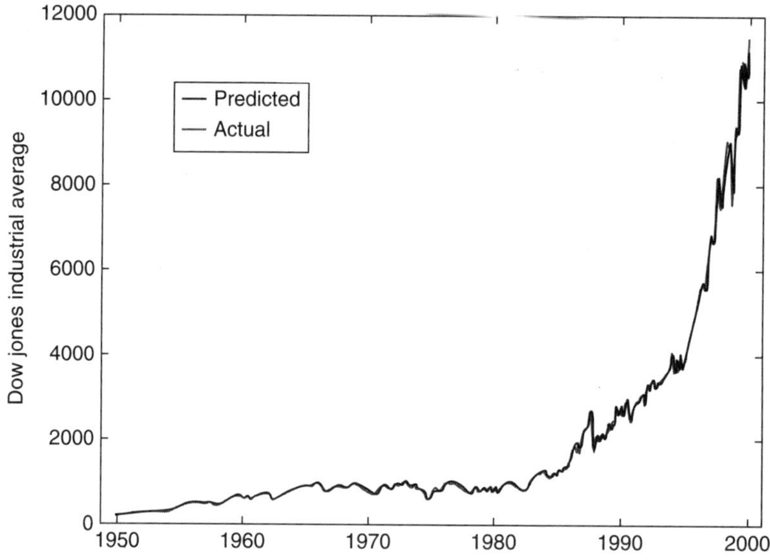

Figure 5.6 Dow Jones Industrial Average, Actual and Predicted, 1950–1999.

A related issue with the third principle is that if trends change dramatically, then even the most robust forecast can be rendered useless. Consider, for example, someone forecasting the future of the stock market at the beginning of 2000. The data on the Dow Jones Industrial Average at this point is shown in **Figure 5.6**. We fit a model that used information on the most recent trends in the data.[3] The predictions our forecast model generated fit the actual data very well. The model's forecast for the end of 2004 (five years into the future at that point) would be 20,135 and 29,591 for the end of 2009. The index's actual value at those points in time was 10,783 and 10,270 respectively. What happened was a massive shift from a mostly strong upward trend to a *martingale*—a zero mean growth pattern.[4] The final forecasting principle states that forecasts for aggregated unit variables is more accurate than for disaggregated units. The reason for this is that although disaggregated units tend to have both systematic and idiosyncratic variation, aggregations of these units "average out" the idiosyncratic variation. Consider the time series data for the four revenue sources that follow (**Figure 5.7**). Each of the revenue sources, when modeled, has sensitivity to overall economic activity and demographic growth in the community. However, each revenue source also has some amount of idiosyncratic risk. Combining the revenue sources into Total Revenue creates a series that has less variation. As idiosyncratic variation is reduced, forecasting becomes much more accurate. Over the long term, greater idiosyncratic variation leads to bigger errors and wider confidence intervals. For this reason, long-term forecasts should be made mostly for highly aggregated variables.

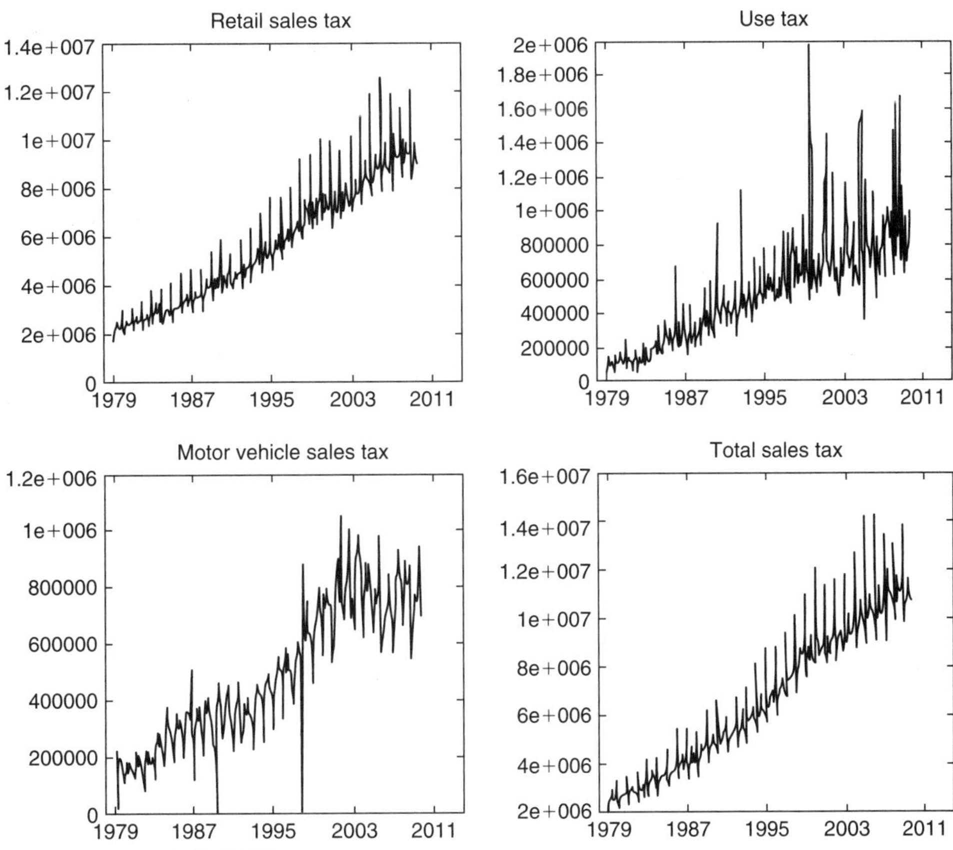

Figure 5.7 City of Omaha, Nebraska Sales Tax Revenue Components, January 1979–October 2009.

Source: Nebraska Department of Revenue.

Forecast Models

Two broad types of forecast models can be used to forecast the value of the variables of interest. *Qualitative* models do not explicitly use quantitative relationships to forecast the value of variables. These models use the judgment, experience, and opinions of individuals or groups to generate forecasts. *Quantitative* models use explicitly quantitative relationships to generate forecasts.

To illustrate the techniques and motivate our discussion, we will use the data on Omaha sales tax revenues shown in Figure 5.7. The data is monthly and runs through October 2009 but for ease of exposition we will often compact it to annual data. Assume that we want a forecast for annual sales tax revenue through 2013 (a four-year forecast).

Qualitative Methods

Qualitative models would involve seeking opinion from experts on the likely annual values and changes over the forecast period. One way to do this is through the use of *expert surveys*. Surveys would be given to a panel of experts and the results analyzed. The survey distribution may include data on past values of the variable of interest or may simply ask for the expert opinion. There are a number of ways that the survey data could be analyzed, using means or medians of forecast values, or even using simulation analysis on the results. Simple arithmetic means may be used, or means may be "trimmed" to exclude or underweight outliers. We will discuss simulation methods under the section "Naïve Quantitative Methods" later in this chapter. Two examples of expert survey methods at the national level are the Survey of Professional Forecasters (SPF) and Livingston Survey (LS), conducted quarterly by staff economists at the Philadelphia Federal Reserve Bank. The surveys ask private and public sector forecasters for their forecasts of several macroeconomic variables in the short term. In addition, the SPF asks for inflation forecasts for five and ten year time frames and the LS asks for real GDP growth and inflation over the next ten years (Croushore, 2010). The responses to the survey are averaged to produce a mean estimate. The results of simple survey methods can be quite impressive in some applications, especially if the pool of experts is large and statistical techniques are applied to the responses. A recent study found that SPF interest rate forecasts, when "shrunk"–adjusted toward the long-term mean–were slightly more accurate over longer forecast periods than much more sophisticated quantitative models (Dorsey-Palmateer and Smith, 2007).

Qualitative forecast methods can have several advantages recommending their use. They tend to be simple to implement and require little in terms of resources or expertise. In essence, these methods "exploit" the knowledge base of a larger group of experts. Results from expert models also tend to be easy to understand. Against these advantages, there are several disadvantages with the use of expert models. First, although the results from expert models are easy to understand, this usually comes at the cost of being somewhat of a "black box." There tends to be little discussion in the results from these models of the factors that drive the results. This may be mitigated by asking for large numbers of variables to be forecast thus leading to a greater level of detail in the model, but at times, one can get the feeling that results simply materialize. The second limitation of the models comes from the first. Oftentimes there are no confidence intervals[5] provided with expert results. Confidence intervals are vitally important in creating and assessing forecast errors. As just discussed, forecast errors are a vital component of long-term forecasts. The final potential disadvantage of expert models is that they can be somewhat prone to the problem of "groupthink," where individuals in groups are led to support a consensus that individually they may not support. Groupthink arises from situations where one or a few individuals are dominant in the group or one opinion is seen as the correct opinion prior to individuals being able to form their own strong opinions (Janis, 1982). In this case, even seemingly separate opinions can be driven by a single undetectable factor that potentially biases the results. An example of groupthink in the forecasting realm is "this time is different" thinking that tends to forecast continued economic growth even in the face of "bubbles" that in retrospect should have been obvious (Reinhart and Rogoff, 2009).

Another qualitative method that has been proposed to circumvent the problem of groupthink is the *Delphi technique*. The Delphi technique is a method of elaborating a consensus among many individuals concerning a decision or forecast. The consensus is reached through an iterative process of information solicitation and structured feedback (Dalkey and Helmer, 1963). An example of this in the Omaha example would be to distribute a survey along with information on past data to a panel of experts. Summary statistics of this first round of surveys would then be calculated (along with anonymous summaries of any comments that might be given by the expert respondents) and distributed to the panel of experts along with a new survey. The experts would then revise their forecasts and resubmit them. Once again, summary statistics and comments would be gathered, and a new round of surveys with information may be distributed. The process iterates until the results of the survey "converge" to a reasonable consensus, which becomes the consensus forecast (one must be careful of using this term in regard to any specific method, as in practice, consensus forecasting has been used to describe unstructured survey or nominal group methods).

As we alluded to earlier, Delphi techniques may mitigate problems of groupthink. The anonymity afforded in the information gathering and revelation process allows individuals to commit to positions that may be unpopular. However, the power of the Delphi technique to improve on individual opinions or survey aggregations of opinions relies on the diffusion of knowledge among experts. If experts are predisposed to certain forecasts, then even the best Delphi methods will not necessarily result in better forecasts, just forecasts that carry more subjective weight. An example of this was a carefully implemented Delphi forecast of solar power market penetration in the United States. Conducted in 1979, the study forecast a range of 0.8 to 50 gigawatts of total solar power output in the United States for 2000 (Sarin, 1979). Aside from the fact that the range of potential forecast outcomes was so great as to make the forecasts meaningless in application, the average forecast of 2.9 gigawatts of solar power output used for electricity production proved to be wildly optimistic. The actual figure was 0.5 gigawatts (U.S. Energy Information Administration, 2010).

Quantitative Methods

Quantitative methods for forecasting most often involve the manipulation of current and past data on the variable of interest. These methods fall broadly into two general approaches. The first approach relies little on past patterns of data but instead on a few "parameters" of significant relationships between current and past data or between elements of a system of variables that form the forecasting space. We will refer to these models as *naïve quantitative models*. The second approach relies heavily on past patterns of data on the variable to be forecasted or a system of variables in order to forecast into the future. We call these *parameterized quantitative models* due to their need for heavy amounts of data and many parameters.

Naïve Quantitative Methods

Many variants of naïve models can be applied in the quantitative realm. The easiest to implement are the *moving average* models. A moving average is simply an average of past observations on a variable that is used to forecast for the next few periods. An example may facilitate understanding of this method. Assume that the last five years of data on property assessed values were $10 billion in 2006, $11 billion in 2007, $12 billion in 2008, $11 billion in 2009, and $10 billion in 2010, respectively. A five-year simple moving average of property values would be found by adding up the values and dividing by five, so ($10 billion + $11 billion + $12 billion + $11 billion + $10 billion)/5 = $10.8 billion. This would become our forecast value for 2011. Then if the actual value for 2011 came in at $11 billion, we would include this in the average and remove the most distant observation ($10 billion in 2006). So our average would now be ($11 billion + $12 billion + $11 billion + $10 billion + $11 billion)/5 = $11 billion. This would become the 2012 forecast value. This process of removing the oldest value and replacing it with the newest value forms the basis for the term "moving" average. If a forecaster feels that more recent data is more valuable in terms of forecasting, she can add "weights" to the observations, creating a *weighted moving average*. For example, if a forecaster in 2010 thought that 40% of the information on future values was contained in the most recent observations, with 30% of information in the next most recent observation and 10% in each of the remaining three years of data, then she would find the product of the weights and the values to find the weighted average: ($10 billion * 0.4) + ($11 billion * 0.3) + ($12 billion * 0.1) + ($11 billion * 0.1) + ($10 billion * 0.1) = $10.6 billion.[6] The weights can be decided in an ad hoc fashion, or they can follow a specific functional form such as with exponentially weighted average forecast.

Moving average models tend to only be used for short-term forecasting of data that has a stable long-term mean. Over longer-term periods, the moving average tends to use increasing numbers of forecasts to generate other forecasts. To see this, consider our example if we are trying to forecast to 2016. In that last year, we would be using data from 2011–2015, all of which is forecast. This tends to amplify forecast errors; errors early in the period compound into the future. Also, the data should have a stable long-term mean to use moving average forecasts. Using these forecasts on data with long-term trends produces forecasts that never "catch up" to the trend (e.g., if the data is trending upward then moving average forecast values will be downwardly biased).

A naïve quantitative model that can be used with longer-term forecasts and on data with trends is the *simple trend model*. The trend model analyzes the long-term trend in the data and forecasts that it will continue into the future (for this reason these models are sometimes called *extrapolation* models). Most often the trend used is a linear trend. This is estimated as a regression of the variable of interest on a time trend variable. For our sales tax data, assume that we want to conduct a linear trend analysis of the Sales Tax variable. Our regression equation for a linear time trend would be:

$$SalesTax_i - \alpha + \beta Time_i + \varepsilon_i \qquad (1)$$

where *SalesTax* is the observation of the sales tax in year *i* and the variable *Time* is the time trend variable that takes the value 1 in 1979 and increments by one each year (taking a final value of 30 in 2008). The results of the regression are shown in **Figure 5.8**. The model predicts the long-term trend of the data fairly well but does not do well in forecasting any one year of data. The measures of the error of the predictions from the regression (the RMSE and MAPE as described in the next section) indicate that in any given year the forecast value can be expected to be about \$3,000,000 (about 5.7%) on average off of the actual value. This is reflected in the forecast errors (shown by the distance from the top band to the bottom band of the forecast range in Figure 5.8), which are relatively large compared to the base forecast.

There are some definite advantages to trend models. First, they are extremely easy to estimate. Modern spreadsheet packages such as Microsoft Excel® have built-in regression

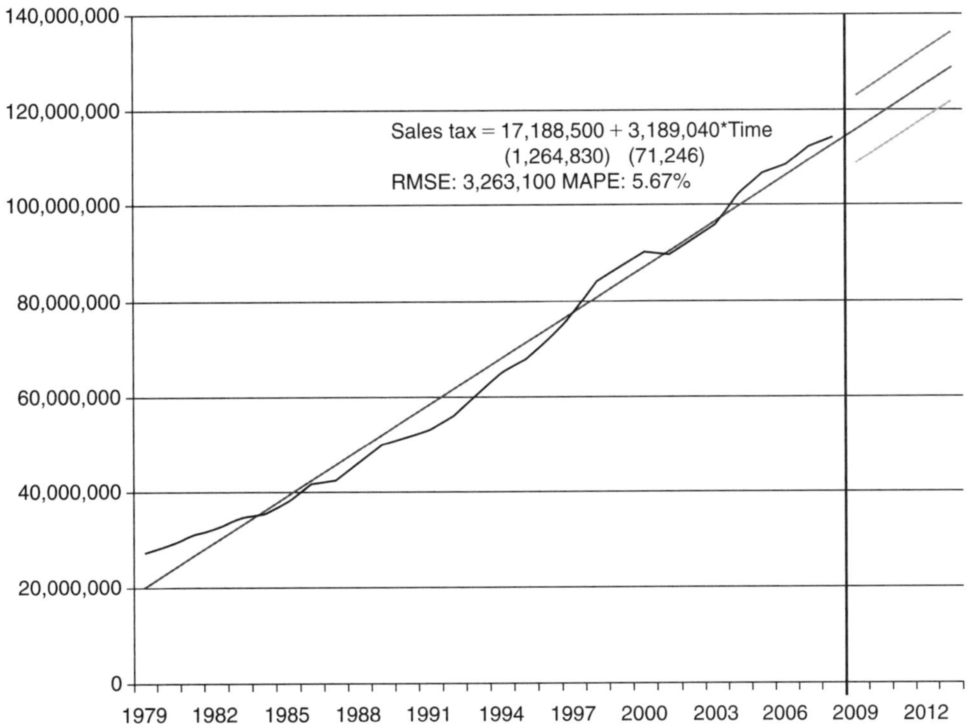

Figure 5.8 Linear Trend Regression Results and Forecasts, Omaha Sales Tax Revenue.

functions. Calculating forecast errors requires some additional computations, but there are numerous "add-on" packages that can be employed to estimate models and compute measures of forecast errors. Second, as discussed earlier, over time the trend in a time series dominates the cyclical components. So getting a handle on the trend in the data is at least a good start in long-term forecasting.

The wide error band shown in Figure 5.8 illustrates a basic weakness of simple trend models. They tend to give a general picture of the overall direction of change in a variable but not capture fluctuations in any one period. As such, they might be appropriate if only a general sense of where the variable is headed over time is necessary. But these circumstances are rarely the case. A second weakness with linear trend models is that their estimated errors tend to be constant over time. As we have just seen, errors should in fact grow over time reflecting greater uncertainty in forecasts that are made over longer time periods. But with linear trend models, as shown in Figure 5.8, the error bands are the same width relative to the base forecast.[7] A final weakness, as discussed earlier, is that if trend changes during the forecast period, then the forecast can be very inaccurate. This is somewhat related to the earlier point about forecast errors. As we will see, in other models the forecast errors are related to the historical volatility in the data. If the variable of interest has had periods of wide fluctuation over time, then the error bands will tend to be much larger than if it has had rather mild fluctuation. This represents a higher ex ante risk of large errors with wide fluctuations in the variable as compared to lower risk of large errors with mild fluctuations over time.

Another naïve quantitative model that captures this notion of ex ante risk well is the *stochastic simulation* forecasting model. In this model, future values of the variable of interest are simulated from the current level of the variable and past changes in the variable. Applying this model to the Omaha data, we observe the following patterns in annual percentage changes in the variable of interest. The mean annual percentage change in sales tax revenue is just under 5% (4.92%). The standard deviation of the changes is about half of the mean annual percentage change. The AR(1) measure (referred to as the first order autocorrelation coefficient), which captures the correlation between the current period value of SalesTax and the immediate past value of the variable (the one-period lagged value), is 0.146 and not statistically different from zero at the 95% confidence level. The AR(2) second order autocorrelation coefficient is 0.003 and again not different from zero. Therefore, we can rule out autocorrelation in our data and say that the annual percentage changes in SalesTax are not correlated across time. We can therefore model the stochastic process of how Sales Taxes evolve over time as a *Markov process*, which means that past percentage changes do not affect the distribution of current period changes (and by extension that the current percentage change will not affect future percent changes). The best way to think about Markov processes would be to imagine someone driving down a road, coming to an intersection, and rolling a die to determine whether to go straight, left, or right. Then at the next intersection, the die is rolled again. The resulting path that the driver would take would be a random stochastic process where the probability of going in any direction at one intersection is independent of the direction taken at the previous intersections.

The most commonly used Markov process for simulating future value changes is Geometric Brownian Motion, expressed as the differential equation (2).

$$dS_t = \mu S_t dt + \sigma S_t dW_t \tag{2}$$

where S is the *SalesTax* realization at time t, d indicates the change in a variable, μ is the mean growth rate in S (called the stochastic drift of the process), and σ is the standard deviation of the rate of change in S (the stochastic volatility). The variable W represents the Weiner process, which is a random process that is distributed with mean 0 and variance t. Equation (2) is technically a continuous time differential equation, but can be made discrete by setting $dt = 1$:

$$S_{t+1} = S_t + \mu S_t + \sigma S_t W_t \tag{3}$$

Equation (3) is usually estimated by sampling from the normal distribution using "Monte Carlo" or other sampling methods (Hull, 1997). What results is a point estimate of our variable of interest along with many potential confidence intervals. The results for a given year can be summarized in a frequency distribution. **Figure 5.9** shows the results for the Omaha sales tax in 2013. The point estimate for sales tax revenue in that year is just over \$145.2 million, with the vast majority of estimates falling into the \$140–\$150 million range.

One big advantage of a Monte Carlo simulation is that many different statistics and confidence intervals can be gleaned from the data. For example, if city officials believe that they must have \$150 million in sales tax revenues by 2013 to support their desired

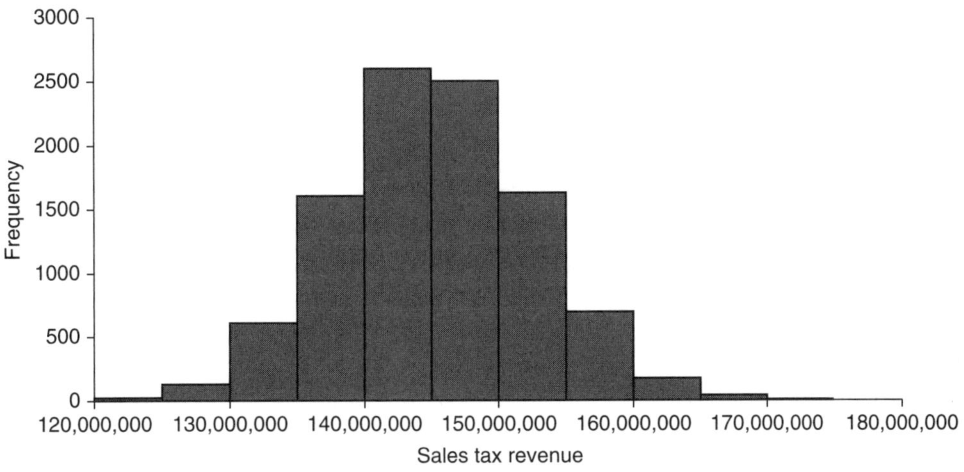

Figure 5.9 Monte Carlo Simulation Results for Omaha Sales Tax Revenues in 2013.

spending growth, we can calculate that there is approximately a 25% probability that revenues will be at least that high in that year.[8] In this way, the risk to decision makers can be quantified. Another major advantage of Monte Carlo simulation is that estimation of the models (if not conceptualization) can also be done on a spreadsheet. Most major spreadsheet packages have functions for generating samples from the normal, lognormal, and other common distributions. And simple methods can be used to glean results from those simulated samples. Additionally, many spreadsheet add-in programs, ranging from very sophisticated and expensive to basic and inexpensive, can be used in simulations to improve speed and output. Finally, the forecast errors are not linear but increase over time.

There are two major disadvantages to the use of stochastic simulation models for forecasting. The first concerns the errors at larger time frames. The 95% confidence interval for the 2013 forecast is nearly $28.5 million. This can be too wide to inform policy makers. This problem derives from the naïve nature of the model. There are not enough parameters to narrow the forecast error. The second disadvantage of simulation models concerns the communication of results. Though the use of result distributions such as Figure 5.9 are more intellectually honest, policy makers often want something more definite in the way of a point estimate compared to a range of potential results.

Parameterized Quantitative Models

In comparison to naïve quantitative models, parameterized models require relatively large amounts of data and employ relatively sophisticated methods to obtain forecasts. Within this group of models, there are actually two subgroups. One subgroup is estimated using statistical methods on historical data with fitted results projected into the future. The second subgroup uses models of the system that underlies that the variable of interest. Although this subgroup of models is informed by previous statistical results, the direct estimation of the models does not rely on statistical model fitting.

There are numerous parameterized statistical models. The simplest is *multiple linear regression*, which is a linear regression model similar to equation (1) but with additional independent or predictor variables on the right hand side of the equation. We will not discuss these methods in detail as there are many statistical textbooks that cover their estimation (Harvey, 1990; Stock and Watson, 2007; Wooldridge, 2003), but a few points about them seem appropriate to this discussion. First, the linear model can be estimated consistently using a trend component (as in (1)) or on data where the trend has been removed by calculating the changes in the observations (to see this, think of the numerical sequence 1,2,3,4 . . . as a series of observations on a variable; the trend is an increase of 1 in each observation, if we calculate the changes between the observations the result is 1,1,1,1 . . . in other words the trend has been removed). However, in terms of forecasting, using a trend component is preferable since there is a loss of information in the model when data is detrended. Also, seasonal effects should be taken into account for data with a periodicity less than annual through using seasonal dummy variables or seasonal differencing. Second, lagged values of the dependent and independent variables can be entered into the regression. The appropriate number of lags should be determined through examination of autocorrelation and partial autocorrelation functions of the original data as well as the residuals or any model estimated (Harvey, 1990). For consistent estimates to be reached and forecast errors minimized, the errors of the estimation must be reduced to "white noise" indicating no serial correlation remains in the data. To demonstrate what is meant by this statement; consider the autocorrelation and partial autocorrelation functions of the sales tax data (**Figure 5.10**, in this case the monthly data). There are several significant lag correlations (as indicated by the bars being above or below the horizontal lines), plus an apparent seasonal correlation at lag 12). Each of these significant lags represents information that forecasts must incorporate to reduce the forecast error to its lowest level. Besides the visual interpretation of autocorrelations, there are several diagnostic tools that can be used to determine when the information in a forecast has been maximized, including error measures, goodness of fit measures, information criteria (such as the Akaike Information Criterion, Schwartz Bayesian Information Criterion, and Hannan-Quinn Criterion), and "portmanteau" tests of the joint significance of autocorrelations (such as the Ljung-Box "Q" statistic, on these points see Mills [1990]).

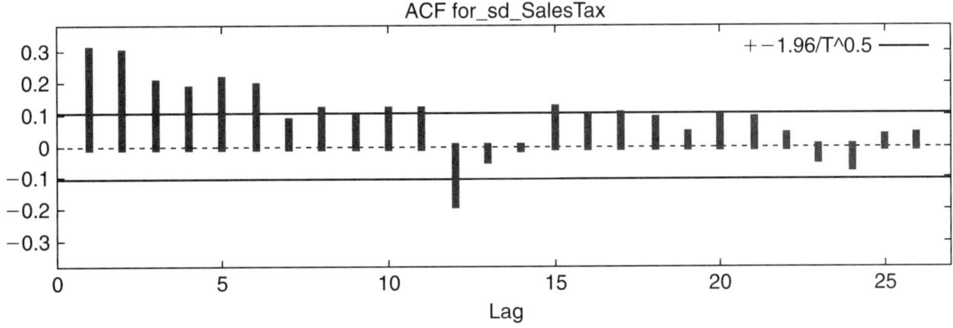

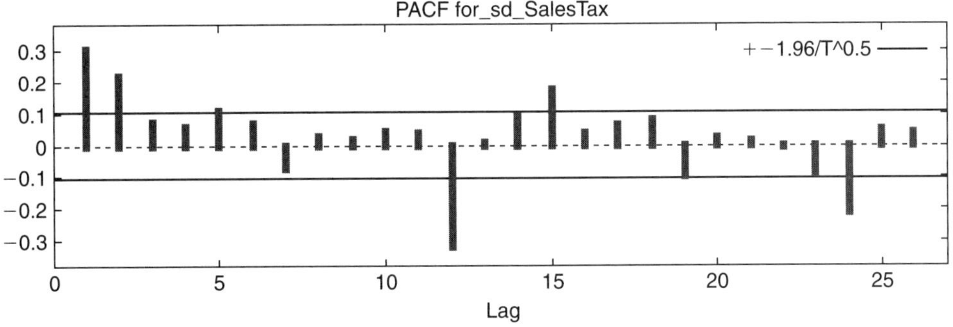

Figure 5.10 Autocorrelation and Partial Autocorrelation Functions, Seasonally Differenced Monthly Omaha Sales Tax Revenue.

There are many advantages to using multiple linear regression models. First, they are easily estimated. Many spreadsheets and even the most basic statistical packages include routines for regression analysis. Second, the results are relatively easy to explain to decision makers. Many decision makers have had at least one statistics course, and most of these courses include some material on regression analysis. Depending on the predictive power of the independent variables, errors can be relatively small (potential independent variables for forecasting sales taxes would include per capita income, employment and unemployment measures, and population and demographic variables). Balanced against these advantages are several potential shortcomings of simple linear regression. Some of these are conceptual, some are found in implementation of the models. One conceptual shortcoming is that good forecasts are needed of the independent variable. For example, assume that we find that city revenue will increase by $5,000,000 for each $1,000 increase in per capita income among city residents. Even if this model is accurate, if the forecasted per capita income is in error, our revenue forecasts are likely to be off, and potentially by an amount greater than the forecast model projects. Another conceptual shortcoming concerns the relationship between the dependent and independent variables. A linear regression model presumes a linear relationship between variables. If the relationship is subtly nonlinear, even a model with a decent fit can produce problematic forecasts. One important implementation shortcoming concerns the point just made about the potential need to incorporate many lags into the model in order to capture all of the information from past data patterns. If analysts are not careful, they may incorrectly specify the model and lead to significantly underestimated errors.

As we incorporate more lags into our model, we begin to approach the next type of parameterized statistical model, the *ARIMA/ARIMAX* model. ARIMA models incorporate potentially many lags of the dependent variable as independent variables in the prediction model, and ARIMAX models incorporate not only lagged dependent variables but also contemporaneous and lagged values of independent variables. ARIMAX is an acronym that stands for AutoRegressive Integrated Moving Average with eXogenous variables. The general estimating equation for the ARIMAX model is shown in equation (4). The model incorporates both autoregressive terms (the term with the phi coefficient, capturing the relation of current values of a variable to past values), moving average terms (with the theta coefficient, capturing the relation of current values to the average of past values), and independent variables (the beta terms).

$$\left(1-\sum_{i=1}^{p}\varphi_t L^i\right) SalesTax_t - \left(1+\sum_{i=0}^{z}\beta_t L^i\right) x_t + \left(1+\sum_{i=1}^{q}\theta_t L^i\right)\varepsilon_t \qquad (4)^9$$

Equation (4) can be estimated using OLS methods as long as the independent and dependent variable data do not violate multivariate normality. However, even if multivariate normality is not present, consistent estimates can be achieved through the use of maximum-likelihood estimation (MLE). ARIMAX models (and their statistical

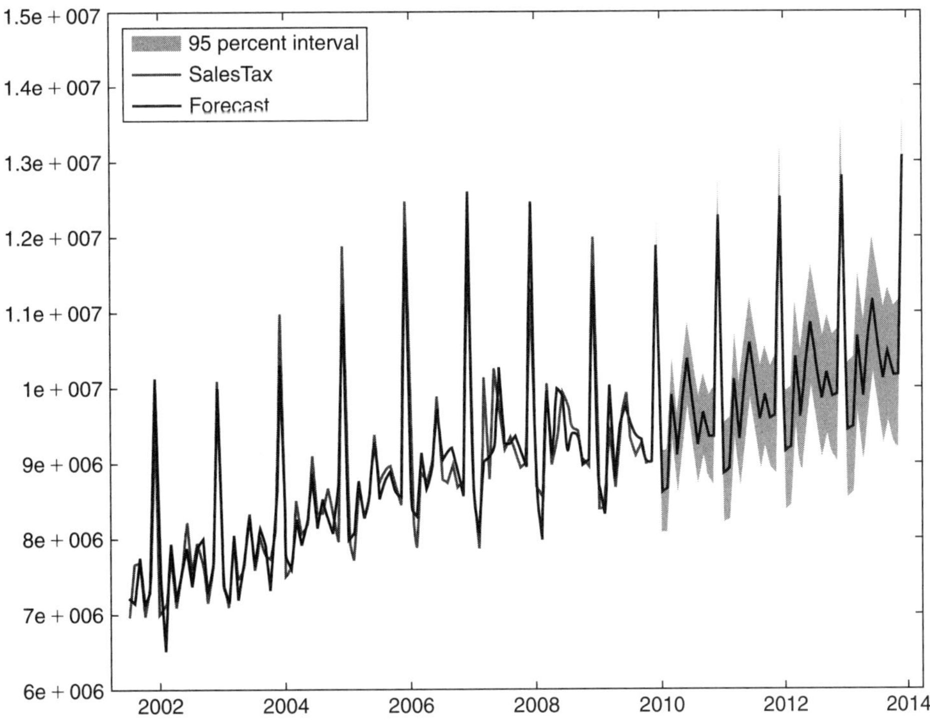

Figure 5.11 ARIMAX (5,0,0)(1,1,0) Estimate of Omaha Sales Tax Revenue.

cousins called *transfer function models*) can be very powerful in terms of fitting past data to develop a forecast (Mills, 1990). **Figure 5.11** shows the model and forecasts for Omaha sales tax revenue (in this case using the monthly data). The model generating this forecast had 5 autoregressive terms ($p = 5$ in equation (4)), 1 seasonal difference and 1 seasonal autoregressive term, and two lagged values of the Nebraska Coincident Economic Index—a measure of economic activity used as an independent variable ($z = 2$). As you can see, the fit of the model is very good. For the annualized estimates, the errors are about half of those from the linear trend model. This illustrates one of the major advantages of using ARIMAX models. The errors from these models tend to be relatively small compared to other methods (specific error measures will be introduced in the final section of the chapter).

The previous statement regarding in-sample errors does not necessarily extend to "out of sample" errors (errors using a model and tracked into the future). What the ARIMAX models do in essence is to use a flexible model building format to build a model that fits as close as possible to past data. To repeat an earlier statement, if future trends and cycles differ dramatically from past patterns, then even the model with the best in-sample fit may not be worth much in terms of future forecasts. Still, the forecasts can be impressive.[10] Another advantage of ARIMA/ARIMAX models is that with some explanation, it can be relatively easy to communicate the patterns found in the data to decision makers. Balanced against these benefits, it is usually necessary to learn specialized statistical software packages to estimate ARIMA models. Further, ARIMA modeling is open to data mining problems. In an effort to minimize in-sample forecast error, some modelers have included lags and variables that in the forecast period have proved to be unrelated to the forecasted variable, causing large out-of-sample errors. Also, similar to multiple regression methods, if an ARIMAX model is used with an exogenous variable, then forecasts are needed of this variable.

There are other parameterized statistical models that are somewhat beyond the scope of this chapter, but we will introduce them and provide references. *Vector autoregressive models* are an extension of ARIMA models where multiple dependent variables are estimated in a system of equations (Lütkepohl, 1991). Variants of these type of models have become very popular in economic forecasting. To get a feel for what these models would consist of, consider a two endogenous variable vector autoregressive system. We would have two variables that would each affect each other in a current and lagged sense (for example, the money supply– we'll call this y_1—would affect economic output—y_2—which in turn would affect the money supply). We can write this in vector form as:

$$Y_t = \Phi_0 + \sum_{i=1}^{p} \Phi_i Y_{t=i} + E_t \tag{5}$$

where Φ_0 is a vector of constants, and each Φ_i is a matrix of lagged coefficients for the effect of one variable on another and itself. For a two variable system such as ours with one lag (referred to as a VAR(1) system), the system of equations can be written in matrix form as:

$$\begin{pmatrix} y_{1t} \\ y_{2t} \end{pmatrix} = \begin{pmatrix} \varphi_{10} \\ \varphi_{20} \end{pmatrix} + \begin{pmatrix} \varphi_{1,11} & \varphi_{1,12} \\ \varphi_{1,21} & \varphi_{1,22} \end{pmatrix} \begin{pmatrix} y_{1,t-1} \\ y_{2,t-1} \end{pmatrix} + \begin{pmatrix} \varepsilon_{1t} \\ \varepsilon_{2t} \end{pmatrix} \tag{6}$$

In the estimation of (6), $\varphi_{1,12}$ is the coefficient measuring the impact of $y_{2,t-1}$ on y_{1t} in the presence of $y_{1,t-1}$. Said another way, the model simultaneously captures the effect of the lags of one of the endogenous variables on the other endogenous variable while controlling for the lagged values of that variable. VAR models are very strong for forecasting. The problem with VAR models lies in their interpretation. Most VAR systems have a large number of parameters compared to the number of variables. Even the slightest problem in measurement or estimation can have drastic consequences for the prediction accuracy of the models. For policy analysis, many structural models have been proposed that put restrictions on the covariance matrix to keep standard errors from exploding. And it is very difficult to explain to decision makers why effects appear in forecasts due to the many effects that are simultaneously estimated. VARs also suffer from the problem of selecting the appropriate lag length, although modern techniques have led to many approaches that yield promising results. Balanced against these shortcomings, a definite strength of VAR is that forecasts are generated of the entire system, so that forecasts of exogenous variables are not needed.

A final parameterized statistical model is the *artificial neural network* (ANN) model. ANN models are multivariate nonlinear nonparametric statistical models (Zhang, Patuwo, and Hu, 1998). By this, it is meant that ANN models impose no restrictions regarding the linearity of models that underlie observed relationships. ANN models seek to reproduce how brains learn and generalize using neural structures in order to "mine" the data for relationships. Similar to VAR models, ANNs are highly parameterized, but in their case the parameters need not follow a linear pattern. Because of this, ANNs are very good at finding hidden patterns in the data. However, this heavy parameterization leads to overfitting problems and lack of parsimony, similar to VARs. Further, ANNs require heavy amounts of time and computing power to estimate. And although the results in some comparisons of forecasts have been favorable, in other instances, the models did no better than and even worse than traditional models already mentioned.

The second subtype of parameterized quantitative models consists of *systems models*. Systems models estimate relationships between variables in a large system, where the effects of variables are not directly determined through statistical analysis. Often, the parameters of systems models are gleaned from previous statistical analysis, but there is no statistical model brought to bear on the system. There are two main types of systems models that we will discuss: systems dynamics models and general equilibrium models.

Systems dynamics models were originally developed to simulate the behavior and operations of industrial organizations (Forrester, 1961) but have come to be used in many areas. At the heart of systems dynamics models is a set of stock and flow equations (sometimes called level and rate equations). The equations typically are arranged in a system that takes a differential equations structure. An example of this is shown in equation (7), which relates changes in the number of households to attractiveness of an area which is in turn determined by two factors.

$$Households_t = Households_{t-1} + Arrivals - Departures \; Arrivals = f(Attractiveness)$$
$$Departures = f(-Attractiveness) \; Attractiveness = f(HousingAvailability - Unemployment) \qquad (7)$$

Simulating the set of equations in (7) will produce a dynamic forecast of the behavior of a system over time. Although systems dynamics models were originally created to simulate the behavior of business organizations, they have become quite popular tools for creating simulations of urban dynamic systems including population and employment simulations and "visioning" of urban form (Waddell, 2002). The main advantage of using systems dynamics models is that they can be made very dynamic and visually appealing. Urban dynamic systems models often have a visual output that represents an urban area (sometimes in 3D), and decision makers can "see" the area change in response to different decisions that are made.

There are two major disadvantages of using systems dynamics models. The first is that specialized software packages generally are required for large-scale problems. Smaller problems can be estimated on spreadsheets or as systems in statistical packages. However, larger problems require the use of software packages. These packages can be relatively low cost if an analyst wants to forego the more attractive output options, but full packages can be prohibitively expensive. The second disadvantage relates to the models' dependency on the assumptions being used. Often the results of an urban dynamics model are very sensitive to the assumptions of functional form and parameters. Also, systems dynamics models rarely produce confidence intervals as they are not built for statistical testing purposes. The confidence intervals allow decision makers to see a measure of the risk of a certain course of action prior to it being implemented (e.g., the results of these type of models may indicate that the number of households in a certain year under a specified set of policy choices would be 100,000 plus or minus 5,000 and from another set of policy choices it would be 95,000 plus or minus 3,000).

General equilibrium models (GE models) are similar to systems dynamics models in that they consist of large systems of equations. The differences are in orientation and parameterization. The orientation of GE models is economic. The modeling framework tends to emphasize economic relationships and the focus of the models is economic results, on variables such as output, prices, and employment. The equations that underlie the models capture the flows of resources within economies. Some of the equations capture input-output relationships, the flow of resources among different parts of a chain of suppliers and manufacturers. Other equations capture the production function for the creation of new finished goods, the demand for goods by households, and the demand for labor in the labor market. The equations are parameterized by adding elasticities that are assumed from the results of past studies or calibrated through examination of existing data (Kehoe and Kehoe, 1994).

There are two general forms of GE models. The first is the applied (or computable) general equilibrium model. The structure of an AGE model is comparative-static, in other words, it does not assume that the different parts of the model will respond to changes in other parts of the model. So businesses will not respond to increased taxes by raising prices to consumers. They therefore represent short-term processes very well at the expense of potentially making errors in the long run. The second type is the dynamic-stochastic general equilibrium (DSGE) model. DSGE models fully model the responses of actors to changes in the economic environment. Therefore, they are more readily suited to generating long-term forecasts.

If the goal of the forecasting exercise is to model economic variables, then there are many advantages to using general equilibrium models. GE models are fully parameterized models of the economy, so very little of the structure of the models is left to assumptions. Even in the most sophisticated VAR models, strong assumptions are made as to what is **not** included in the model. GE models form the most complete models of the economy while retaining some parsimony. The structure of GE models also lends itself readily to explanation. It is straightforward for an analyst to delve into the structure of the model to pick out the variables that seem to be driving forecasts. However, GE models have some striking disadvantages. First, similar to systems dynamics models the estimates from GE models (at least in practice) most often are not accompanied by confidence intervals. Therefore, long-term risk management is difficult. Second and somewhat related, results are not often tested for robustness to differing assumptions regarding elasticities.

To summarize the discussion of the last few pages, there are numerous options for forecasting. The choice regarding the appropriate method is at times simple, with one forecasting method being the clear favorite in terms of its focus, approach, or output needs. More often, it is up to the analyst to work with the decision maker to identify an appropriate approach. There are some guidelines available for deciding. The website Principles of Forecasting has a handy decision chart for picking methodologies as well as short descriptions of each method and references to more resources (*Principles of Forecasting*, 2011).

Model Validation and Error Measurement

The final step in any forecasting exercise is to validate the model. This process involves measuring the error of the model by comparing predicted values with actual values. In some models such as ARIMAX and ANN, an initial validation is done concurrently with the model development. But in other cases, initial model validation occurs after the forecasts are made, as the true values of the forecasted variables are realized (and for models with initial model validation during model development a second validation should occur after the forecasts are made).

There are two important dimensions to model validation. The first is the timing of the model validation. Forecast errors can be measured *in-sample*, *in-holdout sample*, or *out-of-sample*. In-sample errors refer to errors during the time sample over which the model is developed. Referring to Figure 5.11, the time sample over which the model was developed was January 1979 through October 2009. Therefore, the error measures are valid for that period. Forecasters are often dubious of in-sample errors due to the possibility of overfitting. For example, in December 2005 and December 2006, there were higher than predicted sales tax realizations. If the analyst wished, she could enter an "indicator" variable taking the value of one in each of those months. As if by magic, the in-sample error would then decrease, sometimes dramatically. But this would tell us nothing about the likelihood of another "high month" upcoming. For this reason, out-of-sample errors are preferable to in-sample errors as measures of forecast accuracy. Out-of-sample errors occur in periods beyond the sample period. So in our case, we would track the city sales tax revenue in the forecast period (November 2010–December 2013) and compare to our forecast. These errors are theoretically the best measure of the forecasts since the reason we are developing forecasts is to predict future values. However, in a practical sense, out-of-sample errors are more useful for future forecasting projects than for evaluating the current forecasts. In this way we can verify that the approach we are using has a good track record, but we cannot necessarily extend that conclusion to the current forecast.

For this reason, some forecasters use holdout samples to evaluate the accuracy of the current forecast. Holdout samples are a portion of the existing data timeframe that is "held out" of the model development phase in order to assess the forecast. So in our case, instead of using the data from January 1979–October 2009 to develop the model, we may use a shorter timeframe, such as January 1979–October 2006 to develop the model and then use the holdout sample of November 2006–October 2009 for model verification. This would allow us to "test" the model against real data and validate its accuracy. This can be a powerful method of validation; however, it does not solve the problem of structural change during the forecast period.

The second dimension of measuring forecast accuracy is to use appropriate methods to measure and assess error. There are numerous choices for measuring forecast errors. We have already seen two frequently used measures, the *Root Mean Squared Error* (RMSE) and the *Mean Absolute Percentage Error* (MAPE). We will not go into detail about calculating these errors,[11] but the RMSE is essentially the standard error of the forecast, the expected value of the difference between the forecast and actual values. This definition is only true for an unbiased indicator (where the expected value of the forecast error is zero), so there are alternative measures that have been developed to capture errors in biased forecasts. One limitation of the RMSE is that it is an absolute error measure so it is not scale invariant. Therefore if one wants to compare forecasts on data with different scales, the RMSE of the model would not be appropriate. In this case, a measure of the expected percentage error would be useful, and this is the essence of the MAPE. Many other measures of error can be evaluated as part of the model validation process, and Diebold (2007) has a good discussion of the advantages and disadvantages of each measure.

Conclusion

In this chapter, we examined long-term forecasting principles and methods. We explored many different aspects of forecasting and learned the terms associated with forecasts. The chapter began by defining forecasting and exploring elements of a forecast. We then examined some of the components of data that one encounters when forecasting. Then we discussed the four vital principles of forecasting: errors are inevitable and should be included with forecasts, errors grow as forecasts get longer, forecasts are based explicitly or implicitly on past patterns and relationships, and forecasting is more accurate at higher levels of aggregation. We saw several examples of these principles. Then we moved to a discussion of the various types of forecast models, beginning with qualitative models, proceeding to naïve quantitative models and ending with parameterized models. We discussed the strengths and weaknesses of each type of model, and then illustrated ways to evaluate forecast accuracy. We saw that there are numerous techniques and models available for forecasters. These techniques form a "toolkit" from which the forecaster should pick the one that produces the best results and aids decision makers in understanding potential future outcomes.

Endnotes

1. The model used was an ARIMA (9,1,0)(1,0,0).
2. The 1994 report was chosen because it was the most recent report since the last piece of significant legislation affecting the structure of Social Security, the Omnibus Budget Reconciliation Act of 1993, which increased taxes on benefits for higher income retirees (*Social Security CRS Legislative Histories*, 2011).
3. The model estimated was an ARIMA (10,2,5).
4. A similar type of error was incorporated into one of the more unfortunate forecasts of all time, popularized in the book *Dow 36,000* (Glassman and Hassett, 1999).
5. Confidence intervals tell the levels of the forecast variables that correspond to certain confidence in the forecasts. For example, if our forecast is $1,000,000 with a 95% confidence interval of $750,000 to $1,250,000 it means that the forecaster is 95% confident that her result will fall into the range indicated. The relative "width" of the confidence interval imparts knowledge about the level of certainty in the forecasts.
6. One may wonder why we do not divide by five in this case. As long as the weights in the model add to one, then the division by the number of observations is implied.
7. This is not necessarily the case with higher order polynomial trend models, which model nonlinear relationships between the variable of interest and time.
8. Using a similar Monte Carlo simulation framework, Kriz (2003) developed probabilistic estimates of the amount of budget reserves needed by municipalities in Minnesota.
9. Equation (4) can also be modified to add seasonal autoregressive and moving average terms as well as using differenced, log differenced, or seasonally differenced data.
10. As a point of reference, a similar model used to forecast Omaha sales tax revenue for 2010 produced an out-of-sample error of 0.75%.
11. See Diebold (2007) for a good discussion.

Glossary

Cycle: short-term fluctuations in a series of data over time, usually corresponding to a regular pattern such as a business cycle.

Delphi Technique: a method of elaborating a consensus among many individuals concerning a decision or forecast. Consensus is reached through an iterative process of information solicitation and structured feedback.

Error: that part of the fluctuation in time-series data that cannot be explained by trend, cycle, and seasonal cycle components or by changes in explanatory variables.

Expert Survey: surveys given to a panel of experts asking their opinion on future values of the variable of interest as well as any other variable.

Forecasting: the process of making statements about the value of variables whose values have not yet been realized.

In-Holdout Sample Error: the error of a forecast model that is realized over a period where there is actual data but is not part of the period over which the model is estimated.

In-Sample Error: the error of a forecast model that is realized over the period that the model is estimated.

Long-Term Forecasts: forecasts made for periods of more than three years.

Markov Process: a process that a variable moves through to arrive at its ultimate value. Markov processes feature independent observations (i.e., the value of a variable in one period does not change the likelihood of getting another value in the next period).

Medium-Term Forecasts: forecasts made for periods of one-to-three years.

Moving Average: an average of past observations on a variable that is used to forecast for the next few periods. The observations used to calculate the average are updated each period to exclude the oldest observation.

Naïve Model: models that incorporate very little information from past patterns or relationships.

Out-of-Sample Error: the error of a forecast model that is realized in the future (after the model is estimated).

Parameterized Model: models that incorporate much information from past patterns or relationships.

Qualitative Model: models that do not explicitly use quantitative relationships to forecast the value of variables.

Quantitative Model: models that use explicitly quantitative relationships to generate forecasts.

Seasonal Cycle: fluctuations in a series of data that occur at regular time intervals, such as an increase in a series of sales data before the Christmas holiday.

Short-Term Forecasts: forecasts made for periods of less than one year.

Trend: the general direction (increasing or decreasing) of a series of data over time.

Discussion Questions

1. Go to the website of the Congressional Budget Office (http://www.cbo.gov) and download the most recent *Long Term Budget Outlook*. Discuss the economic and/or budget forecast. What methods does the CBO use in its forecasts? How does the agency reflect risk or uncertainty in its forecasts? What criticisms would you have of its methods or presentation? What does the agency do right in their forecasts?
2. Assume that you have been asked to produce a revenue forecast for a local government in your area. Discuss how you would come to a decision regarding which method to use in your forecast? Describe how you would present the forecast to the mayor, city administrator, and/or city council.

3. Discuss the broad types of risks inherent in any forecasting exercise. How should forecasters approach these risks and what types of disclosures should be made to consumers of the forecasts?
4. Download the paper *Standards and Practices for Forecasting* from http://www.forecastingprinciples.com/files/standardshort.pdf. Pick one or two areas and discuss the practices and standards identified in the paper. What do they tell us about the standard approach to forecasting?

Recommended Resources

Books

Diebold, F. X. (2007). *Elements of forecasting.* London: South-Western.

Elliott, G., Granger, C.W.J., and Timmermann, A. (2006). *Handbook of economic forecasting, Volume 1.* Amsterdam: Elsevier.

Lütkepohl, H. (1991). *Introduction to multiple time series analysis.* Berlin: Springer.

Mills, T. C. (1990). *Time series techniques for economists.* Cambridge [England]: Cambridge University Press.

Software

AUTOBOX. Automatic Forecasting Systems, http://www.autobox.com/

Crystal Ball. Oracle, http://www.oracle.com/us/products/applications/crystalball/crystalball-066563.html

ForecasterXL. Alyuda Research, LLC. http://www.alyuda.com/forecasting-excel-software-with-neural-network.htm

gretl. Allin Cottrell and Riccardo "Jack" Lucchetti, http://gretl.sourceforge.net/

NeuroSolutions. NeuroDimension, Inc., http://www.neurosolutions.com/

SAS. SAS Institute Inc., http://www.sas.com/

STATA. StataCorp LP., http://www.stata.com/

Vanguard ForecastServer. Vanguard Software Corporation, http://www.vanguardsw.com/products/forecast-server/

Websites

Principles of Forecasting: http://www.forecastingprinciples.com/

Time Series Analysis for Business Forecasting: http://home.ubalt.edu/ntsbarsh/stat-data/forecast.htm

2010 Forecasting Software Survey: http://www.lionhrtpub.com/orms/surveys/FSS/FSS.html

References

Croushore, D. (2010). Philadelphia fed forecasting surveys: Their value for research. *Business Review (Federal Reserve Bank of Philadelphia)*, 1–11.

Dalkey, N., and Helmer, O. (1963). An experimental application of the Delphi method to the use of experts. *Management Science, 9*(3), 458–467.

Diebold, F. X. (2007). *Elements of forecasting*. London: South-Western.

Dorsey-Palmateer, R., and Smith, G. (2007). Shrunken interest rate forecasts are better forecasts. *Applied Financial Economics, 17*(6), 425–430.

Forrester, J. W. (1961). *Industrial dynamics*. Cambridge, MA: M.I.T. Press.

Gerardi, K., Lehnert, A., Sherlund, S. M., and Willen, P. (2008). Making sense of the subprime crisis. *Brookings Papers on Economic Activity*, 69–145.

Glassman, J. K., and Hassett, K. A. (1999). *Dow 36,000: The new strategy for profiting from the coming rise in the stock market*. New York: Times Business.

Greider, W. (1982). *The education of David Stockman and other Americans*. New York: Dutton.

Harvey, A. C. (1990). *The econometric analysis of time series*. Cambridge, MA: MIT Press.

Hull, J. C. (1997). *Options, futures, and other derivatives*. Upper Saddle River, NJ: Prentice Hall.

Janis, I. L. (1982). *Groupthink: Psychological studies of policy decisions and fiascoes* (2nd ed.). Boston: Houghton Mifflin Company.

Kehoe, P. J., and Kehoe, T. J. (1994). A primer on static applied general equilibrium models. *Quarterly Review (02715287), 18*(2), 2–15.

Kriz, K. A. (2003). The optimal level of local government fund balances: A simulation approach. *Proceedings of the 2002 National Tax Association Annual Conference*. Retrieved January 17, 2011 from http://search.ebscohost.com/login.aspx?direct=true&db=buh&AN=11060956&site=ehost-live

Lütkepohl, H. (1991). *Introduction to multiple time series analysis*. Berlin: Springer.

Mills, T. C. (1990). *Time series techniques for economists*. Cambridge [England]: Cambridge University Press.

Principles of forecasting—ForPrin home. Retrieved June 13, 2011, from http://www.forecastingprinciples.com/

Reinhart, C. M., and Rogoff, K. S. (2009). *This time is different: Eight centuries of financial folly*. Princeton, NJ: Princeton University Press.

Sarin, R. K. (1979). An approach for long term forecasting with an application to solar electric energy. *Management Science, 25*(6), 543–554.

Social security CRS legislative histories. Retrieved June 15, 2011, from http://www.ssa.gov/history/reports/crsleghist2.html

Stock, J. H., and Watson, M. W. (2007). *Introduction to econometrics*. Boston: Pearson/Addison Wesley.

The Board of Trustees, Federal Old-Age and Survivors Insurance and Disability Insurance Trust Funds. (1994). *1994 annual report of the board of trustees of the federal old-age and survivors insurance and disability insurance trust funds* (House Document No. 103-321). Washington, DC: U.S. Government Printing Office. doi:http://www.ssa.gov/history/reports/trust/1994/1994.pdf

U.S. Bureau of Economic Analysis. (2011). *National economic accounts: Real gross domestic product, chained dollars*. Retrieved January 21, 2011, from http://www.bea.gov/national/nipaweb/SelectTable.asp?Selected=N

U.S. Energy Information Administration. (2010). *Electricity net generation: Total (all sectors), 1949–2009.* Retrieved January 21, 2011, from http://www.eia.gov/electricity/data.cfm#generation

Waddell, P. (2002). UrbanSim: Modeling urban development for land use, transportation, and environmental planning. *Journal of the American Planning Association, 68*(3), 297.

Wooldridge, J. M. (2003). *Introductory econometrics: A modern approach.* Cincinnati: South-Western College Pub.

Zhang, G., Patuwo, B. E., and Hu, M. Y. (1998). Forecasting with artificial neural networks: The state of the art. *International Journal of Forecasting, 14*(1), 35–62.

Part III

Pensions and Other Postemployment Benefits

Chapter 6

Postemployment Benefits and Fiscal Analysis[1]

by Dean Michael Mead

Introduction

To the extent that analyzing the fiscal health of governments incorporates the amounts governments owe to others—their liabilities—it tends to be debt centric. In other words, the focus often is placed on outstanding bonds, notes, and loans. This is particularly true in the practice of one form of financial analysis, municipal credit analysis, for obvious reasons: Municipal credit analysts are concerned with a government's ability to repay its outstanding municipal bonds and notes on time. However, municipal credits analysts are nonetheless aware of, and take into account, the existence of other significant liabilities that will require resources to satisfy, such as claims and judgments against a government, accumulated leave for which employees are compensated when leaving the employ of the government, and amounts due to other governments (for instance, aid payments to school districts).

By far the largest nondebt amounts governments owe relate to postemployment benefits—pensions, health insurance, and other benefits employees earn as they work for a government and receive after they retire or otherwise leave the government's payroll. By one account, the total amount state and local governments owe for postemployment benefits surpasses $3.3 trillion, and the cumulative gap between that amount and the assets available to pay benefits exceeds $1 trillion[2] (Pew, 2010). In comparison, total outstanding municipal debt totaled $2.7 trillion at the end of 2008 (Agriss, 2008).

The purpose of this chapter is to describe the postemployment benefits that state and local governments in the United States provide to their employees and how those benefits affect the fiscal health of governments (or contribute to fiscal stress). The chapter is divided into five parts. The first part describes the types of benefits governments provide and the arrangements by which the benefits are provided. The next section explains how the cost of and obligations related to postemployment benefits are calculated. The third section identifies the key pieces of information that are reported about postemployment benefits and how they should be interpreted. The penultimate section considers how this information can be incorporated into the analysis of fiscal health and the pros and cons of alternative approaches. Finally, the chapter concludes by briefly noting looming changes in governmental financial reporting that may significantly alter the information available for fiscal analysis.

Overview of Postemployment Benefits

As employees of state and local governments work, they earn *current* compensation in the form of a salary and benefits, such as health insurance. At the same time, many employees earn *deferred* compensation over their years of service that will not be received until after their employment with the government ends through retirement.[3]

These *postemployment benefits* typically are considered to be in two groups, the most common being a pension. *Other postemployment benefits* (OPEB) are postemployment benefits *other than pensions.* OPEB generally takes the form of health insurance and dental, vision, prescription, or other healthcare benefits provided to eligible retirees, including in some cases their beneficiaries. It may also include some types of life insurance, legal services, and other benefits.

Cash payments to an insurance company for premiums (or to retirees who pay the premiums themselves) are the most obvious way in which OPEB is provided. However, not all OPEB involves an exchange of cash between a government and an insurance company or retiree. Some governments allow retirees to buy their own health insurance through the governments' insurance plan for current employees. Health insurance for retirees tends to be considerably more expensive than for current employees because retirees are older and more prone to require healthcare. Being insured together with current employees can greatly reduce the premiums that retirees pay. The difference between what retirees would pay on their own and what they pay as part of the government's insurance plan is referred to as an *implicit rate subsidy.* The employer government does not make a cash payment to or on behalf of the retirees, but it pays higher premiums for its current employees than it would if only current employees (and no retirees) were included in the insurance plan. The extra amount a government is paying for current employee premiums subsidizes the lower premiums paid by the retirees.

The provision of postemployment benefits usually involves the creation of a pension or OPEB *plan,* of which there are two basic forms. *Defined benefit* plans are those that specify the *amount of benefits to be provided* to the employees after retirement. *Defined contribution* plans stipulate only the *amounts to be contributed by a government employer* to a plan member's account each year of active employment and do not specify the amount of benefits employees will receive after retirement.[4]

Plans may also be distinguished by how many employer governments participate in them. *Single-employer* plans involve only one government, whereas *multiple-employer* plans include two or more governments. In a *cost-sharing multiple-employer* plan, governments *pool or share* the costs of financing benefits and administering the plan and the assets, if any, accumulated to pay benefits. In *agent multiple-employer* plans, benefit costs are not pooled. Separate accounts are maintained in agent plans to ensure that each employer's contributions are used to provide benefits only for the employees of that government. The cost of administering the plan, however, is shared by the participating governments, and they may also combine the plan's assets for investment purposes. Effectively, an agent plan is a collection of many single-employer plans.

The benefits that public employees receive under pension and OPEB plans generally are determined through the collective bargaining process and stipulated in labor contracts. Benefits may also be governed by legislation or, particularly in the case of pensions, provisions in state constitutions. Features such as retirement age, calculation of final salary, even deductibles and copays, can be the subject of negotiation. The actual cost of the health insurance benefits often is the product of negotiations between the government and the insurance company, balancing increases in premium payments from year to year with copays, deductibles, and other coverage features.

In general, postemployment benefits are financed in one of two ways. Some governments follow an *actuarial* approach, which entails paying to an irrevocable trust an amount that is expected to be sufficient, if invested now, to finance the benefits of employees after they are no longer working for the government. This approach is commonly followed for determining pension contributions. For OPEB, however, most governments currently follow a *pay-as-you-go* approach, paying an amount each year equal to insurance premiums or the benefits distributed or claimed in that year.

Measuring Postemployment Benefit Costs and Obligations

To meaningfully use the available information regarding postemployment benefits in analyzing fiscal health or fiscal stress, it is imperative to understand the nature of that information and how it is produced. The external reporting of postemployment benefit information is governed by the following pronouncements of the Governmental Accounting Standards Board (GASB):

- Statement No. 25, *Financial Reporting for Defined Benefit Pension Plans and Note Disclosures for Defined Contribution Plans,* issued November 1994
- Statement No. 27, *Accounting for Pensions by State and Local Government Employers,* issued November 1994
- Statement No. 43, *Financial Reporting for Postemployment Benefit Plans Other Than Pension Plans,* issued April 2004
- Statement No. 45, *Accounting and Financial Reporting by Employers for Postemployment Benefits Other Than Pensions,* issued July 2004
- Statement No. 50, *Pension Disclosures (an amendment of GASB Statements No. 25 and No. 27),* issued May 2007
- Technical Bulletin 2004-2, *Recognition of Pension and Other Postemployment Benefit Expenditures/Expense and Liabilities by Cost-Sharing Employers,* issued December 2004
- Technical Bulletin 2006-1, *Accounting and Financial Reporting by Employers and OPEB Plans for Payments from the Federal Government Pursuant to the Retiree Drug Subsidy Provisions of Medicare Part D,* issued June 2006
- Technical Bulletin 2008-1, *Determining the Annual Required Contribution Adjustment for Postemployment Benefits,* issued December 2008.

Governments also generally adhere to these standards when determining how they will *fund* their benefits; in other words, how they will systematically set aside enough resources to pay benefits when they come due in the future.

A key feature of these standards is the establishment of parameters or boundaries for the assumptions and methods used to produce actuarial estimates of pension and OPEB costs and obligations. The *actuarial valuation* essentially involves the following steps:

1. Project future cash flows related to benefit payments, based on historical experience and assumptions about such factors as number of covered employees, salary amounts and rate of increase, number of years of service of employees, life expectancy, and so on.
2. Discount the projected cash flows to their present value using a discount rate based on the expected long-term rate of return on the invested assets of the pension or OPEB plan.
3. Allocate the present value to past, current, and anticipated future years of service of employees using one of six acceptable cost allocation methods; of the six methods, the vast majority of governments use the "entry age normal" method. (GASB 2008a)

Of course, an actuarial valuation is a much more complex process, but as this is not the place to embark on an explanation of actuarial science, this brief description of the process should be sufficient.

The portion of the actuarial present value allocated to prior years of employment is called the *actuarial accrued liability* (AAL). If a pension or OPEB plan has cash, investments, and other resources, these may be applied to fund the actuarial accrued liability. The value of these resources is referred to as the *actuarial value of assets.* The actuarial value of assets is not the same as fair value; for financial reporting purposes, annual gains or losses in plan assets are averaged over several years (usually three to five).

Employer contributions–irrevocably transferred assets to a trust–are the primary source of pension and OPEB plan assets.[5] The other major sources of plan assets are employee contributions, contributions from other entities (such as state government contributions to a teacher retirement plan), and investment earnings. In addition, employer contributions to an OPEB plan may include payments from the government directly to or on behalf of a retiree or beneficiary, or premium payments to insurers.

The excess of the AAL over the actuarial value of assets is the *unfunded actuarial accrued liability* (UAAL or unfunded liability). The unfunded liability is amortized (systematically attributed) over a period of up to 30 years (approximately equal to a typical public employee's term of employment), either in *level dollar* amounts or as a *level percentage of projected payroll.* Like a home mortgage, the level dollar method divides the liability into equal dollar amounts over the selected number of years; each payment is part interest, part principal. The level percentage method calculates payments so that they equal a constant percentage of payroll over time as payroll increases; most governments currently use this method when reporting their pension benefits.

The *normal cost* (the value of newly earned benefits in the current year) and the portion of the UAAL to be amortized in the current year together make up the *annual required contribution* (ARC) of the employer for the year. Conceptually, the ARC is an amount that, if paid on an ongoing basis, would be expected to provide sufficient resources to fund both the normal cost for each year and the amortized unfunded liability.

For a government in a single-employer or agent multiple-employer plan, the *annual pension/OPEB cost* equals the ARC plus or minus certain adjustments if the employer's actual contributions in prior years differed from the ARC. The annual pension/OPEB cost is the *expense* that a government would report in its accrual-based financial statements—the government-wide statements and the proprietary fund statements. Generally, the cumulative sum of differences between an employer's annual pension cost and the amounts *actually contributed* to the plan since makes up a liability (or asset) called the *net pension obligation* (or *net OPEB obligation*). Governments were not required to report an initial liability related to either the AAL or UAAL on the face of the financial statements when the pension and OPEB standards were first implemented. For an employer government participating in a cost-sharing multiple-employer plan, the annual pension or OPEB expense is equal to the employer's *contractually required contribution* to the plan—the amount assessed by the plan for the period—which may or may not equal the ARC.

Under modified accrual in the governmental fund financial statements, an employer would report OPEB *expenditures* equal to *the amount contributed to the plan or expected to be liquidated with expendable available financial resources*.[6] Because the governmental fund financial statements focus on current financial resources, they do not include the net pension or OPEB obligation or any other long-term liability.

Key Postemployment Benefit Information

The data produced by the actuarial process just described, plus supporting disclosures, constitute the information available about postemployment benefits in audited financial reports. This section of the chapter identifies the key decision-useful pieces of information that can be obtained from the financial reports of employer governments and their pension and OPEB plans.

Difficulties in Collecting Information

As the preceding sentence indicates, in most instances not all of the useful information can be found in one place. Rather, one must use the financial reports of the employer government in concert with those issued by the pension or OPEB plan itself.[7] This leads to an unfortunate juggling act between the two documents and roughly doubles the effort required to collect the information. Government employers are required to disclose how to obtain a copy of the pension or OPEB plan's financial report, but this generally takes the less-than-useful form of providing a mailing address for the plan.

Acquiring these financial reports is relatively easy for large governmental entities. One study found 88% of the annual financial reports of the 50 states and largest (by annual revenue) counties, localities, independent school districts, and special districts on the Internet for fiscal years 2006–2008 (Mead, 2011). However, the smaller a government gets, the less likely it is to post its annual financial report to its website (if it even has a website). The same study was able to obtain online 41% of the annual financial reports of a random sample of 193 governments with annual revenues of $10 million to $100 million for fiscal years 2006–2008. Obtaining a financial report directly from a small government is an ordeal in itself, presuming one can identify the right person in the government to contact. A three-month effort to collect the remaining reports directly from the governments yielded an additional 29%, or 70% of the small-government financial reports overall.

Lastly, the amount of information presented in a government employer's financial report (versus the report issued by its pension or OPEB plan) varies depending on the type of plan the government participates in. The majority of the reporting requirements for cost-sharing multiple-employer plans falls on the plan, rather than on the participating employers, in part because a single actuarial valuation is conducted for the entire plan and not for each individual government. By comparison, governments in single-employer and agent multiple-employer plans shoulder greater responsibility for meeting the overall financial reporting requirements.

Postemployment Benefit Obligations and Funding Progress

The actuarial value of assets, AAL, and UAAL can be found in two places. First, governments are required to disclose these amounts from the most recent actuarial valuation in the notes to the financial statements. Second, one can find the amounts tracked over time in the *schedule of funding progress,* a form of required supplementary information (RSI).[8]

A government participating in a single-employer or agent multiple-employer plan presents RSI covering the last three actuarial valuations, as long as its plan issues its own financial report. However, if the government includes the plan as a trust fund in its own financial report and a separate report is not issued by the pension plan, then the government presents this RSI for the last six fiscal years regardless of what kind of pension plan it participates in. Governments participating in cost-sharing plans do not present this information, unless they are the sponsor of the plan. In plan financial reports, this schedule covers the last six fiscal years.

Figures 6.1 and **6.2** present illustrative schedules of funding progress for pension and OPEB plans, respectively. In addition to presenting the basic data points, the schedule also includes ratios intended to identify the degree to which assets have been set aside to cover the pension or OPEB obligation and to convey a sense of the magnitude of the unfunded liability.

The fifth column of the schedule divides asset value by the AAL, producing the *funded ratio.* A funded ratio can be as low as zero (for a pay-as-you-go system with no assets) and as high as 100% or even higher (for a fully funded system, or one that actually has assets

	[A]	[B]	[C]	[D]	[E]	[F]
Valuation Year	Actuarial Accrued Liability	Actuarial Value of Assets	Unfunded Actuarial Accrued Liability	Funded Ratio (A÷B)	Covered Payroll	UAAL-to-Covered-Payroll (C÷E)
2008	$73,466	$65,315	$8,151	88.91%	$12,801	63.67%
2007	69,734	67,151	2,583	96.30%	12,584	20.53%
2006	66,161	61,296	4,865	92.65%	12,175	39.96%
2005	61,146	54,473	6,673	89.09%	11,806	56.52%
2004	57,604	50,452	7,152	87.58%	11,806	60.58%
2003	54,774	46,746	8,028	85.34%	11,454	70.09%

Figure 6.1 Schedule of Funding Progress, Pension Plan ($ in millions)

	[A]	[B]	[C]	[D]	[E]	[F]
Valuation Year	Actuarial Accrued Liability	Actuarial Value of Assets	Unfunded Actuarial Accrued Liability	Funded Ratio (A÷B)	Covered Payroll	UAAL-to-Covered-Payroll (C÷E)
2008	$29,623	$10,748	$18,875	36.28%	$12,801	147.45%
2007	29,825	12,801	17,024	42.92%	12,584	135.28%
2006	30,748	12,025	18,723	39.11%	12,175	153.78%
2005	31,796	11,470	20,326	36.07%	11,806	172.17%
2004	31,307	11,070	20,237	35.36%	11,806	171.41%
2003	29,479	10,816	18,663	36.69%	11,454	162.94%

Figure 6.2 Schedule of Funding Progress, OPEB Plan ($ in millions)

that exceed the AAL, respectively). All other things being equal, a higher funded ratio indicates a better funded plan.

The second-to-last column in the schedule presents the total payroll of the current employees covered by the plan—the covered payroll. The last column then calculates a ratio dividing the UAAL by the covered payroll. This ratio gives one a sense of the magnitude of the unfunded liability (the government illustrated in Figure 6.1 has an unfunded liability equal to almost 64% of its total annual payroll in 2008). The ratio also allows for comparisons to be made among plans of varying sizes.

A study of state pension systems found them to be 84% funded cumulatively in 2008, but identified 21 state systems with a funded ratio below 80%, an industry rule of thumb

(Pew Center, 2010). Eight states were less than two-thirds funded. It should be noted that these figures do not reflect the major decline in investment values in the latter half of 2008 for the majority of states with actuarial valuations as of June 30. Nevertheless, funded status already was in decline: Half of the state systems were fully funded or better in 2000, but only four were fully funded or better by 2008. For OPEB, only two states had funded ratios above 50%.

If a government has historically contributed less than the ARC to its pension or OPEB plan, then it will report a net pension obligation or net OPEB obligation in the government-wide statement of net position (and proprietary fund statement of fund net position, if appropriate).

Annual Contributions

A second RSI presentation is the *schedule of employer contributions*. It compares a government's actual contributions to its pension or OPEB plan with its ARC. A government is required to present this schedule only if the pension plan does not issue its own financial report, which would include such a schedule covering the last six fiscal years. **Figure 6.3** shows that the illustrative government contributed to its pension plan an amount equal to 100% of the ARC each year. On the other hand, **Figure 6.4** shows a government that

Fiscal Year	Annual Required Contribution	Percentage of ARC Contributed
2008	$1,043,231,908	100%
2007	913,046,745	100%
2006	1,071,049,868	100%
2005	1,110,687,879	100%
2004	1,122,388,137	100%
2003	1,069,594,041	100%

Figure 6.3 Schedule of Employer Contributions, Pension Plan

Fiscal Year	Annual Required Contribution	Percentage of ARC Contributed
2008	$1,698,928,499	25.04%
2007	1,855,720,690	21.83%
2006	2,068,922,571	18.65%
2005	1,990,561,830	18.46%
2004	1,870,435,879	18.71%
2003	1,759,839,056	18.94%

Figure 6.4 Schedule of Employer Contributions, OPEB Plan

has contributed only a fraction of the ARC for its OPEB plan. This is not unusual, considering that very few governments prefunded OPEB to any extent prior to implementing Statement 45. Further, many governments have chosen to continue financing OPEB on a pay-as-you-go basis.

The Pew Center study found that 21 states failed to contribute an average of at least 90% of the ARC to their pension plans between 2004 and 2008. In 2008, Colorado contributed 68% of the ARC, Kentucky and Wyoming 66%, Kansas 65%, Minnesota 63%, Illinois 58%, New Jersey 57%, and Pennsylvania a paltry 40%. In that same year, only four states contributed 100% of the ARC for OPEB. Overall, states contributed slightly more than one-third of the cumulative OPEB ARC for 2008.

If a government or plan is aware of any factors that have a significant effect on the trend information in these two RSI schedules, such as improvements or reductions in pension benefit provisions, expansion or reduction of the eligible population, or changes in the actuarial methods, it adds an explanatory note to the schedules. If a government reports a cost-sharing plan as a trust fund and the plan does not issue its own financial report, then the government adds another note to the schedules that describes the methodology and assumptions for performing actuarial valuations for the pension plan.

Note Disclosures

The notes to the financial statements that relate to pensions and OPEB are quite extensive. **Figure 6.5** illustrates a typical pension note disclosure; an OPEB note disclosure would appear quite similar. All governments, regardless of the type of pension or OPEB plan they participate in, are required to do the following in the notes for each plan:

- Identify and describe the plan and describe the benefits.
- Identify the authority under which benefit provisions and requirements to contribute to the plan were established or may be changed.
- Present the required employer and employee contribution rates.
- Present the required contributions and the percentage actually contributed for the past three years (cost-sharing plans only).
- Explain how to obtain the financial report of the plan, if one was issued.

The following information is disclosed by the plan in its own financial report. If the plan does not issue a report, the information should be disclosed in the notes of the government that reports the plan as a trust fund.

- Number and types of employees covered by the plan
- Number of plan members, distinguishing between current employees, persons already receiving benefits, and persons no longer working for the government who are not yet receiving benefits
- Information about legally required reserves, if any

Plan Description. Whitney Employees' Pension Plan (WEPP) is a single-employer defined benefit pension plan administered by the Whitney Retirement System. WEPP provides retirement, disability, and death benefits to plan members and beneficiaries. Cost-of-living adjustments are provided to members and beneficiaries at the discretion of the State legislature. Article 29 of the Regulations of the State of Whitney assigns the authority to establish and amend benefit provisions to the State legislature. The Whitney Retirement System issues a publicly available financial report that includes financial statements and required supplementary information for WEPP. That report may be obtained by writing to Whitney Retirement System, 4427B Willow Pond Road, Anytown, USA 01000 or by calling 1-800-555-PLAN.

Funding Policy. The contribution requirements of plan members and the State are established and may be amended by the State legislature. Plan members are required to contribute 7.8% of their annual covered salary. The State is required to contribute at an actuarially determined rate; the current rate is 11.9% of annual covered payroll.

Annual Pension Cost and Net Pension Obligation. The State's annual pension cost and net pension obligation to WEPP for the current year ended December 31, 20XX were as follows:

(dollar amounts in thousands)

Annual required contribution	$ 137,916
Interest on net pension obligation	2,867
Adjustment to annual required contribution	(2,089)
Annual pension cost	138,694
Contributions made	(137,916)
Increase in net pension obligation	778
Net pension obligation beginning of year	38,221
Net pension obligation end of year	$ 38,999

The annual required contribution for the current year was determined as part of the December 31, 2009 actuarial valuation using the entry age actuarial cost method. The actuarial assumptions included (a) 7.5% investment rate of return (net of administrative expenses) and (b) projected salary increases ranging from 5.5% to 9.5% per year. Both (a) and (b) included an inflation component of 5.5%. The assumptions did not include postretirement benefit increases, which are funded by State appropriation when granted. The actuarial value of assets was determined using techniques that smooth the effects of short-term volatility in the market value of investments over a four-year period. The unfunded actuarial accrued liability is being amortized as a level percentage of projected payroll on an open basis. The remaining amortization period at December 31, 2009 was 23 years.

(continued)

Three-Year Trend Information

(dollar amounts in thousands)

Fiscal Year Ended	Annual Pension Cost (APC)	Percentage of APC Contributed	Net Pension Obligation
12/31/09	$119,757	99.1%	$37,458
12/31/08	125,039	99.4	38,221
12/31/07	138,364	99.4	38,999

Funded Status and Funding Progress. As of December 31, 2009, the most recent actuarial valuation date, the plan was 88.1% funded. The actuarial accrued liability for benefits was $8.8 billion, and the actuarial value of assets was $7.8 billion, resulting in an unfunded actuarial accrued liability (UAAL) of $1.0 billion. The covered payroll (annual payroll of active employees covered by the plan) was $2.2 billion, and the ratio of the UAAL to the covered payroll was 45%.

Actuarial valuations of an ongoing plan involve estimates of the value of reported amounts and assumptions about the probability of occurrence of events far into the future. Examples include assumptions about future employment and mortality. Amounts determined regarding the funded status of the plan and the annual required contributions of the employer are subject to continual revision as actual results are compared with past expectations and new estimates are made about the future. The schedule of funding progress, presented as required supplementary information following the notes to the financial statements, presents multiyear trend information about whether the actuarial value of plan assets is increasing or decreasing over time relative to the actuarial accrued liabilities for benefits.

Figure 6.5 Pension Note Disclosures

Source: Adapted from Mead, D. M. (2005b). What else you should know about your government's finances: A guide to notes to the financial statements and supporting information. Norwalk, CT: GASB.

As mentioned earlier, governments in single-employer and agent multiple-employer plans disclose the schedule of funding progress information (actuarial value of assets, AAL, UAAL, and ratios) for the most recent actuarial valuation. They also disclose:

- The annual pension/OPEB cost and the contributed to the plan for the current year
- The annual pension/OPEB cost, percentage actually contributed, and net pension/OPEB obligation (if any) for each of the past three years
- The components of the annual pension/OPEB cost, if the government has a net pension/OPEB obligation
- The date of the most recent actuarial valuation, the methods and significant assumptions employed in the valuation, and the methods used for amortization.

What is the purpose of these lengthy disclosures? Having the details of the plans, the benefits they provide, and to whom they apply helps to explain the financial information about pensions and OPEB, such as the annual cost and the unfunded obligation. As mentioned, governments have the leeway to select from multiple methods of cost allocation, amortization, and asset smoothing, and to choose appropriate assumptions within the parameters. Knowing what methods and assumptions have been employed allows an analyst to draw conclusions about the appropriateness of the choices, consider how the actuarial amounts might increase or decrease if other assumptions are employed, and become informed about whether multiple governments are using relatively similar methods and assumptions and, therefore, producing financial information that can be compared.[9]

Separately Issued Plan Financial Reports

Pension and OPEB plans present two financial statements—a *statement of plan net position* and a *statement of changes in plan net position.* The first shows the assets belonging to the plan, any amounts owed by the plan, and the difference between them—net position held in trust for pension/OPEB benefits (See **Figure 6.6**). The second statement shows additions to the plan's net position (such as contributions and investment income) and deductions from the plan's net position (such as benefit payments). (See **Figure 6.7**)

A key piece of information to be found in the statement of plan net position is the fair value of plan investments as of the date of the financial statements. The actuarial value of assets described earlier is not the current fair value but rather essentially a weighted average of the fair value for the past several years. Recent increases and decreases in fair values are only partially reflected in the actuarial value of assets, but the amounts shown for investments in the plan financial statements will be fully up to date.

Larger pension and OPEB plans often prepare a comprehensive annual financial report (CAFR), which adds introductory information, supporting financial schedules, and historical data to the financial statements, notes, and RSI. The historical data is contained in the *statistical section.* In this part of the CAFR, a pension or OPEB plan would present the following schedules:

- Changes in plan net assets position[10] by type for the past 10 years
- Benefit and refund deductions from net assets position by type for the past 10 years (a more detailed presentation of deductions, which may be combined with the first schedule)
- Retired members by type of benefit and amount of monthly benefit for the past 10 years
- Average benefit payments for the past 10 years
- Largest participating governments for the current year and 9 years ago (the last and first years, respectively, in the same 10-year period covered by the other schedules.

Assets	
Cash and cash equivalents	$ 2,765,652
Cash and cash equivalents with trustee	1,607,551
Securities lending:	
Short-term collateral, at market value—	
Corporate and government bonds	127,583,577
Receivables:	
Employer	2,208,857
Interest and dividend	1,906,531
Sales receivable	2,614,542
Total receivables	6,729,930
Investments, at market value:	
Corporate and government bonds	209,010,203
Common stock	401,163,460
International stock	117,646,897
International emerging markets	41,627,350
Real estate	44,071,834
Total investments	813,519,744
Total assets	$ 952,206,454
Liabilities	
Accounts payable	$ 2,430,568
Accrued vacation	59,121
Purchases payable	4,842,249
Liabilities under securities lending	127,583,577
Total liabilities	$ 134,915,515
Net position held in trust for pension benefits	$ 817,290,939

Figure 6.6 Statement of Plan Net Position

Pension and OPEB financial reports may also include other information. Many plans present a section with more in-depth information about the content of their investment portfolio and investment performance. Another section may include more detailed information about the plan's actuarial valuations. Multiple-employer plans also typically list the names of the participating governments.

Additions (decreases)	
Employer Contributions:	
City General Fund	$ 15,334,901
City Contribution—General Fund	1,500,001
Waterworks Fund	1,426,525
School Operating Fund	5,047,143
Other Contributions:	
Income from Leave Exchange	1,541,852
Employee Buy-back	857,645
Medicare Part D—City	529,104
Return of City Health Insurance Surplus	1,589,282
Total contributions	27,826,453
Investment income:	
Net appreciation—bonds	4,072,931
Net appreciation—stocks	88,685,159
Interest	10,096,170
Dividends	12,932,959
Real estate operating income	7,535,139
Commission recapture	108,977
Total investment gain	123,431,335
Less investment expenses:	
Other investment expenses	(4,474,029)
Net investment gain	118,957,306
Total additions	146,783,759
Deductions	
Benefits:	
Service	$ 34,912,466
Occupational death	50,060
Nonoccupational death	65,451
Occupational disability	241,870
Nonoccupational disability	580,956
Retirees insurance benefits	11,984,402
Other benefits	2,281,314
Total benefits	50,116,519

(continued)

Administrative expenses:	
Personal services	446,113
Board fees	5,168
Consultant fees	135,001
Actuary fees	133,091
Legal fees	57,014
Other expenses	2,996
Total administrative expenses	779,383
Total deductions	50,895,902
Net increase	$ 95,887,857
Net position held in trust for pension benefits at June 30, 2010	721,403,082
Net position held in trust for pension benefits at June 30, 2011	$ 817,290,939

Figure 6.7 Statement of Changes in Plan Net Position

The Place of Postemployment Benefits in Fiscal Health Assessments

There are at least four approaches to addressing postemployment benefits when assessing the fiscal health of a government: (1) incorporate information about postemployment benefits by including it in existing financial ratios, (2) incorporate postemployment benefits as a separate factor with its own ratios, (3) consider postemployment benefit information as a qualitative matter, and (4) do not incorporate postemployment benefit information at all.

Incorporate Information into Existing Ratios

This approach involves including pension and OPEB obligation information with other liabilities in the calculation of financial ratios. For instance, a debt-per-capita ratio divides outstanding debt by population; the UAAL (and other long-term liabilities, for that matter) would be added to the outstanding debt in the numerator. The result would be obvious: the ratio would be much bigger, reflecting that residents of the government are indeed on the hook for repaying much more than just municipal debt.

The foremost advantage of this approach is that one of the most significant liabilities of a government would receive scrutiny when assessing the government's financial health. Debt ratios would cover all significant long-term liabilities and more fully measure how much a government owes.

One argument made against this approach is that the UAAL is not really a liability, and if it were, it would be reported in the financial statements. This is a specious argument for several reasons. Postemployment benefit obligations are not the only long-term liabilities not included in debt ratios. And the fact that postemployment benefit obligations are not recognized on the face of the financial statements alone does not mean it is not a liability. The GASB originally intended that its pension standards would be implemented simultaneously with Statement 11 (GASB, 1990), which would have established a basis of accounting under which a long-term liability based on the AAL or UAAL could be recognized (GASB, 1994b). However, Statement 11 never went into effect and there was no place to report a long-term liability until Statement 34 (GASB, 1999) was issued five years after the pension standards.

Since that time, the GASB has established a conceptual definition of a liability against which both the AAL and UAAL can be evaluated. The GASB defines liabilities as "present obligations to sacrifice resources that the government has little or no discretion to avoid" (GASB, 2007a). In 2011, the GASB proposed new standards that state that the unfunded portion of the pension obligation meets the definition of a liability and that it is measurable with sufficient reliability to be recognized in the financial statements (GASB, 2011b).

The second part of that decision defuses another argument against incorporating the AAL or UAAL into ratios—that both are based on assumptions and estimates and therefore are not reliable liability measures. This argument ignores the fact that many assets and liabilities recognized in the financial statements are based on assumptions and estimates, such as capital assets and depreciation (based on assumptions about how long they will be in use and their value afterwards), investments for which there is no readily determinable market price (for which fair value is determined by projecting future cash flows and discounting to present value), and pollution remediation obligations (calculated using a probability-weighted average of possible outcomes).

In the final analysis, the best argument against incorporating postemployment benefit information directly into financial ratios is that it is not practical. Debt ratios work because they only include debt—the various forms of debt all are amenable to coverage ratios, for instance. How would a coverage ratio be calculated for a UAAL or compensated absences? What is the established payment schedule and what is the revenue stream against which it would be compared? However, there seems to be little argument against including the UAAL in broader liability-related ratios, such as the debt-to-assets, debt-to-net-assets position, and other solvency ratios.

Postemployment Benefits as a Separate Factor

This approach entails analyzing postemployment benefits as their own factor in assessing the overall fiscal health of a government, rather than folding it into debt analysis. The former approach certainly is less complicated than the latter, and there is a host of potential ratios available.

The funded ratio and unfunded-liability-as-a-percentage-of-covered-payroll ratio may be the most widely used, but they are by no means the only ratios employed for assessing postemployment benefits. Percentage distributions may be calculated by type of investment, and percentage changes in the fair value of investments by type and in net position held in trust. A measure of overhead costs can be found by dividing deductions for administration by total deductions; in general, the lower the ratio, the more efficient the plan's administration. Ratios similar to those used to make basis financial assessments of a government also can be used for pension analysis, including:

- Plan assets compared to benefits
- Plan receipts additions compared to pension deductions (or, more specifically, contributions compared to benefit payments)
- Plan contributions compared to salaries
- Plan investment earnings compared to benefits. (Mead, 2001)

An interesting take on measuring the sufficiency of plan assets to cover future benefit payments might be dubbed a *depletion ratio.* This is calculated by dividing net position held in trust by deductions for benefit payments. The result is an approximation of the number of years before the plan would run out of money. It is a useful and simple-to-calculate ratio, much like the covered payroll ratio, in that it sets the finances of the plan in context and can be used for comparisons. In this instance, instead of assets being set against the total obligation, assets are set against the consumption of assets via yearly benefit payments.

In its simplicity, however, it is a fairly unrealistic measure, as it ignores at least two key facts—the plan will continue to receive contributions and investment income, increasing net position held in trust, and the amount of the annual benefit payments will increase over time. A more sophisticated and realistic approach would involve extrapolating additions and deductions based on historical experience. The result should be a longer and more accurate calculation of years-to-depletion.

A disadvantage to this approach is that it perpetuates debt analysis that, at best, nods to the existence of other major long-term liabilities and, at worst, ignores them completely. Another issue, though by no means a fatal flaw, is how to incorporate the results of the analysis of postemployment benefits into an overall formula for fiscal health assessment. This is, of course, an issue facing all analytical factors of fiscal health, not just postemployment benefits alone.

Qualitative Indicators of Managerial Ability

Managerial ability generally is a contextual issue considered in conjunction with quantitative analysis of factors such as debt, economics and demographics, and so on. The notion here is that if there are two governments with identical financial ratios across the board, then the government with the more professional and capable leadership has better prospects for continued or improved fiscal health. Financial management is one of the categories of credit worthiness analysis employed by the credit rating agencies.[11]

Indicators that otherwise would inform the financial status of a pension or OPEB plan are interpreted as measures of the ability of a government's officials to manage a government's finances and make choices that maintain and improve its fiscal health. An analyst would look at the progress of the funded ratio over time, for instance, and make judgments about the ability and willingness of officials to provide the resources necessary to satisfy the postemployment obligation or otherwise manage the size of the obligation.

The reaction of the credit rating agencies to the implementation by governments of the OPEB reporting standards is a case in point (Laskey et al., 2007; Mason et al., 2005). The mere appearance in the financial report of an OPEB unfunded liability, where one was not previously reported, did not by itself trigger any change in ratings. The rating agencies were keenly interested in how governments planned to deal with their unfunded liabilities; a viable plan is a ratings plus, a nonviable or nonexistent plan, a minus. Going forward from implementation of the OPEB standards, the rating agencies are looking for progress on funding, with improving funded status a positive and declining status a negative, just as they do for pensions.

However, rating agencies also conduct thorough financial analyses of postemployment benefits as well, and do not treat them as solely indicators of managerial ability. To the extent that qualitative managerial analysis is coupled with the kind of quantitative analysis discussed in the preceding approach, it can be very valuable. However, managerial analysis in the absence of that quantitative analysis has very little to recommend it as a part of assessing governmental fiscal health.

Do Not Incorporate at All

This approach is also known as the stick-your-head-in-the-sand method. There are no arguments in favor of this approach. One cannot convincingly pretend to fully comprehend a government's fiscal health or its exposure to fiscal stress without understanding the effect of a government's postemployment benefit promises. The cons against this approach should, based on the discussion thus far in this chapter, be evident and do not bear repeating.

The Future of Postemployment Benefit Information

In the preceding section, it was mentioned that the GASB released proposed new pension standards for public comment in June 2011. In a Preliminary Views issued the previous year, the GASB advanced the concept that a pension plan is the primary obligor of the pension obligation to the extent that assets are available in the plan; essentially, the funded portion of the obligation (GASB, 2010). The government employer is the primary obligor for the remainder of the pension obligation and the secondary obligor for the funded portion, should the plan assets decline in value or be lost. In its proposed standards, the GASB stated that the portion of the obligation for which the government is primary obligor is a liability (a *net pension liability*) and should be recognized in the accrual-based statements of net position (GASB, 2011b). Furthermore, a government participating in a cost-sharing plan would report a liability in its own financial statements that is equivalent to its proportionate share of the collective unfunded obligation.

The 2011 proposal included many changes to the existing pension standards nearly as momentous as the liability decision, including:

- Governments would no longer have a choice among cost allocation methods but would be required to use entry age normal and level percentage of payroll.
- The basic discount rate would continue to be the long-term expected rate of return on plan investments but only to the extent that plan assets are available to pay benefits; beyond the point at which plan assets are exhausted, benefit payments would be discounted based on a high-quality municipal bond index.
- (1) Pension benefits earned, (2) interest cost on the beginning balance of the net pension liability, and (3) changes in plan net position not related to investments would be reported as expenses each year as they occur.
- Changes in pension plan terms that affect the amount of benefits attributed to past years would be incorporated into expense immediately, rather than the current allowance of up to 30 years.
- (1) Differences between expected and actual changes in relevant economic and demographic factors and (2) changes in assumptions about those factors, as they affect the portion of the pension liability related to *inactive* members (retirees and others no longer working for the government), would be incorporated into expense immediately, rather than over 30 years.
- (1) Differences between expected and actual changes in relevant economic and demographic factors and (2) changes in assumptions about those factors, as they affect the portion of the pension liability related to *active* members (current employees), would be systematically reported as expenses over a period equal to the remaining service periods of employees, a period likely to be much shorter than 30 years.
- Differences between assumed returns on pension plan investments and actual returns would be deferred and introduced into the expense calculation over a five-year period; this is considerably faster than the present requirements, in which changes in investment fair values are introduced into the liability measurement over a three- to five-year period (smoothing) and then introduced into expense over 30 years.
- Ad hoc cost-of-living adjustments (COLAs) would be included in projections of pension benefit payments if they happen with a frequency that makes them essentially automatic COLAs (which are already required to be included in projections)

- The date of the actuarial valuation used to report an employer's net pension liability would have to be no more than 24 months prior to the end of a government's fiscal year; measurements of the net pension liability earlier than the end of a government's fiscal year would be updated to reflect all significant changes between the actuarial valuation date and the fiscal year-end.

The 2011 proposal did not address OPEB, but given the Board's historical approach, which addresses all postemployment benefits in essentially the same way, one can expect most of these changes, if they become final for pensions, to be extended eventually to OPEB.

The effect on postemployment benefit information of these proposed changes would be very significant. First, a potentially sizable liability will be reported in the financial statements for the first time, automatically making the financial position as measured by net position look less healthy. Second, comparability—which is currently hampered by the considerable leeway that governments are given to choose their assumptions and methods—should be improved by the tentative decisions regarding cost allocation methods and recognizing changes in asset values.

Third, the tentative decisions regarding ad hoc COLAs, the discount rate, and the shortening of the amortization period should result in the reporting of larger total and unfunded pension obligations and larger annual pension expenses. Fourth, actuarial valuation information should be more recent and thereby more relevant to present fiscal assessments. Fifth, information approximating the individual pension obligations and costs of governments in cost-sharing plans would be available for the first time.

The sum of these changes, should they be enacted, would be information that is easier to understand, more comprehensive, and more transparent, and should greatly aid fiscal health and stress assessments.

Endnotes

1. The opinions expressed in this chapter are those of the author. Official positions of the Governmental Accounting Standards Board are established only after extensive public due process and deliberation.
2. The Pew Center study is based on hand-collected data from the financial plans of governments and pension and OPEB plans. The funding gap may actually be greater because the information for many of the governments predated the enormous decline in the stock market in the latter half of 2008. Other studies (Bornstein et al., 2010; Novy-Marx and Rauh, 2010) have claimed that the size of the gap is considerably greater than reported in financial reports. However, it should be noted that much of the increase in the gap that these studies cite is the product of using a much smaller discount rate (e.g., 4.14 versus 7.5–8.0% in Bornstein et al.), which mathematically produces a larger present value of the benefit obligation. The authors have changed the assumption based on their belief that it is inappropriate to use a long-term rate of return on plan investments as the discount rate.
3. Some employees earn and ultimately receive retirement benefits from a government employer, even if they are no longer employed by that government at the time they retire. That is the

reason why these benefits are properly referred to as postemployment benefits, rather than retirement benefits. For the purpose of simplification, references to retirees, retirement, and so on should be understood to include these employees as well.

4. Because a government participating in a defined contribution plan has no obligation beyond paying the required contribution, the accounting and financial reporting requirements are relatively simple. Contributions paid or due and payable are reported as expenditures, contractually required contributions are reported as expenses, and the only liability (if any) relates to contributions due but not yet paid. Additionally, the required note disclosures are few. By contrast, the accounting for defined benefit plans is far more complex and the reporting requirements much more extensive. For this reason, this chapter focuses exclusively on defined benefit plans.
5. The GASB's usage of the term *irrevocable trust* refers to a trust in which plan assets are dedicated to providing benefits to retirees and beneficiaries in accordance with the terms of the pension or OPEB plan and are legally protected from creditors of the employer and plan administrator. In other words, the assets are solely dedicated to the provision of benefits and cannot be touched by the government employer.
6. For an explanation of the differences between expenditures and expenses and their relative merits as measures of cost, see Mead (2005a).
7. If a government's pension or OPEB plan does not issue its own financial report, then all of the required information should be found in the employer's financial report.
8. RSI is presented following the note disclosures. Although certain limited auditing procedures are applied to RSI, such as inquiring about how the information was assembled and checking it against the information presented in the financial statements and notes, RSI is not fully audited to the extent of financial statements and notes.
9. Ives (2006) offers an excellent discussion of the implications of different choices of methods and assumptions.
10. As a result of GASB Statement 63 (GASB, 2011a), *net assets* will be referred to as *net position* beginning in fiscal years ending December 31, 2012, and later.
11. For example, see Standard & Poor's (2006).

Glossary

Actuarial accrued liability (AAL): the portion of the actuarial present value of projected benefit payments that is allocated to prior years of employment.

Agent multiple-employer plans: postemployment benefit plans that involve more than one employer, in which the contributions of a government employer may be pooled for investment purposes, but which may be used to make benefit payments only for the employees of that government.

Annual required contribution (ARC): the actuarially determined amount a government should contribute in order to ultimately fully fund a benefit plan.

Cost-sharing multiple-employer plans: postemployment benefit plans that involve more than one employer, in which the contributions of government employers are pooled for investment purposes and which are used to make benefit payments for the employees of any participating government.

Defined benefit plans: postemployment benefit plans that guarantee a specific level of benefits.

Defined contribution plans: postemployment benefit plans that guarantee a specific amount to be contributed by a government employer to a plan member's account but do not guarantee the level of benefits employees will receive.

Funded ratio: an indication of the degree to which assets held by a benefit plan are sufficient to cover the present value of the benefit obligation; it is calculated as the actuarial value of assets held by a pension or OPEB plan for making benefit payments divided by the AAL.

Other postemployment benefits (OPEB): all retirement benefits not provided through a pension plan, most notably retiree health insurance.

Single-employer plans: postemployment benefit plans that involve only a single government employer.

Unfunded actuarial accrued liability (UAAL): the AAL less the actuarial value of assets held by a pension or OPEB plan for making benefit payments.

Discussion Questions

1. What are the differences between defined benefit and defined contribution plans? Which type of plan is more likely to lead to a more costly obligation for a government to provide benefits? Why?
2. One criticism of the information currently reported about pensions and OPEB is that it is difficult to compare across governments. What causes this lack of comparability? How might comparability be improved?
3. "It is not possible to include pensions and OPEB in financial analysis because their related liabilities are not reported in the financial statements." Do you agree with this statement? Why or why not?
4. How are the obligations and costs associated with pensions and OPEB best incorporated into analyses of fiscal health and stress? Support your conclusion.

Recommended Resources

Center for Retirement Research at Boston College, www.crr.bc.edu

Governmental Accounting Standards Board (2011c). Proposed statement of the Governmental Accounting Standards Board: Plain-language supplement, *Pension Accounting and Financial Reporting*. Norwalk, CT: GASB.

Mead, D. M. (2008). Accounting and financial reporting by governments for retirement benefits: Understanding and using the information in audited financial reports. In C. G. Reddick and J. D. Coggburn (Eds.), *Handbook of employee benefits and administration* (pp. 285–308). Boca Raton, FL: Taylor & Francis Group.

National Association of State Retirement Administrators, www.nasra.org

National Conference on Public Employee Retirement Systems, www.ncpers.org

Pew Center on the States. (2010). *Trillion dollar gap: Underfunded state retirement systems and the road to reform*. Washington, DC: Pew Charitable Trusts.

References

Agriss, T. (2008). *Municipal bond market issues: Recent developments*. Hauppauge, NY: Black & Veatch.

Bornstein, H., Markuze, S., Percy, C., Wang, L., and Zander, M. (2010). *Going for broke: Reforming California's public employee pension systems*. Stanford, CA: Stanford Institute for Economic Policy Research.

Governmental Accounting Standards Board. (1990). Statement No. 11, *Measurement focus and basis of accounting—governmental fund operating statements*. Norwalk, CT: GASB.

Governmental Accounting Standards Board. (1994a). Statement No. 25, *Financial reporting for defined benefit pension plans and note disclosures for defined contribution plans*. Norwalk, CT: GASB.

Governmental Accounting Standards Board. (1994b). Statement No. 27, *Accounting for pensions by state and local government employers*. Norwalk, CT: GASB.

Governmental Accounting Standards Board. (1999). Statement No. 34, *Basic financial statements—and management's discussion and analysis—for state and local governments*. Norwalk, CT: GASB.

Governmental Accounting Standards Board. (2004a). Statement No. 43, *Financial reporting for postemployment benefit plans other than pension plans*. Norwalk, CT: GASB.

Governmental Accounting Standards Board. (2004b). Statement No. 45, *Accounting and financial reporting by employers for postemployment benefits other than pensions*. Norwalk, CT: GASB.

Governmental Accounting Standards Board. (2004c). Technical Bulletin 2004-2, *Recognition of pension and other postemployment benefit expenditures/expense and liabilities by cost-sharing employers*. Norwalk, CT: GASB.

Governmental Accounting Standards Board. (2006). Technical Bulletin 2006-1, *Accounting and financial reporting by employers and OPEB plans for payments from the federal government pursuant to the retiree drug subsidy provisions of Medicare Part D*. Norwalk, CT: GASB.

Governmental Accounting Standards Board. (2007a). Concepts Statement No. 4, *Elements of financial statements*. Norwalk, CT: GASB.

Governmental Accounting Standards Board. (2007b) Statement No. 50, *Pension disclosures (an amendment of GASB Statements No. 25 and No. 27)*. Norwalk, CT: GASB.

Governmental Accounting Standards Board. (2008a). *GASB research findings: Pension accounting and financial reporting by plans and employers applying GASB Statements 25 and 27, 1996–2005*. Norwalk, CT: GASB.

Governmental Accounting Standards Board. (2008b). Technical Bulletin 2008-1, *Determining the annual required contribution adjustment for postemployment benefits*. Norwalk, CT: GASB.

Governmental Accounting Standards Board. (2010). Preliminary views, *Pension accounting and financial reporting by employers*. Norwalk, CT: GASB.

Governmental Accounting Standards Board. (2011a). Statement No. 63, *Financial reporting of deferred outflows of resources, deferred inflows of resources, and net position*. Norwalk, CT: GASB.

Governmental Accounting Standards Board (2011b). Proposed statement of the Governmental Accounting Standards Board, *Accounting and financial reporting for pensions, an amendment of GASB Statement No. 27*. Norwalk, CT: GASB.

Governmental Accounting Standards Board (2011c). Proposed statement of the Governmental Accounting Standards Board: Plain-language supplement, *Pension accounting and financial reporting*. Norwalk, CT: GASB.

Ives, M. (2006). *Assessing municipal financial condition*. Croton-on-Harmon and Albany, NY: Martin Ives and David R. Hancox.

Laskey, A. R., Raphael, R., Greene, R. A., Litvack, D. T., Offerman, D., and Doppelt, A. S. (2007). *Tax supported special report: Old promises, emerging bills—Considering OPEB in public finance* ratings. NY: FitchRatings.

Mason, J. D., Doppelt, A. S., Laskey, A. R., and Litvack, D. T. (2005). *Special report: The not so golden years—Credit implications of GASB 45*. NY: FitchRatings.

Mead, D. M. (2001). *An analyst's guide to government financial statements*. Norwalk, CT: GASB.

Mead, D. M. (2005a). "Expenditures versus expenses: Which should you use to calculate cost per student?" In William Fowler (Ed.), *Developments in school finance: 2004*. Washington, DC: National Center for Education Statistics.

Mead, D. M. (2005b). *What* else *you should know about your government's finances: A guide to notes to the financial statements and supporting information*. Norwalk, CT: GASB.

Mead, D. M. (2011). *The timeliness of financial reporting by state and local governments compared with the needs of users*. Norwalk, CT: GASB.

Novy-Marx, R., and Rauh, J. D. (2010). Policy options for state pension systems and their impact on plan liabilities. Paper presented at the National Bureau of Economic Research State and Local Pensions Conference, August 2010.

Pew Center on the States. (2010). *The trillion dollar gap: Underfunded state retirement systems and the road to reform*. Washington, DC: Pew Charitable Trusts.

Standard & Poor's. (2006). *U.S. public finance: GO debt*. NY: S&P.

Chapter 7

Sustainable Approaches to Retiree Benefits

Options and Implementation for Program Design and Financing

by Jun Peng

Introduction

Public employee benefits, pension and other postemployment benefit (OPEB), chiefly health benefits for retirees, are posing a long-term threat to the fiscal health of state and local governments, similar to the threat Social Security and Medicare pose to the long-term fiscal health of federal government.

There are two main reasons for this long-term threat. The first reason has to do with the investment return on assets in public pension funds. Because of the stock market tumble in 2008 and early 2009, the market value of pension assets has been down sharply since the end of 2007. Even though the stock market has recovered significantly since its low in March 2009, at the end of 2009, the total market value of assets held in state and local public pension funds was $2.67 trillion, down from $3.22 trillion at the end of 2007, a loss of 17% in two years.[1] Though this may sound like a lot, the investment loss only tells part of the story because an average pension fund is expected to earn 8% on its investment every year to keep up with the growth in pension liabilities. So instead of earning roughly 16% over these two years, it actually lost 17%, therefore creating a very large gap between assets and liabilities. At the end of fiscal year 2008, the total unfunded liability for all state retirement systems stood at $450 billion (Pew Center on the States, 2010). In one nationwide survey of local government pension plans, Wilshire (2009) found that in fiscal year 2008, 73 city and county retirement systems, with $231 billion in pension assets, had an unfunded liability of $43 billion.[2] The increase in unfunded pension liability will therefore lead to a substantial increase in pension contribution in the years to come.

The second reason is the growth in medical cost. It has been well known that medical cost inflation rate is much higher than the general inflation rate in the economy measured by consumer price index, and it is expected to continue to increase at a higher rate for the foreseeable future. This higher inflation rate is a threat to public finance when it exceeds the government revenue growth rate, taking up an ever larger percentage of government financial resources. This becomes even more problematic when coupled with the aging of the population and increase in life expectancy. An aging population means an increase in the ratio of retirees to current workers, and longer life expectancy means more medical services will be needed (and more pension benefits for the same reason). According to a Government Accountability Office (2009) report, the number of state and local government retirees is likely to grow by about 70% from 3 million in 2009 to 5.1 million retirees in 2050. However, the cost of retiree health benefits is projected to grow more quickly, at an annual rate of 6.7% over that same period, meaning that the spending of $15.8 billion in 2009 on retiree health benefits will grow to $237.3 billion by 2050, in current dollars, and spending on state and local government retirees' health benefits is projected to more than double as a share of total operating revenues by 2050, from 0.9% to 2.1%. Governments that maintain pay-as-you-go funding could see their retiree healthcare costs increase dramatically by midcentury, from about 2% of payroll to 5% by 2050 (Government Accountability Office, 2007). State unfunded liability for retiree health benefits was $555 billion at the end of fiscal year 2008 (Pew Center on the States, 2010). In other words, state governments, not counting some local governments, owe roughly $1 trillion in pension and health benefits.

This $1 trillion gap also exacerbates the effect of the Great Recession of 2008 and 2009 on state and local government finance. Because of the high unemployment rate, the drop in consumer spending, the tightening of consumer credit, and the drop in residential and commercial property value, all major tax bases of state and local government have shrunk. Even though the economy will eventually recover and tax revenues will grow again, they will grow from a base much smaller than the one prior to the recession. What this means is that while the cost of financing employee benefits will grow ever higher, state and local government revenue growth will lag behind. From this perspective, the growth in pension and healthcare benefits is unsustainable in the long run, and changes are needed to make them more affordable and minimize this threat to the long-term structural balance of state and local government finance. The most prominent example of this threat can be found in the city of Vallejo, California. Because of the severe economic recession, tax revenue had fallen sharply for this Bay Area community of 121,000. At the meantime, salary and pension benefits for police and firefighters took up a lion's share of the city budget, making it impossible to balance the book without the union making any concessions. In the end, the city declared bankruptcy in 2008.

The weight of pension and OPEB obligations can also affect state and local government finance through credit rating. In a report (Shields, 2009), Moody's Investors Service said that the fiscal strain of deteriorating pension funding levels on local and state governments could contribute to downgrades in the next several years, especially among those governments that entered the recession with poor funding ratios or have little flexibility in their funding requirements, such as Illinois and New Jersey. As an example, the city of Omaha, Nebraska, lost its top-level credit rating partly due to the pension funding level.

While pension and health benefits share some similarities in the sense that they are all long-term financial obligations, they also exhibit some major differences, from the obvious one such as the benefit design to the not so obvious one such as the level of legal protection. The differences and similarities also lead to differences and similarities in how these two types of benefits can be changed to make them more affordable and sustainable in the long term. Pension benefit reform is discussed first, followed by a discussion of OPEB reform. It is then followed by a section on benefit bonds that apply to both of them. The final section presents the conclusions.

Basic Features of Benefit Plans

Pension benefit plans can generally be divided into two types, defined benefit (DB) plan and defined contribution (DC) plan. In a DB plan, an employer guarantees the amount of pension benefit, defined by a benefit formula at the time of retirement. This formula consists of three elements, years of service, final salary, and benefit multiplier (in percentage). For example, if an employee has worked for 30 years, and the final salary at time of retirement is $50,000, and the benefit multiplier is 2%, then the pension benefit is $30,000 (calculated as 30 X $50,000 X 2%). Although the benefit is well defined and guaranteed in a pension plan, the pension contribution from both employer and employee is not and can change depending on the funding situation of the pension plan itself. DC plan is just the opposite of DB plan. In a DC plan, the pension contribution from both employer and employee is well defined as a set percentage of the employee's salary, but the pension benefit at time of retirement is not guaranteed by the employer.

In the public sector, DB is the predominant pension benefit type. There are two basic methods of funding benefits in a DB plan, pay-as-you-go (PAYGO) and advanced funding. PAYGO means that the funds for pension benefits are provided only at the time when they are due to the retirees and comes out of the current year's budget. Advanced funding means the funds, in the form of pension contribution from both employer and employee, for pension benefits are set aside periodically while the employee is working. These funds are invested, and by the time the employee retires, the pension contributions and the investment return together should be sufficient to pay for all the employee's pension benefits in retirement till death. The employer, not the employee, manages the investment. All major public pension plans in the United States adopt the advanced funding method. In a DC plan, the periodic pension contributions are also invested, although the employee not the employer manages the investment, and thus the final pension benefit is largely dependent on the investment performance.

As for OPEB, the benefit plan can also be divided into two basic types, DB plan and DC plan. In a DB plan, the employer guarantees health benefits to retirees whereas the contribution the employer and employee have to make is not well defined. In a DC plan, the employer guarantees contribution to an employee individual account while working, which will be used to pay for health care after the employee is retired.

Pension Reform

Reforms to prevailing *defined benefit pension plans* in the public sector can fall into three major categories: (1) changes to certain features of the current defined benefit plan, (2) change from a defined benefit to a *defined contribution plan*, and (3) change from a defined benefit to a hybrid plan with features of both defined benefit and defined contribution plans. All these changes are aimed at slowing the growth in pension cost to the government, either by reducing the level of pension benefit or shifting the cost and/or risk to public employees. Before the discussion of pension reform, it is important to first consider what constitutes a fair level of pension benefit to public employees, which sets a benchmark for evaluating pension reform. This benchmark is based on the concept of *income replacement ratio*. Maintaining an adequate and reasonable benefit to employees should be a second goal of benefit reform.

Income replacement ratio refers to the percentage of preretirement income that will be replaced by postretirement income. It is aimed at determining how much income is needed to maintain the same quality of life after retirement. Several changes after retirement will reduce the level of income needed. First, the retiree no longer has to pay payroll tax (Social Security and Medicare taxes), which comes to 7.65% of income. Second, the retiree no longer has to contribute to a pension plan, and the median pension contribution rate to a public defined benefit plan for an employee is 5% (Wisconsin Legislative Council, 2009). Third, Social Security benefit, part of overall retirement income, is partially exempt from federal personal income tax, increasing after tax income. Thus on average about 85% of preretirement income is needed to maintain the same quality of life for a government employee with a median preretirement income.[3] In retirement, Social Security benefit accounts for 24 to 49% of preretirement income, depending on the person's preretirement income level (Government Accountability Office, 2004). It is reasonable to assume that this percentage for an average public employee will be at least 25%, if not higher, given the average income in the public sector. Therefore, it is safe to say that a public sector pension benefit is reasonable and sufficient when it replaces 60% of preretirement income after a full career service of at least 30 years at the age of 65.[4] With that in mind, we can proceed to examine pension reforms in the three major categories mentioned earlier.

Changes within the Current DB Plans

One critical element of current public sector defined pension benefit is the legal protection it enjoys. Public employees' defined pension benefit is guaranteed by state constitutions, statutes, or court rulings. For example, Article XIII, Section 5, of the Illinois Constitution, which pertains to pension and retirement rights, provides that: "Membership in any pension or retirement system of the State, any unit of local government or school district, or any agency or instrumentality thereof, shall be an enforceable contractual relationship, the benefits of which shall not be diminished or impaired." As for an example of statutory protection of pension benefit, Section 692 of Kentucky State Statute 61, *Benefits not to be reduced or impaired-Exception* also stipulates to the same effect. This guarantee applies not only to the benefits already earned by current employees but also to prospective benefits yet to be earned in the future. This is quite different from the private sector where only accrued benefits are guaranteed. This is because the contract agreed to at the time of employment is considered a property right that cannot be violated, and therefore pension benefits cannot be reduced. This guarantee means that any pension reform aimed at reducing pension benefit level can only be applied to new employees but not to current employees. When pension reform is applied to new employees, they are essentially put into a new tier in the pension system. Tiered pension system is a unique characteristic of public pension system due to the guarantee of all accrued and prospective pension benefits for all current workers.

Changes to benefit design.

Changes are targeted at the key elements in the formula that collectively determine the benefit level: benefit multiplier, years of service, and the normal age of retirement. As discussed earlier, for a pension to be sufficient, it needs to replace about 60% of final salary. If 30 years is considered adequate for a full-career service, then a benefit multiplier of 2% will generate a replacement ratio of 60%. Because the average benefit multiplier in the public sector is 2% (Wisconsin Legislative Council, 2009), it suggests that the current pension benefit already meets the sufficiency criterion. Although the sufficiency criterion is satisfied, the current benefit challenges the sustainability side of the benefit, for at least two reasons. The first reason has to do with the normal retirement age. Many pension systems set the normal retirement age below 65. Based on the survey of state pension systems by Wisconsin Legislative Council (2009), 84 of the 87 plans allow normal retirement at age 62 or earlier; only two of the plans in the survey restrict normal retirement to persons who are at least 65; and 28 plans allow employees to retire at the age of 55 after 30 years of service. For a long time, 65 was the normal retirement age for collecting Social Security benefit. With the increase in life expectancy, people spend more years in retirement to draw on Social Security benefit, leading to a funding gap, and that is why the retirement age has been gradually increased to 67. The same logic also applies to public pension benefit. With the retirement age set below 65 and not increased despite the increase in life expectancy, public pension benefits have become increasingly more costly and unsustainable. Therefore an immediate step to reduce pension cost without impairing sufficiency is to increase the normal retirement age to 65 for new employees. And like Social Security, this retirement age should be gradually increased over time to account for longer life expectancy.

The second reason has to do with the limit on the benefit level. According to the Wisconsin survey, the vast majority of plans do not set a cap or set a cap to 70% or above. Only two pension plans in Vermont set the cap to 50% of final salary. Without a cap, it is conceivable that at 2%, someone working in the public sector for more than 30 years, his pension, when combined with social security benefit, can substantially exceed the 85% replacement ratio. One criticism against a cap at 60% after 30 years is that when the limit is reached, it creates a disincentive to people to stay longer on the job. There can be an additional incentive built in to reward longer service without adding significant cost to the government. One example is for the employer to continue making contribution to the employee's pension after 30 years of service. However, the contribution will go into a supplemental retirement account managed by the employee himself, and the entire amount in the account can be withdrawn at the time of retirement. The employee also has the option to contribute to the supplemental account what he normally contributes to the defined benefit plan.

With these changes, the formula for a reasonable normal retirement benefit is as follows: to qualify for a normal retirement benefit, an employee needs to work for 30 years; the normal retirement age is 65; the multiplier factor is 2% for each year of service provided: and the total benefit is capped at 60% of final salary; and after 30 years, employer and employee contributions will go into a supplemental account managed by the employee. Once the normal retirement age is determined, then we can calculate the discount allowed for early retirement. For each year earlier than the normal retirement age of 65, a certain percentage should be taken off the pension benefit based on the formula, say 5% for every year, up to the minimum early retirement age. This is similar to the Social Security system, in which the earliest retirement age allowed is 62, and the discount for someone with a normal retirement age of 67 is 30%, or roughly 6% per year.

It is encouraging to see that some states have already implemented changes to increase the retirement age. For example, New York increased the normal retirement age from 55 to 62 in 2009; Kansas in 2007 increased to age 60 with 30 years of service; and Illinois in 2010 increased the normal retirement age to 67. However, most of these changes still fall short of the minimum retirement age of 65 and therefore do not go far enough in reducing the government's pension cost.

Change to pension contribution.

Although these changes to new employees' pension will bring down and contain the pension cost for government employers and maintain a sufficient benefit level for employees, the decrease in pension cost will come in very slowly when current employees are replaced by new employees. It does not do anything to the pension cost and unfunded liability incurred by current employees. Because nothing can be done on the cost side, more needs to be done on the revenue side in terms of pension contribution from current employees. Even though the benefits are guaranteed, employee pension contributions in many cases are not and therefore employees should be asked to pay higher pension contribution to offset the increasing cost. The logic behind this is relatively simple. The employees benefit from the current pension plan in two ways. First they are shielded from any risk. Their benefit will not be affected even if the long-term investment return is not realized or life expectancy increases, both of which result in higher pension cost and potential unfunded liability. This problem is compounded by the fact that employee pension contribution changes infrequently, if at all. This means any increase in cost to amortize the unfunded liability is borne mostly by the employer and thus taxpayers. Second, employee contribution is lower than that of the employer. Based on the surveys of National Association of State Retirement Administrators (2009), the average employee contribution remained at 5% from 2002 through 2008 whereas employer contribution increased from 6 to 8.7% over the same period.[5] This means that employees, on average, pay for less than half of the pension cost. Even this average rate masks huge variation in the share of employee contribution among all states. Even though employees in a few states pay half of the cost, such as in Arizona and Minnesota, those in many other pension plans pay much less than that. For example, in New York employee contribution rate in 2008 was 3% whereas that for employer was 9.6% (Wisconsin Legislative Council, 2009). Few states do not require employee contribution. Again this is very different from Social Security.[6] For Social Security, the cost is split between employers and employees. Using Social Security as a benchmark, then public employees should also pay for half of the pension cost, and any increase in future pension contribution should also be split between employers and employees. This is fair to both current and future taxpayers. This also means that if there is a decrease in contribution, employees will also get to benefit from that as well. In other words, the employers and employees share the risks and gains in pension financing. Unless a state law specifically says that current employee contribution remains constant and cannot be changed, then the pension cost should be split between employers and all current and future employees for as long as they are in the pension plan.

Retroactive benefit increase.

Enacting benefit increases without proper funding can have severe negative consequences for public pension plans and thus are another factor to control for in sustaining pension benefit. The reason for that is pension benefit increases typically happen when the financial market is doing well. At the peak of a stock market run, most pension plans also tend to do very well and the funding ratio can increase substantially and even exceed 100% in some cases. The overfunding, even though just temporary, provides an illusion that there is surplus in the pension plan that can be used to increase pension benefits. The illusion it creates is that it is cost free to increase the benefit because any increase in pension contribution will be more than offset by the surplus funds in pension plan, at least in the short run. This is what happened in the late nineties when many states increased the benefit at the top of the stock market.

There are two major problems with such pension increase. First, they are retroactive. They not only apply to future benefits but also to benefits already earned in the past for current employees, for which no additional funds have been set aside before. Second, any pension surplus will inevitably turn out to be temporary because no bull market lasts forever and the mean regression of the investment return entails a return below average following a bull market. This means that such surplus will go away sooner or later. The combination of these two factors inevitably results in higher pension contribution in the future.

There are many ways to contain the cost related to retroactive benefit increase. One way is simply to prohibit any increase in benefit and decrease in pension contribution for normal cost when the pension funding ratio is below 100%. In recognition of the impact of stock market on pension funding ratio, a more restrictive version is to prohibit any benefit increase and decrease in pension contribution for normal cost when the pension funding ratio exceeds 100% but falls below a preset percentage, say 120%. This will prevent any temporary overfunding from being used for permanent benefit increase. Short of such limitation, government can be required to disclose the additional cost related to the benefit increase and immediately pay off the cost related to the retroactive portion of the benefit increase.

Since the late nineties, some state governments have taken steps to limit the impact of stock market volatility on pension fund. Even though they are not specifically aimed at preventing pension benefit increase, in an indirect way, they will have some impact to this effect. This can be done in at least three ways. One way, practiced in Florida, is to limit how much the pension contribution can be reduced when the pension plan is overfunded. The second way, done in New York, is to set a minimum pension contribution rate regardless of the funding situation. A third way, done in California, is to extend the smoothing period from 4 to 5 years to a much longer time period such as 10 years when determining the actuarial value of pension assets, which effectively prevents the plan from being overfunded even if the stock market has gone up by a significant margin as much of the gain will be recognized gradually over a much longer period of time.

Switch to Defined Contribution Plan

A far more fundamental pension reform is to completely get out of the current defined benefit (DB) plan and switch to a defined contribution (DC) plan. Because it is established earlier that the twin goals of any reform are to contain the cost for the government employers and provide sufficient income for retirees, this switch should also be evaluated against these goals.

As in the case of DB plan, 60% replacement ratio should also be used as a benchmark in designing a DC plan in terms of setting the contribution rates for both employer and employee. This means that the rate should be set in such a way that after 30 years of service, assuming a certain investment return and salary growth, should generate sufficient income to replace 60% of final salary. In this case, if all the assumptions are the same in both DB and DC plans, in order to generate a 60% replacement ratio after 30 years of service, then the combined pension contribution rates should be the same and the assets accumulated at the end should also be the same for both DB and DC plans. Therefore, in an ideal world when DB and DC plans are rationally designed based on reaching a certain benefit benchmark, then employers and employees will be indifferent between the two plans. However, two major risks with DC plans, investment and longevity, have made it far more difficult to assess and guarantee the sufficiency of DC plan to employee whereas the sustainability to employer is ensured.

Investment risk.

There are at least three kinds of investment risk in a DC plan, one common to both DC and DB plan, and two unique to DC plan. First, the risk common to both DB and DC plans is simply the potential that expected long-term rate of return cannot be realized over time. The only difference is that this investment risk is almost entirely borne by employers in DB plans whereas it is entirely borne by employees in DC plans. It is this shift in investment risk that guarantees funding certainty and thus sustainability to employers whereas it renders uncertain the sufficiency of retirement benefit to employees.

The second investment risk, unique to DC plan, is whether individual employees can achieve a long-term return similar to that of the employer. Many individuals do not have the knowledge or the discipline to invest and accumulate sufficient assets over a very long period of time. Some people may be too risk averse and invest conservatively, and others may take on too much risk and invest aggressively. Still many others are emotional in investing, buying stocks on the rise (performance chasing) or selling stocks when they are going down (the fear factor). All of these actions can have a negative effect on the long-term investment return. Over a long period of time, individuals collectively tend to lag large public pension funds in investment performance (as in the case of Nebraska public pension plan discussed in the next section.) At the very least, the cost of investment is lower for large pension funds than for individuals due to the economies of scale.

The third investment risk unique to DC plan is that even if the employee achieves the long-term return during much of his working life, a significant downturn in the stock market at or close to retirement can still severely disrupt his retirement plan. Even though this is also a risk for the employer in a DB plan, it is not as important because the investment horizon for the employer is infinite. It does not face any critical time like the date of retirement as not everyone in a DB plan retires at the same time. Any temporary setback can be smoothed out. Besides new employees continue to enter into the DB plan and contribute, providing a steady cash flow for investment, especially rewarding when the stock market is down. Individual employee in a DC plan does not have such luxury. He may not have sufficient time to recover from a major market downturn, and there will be no more fresh contribution after retirement.

Longevity risk.

Another risk facing individuals in a DC plan is longevity. A DB plan guarantees lifetime benefit to a retiree who does not have to worry about outliving his income. A DB plan can provide this kind of guarantee due to its group insurance nature. Given a large number of retirees, it can count on the average life expectancy, meaning someone with longer life expectancy can be offset by another person with shorter expectancy. An individual in a DC plan, however, does not have such guarantee. If he lives longer than expected, then there is a serious possibility that he may actually outlive his income. Purchasing an annuity from a commercial insurance company can alleviate this longevity risk. However, this option will be a lot more costly than if it is provided by a public defined plan due to the lack of profit motive. This can be further exacerbated by a sudden drop in asset value just prior to the purchase of annuity, and the interest rate movement will also make the cost of annuity hard to predict.

In all, the various investment risks and longevity risk make it far more difficult to determine the sufficiency of retirement benefit to employees. In the worst case scenario, it is not even certain what the minimum level of replacement ratio will be, let alone 60%.

DB or DC?

If the switch to a DC plan reduces pension cost to the employer because the original DB plan is too generous and unsustainable, then a less generous DB plan can achieve cost savings without switching to DC. If a DB plan provides a reasonable and sufficient benefit to begin with, then a switch to DC plan in order to save cost will put in jeopardy the financial security of employees. In other words, savings is achieved at the expense of sufficiency. If the goal is to reduce long-term risks to the employer, such as investment and longevity risk, then this goal is only achieved through a transfer of risk from the employer to the employee. If the assumed rate of return is reasonable to begin with, then the DB plan is better at handling investment risk and longevity risk than individual investors due to its infinite investment horizon, economies of scale, investment expertise, and group insurance nature.

Because of these risks to employees, there is strong resistance to this switch in the public sector, and so far there are only two mandatory DC plans at the state level and one in Washington, DC.[7] In 2005, the Alaska legislature voted to close its defined benefit plans to new employees and anyone hired after July 1, 2006, will be enrolled in a DC plan. In Michigan, employees hired after March 31, 1997, have to be enrolled in a DC plan. A few other states, such as Florida, Colorado, Montana, Ohio, and South Carolina, also opened DC plan for general employees (Snell, 2009). These are only optional DC plan, however, meaning the employees can choose between the DB plan and the DC plan.

The one risk that a DC plan can avoid is political risk, meaning the elected officials increasing benefit level without putting in sufficient money to pay for them. The only way to increase benefit level in a DC plan is to increase the employer matching contribution rate. The cost is immediate to the employer whereas the benefit to the employee is more difficult to estimate than for DB plan, making such increase more unlikely. Another type of political risk that can be avoided in DC plan is that elected officials no longer have the luxury of postponing pension contribution in time of fiscal distress.

Hybrid Pension Plans

A less radical reform, when compared to the DC plan, is switch to a hybrid plan that combines the features of both DB and DC plans. A *hybrid plan* has the advantage of making pension both more sustainable to the employers than in the case of DB plan and more sufficient to the employees than in the DC plan. This is achieved, in essence, through the sharing of risks between employers and employees.

There are two types of hybrid plans. The first is a combination of both DB and DC plans, and the second is a *cash balance plan*.

DB-DC combination.
As the name suggests, this kind of hybrid plan consists of two parts, a DB part and a DC part. The DB part works just like a regular DB plan with formula-based benefits, and the DC part works like a regular DC plan. The hybrid plan results from the split in the distribution of pension contribution. The employer's contribution typically goes into the DB part of the hybrid plan, and employee's contribution goes into the DC part of the plan. Because the employee's contribution no longer supports the DB plan, the benefit level in the DB part of the hybrid plan will be lower than that in a pure DB plan. The reduction in the benefit level is supposed to be made up by the DC part. Ohio pension plans illustrate this best. Ohio state government offers three different pension plans, all optional: a traditional DB plan, a traditional DC plan, and a hybrid DB-DC plan. The benefit formula for the traditional DB plan is 2.2% for the first 30 years and 2.5% for each year in excess of 30 years. The multiplier in the DB part of the hybrid plan is 1% for the first 30 years and 1.25% for each year after that. The employer contribution rate of 14% goes into the DB part and the employee contribution of 10% goes into the DC part.

Compared to a pure DB or DC plan, this hybrid plan improves in both containing cost for employer and maintaining some level of sufficiency for the employee. Because the defined benefit level is reduced, typically by half, it goes without saying that the employer's future cost is also reduced, making it more affordable to the government. And because this part also provides a guaranteed benefit level for the employee, he will also have a more secure income flow in retirement than in a pure DC plan, regardless of what happens to the account balance of his DC plan. The key to the advantage of the hybrid plan over both traditional DB and DC plans lies in sharing investment risk and gain. If the investment return does not materialize, then both the employer and employee will bear the risk. The employee bears the risk obviously in the DC part of the plan. The employer bears the risk because it will have to increase the pension contribution to make up for the investment loss in the DB part. However, this increase will not be as large as in a pure DB plan. The employee is also protected to some extent if there is a substantial drop in the market at the time of retirement because such a drop does not affect the benefit in the DB part. When the market goes up, employee shares the gain as the value of his DC plan balance goes up, and the employer shares the gain in the form of reduced pension contribution to the DB plan.

Such sharing of risk and gain to achieve sustainability and sufficiency, however, can also be achieved in a pure DB plan. As discussed before, if the pension contribution in a DB plan is split in half between employer and employee, including any increase or decrease due to investment performance, then it will achieve the same purpose.

In addition to Ohio, several other states have hybrid plans, some mandatory and some optional. Indiana has adopted the earliest mandatory hybrid state plan in the United States. Its retirement plan consists of an Annuity Savings Account (a DC plan) made up of employee contribution and a defined benefit plan made up of employer contribution. Oregon has a hybrid plan for state employees, and Washington has one for teachers hired after 1998. Georgia opened a mandatory hybrid plan for state employees hired after January 1, 2009. For the DB part, the formula is 1% for each year of service, and the employee has to contribute 1.25%. For the DC part, the employer matches the first 1% of employee contribution, and then 50% of employee contribution above the 1%, up to 3% total of employer match.

Cash balance.

The essence of cash balance (CB) plan also lies in risk sharing, although the setup is quite different. The basic setup is a notional individual account within a group guaranteed plan. The feature of this plan that resembles a DB plan is that it also provides some type of guarantee to the employee. This guarantee, however, does not apply to the benefit level, bur rather to a minimum final balance in the notional individual account.[8] The feature of a CB plan that resembles a DC plan is that all employer and employee contribution goes into the notional individual account, with two major differences. First, the employer guarantees a minimum rate of return on the account balance every year, regardless of the actual investment return. Second, the investment is managed by the employer rather than the employee himself. This begs an immediate question: how is it different from a DB plan if the employer guarantees the return on pension contribution? The answer is that if the guaranteed rate of return is 8%, then theoretically there is no difference between this plan and a traditional DB plan, as the ending value of asset set aside for each individual should be the same and the employer still bears the same level of investment risk in both plans. The difference is that the guaranteed rate of return is much lower in the CB plan, which is set around 5%. If the actual investment return for the year is higher than the guaranteed rate, the employer has the option to share the excess return with the employee by giving a one-time credit to the individual account. By keeping some of the excess return, the employer can hope to offset any future return that will be below the guaranteed return. That is how the sharing of investment risk is done. By guaranteeing a lower return, the employer has a much better chance of meeting the expectation and not being forced to pay a higher contribution rate in the future. If the long-term rate is consistently higher than the guaranteed return, the employer and employee can share in the gain, thus boosting the overall guaranteed return and balance of individual account. If the realized long-term rate is lower, say between 5 and 8%, then the employees will bear the burden of this lower return, in the form of lower final benefit level, when compared to employees in a traditional DB plan that guarantees an 8% return. If the realized long-term return falls below the 5%, then the employer will bear the risk, but still the risk is much lower when compared to a traditional DB plan.

The group insurance nature also offsets one vital investment risk for the employee. Unlike a pure DC plan, the account balance at the time of retirement is not affected at all by the volatility in financial market because the return is guaranteed on the account balance at anytime. This therefore provides more financial security to the employee. The group insurance also negates longevity risk to the retiree. At retirement, the employee has the option of taking out the lump sum in the individual account, or taking out a life-time annuity based on the account balance. He therefore does not have to fear running out of income in retirement.

Despite all these potential advantages of CB plan when compared to a traditional DB and DC plan, one unavoidable downside is that the benefit level is not as guaranteed and likely will not be as high as in the DB plan. Because the guaranteed interest rate is lower than the assumed rate of return in a traditional DB plan, if the combined contribution rate is exactly the same, then the CB benefit level will be lower. Although it can potentially be compensated by higher return in the future, it is not guaranteed and creates uncertainty. The major implication of this is that it is more difficult to assess the income replacement ratio. So the critical issue when designing a CB plan is to estimate what the final replacement ratio will be under different rate of return scenario and find out what a reasonable combination of guaranteed return and employer and employee contribution will be that will lead to a replacement ratio of 60%.

While the CB plan remains fairly popular in the private sector, with many companies switching from a traditional DB plan to a CB plan, only one state government so far has adopted it. Nebraska had a DC plan from 1967 through 2002. In 2003, a cash balance plan replaced it after study showed that average investment return in the DC plan was far below that in an average state DB plan. The employee contributes 4.8% and employer contributes 7.5% to the CB plan. The interest credit rate is defined in statute as the greater of 5% or the applicable federal mid-term rate plus 1.5%. The retirement system board can also award a dividend to employee based on investment performance. **Table 7.1** shows the history of interest rate credit and dividend since its opening:

To ensure the system's long-term health, effective 2007, any dividends granted in the future will conform to the retirement board's new policy, which states that a dividend plus the annual interest credit cannot exceed 8% unless a majority of the retirement board agrees. At the time of termination, the employee can take either a lump sum or one of several different types of annuity based on the account balance.

TABLE 7.1 Nebraska CB Plan Interest Rate

Year	Interest Rate Credit	Dividend	Total
2009	5.00%	N/A	5.00%
2008	5.02%	0.00%	5.02%
2007	6.12%	5.18%	11.30%
2006	6.27%	2.73%	9.00%
2005	5.45%	13.50%	18.95%
2004	5.19%	2.80%	7.99%
2003	5.04%	3.09%	8.13%

Source: Nebraska Public Employees Retirement System

Summary

After examining the various methods of reforming public pension, it is clear that any successful effort will involve reduction in benefit level from the current level based on an appropriate replacement ratio and retirement age and a sharing of investment risk between employer and employees. There is no free lunch in pension funding. The two goals of sufficiency and sustainability entail trade-off between the level of benefit guarantee to and the risk borne by the pension beneficiary. In a sense, this is analogous to one fundamental principle of investment, which is the tradeoff between risk and return: to achieve a higher return, you have to bear more risk. Politically, the easiest reform to implement is to create a new tier for new employees to reduce government pension liability in the long run, although it will have the least affect on reducing the current pension liability. It is also relatively easy to gradually increase current employees' pension contribution, if it is not specifically prohibited by statutes. This will have a more immediate impact on reducing the current liability and budget pressure on the government employer. Politically, switching to a DC plan is the most difficult reform to be carried out.

OPEB

OPEB shares both similarities and differences with pension benefit and the solutions to containing OPEB cost also exhibit both similarities and differences when compared to those for pension cost.

For differences, first, while pension benefit is guaranteed legally, OPEB is not. Because the OPEB is not as well protected legally as pension benefit, it then is a lot easier, at least theoretically, to reduce OPEB cost than pension cost, as any change can apply not only to new employers, but also to current employees and retirees as well, an option not available to pension cost containment.[9] Second, although almost all major pension plans have prefunded their pension plans for many decades and have accumulated considerable amount of assets and achieved a substantial funding level, very few governments have prefunded OPEB by setting assets aside. This requires a more comprehensive solution to OPEB cost containment than in the case of pension benefit. Third, OPEB liability is more difficult to predict than pension liability due to the assumption about future healthcare inflation rate. As there is more uncertainty and volatility in healthcare cost inflation than in general inflation, employers bear more risk in OPEB than in pension, making containing the OPEB cost even more important. To add to this risk, the aging of population is more critical to OPEB than pension because OPEB cost has not been prefunded. Fourth, although there is a benchmark for evaluating pension reform in terms of arriving at an income replacement ratio, there is no such benchmark for OPEB, making it more difficult to evaluate the sufficiency of OPEB benefit to employees.

The most obvious similarity between pension and OPEB is that both are long-term financial obligations of government, the cost of which will escalate in the future without any meaningful reforms. Another major similarity between the two is that just like there are two types of pension plans, DB and DC, there are also two types of OPEB plans, DB and DC. Therefore the solutions to OPEB cost containment also fall into two categories, changes to features of current existing DB OPEB plan and switch to DC OPEB plan.

Changes to DB OPEB Plan

As the term implies, a DB OPEB plan guarantees the amount of healthcare benefits to retirees during retirement. Unlike defined pension benefit, OPEB benefit can be defined in more than one way. It can be defined in dollars, such as a flat dollar amount, or as a level of coverage, such as a percentage of health insurance premiums paid by the employer. The solution to DB OPEB cost containment consist of reducing the benefit level through shifting the cost and/or risk to employees, and setting up a prefunding mechanism.

Reducing OPEB benefit level.
Reducing OPEB benefit level through cost and/or risk shifting can be achieved in a number of ways. The cost can be reduced by increasing retiree's deductibles and copays. The most effective way, however, is to reduce the share of insurance premium paid by the government. The government can also establish an annual cap (either in hard dollars or linked to the Consumer Price Index) on increases in insurance premium paid by the government. As healthcare cost goes up faster than general inflation, setting a cap thus shifts future increase in cost and risk to the employees.

Another method is to increase vesting requirements for retiree medical benefits by requiring a full career of service to receive full benefits. For example, in South Carolina, the state reduced the level of government contribution for employees hired after May 1, 2008. Employees hired before that date qualified for the full amount of government contribution, approximately 71% of the premium, if they retired with at least 10 years of service. Under the new requirements, to qualify for the full government contribution, such employees hired on or after May 1, 2008, must have 25 years of service. Individuals with 15 to 25 years of service qualify for half of the government contribution, although no contribution is provided to employees with less than 15 years of service. This more stringent vesting requirement has effectively eliminated retiree medical benefits for some employees, thus substantially reducing the government's OPEB cost. Another example is Vermont. Employees hired before July 1, 2008, qualify for full coverage, equal to 80% of premium, after 5 years of service. For employees hired after that date, they have to work for 20 years to qualify for full coverage and work for 10 years to qualify for half the coverage.

This reduction in OPEB cost can also be accomplished by requiring current employees to contribute towards their future OPEB benefit at a level so that the overall contribution rate will be roughly split between the employer and employee, just like in the case of pension contribution.

Setting up a prefunding mechanism.
Requiring current employees to pay toward their future OPEB, however, entails establishment of an irrevocable trust fund because it amounts to a prefunding of future OPEB cost and thus employee contribution has to be protected and invested in an irrevocable trust

fund, along with employer contribution. The combination of employee and employer contribution, when fully paid every year and invested over the employee's working career to earn an expected rate of return, should be sufficient to pay for all future OPEB benefit. Even though government employers are not required to prefund its OPEB liability and thus can continue their current pay-as-you-go (or PAYGO) practice, GASB 43 provides two incentives to encourage employers to start prefunding OPEB benefit. First, GASB 43 requires that unfunded OPEB liability, once it is determined, has to be included in the Statement of Net Assets as part of government's annual comprehensive annual financial report. If the government continues to fund OPEB on a PAYGO basis, which is likely to be less costly than paying the actuarially required amount (ARC), then OPEB liability will continue to grow. This can lead to a decrease in the government's net assets shown in the Statement of Net Assets, an indication of worsening fiscal health. If left unaddressed, this eventually will have a negative impact on the government's credit rating and thus its future borrowing cost. For example, in the comprehensive annual financial report for fiscal year 2009, New York City showed a negative net asset value of $96.7 billion, of which $65.5 billion belonged to OPEB liability, an increase of $2 billion over the previous year.[10]

This incentive is further accentuated by a second one in the choice of discount rate. It is already known that future pension benefits are discounted to present value, with the discount rate being the assumed long-term rate of return, which averages about 8%. When it comes to OPEB liability, however, actuary has three options. If the government funds the OPEB on a PAYGO basis, the actuary must use a discount rate equal to the expected rate of return on the government's short-term cash investment. The actuary can use the long-term rate of return as the discount rate only if the employer has established an irrevocable trust and contributes the ARC every year. If the government establishes an irrevocable trust but does not contribute the full amount of ARC, then a blend rate of the short-term and long-term rates will be used as the discount rate. Because the short-term rate is much lower than the long-term rate, with the blend rate in between, the actuarial accrued liability (AAL) and the ARC in the case of PAYGO will be higher than they would be if the plan were properly prefunded funded in an irrevocable trust. Therefore PAYGO funding makes OPEB a lot more costly in the long run.

PAYGO funding is costly due to the loss of investment income that would have been earned if ARCs were made and invested. The financial loss is most apparent when compared to a pension fund. For a mature and well-funded pension plan, investment return on average accounts for 70 to 75% of its annual revenue, with the rest coming from contribution. By delaying the prefunding of OPEB cost, the government thus substantially increases its cost in the long run, as it will be funded more out of taxpayer dollars rather than investment return.

Thus to reduce the cost in the long run, the course of action is to establish a trust fund, contribute ARC into the trust fund, and invest based on an asset allocation strategy similar to that for the pension trust fund due to its long-term horizon. Although a governance structure also needs to be designed, in reality it is fairly easy to merge this plan with an existing public pension plan, and thus no separate governance structure needs to be created.

So far, only a few states, such as Alaska, Arizona, Georgia, and Ohio, have set up trust funds to prefund OPEB liability. Ohio state government has the largest OPEB trust fund by far. It established an OPEB trust fund back in 1974, and it is administered by the Ohio Public Employee Retirement System. In 2007, it had an OPEB liability of about $30 billion, with assets valued at $12.8 billion, resulting in a funding ratio of 43% (Ohio Public Employee Retirement System, 2008). Arizona has the highest funding ratio for OPEB among states with OPEB liability. In FY 2008, it had $1.24 billion in assets against $1.45 billion in OPEB liability, resulting in a funding ratio of 86% (Arizona State Retirement System, 2009).

DC OPEB Plan

As in a DC pension plan, a DC OPEB plan stipulates only the amounts to be contributed by a government employer to an employee's individual account during each year of active employment. Once the employee is retired, he can withdraw from the individual account to pay for healthcare cost. With this DC plan, the employer has completely shifted risks to the employees. There are three risks, two similar to the risks in a DC pension plan and one unique to a DC OPEB plan. The two similar ones are investment risk and mortality risk. The one more unique to OPEB is the healthcare cost inflation risk, making it more difficult for the individual to predict how much is needed to finance health care in retirement. With the absence of all these uncertainties, a DC OPEB plan will be a lot less costly to government employers.

Just as for DC pension plan because of all these risks to employees, very few governments have adopted DC OPEB plan. One prominent example can be found in Oakland County, Michigan. In 2005, it adopted a new defined contribution retiree health benefit plan for eligible individuals hired after December 31, 2005 (Oakland County Michigan, 2005). The defined contribution plan replaced the county's defined benefit plan, under which the county paid from 60 to 100% of the premium for eligible individuals hired before 2006. Under the defined contribution plan, the county contributes $1,300 per year to a retirement health savings plan. Employees can also volunteer to contribute to the health savings account. Upon retirement, employees with 15 years of county service can access 60% of the funds the county contributed to their health savings plans for eligible medical expenses. With each additional year of service, the employee has access to another 4% of the contributed amount, meaning an employee with 25 or more years of service can access to the full amount of funds.

Benefit Bonds

One method in reducing cost that is common to both pension benefit and OPEB is to issue benefit bonds, *pension obligation bonds* (POB) and *OPEB benefit bonds*, to pay off unfunded pension and OPEB liabilities and then pay debt service on the benefit bonds to investors. This transaction, by switching unfunded benefit liabilities owed to pension and OPEB trust funds into debt owed to investors, is to achieve savings through arbitrage. For any unfunded liability, the government also owes interest on it, with the interest rate set at the assumed rate of return on the investment. The logic behind the benefit bonds is that if the government can issue them at an interest rate less than 8% minus the issuance cost, then it can save on interest cost. This transaction is particularly beneficial to OPEB. Because most governments have not started prefunding OPEB, there is no or very little asset in a trust fund if one exists. An infusion of proceeds from OPEB bond will lead to an immediate increase in funding ratio and a substantial amount for investment.[11]

This savings in interest cost, however, is not achieved without any risk. The chief risk comes from investment. As the previous discussion and the first decade of the 21st century have clearly demonstrated, there is substantial risk in investing and achieving an assumed rate of return, even over a long period of time. If the assumed rate of return cannot be achieved, then new unfunded liability will emerge on the bond proceeds put into the trust funds for investment. However, this transaction is still worthwhile even if the actual return is less than the assumed return of 8% because as long as the actual return is higher than the interest rate on the benefit bond, there is still a net gain to the government issuer. Therefore the lower the interest rate on the benefit bond and the greater the margin between the interest rate and the assumed rate of return, the more likely the issuance of benefit bond is going to help the government in reducing cost.

Because the success of a benefit bond depends on the market interest rate and the performance of the financial market, the timing of bond issuance is essential. This entails that the bond should be issued when the overall interest rate is fairly low and the stock market should be in the downside of an investment cycle rather than in the upside. These two conditions usually occur during the early stage of an economic recession (Miller, 2009). Although the first condition is easy to understand and observe, the second one is not quite as intuitive. The reason for the second condition is the regression to the mean, meaning that the rate of return over time regresses to its historical mean. A bull market inevitably will be followed by a correction or a bear market. If the benefit bond is issued in a bull market, there is a much better chance that the investment return in the future will lag the assumed rate of return. If the bond is issued during a market correction, measured by at least a 10% drop from its recent peak, or preferably in a bear market, measured by a 20% drop from the recent peak, then it has a much better chance of realizing, if not beating the assumed return. Such a strategy calls for strong investment discipline. Although this general strategy will increase the chance of meeting or beating the assumed rate of return, it does not guarantee its success, which will not be known until the benefits bonds are paid off, some 20 or 30 years later.

Conclusion

Just like Social Security and Medicare that pose a threat to the long-term fiscal health of the federal government, pension benefit and OPEB for retirees also pose a long-term challenge to the state and local governments due to the uncertainty in the financial market, aging workforce, increase in life expectancy, and high healthcare cost. The collective unfunded liabilities of the two benefit programs have approached $1 trillion and are still rising. No state and local governments are in immediate danger of running out of funds to pay these benefits, and they have, in most cases, 30 years to come up with the funds to cover these unfunded liabilities. This, however, can provide a false sense of complacency. Unless steps are taken to rein in the future cost and a long-term plan is put in place to fund these cost in the near future, they will become increasingly more burdensome, and those who retire soon with benefits can avoid paying their fair share of the cost, leaving the bill to the future generation of employees and taxpayers. In this chapter, several reform proposals are suggested to make them sustainable, with the aim of striking a balance between being fair to the employees and the taxpayers. There is no free lunch in benefit reform as lower government cost inevitably means either lower employee benefit or shifting of risks to employees. A best system should involve sharing of risk and gain between the employers and employees while maintaining some minimum level of guarantee to employees.

Endnotes

1. The data are from Table L. 119 of the Federal Reserve's Flow of Funds Account of the U.S., released on March 11, 2010. It can be reached at http://www.federalreserve.gov/releases/z1/Current/z1r-4.pdf.
2. While this chapter is about benefit program issues at the local level, many examples and data used here are from state-level governments. There are two main reasons for this. First, there is almost no difference between state and local governments in terms of how they are affected by benefit issues and how they should address these issues in the long run. They all face the same problems, legal constraints and risks in managing these benefit programs. Anything that applies to state government should apply to local government as well. Second, state retirement systems, even though relatively small in number versus local retirement systems, account for the vast majority of public pension assets and in many states, local governments are included in state-wide retirement systems, such as in California and New York. Therefore data on state pension systems also cover many local governments. Due to the prominence of state-level pension plans, few nationwide data or surveys are available on local retirement systems.
3. It is more difficult to quantify on the spending side. On the one hand, some expenses will go down, such as cost related to work like commuting. On the other hand, other costs like healthcare spending may go up. Therefore, spending is assumed to hold constant after retirement. For more details on arriving at a replacement ratio, see Aon Consulting (2008).
4. The 60% replacement arrived at in this case and used in this chapter only applies to public employees covered by the federal Social Security program. About a quarter of public employees are not covered by Social Security, and therefore the replacement ratio will certainly be different for them.
5. It should be noted that in some states when the pension plans were overfunded, some governments also took a pension holiday. However, they are usually more than offset by larger increases in pension contributions in later years.
6. Although employees do not contribute to defined benefit plans in the private sector, this is because the benefit level is much lower in the private sector than in the public sector.
7. A third state, West Virginia, enrolled new teachers in a mandatory DC plan in 1991. It was closed in 2005, and any in the DC plan were given the option to join the state's DB plan.

8. This individual account is notional because in reality there is no such separate individual account set up in the group plan. It exists in theory for personal record keeping so that an employee will know at any given time how much he has in the account.
9. However, although this is generally the case in many states, retiree health care in labor contracts can become legally binding in some cases in some states.
10. The comprehensive annual financial report can be retrieved from New York City Comptroller's website at http://www.comptroller.nyc.gov/bureaus/acc/cafr-pdf/cafr2009.pdf.
11. However, issuing OPEB bonds and investing the proceeds in an irrevocable trust fund can create one potential problem. If OPEB is not legally guaranteed, bonding for it may implicitly and perhaps explicitly guarantee those obligations, thus taking away the flexibility in reducing or eliminating such benefits.

Glossary

Cash balance plan: a type of hybrid pension plan in which employer contribution goes into a notional employee retirement account and guarantees a certain investment return on the account balance, which can be used to purchase a life annuity from the employer at time of retirement.

Defined benefit pension plan: a pension plan in which the final pension benefit is determined by a benefit formula based on years of service, final salary, and a multiplier.

Defined contribution plan: a pension plan in which the employer contributes a set percentage of employee's salary to his individual retirement account and otherwise is not responsible for his retirement benefit, which is based on the final account balance.

Hybrid pension plan: a pension plan that combines features of both defined benefit plan and defined contribution plan.

Income replacement ratio: the percentage of preretirement income that is replaced by postretirement income.

OPEB benefit bond: debt issued by government to pay off all of part of unfunded OPEB liability owed to the OPEB trust fund and the government issuer then pays debt service to the purchase of bond.

Pension obligation bond: debt issued by government to pay off all or part of unfunded pension liability owed to the public pension fund and the government issuer then pays debt service to the purchaser of bond.

Discussion Questions

1. Why do pension and OPEB benefit programs pose a long-term threat to the fiscal health of state and local governments?
2. What are the similarities and differences between pension and OPEB benefit programs?

3. What are the major strategies in reforming pension benefit programs in the public sector to contain the cost?
4. What are the criteria that you can use to evaluate any pension reform?
5. Why normal retirement age has become a major focal point in defined pension benefit reform?
6. What are the pros and cons in switching from a defined benefit pension plan to a defined contribution plan?
7. What do the two different types of hybrid plans have in common? What is the implication of this common feature for reforming defined pension benefit in the public sector?
8. What are the main strategies for reforming OPEB benefit program in the public sector?
9. What are the pros and cons of issuing benefit obligation bonds?
10. If you were an elected official for a local government, what is your likely action in dealing with public employees' pension and OPEB benefits?

Recommended Resources

National Association of State Retirement Administrators, http://www.nasra.org/. (It has many research reports on public pension and OPEB.)

Center for Retirement Research at Boston College, http://crr.bc.edu/index.php. (It has many working papers on state and local public pension plans.)

Center for State and Local Government Excellence, http://www.slge.org/. (It has research reports on pubic pension and OPEB plans.)

Girald Miller's Public Money column on public pension and OPEB in *Governing* magazine, http://www.governing.com/columns/Public-Money.

Government Finance Officers Association, http://www.gfoa.org/. (It contains best practices on retirement and benefits administration.)

Peng, J. (2008). State and local public pension plan management. Taylor & Francis: Boca Raton, FL.

References

Aon Consulting. (2008). Replacement ratio study. Retrieved from http://www.aon.com/about-aon/intellectual-capital/attachments/human-capital-consulting/RRStudy070308.pdf. Accessed October 2, 2010.

Arizona State Retirement System. (2009). Comprehensive annual financial report for fiscal year ended June 30, 2009. Retrieved from https://www.azasrs.gov/content/pdf/financials/2009_CAFR.pdf. Accessed October 3, 2010.

Government Accountability Office. (2004). Social Security: Distribution of benefits and taxes relative to earnings levels. (GAO-04-747) (2007, September). State and local government retiree benefits: Current status of benefit structures, protections, and fiscal outlook for funding future costs. (GAO-07-1156) (2009, November). State and Local Government Retiree Health Benefits. (GAO-10-61).

Miller, G. (2009, January 15). Bonding for benefits: POBs and "OPEB-OBs": New strategies to shatter the old POB paradigm. Retrieved from http://www.governing.com/columns/public-money/Bonding-for-Benefits-POBs.html. Accessed September 3, 2009.

National Association of State Retirement Administrators. (2009). Public Fund Survey Summary of Findings for FY 2008. Retrieved from http://www.publicfundsurvey.org/publicfundsurvey/pdfs/Summary_of_Findings_FY08.pdf. Accessed October 3, 2010.

Oakland County Michigan. (2005). Oakland County Michigan: 2005 Financial summary. Retrieved from http://www.oakgov.com/fiscal/assets/docs/2005_financial_summary.pdf. Accessed September 3, 2010.

Ohio Public Employees Retirement System. 2008. The comprehensive annual financial report for the years ended December 31, 2008 and 2007. Retrieved from https://www.opers.org/pubs-archive/investments/cafr/2008-cafr-hires.pdf#zoom=80. Accessed November 5, 2010.

Pew Center on the States. (2010). The trillion dollar gap: Underfunded state retirement systems and the roads to reform. Retrieved from http://downloads.pewcenteronthestates.org/The_Trillion_Dollar_Gap_final.pdf. Accessed November 6, 2010.

Shields, Y. (2009, November 6). Moody's: Pension strains put pressure on ratings. *The Bond Buyer*, 14.

Snell, R. (2009, September). State retirement system defined contribution plans. Retrieved from http://www.ncsl.org/Portals/1/Documents/employ/StateGovtDCPlansSept2009.pdf. Accessed September 8, 2010.

Wilshire Consulting. (2009, September 8). 2009 report on city & county retirement systems: Funding levels and asset allocation.

Wisconsin Legislative Council. (2009, December). 2008 comparative study of major public employee retirement systems. Retrieved from http://www.legis.state.wi.us/lc/publications/crs/2008_retirement.pdf. Accessed October 10, 2010.

Part IV

Revenue Elasticity and Adequacy

Chapter 8

Public-Finance and Fiscal-Federalism Perspectives on Local Government Revenue Bases and Fiscal Sustainability

by Donijo Robbins

Introduction

Governments are responsible for producing a variety of goods as well as providing services. The production [who produces] and provision [who pays] of these many activities is divided among different levels of government. In this regard, all governments play a role in the economy, and decision makers—those who allocate scarce resources—must understand public finance and fiscal federalism. In addition, public officials, decision makers, and stakeholders alike, must appreciate the effect of a recession on revenue bases.

To understand the effect an economic crisis has on a local government, first we must understand government's role in the economy and Gruber (2005) suggests we ask four questions: when, how, and why does the government intervene, and what is the effect of its involvement? Typically, the discussion compares the public sector to the private sector; for example, the government gets involved when the market fails, that is, when the provision and production of a good or service is unprofitable for the private sector. As such, the government raises revenue and allocates those resources for the production of a good or service; for example, public safety. In the end, governments provide services often unprofitable to the private sector by allocating resources and funding programs to improve disparities. However, our purpose here is not to ask and answer these questions in the context of public versus private sectors, but rather to answer these questions from the perspectives of fiscal federalism. We change the fourth question slightly and ask not what the effect of government involvement in the economy is but what the influence of fiscal federalism on subnational governments is, particularly local governments.

Why Government Does What It Does

To answer these questions, we start by asking: why do governments intervene, or more specifically, why does the federal government fund certain services and not others? For example, the federal government funds national defense and income security, while state and local governments produce other services, such as education and parks and recreation programs. Still other functions are funded by the central government but administered by state and local governments, for instance Medicaid and infrastructure. So why do different layers of government provide certain services and other layers do not? The answer rests in the concept of *federalism*.

When you think of federalism, what comes to mind? Perhaps you think of enumerated or reserved powers, hierarchy, division of responsibilities or fragmentation, constitutional authority, cooperation or independence, centralization or *decentralization*, or maybe even Alexander Hamilton, a Federalist, or Thomas Jefferson, an anti-Federalist. All of these words seemingly encapsulate federalism.

From a traditional, legal definition, federalism is a centralized system where the constitution enumerates certain powers—those directly expressed in the constitution, such as the collection of taxes, the declaration of war, and the regulation of interstate commerce—to the federal government and relinquishes all other powers to the states. In the U.S. Constitution, Article 1, Section 8 enumerates powers to Congress to tax, borrow, coin money, regulate commerce, declare war, to name a few, but it is the Tenth Amendment that reserves those powers not delegated to the federal government to the states or to the people. In the United States, the constitutional definition provides a clear separation of powers where different levels of government operate independently; a system of *dual federalism*. From this constitutional model of dual federalism emerges the concept of fiscal federalism, where different layers of government (federal, state, local, and tribal governments) exist, and each is responsible for the provision (taxing) and production (allocation of expenditures) of a different set of goods and services. Those powers not assigned to the federal government are decentralized to subnational governments that then become the sole decision maker.[1]

Interpretations of the constitutional definition abound. A philosophical reading of federalism stems from a decision-maker's attitude toward government's role in society. This theory is grounded in the centralization of power, or more specifically, who or what level of government should hold the decision-making power. Proponents of centralization argue that the central government decision maker is best at defining and achieving broad national goals that result in uniform quality across the country (Mikesell, 2007). Opponents of centralization suggest that many benefits are constrained to a geographic location, and as such, decision-making powers should rest with states and local government officials who better understand the needs and demands of their residents.

Applied to the perspectives of local public finance then, a decentralized approach is likely to achieve economic efficiencies, where local governments produce goods and services specific to their communities' demands and tax their residents accordingly, such that the benefits received principle—those who pay, benefit—is achieved. That is, citizen demand and preferences drive the local production of certain goods and services. Moreover, residents are likely to move to a community that provides services that reflect their needs. Tiebout (1956) proposed this theory of "vote with your feet," and often we find communities with homogenous populations where some local governments provide many services and levy high taxes while other governments provide minimal services and impose smaller tax rates.

Which Layer of Government Provides Goods and Services

Simply put, the central government provides goods and services at the national level that yield benefits, economic or social, to all citizens equally; for example, national defense. On the other hand, state, regional, or local governments supply, or tailor, services to their respective regions based on demand and efficiency such that a link between tax dollars and benefits exist (Oates, 1972). For example, local residents pay for and are direct benefactors of parks and recreation programs, street lighting, garbage collection, street cleaning, to name a few, and these benefits do not extend beyond the jurisdiction.

From the perspectives of local governments, then, expenditures should result in low *economies of scale* and few externalities or spillovers thus achieving an optimal level of fiscal federalism. Economies of scale is achieved when average costs are reduced at the margin as more goods and services are produced. For example, the costs to a school district to educate 100 students or even 10,000 students might be higher than the costs of educating 1,000 students. As costs remain low, economies of scale are achieved regardless of the level of government. However, because local governments are better able to understand local demand, they should provide the service rather than a higher level of government. In other words, if the economics of scale is no different between the local government and the national government, the provision of the service should default to the local government as localities better understand taxpayers' demands.

Externalities exist when constituents from one locality benefit from a service provided by another locality whose residents bear the financial costs via taxes. Say, for example, residents from Eastern use the park system in Western. The constituents of Western fund the park system but the citizens of Eastern do not. In this instance, benefits spillover to other communities, but the tax burden falls to one community.

When spillovers exist but do not justify a more centralized approach because the economies of scale are no different, the local government can charge the other localities. For example, Western can charge the residents of Eastern to use the park system through park fees. However, if these externalities are large enough to create diseconomies of scale and charging fees is not an option, three outcomes are possible. First, the city may stop offering the service altogether because it does not have the fiscal capacity—a large enough tax base—to fund the service; second, the central government (regional, state, or national) could provide intergovernmental funding such that the local provision of the service is possible; or third, the service could become a centralized function and funded completely by the regional (i.e., county) or state government.

As the economy booms and busts, we see the argument of decentralization wax and wane. In good times, local governments are less likely to consider economies of scale, but as the bust cycle approaches and the economy bottoms out, local officials look for ways to improve fiscal capacity (e.g., save money). One strategy to improve capacity is to collaborate with other regional governments. For example, a 911 dispatch office might be more cost effective if shared by a number of communities, rather than each community building, maintaining, and allocating resources to its own office. In 2010 the 911 system in Kent County, Michigan, was consolidated. The city manager of Grand Rapids, Michigan estimated that the city alone would save $1.8 million annually.[2] In this instance, consolidation improved the economies of scale and the fiscal capacity of the participating governments.

How Government Intervenes

The next question to consider is: how do the different levels of government intervene? Governments have three main functions—allocation, distribution, and stabilization. Allocation policy exists whenever governments raise revenue through taxes and charges to provide goods and services. The distribution function takes place when governments impose taxes on some and redistribute the monies to social welfare programming. Stabilization occurs when governments change their tax and spend policies to stimulate the economy; that is, the federal government may spend more money on allocation type projects in an attempt to put more money into the economy. Each of these functions is discussed in turn. It is important to note that the data provided throughout come from two different sources. One source is the Bureau of Economic Analysis (BEA), which provides data for the federal government and combined totals for state and local governments as of 2009. The other source is the U.S. Census Bureau 2007 Census of Government Finance and provides data separately for county, municipal, township, special district, and school district governments but does not provide state data. As a result, the numbers do not equal and should not be used comparatively. The information in this section alone comes from the BEA whereas the data in remaining sections come from the U.S. Census of Government and Finance.

National and subnational governments collect revenues from their citizens and then allocate these dollars to produce government services, such as defense, infrastructure, public safety, parks and recreation, garbage collection, and so forth. In fact, 70% of state and local expenditures, compared to 28.5% of federal expenses in 2009, were allocation type expenditures (U.S. Bureau of Economic Analysis, 2010).

Governments also collect revenues from their citizens and then distribute these dollars via transfer payments to social programs to provide income security for individuals or improve disparities among local governments. For example, the federal government provides income security to the elderly by way of social security payments, which are funded through payroll taxes. Furthermore, the federal government transfers monies to subnational governments through grants-in-aid. In 2009, the majority (62.4% or $2.16 trillion) of federal expenditures was transfer payments, and 75% (or $1.62 trillion) was distributed to fund social benefits. State and local governments, on the other hand, spent $492 billion, or one-quarter of their expenditures, on social benefits (U.S. Bureau of Economic Analysis, 2010).

Central governments can improve funding mechanisms to reduce disparities and inequalities among districts. Consider elementary and secondary education. Historically,

K-12 education has been funded through property tax revenue, and in Michigan, per-pupil funding disparities between poor and wealthy school districts were more than $7,500 (Van Beek, 2010). To improve equity and fiscal capacity and reduce disparities, the state of Michigan, through the passage of Proposal A in 1994, centralized education funding by lowering and capping property taxes, increasing and earmarking sales taxes, state income tax, and a few others. Today, based on an allocation formula, the state distributes monies back to the school districts. According to the Michigan House Fiscal Agency, currently "80 percent of all [Michigan] school districts receive between $7,100 and $7,400 per student; 94 percent fall between $7,100 and $8,500" (Van Beek, 2010). Moreover, additional funding from grants from the state and federal governments further reduces the disparities, sometimes resulting in poorer schools receiving more per-pupil funding than neighboring wealthier districts.

Governments use stabilization to improve the fiscal capacity of subnational governments and to stimulate the economy. The central government can provide assistance to subnational governments to improve economic capacity (Mikesell, 2007); that is, the central government attempts to improve the mismatch between citizen demand and capacity. For example, central governments assist local governments that have extensive infrastructure and declining populations and as a result struggle to maintain the current level of services with an ever shrinking revenue base. These communities receive grants-in-aid from governments to improve fiscal capacity.

Second, in times of economic recession, governments attempt to stabilize or stimulate the economy through monetary and fiscal policies. The federal government is the sole regulator of monetary policy but all governments can use fiscal policy—altering their tax and spend policies—to grow the economy. For example, in 2009, the federal government spent $5.5 trillion while receipts totaled $4.2 trillion. The overexpenditure was an attempt by the federal government to stimulate the economy. This policy is generally reserved for the federal government as most states and local governments are mandated to balance their budgets. Furthermore, subnational government efforts to stimulate the economy often are countercyclical to the boom-bust cycle—in a recession, state and local governments are increasing tax rates and/or cutting expenditures in an effort to balance their budgets.

Overall, governments at all levels and for all functions in the U.S. spent $5.48 trillion and generated $4.21 trillion in revenue in 2009 (Bureau of Economic Analysis, 2010). The majority of revenues (52.4%) and expenditures (63.1%) were raised and expended by the federal government whose largest revenue source is the income tax and largest expenditure is transfer payments—payments to individuals for social benefits as well as grants-in-aid to state and local governments. On the other hand, state and local governments received slightly more than $2.01 trillion in receipts, mainly from intergovernmental transfers, property taxes, and sales taxes. In addition, state and local government spent roughly $2.03 trillion in expenditures, which are composed mostly of education, health, general services, and public safety.

The Effect of Fiscal Federalism on Local Governments

So far we have discussed fiscal federalism and the philosophical reasons for centralization and decentralization. In either case, one layer of government is the sole provider of a good or service, and as such is the sole funder. Therefore, the central government provides goods and services at the national level that yield benefits, economic or social, to all citizens equally. For example, the federal government provides national defense whereas state, regional, or local governments supply, or tailor, services to their respective regions based on demand and efficiency such that a link between tax dollars and benefits exist. As a result, and for Tiebout's theory to hold true, subnational governments should not intervene in national goals such as the redistribution of wealth or the stimulation of the economy; these should be reserved for the federal government. However, in reality, deciding which layer of government is the responsible party is not as simple as efficiencies and externalities.

The debate surrounding government power and responsibility continues today and not just among academics, but within the different levels of government as the federal government duels with state governments, and both battle with local governments as to which layer of government holds the power. It is fair to say that the U.S. federal government clearly provides more for its citizens than is mentioned directly in the Constitution, for example, Social Security, Medicare, Medicaid, unemployment, to name a few. Given the broad language of the document that amounts to limitless responsibilities, most anything the federal government pursues can be considered for the defense or general welfare of the people; the federal government can do whatever the federal government wants to do. In doing so, it can delegate certain responsibilities to states; for example, the federal government creates income redistribution laws such as unemployment compensation and Medicaid and then delegates the power of collecting and distributing funds to the states. In the end, power is devolved not decentralized as states become managing agents rather than the sole decision makers for government programs.

Education, housing, health, infrastructure, and transportation have become increasingly a national interest, from No Child Left Behind and Race to the Top, to the Affordable Care Act and investment in highways, railways, and seaports. However, the majority of local governments budget resources for these very programs. In 2007, as **Figure 8.1** demonstrates, local governments spent most ($571 billion or 40%) of their budgets on education; 21% on social services such as public welfare, hospitals, health, housing, and the environment; and roughly 6% on transportation expenditures, which consists of highways, airports, water/seaports, and parking facilities.

All told, local governments spent $1.4 trillion, and approximately 67% of these expenditures were allocated for ostensibly national goals that, we could argue, are either decentralized or devolved to the local governments. Many of the benefits from local governments' allocation functions spill over not only into neighboring jurisdictions but spread across an entire state or even the whole country. As a result, the federal government provides fiscal resources to fund these expenditures, but is it enough? What is the effect of fiscal federalism and devolution on local governments' revenue bases?

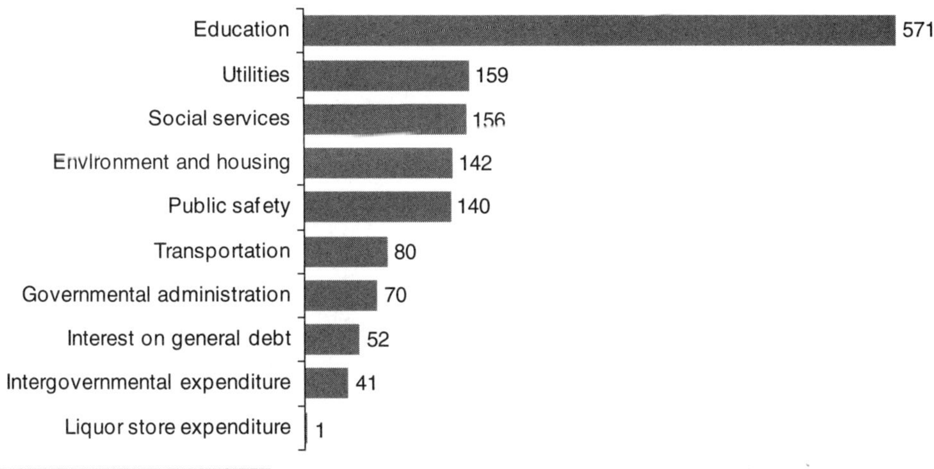

Figure 8.1 Local Government Expenditures (Billions of Current Dollars), 2007

Source: U.S. Census Bureau, 2007 Census of Government Finance. Total local government expenditures for 2007 were $1.4 trillion. Insurance trust expenditures are not included in the figure or the $1.4 trillion. Data are available at http://www.census.gov/govs/estimate/historical_data_2007.html.

Before we answer this question, let us look briefly at the different revenue sources for local governments. Local governments generate revenues from a number of sources and bases. Local governments rely on their own sources of revenue, which consist of taxes on property, consumption, and income; and charge fees for services. Typically, the taxes preserve the ability to pay principle—they are equitable—while charges and fees uphold the benefits received principle.[3] In addition, governments receive revenues from intergovernmental sources to offset the effects of spillovers, to fund those responsibilities devolved to them, or to improve fiscal capacity. In the analysis that follows, we classify taxes as own-source, general revenues, whereas charges and fees are labeled own-source, earmarked revenues. **Figure 8.2** depicts the composition of all local revenue sources in 2007. We begin with own-source revenues.

The major own-source revenues that local governments typically use to fund general fund expenditures come from taxes on property, consumption, individual and corporate income, motor vehicle licenses, to name a few. Property tax revenue is the largest tax source for local government, generating $376.9 billion in 2007. This particular tax generates an incredible amount of attention. Many argue that the property tax is the incredibly shrinking tax, and its importance is declining because of tax revolts (McCabe, 2000) and state restrictions on rates (Saxton, Hoene, and Erie, 2002). Moreover, Krane, Ebdon, and Bartle (2004, p. 523), provide a comparison of 1902 revenue sources to 1997 revenue sources. In 1997, local government revenues made up only 38% of all local revenues, but

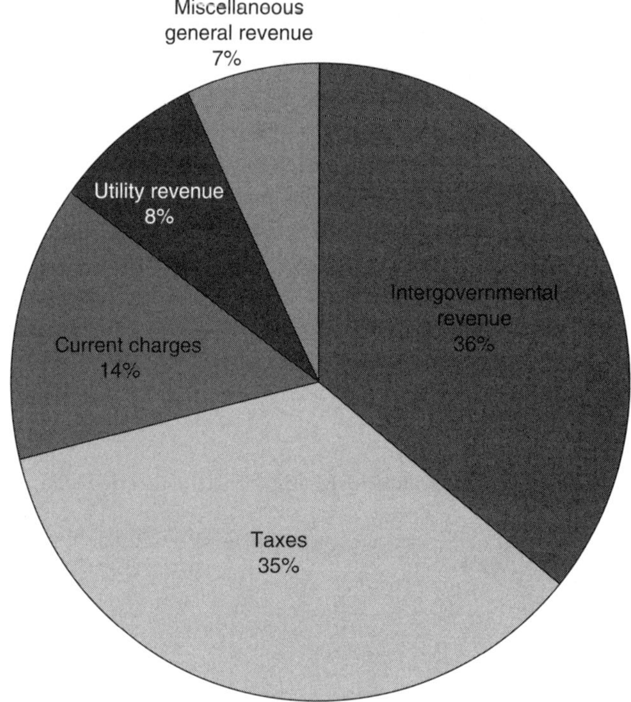

Figure 8.2 Local Government Sources of Revenue, 2007

Source: U.S. Census Bureau, 2007 Census of Government Finance.

in 1902, its proportion was 82%. In addition, revenues from the property tax declined in this same time frame from 73% in 1902 to 27% in 1997.

This may be true, but to suggest that the importance of the property tax is decreasing is misleading for three reasons. First, the composition of revenue sources has changed in 100 years because of revenue diversification. Second, much of the argument about the role of certain taxes is lost in translation; just as the composition of revenues has changed, so too has the composition of expenditures, and property taxes might be an inappropriate funding method for many of these services. Third, revenue sharing was seemingly nonexistent 100 years ago, as was the devolution of responsibilities.

Consider **Table 8.1**. From 1997 to 2007, local tax revenue (in constant dollars) has increased 43% and property tax revenue has increased 40%. In addition, this supposedly shrinking property tax constitutes 72% of all local taxes, 45% of all local own-source revenues (taxes, charges, fees, and other miscellaneous revenue sources), and 25% of all revenue, including intergovernmental. Over a decade, property taxes have remained stable and an important funding source for general government expenditures. In fact, the property tax's composition of local own-source revenues has increased 14% from 1997 to 2007.

TABLE 8.1 All Local Governments' Revenue Sources (Thousands of Constant 1997 Dollars) and Percentage Change for Selected Years

Revenue Source	1997	2002	2007	%Chg 1997–2002	%Chg 2002–2007	%Chg 1997–2007
Intergovernmental revenue	287,002,819	377,625,961	415,413,867	31.58	10.01	44.74
From Federal government	28,767,625	38,330,583	44,714,894	33.24	16.66	55.43
From State government	258,235,194	317,321,703	345,738,324	22.88	8.96	33.89
From local governments	-	21,973,675	24,960,648		13.59	
General revenue from own sources	460,027,471	532,744,583	650,555,666	15.81	22.11	41.42
Taxes	284,397,653	330,019,441	407,023,058	16.04	23.33	43.12
Property	208,524,416	240,428,012	291,792,103	15.30	21.36	39.93
Sales and gross receipts	45,307,452	55,101,633	67,252,668	21.62	22.05	48.44
General sales	31,332,742	38,649,747	47,486,974	23.35	22.86	51.56
Selective sales	13,974,710	16,451,886	19,765,694	17.73	20.14	41.44
Motor fuel	880,679	960,157	1,053,264	9.02	9.70	19.60
Alcoholic beverage	318,888	313,103	350,710	(1.81)	12.01	9.98
Tobacco products	181,087	170,267	414,234	(5.98)	143.29	128.75
Public utilities	7,598,359	8,926,774	9,886,568	17.48	10.75	30.11
Other selective sales	4,995,697	6,081,586	8,060,917	21.74	32.55	61.36
Individual income	14,119,854	15,332,417	18,550,371	8.59	20.99	31.38
Corporate income	3,102,561	2,702,114	5,942,267	(12.91)	119.91	91.53
Motor vehicle license	1,188,379	1,182,194	1,217,714	(0.52)	3.00	2.47
Other taxes	12,154,991	15,273,069	22,267,936	25.65	45.80	83.20
Charges and miscellaneous general revenue						
Current charges	118,380,881	136,479,352	162,751,734	15.29	19.25	37.48
Education	12,409,896	15,375,976	18,234,728	23.90	18.59	46.94
Institutions of higher education	4,426,946	6,135,160	7,255,200	38.59	18.26	63.89
School lunch sales (gross)	4,490,992	5,296,464	5,339,438	17.94	0.81	18.89
Hospitals	33,099,990	36,625,007	44,582,491	10.65	21.73	34.69
Highways	2,198,622	2,772,375	3,524,941	26.10	27.15	60.33
Air transportation (airports)	8,291,133	10,294,662	11,894,952	24.16	15.54	43.47
Parking facilities	1,195,042	1,251,028	1,399,620	4.68	11.88	17.12
Sea and inland port facilities	1,508,848	1,739,058	2,113,515	15.26	21.53	40.07
Natural resources	967,209	790,287	1,212,878	(18.29)	53.47	25.40

(continued)

TABLE 8.1 All Local Governments' Revenue Sources (Thousands of Constant 1997 Dollars) and Percentage Change for Selected Years (cont.)

Revenue Source	1997	2002	2007	%Chg 1997–2002	%Chg 2002–2007	%Chg 1997–2007
Parks and recreation	4,272,517	5,193,928	5,664,203	21.57	9.05	32.57
Housing and community development	3,468,788	3,360,316	3,684,586	(3.13)	9.65	6.22
Sewerage	21,994,668	24,158,694	27,954,857	9.84	15.71	27.10
Solid waste management	9,005,570	9,655,111	10,856,572	7.21	12.44	20.55
Other charges	19,968,598	25,262,911	31,628,391	26.51	25.20	58.39
Miscellaneous general revenue	57,248,937	66,245,790	80,780,873	15.72	21.94	41.10
Interest earnings	30,932,396	31,416,446	34,810,942	1.56	10.80	12.54
Special assessments	3,435,888	4,158,068	5,626,327	21.02	35.31	63.75
Sale of property	1,202,178	1,202,996	2,669,382	0.07	121.89	122.05
Other general revenue	21,678,475	29,468,280	37,674,223	35.93	27.85	73.79
Utility revenue	70,278,577	80,666,369	91,090,441	14.78	12.92	29.61
Water supply	26,792,031	29,510,143	33,613,655	10.15	13.91	25.46
Electric power	33,318,168	39,524,284	43,563,879	18.63	10.22	30.75
Gas supply	4,086,174	5,129,935	6,720,259	25.54	31.00	64.46
Transit	6,082,204	6,502,008	7,192,648	6.90	10.62	18.26
Liquor store revenue	603,035	693,443	792,712	14.99	14.32	31.45
Total Revenue	817,911,902	991,730,356	1,157,852,686	21.25	16.75	41.56

Source: U.S. Census Bureau, 2007 Census of Government Finance.

One reason the property tax is a smaller proportion of all revenue than it was 100 years ago is a result of local governments diversifying their revenue bases. Over time, states have eased restrictions on consumption and income taxes and, accordingly, these compose the second and third largest sources of tax revenue for local governments, 17% and 6%, respectively. Local governments use these own-source revenues, such as those from property taxes, to fund general government services.

Today, local governments provide many charge-based services that did not exist 100 years ago such as refuse collection, parking, water, and sewer services; parks and pools; and even cemeteries and golf courses. As a way to improve economic efficiencies, meet citizen demands, and achieve the benefits received principle, local governments charge fees and earmark the revenue to fund all or a portion of the costs associated with these services. In 2007, local governments collected more than $328 billion (or 22% of local government revenues) from fees and charges (including utility revenue), as shown in Figure 8.2.

Those services that are business type, should charge a price large enough to cover 100 percent of the costs; however, local governments were unable to accomplish this goal in 2007. Local government utilities, which are typically business-type activities, generated $118 billion in revenue but expended $162 billion. However, not all charges pay for these services; for example, the revenue from the other charges account for one-quarter of the total budget. **Table 8.2** presents differences between revenues and expenditures for those services with a charge. Of the 16 items listed, only 3 of the services charged enough to cover expenditures. However, local governments use funds from property, consumption, and income taxes as well as revenue sharing and borrowing to cover the $727 billion budget gap.

Krane, Ebdon, and Bartle (2004, p. 513) summarize it best when they say, "[t]he revenue side of the ledger is politically more interesting because it has become the fiercest policy battleground of state-local relations." As government activities devolve from the federal level to states and then to local governments, the fiscal capacity of the subnational governments

TABLE 8.2 Local Government Charges and Expenditures for Selected Services, 2007 (in 1000s of dollars)

Type of Service	Revenues	Expenditures	Difference
Education	23,556,542	560,505,165	–536,948,623
Highways	4,553,697	56,380,496	–51,826,799
Housing and community development	4,759,934	37,224,969	–32,465,035
Transit	9,291,826	37,323,243	–28,031,417
Parks and recreation	7,317,303	32,345,275	–25,027,972
Water supply	43,423,816	56,954,701	–13,530,885
Hospitals	57,593,912	70,923,181	–13,329,269
Natural resources	1,566,857	8,964,355	–7,397,498
Sewerage	36,113,495	42,833,588	–6,720,093
Solid waste management	14,025,068	20,592,916	–6,567,848
Gas supply	8,681,570	12,060,562	–3,378,992
Air transportation (airports)	15,366,499	18,447,596	–3,081,097
Sea and inland port facilities	2,730,345	3,274,532	–544,187
Liquor store revenue	1,024,066	938,770	85,296
Parking facilities	1,808,100	1,434,329	373,771
Electric power	56,278,017	55,846,829	431,188
Total	288,091,047	1,016,050,507	–727,959,460

Source: U.S. Census Bureau, 2007 Census of Government Finance.

diminishes. That is, in addition to the provision and production of the goods and services local governments traditionally provide—those decentralized services such as police, fire, refuse collection—local governments have to administer programs central governments initiate. This process influences the fiscal capacity and stability of municipal governments, particularly in times of economic recession. As the federal government mandates subnational governments to produce certain services, local governments have to find ways to fund current decentralized responsibilities as well as those devolved to them. In times of fiscal austerity, devolution expands, local revenue bases contract, and local demands increase.

Local government receive monies through grants-in-aid from the federal, state, and sometimes from other local governments to improve fiscal capacity, reduce the effects of externalities (e.g., spill over benefits into other jurisdictions), and fund devolved responsibilities—many of which are listed in Table 8.2.

According to the U.S. Census 2007 survey of local government finance, revenue sharing (i.e., grants-in-aid) represented 36% of local government revenues (see Figure 8.2). States supplied more than 80% of this funding as depicted in **Figure 8.3**. Overall, intergovernmental revenues have increased 45% since 1997, yet their proportion is roughly the same since 1997, when 35% of local government revenues were from intergovernmental sources.

Recall Figure 8.1. We approximated that 67% (or $948 billion) of local government expenditures could be classified as national interests—education, social services, and environment

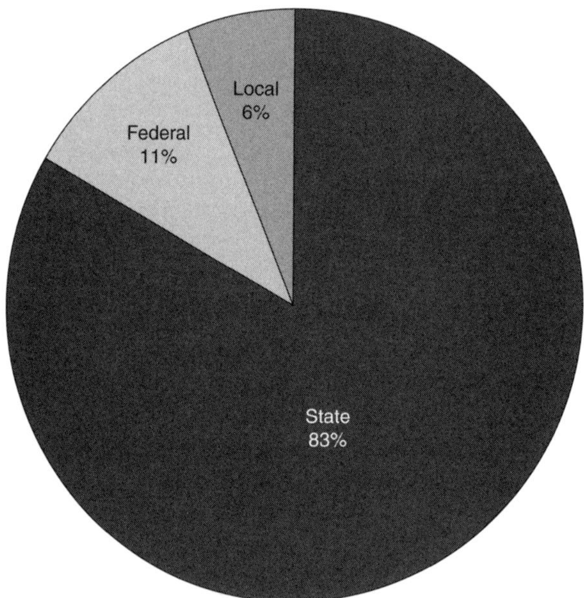

Figure 8.3 Direct Revenue Sharing to Local Governments By Government Type, 2007

Source: U.S. Census Bureau, 2007 Census of Government Finance. Percentages based on $537 billion.

and housing. As such, the federal government provides funding mainly to states but also to local governments to fund these national interests, and these payments have increased over time. For example, in 1960, revenue sharing for capital investments was approximately 4% of the federal budget whereas in 2009 it comprised 3% of federal outlays. However, when we compare intergovernmental revenues distributed to local governments, which totaled $536 billion in 2007, to the costs of the services listed in Figure 8.1 and in Table 8.2, we find that transfer payments nearly support education alone (Figure 8.1) and fix the budget gap when fees are included (Table 8.2) yet leave a large budget gap of $191 billion. Even if we removed those decentralized services from Table 8.2, a budget gap of $109 billion remains. This means local governments must fund the budget gap as well as the local government services—those that result from citizen demand and account for the remaining 32% (or $463 billion) of local budgets.

In 2007, local governments generated $526 billion in own-source, nonearmarked revenues, and collected another $146 billion in other charges, fees, and taxes. These revenues are used to fund the $463 billion for local expenditures and the $191 billion budget gap between intergovernmental revenues and devolved responsibilities. In the end, local government revenues exceeded their expenditures.

Over a decade, from 1997 to 2007, local revenues increased 41.6% while expenditures increased 40% and outstanding debt has increased 49.3% . In fact, in 2007, local governments generated $1.158 trillion, spent $1.157 trillion, and accumulated interest $1.142 trillion in debt (see **Figure 8.4**).

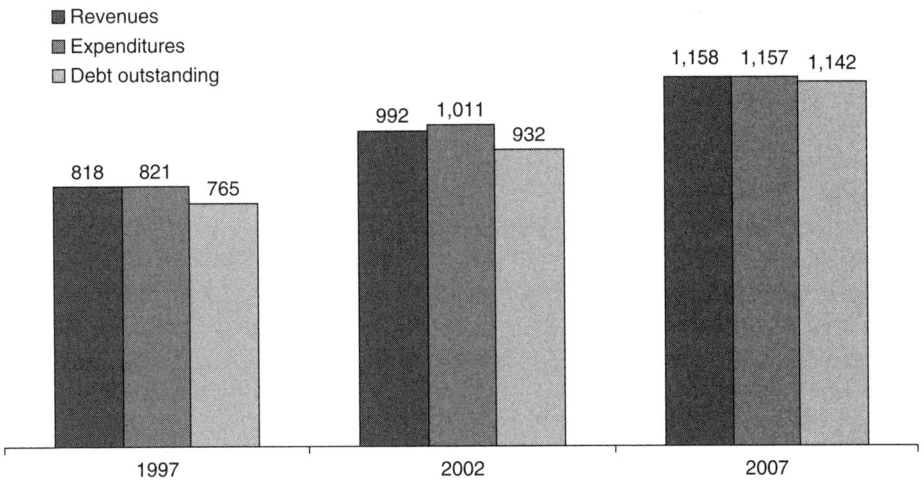

Figure 8.4 Total Revenues, Expenditures, and Debt Outstanding for All Local Governments for Selected Years Billions of Constant (1997) Dollars

Source: U.S. Census Bureau, 2007 Census of Government Finance.

The growth in all three could be partially attributed to decentralization and devolution. As local governments take on additional responsibilities, they look for new, innovative strategies to fund the new services. One approach is revenue diversification. Over time, local governments are instituting new charges for services and levying additional taxes on new bases to fund the services demanded by its local citizenry and to fund the new found responsibilities passed on by the central governments creating a catch-22 of sorts for local governments. Local governments are better able and seemingly more capable to adapt their revenue structures to fund expenditures as state governments lift historic restrictions on taxing ability. For example, Mackey (1997) suggests that the number of state governments allowing municipalities to use local sales taxes has increased from 1 in 1950 to 33 in 1997. Moreover, public officials representing central governments might find this more politically palatable than increasing state or national tax rates or adopting new taxes altogether. Therefore, the central government will continue to devolve responsibilities to the states which in turn pass them off to municipalities all the while providing intergovernmental transfers and improved taxing capability to local governments as they remain innovative change agents.

For example, in 1960, federal government payments to states and local government for individuals (social benefits) were less than 3% of the federal budget but increased to more than 10% by 2009. **Figure 8.5** depicts these changes over time. In addition, over the past decade, grants have increased 128% (see **Table 8.3**), with the largest dollar increases

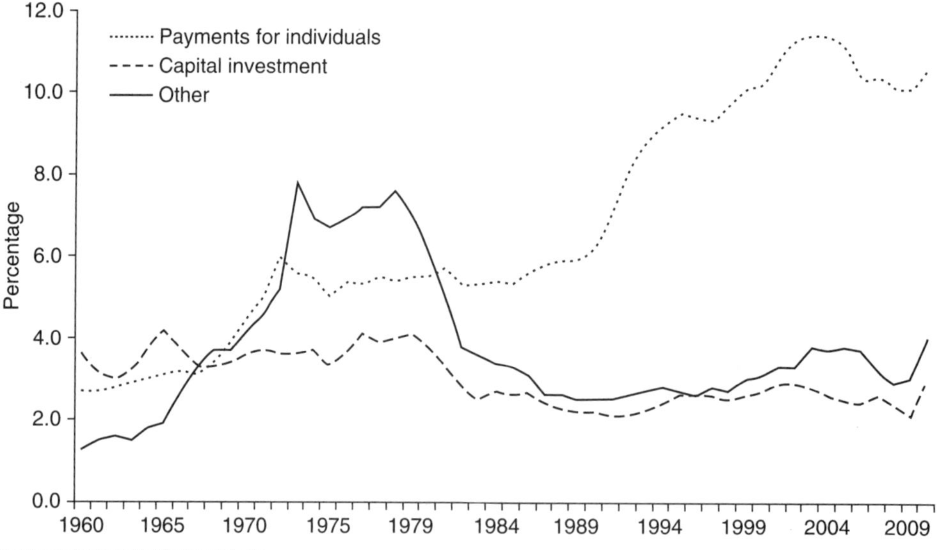

Figure 8.5 Percentage of Federal Outlays to State and Local Governments, 1960–2010

Source: U.S. Office of Management and Budget, Historical Table 12.1. Available at http://www.whitehouse.gov/omb/budget/Historicals/

Table 8.3 Federal Grants to State and Local Governments by Function and Fund Group, 1940–2010 (millions of dollars)

Function and Fund Group	1940	1950	1960	1968	1970	1980	1990	2000	2010 estimate
Health	22	122	214	2,706	3,849	15,758	43,890	124,843	294,613
Income security	341	1,335	2,635	4,188	5,795	18,495	36,768	68,653	121,818
Education	28	150	525	5,170	6,417	21,862	21,780	36,672	111,715
Transportation	165	465	2,999	4,340	4,599	13,022	19,174	32,222	72,249
Community and regional development	277	1	109	862	1,780	6,486	4,965	8,665	21,221
Natural resources and environment	2	18	108	320	411	5,363	3,745	4,595	8,836
General government	10	36	165	338	479	8,616	2,309	2,144	7,104
Energy	....	2	6	18	25	499	461	433	5,927
Administration of justice	....	....	....	12	42	529	574	5,263	5,783
Commerce and housing credit	....	....	2	9	4	3	....	1,218	2,125
Agriculture	25	106	243	542	604	569	1,285	724	1,231
Veterans benefits and services	1	18	8	13	18	90	134	434	935
National defense	....	....	5	27	37	93	241	2	82
Social security	....	....	....	....	....	....	....	6	26
International affairs	....	....	....	6	5	....	....	....	....
Total	872	2,253	7,019	18,551	24,065	91,385	135,325	285,874	653,565

Notes: * $500 thousand or less

Source: U.S. Office of Management and Budget, Historical Table 12.1. Available at http://www.whitehouse.gov/omb/budget/Historicals/

in health, education, and income security as well as a large percentage increase in defense, energy, and general government. One of the reasons for this dramatic increase in grants is to improve the fiscal capacity of states and local governments so to provide these services such that national goals can be accomplished.

Conclusion

We began our discussion by asking four questions. First, why government intervenes or more specifically, to whom do different layers of government offer different services? The answer rests in the U.S. Constitution. Constitutional authority yields certain powers to the federal government, and those not delegated are passed on to the subnational governments. From this emerges the idea of fiscal federalism.

Economic efficiencies, citizen demand, fiscal capacity, and national goals drive the availability of local government services, or government intervention. Economies of scale help answer the first question and settle the argument between centralization proponents and critics. Local government provide services when local residents are the direct benefactors whereas central governments are best at meeting national goals when all citizens benefit equally. As a result, certain functions are more suitable for the different levels of government. Economic efficiencies guide the decision-making process as to which government should offer goods and services yet power struggles, devolution, and funding issues add complications.

Today, local governments have become increasingly more involved in national goals as they develop into managing agents for the federal government programs. Not only are local governments responsible for meeting the demands of their local consistencies, they are now also responsible to manage programs that benefit other jurisdictions as well as other states. Local governments have responded by diversifying their revenue structures and finding economic efficiencies such as consolidation and collaboration with neighboring governments.

Endnotes

1. For a succinct historical overview of federalism, read Kathleen Anders and Curtis Shook's 2003 article, New federalism: Impact on state and local governments in the *Journal of Public Budgeting, Accounting, and Financial Management* and David A. Super's Rethinking fiscal federalism in the 2005 *Harvard Law Review*. Available at http://www.harvardlawreview.org/media/pdf/super.pdf
2. http://www.mlive.com/news/grand-rapids/index.ssf/2010/03/consolidation_of_kent_county_e.html
3. An equitable tax is almost impossible to define because of the endless debate surrounding an agreeable meaning of "fair." For all practical purposes, an equitable tax treats groups in similar economic conditions equally. That is, those on the same horizontal earning plane are treated similarly—horizontal equity—but differently from those on other earning planes—vertical equity. We could say that the property tax is equitable because someone with a large

expensive house will pay more in property taxes than someone with a small, inexpensive house. Broad-based taxes such as property as well as income and sales taxes are used to fund general government expenses, those without charges and fees. When the benefits received are exclusive and can be linked directly to a voluntary payment, like a market system, the government charges only the users—those who are the direct recipients of the benefits. These are benefit-based taxes, and some examples include: charges for garbage collection, water, sewer; driving on roads and over bridges; and swimming in city pools and hiking in the parks.

Glossary

Decentralization: the delegation of decision-making authority to lower levels of government.

Dual federalism: a separation of powers where different levels of government operate independently from the other.

Economies of scale: the marginal cost of producing a good or services decreases as more of the good or service is produced.

Federalism: a centralized system where the constitution enumerates certain powers to the national government.

Discussion Questions

1. Discuss the pros and cons of nationalizing public education in the context of economies of scale and externalities. Is it fair that local residents fund education when benefits spillover to the region, state, or even nation?
2. Discuss the differences between decentralization and devolution. What are some potential funding implications of each to local governments?
3. Is devolution an excuse or the root cause for local governments fiscal stress? Explain.
4. What could local governments do to improve revenue diversification?

Recommended Resources

Anders, K., & Shook, C. (2003). New federalism: Impact on state and local governments. *Journal of Public Budgeting, Accounting, and Financial Management, 15*, 466–486.

Oates, W. (1972). *Fiscal federalism*. New York: Harcourt Brace Jovanovich, Inc.

Oates, W. (2008). On the evolution of fiscal federalism: Theory and institutions. *National Tax Journal, 61*, 313–334.

Super, D. A. (2005). Rethinking fiscal federalism. *Harvard Law Review, 118*, 2544–2652.

References

Gruber, J. (2005). *Public finance and public policy*. New York: Worth Publishers.

Krane, D., Ebdon, C., and Bartle, J. (2004). Devolution, fiscal federalism, and changing patterns of municipal revenues: The mismatch between theory and reality. *Journal of Public Administration Research and Theory, 14*(4), 513–533.

Mackey, S. (1997). *Critical issues in state-local fiscal policy*. Denver: National Conference of State Legislatures.

McCabe, B. C. (2000). State institutions and city property taxes: Revisiting the effects of the tax revolt. *Journal of Public Budgeting, Accounting, and Financial Management, 12*, 205–229.

Mikesell, J. L. (2007). *Fiscal administration: Analysis and applications for the public sector* (7th ed.). Boston: Wadsworth.

Oates, W. (1972). *Fiscal federalism*. New York: Harcourt Brace Jovanovich, Inc.

Saxton, G. D., Hoene, C. W., and Erie, S. P. (2002). Fiscal constraints and the loss of home rule: The long term impacts of California's post-Proposition 13 fiscal regime. *American Review of Public Administration, 32*, 423–454.

Tiebout, C. M. (1956). A pure theory of local expenditures. *Journal of Political Economy, 64*, 416–424.

United States Bureau of Economic Analysis. (2010, August). Survey of Current Business Online. Retrieved on December 15, 2010 at http://www.bea.gov/scb/#chartsandtables

Van Beek, M. (2010, July 6). The unequal funding myth. *Mackinac Center for Public Policy*. Midland, Michigan.

Chapter 9

Understanding and Measuring Elasticity, Volatility, and Implications for Local Government Fiscal Health

by Deborah A. Carroll and Christopher B. Goodman

Introduction

The most recent fiscal crisis and resulting economic environment has posed serious implications for the fiscal health of local governments. Local governments have been struggling with manipulating revenue structures in response to shrinking tax bases and decreased consumer demand for taxable goods and services. Some local property markets have seen significant decreases in home values; something that was never expected to happen. Assessed values have fallen and tax delinquency has risen, thereby leading to decreased property tax revenues. Demand for both consumer goods and fee-based government services has declined as unemployment is up and consumers have tightened their belts to deal with the economic crisis, which has led to significant shortfalls in sales tax and user fee revenues. All of these effects of the economic crisis and state of the economy directly influence the performance of local government revenue structures and consequently affect local government fiscal health.

Fiscal health reflects the ability of a government to meet its ongoing financial, service, and capital obligations. In large part, fiscal health is affected by the volatility of a government's overall revenue structure, which is significantly driven by its aggregate income elasticity. *Income elasticity* measures the change in revenue given a change in the economy; it is a measure of the sensitivity of revenue sources or bases to changes in income.[1] *Revenue volatility* occurs when there is a mismatch between expected and actual revenues; the larger the difference, the greater the volatility. The income elasticity of individual revenue sources/bases directly affects the volatility of a government's overall revenue structure to the extent that the revenue structure is composed of revenue sources/bases that income changes in the economy affect differently. Although the income elasticities of individual revenue bases/sources are largely outside the control of government, local governments can somewhat control the aggregate elasticity of its overall revenue structure. The aggregate income elasticity of a government's revenue structure is likely to produce relatively stable revenue growth unless a jurisdiction significantly varies its tax/fee rates imposed upon its revenue bases from year to year. However, because public service demands and related expenditure requirements typically do not diminish over time, local governments can position themselves for better fiscal health through other means such as building up a stock of slack resources in economic booms and drawing it down in recessionary periods. This approach in combination with consideration of the income elasticities of individual revenue sources or bases when comprising an overall revenue structure can help maintain financial solvency and adequacy of resources for delivering public services constituents desire.

There is much ambiguity with respect to defining and measuring the concepts of fiscal health, elasticity, and volatility, as well as about how these features of local government financial management are interrelated. This chapter offers some resolution to the treatment of these concepts by explaining how fiscal health might be partially improved by managerial considerations of elasticity and actions to reduce overall volatility within the revenue structure. The next section of this chapter illustrates the interconnectedness of factors influencing local government fiscal health, which the composition of a government's revenue structure and its associated volatility mediate. The diagram presented in **Figure 9.1** serves as the basis for subsequent sections of the chapter and information presented herein. After explaining each component of the illustration presented in the figure, the remaining sections of this book chapter provide more detailed discussion of the concepts of elasticity and volatility and their relation to local government fiscal health.

An Illustration of Fiscal Health

Figure 9.1 offers a depiction of how a local government's fiscal health is affected by both controllable and uncontrollable factors stemming from the condition of the overall

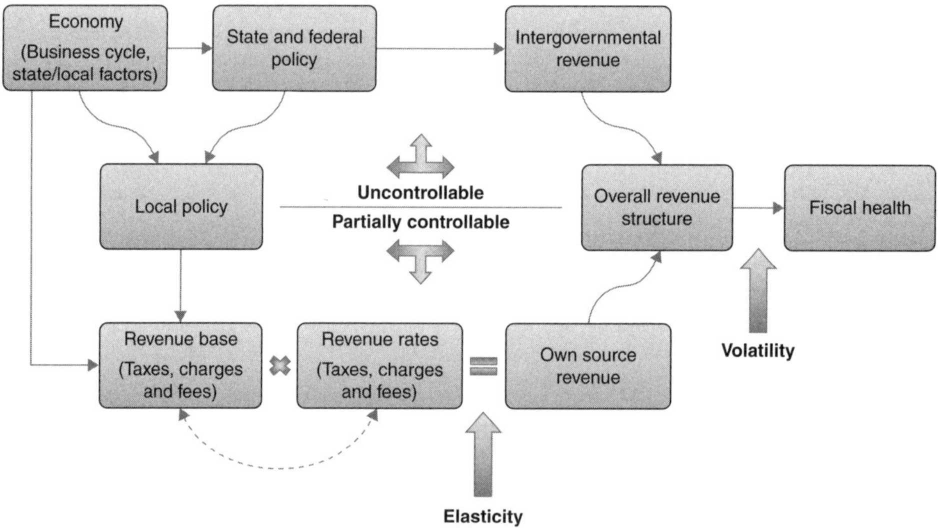

Figure 9.1 Illustration of Fiscal Health

economy and mediated through the composition of its overall revenue structure and consequent volatility, which depends upon the elasticity and covariation of individual sources/bases composing the aggregate structure of its revenue portfolio.

As shown in the upper left corner of Figure 9.1, economic conditions and federal/state revenue policy, both of which are uncontrollable factors for local governments, directly affect local revenue policy.. In turn, local revenue policy, which local governments directly control but legal and/or institutional limits constrain, directly influences a local government's revenue base along with the direct and uncontrollable influence of the economy. A local government's revenue base consists of the value within its jurisdiction upon which taxes, nontax charges, and other miscellaneous fees are imposed. Such value is derived from individuals in cases of direct taxation in terms of their earnings, consumption, or property ownership, but also from the items owned and consumed when taxation is indirect. A local government's revenue base provides the foundation for levying all tax and nontax revenue and is multifaceted in nature as each type of tax, nontax charge, and miscellaneous fee is imposed upon a uniquely defined portion of the overall base. The policy decisions of local government officials affect this revenue base in primarily two ways. First, policymakers identify and define the revenue base as a direct result of their decisions to impose and the extent to which to impose taxes, nontax charges, and other fees upon individuals and goods/services. For example, many local governments directly impose taxes upon property owners based upon the value of real property owned; some jurisdictions tax all or a portion of personal property owned on an ad valorem basis as well. In such cases, the local government's revenue base is at least partially composed of the value of real and/or personal property owned within the jurisdiction. However, if the local government decides to impose the tax on property valued less than 100% of market value, or to offer exemptions for particular uses of real and/or personal property, then the value pertaining to this particular aspect of the government's revenue base is effectively reduced. Conversely, a policy decision to impose an ad valorem tax on personal property in addition to that imposed upon real property or to offer fewer exemptions and therefore impose the personal property tax on a greater number of goods and services would have the opposite effect and consequently increase taxable value or broaden the revenue base.

Second, policy decisions affect the revenue base to the extent that the taxes, nontax charges, and miscellaneous fees imposed upon the base are distortionary and alter individuals' behaviors in attempts to reduce their liabilities. More frequently, local governments indirectly impose taxes on goods and/or services that individuals purchase for consumption within the jurisdiction through a local option to levy an additional percentage tax rate above the state's general sales tax rate. In such cases, the revenue base already consisting of the value of taxable real and/or personal property within the jurisdiction would be supplemented with the value of residents' consumption of taxable goods and services, assuming the local option sales tax is also imposed on an *ad valorem* basis. However, a local government that imposes a local option sales tax might become victim to cross-border shopping and subsequent (albeit perhaps unintentional) evasion of its use tax as residents of the jurisdiction purchase goods and services elsewhere to reduce their tax liabilities, resulting in a reduction of the jurisdiction's revenue base pertaining to the value of taxable goods and services.

As just described, local governments, within the confines of statutory and institutional constraints, generally control changes to the value of particular aspects of a local government's revenue base that result from local policy decisions. However, changes to a local government's revenue base might also result from changes within the economy, and these effects are largely uncontrollable. Such influences can be both positive and negative and also stem from conditions pertaining to the local, state, or national economy. In good economic times, a government's revenue base is likely to expand or broaden, and vice versa. For example, a recession might affect a local economy negatively as businesses are not able to stay afloat and in turn leave vacant properties amid the jurisdiction, thereby depressing taxable property values or perhaps leading to tax delinquency on the part of property owners. Conversely, a local government might benefit from a business that decides to expand or relocate to its jurisdiction during an economic boom as the business occupies formerly vacant property and returns it to the jurisdiction's tax roll and/or makes improvements to a property and consequently raises its taxable value. Related examples of revenue base expansion and contraction might also occur as a result of economic conditions affecting the state more broadly if, for example, a local jurisdiction maintains a local option to draw a percentage from a state-imposed sales tax and consumption of taxable goods and services either increases or decreases commensurate with employment levels and consumers' relative spending patterns. Similarly, economic conditions at the national level might also affect the revenue base of local governments as the positive effects of economic booms, and the negative effects of economic recessions often trickle down from the federal government through states to local communities. Such influences are important because a broader revenue base is preferred as it allows for lower marginal tax/fee rates to be imposed for the same amount of revenue generated. In addition, a stable revenue base is preferred as it provides for more accurate predictions regarding revenue generated to finance necessary public service provision.

As shown on the bottom left of Figure 9.1, each relevant component of a local government's revenue base multiplied by its associated tax/fee rate in aggregate equals a local government's own source revenue. As both revenue policy and economic conditions alter the value of a local government's revenue base, policymakers must determine the types of tax, charges, and fee revenue that can be levied within their legal and institutional constraints, as well as the amounts such revenues can be leveraged from each particular aspect of the overall revenue base. Although there are a multitude of taxes and fees levied from various aspects of a local government's revenue base, the most common are: property taxes, local option sales taxes, license taxes, and general charges/fees.

Moving up and toward the right in Figure 9.1, a local government's overall revenue structure is composed of its total own source revenue plus federal and state intergovernmental revenue (IGR). State and federal intergovernmental revenues are considered uncontrollable sources for local governments as the higher-level governments primarily establish amounts of IGR at their discretion. During economic downturns, intergovernmental revenue, and particularly state aid to local governments, typically declines as state governments struggle to balance their budgets and meet expenditure needs to maintain service provision. Any changes in amounts of state or federal intergovernmental revenue a local government receives must be offset by changes in own source revenue, *ceteris paribus*. Because intergovernmental revenue is an uncontrollable source and contributes to the vulnerability of local governments as it becomes unreliable during fiscal crises, local governments with the capacity to generate greater amounts of own source revenue from their revenue base might choose to do so to intentionally limit their dependence upon IGR.

Also illustrated in Figure 9.1, the elasticities of each individual source influences the amount of own-source revenue yielded from tax/fee rates imposed upon particular aspects of the revenue base . Elasticity refers to the extent to which revenue changes in response to a change in the economy (i.e., income elasticities) or policy decisions (i.e., rate elasticities) that redefine or distort the revenue base. In essence, elasticity represents the sensitivity of revenue relative to its particular base. As noted earlier, changes in revenue resulting from changes in the economy are largely outside the control of local governments, while revenue changes in response to policy decisions are partially controllable. For example, during an economic boom, consumer demand for taxable goods and services is higher as individuals at least perceive they have more disposable income and consequently increase their consumption, thereby leading to greater amounts of sales tax revenue collected by governments with a local option. The reverse effect occurs during a recession in which sales tax revenue declines as consumers reduce their purchasing either because they lack the income formerly at their disposal or they desire to save more of their income as a safeguard against the adverse economic climate. The extent to which sales tax revenue increases commensurate with the tax base expansion that occurs during the economic boom relative to the decline in revenue resulting from the tax base contraction during the recession represents the income elasticity of this particular revenue source.

Each tax/fee comprising a local government's revenue structure is unique in terms of its income elasticity as each source is derived from a particular aspect of the overall revenue base. As such, some taxes/fees will produce great amounts of revenue during economic booms, but also decline dramatically during economic downturns. Other sources will produce less dramatic swings in revenue production as a result of changes to relative aspects of the revenue base, thereby generating less revenue during economic booms but also waning less severely during a recession. The extent to which taxes/fees change concomitantly depends upon how closely their particular bases are associated. Elasticity is important because local governments need to generate sufficient revenue to meet expenditures in the least distortionary way so that residents' actions to reduce their tax/fee liabilities do not diminish the revenue base. This is typically accomplished by either imposing taxes/fees in such a way that residents are unable to avoid their liabilities, which is difficult at the local level because consumer mobility is more prominent and most localities are bound by state-imposed restrictions targeting property taxation, or by deriving revenue from several sources so that relatively low marginal rates are imposed. In the latter case, each tax/fee a government uses to generate revenue will also have a different income elasticity associated with it and therefore respond to income changes in the economy differently. In turn, the elasticities of each individual tax/fee directly affect the volatility of a government's overall revenue structure. Revenue volatility occurs when there is a mismatch between expected and actual revenues; the larger the difference, the greater the volatility. In addition to taxes/fees with adequate growth potential, local governments desire relatively stable sources so that revenue amounts are more easily predicted and service provision is not disrupted during economic downturns. However, more stable sources (i.e., those with lower income elasticities) tend to grow slower over time and might not keep pace with service demands and associated expenditure requirements.

Fiscal managers can construct revenue structures to minimize overall volatility using information about the income elasticities of individual taxes/fees comprising own source revenue. In particular, local governments ideally compose their revenue structures with a mix of sources with varying income elasticities such that some taxes/fees will grow faster and consequently produce greater amounts of revenue during economic booms and others will remain more constant or fall slower during economic downturns but produce relatively less revenue during good economic times. In effect, a combination of sources with varying income elasticities helps to insulate the overall revenue structure and reduce associated volatility. In addition to considering the income elasticities of individual taxes/fees comprising own-source revenue, however, local governments might also take alternative precautions like accumulating reserve slack resources that can be relied upon during economic downturns if revenue growth is unable to meet necessary service provision. Such a combination of approaches can help local governments maintain better fiscal health over the long term. The remainder of this chapter provides more detailed discussion of how income elasticities are defined and measured, how income elasticities of individual sources affect the volatility of a government's overall revenue structure, and how these factors contribute to fiscal health.

Revenue Elasticity and Implications for Volatility

Defining and Measuring Elasticity

Income elasticity is fundamentally defined as the change in revenue in response to a change in the economy. As this definition suggests, elasticity is constructed from two components: a measure of the economy and a measure of revenue. First, the measure of the economy is of prime importance to the construction of elasticity and should reflect the state of the economy as well as indicate resources available to fund government services. As such, the most commonly used measure of the economy is personal income. Second, the measure of revenue presents a choice between using revenue or base values. Each of these has strengths and weaknesses. Revenue values are easily gathered and readily available; however, changes in local policy and tax rates are inherently captured in this measure, muddying the effect changes in personal income has upon revenue as it is difficult to isolate the income elasticity of revenue from the rate elasticity. Using base values resolves the problem of not being able to isolate the effect of income changes from changes in policy or tax rates and therefore represents a more ideal measure; however, revenue base information might be unavailable or difficult to calculate, particularly for users of financial information external to the government. Therefore, both base elasticities and revenue elasticities are commonly used in the literature.[2] In light of this information, we can more narrowly define income elasticity as the change in a revenue or base in response to a change in personal income.

To demonstrate the process of constructing an elasticity measure, a hypothetical situation is useful. Assume that in year 1 a local property tax base is valued at $100,000 and total personal income for residents of this community is $50,000. In year 2, the value of the property tax base increases to $104,250 and personal income increases to $53,000. From year 1 to year 2, property value increased $4,250 and personal income increased $3,000. To construct the income elasticity, the percent changes over time must first be calculated. This would be [($104,250-$100,000)/$100,000] × 100 = 4.25% change for the property tax base and [($53,000-$50,000)/$50,000] × 100 = 6.00% change for personal income.[3] By dividing the percent change in property tax base (4.25%) by the percent change in personal income (6.00%), we get an income elasticity for the property tax base of 0.708.

It is typical to characterize elasticity values greater than one as elastic, values equal to one as unit elastic, and elasticity values less than one as inelastic (Berne and Schramm, 1986).[4] In addition, elasticity values can be negative, indicating that a revenue or base increases when the economy contracts, and vice versa. A negative elasticity might suggest that the revenue or base is counter-cyclical or that there was a change in local policy to offset economic effects. In the earlier hypothetical scenario, the income elasticity of 0.708 would be considered inelastic, meaning that changes in personal income minimally affect the property tax base . This example outlines a simple case of income elasticity for a property tax base. However, what happens if tax (or other revenue) base information is unavailable? This situation is unlikely to occur to those operating inside government; however, individuals or organizations operating outside government and relying on comprehensive annual financial reports or single audits for data might not have access to base data. For users of financial information without base data at their disposal, elasticity calculations become somewhat convoluted.

Consider the previous example using revenue rather than base information. A 2 mill tax rate applied in year 1 would yield $200 in property tax revenue (i.e. [$100,000*2]/1,000 = $200). Assuming the same growth rate for the tax base, an increase to 2.5 mills in year 2 would yield $260.63 in revenue (i.e., [$104,250*2.5]/1,000 = $260.63). Using the same calculation method as before but substituting revenue for the base values, the percent changes would be [($260.63–$200)/$200] × 100 = 30.32% for property tax revenue and remain [($53,000–$50,000)/$50,000] × 100 = 6.00% for personal income. Dividing the percent change in property tax revenue (30.32%) by the percent change in personal income

(6.00%) yields an income elasticity of 5.05, which would be considered highly elastic (i.e., sensitive to changes in personal income). This revenue elasticity is significantly larger than the base elasticity of 0.708 because the elasticity value absorbs both the change in personal income (i.e., income elasticity) and the change in millage rate (i.e., rate elasticity).

This example is certainly an oversimplification in light of an increasingly complex literature on measurement of elasticities. However, the example highlights the importance of accounting for changes in tax rates or other policy decisions prior to constructing elasticity measures. In most cases, income elasticities calculated for a revenue base are more accurate as this approach removes many of the policy decision influences from estimation (though not all). Without using more powerful regression techniques, revenue is often not appropriate for measuring elasticity. Therefore, we suggest that income elasticities be constructed using base values rather than revenue values whenever feasible.

Defining and Measuring Volatility

At the most basic level, revenue volatility is a short-term concept that measures the deviation of actual revenue from a predicted trend (White, 1983). The extant research conceptually begins with Williams et al. (1973) and is later extended by White (1983) to suggest that revenue volatility be measured as the amount of deviation in actual revenue from expected revenue. This same concept has been adapted in both Carroll and Stater (2009) and Carroll (2009) to allow for cross-sectional as well as time series variation in revenue volatility. Based upon these conceptualizations, we define revenue volatility as the median percent deviation of annual revenue from a predicted trend over an economic cycle.

Again, an example helps illustrate this measure.[5] For a six-year economic cycle, assume that year 1 total revenue is $100,000; year 2 total revenue is $102,500; year 3 total revenue is $105,500; year 4 total revenue is $110,000; year 5 total revenue is $111,500; and year 6 total revenue is 115,000. By calculating annual percent changes in total revenue as current-year revenue minus prior-year revenue divided by prior-year revenue and then averaging the annual values over the economic cycle, we can determine that the average annual percent change in total revenue is 2.84%. Next, predicted revenue values are calculated for each year by multiplying the prior-year predicted value to one plus this average percent change value. The exception is year 1 in which the actual revenue value serves as the predicted value. For each subsequent year, the annual predicted value is calculated as $PR_{n-1}*(1 + \Delta\%)$ where PR represents predicted revenue and Δ% is the average annual percent change in total revenue over the economic cycle. Using this approach, predicted revenue values would be $100,000 in year 1; $102,838.98 in year 2; $105,758.55 in year 3; $108,761.01 in year 4; $111,848.71 in year 5; and $115,024.07 in year 6.[6] Finally, we use this information (actual and predicted values) to calculate the percent deviation and determine revenue volatility. Similar to the first step, we calculate annual percent deviations by subtracting the predicted value from actual revenue and dividing by predicted revenue for each year. We then calculate the median of the annual percent deviations over the economic cycle to arrive at the measure of revenue volatility. In this example, the percent deviation for year 1 is 0% because actual revenue is used as the predicted value in the first year; year 2 percent deviation is -0.33%; year 3 is -0.24%; year 4 is 1.14%; year 5 is -0.31%; and year 6 is -0.02%. As can be seen, actual revenue varies both positively and negatively from predicted revenue over the economic cycle. The average of these annual percent deviations is 0.04% while the median is -0.13%. Due to the large deviation observed in year 4, the median value serves as a better representation of revenue volatility.[7]

This measure of revenue volatility is a simplification of methods used in extant scholarly literature. However, because the computing resources required for calculating revenue volatility as defined in academic literature might be unavailable to practitioners or external users of financial information, we offer this simplified approach that is equally valid but offers an ease of calculation and interpretation.

Interrelating Elasticity and Volatility

A stable revenue source should follow a predictable trend over time giving a local government the ability to plan in the long term. Ideally, local governments want to generate revenue from sources that behave in steady and dependable ways to minimize the divergence between expected and actual revenues. On the other hand, fiscal managers also desire to use sources that will keep pace with service demands and associated expenditure requirements, which might not occur with stable revenues or bases (i.e., those with lower income elasticities) because of the tendency for these sources to grow slower over time. Elasticities can help fiscal managers better understand how their local government's revenue sources should be expected to respond to income changes in the economy. Each tax/fee a local government uses to generate revenue is unique in terms of its income elasticity. Generally speaking, however, elastic sources grow faster than the economy as a whole and therefore provide a fiscal dividend in good economic times. However, these same sources will likely experience severe revenue shortfalls in economic downturns because revenues from elastic sources generally fall at a greater rate than the rate of decline in the economy. Typically, there is a *tradeoff* between *growth and stability* (White, 1983). Unit elastic sources are roughly commensurate with changes in the economy; revenues will rise and fall along with the growth and contraction of the economy. Finally, revenues from inelastic sources grow slower than the economy as a whole. And, the economic conditions that affect a portion of a government's revenue base might impact the revenue production of some sources but not others; the extent to which revenues change concomitantly depends upon how closely their uniquely defined bases are associated. In essence, individual revenue sources are affected by different circumstances and in different amounts due to their particular income elasticities.

Table 9.1 provides a summary from the academic literature of income elasticities for property and sales tax bases.[8] Estimated elasticities for the property tax base are long-term elasticities while the elasticities reported for the sales tax base are divided between short and long term. Turning first to the property tax base, Table 9.1 shows estimated income elasticities ranging from a low of 0.22 to a high of 1.526. Simply, these elasticities range from inelastic to elastic. Something that is important to note, however, is that the study by Sexton and Sexton (1986) that reported elasticity values greater than one only included

Table 9.1 Revenue Elasticities from Academic Literature

Tax Base	Estimated Elasticity	
Property Tax Base		
Groves and Khan (1952)	0.22	
Netzer (1958)	1	
Kurnow (1963)	0.941	
Bridges (1964)	0.95 to 0.98	
Sexton and Sexton (1986)	1.174 to 1.526	
Sales Tax Base	*Short Term*	*Long Term*
Fox and Campbell (1984)	0.16 to 0.92	0.58
Sobel and Holcombe (1996)	1.039 to 1.084	0.660 to 0.691
Holcombe and Sobel (1997)	0.97 to 1.076	0.637 to 0.692
Otsuka and Braun (1999)	0.76 to 0.96	0.88
Bruce, Fox, and Tuttle (2006)	0.149 and 1.804	0.811

residential property while the other studies focused on all property. Overall, these studies show the income elasticity of the property tax base is roughly unit elastic, suggesting that the property tax base changes in a similar manner to the economy. Therefore, local government fiscal managers should expect the property tax base to grow and contract at roughly the same rate and direction as the economy over the long term.

Turning to the sales tax base, findings from the literature exhibit large differences between short-term and long-term income elasticities. Long-term elasticities reflect changes to the sales tax base over an entire business cycle, and short-term elasticities describe sales tax base changes within an economic cycle. As seen in Table 9.1, the sales tax base is fairly inelastic in the long term with elasticities ranging from 0.58 to 0.88. This suggests that consumption is fairly stable over the business cycle and that economic conditions, for the most part, do not affect it. In the short term, research has found elasticities to vary significantly depending on the estimation technique with a range of 0.16 to 1.804. Within the business cycle, short-term income elasticities of the sales tax base are procyclical and consequently fall as the economy contracts and rise as the economy expands (Fox and Campbell, 1984; Otsuka and Braun, 1999). In addition, Fox and Campbell (1984) and Otsuka and Braun (1999) demonstrate that different components of the sales tax base react differently to changes in the economy. Depending on the estimation method used (the two papers just cited differ somewhat), factors of the sales tax base such as automobiles, durable goods, and manufacturing tend to be procyclical. However, sales tax base components such as lodging, utilities, and liquor tend to be countercyclical.

The behavior of the sales tax also changes when the base is narrowed as Holcombe and Sobel (1997) show. Removing food purchases from the sales tax base (an extremely stable element) often leads to greater short-term and long-term income elasticities.[9] This suggests that a broad sales tax base would be the most stable over time.

Expanding upon this earlier work, Bruce, Fox, and Tuttle (2006) argue that revenue volatility should be measured in the context of how an actual tax base (or revenue) behaves relative to its long-term equilibrium. In particular, the authors contend that because long-term equilibrium changes instigated by income changes might not be immediately realized, it is important to assess deviations of a tax base or revenue from its equilibrium during shorter time periods or different segments of the business cycle. With long-term equilibrium serving as the expectation for a tax base or revenue, the sales tax base in particular tends to rise above its long-term equilibrium during periods of strong economic growth, and vice versa, as the immediate effect of a change in personal income is often different from the long-term effect (Bruce, Fox, and Tuttle, 2006). Overall, the authors find that when the current sales tax base is above its long-term equilibrium, the short-term income elasticity is rather elastic (1.807). Conversely, when the base is below its long-term equilibrium, the short-term income elasticity is rather inelastic (0.149). These results are similar to those found in Fox and Campbell (1984) and Otsuka and Braun (1999). These findings suggest that tax bases below expected levels (i.e., long-term equilibrium) respond more slowly to increases in personal income, which typically occurs during a recession or sluggish economic growth period. In such cases, base or revenue rebound is largely unaffected by the rate of personal income growth during the recovery period. However, when the current base is above its long-term equilibrium, larger elasticity values suggest the base is more responsive to changes in personal income when it is readjusting downward from the disequilibrium. As a result, in the short term, revenues are more likely to rise noticeably above expectations than to fall below them (Bruce, Fox, and Tuttle, 2006). Therefore, greater volatility might actually benefit a government in the short term if the surplus revenues can be put into reserve or used to fill budgetary gaps.

Case Study: Mecklenburg County, North Carolina

We use data on Mecklenburg County, North Carolina, to offer a better understanding of the concept of elasticity, demonstrate how income elasticities are constructed, and suggest how fiscal managers can use elasticities to better predict revenues. We chose Mecklenburg County primarily because of its size. With a population in 2008 of just over 890,000 and personal income topping $40 billion, Mecklenburg County is the largest county in North Carolina in terms of population and economic resources. Mecklenburg County is also home to the city of Charlotte, an economic driver for the state of North Carolina. In terms of public service delivery, infrastructure, and social service demands, Mecklenburg County is representative of large, metropolitan counties across the United States.

Table 9.2 presents data on Mecklenburg County from fiscal years 2001–2002 through 2006–2007, which most closely correspond with the most recently completed peak-to-peak

TABLE 9.2 Revenue Structure for Mecklenburg County, North Carolina

	2002	2003	2004	2005	2006	2007
Personal Income	$28,145,401,604	$27,435,243,368	$29,363,969,940	$31,448,201,673	$33,522,400,327	$35,065,148,685
Property Tax Base[1]	$64,648,399,397	$65,188,364,769	$67,687,456,824	$76,253,134,484	$77,812,232,205	$80,171,318,178
Sales Tax Base[2]	$14,760,225,680	$14,707,325,683	$15,626,017,151	$17,392,452,604	$17,541,955,584	$18,432,577,536
Property Tax Revenue	$535,669,069	$543,632,385	$562,755,743	$579,178,203	$662,440,466	$658,115,155
Other Tax Revenue	$24,189,558	$27,948,060	$32,240,892	$31,077,748	$32,765,840	$34,741,841
Sales Tax Revenue	$137,820,982	$138,203,616	$168,439,255	$185,752,177	$197,991,821	$218,146,420
Sales & Services Revenue	$61,381,674	$66,654,879	$62,744,768	$68,246,069	$74,769,824	$67,883,936
Intergovernmental Revenue	$184,206,456	$158,221,235	$146,097,935	$149,955,396	$144,934,431	$156,319,925
Other Miscellaneous Revenue	$43,268,899	$38,538,396	$41,740,484	$48,053,387	$60,589,553	$71,752,293
Total Revenue	$986,536,638	$973,198,569	$1,014,019,076	$1,062,262,980	$1,173,491,933	$1,206,959,570

Note: All data are reported in real dollars adjusted for inflation using the Consumer Price Index (CPI).

[1] Real and personal property is valued as of January 1.

[2] Defined as gross retail sales. Data is only available from 2002-2005. Data for 2006 and 2007 is imputed using a linear projection.

economic cycle.[10] The data include financial information on personal income, the property tax base, the sales tax base, and the revenue structure of the county. From this data, we can get a sense of the economic and fiscal landscape of Mecklenburg County over the economic cycle. Between 2002 and 2007, Mecklenburg County saw solid growth in personal income, the sales tax base, and the property tax base. In real terms, the county gained just under $7 billion (roughly 24.6%) in personal income in six years. The property tax base increased about $15.5 billion, equaling just over 24%. The sales tax base increased nearly $3.7 billion or approximately 25%. In terms of its revenue structure, the county derived much of its overall revenue from the property tax. On average, Mecklenburg County generated a little over $590 million per year of property tax revenue or about 55% of total county revenue. The remainder of Mecklenburg County's revenue was derived from a variety of sources including taxes (other taxes and sales taxes), sales and services revenue, intergovernmental revenue, and miscellaneous revenue. These sources varied in the amount of revenue generated from year to year; however, there is a discernable trend in the data presented in Table 9.2. Overall, the remaining five sources (other tax revenue, sales tax revenue, sales and services revenue, intergovernmental revenue, and miscellaneous revenue) were fairly stable with few large changes in revenue. All of these sources experienced growth in real terms over the 2002–2007 economic cycle; however, such growth fluctuated within the economic cycle with some sources exhibiting growth and others showing decline. Despite these fluctuations, the relative shares of these five sources remained fairly constant with other tax revenue equaling 2.9% of total revenue on average, sales tax revenue at 16.2% of total revenue on average, sales and services revenue at 6.3% of total revenue on average, intergovernmental revenue at 14.8% percent of total revenue on average, and miscellaneous revenue equaling 4.7% of total revenue on average.

Given this information, what could a fiscal manager expect about the affect of the economy on the county's revenues or bases? A first step would be to construct income elasticities for each of the sources to better understand their relationship with changes in the economy. Using the method just outlined (i.e., percent change from prior year in revenue or base divided by the percent change from prior year in personal income), **Table 9.3** provides annual calculated elasticities between FY2002 and FY2007 as well as the six-year median elasticity for the fiscal data presented in Table 9.2.[11] We chose the median as our measure of central tendency because the data fluctuate a large amount from year to year, which produces outliers in the data that skew the mean value. The first two rows of data in Table 9.3 show elasticities for the property tax base and the sales tax base, while the remainder of data illustrates elasticities for the tax and nontax revenues presented in Table 9.2.

Overall, Table 9.3 suggests that the property tax base, the sales tax base, and each revenue source maintain unique relationships with the economy as demonstrated by the median income elasticities calculated for the six-year economic cycle. With noticeable variation among the sources, some revenues are inelastic (property tax base, sales tax base, property tax revenue, and intergovernmental revenue), while others are unit elastic (other tax revenue and sales and services revenue), and other revenues are elastic (sales tax revenue and other miscellaneous revenue). In addition, there is variation within

TABLE 9.3 Revenue Elasticities for Mecklenburg County, North Carolina

	2002	2003	2004	2005	2006	2007	Median
Property Tax Base	0.924	–0.331	0.545	1.783	0.310	0.659	0.602
Sales Tax Base[1]	–2.069	0.142	0.889	1.593	0.130	1.103	0.515
Property Tax Revenue	4.567	–0.589	0.500	0.411	2.180	–0.142	0.456
Other Tax Revenue	9.367	–6.158	2.185	–0.508	0.824	1.310	1.067
Sales Tax Revenue	–1.301	–0.110	3.112	1.448	0.999	2.212	1.224
Sales & Services Revenue	–0.639	–3.405	–0.834	1.235	1.449	–2.001	–0.737
Intergovernmental Revenue	–2.241	5.591	–1.090	0.372	–0.508	1.707	–0.068
Other Misc. Revenue	–7.475	4.333	1.182	2.131	3.955	4.003	3.043

Note: Data are calculated using real dollars adjusted for inflation using the Consumer Price Index (CPI).

[1] Defined as gross retail sales. Data is only available from 2002 to 2005. Data for 2006 and 2007 is imputed using a linear projection.

revenue sources during the time period as shown by the annual income elasticities. These fluctuations are primarily the result of either policy decisions or the economy affecting the revenue source or base. For instance, the property tax base was fairly inelastic over the economic cycle with a median income elasticity of approximately 0.60. However, in 2005, the elasticity spiked into the elastic range with a value above 1.25. This anomaly is likely due to a mass revaluation of real property that increased the value of the property tax base to 100% of market value. Specifically, in the mass revaluation year of 2005, the property tax base was highly elastic (> 1.25); however, in a nonrevaluation year like 2006, the base returned to its usual inelastic state (< 0.50). Shocks to the base like these are temporary and abnormal to the long-term trend in elasticities that are related to economic changes. A similar occurrence is apparent with property tax revenue. Changes to the millage rate resulted in dramatic fluctuations in annual elasticity values as property tax revenue increased or decreased commensurate with the policy changes. In particular, property tax revenue in 2006 was highly elastic (2.180) and significantly higher than the two previous years of inelastic values (0.500 and 0.411). The reason for this large increase from 2005 to 2006 is a millage rate increase from 0.7567 mills to 0.8368 mills. In addition, the negative elasticity value for 2007 is likely the result of a decrease in property tax revenue resulting from a decrease in the millage rate from 0.8368 mills to 0.8189 mills.

Over the six-year economic cycle, the sales tax base, as measured by retail sales, was fairly inelastic at about 0.50. This is close to the long-term elasticities found in the scholarly literature. However, there is wide variation in the annual income elasticity values as gross retail sales expanded and contracted with the economy within the economic cycle. The sales tax base was countercyclical in 2002 (–2.069) while it was highly elastic in 2005 (1.593).

There is little explanation other than these changes probably result from changes in consumption because the definition of the sales tax base remained the same during these fiscal years.[12] These swings in annual income elasticities show that there is a varying correlation between consumption and personal income. Had the growth in gross retail sales and the growth in personal income been similar in all years, the annual income elasticities for the sales tax base would have remained relatively stable over the economic cycle.

The remaining own source tax revenues (other tax revenue and sales tax revenue) and nontax revenues (sales and services revenue and other miscellaneous revenue) in Table 9.3 are composed of myriad sources making a direct connection between changes in revenue and changes in personal income difficult. However, the sources comprising single revenues are often similar enough to draw some conclusions regarding what is driving the changes in income elasticities over time. For example, Mecklenburg County's other tax revenue consists of many different miscellaneous taxes including special tax districts, animal taxes, deed stamp excise taxes, real property transfer taxes, scrap tire disposal taxes, local occupancy taxes, and a variety of other taxes. Similarly, sales and services revenue includes nontax charges and fees related to parking, rents and royalties, airport, fire protection, solid waste, ambulance and rescue squad, cemetery, cultural and recreational, library, health and mental health, social services, nursing home services, mass transit, and water/sewer. Other miscellaneous revenue consists of nontax revenue related to the issuance of building permits and the sales of materials, fixed assets, and real property. For these three broader revenue categories (i.e., other tax revenue, sales and services revenue, and miscellaneous revenue), a change in the underlying demand for any of these goods or services upon which taxes/fees are imposed will change the income elasticity of the revenue from year to year. Although the revenue derived from many of these underlying goods and services is relatively stable over time (like solid waste charges and water/sewer charges), other revenue producing activities are more inconsistent and result in more volatile revenues. In such cases, associated revenues will exhibit greater year-to-year income elasticities and less predictability in the related revenue trends. In particular, the elasticity of Mecklenburg's other tax revenue ranged from highly elastic with a maximum value of 9.367 in 2002 to a minimum value of -6.158 in 2003, suggesting a rather volatile revenue source. However, the median value of other tax revenue over the six-year economic cycle was almost unit elastic at 1.067, suggesting the revenue source both increases and decreases commensurate with economic changes; in the long term, the net effect reflects relative stability of this revenue source. For sales and services revenue, the majority of years exhibit a negative income elasticity, ranging from -3.405 to -0.639. In the remaining years, sales and services revenue was generally elastic ranging from 1.235 to 1.449. Over the six-year economic cycle, sales and services revenue had a median income elasticity of -0.737. Finally, Mecklenburg's category of miscellaneous revenue consisted of sources typically growing faster than personal income during the six-year economic cycle and therefore was more elastic. Specifically, between 2005 and 2007, miscellaneous revenue had an income elasticity above two and significantly higher in some years. Although the yearly income elasticity was approximately unit elastic in 2004 and negative in 2002, the overall median income elasticity for other miscellaneous revenue for all years was highly elastic at 3.043.

Sales tax revenue is similarly composed of multiple sources. North Carolina legislation enables local governments to impose four separate sales and use taxes. The maximum allowable 1% plus three 0.5% local general sales and use taxes would amount to a 2.5% levy above the state-imposed sales and use tax rate. However, one of the 0.5% tax levies was not implemented until FY2004 and therefore accounts for the highly elastic (3.112) nature of the sales and use tax in 2004. From 2005 to 2007, income elasticity of the sales and use tax fluctuated from elastic to unit elastic and back to elastic as the economy changed. These variations are likely because of changes in the sales tax base expanding and contracting at different rates than personal income. For Mecklenburg County, it appears that the sales and use tax was somewhat elastic over the economic cycle, which differs from the academic literature reported earlier.

Composition of Revenue Structures

As noted earlier and illustrated by the Mecklenburg case study, each tax/fee composing a local government's revenue structure is unique in terms of its income elasticity as each source is derived from a particular aspect of the overall revenue base; therefore, individual taxes/fees respond to income changes in the economy differently. Due to this variation, fiscal managers can construct revenue structures to minimize overall volatility using information about the income elasticities of individual taxes/fees comprising own source revenue. Ideally, local governments compose their revenue structures with a mix of sources with varying income elasticities such that some sources will grow faster and consequently produce greater amounts of revenue during economic booms and others will remain more constant or fall slower during economic downturns but produce relatively less revenue during good economic times. In effect, a combination of sources with varying income elasticities helps to insulate the overall revenue structure and reduce associated volatility.

Balancing Elasticity of Revenue Sources

The Advisory Commission of Intergovernmental Relations (ACIR) suggested that the revenue structure of local governments be roughly unitary (Shannon, 1987). All of the revenue sources a local government uses should have an aggregate elasticity of close to one; therefore, total revenue should rise and fall commensurate with changes in the economy. Individual sources may rise and fall at different rates in response to economic changes, but the growth trend for aggregate revenue should roughly approximate an income elasticity of one. However, Ladd and Weist (1987) contend that the ACIR's suggestion of aggregate unitary income elasticity makes governments susceptible to insufficient revenue when the economy contracts. Generally speaking, unit elastic sources typically rise and fall with changes in the economy. As such, a revenue structure with unitary elasticity will decline at roughly the same rate as an economic contraction. This situation poses a problem for local government fiscal managers because service demands generally do not diminish accordingly (Borcherding and Deacon, 1972). On the other hand, elastic sources that exhibit greater growth potential and consequently produce greater amounts of revenue are also the most volatile or unpredictable. As such, given the typical behaviors of revenue sources with specific income elasticity characteristics, it is possible to construct a revenue structure that balances these differences to achieve adequate revenue production while also insulating resources from economic downturns to maintain service provision.

Considering Covariation of Revenue Sources

In addition to the concept of balance among sources, potential correlations and covariations between revenue bases should be considered in the composition of a revenue structure. Certain revenues behave concomitantly because they utilize the same or similar aspects of the government's revenue base. Other sources antithetically produce revenues, and there are varying correlations among revenues between these two ends of the spectrum. The manner in which individual revenue sources behave in response to changes in the economy and are related to other sources within a revenue structure has a direct effect upon a government's revenue volatility and subsequently its fiscal health as it relates to the government's ability to meet its ongoing obligations.

Turning back to Mecklenburg County, Tables 9.2 and 9.3 also suggest some covariation of the various revenue sources. Table 9.2 shows total revenue increasing during the 2002–2007 economic cycle. Within this generally increasing trend, however, the proportions of individual revenues comprising the overall structure change from year to year. For example, sales tax revenue rises from 13.97% of total revenue in 2002 to 18.07% of total revenue in 2007. However, property tax revenue remains fairly constant, increasing only slightly from 54.30% of total revenue in 2002 to 54.53% in 2007. This divergent growth in importance to total revenue might reflect their different income elasticities and corresponding revenue growth potential. Over the six-year economic cycle, property tax revenue (and the underlying base) was inelastic while the sales tax was slightly elastic. This difference in income elasticities likely affected revenue growth between these sources and might account at least in part for the gain in relative importance of sales tax revenue to total revenue. However, although the remaining revenues remained fairly stable over the six-year economic cycle in terms of their relative proportions of total revenue, the elasticity values varied such that some resources were inelastic and others elastic.[13] As this case illustrates, if the income elasticities of individual revenue sources vary in a complementary manner, the overall revenue structure can produce consistent amounts over time.

Case Study: Comparing Revenue Structures of Five Counties

To illustrate how the composition of a revenue structure and the income elasticities of sources comprising own-source revenue influence volatility, we explore the revenue structures of five North Carolina counties. **Table 9.4** reports the six-year (2002–2007) median elasticities for the property tax base, sales tax base, and each major revenue source of each county. We chose these counties because they represent the five most populous counties in North Carolina. Collectively, these counties represent roughly one-third of the total population of the state of North Carolina. However, their sizes vary enough as to have a diversity of revenue policies, revenue bases, and somewhat different economic conditions. To arrive at the median values, annual elasticities were first calculated in the same manner just outlined as the prior-year change in revenue or base divided by the prior-year change in personal income; the median of the six annual elasticities was then calculated. Again, median values were calculated to reduce the effects of outliers in the data.

Table 9.4 highlights some similar trends to the Mecklenburg County case study presented earlier. First, the property tax base and the sales tax base in most of the counties are relatively inelastic. However, there is variation across the counties. Second, the five counties have significant variation in the income elasticity values of their revenue sources with each county exhibiting a mix of inelastic, unit elastic, and elastic sources. However, this combination is not uniform among the five counties with the exception of the property tax base, the sales tax base, and sales tax revenue; all other revenues vary from county to county in terms of elasticity with little congruence. To illustrate how varying mixtures of income elasticities might influence the overall performance of a revenue structure, examination and comparison of the five counties are helpful.

TABLE 9.4 Six-Year (2002–2007) Median of Income Elasticities for Major Revenue Sources

	Durham County	Forsyth County	Guilford County	Mecklenburg County	Wake County
Average Population[1]	243,105	324,233	444,490	793,481	746,525
Property Tax Base	0.303	0.642	0.070	0.602	0.322
Sales Tax Base[2]	0.660	–0.193	0.416	0.515	0.657
Property Tax Revenue	0.477	0.725	0.601	0.456	0.365
Other Tax Revenue	3.696	1.108	0.079	1.067	0.735
Sales Tax Revenue	1.296	1.427	2.020	1.224	1.841
Sales & Services Revenue	–1.013	0.748	–1.063	–0.737	–1.734
Intergovernmental Revenue	1.684	–0.394	3.048	–0.068	0.353
Other Miscellaneous Revenue	5.603	3.803	4.553	3.043	2.908

Note: Data are calculated using real dollars adjusted for inflation using the Consumer Price Index (CPI).

[1] Population is calculated as a six-year (2002–2007) average.

[2] Defined as gross retail sales. Data is only available from 2002–2005. Data for 2006 and 2007 is imputed using a linear projection.

TABLE 9.5 County Revenue Structures

	Property Tax Revenue	Other Tax Revenue	Sales Tax Revenue	Sales & Services Revenue	Intergov-ernmental Revenue	Other Misc. Revenue
Durham County	29.56%	2.21%	7.75%	6.13%	50.30%	4.05%
Forsyth County	55.02%	2.70%	18.14%	5.88%	14.75%	3.51%
Guilford County	49.86%	3.70%	14.88%	6.43%	20.55%	4.58%
Mecklenburg County	55.19%	2.85%	16.20%	6.28%	14.79%	4.68%
Wake County	50.82%	6.33%	14.07%	10.30%	14.40%	4.08%

Table 9.5 shows the six-year average proportion of revenue derived from each source for each county. These values were calculated by dividing the dollar amount of revenue derived from each source by total revenue; the proportions were then averaged over the six-year economic cycle (2002–2007). Common among local governments, Table 9.5 shows the counties derived much of their revenue from the property tax with every county except Durham County generating approximately 50–55% of total revenue from property taxation. The remainder of revenue for the counties varied in the proportions of other tax revenue, sales tax revenue, sales and services revenue, intergovernmental revenue, and other miscellaneous revenue comprising each county's aggregate structure. For example, Durham County generated an average of about 8% of total revenue from sales taxation, while the other four counties derived approximately 14 to 18% of total revenue from the sales tax. These proportions are useful for calculating aggregate income elasticities for the counties' revenue structures.

By weighting the elasticities of each revenue source by the proportion of total revenue derived from that source, the aggregate income elasticity of a local government's revenue structure can be determined. Based upon the method of Ladd and Weist (1987), each county's aggregate revenue income elasticity was calculated as $\sum_1^n p_{it} \times \varepsilon_{it}$ where p is the proportion of total revenue derived from each source (i) in a particular year (t) and e is the income elasticity relative to each source (i) in a particular year (t). For each county (n), the summation of all proportions multiplied by the associated elasticities yields the aggregate income elasticity of the county's revenue structure for each year. The median of these yearly aggregate income elasticities was then calculated and is reported in **Table 9.6**. Again, the median is used instead of the mean to control for outliers in the data.

As can be seen from the first column of Table 9.6, most revenue structures vary from inelastic to unit elastic. With the exception of Durham County that has a revenue portfolio of 1.145, all median aggregate income elasticities are below one. The first column of Table 9.6 reveals variation in the median elasticities across counties with three counties

Table 9.6 Median Income Elasticities and Median Percent Deviation

	Median Income Elasticity	Median Percent Deviation (Total Revenue)
Durham County	1.145	–3.19%
Forsyth County	0.547	3.45%
Guilford County	0.978	0.27%
Mecklenburg County	0.562	–5.27%
Wake County	0.647	6.46%

Note: Data are calculated using real dollars adjusted for inflation using the Consumer Price Index (CPI).

having inelastic revenue portfolios (Forsyth, Mecklenburg, and Wake Counties) and two having unit elastic revenue portfolios (Durham and Guilford Counties).

Taken together, Tables 9.4, 9.5, and 9.6 provide indication of the relationship between the income elasticity of individual revenue sources and the aggregate elasticity of a revenue structure. Overall, a revenue structure is most likely to exhibit aggregate income elasticity commensurate with the elasticity of individual sources comprising the largest portion of the structure. For example, Forsyth County generates approximately 55% of its total revenue from property taxation. With a median income elasticity of 0.725, property tax revenue is an inelastic source for this county. Accordingly, Forsyth County's revenue structure is the most inelastic among the counties with an aggregate median income elasticity of 0.547. This suggests that the county's resources are far less susceptible to changes in the economy affecting personal income and therefore likely produce more stable and predictable amounts of revenue; however, the growth potential of this revenue structure is more limited.

Counties that balance a variety of inelastic, unit elastic, and elastic revenue sources are likely to have a revenue structure with aggregate income elasticity closer to the unit elasticity the ACIR suggests. For example, Guilford County's revenue structure is relatively balanced as it consists of about one-fourth elastic sources (sales tax revenue, intergovernmental revenue, and miscellaneous revenue), one-half inelastic sources (property tax revenue and other tax revenue), and the remainder counter-cyclical sources (sales and services revenue). Accordingly, the county's revenue structure has aggregate median income elasticity nearly unit elastic at 0.978. This suggests the revenue growth of Guilford County should be roughly commensurate with economic changes affecting personal income and perhaps provide some protection from revenue declines during economic downturns. All else equal, inelastic or unit elastic revenue structures should be more stable than elastic revenue structures but will be more limited in terms of revenue growth.

The last two columns of Table 9.6 provide our measure of revenue volatility for each of the five counties. Revenue volatility is measured as the median percent deviation of annual revenue from the predicted trend for the 2002–2007 economic cycle. A larger median percent deviation (positive or negative) reflects greater revenue volatility or extent to which a county's total revenue deviated from what was expected. According to Table 9.6, the median percent deviation of total revenue varies significantly, ranging from -5.27% to 6.46%. Mecklenburg County has the greatest negative revenue volatility with a median percent deviation of -5.27; this county also has a revenue structure nearly most inelastic with aggregate median income elasticity of 0.562. The negative volatility indicates Mecklenburg County's total revenue maintained an annual average of roughly 5% lower than expected over the economic cycle. Conversely, the county with the least volatile revenue structure as evidenced by the median percent deviation of 0.27% has a revenue structure closest to unit elastic, which is Guilford County with an aggregate median income elasticity of 0.978. Table 9.6 provides limited evidence that counties with revenue structures close to unit elastic will likely experience lower revenue volatility.

Volatility of Resource Flows and Fiscal Health

The volatility of a local government's revenue structure negatively affects its fiscal health to the extent that the unpredictable revenues disrupt the government's ability to meet its ongoing financial, service, and capital obligations. Fiscal health is indicated by both a government's *resource flow* as well as its *resource stock*. Resource flow represents the cumulative inflows and outflows of resources over a period of time and is reported by state and local governments on the statement of activities. Resource stock represents accumulated resources, obligations, and net worth at a particular point in time and is reported by state and local governments on the statement of net assets. Assessing fiscal health on the basis of resource stock offers insight into a government's liquidity, solvency, and leverage (Rivenbark et al., 2008). However, using information pertaining to resource flow to determine relative fiscal health provides better indication of a government's dynamic ability to live within its means during the fiscal year, generate revenues sufficient to meet expenditures, avoid overreliance upon other governments for resources, and maintain service flexibility with the amount of resources committed to annual debt service (Rivenbark et al. 2008). This is because resource flow relates more directly to a government's operating or cash budget, reflects a government's financial position over the course of the fiscal year, and results from decisions made regarding sources comprising the revenue structure and expenditures for service provision. For example, cash flow measures the difference between cash sources and cash expenditures and is a key indicator of fiscal health (Swanson and Kavanagh 2009). The volatility of a local government's revenue structure has the greatest influence on the government's flow of resources as opposed to its resource stock. Local governments rely on the performance of their revenue structures to provide them with a stable and predictable flow of resources to finance necessary public service provision. In this regard, the composition of a local government's revenue structure is integral to its fiscal health.

Turning back to the volatility measures reported in Table 9.6, it is important to note that some of the median percent deviations are negative while the majority of values are positive. Positive deviations indicate total revenue exceeded predicted values on average over the six-year economic cycle, and negative deviations represent shortfalls on average. The latter outcome is less desirable as it creates the potential for service disruptions or might inhibit a local government from meeting its ongoing obligations, thus diminishing its fiscal health. Table 9.6 shows the two counties with revenue structures nearly unit elastic and slightly elastic (Durham and Guilford Counties) had the least revenue volatility of the five counties as measured by the median percent deviation. Meanwhile, the counties with the most inelastic revenue structures (Forsyth, Mecklenburg, and Wake Counties) had the greatest amounts of revenue volatility. A caveat, however, is that although Durham County's slightly elastic revenue structure exhibited lower volatility than the three counties with inelastic revenue structures, Durham County's actual revenue was less than expected as indicated by the negative median percent deviation. Conversely, although Forsyth and Wake Counties had greater revenue volatility over the six-year economic cycle, these inelastic revenue structures produced unexpectedly higher revenue on average. However, this pattern is not universal as Mecklenburg County with an inelastic revenue structure also had among the highest revenue volatility but also generated revenue amounts below expectations on average. The findings from Table 9.6 reiterate that unit elastic revenue structures are likely to produce more stable and predictable resource flows as the revenues comprising the structures are most likely to change commensurate with changes in the economy. This suggests at least a reserved implication that unit elastic revenue structures might help achieve more favorable outcomes regarding revenue volatility such that local governments are better able to maintain operations, meet obligations, and consequently improve fiscal health. And, departures from unit elasticity can lead to greater revenue volatility. However, the positive and negative volatility values suggest that volatile revenue structures might prove less harmful and perhaps beneficial in the short term if surplus revenues can be put into reserve or used to fill budgetary gaps. Overall, the evidence suggests that a local government's aggregate revenue income elasticity is directly linked to the volatility its revenue structure.

Among other factors, the flexibility and constraints imposed upon the revenue-generating capacity of local governments provide indications of fiscal well being (Pagano 1990). A key component and particular challenge for local governments' abilities to generate revenue and maintain good fiscal health is the adequacy of the base from which revenue is derived (Maher and Deller 2007). As such, a local government's fiscal health is affected by myriad controllable and uncontrollable factors stemming from the condition of the overall economy and mediated through the composition of its overall revenue structure and consequent volatility of its resource flows. As discussed throughout this chapter, with consideration of the elasticity and covariation of individual sources, a local government can design its revenue structure to minimize the volatility of its resource flows. In effect, a combination of taxes/fees with varying income elasticities helps to insulate the overall revenue structure and reduce associated volatility. In addition, local governments might also take alternative precautions like accumulating reserve slack resources that can be relied upon during economic downturns if revenue growth is unable to meet necessary service provision. Such a combination of approaches can help local governments maintain better fiscal health over the long term.

Endnotes

1. The income elasticity of a revenue source or base differs from the rate elasticity of a revenue base, which measures the response of the base to a change in the tax/fee rate applied to it. The discussion throughout this chapter focuses primarily on the income elasticity of revenue sources/bases, which is the response of a source/base to a change in income within the economy.
2. Elasticities may be calculated for any revenue source (i.e., taxes, charges and fees, and intergovernmental revenue); however, the most common calculations in the literature deal with tax sources.
3. Actual elasticity calculations should use real dollar values adjusted for inflation.
4. However, this classification scheme is rather rigid and a looser interpretation of elasticity values might be warranted. In such a case, it is reasonable to classify elasticity values greater than 1.25 as elastic, values between 1.24 and 0.76 as unit elastic, and elasticity values less than 0.75 as inelastic.
5. Real dollars adjusted for inflation should be used for calculations.
6. Necessarily, this is a linear projection of total revenue over time. If we assume that revenue grows at a steady and predictable rate, a linear growth trend is appropriate. However, it may be useful to adapt that assumption given local conditions.
7. Any central tendency statistic can be calculated to develop the overall measure of revenue volatility during a specified time period. The measure of central tendency that best fits the distribution of the data should be chosen.
8. Most of the academic literature on elasticities focuses on the big three taxes (i.e., property, sales, and income); however, because income taxes are not available to or not levied by most local governments, they are excluded from this discussion and we focus exclusively on property and sales tax elasticities. In summary, the extant research on state income taxes suggests the income tax base is unit elastic or somewhat elastic in the short term (0.857 to 1.392) and slightly inelastic in the long term (0.83 to 0.89), depending on the estimation technique. Income tax revenue is roughly the same as the base in the short term (0.857 to 1.392) but rather elastic in the long term (1.924 to 1.897). Overall, these findings suggest that the income tax is rather unstable in the long term. See Holcombe and Sobel (1997) and Bruce, Fox, and Tuttle (2006).
9. Because local options for sales taxes are typically imposed upon a state's predefined base, exemptions from taxation are usually a matter of state policy and not the discretion of local governments. Of the 45 states imposing a sales and use tax, 32 states provide an exemption for and 7 states tax at a lower rate the sales of nonprepared food from a grocery store that is intended for at-home consumption (CCH Editorial Staff, 2008).
10. Mecklenburg County's budgetary information is reported on a July 1 through June 30 fiscal year. The National Bureau of Economic Research (NBER) dated the most recently completed peak-to-peak economic cycle between March 2001 and December 2007. See NBER, U.S. Business Cycle Expansions and Contractions: http://www.nber.org/cycles.html.

11. Elasticities reported for a particular year were calculated using percent changes from the prior year. For example, the 2004 elasticities used percent changes between 2003 and 2004 for calculation. The median is for the six-year time frame and represents the expected elasticity over an economic cycle.
12. Beginning in FY2006, the State of North Carolina changed the reporting of the sales tax base from gross retail sales to total taxable sales. For comparison purposes, we continued with the original definition of gross retail sales by imputing FY2006 and FY2007 values using a linear projection of the trend in gross retail sales.
13. Intergovernmental revenue remained fairly constant in absolute terms, but increasing amounts of total revenue lead to a decline in the importance of this revenue source.

Glossary

Fiscal Health: the ability to continue to deliver services at current levels; the ability of a government to live within its means during the fiscal year, generate revenues sufficient to meet expenditures, avoid overreliance upon other governments for resources, and maintain service flexibility with the amount of resources committed to annual debt service.

Growth and Stability Tradeoff: Often, revenue sources that exhibit strong positive growth are also associated with increased instability in that growth trend over time. Conversely, slower growing revenue sources are often more stable in the face of economic turmoil. Therefore, local governments face a tradeoff between fast growing, but unstable revenue sources and slower growing, but stable revenue sources.

Income Elasticity: the change in revenue in response to a change in the economy; specifically, the change in a revenue or base in response to a change in personal income.

Resource Flow: the cumulative inflows and outflows of resources over a period of time; reported by state and local governments on the statement of activities.

Resource Stock: the accumulated resources, obligations, and net worth at a particular point in time; reported by state and local governments on the statement of net assets.

Revenue Diversification: a revenue structure that relies on a variety of revenue sources with no imbalanced use of one revenue source at the expense of other revenue sources.

Revenue Volatility: a short-term concept that measures the deviation of actual revenue from a predicted trend; the median percent deviation of annual revenue from a predicted trend over an economic cycle.

Discussion Questions

1. Which factors affecting its overall revenue structure are uncontrollable for a local government? Which factors are partially controllable? How do these factors shape the revenue structure of a local government?
2. How are tax base and revenue information used to calculate revenue elasticity? Does it matter which is used? Why or why not?

3. What is revenue volatility and why is it a concern for local governments? How is revenue volatility connected to elasticity?
4. What considerations should be given in determining the composition of a local government's revenue structure? How are these factors related to elasticity and revenue volatility?
5. What is local government fiscal health and why is it an important concern? How do resource stocks and flows provide different indications of fiscal health? How is revenue volatility connected to local government fiscal health?

Recommended Resources

Bahl Jr., R. W. (2004). Local government expenditures and revenues. In J. R. Aronson and E. Schwartz (Eds.) *Management policies in local government finance* (5th ed.). Washington, D.C.: International City/County Management Association.

Bland, R. L. (2005). *A revenue guide for local government* (2nd ed.). Washington, D.C.: ICMA Press.

Groves, S. M., Valente, M. G., and Nollenberger, K. (2003). *Evaluating financial condition: A handbook for local government* (4th ed.). Washington, D.C.: International City/County Management Association.

Hendrick, R. M. (2011). *Managing the fiscal metropolis: The financial policies, practices, and health of suburban municipalities*. Washington, D.C.: Georgetown University Press.

Schroeder, L. D. 2004. Forecasting local revenues and expenditures. In J. R. Aronson and E. Schwartz (Eds.). *Management policies in local government finance* (5th ed.). Washington, D.C.: International City/County Management Association.

References

Berne, R., and Schramm, R. (1986). *The financial analysis of governments.* Englewood Cliffs, NJ: Prentice Hall.

Borcherding, T. E., and Deacon, R. T. (1972). The demand for service in non-federal governments. *American Economic Review*, *62*(5), 891–901.

Bridges, B., Jr. (1964). The elasticity of the property tax base: Some cross-section estimates. *Land Economics*, *40*(4), 449–451.

Bruce, D. J., Fox, W. F., and Tuttle, M. H. (2006). Tax base elasticities: A multi-state analysis of long-run and short-run dynamics. *Southern Economic Journal*, *73*(2), 315–341.

Carroll, D. A. (2009). Diversifying municipal government revenue structures: Fiscal illusion or instability? *Public Budgeting and Finance*, *29*(1), 27–48.

Carroll, D. A., and Stater, K. J. (2009). Revenue diversification in nonprofit organizations: Does it lead to financial stability? *Journal of Public Administration Research and Theory*, *19*(4), 947–966.

CCH Editorial Staff. (2008). *2009 State tax handbook*. Chicago: CCH.

Fox, W. F., and Campbell, C. (1984). Stability of the state sales tax income elasticity. *National Tax Journal, 37*(2), 201–212.

Groves, H. M., and Kahn. C. H. (1952). The stability of state and local tax yields. *American Economic Review, 42*(1), 87–102.

Holcombe, R. G., and Sobel, R. S. (1997). *Growth and variability in state tax revenue: An anatomy of state fiscal crises.* Westport, CN.: Greenwood Press.

Kurnow, E. (1963). On the elasticity of the real property tax. *The Journal of Finance, 18*(1), 56–58.

Ladd, H. F., and Weist, D. R. (1987). State and local tax systems: Balance among taxes vs. balance among policy goals. In Frederick D. Stocker (Ed.), *The Quest for Balance in State-Local Revenue Structures* (pp. 39–69). Cambridge: Lincoln Institute of Land Policy.

Maher, C., and Deller, S. (2007). Fiscal health of Wisconsin municipalities: An update for 2007. University of Wisconsin, Agricultural and Applied Economics, Staff Paper Series.

Netzer, D. (1958). The outlook for fiscal needs and resources of state and local governments. *American Economic Review, 48*(2), 317–327.

Otsuka, Y., and Braun, B. M. (1999). The random coefficient approach for estimating tax revenue stability and growth. *Public Finance Review, 27*(6), 665–676.

Pagano, M. A. (1990). State-local relations in the 1990s. *Annals of the American Academy of Political and Social Science, 509*, 94–105.

Rivenbark, W. C., Roenigk, D. J., and Allison, G. S. (2008). *Conceptualizing financial condition in local government.* Paper presented at the *Southeastern Conference on Public Administration.*

Sexton, T. E., and Sexton, R. J. (1986). Re-evaluating the income elasticity of the property tax base. *Land Economics, 62*(2), 182–191.

Shannon, J. (1987). State revenue diversification—the search for balance. In Frederick D. Stocker (Ed.), *The quest for balance in state-local revenue structures* (pp. 9–37). Cambridge: Lincoln Institute of Land Policy.

Sobel, R. S., and Holcombe, R. G. (1996). Measuring the growth and variability of tax bases over the business cycle. *National Tax Journal, 49*(4), 535–552.

Swanson, C. J., and Kavanagh, S. C. (2009). Identifying Shortfalls: The Importance of Cash Flow Analysis in Times of Fiscal Stress. *Government Finance Review, 25*(2), 34–38.

Williams, W. V., Anderson, R. M., Froehle, D. O., and Lamb, K. L. (1973). The stability, growth, and stabilizing influence of state taxes. *National Tax Journal, 26*(2), 267–274.

White, F. C. (1983). Trade-off in growth and stability in state taxes. *National Tax Journal, 36*(1), 103–114.

Part V

Business Cycle, Bubbles, and Reserve Funds

Cutback Management for the 21st Century

Chapter 10

Fiscal Stress and Cutback Management Among State and Local Governments[1]

What Have We Learned and What Remains to Be Learned?

by Christina Plerhoples and Eric A. Scorsone

Introduction

Throughout much of our history, state and *local government* budgeting in the United States has been based on the assumption that public revenues and expenditures will grow continuously. This changed during the 1970s, however, when city and state budgets underwent widespread contractions. This was the first time in the post-WW II era when state and local governments were forced to address revenue constraints on a major scale. During this time, budgeting shifted from a "do anything at any cost" attitude to an "era of limits," and cutback management emerged (McTighe, 1979). *Cutback management* was defined during this period as the management of "organizational change toward lower levels of resource consumption and organizational activity" (Levine, 1979). Since that time, it has become almost an article of faith that every few years state and local governments will face some type of fiscal crisis. Some even argue that we have entered a "period of permanent fiscal crisis" (Osborne and Hutchinson, 2004).

From the 1970s until the early 2000s, cutback management was coupled with increased revenue actions in order for governments to respond to fiscal crises. During the recession of the early 2000s, however, governments in the United States chose to predominantly cut services and to implement only minimal and targeted increases to taxes, possibly because of the greater availability of reserve and savings funds.

The Great Recession of the late 2000s, the largest recession since the Great Depression, has threatened fiscal security at all levels of government, sending cutback management into a new and even more extreme phase among state and local governments. Government officials are being forced to adapt to an environment where service demands are rising as both short- and long-term prospects for revenue are among the bleakest in modern history. Because they are required to balance their budgets under state law, city governments will have to confront decisions in the coming years about cutting spending, raising additional revenues, taking on additional debt, or drawing down reserves that have predominantly run dry.

An important question that will emerge from the Great Recession is whether it has followed the trend of the early 2000s by involving mainly cuts to spending and only minimal increases to taxes, which would signify a breakpoint between previous cutback management strategies and those of the 2000s. If so, another important question is how this new method of recessionary budgeting will affect long-term growth and fiscal sustainability.

This chapter examines these questions in three ways. First, it outlines the history of thinking on cutback management in the United States among state and local governments. Second, it assesses the preliminary evidence and explanations for a shift in state and local government responses to fiscal stress in the 2000s. Finally, it advances proposals for a future research agenda to further our understanding of this potential phenomenon and its policy implications.

Cutback Management and Budgeting

Before fully assessing the role of cutback management and budgeting in the last decade, a review of the relevant literature is useful. Since the 1970s, scholars have begun to seriously engage in understanding the how and why of cutback management in government, using both a positive and a normative approach. This section describes the evolution of budgeting theory from the late 1970s through the early 2000s.

Cutback Management's Origins

In 1978 and 1979, in a series of books and articles, Charles Levine began the modern study of cutback management and budgeting. Levine (1978) argued that "we know very little about the decline of public organizations and the management of cutbacks." In attempting to address this shortcoming, Levine analyzed both the causes of and responses to fiscal stress and decline. He named four major causes: political vulnerability, organizational atrophy, problem depletion, and environmental entropy. Political vulnerability refers to the high level of fragility within a governmental organization that limits its capacity to resist budget decrements. Organization atrophy occurs when there is declining performance and internal atrophy, a situation that can often go unnoticed in public organizations because they lack the market-generated revenues to signal a malfunction. Problem depletion is when the government entity is involved in solving a short-, medium-, or long-term problem such as a natural disaster or a war that puts stress on its fiscal capacity. Finally, environmental entropy refers to the erosion of the capacity of the government to support public organization, such as with a declining economic base that is common in today's state and local governments. Political vulnerability and organizational atrophy were envisioned as internal forces that threatened an organization to restructure or eliminate services or programs. Problem depletion and environmental atrophy represent external threats to organizational fitness.

More importantly, this was one of the first modern attempts to create a taxonomy or set of categories for understanding cutback responses. One of the most important distinctions that Levine made was between efficiency and equity cuts. Efficiency cuts represent the type of rational management thinking where choices are made based on evidence of performance or cost savings. Equity cuts represent a political type of calculus where the pain is shared across the organization. He also laid out a range of cutback tactics such as implementing hiring freezes, renegotiating long-term contracts, improving productivity, establishing study commissions, adopting new user charges, and threatening to cut vital or popular programs. All of these tactics are familiar on the cutback management stage of today. However, Levine made no attempt to determine which tactics will be used under what circumstances or with what frequency. Thus, the taxonomy was created but no attempt was made to create a cause-and-effect framework.

A year later, Levine (1979) reviewed these issues again. In this article, he identified nine reasons why managing cutbacks are so difficult, focusing on how they force management to rethink the process of organizational development and growth. In the conclusion, Levine proposed that research was needed in four areas of cutback management: the development of a baseline inventory of tools and techniques for managing cutbacks, the creation of methods that can perfect the democratic processes for allocating cuts making them effective yet equitable, thorough analysis of the ethical dimensions of cutbacks, and a greater understanding of how cuts affect the public expectations and support for government.

Allen Schick (1983) was another influential author in this early period. He wrote that incremental budgeting was facing a period where budgets would be constrained if not declining. An important question that Schick raised was whether decremental budgeting was just incremental budgeting in reverse. In other words, can cuts be made in the same increments and manner in which they were budgeted in the first place? Schick argued, in fact, that decremental budgeting was much more difficult and likely to elicit conflict between agencies and stakeholders and also likely to be far more unstable than incremental budgeting. He also felt that a theory was needed to determine not only which cutback strategies would be used when, but also why certain programs and agencies were favored over others.

Following closely on the heels of Levine, Jick and Murray (1982) set out to understand cutback management. In their framework, they argued that several forces drive cutback decisions. One main force is the rational paradigm in which decision makers use information and knowledge to prioritize and determine the most efficient approaches to cutting. A second paradigm is described as a political approach where the relative internal and external collations are assessed and decisions are made on the basis of this relative political power. Jick and Murray claim that the source of cuts along with the distribution of power among agencies and groups within a government is the key to explaining the approaches managers and politicians take. Here we see the first attempt to build an explicit framework with decision variables and explanatory variables, although no empirical work accompanied the framework.

Downs and Rocke (1983) attempted to use the occurrence of municipal revenue decline to test alternative theories of budgetary decision making. They test three theories: interest group strategies, managerial strategies, and bureaucratic process theories. Interest group theory is tied to the notion that budgetary outcomes are based on the distribution of power. Managerial theory suggests that budgetary decisions are made based on mandated expenditures. And finally, bureaucratic process theory implies that budgetary decisions are made by bounded rationality-driven incrementalism. They tested these theories using longitudinal budget change data from two major cities, Pittsburgh and San Diego. Their findings indicated support for the managerial theory, implying that given that much of the budget is uncontrollable in the short or medium term, governments will seek to address the controllable part of the budget in cutback strategies. This will consist of random processes across governments implying that no budget cutting algorithm exists in a consistent fashion as predicted by a bureaucratic process or incrementalist type approach.

A 1983 article by Miller reviewed the various practices that states adopted to deal with the severe recession of the early 1980s. The list includes many of the items we now take for granted such as travel restrictions, physical space strategies, hiring freezes, across-the-board cuts, and the use of bonds among other things. Although Miller reports some basic data concerning usage of these strategies, which is fairly mixed across states, no empirical evidence is provided as to why certain strategies are used by certain states or the relative effectiveness of these strategies.

Also in 1983, Wolman laid out a theoretical model for responses to fiscal stress at the local level and tested it through a series of case studies in the United States and the United Kingdom. Wolman's model suggested that a governmental unit will attempt to balance expenditures and revenues through means that minimize the decline in services to the public and the loss of employment of existing employees. In his case study analysis used to test this hypothesis, Wolman found that local governments first attempt to buy time in the face of fiscal stress through the use of devices that in the short run require neither expenditure and service reductions nor revenue increases. This is commonly achieved through the drawing down of existing surpluses. When time runs out and these devices are no longer available, local governments must then make decisions about either cutting spending or increasing revenues. Wolman found that governments that are not required to consult the electorate in a referendum are more likely to raise own-source revenues than to cut spending. Also, the farther in time the government is from an election, the more likely it is to increase revenue rather than cut spending. If expenditure cuts are necessary, Wolman found that local governments attempt to make these cuts in ways that least disrupt aggregate service levels, such as through efficiency gains or through privatization of services. He argued that these findings verify his belief that governments behave as organizations concerned with maintaining an equilibrium relationship with their external and internal environments.

Later, Wolman (1986) used the concept of innovation diffusion, developed in the sciences and technology literature, to assess cutback strategies in government. He argued that the prevailing cutback literature had failed to clearly define innovation and thus it was unclear if governments under fiscal stress were more or less innovative. It could be argued, as Cyert and March (1963) did that a stress or performance gap could lead to searches for more innovative behavior. At the same time, surplus or slack resources are key to investing in innovative new practices and strategies. One tentative conclusion Wolman reached is that governments under fiscal stress will seek out productivity or internal enhancements of existing services as opposed to adopting services, which requires slack resources. Again, an attempt is made to ascertain important contextual factors for cutback management but no empirical evidence is brought to bear on the problem.

A few years later, West and Davis (1988) discussed a different angle concerning the role of administrative values in cutback management. Their base argument was that conflicting value systems in public administration are at play in determining the course of action that will be taken during a retrenchment process. They depicted these value systems as consisting of administrative efficiency, political responsiveness, individual rights, and social equity. Using survey data from more than 1,000 personnel directors in municipal governments, West and Davis found that public safety is targeted least for cuts as compared with program areas such as leisure and social services. They found that administrative value systems do not appear to explain the types of cuts being enacted. More prominently, a preferred policy hierarchy appears to be a better explanatory variable for retrenchment decisions.

By the end of the 1980s, more than a decade of research had been conducted on cutback management and budgeting. Over the course of the decade, a strong taxonomy had been built regarding the types of actions or measures that managers and politicians might exercise in addressing fiscal stress. Furthermore, an attempt had been made to understand the contextual factors that would drive which types of cutback decisions were to be made. However, lacking from the knowledge base were the short- and long-run implications of these cutback decisions as well as concrete empirical evidence to back up the conceptual and theoretical frameworks.

Berne and Stiefel (1993) took one of the first attempts to understand the effects of cutback management on long-term public sector outcomes. The study was aimed at understanding the impact of education cuts New York City made on relevant variables throughout the 1980s. Their findings indicated that in many cases, the effects of cutbacks were short term only such as those relating to teacher salaries and operating budgets. In some areas however, such as capital expenditures, maintenance, and total teacher positions, the cuts did have a long-term impact. The researchers warned that decision makers should be cautious in making cutbacks to address short-term budgetary problems and be conscious of the potential negative ramifications of some of those decisions on long-term viability. Further research of this nature was clearly needed to confirm and assess these findings in the context of other geographies and service areas.

Bartle (1996) examined the cutback responses of cities in New York State, excluding New York City. He stated that there were three prevailing theories to explain budgetary cutbacks. One is the familiar incrementalism in which a type of "decrementalism" takes over during a decline. In the second approach, administrators follow a specified set of actions to reduce expenditures depending on the degree of the downturn. The final framework relates to the "garbage can theory of administrative decision making," saying that given the last of set goals or objectives, there will be a hodgepodge of fairly random responses across governments in response to revenue declines. Bartle finds little "systemic responsiveness" among cities in addressing cutbacks. He argues in the conclusion that his findings support Downs and Rocke (1984) in that there is "little evidence of any budget cutting algorithm based on stable account priorities."

The literature from the 1970s to the 1990s was inconclusive as to whether there was a rhyme or a reason to be found in cutback management strategies. Strategies during this era did, however, include both expenditure cuts and revenue increases. Some evidence suggests that a shift occurred in strategies between that period and the post-2001 era, during which time cutbacks began to be focused mainly on expenditure cuts with little changes to revenues. The next section discusses thinking on this issue.

A New Era in Cutback Management: Post 2001 and the Great Recession

The recession that began in 2007, or the Great Recession, has been deemed the worst economic downturn since the Great Depression of the 1930's. In fiscal year 2010 alone, states faced the largest budget gap on record, and this gap is expected to grow in 2011 to greater than $200 billion. In total, states will have dealt with a budget shortfall of at least $380 billion for 2010 and 2011 (Johnson, Oliff, and Williams, 2009). The Great Recession will affect state governments long after it has subsided at the federal level. In fact, state governments are expected to suffer the effects of the recession for ten years in total—what some are beginning to call the lost decade.

State finances and their cutback budgeting decisions affect local governments because local government revenue sharing is often one of the first things to be cut at the state level. City and other local governments will also feel the effects of the recession directly. This effect lags behind that at the federal and state level because of property tax assessment cycles in which it takes several years for property tax revenues to accurately reflect the totality of changes in housing values. Property tax bills typically reflect the values of property taxes anywhere from 18 months to several years prior to the date. It can also take several months for city sales tax revenues to reflect changes in consumption, largely because of collection and administration issues (Hoene and Pagano, 2009). Many cities rely solely on property taxes as their main source of revenue, while others have more diversified revenue streams including local sales and income taxes. Therefore, the severity and timing of the recession on different local governments will depend upon their specific tax structure. Some evidence suggests that both the Great Recession and that of the early 2000s signified a shift in cutback responses away from revenue increases and toward expenditure reductions. The next section analyzes this hypothesis in more detail.

A Shift in Cutback Responses?

State and local government reactions to the recession of the early 2000s favored budget cuts and restructuring over tax increases to a much greater degree than previous recessions. The increasing adoption of *budget stabilization funds* and other government savings may help to account for this shift in behavior. State and local government savings only began to slowly increase after WW II. The pattern began to change during the mid-1970s, as can be seen in **Figure 10.1**.[2] This was the period when states began to adopt so-called countercyclical or budget stabilization funds. Starting in 1991, but particularly accelerating in the 2000s, savings and dissavings swings were much larger than before and correlated with periods of recessions and prosperity. This signified the use of stabilization funds during times of fiscal stress.

Figures 10.2 and **10.3** break governments savings into state government savings and local government savings. As can be seen in Figure 10.2 state government savings accounted for much of the dramatic swings in total state and government savings. Figure 10.3 shows that local government swings in savings were not as drastic as those of state governments. In fact, there were no periods of aggregate dissaving at the local government level. Reserves were built up dramatically in the late 1990s and early 2000s and then partially used up during the recession of the early 2000s and nearly finished off by the Great Recession.

Revenue increases.

Stabilization funds may only be part of the explanation for how governments responded to the most recent recessions. A second set of factors affecting cutback decisions are the challenges state and local governments face when attempting to implement tax increases

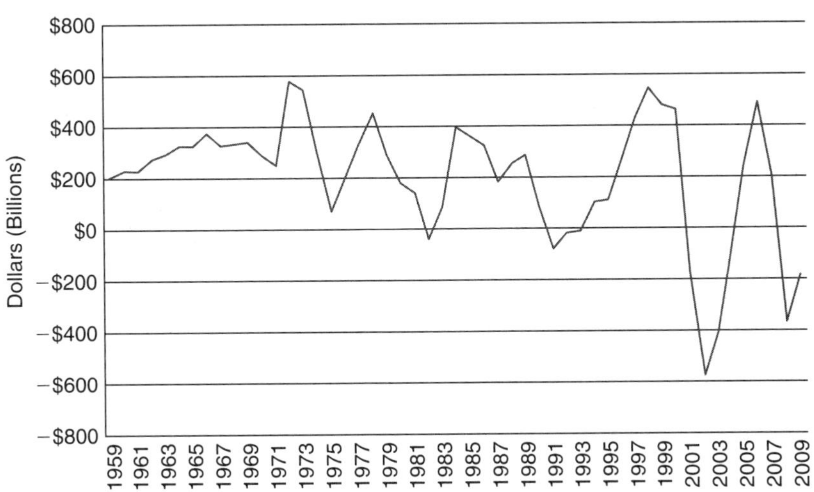

Figure 10.1 Real State and Local Government Net Savings, 1959–2009

Data source: Bureau of Economic Analysis, 2008

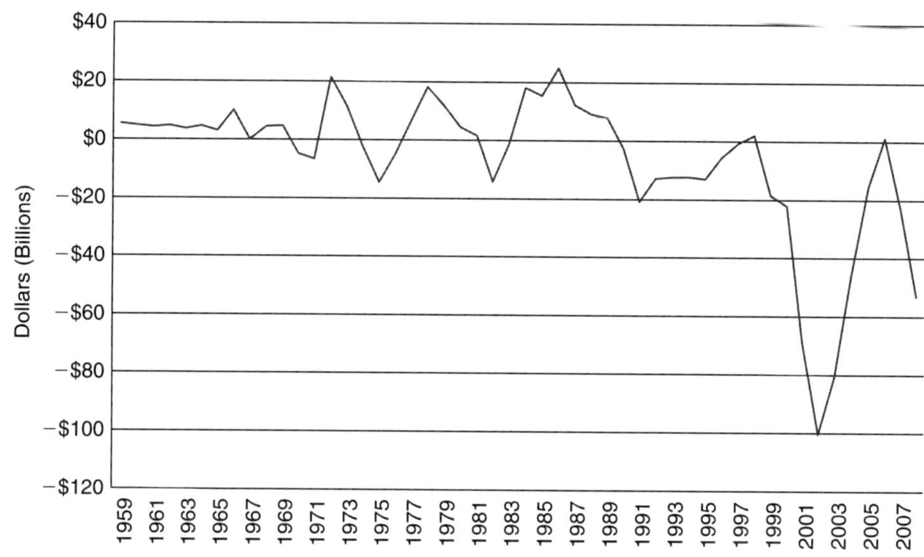

Figure 10.2 Real State Government Net Savings, 1959–2008

Data source: Bureau of Economic Analysis, 2008

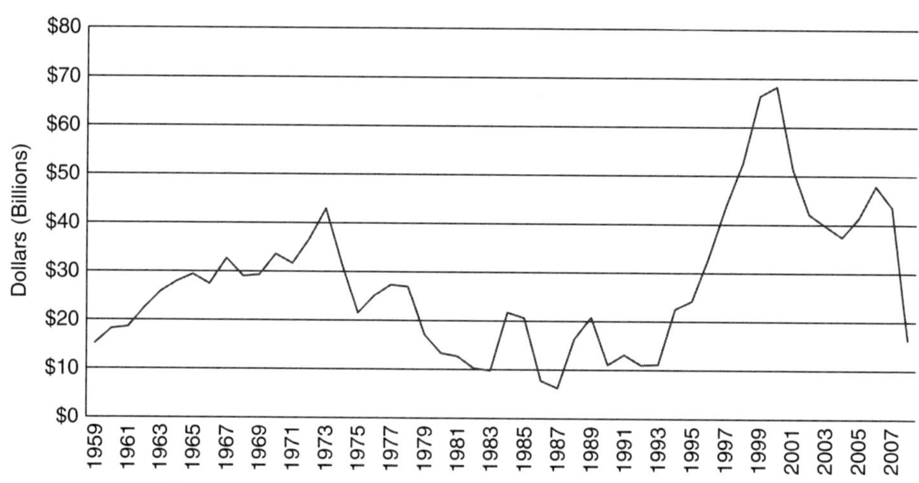

Figure 10.3 Real Local Government Net Savings, 1959–2008

Data source: Bureau of Economic Analysis, 2008

and revenue enhancements. Maag and Merriman (2003) found extensive empirical evidence to support the fact that states were far less reliant on tax increases during the recession of the early 2000s than during previous recessions. Their argument was that states face political and legal challenges in raising taxes and that large reserve or rainy-day funds make it less likely in the short term that states need to raise taxes. They estimated that states had only increased taxes one-third as much in the 2001 recession and the aftermath as they had in the recession of the early 1990s. **Figures 10.4** and **10.5** show an increasing

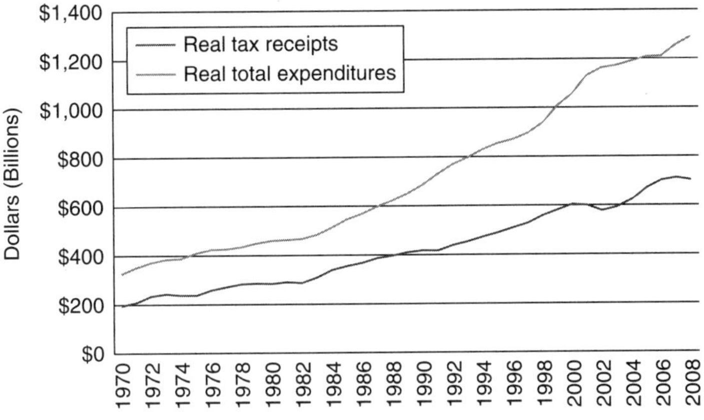

Figure 10.4 Real State Government Tax Receipts and Expenditures, 1970–2008

Data source: Bureau of Economic Analysis, 2008

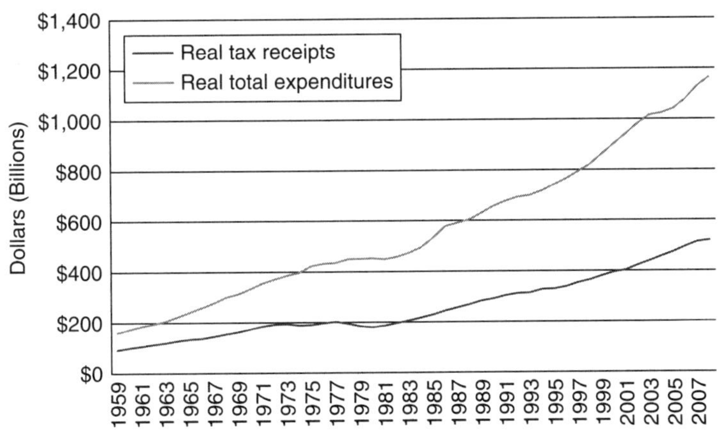

Figure 10.5 Real Local Government Tax Receipts and Expenditures, 1959–2008

Data source: Bureau of Economic Analysis, 2008

spread between tax receipts and total expenditures at both the state and local government level since the 1970s. The state government tax receipts show a decrease in tax receipts during the recession of the early 2000s and then another decrease during the early years of the Great Recession. Expenditure increases, on the other hand, appear to have slowed during the recession of the early 2000s more than during the recessions of the 70s, 80s, and 90s. This implies that state governments may have leaned more toward reducing expenditures than toward raising revenues during times of fiscal stress post 2000.

A closer look at the change in state and local government tax receipts during the beginning of the Great Recession shows a dramatic decrease from 2005 to 2008 for state government tax receipts and from 2006 to 2008 for local government tax receipts as can be seen in **Figure 10.6**. The end of 2008 and the beginning of 2009 were considered to be the worst period in the last 50 years for state revenues.

According to a report by the Rockefeller Institute, total state tax collections declined for five consecutive quarters through April 2010, and total revenues were down 8.6% from the same quarter two years earlier, or 18% less than what would be expected based on normal growth patterns. After adjusting for inflation, state tax revenues are at about the same level as they were 10 years ago even though the nation's population has increased by approximately 10% during that period (Boyd and Dadayan, 2010). Local taxes have not been hit quite as hard and have shown a relatively strong growth of 4.6% in 2011 according to the Rockefeller report. Property taxes actually rose by 5.6% during that quarter.

As of early 2009, some states had taken measures to increase revenues during this most recent crisis, yet on a smaller scale than expenditure cuts as can be seen in **Figure 10.7**. By that time, 30 states had raised taxes in one or more areas and another 7 are considering such measures. These increases include vehicles taxes and fees (12 states), increases to

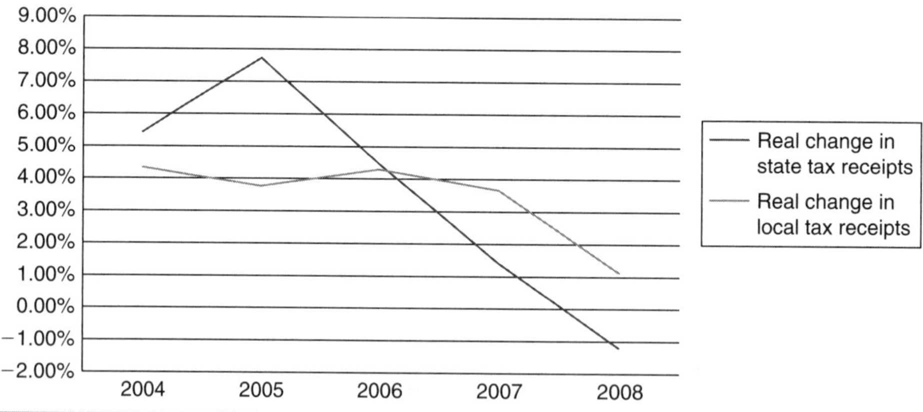

Figure 10.6 Real Change in State and Local Government Tax Receipts, 2004–2008

Data source: The Federal Reserve, 2010

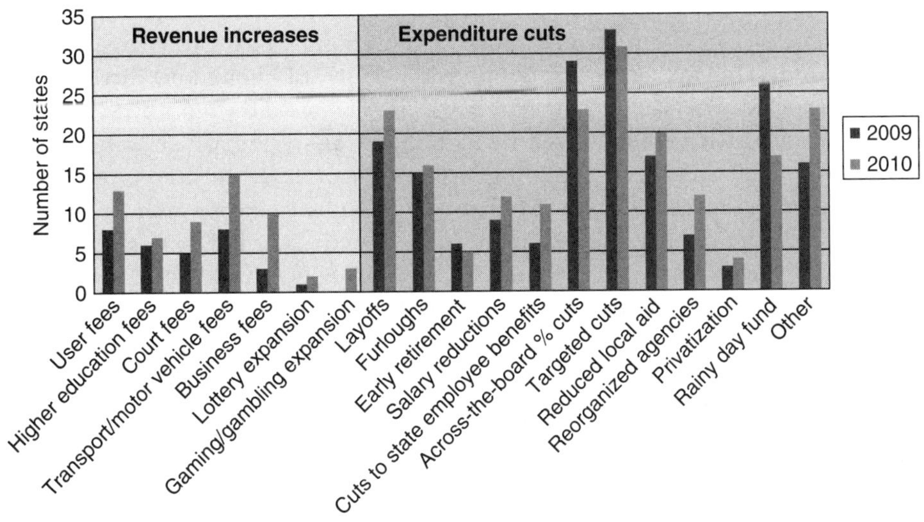

Figure 10.7 Strategies Used by States to Reduce or Eliminate Budget Gaps, 2009–early 2010

Data source: Fiscal Survey of States, 2009

personal income taxes either by the addition of new upper income tax brackets or reductions in various credits, exemptions, or deductions (11 states), increases in sales taxes (12 states), increases in business taxes (11 states), and increases to tobacco and alcoholic beverage taxes (15 states). These tax increases, similar to those in the early 2000s, have been narrow and targeted and have not been great enough to solve state budget shortfalls (Johnson, Nicholas, and Pennington, 2009).

Cities have also attempted to increase revenues to balance budgets, the most common method being increases to the levels of fees for services. At least one in five cities reported increases in the number of fees or the level of impact and development fees. The NLC survey showed that one in four cities increased their property tax rates whereas increases in sales tax rates, income tax rates, and other tax rates were less common (Hoene and Pagano, 2009). A recent Pew study of 13 major cities throughout the United States showed that only four of the cities studied sought to enact major tax increases as part of their budget balancing. Although all four of those cities ultimately enacted the increases, they all involved controversy and delay. Most of the other cities in the study decided not to consider tax increases even as their fiscal situations continued to worsen (The PEW Charitable Trust [PEW], 2009). Therefore, it seems that cities are also focusing more on expenditure cuts than on revenue increases, similar to state governments.

However, a state tax update by the National Conference of State Legislatures (NCSL) shows that numerous states have increased taxes and fees to help fill budget gaps, resulting in a net tax increase of $28.6 billion for fiscal year 2010. According to the report, the tax increases represent 3.7% of prior year total tax collections, which is the largest increase since 1991. In fact, all tax categories monitored by the NCSL showed net increases in FY 2010. These included personal income taxes, which were raised the most by $11.4 billion; business taxes, which were increased by $2 billion; sales taxes, which were raised by $7.2 billion, and all other areas including health industry taxes, tobacco taxes, taxes on alcoholic beverages, motor vehicle and fuel taxes, other miscellaneous taxes, and property taxes. States also approved numerous nontax revenue actions including fees and accelerations bringing the combined revenue increase to $33.7 billion for FY 2010 compared to $9.2 billion in FY 2009 (Waisanen and Haggerty, 2010).

Many of these changes may be accounted for by a few large states that disproportionately altered their taxes in FY 2010. These states include California, which raised nearly $11 billion in new taxes, New York, which enacted $6.9 billion in tax increases in FY 2010, and Florida, which approved excise tax and fee increases that represented a substantial portion of the net increases in those categories (Waisanen and Haggerty, 2010). California and New York alone account for more than half of the recent tax increases. Therefore, it is unclear how much of these increases are due only to these few states and how much represent increases in all states in general. In addition, the total revenue increases of $33.7 billion account for only 17% of the 2010 state budget gap of $196 billion. The rest of the budget gap will still need to be closed through other means.

These recent tax increases may imply that state governments are returning to revenue increases as a major source of managing fiscal stress during the Great Recession, but this is very preliminary evidence. The effects seem to be isolated to a few large states and by no means fill the budget gap that states face. We will have to wait to see whether this shift will be widespread.

Expenditure reductions.

State and local governments have also taken actions to reduce expenditures to deal with the Great Recession. According to the Center on Budget and Policy Priorities, midyear state budget gaps were closed predominantly by gubernatorial spending cuts, with at least 43 states having imposed cuts that target vulnerable residents. For the states that made cuts, employee layoffs and furloughs were among the most common response (7 states), as were reductions in funding to K-12 education (3 states); cuts to higher education (2 states); cuts in rates to Medicaid providers (2 states); cuts in school transportation, child care, and mental health services (1 state); and cuts pending for significant reductions in funding to local governments (1 state) (Johnson, Nicholas, and Pennington, 2009). These changes as well as the early revenue actions can be seen in Figure 10.7 (note: this graph does not account for the most recent revenue measures taken by the states, which would drastically increase the amount of revenue increases).

City governments have also had to make drastic budget changes to survive the current crisis. Most cities have instituted hiring freezes and layoffs as well as delays and cancellations of planned infrastructure projects. One in three cities has made cuts in services other than public safety and human social services. As of the most recent survey from the National League of Cities (NLC) from 2008 to 2009, 9 in 10 cities made spending cuts in 2009, and 82% predicted that their cities would make further cuts in 2010 (Hoene and Pagano, 2009).

Debt financing.
State and local governments may also use debt financing as a fiscal stress management tool. Government borrowing (and similarly government saving) enables governments to detach the flow of current revenues from the flow of current expenditures. This helps to smooth taxes and expenditures over time (Wildasin, 2009).

The ability of state and local governments to borrow money depends upon their fiscal health and the confidence that people have in their ability to repay their debt. The faith in municipal bonds, for instance, has fluctuated during the course of the Great Recession, and rating agencies are downgrading some cities because of fiscal stress (The Bond Buyer, 2010). The municipal bond market in particular was depressed at the end of 2008, which can be seen to influence total state and local government lending and borrowing in **Figure 10.8**.

Figures 10.9 and **10.10** break net lending into state government and local government lending. As can be seen in Figure 10.9, state government borrowing increased drastically during the recession of the early 2000s, and is beginning to increase during the Great Recession as well. Figure 10.10 shows that local government borrowing never recovered from the recession of the early 2000s, and may be headed even further down during the Great Recession.

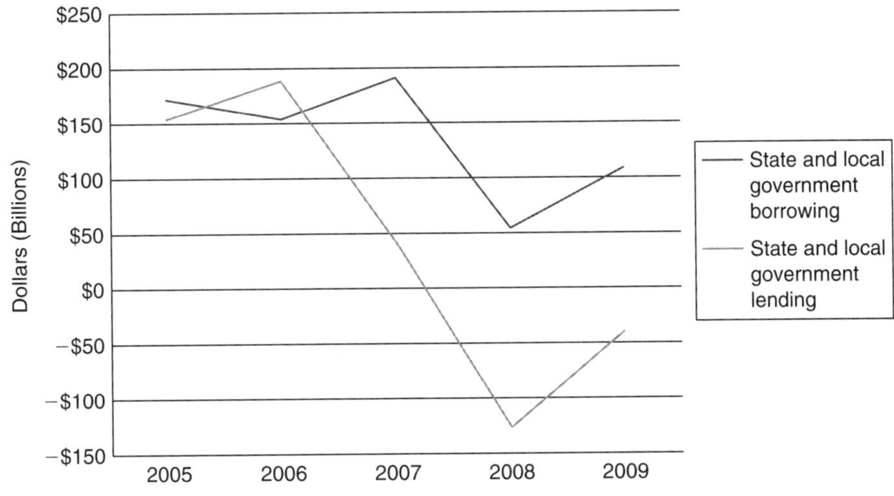

Figure 10.8 State and Local Government Lending and Borrowing, 2005–2009

Data source: The Federal Reserve, 2010

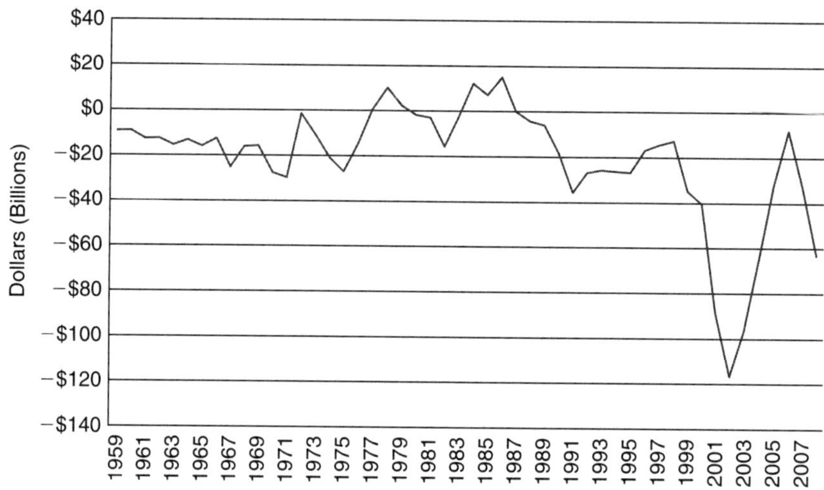

Figure 10.9 Real State Government Net Lending (or Borrowing), 1959–2008

Data source: The Bureau of Economic Analysis, 2008

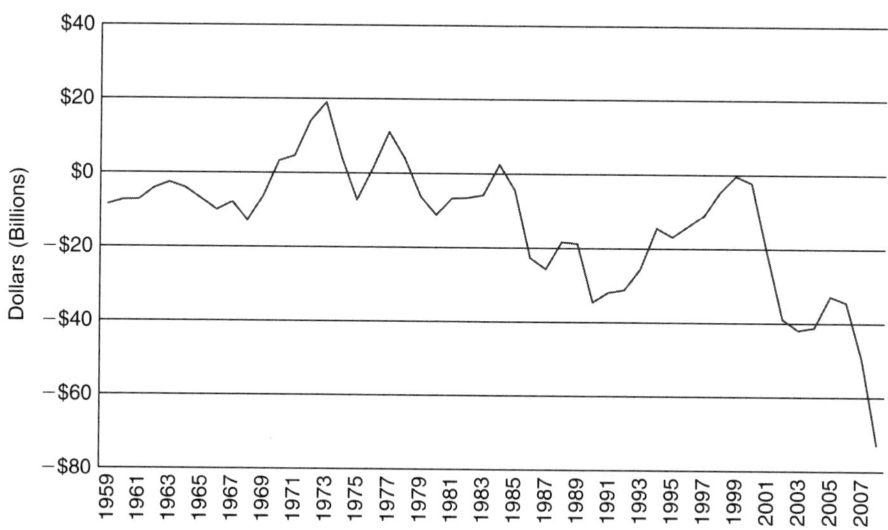

Figure 10.10 Real Local Government Net Lending (or Borrowing), 1959–2008

Data source: The Bureau of Economic Analysis, 2008

Municipal bond yields are still at historically low rates, even though the market rebounded a bit from its 2008 low. AAA-rated municipal bond yields ended in the third quarter of 2009 at 2.96%, down from 3.37% at the end of the second quarter and 4.16% at the end of the same year-earlier period and the SIFMA Municipal Swap Index, a short-term yield of tax-exempt variable rate demand obligations rose slightly to .34% at the end of September from .3% at the end of June (Rainy, 2010).

A recent report and survey by the Securities Industry and Financial Markets Association (Brandon, 2009) forecast that total municipal issuance will increase by 14% in 2010. This is mainly because of the issuance of several new taxable bonds in 2009 including the Build America Bonds (BABs), which were predicted to help taxable bonds alone to increase by 45% in 2010 (Brandon, 2009). Issuance of BAB's amounted to $20 billion in the third quarter of 2009 with more than a quarter of the proceeds going to public works projects, slightly less going to the building and repairing of roads, streets and highways, and a smaller portion going to higher education (Rainy, 2010).

The vast majority of municipal bonds, which are the major source of local government debt financing, are for capital projects that have a specific revenue source that is dedicated to paying off the debt. Therefore, they are not a widely used tool for fiscal stress management so they will not have anything to do with deficits. However, there are some exceptions, and some governments try to issue debt to deal with deficits. However, this method tends to be fairly isolated, and in some places, it is not even legal. More research needs to be done to see which kinds of debt are fiscally sustainable and which are not.

Government transfers.

Cutback budgeting and management must take place in the context of intergovernmental aid, which is often a critical source of revenues for many local governments. Historically, federal and state aid to local government has made up to one third of all local government revenues. State aid in particular has been subject to many cutbacks as legislators and governors have faced red ink through various recessions. Unlike the federal government, almost every state must act to balance its budget every year. In the early 2000s, states cut nearly $2.3 billion in aid to local governments (Hoene and Pagano, 2003). It is difficult, especially in an environment of tax limitation policies, to adequately offset state aid cuts with increased revenues.

Federal aid is typically more resilient than state aid, especially during recessions. During the Great Recession, in fact, the federal government pumped a significant amount of money into state and local governments through a stimulus plan. The stimulus totaled nearly $282 billion in aid to state and local governments (GAO, 2010). This aid was targeted at programs such as Medicaid, infrastructure, and public safety payroll. The goal of such aid is to help to alleviate the effects of the recession by strengthening aggregate demand, increasing the ability of subnational governments to repay their debt obligations in a timely manner, and allowing state and local governments to maintain expenditures and the provision of public goods and services and investment in public infrastructure (Wildasin, 2010).

Despite such aid, state and local government spending nevertheless declined during the Great Recession and actually led to a negative impact on GDP. It is likely that state and local government spending would have been cut further in the absence of the stimulus plan.

The overall reliance on government transfers has increased over the past 50 or so years as can be seen in **Figures 10.11** and **10.12**. In these figures, transfers are broken down into

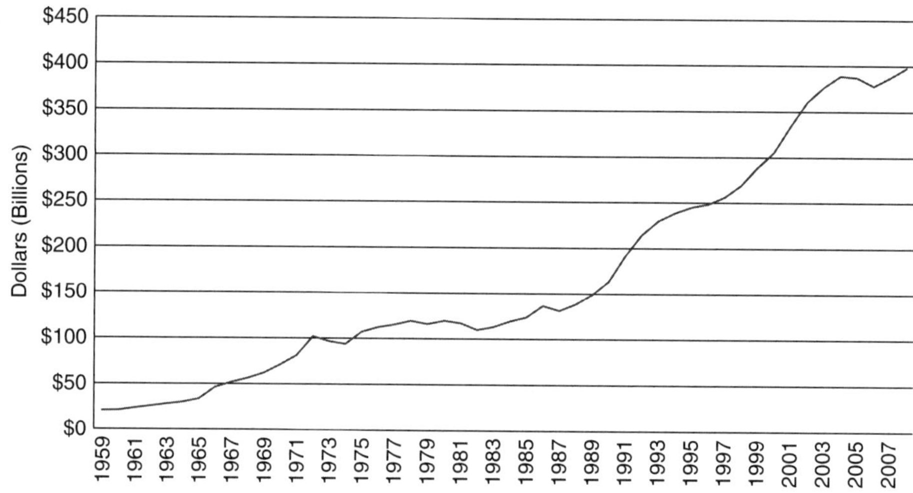

Figure 10.11 Real State Government Transfer Receipts, 1959–2009

Data source: The Bureau of Economic Analysis, 2008

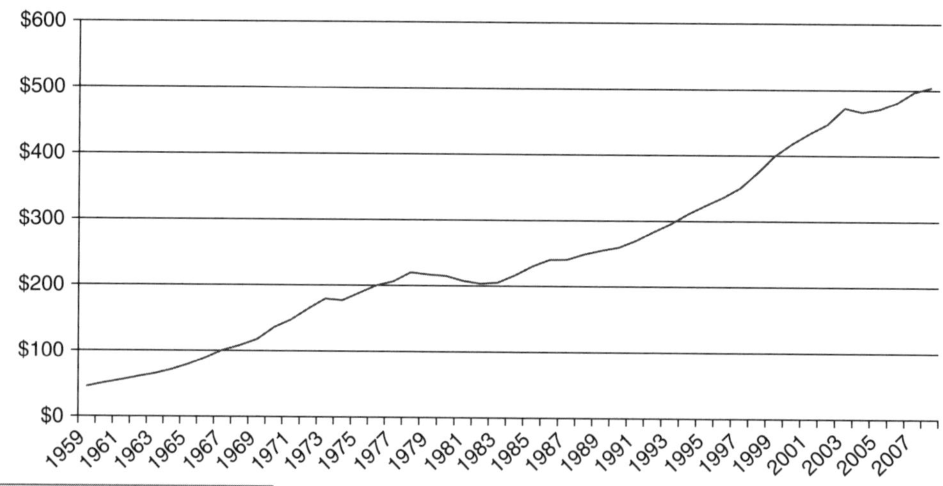

Figure 10.12 Real Local Government Transfer Receipts, 1959–2008

Data source: The Bureau of Economic Analysis, 2008

state government transfer receipts and local government transfer receipts. In 2005 and 2006, federal transfers to state and local governments accounted for 22% and 4% of their revenues, respectively, while state transfers to localities amounted to 30% of local revenues (Wildasin, 2010). This includes regular transfers as well as federal stimulus funds. This increased reliance on transfer receipts at both the state and local level have made governments more vulnerable to stress when these funds are not available.

There are some general lessons that have been learned from previous stimulus packages and transfer programs. First, it is argued that tax increases have less of an effect than cash grants to localities. Second, capital project support has a greater effect than operating expenditure support. And third, higher level government project and block grants speed recovery more so than do formula grants (Miller and Svara, 2009).

Case Studies: New York City, Chicago, and Los Angeles

Because aggregate data at the local level is not available for cutback responses to the current or previous recessions, we instead look at case studies of the three largest cities in the United States: New York City, Chicago, and Los Angeles. This next section reviews how each of these cities has responded to the current and previous recessions, and how their histories have helped shape not only how hard they were hit by each recession but also how they responded to each recession.

New York City.

The Great Recession was not New York City's first fiscal crisis, nor its worst. New York City underwent a major fiscal crisis in 1975, as examined by Brecher and Horton (1985). Between 1969 and 1977, NYC lost more than 600,000 jobs, or one-sixth of its employment base, and its population fell by more than one-tenth. In 1977, the local economy began to recover, and job gains were posted each year through 1982. New York City's unique position in the international economy contributed to its growth but so did changes in local policies including the lack of new tax measures, lowered rates on selected business taxes, and frozen property tax rates. During its fiscal crisis, redistributive functions (those that shift resources from one group to another) were accorded the highest priority, developmental functions (those that are designed to make the city a more competitive location for business activity) were assigned the lowest priority, and allocative functions (those that provide benefits to the community as a whole) received a slightly increased share of funds. During the recovery period of 1978–1982, municipal priorities were altered significantly: developmental functions went from least favored to most favored, redistributive functions shifted to the lowest priority, and allocative functions continued to receive a slowly growing share of city services. The New York City fiscal crisis of the 1970s followed the pattern of no longer budgeting based on increments but rather based on targeted goals of what is most important at the time.

The fiscal crisis of 2007–2010 was different from that of the 1970s not only because of its reach beyond New York City, but also because it was caused by drastically different actions than the fiscal crisis of the 1970s. City policies (mainly borrowing too much) caused the crisis of the 1970s, whereas the 2007–2010 crisis was the result of the worldwide financial crisis. In the 1970s, the state had to help the city to recover from fiscal crisis, whereas in the 2010s the city is helping the state. The city seems to have learned from the crisis of the 1970s, and the mayor of the late 2000s, Mayor Bloomburg, followed the same methods used to recover from that crisis although with additional policies enacted before the crisis in order to lessen the effect of potential crises. For instance, he created reserve funds during times of economic boom to use during times of fiscal stress. He also ordered periodic reductions across the board in all city agencies (American Public Media, 2010).

Laws created since the crisis of the 1970s have also helped New York City to weather subsequent fiscal crises better than other cities. After the 1970s, laws were created mandating that the city must balance its books. The city can no longer borrow for day-to-day operations (American Public Media, 2010). The City also took steps to diversify its economy before the recession hit (NYC.gov, 2010). The breakdown of projected taxes by type for 2010 can be seen in **Figure 10.13**.

In addition, New York City has been fairly steadily increasing its residential property tax rates over the past 30 years as depicted in **Figure 10.14**. The laws in the city are such that it may levy as much real property tax as necessary to cover debt service expenses, but the levy to cover operating expenses may not exceed 2.5% of the full valuation of taxable real property.

Because of these management choices, the mayor has been able to close the $4.9 billion deficit for FY 2011 with no tax increases for New Yorkers (NYC.gov, 2010). This has been possible due to $1.6 billion in new agency gap closing actions and reductions to growth in teacher and city employee salary costs. The gap closing actions created a surplus in FY 2010 that was used to achieve a balanced budget in FY 2011. Also involved in the cutback management policies for New York were employee productivity increases, pension reform, and mandatory health care premium contributions in exchange for future salary increases.

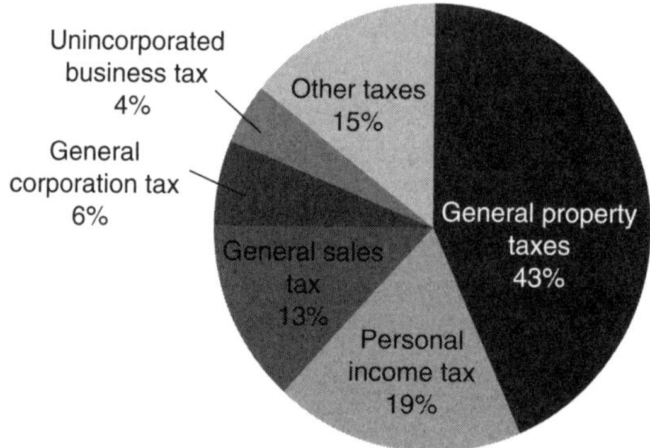

Figure 10.13 Projected Taxes by Type for New York City, 2010

Data source: New York City Budget, 2010

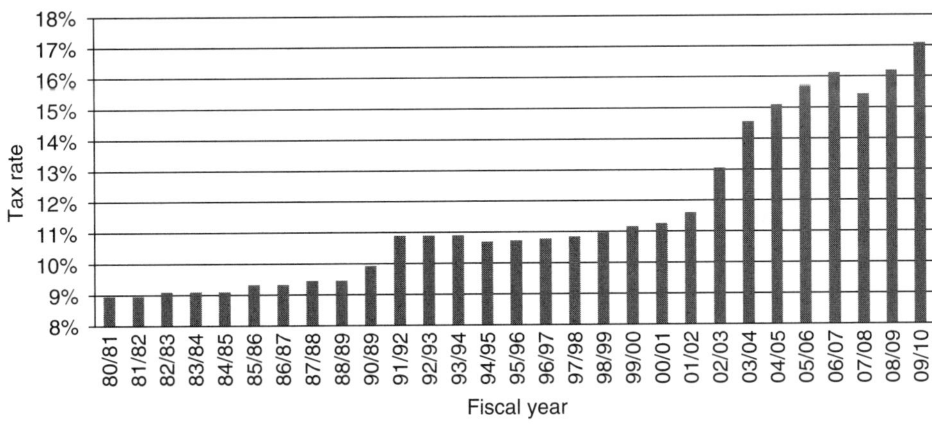

Figure 10.14 Residential Property Tax Rates for New York City, 1980–2010

Data Source: Grathwol, J., and Chun R. (2010). Tax revenue forecasting documentation. The City of New York Office of Management and Budget.

Although New York City was better prepared for the Great Recession relative to other cities in the United States, policymakers still had to reduce expenditures to weather the storm. Controllable expenses in FY 2011 were reduced by 1.8% from FY 2010, the result of cumulative cost-cutting and agency actions taken by the administration.

New York City appears to have learned from its fiscal crisis in the 1970s. Diversifying their income stream, building up rainy-day funds, and minimizing the amount of tax increases during the recession have been their main policies for managing cutbacks.

Chicago.

Chicago is also relatively better off than other cities, similarly because of substantial reserves that were set aside during times of economic boom. These reserves are mainly from infrastructure asset leases including the Chicago Skyway and the citywide parking meter system. Chicago used $400 million of the $1.03 billion reserves in their 2010 budget and used tax increases as a last resort (they did not raise property taxes in 2010). And as with many other cities, public safety remains Chicago's top priority (2010 Budget).

Still, personnel costs are growing as they are in all cities, and Chicago must therefore spend more for salaries and benefits even though that have reduced wages for nonsworn employees and cut positions. These expenditures related to employee wages, benefits, and pension costs compose more than 80% of the city's corporate budget.

Specific actions the municipal government in Chicago took to deal with cutbacks included reducing expenditures in the budget by $168 million in 2009 through layoffs, government shutdown days, and the elimination of five departments. In the 2010 budget, expenditure reductions included $24 million in personnel reductions and $20 million in nonpersonnel reductions. On the revenue side, the government closed *tax increment financing (TIF)* districts to get $8 million, used debt financing and restructuring to get $118 million, and used additional asset lease proceeds for $350 million (including those borrowed from the Parking Meter Long-Term Reserve).

Chicago's main focus during this recession has been on expenditure cuts over revenue increases, the use of reserve funds, and keeping public safety a main priority. It has also fared relatively well compared with other cities such as Los Angeles, which we look at in the next section.

Los Angeles.

As the United States' second-largest city, Los Angeles (L.A.) is an important player in municipal policy. However, L.A. has not fared as well as New York or Chicago has during the Great Recession. Although crime has been falling in L.A. for the past two decades, unemployment has increased substantially and revenues have been declining (LAcity.org, 2009). The city faced a budget deficit of at least $212 million in the 2010 fiscal year and $484 million in FY2011 ("Calling on the Angels," 2010).

Los Angeles has the added problem of being in California, a state that has been suffering the biggest budget crisis and one of the worst housing busts in the United States. California's voting system over the past few decades has also added to the city's problems in that all money matters are now more complicated than necessary. Proposition 13 of 1978 cut and capped property taxes, which are still the biggest source of city revenue, and Proposition 218 of 1996 made it such that explicit voter approval is needed to raise most other city fees and revenues. Cutting spending is also more difficult in L.A., because of a weak mayor and a strong city council. This is common in western cities, but not as much in large Eastern ones ("Calling on the Angels," 2010).

Under these restrictions and obstacles, the current mayor, Mayor Villaraigosa, has proposed to keep expenditures down by giving no additional funding to most city departments, by eliminating 4,000 of the city's 48,500 jobs and by cutting pay. He will also consolidate several smaller departments and even get rid of entire other departments such as personnel, discontinue contracts, and shutting most city agencies for two days a week. However, the City Council will not easily approve most of these proposed actions. On the revenue side, the mayor has proposed to increase public-private partnerships and advertising opportunities to increase revenues over the next few years (budget).

The struggle of power in L.A. reached extreme levels when the City Council and the city's Department of Water and Power (DWP), the largest municipal utility in the United States, fight over payments to the city's treasury and municipal rates. DWP had made commitments to give $73.5 million to the city, which they are now saying that they cannot do without drastic rate increases for municipal residents. The city council denied these rate increases, and therefore DWP is refusing to fulfill its committed payment. The city's chief accountant is now requesting $90 million be transferred from the city's reserve fund to its general fund to ensure the fiscal solvency of the city. However, this move will not only leave the city without reserves in the case of future emergencies but it may also trigger another downgrade in its Wall Street credit ratings.

Los Angeles has not been able to weather the storm of the fiscal crisis of 2007–2010 as well as New York and Chicago have, mainly due to policies that were in place before the crisis occurred such as Proposition 13 and Proposition 218. These three case studies suggest that cutback management strategies for municipal governments depend upon the institutional structure of the system as well as policy taken during economic boom more so that specific goals of policy makers during times of fiscal stress.

Current Literature

Other authors have also attempted to analyze the change in strategies pre- and post-2000. Bowling and Burke (2006) conducted empirical analysis investigating the differences in strategies between 1984 and 2004. They used the American State Administrators Project to determine differences in responses across the two time periods. Their findings were that, in general, few differences could be uncovered between the time periods and types of cutback strategies used. However, there were some important differences in the scope and extent of strategies used by states that had tax and expenditure limits versus those that did not have such limits. Those states with tax limits did engage in a broader and deeper set of cutback strategies than those without. Overall, findings seem to indicate that general cutback strategies, such as hiring freezes, pay freezes, layoffs, and productivity improvements, are used at about the same rate and scope across both time periods. On the expenditure side, this study lacks evidence of a major structural change in approaches to cutback management.

Dougherty and Klase (2008) also examined modern cutback management strategies. After reviewing the literature, they provided a survey of cutback strategies in eight mid-Atlantic and Eastern states. They believe the evidence supports the model of phased-in responses as articulated by Levine et al. (1981). In essence, in the first phase, governments engage in broad across-the-board cuts. In the second phase, as the severity increases, targeted eliminations and major reductions are deployed. Thus, we have evidence for a budget cutting algorithm Levine and coauthors discussed in the earlier literature , as well as conflicting evidence as to whether Levine's model accurately describes the cutback management strategies employed.

Most recently, Rubin and Willoughby (2009) discussed the future of state budget balancing strategies and the differences in responses based on a state's economic difficulties. Using classifications of national and state recessions, they attempted to determine if states' cutback responses varied due to the severity of the economic problem, the theory being that a state facing more significant economic and fiscal stress will be forced to undertake a wider variety of cutback strategies. Generally, they find that states with the longest economic downturns employed a broader array of strategies. On the other hand, all states, regardless of the severity of the downturn, employed some strategies.. Thus, we have evidence that socioeconomic-contingent conditions do matter in the choices state executive and legislative branches make to address budgetary problems.

In the two recessions following the new millennium, we face a body of mixed evidence regarding cutback management among state and local governments. With the aforementioned three relatively recent studies, there does appear to be cumulating evidence of a type of budget cutting algorithm. This consists of phased in response to fiscal stress varying across states depending on formal authority structures and the severity of the crisis. On the revenue side, public finance economists have found that states have engaged much less in revenue enhancement behavior and relied more on rainy-day reserve funds and other savings and spending cuts.

The Effects of Different Cutback Strategies

Some research has been done on the effects of cutback strategies and other responses to fiscal stress and their effects on fiscal health and economic growth. Poterba (1994), for instance, analyzed the short-term effects of different cutback strategies. He found that fiscal institutions affect the short-run patterns of taxes and expenditures when states experience unexpected fiscal shocks. For example, states with weak antideficit rules adjust spending much less in response to positive deficit shocks than do their counterparts with strict antideficit rules.

There are also several studies on the long-term effects of cutback strategies, but they are often narrow in focus. Berne and Stiefel (1993), for example, look at the effect of New York City's mid-1970s fiscal crisis on education services in the city. They find that the budgetary cutbacks of 1976 and 1977 permanently affected some dimensions of public education in the city. They find that better times did not result in enough expenditure growth to both preserve competitive salaries and to recover cut positions. This implies that certain types of education cuts can rebound after a crisis and others cause permanent damage. More research such as this is needed on broader cutback management and other fiscal stress policies and their long-term effects, comparing and contrasting different policies and policy packages.

The Effects of Spending Cuts Versus Tax Increases

There is some debate as to the effectiveness of spending cuts versus tax increases. Most economists argue that spending cuts reduce overall demand and can make downturns deeper because they usually involve laying-off employees, canceling contracts with vendors, eliminating or lowering payments to businesses and nonprofit organizations, and cutting benefit payments to individuals. The organizations and individuals that would have received government payments or salaries therefore have less money to spend. Tax increases can also remove demand, but if they are directed toward upper income residents, the negative effects on an economy are small because much of the money lost comes from savings (Johnson, Oliff, and Williams, 2009). Therefore, if tax increases are designed in such a way to impose little or no costs on the most vulnerable citizens, they can be less harmful to the overall economy than spending cuts.

Orszag and Stiglitz (1991) draw a distinction between transfer programs and direct government spending on goods and services, arguing that a reduction in government spending on goods and services is likely to be more harmful to the economy in the short run than an increase in taxes or a reduction in transfer program spending. However, they argue that *any* state spending reductions or tax increases during a time of recession are counterproductive and that balanced budget rules force such counter-productive fiscal policies.

Recommending Strategies for Cutback Management

There have been several attempts in the literature to build explicitly normative models to guide policymakers when making cutback decisions. Mctighe (1979), for example, recommends strategies such as performance-based budgeting and management by objectives, encouraging employee participation in cost cutting strategies, cultivating political and citizen support for change, clarifying mission and eliminating or divesting from marginal programs. These recommendations are consistent with many authors of the time.

Plant and White (1982) take a different approach by specifically focusing on the political alliance aspects needed to engage in cutback budgeting. They also identify cutback strategies including: (1) across-the-board cuts, (2) productivity improvements, (3) cuts of marginal programs, (4) outsourcing or market driven strategies, and (5) clarifying/focusing on the organizational mission. The authors then proceed to outline two alliance building tactics to accomplish some of these cutback strategies. One approach consists of building support among technical and financial staff within government plus the external business community with an emphasis on productivity and efficiency. A second approach is to focus on citizen support and determine which programs have widespread public support. Using this basic outline, they suggest, for example, that a strategy that focuses on specific program cuts may lead to mobilizing active client oppositions whereas a general broad strategy may have less opposition. On the flip side, it will be more difficult to garner active support for a more general strategy. Therefore, politicians and government executives face a difficult balancing act in determining an appropriate strategy.

In 1980, Robert Behn weighed into the subject. Behn argued that the main challenge for an organization in this kind of fiscal crisis is to craft and implement a new corporate strategy. Behn defined corporate strategy as, "more than the selection of means to an end. . . . It also includes the definition of those ends." He focused on this issue because through cutbacks, an organization must not only downsize but must also ensure success in the future. Behn emphasized cooperation with both internal and external audiences to ensure a successful implementation. Further, he argued that leadership must be "active, but subtle" in guiding employees and constituents of services toward a different end.

More recently, Jonathan Justice (2009) summarized some of the past findings and current thinking on cutback strategies in a period of fiscal stress. Justice discussed some of the common sense strategies that have held up well such as avoiding fixed expenses, improving efficiency, long-term financial planning and deploying a range of revenue sources to fund government. He also highlighted the dangers of politically expedient but short-term solutions such as deferring maintenance, shifting expenses across fiscal years and postponing the funding of long-term commitments. He ends the piece with several important recommendations: avoid short-term band aid approaches, understand and generate a full range of options for policymakers to consider, and convey the stress facing the government to all stakeholder groups.

Overall, there does appear to be a general consensus as to the types of normative recommendations that have emerged from the cutback management literature. One important theme is that government managers and officials need to seek out a basic understanding of an organization's reasons for being and then guide resource allocation decisions on that basis. This type of rational planning is commonplace in the literature. However, there is a second strand to that theme. To successfully implement such an approach, internal and external stakeholders must be engaged and brought along throughout the process. This will ensure the necessary buy-in to cutback strategies. As we have seen in other work, however, a strategy of building alliances is neither easy nor quick when dealing with decremental budgeting and persistent fiscal problems.

As governments face the difficult need to prioritize resources, certain budgeting strategies may become more useful. Strategies such as zero based budgeting, budgeting for outcomes, performance based budgeting and many other similarly named programs are part of the toolbox that may be utilized in addressing the challenges of cutback management. At the top of the list, budgeting for priorities or outcomes is the most popular and advanced set of budgeting strategies currently available. The focus of these budgeting strategies is to assist policy makers in prioritizing among scarce resources among the nearly unlimited demands of delivering services and enforcing regulations in a complex society. The academic evaluation of these strategies has not always been kind, but it does point to certain benefits in employing such tools.

However, even these tools have their limits and still require human judgment and choice over which areas to prioritize. Many externally imposed mandates and constraints mean certain budget areas are off limits for cuts. Political motivations and other concerns also often trump the supposed "rational" approaches that these types of budget strategies represent. However, they remain a useful part of the toolbox for managers facing the need to engage in the process of cutback budgeting and management. Most importantly for public managers, they are an important form of discourse that represents a counternarrative to the traditional political discourse that does not address the fiscal stress facing many state and local governments.

What Have We Learned?

All of this review and discussion leads to a natural question about the current state of knowledge and research on cutback management and budgeting. In the early period of the cutback management literature, several competing theories were proposed to explain the types of strategies used. These theories generally coalesced around explanations relating to efficiency or rational type approaches versus political and equity based approaches. Importantly, a set of phases as to the types of approaches that would be used over time was presented by Levine et al. (1981). The accumulation of empirical evidence does not point to any definitive answers or knowledge regarding cutback management, but certain trends are discernable. The most recent empirical evidence does suggest some form of budget cutting algorithm, but it is not always clear as to the link or association between the empirical evidence and the proposed theories.

The most recent evidence makes it difficult to ascertain if, in fact, a break point has occurred in cutback management. Looking at the totality of tax increases, spending cuts and the use of reserves, states appear to have shifted to a greater reliance on rainy-day funds and reserves as opposed to tax increases during periods of recessions, as can be seen in **Figure 10.15**. In essence, states and localities have kept taxes higher than they otherwise would need to during periods of economic prosperity to build up reserves and avoid major tax increases during a recession. This is good news from the standpoint of national stabilization policy where traditionally state tax hikes have partially offset federal stimulus efforts.

In terms of expenditure reductions and service restructuring, evidence is building that there is some type of budget cutting algorithm or pattern that does exist between and among state and local governments in dealing with fiscal stress. Theoretical and empirical work from the 1970s and 1980s certainly suggested that different rationalities, including both political and managerial, may be at work in determining cutback management strategies. The two most recent empirical studies provide corroborating evidence that

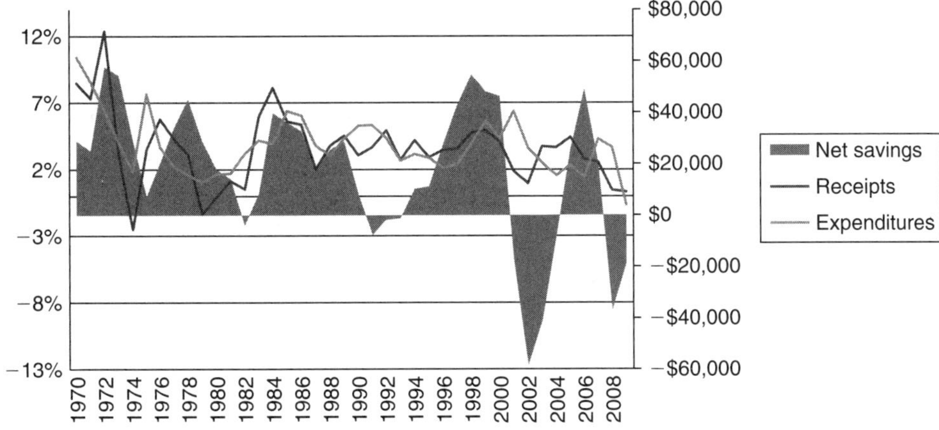

Figure 10.15 Change in Real State and Local Government Receipts and Expenditures (in Percent Change) and Total Net Savings (in Dollars), 1970–2008

Data Source: Fiscal Survey of the States, 2009

such a pattern exists (Bolwing and Burke, 2006; Rubin and Willoughby, 2009). The 2007–2009 recession provides a new natural experiment for assessing these theories and placing past evidence into a new context.

What Remains to be Learned?

One major problem with the prevailing literature is the lack of a time element in the discussions of both strategies implemented and strategy effectiveness. It is often unclear, although perhaps implicit in Levine's original definition, whether organizational cutbacks are to be permanent or whether they represent short-term responses to a budget problem that is only temporary in nature. Certainly, the element of time matters in terms of what strategies are and should be undertaken. Some strategies such as hiring freezes are likely to be considered as temporary in nature while program elimination or asset sales are more long term. This time element represents an important gap in the literature.

In addition, there is a lack of understanding of the long-term effects of different cutback management strategies. Most of the literature at the state and local government level that deals with the effects of different strategies focuses solely on the short-term effects of such strategies. More long-term analyses of the effects of different cutback strategies and packages needs to be completed, comparing their effects on long-term grown and fiscal sustainability.

Conclusion

State and local governments rely on many different strategies to address fiscal stress and cutback management. There are revenue side strategies, such as tax increases and increases in fees and there are expenditure side strategies, such as layoffs and across-the-board cuts. However, neither tax increases nor expenditure cuts are best in times of recession. The best tools that state and local governments can use to manage cutbacks is to prepare for them before fiscal stress becomes apparent. This includes tools such as building up reserve funds and creating laws that reduce the ability of government to get into fiscal stress while at the same time keeping open options for cutback management policy changes. If these strategies do not work to completely prevent fiscal stress, however, tax increases and expenditure cuts can be managed in a manner that do the least harm to vulnerable populations and do not prolong the local recession. These policies include targeting tax increases toward upper income residents and targeting expenditure cuts toward transfer programs instead of toward direct government spending on goods and services. However, *any* state spending reductions or tax increases during a time of recession are counterproductive.

Historically, state and local governments in the post WW II eras relied on a combination of tax increases and spending cuts to address fiscal problems. Starting in the 1990s, the use of strategies shifted as tax and expenditure limits and rainy-day funds became more predominant. In the 2000s, the use of tax increases, outside of very selective excise tax increases, became far less common. The most recent crisis, the Great Recession of 2008 and 2009, will test whether this new paradigm holds. It appears, however, that state and local governments are moving more toward expenditure reductions and the use of rainy-day funds post 2000, although recent tax increases may imply that this shift is not permanent.

Future research needs to better integrate its examination of the use and implications of these alternative approaches to cutback management across different types of governments facing different situations. Cutback management and budgeting strategies should be analyzed closely both in times of recession and in times of economic boom. Most importantly, as the Great Recession and the associated fiscal crisis winds down it will be important to assess whether a new set of cutback management strategies has emerged. From the managerial perspective, state and local fiscal stress is likely to be a recurring problem and therefore an organized strategy of dealing with this stress must be planned in advance in order to minimize both short- and long-term negative effects.

Endnotes

1. This chapter is an extension and revision of Scorsone, E., and Plerhoples, C. "Fiscal stress and cutback management amongst state and local governments: What have we learned and what remains to be learned." doi: 10.1177/0160323X10378826 State and Local Government Review August 2010 vol. 42 no. 2 176–187.
2. All graphs that are in real dollar terms were deflated using the Gross Domestic Product Implicit Price Deflator from the U.S. Department of Commerce's Bureau of Economic Analysis (2008).

Glossary

Budget stabilization fund (BSF): the budget stabilization fund, popularly called the "rainy-day fund" (RDF), is a fiscal device used by subnational governments to store extra revenues during economic booms for use in economic downturns to supplement inadequate resources for meeting outlay demands. Since the early 1980s, this countercyclical device has attracted increasingly more academic attention (Hou, 2008).

Cutback Management: the management of organizational change toward lower levels of resource consumption and organizational activity (Levine, 1979).

Local Government: administrative authorities over areas that are smaller than a including municipal governments, county governments, village governments, and township governments, among others.

Tax Increment Financing (TIF): tax increment financing is a public financing method that has been used for redevelopment and community improvement projects in many countries including the United States for more than 50 years. The TIF is mechanism through which, starting from a base year, the growth in taxes within a certain boundary are sequestered and can only be used for services or infrastructure within that boundary and not for the rest of the governments jurisdictional boundary. This deprives tax revenues from the general purpose governments that would have collected those taxes. The goal is to stimulate economic development through concentrating resources in one specific geographic area. With federal and state sources for redevelopment generally less available, TIF has become an often-used financing mechanism for municipalities (Wikipedia).

Discussion Questions

1. How can cutback management methods be created and implemented in a way that uses the democratic process to allocate cuts making them effective yet equitable?
2. How might policies be designed by the federal government to incentivize cutback management methods at the state and local government levels that are effective for both short-term and long-term fiscal health?

Recommended Resources

Bland, R. L. A budgeting guide for local government, 2nd Edition. *International City/County Management Association Press.* May, 2007. http://bookstore.icma.org/A_Budgeting_Guide_for_Local_Go_P1745C29.cfm

Miller, Gerald J., and James H. Svara. Navigating the fiscal crisis: Tested strategies for local leaders. *International City/County Management Association White Paper.* http://www.sonomacity.org/uploads/City_Manager/Navigating_Fiscal_Crisis.pdf

Thomas, Edwin C., Jon B. Pierce, and William E. Tomes. The challenges of cutback management. *Institute for Public and Policy Research Publication.* http://ipspr.sc.edu/publication/Cutback.pdf

Wong, John D., and Michael Woodrum. Cutback management: Techniques for a down time. *Kansas Government Finance Officers Association 10th Annual Fall Professional Conference Presentation.* http://www.ksgfoa.com/documents/09KSGFOA/Cutback%20Management-%20Techniques%20for%20a%20Down%20Economy%20Part%20II.pdf

References

American Public Media. (2010). NYC spending makes some nervous. *Marketplace.* April 12.

Behn, R. D. (1980). Leadership for cut-back management: The use of corporate strategy. *Public Administration Review, 40*(6), 613–620.

Bartle, J. R. (1996). Coping with cutbacks: City response to aid cuts in New York State. *State and Local Government Review, 28*(1), 38–48.

Berne, R., and Stiefel, L. (1993). Cutback budgeting: The long-term consequences. *Journal of Policy Analysis and Management,* 12(4), 664–684.

Bowling, C. J., and Burke, B. F. (2006). Levine's legacy: Comparing state administrator strategies to treat fiscal stress, 1984 and 2004. Prepared for *7th State Politics and Policy Conference.*

Boyd, D. J., and Dadayan, L. (2010). State revenue report: Revenue declines less severe, but states' fiscal crisis is far from over. The Nelson A. Rockefeller Institute of Government. University at Albany. No. 79 Retrieved from http://www.rockinst.org/pdf/government_finance/state_revenue_report/2010-04-16-SRR_79.pdf. Accessed February 5, 2011.

Brandon, K., (2009). SIFMA 2010 municipal issuance survey. The Securities and Financial Markets Association Retrieved from http://www.sifma.org/uploadedFiles/Research/ResearchReports/2009/Municipal_MunicipalIssuanceSurvey2010_20091207_SIFMA.pdf. Accessed November 18, 2010.

Brecher, C., and Horton, R. D. (1985). Retrenchment and recovery: American cities and the New York experience. *Public Administration Review*, *45*(2), 267–274.

Budget summary. (2009). LAcity.org

Bureau of Economic Analysis National Economic Accounts. (2009). Table 3.20. State government current receipts and expenditures. Retrieved from http://www.bea.gov/national/nipaweb/TableView.asp?SelectedTable=124&Freq=Year&FirstYear=2007&LastYear=2008. Accessed July 14, 2010.

Bureau of Economic Analysis National Economic Accounts. (2009). Table 3.21. Local government current receipts and expenditures. Retrieved from http://www.bea.gov/national/nipaweb/TableView.asp?SelectedTable=125&Freq=Year&FirstYear=2007&LastYear=2008. Accessed November 17, 2010.

Calling on the angels. (2010, April 8). *The Economist.* Retrieved from http://www.economist.com/node/15867930. Accessed August 1, 2010.

Chicago City Clerk. (2009). 2010 Budget Overview and Revenue Estimates. Retrieved from http://www.chicityclerk.com/citycouncil/budget/2010/2010_Budget_Overview_and_Revenue_Estimate.pdf. Accessed January 1, 2010.

Cyert, R. M., and March, J. G. (1963) A Behavioral Theory of the Firm (2nd ed.). Cambridge, MA: Blackwell Publishers.

Downs, G. W., and Rocke, D. M. (1984). Theories of budgetary decision-making and revenue decline." *Policy Sciences*, *16*, 329–347.

Fitch downgrades $3.4 billion of Los Angeles debt. (2010, April 22). *The Bond Buyer*, 371.33302, 20. *General OneFile*.

Grathwol, J., and Chun R. (2010). Tax revenue forecasting documentation. The City of New York Office of Management and Budget.

Hoene, C. W., and Pagano, M. A. (2003, October). Fend-for-yourself federalism: The impact of federal and state deficits on America's cities. *Government Finance Review*, *19*(5), 36–42.

Hoene, C. W., and Pagano, M. A. (2009). Research brief on America's cities: City fiscal conditions in 2009. *National League of Cities,* Issues 2009-2.

Jick, T. D., and Murray, V. V. (1982). The management of hard times: Budget cutbacks in public sector organizations. *Organization Studies*, *3*(2), 141–169.

Johnson, N., Nicholas, A. C., Pennington, S. (2009). Tax measures help balance state budgets: A common and reasonable response to shortfalls. *Center on Budget and Policy Priorities*, Special Series Dealing with Deficits: How States Can Respond. Retrieved from http://www.cbpp.org/files/5-13-09sfp.pdf. Accessed June 29, 2010.

Johnson, N., Oliff, P., and Williams, E. (2009). An Update on State Budget Cuts. *Center on Budget and Policy Priorities*. Retrieved from http://www.cbpp.org/cms/index.cfm?fa=view&id=1214. Accessed April 2, 2010.

Justice, J. B. (2009, January). Coping with fiscal stress. In G. J. Millerand J. H. Svara (Eds.), *Navigating the fiscal crisis: Tested strategies for local leaders*. Retrieved May 27, 2010, from http://icma.org/en/icma/knowledge_network/documents?s=navigating%20fiscal%20crisis.

Layoffs, furloughs and union concessions: The prolonged and painful process of balancing city budgets. (2009). *The PEW Charitable Trust*. Retrieved from http://www.pewtrusts.org/uploadedFiles/wwwpewtrustsorg/Reports/Philadelphia-area_grantmaking/Layoffs,%20Furloughs%20and%20Union%20Concessions%20FINAL.pdf?n=7888. Accessed September 24, 2010.

Levine, C. H. (1979). More on cutback management: Hard questions for hard times. *Public Administration Review*, *39*, 182.

Levine, C. H. (1978). Organizational decline and cutback management. *Public Administration Review*, *38*, 316–325.

Levine, C. H., Rubin, I. S., and Wolohojian, G. G. (1981). Resource scarcity and the reform model: The management of retrenchment in Cincinnati and Oakland. *Public Administration Review*, *41*(6), 619–628.

Maag, E., and Merriman, D. (2003). Tax policy responses to revenue shortfalls. Prepared for State Fiscal Crises: Causes, Consequences, and Solutions. Urban Institute. Retrieved http://www.taxpolicycenter.org/UploadedPDF/410798_tax_policy_responses.pdf. Accessed October 10, 2010.

Mayor Bloomberg Presents FY 2011 Preliminary Budget. (2010). NYC.gov

McTighe, John J. (1979). Management strategies to deal with shrinking resources. *Public Administration Review*, 39(1), 86–90.

Miller, Gerald R. (1983). Taking stock of a discipline. *Journal of Communication*, *33*(3), 31–41.

Osborne, D., and Hutchinson, P. (2004). *The price of government: getting the results we need in an age of permanent fiscal crisis*. New York: Basic Books.

Orszag, P., and Stiglitz, J. (2001). Budget cuts versus tax increases at the state level: Is one more counter-productive than the other during a recession? *Center on Budget and Policy Priorities*. Retrieved from http://www.ocpp.org/2009/20011106StiglitzOrzag.pdf. Accessed May 10, 2010.

Plant, J. F., White, L. G. (1982). The politics of cutback budgeting: An alliance building perspective. *Public Budgeting & Finance*, *2*(1), 65–71.

Poterba, J. M. (1994). State Responses to Fiscal Crises: The Effects of Budgetary Institutions and Politics. *The Journal of Political Economy*, *102*(4), 799–821.

Rainy, P. (2010). Municipal Bond Credit Report. Securities Industry and Financial Markets Association. Retrieved from http://www.sifma.org/research/pdf/RRVol4-12.pdf. Accessed January 1, 2011.

Recovery act: One year later, states' and localities' uses of funds and opportunities to strengthen accountability." (2010, March). GAO Report to Congress. GAO-10-437.

Rubin, M. M., and Willoughby, K. G. (2009). State budget balancing strategies: Riding into the future on lessons learned from the past. Prepared for *5TAD Conference, Washington, D.C.*

Schick, Allen. (1983). Incremental budgeting in a decremental age. *Policy Sciences 16*(1). 1–25.

State Budget Update: July 2009. (2009). *National Conference of State Legislatures.*

Tax increment financing. (2011). In Wikipedia, The Free Encyclopedia. Retrieved from http://en.wikipedia.org/w/index.php?title=Tax_increment_financing&oldid=475044984. Accessed September 16, 2011.

U.S. Department of Commerce Bureau of Economic Analysis. National economics accounts. (2008) Retrieved from http://www.bea.gov/national/nipaweb/TableView.asp?SelectedTable=88&ViewSeries=NO&Java=no&Request3Place=N&3Place=N&FromView=YES&Freq=Qtr&FirstYear=2000&LastYear=2009&3Place=N&Update=Update&JavaBox=no. Accessed February 26, 2010.

Waisanen, B., and Haggerty, T. (2010). State Tax Actions 2009 Special Fiscal Report. National Conference of State Legislatures.

West, J. P., and Davis, C. (1988). Administrative values and cutback politics in American local government. *Public Personnel Management, 17*(2), 2.

Wildasin, D. E. (2009). State and Local Government Finance in the Current Crisis: Time for Emergency Federal Relief? IFIR Working Paper No. 2009-07.

Wolman, H. (1986). The Reagan urban policy and its impacts. *Urban Affairs Review, 21*(3), 311–335.

Chapter 11

A Framework for Deciphering and Managing the Fiscal Environment

by Josephine M. LaPlante

Managing for fiscal health requires an understanding of the linkages between a government's finances and the fiscal context within which it operates. Achieving and maintaining fiscal health obliges local decision makers to understand and respond effectively to multiple and often interdependent forces that shape and reshape local budgetary options, opportunities, and constraints. To accomplish this, local managers need sound data and a comprehensive, cohesive framework for making sense of multiple fiscal effects and interconnections. This chapter begins with a review of the research that has contributed to our understanding of the relationship between fiscal factors and local finances. Next, financial indicator systems designed to assist local managers with monitoring and evaluating financial condition are considered and limitations identified. Then, to provide context for measurement and strategy development, a visual fiscal framework is presented and explained. The framework identifies fiscal factors that create local spending pressures and determine potential revenue capacity, highlights interdependencies among characteristics, delineates likely paths of influence, and pinpoints areas where feedback from policy choices may affect long-term financial condition. Armed with knowledge of complex forces that shape the decision environment, local officials are equipped to plot a course for robust fiscal health.

Introduction

Managing for fiscal health is a complex undertaking made more challenging by the Great Recession's exacerbation of chronic gaps between *fiscal capacity* and expenditure needs and revelations of neglected and emerging budgetary claims (LaPlante and Honadle, 2011). Jurisdictions seeking to adapt effectively to new fiscal realities and achieve sustainability will need to align "the scope of spending commitments and the accompanying price tag" with "real and lasting revenue constraints" (LaPlante, 2011, p. 216). Determining what is truly affordable and prioritizing and controlling spending will be aided by knowledge of factors that influence government finances. The economy; community socioeconomic and demographic characteristics; tax base size, composition, productivity, and access; federal and state mandates and aid policies; long-term financing and deferred spending commitments; the timing and extent of new budgetary demands; citizens' views about spending and taxes; and tax levels and burdens change and interact to shape and reshape budgetary pressures, opportunities, and constraints. Achieving sustainability requires managers to gauge recent financial performance, identify and evaluate emerging trends, delineate opportunities and constraints, and recognize pitfalls and tradeoffs embedded in policy choices.

Historically, governments seeking greater control over local finances turned to a variety of turnkey *financial condition* measurement systems or developed community-specific indicators. Common to the numerous methodologies is an expectation that implementing and using an indicator system advances fiscal health. However, monitoring systems may fall short of their potential in increasingly difficult local fiscal settings. First, indicator systems usually examine performance and position using financial statements and, as such, place an emphasis on a narrow view of recent events. A lack of prospective analysis may provide policymakers with an inaccurate sense of ability to pay. At the same time, an abbreviated historical view may miss important cyclical changes in spending needs and tax receipts. A resulting myopic view promotes unsustainable budget decisions (LaPlante, 2011). Second, indicators tend to be viewed in isolation from each other and from variables that affect their levels and trends. Even elaborate monitoring approaches may neglect interactions among fiscal variables and interdependencies among clusters of variables. Third, monitoring data rarely is used to forecast effects of policy choices and budgetary outputs on future fiscal position. In the absence of good knowledge, policymakers may repeat past mistakes and push taxes to a point where citizens revolt. Finally, monitoring systems tend to focus primarily on internal factors over which financial managers and policymakers have direct control and may fail to consider adequately the linkages between a government's finances and the complex *fiscal environment* within which it operates (Berne and Schramm, 1986).

In an extended white paper prepared for the Governmental Accounting Standards Board (GASB) in 1992, Berne called attention to the importance of the state of and trends in the fiscal environment to governmental financial condition. He identified economic and fiscal trend data that could be compiled and included in government financial statements and provided a foundation for the development of economic condition reporting guidelines codified in the GASB's Statement 44. As Gauthier (2007) explained, deliberate consideration of the multiple forces that influence budgets and *financial position* provides "necessary context" for sound interpretation of indicators and facilitates good finance decisions.

The data needs of expanded fiscal measurement and the expertise required to conduct analyses are significant. Lewis (2003) argued that maturing practice and unprecedented fiscal challenges are increasing both the need for and capacity to grapple with multiple measures. Nonetheless, assessing fiscal forces and trends and integrating this information with internal financial indicators is challenging at best, with assessments complicated by an absence of "how-to" guidance. As Clark (1994, p. 27) described, even municipal bond analysts have difficulty explaining how various fiscal measures may be combined to produce a considered opinion of local credit worthiness: when pressed for specifics, interviewees could answer only in vague generalities. Berne (1996) confirmed the dominance of art over science in the determination of bond ratings; he explained that quantitative analysis is used to arrive at a sound qualitative judgment about future financial condition. Though the knowing-pornography-when-they-see-it school of analysis may work for Wall Street investment gurus (or not), local managers need guidance deciphering and considering prospectively the likely trends and effects of multiple, interdependent fiscal forces. This chapter helps fill this knowledge gap by presenting a visual map of the fiscal environment.

The remainder of this chapter begins with a review of research on the fiscal status of local governments, with attention to two parallel threads of work. First, a large research base developed over many years emerged initially from concerns about city fiscal distress; this literature provides substantial information about and insight into linkages between external fiscal influences and local finances. Recent work is addressing theoretical and practical concerns including how state aid to municipalities and schools might be distributed more equitably without sacrificing efficiency. Second, over the past three decades, public management and accounting researchers and professionals developed a variety of approaches to evaluating financial position and condition. These systems represent an important advance in the management of fiscal health, but complexities and conceptual limitations reduce their capacity to gauge fiscal strength reliably. In particular, a lack of attention to the connections between indicators and the fiscal environment that shapes and reshapes measures undermines their utility for forecasting and strategy development.

Next, the visual fiscal framework is introduced and explained. The framework for fiscal analysis delineates variables that create local spending pressures and determine potential *revenue capacity*, highlights interdependencies among characteristics, shows likely paths of influence, and pinpoints areas where feedback from policy choices may affect longterm financial condition. Armed with this roadmap, local government managers will be prepared to decide upon and compile data for the most appropriate measures, select a *reference set* of communities and employ comparative fiscal analysis to improve measurement, and integrate information into a comprehensive and coherent appraisal of fiscal health. Furthermore, the framework will enable local officials to project the likely effects of changes and trends in key indicators; identify and evaluate options for redirecting trends; and explain method and results to stakeholders.

Research on the Fiscal Status of Local Governments

Interest in deciphering the fiscal forces that influence governmental finances traces back to the 1930s, when widespread concern about depressions produced a fledgling literature (Clark, 1994). However, recognition of a need for an urban research agenda did not emerge until the 1960s, when affluent families abandoned cities for suburbs and social problems left behind stressed city tax bases. The first "window" into the fiscal status of local governments gained momentum during the latter part of the decade, when growing awareness of central city decline and consequent fiscal distress catalyzed research on social, economic, demographic, and structural factors that affect local expenditure demands and revenue capacity (Burchell, Listokin, Sternlieb, Hughes, and Casey, 1980). A large subset of these urban hardship studies focused on mismatches or "fiscal disparities" between spending needs and available resources within individual cities and across cities, between central cities and surrounding suburbs, and between city and suburban schools. More than five decades of work has built a rich body of research that describes the fiscal environment and its many effects upon local finances.

A second lens on the fiscal status of local governments was prompted by the near bankruptcy of New York City in 1975. Before this time, many viewed municipal bonds as virtually risk free, but the sudden onset of fiscal crises in New York and several other large U.S. cities reversed that perception and brought attention to the importance of managing for financial health (Clark, 1994). This second line of inquiry has been more applied in focus and has both developed and assessed practical strategies for examining local finances. And like the urban hardship literature, this body of work developed along two main paths. First, financial indicator systems were created and refined through application in state and local governments; these approaches tend to emphasize financial position and rely upon ratio analysis of annual financial statements (McKinney, 1995). A second and related group of studies examined aspects of local fiscal structure over which managers have at least some control, such as management practices, expenditure levels, revenue reliance, and related trends (Hendrick, 2004).

Berne and Schramm (1986) made a strong case that managing for fiscal health requires local officials to understand the dynamic relationship between a government's finances and the fiscal environment within which it operates. Although the two paths of inquiry into the fiscal status of local governments have converged somewhat, the overlap remains shallow. Let us consider research on the fiscal context more closely, after which we will study the visual framework, which maps the fiscal environment.

Research on the Fiscal Environment and Local Finances

The literature on the fiscal environment and local finances may be traced to the groundbreaking publication in 1967 of Campbell and Sacks' book titled *Metropolitan America: Fiscal Patterns and Government Systems*. Campbell and Sacks considered the causes of urban distress, with particular attention devoted to the fiscal effects of changing patterns of settlement. They credited the departure of affluent households from cities with producing a simultaneous increase in service needs and reduction in ability to pay in central cities. Of particular concern to Campbell and Sacks were differences in the mix and levels of services that emerged between cities and suburbs. City government services revealed necessary responses to economic functioning and high-need populations. In contrast, suburban governments catered to tastes and preferences of their more affluent taxpayers.

Sacks (1968, 1972) extended his and Campbell's 1967 disparities research by examining differences in the fiscal circumstances of urban and suburban schools. Sacks maintained that city schools would need to spend more, not less, than suburban schools because they served needier student populations and operated in older physical plants. However, he found that city schools often spent less than their suburban counterparts. He attributed the gap between expected and actual service levels to a reduction in spending for learning resources caused by the higher taxes required to support economic activity and address the greater social needs of city residents. Sacks' (1972) conclusions were grounded in the *municipal overburden hypothesis*, a model based on a set of assumptions about non-education and education financing and their interaction (Peterson, 1971). First, the municipal overburden hypothesis contends that higher than normal demand for non-school public services causes higher taxes for these purposes in cities as compared with suburbs. Second, it is supposed that urban schools will need to spend more than suburban schools because their needier student populations require specialized programming, higher teachers' salaries, and support services. Third, a maximum local tax level is assumed to exist, especially in the face of dwindling tax base value and the regressive incidence of the property tax. Fourth, the consequent resource constraint will force less than optimal spending levels for at least some public functions. Finally, under an inflexible own-source revenue constraint and in the absence of adequate intergovernmental aid, it is expected that cities will spend less than needed for educational programming and related learning resources. Each proposition fostered research, with examination of key ideas extending to the present. Although the suggestion that high taxes for noneducation responsibilities might crowd out spending for education produced controversy in the academic literature, legal and education practitioners embraced the concept.

Attorneys for plaintiffs in school finance challenges have used the elements of the municipal overburden hypothesis to explain learning resource deficits in urban school districts. In turn, courts have accepted as valid the notion that municipal overburden reduces school resources (Dayton, 1993.) In 1986, Brazer and McCarty published an influential study disputing the existence of municipal overburden; they based their conclusions on their inability to demonstrate empirically the existence of reduced resource allocations to urban schools. The dichotomy between the economists' and legal views may be attributable to Brazer and McCarty's partial view of the hypothesis, which focused on the issue of whether education resources are crowded out by nonschool services overburden, and their acceptance of per pupil expenditures as a valid gauge of the availability of learning resources.

Achieving per pupil spending equalization is a goal of many states' school finance formulas, and the degree of equalization is used by states and researchers to determine the efficacy of funding distributions. Yet as LaPlante (2011, p. 242) described, "the unexamined belief that equal funding per pupil produces equitable and efficient school systems has guided education finance policy development and research for many years." Evaluating whether learning resource disparities exist requires improved measurement. LaPlante explained that "the presumption of cause and effect and circular reasoning went unchallenged for many years," but in the early 1990s, justices hearing school finance system lawsuits claiming unequal resources implicitly rejected the comparison of per pupil expenditures as the sole means of establishing resource differences. Instead, justices began asking for detailed information about curricular extensity and intensity, teachers' salaries, technology, and other indicators of student learning opportunities (Dayton,

1993; LaPlante, 2011). LaPlante's 1994 study of learning resources in Maine schools and Betts and Danenberg's 2001 California study suggested that equalizing per pupil expenditures actually may increase disparities in learning resources when school district and pupil circumstances differ widely. Downes and Pogue (2002) have argued that dissimilar spending is required when conditions differ.

The plight of cities continued to attract significant research attention after the publication of Campbell and Sacks' 1967 study. In 1973, the Advisory Commission on Intergovernmental Relations (ACIR) contributed to the momentum when they released a report on city financial emergencies that documented severe fiscal problems and projected a potential for financial default by some cities. New York's 1975 financing crisis prompted significant research into the City's financial practices and causes of decline and encouraged similar analyses of other cities, sets of cities in comparison to New York and, eventually, cities in general (Gramlich, 1977). Burchell, Listokin, Sternlieb, Hughes, and Casey (1980) present an exhaustive catalogue of the numerous urban need and hardship indices and resource allocation approaches presented during the 1970s; their detailed and thoughtful review defined variables used in each study and categorized expenditure need factors as social, economic, or fiscal.

Researchers from political science and sociology aided the growing comprehension of expenditure determination by adding politics, political culture, voting preferences, and state statutes as explanatory variables (Hendrick, 2004). In 1976, sociologist Liebert presented compelling evidence that total city spending was explained by the range of functions performed, which in turn was related to city age. Liebert (1976) explained that older cities were founded at a time when government viewed itself as serving a paternal role toward citizens, which produced a broad array of services ranging from education and common municipal functions to hospitals and sanitariums. Cities founded at a later date performed a narrower range of functions, often leaving service provision to special districts or the private sector. Liebert attributed the conflicting research findings and lack of synthesis that troubled the literature to overly aggregated data problems. His findings encouraged expenditure determination researchers to model individual functions and matched sub-functions rather than total spending. Liebert's path-breaking work is especially noteworthy for identifying citizens' frames of reference and experiences as determinants of spending expectations.

In 1983, Bradbury introduced the concept of *structural distress*, which is a long-term imbalance among a government's functional responsibilities, service demands, capital investment needs and revenue raising capacity. Far from being a simple budget gap to be closed with short-term spending reductions and revenue increases, a structural gap reflects a persistent difference between revenue capacity and spending pressures. Bradbury, Ladd, Perrault, Reschovsky, and Yinger (1984) advanced thinking about structural imbalances by identifying and documenting differences in costs that emerge from community level service production characteristics. Service production characteristics include population density, program level and facility physical and operational *scale*, the presence or absence of untapped service and infrastructure capacity, age of housing, weather conditions, infrastructure age and condition, and crime rates. These conditions vary across local governments, even within the same state. A community's unique service production situation affects how much it will cost to produce a unit of service of average quality

During the 1980s and 1990s, continued study and careful comparative analysis brought depth to our understanding of the relationship between the fiscal environment and local finances (Bradbury, 1983; Bunce and Neal, 1984; Ladd and Yinger, 1989; Bahl, Martinez-Vasquez, and Sjoquist, 1992; Bahl, 1994). A particularly important policy application emerged from this literature when Bradbury et al. (1984) applied cost differences concepts to the design of a municipal aid formula for Massachusetts. Recent work is focusing on refining this literature base by improving conceptualization and measurement of disparities in nonschool spending requirements and financing capacity (Bradbury and Zhao, 2009; Zhao and Bradbury, 2009). In addition, the fiscal stress literature has been extended to the study of conditions in rural and suburban communities, with similarities and differences with cities identified and explored (Dougherty, Klase, and Song, 1999; Hendrick, 2004; Kloha, Weissert, and Kleine, 2005). Hendrick (2004) examined adaptation or balance between a government's fiscal structure and its environment by considering the extent to which revenue resources have been captured and whether adequate services are provided to constituents; this analytical approach links explicitly consideration of the fiscal environment and local finances.

The literature on urban hardship and city-suburban disparities identified key fiscal factors that influence local government spending and revenues and explained both how they exert influence and how they interact with each other and with policy choices to shape a community's fiscal fortunes. More than five decades of study have provided a rich foundation of knowledge that once organized and integrated produces a model for deciphering the complex forces and interactions that characterize the intersection of the fiscal environment and local finances. Before turning to the ensuing fiscal framework, let us consider the second line of inquiry into the fiscal status of government.

Research and Developmental Efforts Aimed at Gauging Financial Condition

Interest in measurement in budget and finance has roots in the early part of the twentieth century, when John Moody developed a rating system for railroad bonds (Lewis, 2003). However, it was the near default of New York City in 1975 that prompted accounting and finance professionals to seek improved methods for measuring financial position of governments; this work focused primarily on ratio analysis of financial statements (Clark, 1994). In 1978, the Municipal Finance Officers Association's publication of Rosenberg and Stallings' manual, *Is Your City Heading for Financial Difficulty*, considered both internal indicators of financial position and external fiscal characteristics that influence financial condition. Economic base vitality, income trends, employees per capita, revenue shortfalls, and assessment ratios supplemented traditional financial position ratios and brought a more comprehensive perspective to the measurement of financial condition.

In 1980, Groves developed the International City Management Association's Financial Trend Monitoring System (FTMS), the first comprehensive financial assessment tool available to local managers. In 1983, Clark and Ferguson released a book that offered significant insight into the linkages between the fiscal environment and financial condition and, by doing so, connected the formerly divergent government finance literature bases. They developed 28 indicators of fiscal strain, applied them to a national sample of cities to analyze causes of strain, and concluded that distress represented a lack of adaptation to the external fiscal environment.

In 1986, Berne and Schramm's *Financial Analysis of Governments* advanced thinking with its emphasis on examining financial condition analysis within the context of the fiscal environment. They differentiated *financial position*, with its emphasis on explicit obligations of government, from *financial condition*, which includes implicit obligations left unrevealed in financial statements. Implicit or invisible obligations include any future obligations not considered in financial statements, deferred capital maintenance, unmet capital needs, and unaddressed and emerging service demands. Viewed from the financial position perspective, a local government with substantial cash reserves would be viewed as fiscally healthy. However, the same jurisdiction might have pent-up service demand and inadequate infrastructure investment, so financial condition would be weaker than financial position ratios suggests. Berne and Schramm (1986) emphasized that financial condition cannot be assessed solely on the basis of a government's financial obligations to creditors but must encompass obligations to all government clientele providing or receiving resources.

Despite the developing view among public finance experts that financial condition management requires knowledge of the fiscal context, during the late 1980s and early 1990s substantial effort was devoted to developing brief measurement tools that could provide an easily applied gauge of financial performance. Brown's (1993) 10-point test became a popular means for regular, quick analysis of financial condition. In 1995, McKinney lamented that public financial management had become preoccupied with short-term financing concerns such as the adequacy of cash relative to immediate financial obligations while ignoring long-term issues that ensure the fiscal health of the community.

Concurrently, FTMS was expanded to include some crucial fiscal variables (Groves and Valente, 1994). The diagram that accompanied the system showed three columns of variables. The first column showed clusters of variables including community needs and resources, external economic conditions, intergovernmental constraint, and political culture. Factors in the first column were diagrammed as setting the stage for management practices and legislative choices (the second column), which in turn influenced the last column, budgetary and financial outputs of policies and practices. The third column included revenues, expenditures, debt structure, condition of infrastructure, and operating position. Major shortcomings of the improved but underdeveloped Groves and Valente fiscal model are similar to those discussed in the Introduction and include an emphasis on individual indicators viewed and interpreted in isolation and oversimplification of relationships between and among factors. Nollenberger's 2003 version of the FTMS continued to disregard interactions between variables, among clusters of variables, and across input and output clusters. Perhaps even more importantly from a policy pitfall perspective, feedback on fiscal factors produced by spending and tax choices is ignored. This is a crucial flaw because the mix, levels of services, and service quality that expenditures purchase combine with revenue capacity to determine required tax effort, which in turn influences population and income trends in the community, business location, property values, and ability and willingness to pay.

Implementation during the mid-1990s of the Governmental Accounting Standards Board's Statement No. 34 for basic financial statements expanded reporting requirements and the number of financial ratios that might be computed (Chase and Philips, 2004). Statement 34 recommended a more comprehensive assessment of financial health and introduced a new requirement for management analysis and discussion of finances, shifting responsibility for analyzing and explaining finances from accounting and finance professionals to public managers (Chase and Philips, 2004; GASB Basic Facts, undated). The GASB's Statement No. 44 on Economic Condition and Fiscal Sustainability expanded the range of fiscal factors for which data should be collected and reported and requires governments to synthesize information into a composite picture of a government's ability and willingness to meet its financial obligations and service commitments in the current period and in the future (GASB Basic Facts, undated).

Although it is too soon to know how and to what extent Statements 34 and 44 will change financial management analysis and reporting practices (Jung, 2008), the new models address long standing measurement issues that have limited the utility of indicators systems. In addition, the new managerial perspective, an implicit accountability mandate, and a focus on synthesis of environmental fiscal information with financial indicators raise the bar for local officials by requiring of them a working knowledge of the fiscal forces behind the numbers. However, to decipher and direct change successfully, local government decision makers need a framework to help them to identify and monitor the diverse and interconnected fiscal forces that drive local spending pressures and revenue capacity, understand interdependencies among factors, and pinpoint areas where feedback from policy choices may affect future conditions. As Rivenbark and Roenigk (2010, p. 149) pointed out, despite the "more robust financial reporting model" of Statement 34, "local government managers continue to struggle with defining financial condition, interpreting it..., and communicating it...". The remainder of this chapter presents and discusses a visual framework that maps the fiscal terrain.

The Visual Fiscal Framework

A multifaceted relationship exists between community characteristics, demand for services, timing of budgetary pressures, local ability to finance services and infrastructure, and policy choices about spending and taxing. **Figure 11.1** presents a visual model that

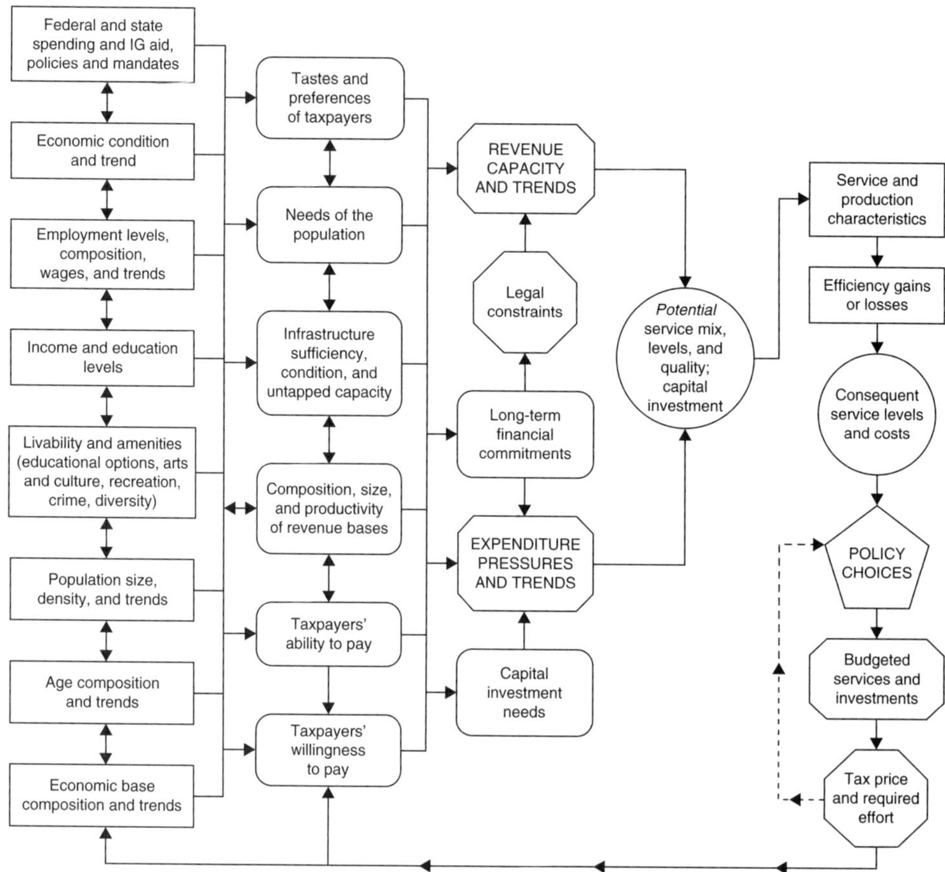

Figure 11.1 Framework for Deciphering and Monitoring the Fiscal Environment

may be used to decipher the complex array of fiscal forces and optimize finance policy choices. The framework illustrates paths of influence, including interactions among variables and the dual effects of many key indicators on revenues and expenditures. In addition, the model shows the role of production and service characteristics, which may create a gap between the mix, level, and quality of services desired at a given price and what actually may be produced at that price, given local circumstances that affect production costs and the potential efficacy of services. Finally, the framework traces the effects of policy choices first as they determine service mix, levels, and quality; capital investments; and tax burden; and then as they loop back and influence factors that in turn affect future revenue capacity and expenditure pressures.

At first glance, the visual framework can be intimidating because there are many variables and multiple connections among the fiscal factors. However, considering in turn the various sections of the framework, for example, factors that influence revenue capacity, helps to make it comprehensible and usable. Readers who work with local finance issues regularly will find the map instinctive because it shows systematically the effects and counter-effects that affect day-to-day problem solving and decision making. Let us review the framework briefly to gain a sense of its components and then turn to closer examination of key sections.

Inspection of Framework Segments

Beginning with the first two columns of fiscal factors that are shown on the left, we see many of the expenditure and *revenue determinants* identified by fiscal distress and disparities researchers plus other variables documented and investigated in more recent studies. The intergovernmental dimensions and local social, economic, political and livability characteristics shown in the first column connect with and affect each other, which creates a dynamic environment that is influenced by and at the same time influences the fiscal direction of a jurisdiction. As modeled by the connections between the first and second columns, fiscal traits in the first column influence community characteristics such as needs and tastes of residents, the composition and productivity of revenue bases, and taxpayers' ability and willingness to pay for government programs. Substantial interaction occurs between factors within column two and in the case of the composition, size and productivity of the revenue base, between factors in column two and column one.

Some aspects of the fiscal environment depicted in columns one and two are beyond the control of local policymakers, for example, federal and state spending and aid policies and the national and regional economies. However, the relationships between and the directions of trends in many of the fiscal variables are affected directly and importantly by policy choices about spending and taxing, as the feedback loop at the bottom of the diagram portrays. In the third column, we see that the very same sets of fiscal factors affect both expenditure pressures and revenue capacity, but legal constraints moderate revenue capacity and trends in capacity. Long-term financial commitments and capital investment needs also influence expenditure pressures.

Changing our view to the center of the framework reveals that expenditure pressures and revenue constraints combine to produce a *potential* mix of services and infrastructure investment and service levels and quality, with spending either constrained or facilitated by revenue capacity. Moving to the last column, we see that the outputs of simultaneous expenditure and revenue determination must be filtered through the particular production characteristics that characterize the locality where services will be produced. Production characteristics range from labor costs to weather conditions to frequency of natural disasters to population density to age of infrastructure. Physical and operational scales and *capacity utilization* are important features of the production environment. At a given funding level, the actual services that may be produced and delivered may differ slightly or greatly from the anticipated level because of the conditions under which programs operate. For example, even with a comparatively high per pupil expenditure, a rural or island school may be able to purchase only modest learning resources for its students because of a high combined fixed and semifixed *cost threshold* and *diseconomies of small scale*. As the fiscal model shows, the potential or expected mix, levels and quality of public services are adjusted by efficiency gains or losses and other production conditions facing a particular community. The effect of production characteristics on service costs may force policymakers to reconsider spending priorities and choices as the loop back to policy choices illustrates. Once decisions about spending and taxes have been made, the model shows the feedback of these choices on fiscal variables.

Let us now consider a few key sections of the framework more closely, beginning with the critical matter of factors that influence spending pressures.

Sources of Expenditure Pressures

Federal and state spending, aid levels and policies, and mandates are crucial sources of spending pressure. Though many policymakers think about intergovernmental fiscal relationships from the perspective of revenue capacity, important direct and indirect spending pressures also derive from federal and state policies. First, each state decides the *functional assignment* of service responsibility when it determines which services it will provide directly and which services will be delivered locally. Second, the federal government and states often place mandates on local government, which can increase spending pressure dramatically (Baicker, 2001). For example, the No Child Left Behind federal initiative, with its emphasis on student performance, is raising costs in some schools (Imazeki and Reschovsky, 2004). Many local governments apply for grants from the federal and state governments, which may require matching funds or development of activities in specified areas. Hall (2010) compared the burden of federal grant match requirements on local governments and found the burden to be notably higher in nonmetropolitan areas. Indirect spending pressure occurs when federal or state aid stimulates local expenditures for aided functions (Sacks, Palumbo, and Ross, 1980). Finally, many grants-in-aid are designed to phase out over time, which requires local governments to pick up the financing or end the program, a difficult but not impossible action. Similarly, grants from foundations or gifts from individual benefactors may require increased local spending.

A broad array of spending pressures derives from the fiscal environment of the community. The total amount expended, the particular array of services offered, the extensiveness of each service, and the resulting balance among programs within the total budget plan are influenced by the fiscal characteristics of a community, as delineated in the first two columns of the framework. Overall demand for public spending is the sum of multiple demands for services and infrastructure provision required first, to meet citizens' needs; second, to satisfy citizens' desire for public services at a specified quality level and preferences among service types; third, to support economic, political, and social functioning in the community; and fourth, to increase the provision of services and goods beyond the level required by citizens and businesses in order to serve a nonresident user population. Let us consider each of these four components of public service demand.

First, a class of service demands known as "needs" arise because some citizens require assistance to enable them to reach a society-determined acceptable quality of life or to access opportunities such as learning in a manner that is reasonably similar to their unassisted peers (Lewis, 1981). Addressing needs involves compensatory expenditures aimed at correcting or responding to problems, redressing limiting conditions, or leveling the playing field among individuals or households. Head Start preschool programs, special education, and vocational rehabilitation services are examples of public efforts to redress inequities. In some communities, needs are quite extensive because there are high levels of poverty, low educational levels, high proportions of low-income elderly, and children who require special assistance in school. Research on fiscal disparities was prompted in part by concern for people of limited means who were being left behind in cities when people of means moved to the suburbs. Today, many communities are confronting poverty issues for the first time because of a more rapid increase in poverty outside cities, a phenomenon that is being called the *suburbanization of poverty* (Kneebone and Garr, 2010).

National, regional, and local economic conditions are major forces affecting needs of the populace. Although the federal government and states are the principal responders to needs arising from job losses and unemployment, some counties and cities provide public welfare programs, corrections, and mental health services, all of which see increased need for services when the economy is down. Even local governments that do not have responsibility for social programs may feel pressure to respond to heightened need levels by offering tax abatements, short-term income replacement or assistance, subsidized housing, and shelters for homeless persons. Funding requests from nonprofit charitable organizations tend to escalate during bad economic times because those agencies see client needs increasing and available resources dwindling. Contractual arrangements under which governments reimburse nonprofit organizations for services provided to specified beneficiaries become more costly and may be unaffordable during recession.

Population size and trends and the density of settlement are two important influences on needs-based expenditure pressures, although the precise effect depends upon service production characteristics such as scale of operations and capacity utilizations (Ladd, 1980, 1984, 1992). Growing populations eventually stress services; how soon the effect is felt depends upon whether service and physical infrastructure capacities are adequate to absorb growth and how many additional users may be served. Small communities may see little pressure for services common in cities, for example, garbage pickup and street sweeping. The smallest places may be able to deliver a service such as firefighting using volunteers primarily, but growth or diversification of the economic base may necessitate a change to mostly paid firefighters. In contrast, even in a small town, high population density may call for professional firefighters because risk increases when buildings are close together. Large cities will see increased pressure to spend for services that keep the community safe, clean, and healthy. High population density exacerbates these demands, although larger scale operations may reduce the *unit cost* of service provision. Although not limited to large, dense places, crimes rates tend to be higher in cities and require larger expenditures for police patrols and investigation. Unacceptably high crime rates not only produce pressure to spend more for crime prevention and enforcement but also create a production environment that makes it more expensive to deliver a unit of service of acceptable quality, as will be discussed further later in this chapter.

What constitutes *unacceptably* high in the minds of citizens and businesses crosses over into the second area of demand for spending: taxpayers' tastes and preferences for public services. Crime creates need-based demand for public services to ensure public safety, but the level of crime expenditures also depends on taxpayers' tastes for safety and preferences for spending for crime prevention relative to other service areas. Whether crime is comparatively high or low is a separable issue from what people think about crime level. Sense of safety, personal experiences with crime, viewpoints about criminal activity, and other factors that are distinct from the actual level of crime will determine how much crime prevention and enforcement is desired.

When citizens have a taste for a particular service or good, it means they desire it, would like to see it provided publicly, and may want more than just a minimum level of service. For example, some citizens might like a state or a local government to purchase waterfront property and build a park. Other citizens might agree and then up the ante by arguing for a swimming pool and playing fields with artificial turf. A contrasting example may help to distinguish between needs and tastes for services. Citizens may have a taste or preference for high quality education, but children who do not speak English need academic support to gain the same chance to achieve as their English-speaking peers. The distinction rests upon the idea that a needs-based service supplies a remedy for an identified gap, while a taste-based service simply responds to citizens' wishes and requests.

Tastes and preferences for public spending vary with income and educational levels, age, employment, and across economic cycles. Although a large proportion of low-income residents always points to high need-based demand for services, a small proportion of low-income residents does not necessarily mean there will be little or no spending pressure. Affluent communities often see heightened demand for spending on amenity services and education because residents have both a taste for service enhancements and the ability to pay for additional spending. When high educational levels accompany high incomes, demands for improvements to educational programs are likely to be intensified beyond what income levels alone would predict.

Tastes for services are shaped in part by experiences. As Liebert (1976) identified, older cities provide a broader array of services than newer cities, so where someone has lived will influence expectations about service types and levels. People who move to a different part of a state or to another state tend to bring their tastes with them when they relocate. In-migration into a nonmetropolitan area, a small town or even a small city of new residents who lived previously in densely populated places can exert significant expenditure pressure on local budgets because the new citizens are used to a broader array of services than offered locally and higher levels of existing services. This effect will be magnified when the newly arrived have higher income and educational levels than long-time residents.

For example, in the mid-1980s, Maine saw a large influx of affluent households from other states who settled in southern and coastal regions; higher expectations about educational programming and services contributed to enactment of the School Finance Reform Act of 1985, which brought sweeping educational reforms and propelled both the price of public education and local property taxes (LaPlante, 1993). However, not everyone shared the higher taste for services of people new to Maine: in 1988 and 1989, a large number of tax and expenditure limitation measures appeared on local ballots (LaPlante, 1990).

The economy and economic base composition and trends are important influences on citizens' tastes for services. When times are good and employment opportunities prevalent and growing, people may be more interested in new and expanded programs and maintaining quality of services. Similarly, referenda for approval of the issuance of debt for capital improvements may pass easily. In contrast, when times are tight, people tend to constrain their own spending and pay down debt and expect government to behave similarly.

Last but far from least, taxpayers' values shape their taste for specific services, preferences among service options, and willingness to support governmental spending. As has become increasingly clear over the past three decades, some taxpayers feel antipathy toward government spending; they may wish to see lower taxes, more return on the investment of tax dollars, or the transfer of service production to the private and nonprofit sector. Values combine with ability to pay to determine the specific needs of the populace taxpayers will choose to address and at what level they will elect to address the problems. Leonard (1992) traced the transformation of state and local spending in Massachusetts over the course of the 1980s and found that public spending grew rapidly but the increase was less than would be predicted based on the high education and income levels of residents. Leonard determined that the lower than expected total growth was explained by radically different rates of growth within budget components, with some such as corrections and especially human services increasing more than expected, and elementary and secondary education, public safety, and highway operations growing at a far slower rate. The redistribution of spending was unexpected in a decision environment traditionally characterized by incremental change and fair share allocation of new dollars. Leonard concluded that the clear shift in priorities and reduction in the overall priority formerly exhibited toward public spending were explained by changed values linked with very rapid income growth and a new political culture.

The third area of demand is service requirements originating from the business sectors of the economic base. When a local economic base diversifies from largely residential to partly business, industrial or commercial, the level of services required increases, but even more importantly, the types of services demanded and viewed as necessities change. Initial business activity adds new demands to traditional priorities like schools. The types of businesses make a difference to the level and mix of service demands. When there are many retail shops and restaurants, for example, citizens and businesses alike will expect traffic lights to be in place and operational, crimes to be responded to and investigated, cars to be towed when they are blocking exits, health laws to be enforced, and fires to be put out.

A new mall may escalate policing time because of shoplifting investigations and arrests. In contrast, a paper company or manufacturing plant may require traffic control only at predictable times of the day and place little other stress on public services. The location and volume of activity determine whether congestion occurs and in turn the extent of fiscal impact. Tax base diversification may require a community to provide infrastructure that would not have been needed in the absence of business activity, for example, traffic lights and sidewalks. Construction of a tall building may necessitate the purchase of specialized firing fighting equipment. Finally, demands for public service and infrastructure provision derive from service use by nonresidents who visit a community to work, to go to college, to visit government offices and nonprofit agencies, and to pursue social, arts and culture, recreation and other leisure activities. Services and employment hub communities see service user populations increase, in some cases dramatically (Bradbury and Zhao, 2009; LaPlante, 1990). When a community serves as a county seat or is home to large governmental properties such as district courts, prisons, and office buildings, the daily influx of nonresidents can be quite large, which places strain on local services. A jurisdiction with a large mall or other shopping opportunities, lodging, restaurants, entertainment venues, recreational opportunities, and arts and cultural activities also will see many people come into the community. Although the fiscal impact of nonresidents has been documented for cities (Bradbury, 1983; Bradbury and Zhao, 2009; Ladd and Yinger, 1989), the spending pressure impact on small places can be quite severe because either services, physical infrastructure, or both are inadequate; adding initial capacity can be extremely expensive relative to what a community would have spent for its residents alone (LaPlante, 1990).

At the center of the framework, you may notice that long-term financial commitments and capital investment needs are influenced by many of the same variables that produce spending pressure and also exert spending pressure. Although capital investment needs are a direct influence on spending, budgetary effects may be delayed, in some cases indefinitely. By renting portable classrooms, construction of a planned new school may be postponed. Because capital projects often may be deferred for some time without serious consequence, these spending requests commonly are among those denied when resources are tight (Pagano, 2001; Hoene and Pagano, 2003).Unfortunately, policy choices that defer investments add to spending pressure because unmet capital needs do not disappear but instead grow more costly the longer they are shelved and may require interim expenditures. Compounding the problem is the potential for inadequate infrastructure investment to limit the types and extent of new development.

Prior financial commitments including debt and postretirement pension and health care obligations also are important sources of spending pressure. Long-term financial obligations often create claims against resources that grow over time. In times of resource constraint, local governments and states are likely to feel more acutely the burden of past commitments and may look for ways to postpone paying toward these obligations. However, a decision to sidestep payment responsibilities for the short term may produce long-term financial consequences, such as a downgrade of the jurisdiction's credit rating or reduced access to credit markets. Pension financing difficulties revealed during the Great Recession drew attention to the importance of making decisions that obligate resources far in advance with great care because in the future meeting commitments may preclude funding new programs or capital investments, spending to reduce outstanding financial obligations, responding to emergencies, or stabilizing or reducing taxes (LaPlante, 2010).

Revenue Capacity

Revenue capacity is the total value of resources that reasonably may be raised by a local government to support public services, pay for long-term financial commitments, and finance capital investment. State laws that specify which types of revenues local governments may use and how deeply they may tap those resource bases are an important determinant of revenue capacity. Since the passage of the highly restrictive Proposition 13 in 1978 in California, citizens across the United States have been constraining policy makers' access to tax bases, with the unpopular property tax a particular target for limitation. In response to antitax voter sentiment, some state legislatures have enacted statutes that limit tax growth and restrict total tax collections to a specified percentage of local tax bases. Some states reserve income and sales taxes for their own purposes, permitting local government access only to the property tax. Because property tax collections are relatively unresponsive to economic growth while service demands often escalate in the face of population increases and business development, a lack of authority to levy other taxes may place a severe and potentially insurmountable revenue constraint on local governments (LaPlante, 1990, 1993; Hoene and Pagano, 2008). Further reducing potential revenues, state governments often approve exemptions from property taxes for charitable and nonprofit organizations, among other beneficiaries. Reductions in tax base value and tax collections may be offset partially with payments in lieu of taxes and fees for services provided, but affected locales often find that exemptions contribute to fiscal stress (Mullen, 1990).

Functional assignment of service responsibility is the second primary determinant of revenue capacity because what a government does in part determines what types of revenues are feasible (Hoene and Pagano, 2008). The first division between revenue types is intergovernmental assistance and own-source revenue. State and federal spending decisions and intergovernmental aid policies are important determinants of local revenue capacity (Downes, 1987). As the Great Recession underscored, the fiscal condition of local governments rises and falls on the basis of federal and state decisions about the amounts of financial assistance they will provide (Downes, 1987; Reeder, Bagi and Calhoun, 1996; Hoene and Pagano, 2003). When provided locally, very costly services like corrections or public welfare may receive significant state financial assistance. Other programs like elementary and secondary education receive varying amounts of intergovernmental aid, with the proportion of spending subsidized ranging from very low in affluent places to quite high in poor places. The influence of federal and state aid is unusually complex because it produces both revenue and expenditure effects, some of which are not visible immediately or easy to forecast (Berne and Schramm, 1986). McKinney (1995) found that aid does not help local governments avoid fiscal strain because over time external assistance may cause local governments to increase use of their own resources. First, state and federal aid often is provided with an expectation that the local government will match the aid with higher spending or at least maintenance of effort. Second, intergovernmental aid stimulates local spending, producing a higher level of spending than would exist in the absence of aid (Sacks, Palumbo, and Ross, 1980). Third, intergovernmental aid usually stays where it is targeted, a phenomenon known as the flypaper effect, which can make it more difficult to allocate resources efficiently. Fourth, some intergovernmental grants are designed so that assistance is phased-out over time, leaving the local government with full financing responsibility. Although few are willing to turn down an offer of assistance, dependence on intergovernmental revenue makes a local government vulnerable to changed policies and aid levels (Morgan and Hirlinger, 1993; Reeder, 1989; Reeder, Bagi, and Calhoun, 1996). Vulnerability has both fiscal and behavioral dimensions; MacManus (1995) established that growing taxpayer animosity toward school districts in Florida was attributable to state policy choices to divert funding from local schools to prisons and other state programs.

The majority of revenues often is raised from local governments' own sources, which fall into two broad classes: taxes and charges or fees paid by service beneficiaries. In the southwest, special districts provide services such as firefighting that are a municipal government responsibility in other parts of the United States. When services are provided to residents and businesses that benefit directly, fee-based finance may recoup some or all of the cost of service production. Local governments that produce and sell a service to neighboring jurisdictions, for example, a regional crime lab, may price their product and receive payment. When fee-based finance is not feasible or must be subsidized, governments must turn to taxes to fill the gap.

As the framework shows, many of the same variables that influence demand for spending simultaneously determine the tax capacity of a government. The composition of a tax base, the values of tax base components, and the responsiveness of tax bases to economic changes are key determinants of revenue potential. When local governments have access to point of origin sales tax revenues, a strong retail sector will produce strong revenues in good economic times. However, retail sales often drop sharply with the onset of recession and recover slowly as consumers pay down debt and defer purchases. The property tax base historically has been quite stable across economic cycles, but recent experience has shown the new vulnerability of this base to economic conditions.

The values of tax bases depend upon the nature of the economic base, that is to say the mix between residences, businesses, farmland, and tax-exempt properties. Homes with high values and a large business valuation create substantial resource capacity. However, high valuations may increase taste-based spending demand and reduce state financial assistance for K–12 education. Low property valuations may increase state school aid, helping to offset lower own-source resource capacity. Good jobs with good wages and benefits produce a more productive tax base and encourage citizens to support government.

Two components of demand for public services and infrastructure discussed in the last section, diversification of the tax base and an influx of service users who do not pay for services also are important considerations when discussing revenue capacity. A sizable increase in the daily service user population necessitates a commensurate increase in service levels. Depending on state laws and aid policies, revenues may or may not offset the costs imposed by nonresident service users. For example, a community with a local sales tax is better able to recover some of the costs of serving nonresidents than a community that is wholly dependent on property taxes. When state aid policies do not address directly the costs imposed on local governments for serving nonresidents, high local tax effort is required and budget deficits and eventually structural fiscal distress may result (Bradbury, 1983; Bradbury and Zhao, 2009; Bradbury, Ladd, Perrault, Reschovsky and Yinger, 1984; Ladd and Yinger, 1989; Zhao and Bradbury, 2009). LaPlante (1990, 1993) found that as a consequence of narrow local tax authority and a state aid program that failed to address cost differences, property tax effort in Maine's small employment and services hub communities often reached double the state average.

Factors beyond statutes and constitutional provisions may limit local officials' access to tax bases. Citizens' willingness to pay taxes is a crucial determinant of resource capacity. Citizens with higher educational levels and greater ability to pay tend to be more willing to finance services, but other variables may moderate the anticipated positive relationship (Berne and Schramm, 1986; Steel and Lovrich, 1998). Steel and Lovrich (1998) determined that cynicism, perceptions about government waste, and party identification influence judgments about preferred service levels, and these symbolic factors are centrally important in voting on spending and tax limitation measures. When businesses share financing responsibility and the economic base is vibrant, citizens may be more willing to pay higher taxes, especially for schools. On the other hand, if those taxes support services that do not benefit residents, willingness to pay may be reduced (Simonsen and Robbins, 1999).

Community values may dictate against high tax levels or permit reasonable access to tax bases, either as a consequence of views about and personal experiences with services to be funded or as a general stance (Glaser and Hildreth, 1999; Leonard, 1992; Robbins, Simonsen, and Feldman, 2004). Citizens often demand services but are reluctant to pay, which creates a tax-demand discontinuity that Glaser and Hildreth (1996) predicted will intensify if fiscal constraints increase.

Policymakers' own perceptions about the appropriateness of the local tax burden, the ability of local citizens to afford tax increases, and tax competitiveness affect their willingness to increase taxes, and in turn, their willingness to spend (Berne, 1996). Absence of a circumstance such as poverty impaction, which can make it distasteful to increase revenue burdens, makes increasing use of a tax or implementing a fee hike easier. Most public officials understand that the quality of public services and infrastructure sufficiency, condition, and untapped capacity influence revenue capacity by facilitating or inhibiting residential and business location, so their willingness to invest in the economic future of the community may temper the effects of other variables. Political views and aspirations also play a role in whether policymakers will increase taxes, whether they will diversify revenues to include more charges for services, and whether they will price amenable services to recover most or all of the full cost of service provision.

Service Production Conditions

Although revenue capacity imposes a constraint on spending, a difference between the potential and actual level of services may emerge as a consequence of characteristics of the service production environment. *Service production conditions* include costs of inputs including labor, supplies, and materials; population density; and other factors such as weather conditions that may require higher expenditures (Bradbury, 1983; Ladd, 1992). When unfavorable production characteristics exist, the cost of producing a unit of service will be higher than average without any commensurate increase in quantity or quality. Conversely, when production characteristics are favorable, a community may achieve above average service quantities or quality while spending only an average amount.

Infrastructure availability and sufficiency are important production characteristics. Cities and larger suburbs are likely to have invested in service capacity and infrastructure in earlier decades and often can absorb new growth or increased business activity within existing capacity. When service capacity or facilities must be provided for the first time, growth and development will have profound budgetary effects. Fiscal impact models based on average costs in other communities will understate direct costs greatly. Even in larger communities, growth often necessitates expansion at some point.

Public Service Cost Structures

Public services such as jails, schools, and water systems deliver many services collectively to many users at the same time. Most collective consumption services are characterized by high fixed costs, which means the bulk of expenses do not vary with use. For example, a school built to house 300 pupils requires heat, lighting, and debt repayment regardless of the number of students who actually attend. These types of public services also often have a high semifixed cost component, which includes expenses such as teachers' contracts that do not vary in the short or even the intermediate term. Although labor usually is viewed as a variable expense, teaching staff work under annual contracts and the staffing level cannot be reduced until a classroom can be closed.

Utilization of capacity.

The size of a facility and staffing together determine the capacity of a service system. There is an important relationship between capacity and unit costs: unit costs fall as capacity utilization increases, up to the point of crowding. When a school is staffed to serve 400 pupils but serves only 200, its capacity utilization is only 50% and the unit cost will be high because total costs are divided across a small number of users. As the number of students served increases, more capacity will be used and unit costs will decline. On the other hand, a school that traditionally has had high capacity utilization but sees its enrollment declining will see unit costs increasing even if spending is held steady or cut modestly.

Because most states fund local schools on the basis of a per pupil allocation based on statewide average unit costs, understanding capacity utilization is fundamental to financing education and forecasting state aid. Education aid usually is based on the number of pupils in a district and local ability to pay. School districts that are experiencing declining enrollments often see their unit costs increasing, sometimes sharply, as a consequence of lower utilization of capacity, but may have few real opportunities to reduce spending. Schools with declining enrollment often see their state aid evaporating, while at the same time the smaller number of pupils left behind are needier (Sacks, 1972). While these linear funding issues typically are associated with urban schools, recent studies have demonstrated that rural schools are similarly adversely affected (Thorson and Edmundson, 2000, 2005).The impact of pupil count on state aid is exacerbated in many states by the use of per pupil valuation as the prime measure of local ability to finance education. Enrollment losses increase per pupil valuation, providing a sense that there is more ability to pay, so the affected district faces greater financing responsibility.

Many communities make the mistake of assuming that growth of the business tax base always is superior to residential growth because businesses do not increase school costs. However, the actual budgetary impacts of residential and nonresidential growth depend on whether there is available capacity. If new pupils may be accommodated within existing capacity, the cost impact of residential growth will be modest. In contrast, if residential growth will cause a school to exceed capacity, the marginal cost of growth will be high because expanding capacity will be expensive.

Scale of facilities and operations.

Though capacity utilization is a key determinant of unit costs for all infrastructure and most services, scale of operations and facilities also needs to be considered. Physical scale refers to size, for example the number of people who fit comfortably in a community center or the amount of water a system can deliver. Service scale refers to the number of people or households that can be served with existing staff, such as police officers or teachers. An *economy of scale* occurs when a facility is built large enough that the average cost of construction per square foot is reduced by discounted price for square footage purchased beyond a certain threshold. Economies of scale also occur in operations because of quantity discounts and more efficient use of inputs. When scale is large but not ultra large, economies result. For example, a larger enrollment permits teacher specialization, more economical meshing of personnel assignments, and volume discounts for books and materials (Riew, 1986). Achieving the learning resource levels available in a large secondary school would be very costly in a small or medium-sized school (LaPlante, 1994).

However, bigger is not always better. Very large scale operations often are more expensive on a unit cost basis than their large counterparts because more personnel are needed to manage operations and connect multiple levels of organizations.

Whether economies are achieved when scale is increased depends in part upon the composition of services and programs. When scale is increased, services tend to be diversified and expanded, specialized equipment is purchased, and additional, more highly educated and more highly paid staff recruited. For example, a very large hospital is likely to have specialty services not found in a smaller facility and may conduct research. A large urban school may spend more per pupil than a large school because the student body is more diverse and requires an expansive array of programs and support services not required in a large but more homogenous suburban school.

In schools that serve students with more diverse educational needs and paths, needs-based demand characteristics may combine with service production characteristics to raise appreciably the cost of providing education. Large schools often sacrifice economies of scale because they must mount multiple small programs to address the needs of heterogeneous student populations. The most serious effects of student heterogeneity are likely to occur in rural secondary schools, where diseconomies of small scale, a small number of teachers with only a limited array of credentials, and low wealth tax bases may preclude mounting the programming and support required to address student needs adequately (Riew, 1986). Use of per pupil expenditures to gauge the adequacy of learning resources may miss deficiencies because unit costs of education can be quite high in very small schools.

LaPlante's 1994 analysis of resources and programming in Maine schools determined that a secondary school size of approximately 400 pupils was a prerequisite for mounting the full range of programming and learning support services found in highly resourced schools in the state. However, size alone did not determine the level of learning resources. LaPlante found that many medium-sized secondary schools were able to offer breadth and depth of curriculum suggestive of larger schools because student bodies were largely college-bound and citizens were willing to exert more tax effort. Large schools with diverse student populations were unable to achieve as full an array of learning options for college-bound students because other types of programming competed for funding and funding was not incremented to the extent observed in more affluent places. The interplay of who was being educated with taxpayer willingness to pay exacerbated learning resources deficiencies in poorer places and enhanced educational opportunities in the already better-resourced affluent districts. As LaPlante (2011) described, state aid minimums paid to affluent districts aggravate inequities.

Community attributes as production conditions.

Community attributes are an additional but often neglected aspect of the service production environment. When a community is home to affluent households, the production environment is likely to yield unexpected fiscal pluses because homeowners coproduce some services. For example, even though the presence of expensive homes might suggest a need for higher fire prevention expenditures, homeowners are more likely to take responsibility for avoiding fires in their homes. Schools serving children of the affluent often have more motivated students who receive family financial and academic support. In these settings, high achievement may promote inaccurate conclusions that schools must be truly excellent, but the tax base benefits nonetheless from the image of quality. In contrast, some governments must produce services in the face of one or more negative community characteristics.

Variables such as poverty and crime create demand for spending, but when conditions become entrenched, they also may interfere with achieving an acceptable result, even if tax effort is increased appreciably (Bradbury, 1983; Berne and Schramm, 1986; Sacks, 1972; Schwab and Oates, 1991). Schwab and Oates (1991) explained that residents of a poor community burdened with a large number of people who have a propensity to commit crimes will feel less safe, regardless of the relative success of public safety programming. The difference between what is achievable with an average or even an above average level of service effort and what it would take to attain higher levels of community satisfaction creates a structural cost difference (Berne and Schramm, 1986; Bradbury, 1983; Bradbury and Zhao, 2009).

When input prices are low and production characteristics conducive to lower unit costs, the fiscal dividend may be used to increase service levels, add additional services, improve quality, or reduce spending and taxes. In contrast, where input prices are high and production characteristics less than ideal, it will be much more costly to produce a unit of service. Higher costs and efficiency losses may create a gap between potential levels and the consequent feasible mix, level, and quality of services. The gap may be addressed through cutbacks in service levels or quality, higher fees or taxes, or a combination of spending and revenue strategies. In sum, production characteristics may reduce or exacerbate disparities between anticipated and actual service outputs.

Policy Choices, Spending and Tax Outputs, and Fiscal Feedback

The remaining items on the right hand sections of the framework emphasize the budget decision process, during which policymakers review options and then allocate resources to services, long-term financial obligations, and new capital investments. This is a complicated process because individuals bring their own values and goals to the process and they represent constituents including people and businesses who may benefit from some services, have expressed a desire to see new or expanded services, may have asked for less government and lower taxes, or may wish to see a particular capital project funded. Once an initial agreement has been reached on capital and operating budgets, it is not unusual for policymakers to deem excessive the tax price and accompanying required effort so one or more additional iterations may occur. Eventually, budgetary outputs are decided and establish the mix, levels, and potential quality of public services; capital investment; likely borrowing; and taxes and other revenues.

Policy makers' priorities explain a portion of differences observed between needed and actual funding levels. Rich (1982) identified a tradeoff across business-oriented spending and expenditures aimed at addressing human needs; he observed that local governments respond selectively to known needs and as a consequence fail to supply the services at the level required to improve conditions. Rich concluded that businesses' concerns are central to local policy makers, who view ensuring that business activities can go on as their top priority, while keeping the effects of human problems within acceptable limits. A second and potentially even more important explanation for divergence between anticipated and actual spending is the existence of a *fiscal opportunity constraint*, which is the intersection of a local government's revenue capacity, needs of the populace and other demands for services, infrastructure investment requirements, long-term financing obligations, and service production characteristics. The opportunity constraint influences the particular array of services that may be scheduled, the extensiveness and quality of each service, the balance among various services within the overall service mix, and the total expended. When circumstances are favorable, the opportunity constraint is flexible and permits substantial budgetary choice. When circumstances are unfavorable and include structural imbalances between spending requirements and resource capacity, adverse cost differences, or both, the opportunity constraint will obstruct choices.

Research on central-city-suburban fiscal disparities provides insight into why actual spending may diverge from expected spending (Campbell and Sacks, 1967; Sacks and Callahan, 1973; Bahl, Martinez-Vasquez, and Sjoquist, 1992; Bahl, 1994). A discrepancy often emerges because many of the factors in the first column of the fiscal framework have both demand and supply characteristics, which means they exert pressure to spend for services while simultaneously influencing the local government's capacity to finance services. For example, the size and composition of the economic base affects spending demands but also contributes to revenue potential. This duality produces the classic *fiscal disparity* dilemma: the places with the highest levels of needs often have inadequate resources to finance the required services, while places with abundant resources may have lower need. Although one would expect higher spending in cities and other older communities with needy residents, actual spending in disadvantaged places may not differ appreciably from spending in more affluent and homogenous places because, as Campbell and Sacks identified in 1967, the mix and levels of services differ. In a city or rural community, in the absence of adequate resource capacity and often despite higher than average tax effort, spending may be diminished to a point beneath the level required to address needs adequately. While a jurisdiction with greater ability to pay may not have as much need for services as an older community with needy residents, excess revenue capacity permits larger investments in preferred services, such as funding more extensive college preparatory programming in schools and more highly paid teachers. Total spending in an affluent place may be almost as high as expenditures in a nearby city, but the distribution of financing will favor schools and amenities in suburbs (Sacks, 1972; Bahl, 1994). Bahl (1994, p. 297) concluded that "central-city budgets have become more weighted toward non-education responsibilities, and there is no evidence that education spending disparities have narrowed...."

A key element of the framework is the connection between decisions about the mix and levels of public services, long-term financing commitments, capital investments, and tax price and effort with the expenditure and revenue determinants shown in the first two columns. Feedback onto choices on the left side of the framework can be either negative or positive and contributes to shaping the fiscal future of the community. Areas of particular concern include first, the influence of spending choices and tax burden on the willingness of citizens to pay for services; second, whether spending and capital investments facilitate economic functioning and development; and third, whether schools are receiving funding adequate to reach high quality. Public officials may assume that school quality is important only to households with children, but in fact residential property values are linked with generalized perceptions of local school quality (Oates, 1964). Recent research is revealing that the value of more expensive homes in particular is affected by school quality (Ries and Summerville, 2010).

Berne and Schramm (1986) advised that it is essential to examine critically a jurisdiction's revenue position with respect to the extent to which own source, locally raised revenue collections are over or under *prudent* revenue capacity. The authors called the difference between actual and target revenues a revenue reserve; a reserve may be negative or positive.The local revenue reserve is computed by applying the average tax rate for jurisdictions within a specified area, perhaps a county, or across a set of municipalities against the local tax base and comparing the resulting revenue level to the actual revenues collected by the local government. For example, if the average property tax mil rate in the area is $10.00 per $1,000 of property value and a local government is raising $15.00 per 1,000 of value, the revenue reserves analysis will reveal that tax collections are 50% higher than a prudent level. Berne and Schramm (1986) noted that the direction and size of a divergence between budgetary demands and fiscal capacity is an important indicator of financial condition. A positive revenue reserve suggests untapped fiscal capacity and a negative reserve reveals overuse. Ideally, revenue reserves analysis will divulge some resource slack, which would suggest untapped revenue capacity (Berne and Schramm, 1986; Hendrick, 2004). However, a determination that there may be untapped capacity does not necessarily mean additional tax dollars may be raised easily (Berne and Schramm, 1986).

There is a delicate balance between the service mix, levels, and quality and the tax effort required to finance governmental programs. High tax effort is symptomatic of fiscal stress (Benson et. al., 1988), but what may be considered "too high" depends on factors specific to the community. Throughout the fiscal environment literature, there is explicit and implicit acknowledgment that policy choices about budgetary outputs shape a community's fiscal future. Citizens will tolerate somewhat higher taxes when those revenues support a higher level of services from which they benefit and when the dollars produce high quality schools (Luo and Douglas, 1996). However, how much higher taxes may rise before an effective tax limit is reached and the local tax base begins to erode depends on the views of taxpayers. Citizens' sense of the place in which they live, experiences and satisfaction with public services and government, and perceptions of circumstances in other places they might live influence what constitutes an unacceptable tax burden. Research on the fiscal plight of cities provides us with substantial evidence that people of means will relocate to achieve the mix and quality of public services they prefer at a tax price with which they feel comfortable. A community with attractive amenities such as beaches or parks and arts and culture, excellent schools, and low crime rates is likely to see its population growing. These same features tend to attract residents with higher educational levels and higher incomes. Citizens who are drawn to a community's amenities often have more ability to pay for public services and more willingness to pay. In contrast, deteriorating infrastructure, failing schools, and concentrating poverty are likely to plague an older community that is not revitalizing.

When the attractiveness of a community declines and public services do not make enough difference in the quality of life, more affluent residents become less willing to pay and may migrate to nearby places that better fit their vision for a good place to live. At the same time, households of means locate in other places. Because local amenities such as restaurants, arts, and culture may be accessed by nonresidents but schools are local, a community cannot count on amenities holding households within its boundaries. The combination of mismatched services and preferences with high taxes creates a fiscal time bomb that eventually may lead to taxpayer revolt, while ticking influences negatively the many fiscal factors that shape and reshape spending pressures and resource capacity. Unabated, sequential *"fiscal feedback"* may harm irreparably the tenor of the community and its tax base, especially if policymakers address budget gaps with round after round of tax increases.

Fiscal feedback may be worsened by decisions of businesses and on behalf of businesses. Retail and hospitality providers and other service sector firms will be sensitive to parking availability and traffic congestion issues. Interlocal differences in general sales taxes, hospitality taxes, and property taxes are not the most important influences but do play a role in location choices. In the worst-case scenario, a prolonged cycle of tax increases that do not benefit businesses adequately are likely to promote relocation. Local officials concerned about business retention are likely to offer incentives to stay, further stretching available resources and weakening the capacity to meet other spending demands.

Comparative Analysis

In 1996 Berne pointed out that most fiscal variables and budgetary outputs have no absolute or ideal value. He suggested that evaluation should be augmented with comparison of local budgetary outputs to those of similarly situated governments. Rivenbark and Roenigk (2011) made a case that comparative analysis actually is a prerequisite for financial condition analysis because accurate interpretation of indicators is possible only within a meaningful context. Changes to financial reporting implemented under the

GASB's Statement 34 are enhancing "local government's ability to compare itself ... with other local governments" (Rivenbark, Roenigk, and Allison, 2009, p. 4) and should help to make comparison more routine.

Lewis (1984) cautioned that the amount expended should be assessed with respect to the scope of the problem being addressed and what is being accomplished. A "yardstick" with which to assess a local government's relative fiscal and budgetary position may be fashioned by carefully selecting a reference set of communities that on average share fiscal circumstance with the jurisdiction being studied. The underlying premise of the method is that the reference group average will provide a reference point or benchmark against which a jurisdiction's fiscal outputs, constraints, and opportunities may be assessed. Berne (1996) advised that there are no ironclad rules for selecting a reference set, but guidelines may be developed from the literature. The fiscal framework provides a sound starting point for selecting a reference set.

If a reference set average is to yield a meaningful benchmark, the set of communities selected must share characteristics of importance. For expenditures, a good expenditure reference set will share: cost factors that affect the price and potential efficiency of service delivery, variables that influence demands for service, revenue capacity determinants, the willingness of taxpayers to finance services, and legal constraints. Berne and Schramm (1986) suggested a one-state reference set to minimize differences in functional assignment, permitted revenue sources, and state aid policies. The relevance and quality of comparisons may be improved further by focusing on functions and sub-functions rather than aggregate expenditures (Liebert, 1976). It is common to use the same set of communities to evaluate both spending and revenue policies. However, because affluent residents may shop for the best mix of taxes and services, local governments should compare their tax levels, trends, and burdens to those of places with which they compete for residential location.

Consideration of special circumstances enhances the utility of comparative analysis. A special circumstance might be the presence of a large college within the jurisdiction, which might be addressed by including at least one college town in the reference set. However, care should be taken to avoid distorting reference set averages for key criteria such as population density and income. In the event no comparable town exists, the effects of the college on local finances can be considered during discussion of differences between the reference set averages and local conditions. Sometimes a special circumstance cannot be addressed directly through the reference set. For example, the state of Maine has a lengthy coastline, with many peninsulas and islands, which produces dramatic structural cost differences (LaPlante, 1990). No other state fully shares this circumstance so the higher costs inherent in service delivery would need to be discussed and used to moderate comparative findings.

Maintaining fiscal health in the face of complexity and change is aided by having a sound sense of how taxpayers view the jurisdiction in relationship to other places they might choose to live or run their businesses. Peer effects should be considered when selecting a reference set. Peer effects are policies and directions of nearby governments or communities with which the jurisdiction under study competes for residential and business location. Peer effects influence state and local spending choices because jurisdictions look to see what others are doing and measure the success of local efforts against outputs for other communities such as test scores. Even more importantly, there usually are leaders among peer places, to which others look for innovative ideas and strategies. At the local level, vibrant communities with excellent schools often set the path for others to follow. Within a reasonably large reference set, for example eight to ten towns, including two towns that are considered leaders will incorporate peer effects on spending pressures. Including smaller or larger places to account for peer effects can distort averages for the fiscal indicators being used for selection so it may be necessary to expand the comparison group to achieve reference set averages for indicators that mirror conditions in the place of study. Finally, communities interested in attracting new residents and retaining current residents also will want to compare their amenities and services to those in neighboring and competitor towns, with an eye toward both continual quality improvement and marketing.

The use of the reference group approach to study trends in fiscal factors and budgetary outputs permits us to control partially for the extent of problems being faced. By permitting the direct comparison of apples and apples, rather than apples, oranges, and grapefruit, the use of a reference set enables us to separate out at least some of the influences on spending that lie beyond the control of policymakers and implicitly acknowledges constraints placed upon policymakers by their jurisdiction's relative ability to pay. However, it is important to understand that the reference set approach does not evaluate the effectiveness of programs nor attempt to establish a goal for the mix and levels of local public services.

Monitoring fiscal conditions by comparing indicators to the average for a carefully selected reference set helps policymakers to pinpoint budget and financial issues that require further study, enables a preliminary assessment of budgetary flexibility, assists with the identification of areas in the budget where efficiency gains may yield cost savings or at least constrain future increases, and assists with the identification of potential time bombs. However, the strength of the reference set method, its reliance on comparison of a jurisdiction with similarly situated places, can be its Achilles' heel if users do not ask the questions the approach leaves unanswered. First, the reference set approach provides no guidance on what local taxpayers think about spending including the mix, levels, and perceived quality of services; who benefits from services; and the balance between current spending and capital investment. Second and even more importantly, the reference set approach may lead to complacency about tax levels because similarly placed communities often have fairly similar tax burdens.

Sohl et. al. (2009, p. 88) advised: "comparative studies are certainly not 'plug-and play'... analysts should plan time and resources for adequate qualitative research." Using relevant complementary indictors can enhance comparative analysis by connecting what government does with those it seeks to serve. Service efforts and accomplishments reporting extends fiscal and financial analysis (Lewis, 2003). Taxpayer surveys can help evaluate whether the mix and levels of services are satisfactory to taxpayers, whether the balance between current spending and capital investment is appropriate, and whether the tax effort required to finance programs is acceptable. However, citizen surveys are time consuming and can be costly. Some jurisdictions have used focus groups to establish priorities and avoid across-the-board budget cutbacks (McAskill and Bond, 2011). A quick method for regularly taking the pulse of the town and for generating questions for a survey is to compare local livability factors against those in places with which the jurisdiction under study competes for residential and business location. Engaging citizens through web portals and blogs is a growing means for listening and learning about what citizens think.

Conclusion

Among the most serious of deficiencies identified with current financial condition measurement approaches is their lack of attention to first, the interdependencies and interactions among the many factors that contribute to financial condition and second, the fiscal feedback impact of day-to-day policy choices on those variables. As discussed in this chapter, both demand for spending and the tax effort required to support expenditures flow from complex and interconnected fiscal factors that lie beyond the direct control of government managers, yet can be deciphered and synthesized into a coherent picture of current and emerging conditions. Economic, social, and demographic circumstances and trends; production and service characteristics that make it more or less costly to provide services in a given locale; the nature, size, and productivity of tax bases and access to revenue bases; and federal and state spending, mandates, and intergovernmental aid policies are among the multiple sets of variables that interact and influence what a local government needs to spend and how much it realistically can afford to spend. To complicate matters further, policy choices that determine the level and mix of services and capital investments and the tax burden imposed affect both future revenue capacity and expenditure pressures.

The visual framework shows fiscal forces that drive local spending pressures and revenue capacity, highlights interdependencies among factors and paths of influence, and pinpoints areas where feedback from policy choices may affect long-term financial condition. The fiscal environment framework may be used with measures of financial position and fiscal health to identify and assess underlying factors and influential fiscal relationships and trends. The inclusion of livability and amenity factors acknowledges explicitly that not just quantitative but also qualitative dimensions of place and budgetary outcomes matter greatly to citizens and influence tastes and preferences for services, willingness to pay, and trust in government. Drawing upon the words of George Bernard Shaw, Lewis (2003) advised that the welfare of a community should not be reported just in figures and requires *counters* of a more spiritual kind and the imagination and conscience to sum them.

Engaging public officials and citizens in deliberating their community's fiscal future and evaluating potential consequences of policy choices requires local managers to communicate effectively how and why these forces matter. As Rivenbark and Roenigk (2011, p. 263) explained, the results of financial condition analyses "must be presented in a manner that increases the likelihood that the information will be used for making policy decisions." Armed with knowledge about complex fiscal forces, local managers are equipped to decipher, manage, and communicate financial condition; project likely effects of policy choices; and work with stakeholders to plot a path for robust fiscal health.

Glossary

Capacity: service capacity refers to the maximum number of customers who may be served by a program, and physical capacity refers to total physical space in a facility or other type of infrastructure. The facility size and staffing together determine maximum capacity of a public service.

Capacity utilization: the percentage of service or physical capacity used at a given time.

Cost threshold: the minimum amount that must be expended if a program or facility is to be made available, even if there is only one user. Public services such as education are troubled by high cost thresholds because both a facility and staff are needed, even when the number of children to be educated is small.

Diseconomy of scale: an increase in unit costs due to either unusually small or unusually large operations and/or facilities. Very small scale operations or facilities often cost more on a unit basis because of high cost thresholds and inability to access discounts, and very large scale entities may incur extra communication costs and duplicate effort.

Economy of scale: a reduction in unit costs that accrues from the larger size of an operation and/or a facility. Larger sized operations and facilities are able to spread the cost threshold over more users, obtain quantity discounts, and achieve other efficiencies.

Expenditure determinant: social, economic, economic base, and demographic characteristics that intersect to affect the needs, tastes, and spending preferences of taxpayers and service demands from the business sector.

Financial condition: places financial health of a local government within a broadened context that encompasses current financial position, obligations to constituencies not reported in financial statements, and the evolving fiscal environment.

Financial position: determination of a local government's capacity to meet its financial obligations based upon audited financial statements prepared in conformity with generally accepted accounting principles (GAAP) and presenting, in all material respects, the jurisdiction's financial obligations.

Fiscal capacity: aggregate resources available to support government spending.

Fiscal disparity: when viewed within a single government, a mismatch between spending needs and resources. Across units of government, describes differences in the degree of imbalance between spending needs and resource availability.

Fiscal environment: the social, economic, economic base, and demographic characteristics that interact to affect needs, tastes, and taxpayer ability and willingness to pay, which together with political culture, values, and other factors influence the total amount expended, the particular array of services offered, the extensiveness of each service, the resulting balance among programs within the total budget plan, and required tax effort.

Fiscal feedback: a process wherein declining tax revenues are met with a tax rate increase, which in turn reduces tax base value, necessitating another tax rate increase and additional tax base losses.

Fiscal opportunity constraint: intersection of a local government's revenue capacity, needs of the populace and other demands for services, infrastructure investment requirements, long-term financing obligations and service production characteristics; influences the particular array of services that may be scheduled, the extensiveness and quality of each service, the balance among various services within the overall service mix, and the total amount spent.

Functional assignment: the determination of which level of government in a federal system performs and/or finances specific governmental functions.

Municipal overburden hypothesis: a set of ideas that suggest that urban governments will face heavier demands for services than suburbs, resources inadequate to finance needed services and other obligations, many low income taxpayers for whom increased taxes could become excessively burdensome, and unfavorable tradeoffs when allocating available revenues.

Reference set: a group of local governments selected to mirror the fiscal environment facing a local government. The reference set average for each indicator is expected to serve as a benchmark for a typical response to circumstances, which may be used to assess position and trends in the local government under study.

Revenue capacity: the total value of resources that reasonably and legally may be raised by a local government to support public services, pay for long-term financial commitments, and finance capital investment.

Revenue determinant: social, economic, economic base, labor force, and demographic characteristics that influence local revenue capacity.

Scale: the size of a facility or operations.

Service production condition: characteristics that influence how much it costs to produce a unit of service of average quality. Examples include population density, program level operational scale, physical facility scale, the amount of untapped service and infrastructure capacity, age of housing, weather conditions, and infrastructure age and condition. These factors vary across governments and make it more or less expensive to deliver services.

Structural distress: a long-term imbalance between a government's functional responsibilities, service demands, capital investment needs, and revenue raising capacity. Far from being a simple budget shortfall to be closed with spending reductions and revenue increases, structural distress reflects a persistent gap between spending pressures and revenue capacity.

Suburbanization of poverty: once thought to be an urban problem, recent socioeconomic trends have revealed a sharp rise in the number of households in poverty that are living in suburbs.

Unit cost: total cost of an operation or facility divided by the number of users.

Discussion Questions

1. What is meant by the *local fiscal environment*?
2. How does the fiscal environment affect expenditure pressures?
3. What fiscal factors influence revenue capacity and how?
4. Why is it important for local managers to understand the fiscal environment?
5. What pitfalls exist in viewing indicators in isolation from each other and from the fiscal environment?
6. What towns would you use as a reference set for your local government? When selecting these reference towns, did you include any communities to address special circumstances your town faces (e.g., being a "college town" or "services and employment center")? Which jurisdiction(s) might be included to capture peer effects?

Recommended Resources

Honadle, B., Cigler, B., and Costa, J. (2003). *Fiscal health for local governments.* Boston: Elsevier.

Governor's Center for Local Government Services. (2008). *Fiscal monitoring workbook.* Harrisburg, PA: Governor's Center for Local Government Services, Department of Community and Economic Analysis. Available at http://www.newpa.com/get-local-gov-support/publications/index.aspx

Hustedde, R.J., Shaffer, R., and Pulver, G. (2005). *Community economic analysis: A how-to manual* (Rev. ed.). Ames, Iowa: North Central Regional Center for Rural Development.

References

Bahl, R. (1994). Metropolitan fiscal disparities. *Cityscape, A Journal of Policy Development and Research, 1*, 293–306.

Bahl, R., Martinez-Vasquez, J., and Sjoquist, D. L. (1992). Central-city suburban fiscal disparities. *Public Finance Quarterly*, *20*(4), 420–432.

Baicker, K. (2001). Government decision-making and the incidence of federal mandates. *Journal of Public Economics, 82*(2), 174B94.

Benson, E. D., Marks, B. R., and Raman, K. K. (1988). Tax effort as an indicator of fiscal stress. *Public Finance Quarterly, 16*, 203–218.

Berne, R. (1996). Measuring and reporting financial condition. In J. L. Perry (Ed.), *Handbook of Public Administration* (2nd ed.) (pp. 332–347). San Francisco: Jossey Bass.

Berne, R. (1992). *The relationships between financial reporting and the measurement of financial condition.* Norwalk, CT: Governmental Accounting Standards Board.

Berne, R., and Schramm, R. (1986). *The financial analysis of governments.* Englewood Cliffs, NJ: Prentice Hall.

Betts, J. R., and Danenberg, A. (2001). An assessment of resources and student achievement. In J. Sonstelie and P. Richardson (Eds.), *School finance and California's master plan for education* (pp. 47–80). San Francisco: Public Policy Institute of California. Retrieved March 12, 2010, from http://www.ppic.org/content/pubs/report/R_601JSR.pdf

Bradbury, K. L. (1983). Structural fiscal distress in cities: Causes and consequences. *New England Economic Review* (January/February), 33–44.

Bradbury, K. L., and Zhao, B. (2009). Measuring non-school fiscal disparities among municipalities. *National Tax Journal, 62*, 25–56.

Bradbury, K. L., Ladd, H. F., Perrault, M., Reschovsky, A., and Yinger, J. (1984). State aid to offset fiscal disparities across communities. *National Tax Journal, 37*, 151B70.

Brazer, H. E., and McCarty, T. A. (1986). Municipal overburden: An empirical analysis. *Economics of Education Review, 5*, 353–361.

Brown, K. W. (1993). The 10-point test of financial condition: Toward an easy-to-use assessment tool for smaller cities. *Government Finance Review, 9*, 21–26.

Bunce, H. L., and Neal, S. G. (1984). Trends in city conditions during the 1970s: A survey of demographic and socioeconomic changes. *Publius: The Journal of Federalism, 14*(2), 7–19.

Burchell, R. W., Listokin D., Sternlieb, G., Hughes, J. W., and Casey, S. C. (1980). Measuring urban distress: A summary of the major urban hardship indices and resource allocation systems. In R. W. Burchell and D. Listokin (Eds.) *Cities Under Stress: The Fiscal Crises of Urban America* (pp. 159–229). Piscataway: Center for Urban Policy Research at Rutgers, The State University of New Jersey.

Campbell, A. K., and Sacks, S. (1967). *Metropolitan America: Fiscal patterns and government systems.* New York: The Free Press.

Chase, B. W., and Phillips, R. H. (2004). GASB 34 and government financial condition. *Government Finance Review, 20*(2), 26–31.

Clark, T. N. (1994). Municipal fiscal strain: Indicators and causes. *Government Finance Review, 10*(3), 27–29.

Clark, T. N., and Ferguson, L. C. (1983). *City money: Political processes, fiscal strain, and retrenchment.* New York: Columbia University Press.

Dayton, J. (1993). Correlating expenditures and educational opportunity in school funding litigation: The judicial perceptive. *Journal of Education Finance, 19*, 167–182.

Dougherty, M. J., Klase, K., and Song, S. G. (1999). The needs and financial problems of small and rural localities: The case of West Virginia. *Public Budgeting and Finance, 19*(3), 16–30.

Downes, B. (1987). The fiscal consequences of federal and state revenue policies: The case of small Oregon cities. *Publius: The Journal of Federalism, 17*, 189–205.

Downes, T. A., and Pogue, T. F. (1994). Adjusting school aid formulas for the higher cost of education disadvantaged students. *National Tax Journal, 47*(1), 89–110.

Downes, T. A., and Pogue, T. F. (2002). How best to hand out money: Issues in the design and structure of intergovernmental aid formulas. *Journal of Official Statistics*, 18(3), 329–352.

Finkler, S. A. (2001). *Financial management for public, health and not-for-profit organizations*. Englewood Cliffs, NJ: Prentice Hall.

Gauthier, S. J. (2007). Interpreting local government financial statements. *Government Finance Review*, 25(3), 8–14.

Glaser, M. A., and Hildreth, W. B. (1996). A profile of discontinuity between citizen demand and willingness to pay taxes: Comprehensive planning for park and recreation investment. *Public Budgeting and Finance, 16*(4), 96–113.

Glaser, M. A., and Hildreth, W. B. (1999). Service delivery satisfaction and willingness to pay taxes. *Public Productivity and Management Review, 23*, 48–67.

Gramlich, E. M. (1977). This way to the morass: A guide to New York's fiscal crisis. *Intellect, 106*, 227–230.

Groves, S. M. (1980). *Evaluating local government financial condition*. Washington, DC: International City Management Association.

Groves, S. M., and Valente, M. G. (1994). *Evaluating financial condition: A handbook for local government* (3rd ed.). Washington, DC: International City/County Management Association.

Governmental Accounting Standards Board. *Basic facts about GASB's project on economic condition reporting: Fiscal sustainability*. Norwalk, CT: Governmental Accounting Standards Board. Retrieved on April 1, 2010, at http://www.gasb.org/cs/ContentServer?c=Document_C&pagename=GASB%2FDocument_C%2FGASBDocumentPage&cid=1176156740802

Hall, J.L. (2010). Giving and taking away: Exploring federal grants differential burden on metropolitan and nonmetropolitan regions. *Publius: The Journal of Federalism, 40*(2), 257–274.

Hendrick, R. (2004). Assessing and measuring the fiscal health of local governments: Focus on Chicago suburban municipalities. *Urban Affairs Review, 40*(1), 78–114.

Hoene, C. W., and Pagano, M. A. (2003). Fend-for-yourself federalism: The effect of federal and state deficits on America's cities. *Government Finance Review, 19*(5) , 36–42.

Hoene, C., and Pagano, M. (2008). *Cities and state fiscal structure*. Washington, DC: National League of Cities. Retrieved on April 4, 2010, at http://www.nlc.org/ASSETS/B151C0A433854A8098A3950B51EE14B4/rmproundtablerptmay03.pdf

Imazeki, J., and Reschovsky, A. (2004). Is no child left behind an un(or under)funded federal mandate? Evidence from Texas. *National Tax Journal, 57*, 571–588.

Jung, C. (2008). Practices of assessing financial conditions and fiscal health in local governments in the United States. *Governmental Accounting Research, 6*(1), 89–106.

Kloha, P., Weissert, C. S., and Kleine, R. (2005). Developing and testing a composite model to predict local fiscal stress. *Public Administration Review, 65*, 313–323.

Kneebone, E., and Garr, E. 2010. The suburbanization of poverty. Washington, DC: Brookings Institution. Retrieved on April 4, 2010, at http://www.brookings.edu/~/media/Files/rc/papers/2010/0120_poverty_kneebone/0120_poverty_paper.pdf

Ladd, H. F. (1980). Municipal expenditures and the rate of population change. In R. W. Burchell and D. Listokin (Eds.), *Cities under stress: The fiscal crises of urban America* (pp. 351–367). Piscataway: Center for Urban Policy Research at Rutgers, The State University of New Jersey.

Ladd, H. F. (1984). Fiscal impacts of local population growth: A conceptual and empirical analysis. *Regional Science and Urban Economics, 24*, 661–686.

Ladd, H. F. (1992). Population growth, density and the costs of providing public services. *Urban Studies, 29*(April), 273–295.

Ladd, H. F., and Yinger, J. (1989). *America's ailing cities: Fiscal health and the design of urban policy.* Baltimore: Johns Hopkins University Press.

LaPlante, J. M. (1990). Property taxes in Maine: Understanding the problem and seeking solutions. In R. Barringer (Ed.), *Changing Maine* (pp. 181–195). Portland: Muskie Institute, University of Southern Maine.

LaPlante, J. M. (1993). *Dollars and sense: Maine state budgeting at a crossroads.* Portland: Muskie Institute, University of Southern Maine.

LaPlante, J. M. (1994). *Analysis of resources and programming under budget scarcity in Maine schools.* Report to the Maine State Legislature, Joint Committee on Education. Portland: Muskie Institute, University of Southern Maine.

LaPlante, J. M. (2010). Debt financing and capacity. In E. Berman (Ed.), *Encyclopedia of public administration and public policy* (2nd ed.). New York: Taylor & Francis.

LaPlante, J. M. (2011). Seven habits of unsustainable budget building: A state policy perspective. *Journal of Public Budgeting, Accounting and Financial Management, 23*(2), 215–267.

LaPlante, J. M., and Honadle, B. W. (2011). Beyond the storm: Surmounting challenges of the new public finance. *Journal of Public Budgeting, Accounting and Financial Management, 23*(2), 189–214.

Leonard, H. B. (1992). *By choice or by chance? Tracking the values in Massachusetts public spending.* Boston: Pioneer Institute for Public Policy Research.

Lewis, C. (1981). Service needs and municipal expenditures. *Policy Studies Journal, 9,* 1021–1030.

Lewis, C. (1984). Interpreting municipal expenditures. In Richard Rich (Ed.), *Analyzing urban services* (pp. 203–218). Lexington, MA: D.C. Heath and Company.

Lewis, C. (2003). Updating state and local financial indicators. *Municipal Finance Journal, 24,* 17–35.

Liebert, R. J. (1976). *Disintegration and political action: The changing functions of city governments in America.* New York: Academic Press.

Luo, H., and Douglas, J. W. (1996). Revenue effort of local governments: Determinants, impacts, and policy implications. *Public Budgeting and Financial Management, 8*(1), 47–68.

MacManus, S. A. (1995). The constituents are mad: Just ask Florida's local government_budget chiefs. *Government Finance Review, 11*(4), 11–15.

McAskill, F. and Bond, T. (2011). Funding the services citizens want: Polk county's BFO process. *Government Finance Review, 27*(6), 34–39.

McKinney, J. B. (1995). *Effective financial management in public and nonprofit agencies* (2nd ed.). Westport, CT: Quorum Books.

Morgan, D. R. and Hirlinger, M.W. 1993. The dependent city and intergovernmental aid. *Urban Affairs Review, 29*(2), 256–275.

Mullen, J. K. (1990). Property tax exemptions and local fiscal stress. *National Tax Journal, 43*(4), 467–479.

Nollenberger, K. (2003). *Evaluating financial condition: A handbook for local government* (4th ed.). Washington, DC: International City Management Association.

Oates, W.E. (1969). "The effects of property taxes and local public spending on property values: An empirical study of tax capitalization and the Tiebout hypothesis." *Journal of Political Economy, 77*(6), 957–971.

Pagano, M. A. (2001). *City fiscal conditions in 2001.* Washington, DC: National League of Cities.

Peterson. L.J. (1971). *Municipal overburden.* Washington, DC: National Center for Education Research and Development.

Reeder, R. J. (1989). Targeting state aid to distressed rural communities. *Publius: The Journal of Federalism, 19,* 143–160.

Reeder, R., Bagi, F., and Calhoun, S. (1996). Who's vulnerable to federal budget cuts? *Rural Development Perspectives, 11*(2), 36–42.

Rich, R. C. (1982). The political economy of urban-service distribution. In R. C. Rich (Ed.), *The politics of urban public services* (pp. 1–16). Lexington, MA: D.C. Heath and Company.

Ries, J. and Summerville, T. (2010). School quality and residential property values: Evidence from Vancouver rezoning. *Review of Economics and Statistics, 92*(4), 928–944.

Riew, J. (1986). Scale economies, capacity utilization, and school costs: A comparative analysis of secondary and elementary schools. *Journal of Education Finance, 11*(Spring), 433–446.

Rivenbark, W. C. and Roenigk, D.J. (2011). Implementation of financial condition analysis in local government. *Public Administration Quarterly, 35*(2), 238–264.

Rivenbark, W.C., Roenigk, D.J., and Allison, G.S. (2009). Communicating financial condition to elected officials in local government. *Popular Government, 75*(1), 4–13.

Rivenbark, W. C., Roenigk, D. J., and Allison, G.S. (2010). Conceptualizing financial condition in local government. *Journal of Public Budgeting, Accounting & Financial Management, 22*(2), 149–177.

Robbins, M., Simonsen, B., and Feldman, B. (2004). The impact of tax price on spending preferences. *Public Budgeting and Finance, 24*(3), 82–97.

Sacks, S. (1968). Central city and suburban public education: Fiscal resources and fiscal realities. In R.J. Havinghurst, *Metropolitanism: Its Challenge to Education* (pp. 148–172). Chicago, IL: University of Chicago Press.

Sacks, S. (1972). *City schools suburban schools: A history of fiscal conflict.* Syracuse, NY: Syracuse University Press.

Sacks, S. and Callahan, J. (1973). Central city-suburban fiscal disparity. In Advisory Commission on Intergovernmental Relations (Ed.), *City financial emergencies: The intergovernmental dimension* (pp. 91–161). Washington, DC: Advisory Commission on Intergovernmental Relations.

Sacks, S., Palumbo, G., and Ross, R. (1980). The determinants of expenditures: A new approach to the role of intergovernmental grants. In R. W. Burchell and D. Listokin (Eds.), *Cities under stress: The fiscal crises of urban America* (pp. 369–385). Piscataway: Center for Urban Policy Research at Rutgers, The State University of New Jersey.

Schwab, R. M., and Oates, W. E. (1991). Community composition and the provision of local public goods: A normative analysis. *Journal of Public Economics, 44*, 217–237.

Sohl, S., Peddle, M. T., Thurmaier, K., Wood, C. H., and Kuhn, G. 2009. Measuring the financial position of municipalities: Numbers do not speak for themselves. *Public Finance and Budgeting, 29*(3), 74–96.

Simonsen, B., and Robbins, M. D. (1999). The benefit equity principle and willingness to pay for city services. *Public Budgeting and Finance, 19*(2), 90–110.

Steel, B. S., and Lovrich, N. P. (1998). Determinants of public support for tax and expenditure initiatives: An Oregon and Washington case study. *Social Science Journal, 35*, 213–229.

Thorson, G. R. & Edmondson, J. (2000). *Making difficult times worse: The impact of per pupil funding formulas on rural Minnesota schools.* Minnesota State University. Mankato, MN: Center for Rural Policy and Development.

Thorson, G. R. & Edmundson, J. (2005). *Towards a better understanding of the origins and consequences of inequality in public school funding: Measuring the consequences of fixed per-pupil funding formulas on small, rural schools.* Paper presented at the annual meeting of the Midwest Political Science Association, 4-7-2005, Chicago, Illinois.

Zhao, B., and Bradbury, K. L. (2009). Designing state aid formulas. *Journal of Policy Analysis and Management, 28*, 278–295.

Chapter 12

Fiscal Slack, Reserves, and Rainy Day Funds

by Justin Marlowe

Conventional wisdom in public financial management suggests that some level of slack resources is essential to sound local government financial health. But beyond the "five percent rule" and other simple platitudes, we know little about how slack resources do affect or should affect local fiscal health. This chapter presents a review of the theory and empirical evidence on the slack–financial condition link. The main conclusion is that, in fact, little empirical evidence shows that slack resources affect financial condition in any uniform way. This lack of a systematic relationship is likely because of differences in how slack resources are created, managed, and reported. Recent changes in accounting standards are likely to homogenize those differences, and could in turn establish a clearer link than the evidence currently suggests.

Introduction

In the spring of 2009, in the throes of the "Great Recession," Minnesota Governor Tim Pawlenty proposed a state budget that cut state aid to local governments by $245 million. Local governments were well positioned to absorb those cuts, Pawlenty believed, because at that time they held an estimated $1.5 billion—or 40% of annual local revenues for a typical jurisdiction—in reserve funds. Pawlenty's supporters in the state legislature agreed. "We're all in this together, and my hope is that [local governments] will do their part in sharing in it," said Minnesota House Minority Leader Marty Siefert. "This is what budget reserves are for, to kind of ride out tough times until the economy improves" (Scheck, 2009).

Local government leaders quickly produced a multifaceted counterargument. First, they suggested spending down reserves would leave them vulnerable if the recession stretched beyond the current fiscal year. "When the money is gone, then what?" asked City of Wadena, Minnesota Mayor Wayne Wolden (Scheck, 2009).

They also argued that spending down reserves would create a local government cash flow crisis. Most local governments in Minnesota, and in many other states, derive the majority of their revenue from property taxes received in large, annual inflows. Most jurisdictions need large pools of liquid resources to meet cash flow needs in between those infrequent but critical inflows. Wolden and others said that asking local governments to sacrifice predictable cash flow to stabilize near-term expenditures would do more harm than good. "We are protecting that reserve because it is cash flow," Walden said. "We do not have other pots to dip into. We use that cash flow, so we are making serious cuts. It's prudent financial management." Siefert replied, "Rainy Day funds are to get through tough times, and right now it's raining" (Scheck, 2009).

Other local officials argued the $1.5 billion figure was misleading because it overstated the amount actually available to backfill Pawlenty's proposed cuts. They suggested those numbers did not show that many local governments had spent down much of their reserves a few months earlier in response to a round of similar cuts to local aid brought on by midyear adjustments to the state budget. Moreover, these local leaders pointed out, figures on "average" reserves concealed substantial variation across jurisdictions; some had nothing, while a few outliers had reserves in excess of 300% of annual revenues. Many jurisdictions with little or no reserves faced major cuts in basic services if Pawlenty's proposed cuts were enacted, they argued (Scheck, 2009).

Wolden and other local leaders also pointed out that the $1.5 billion estimate was based on technical accounting assumptions that did not recognize the centrality of reserves to local capital budgets. For instance, according to figures from the Minnesota Office of the State Auditor, roughly half the funds Pawlenty classified as general fund reserves were actually designated by local officials for local capital projects. Diverting reserves from capital projects to operating needs, Wolden and others said, would stall those projects and slow the delicate economic recovery underway in many of their jurisdictions (Helgeson and Von Sternberg, 2009).

After a protracted debate, Pawlenty tabled the proposed cut. He proposed similar cuts two more times in the next year. A similar debate unfolded both times, and both times the proposed cuts were either tabled or significantly reduced (Helgeson and Von Sternberg, 2009).

The Minnesota episode illustrates the central point of this chapter: the relationship between *slack* financial resources and local fiscal health is simple in principle but complex in practice. This chapter provides a more nuanced explanation of that relationship, with an emphasis on the growing body of empirical research in this area and how recent changes to the accounting treatment of slack resources will likely affect the slack–financial condition relationship going forward.

This discussion proceeds in six parts. The next section presents several definitions of local slack resources. The third section presents slack resource levels, both in the past and the present. The fourth section is a discussion of the three main ways that slack is thought to bolster fiscal health: expenditure stabilization, credit quality maintenance, and protection from revenue volatility. Throughout this discussion, the theory and empirical evidence behind each of these proposed relationships is emphasized, and then the new accounting standards around slack resources and their likely implications for slack resource management are highlighted. The final section presents some conclusions and suggestions for future research.

Types of Slack

The slack resources–financial condition link is difficult to understand because both sides of the relationship have been defined several different ways. The concept of financial condition has been explicated elsewhere, including in this volume (Jacob and Hendrick), and does not require exposition here. To be clear, the focus of this chapter is slack in terms of liquid financial resources. This is an admittedly narrow focus given that slack has many other dimensions such as unused physical resources, underdeveloped human capital, untapped potential to generate new revenues, and many other assets that could potentially improve financial condition. That said, liquid financial resources are the traditional conception of the term. Liquid financial slack is most often equated with three different types of financial resources.

Fund Balance

The first financial resource is drawn from generally accepted accounting principles (GAAP). Local governments that follow GAAP accounting and reporting identify two main types of slack: *fund balance* and *net assets*. Fund balance is the difference between current assets, or resources a local government owns, and current liabilities, or others' claims against those assets. Fund balance is usually reported on the "modified accrual" basis of accounting, which is designed to show how transactions affect an organization's financial position in the most recent fiscal year.

Fund balance is currently classified one of three ways (see the later section for a discussion of forthcoming changes). "Reserved" fund balance is for a specific purpose and is therefore not available for appropriation in the next fiscal period. It represents slack that the jurisdiction's governing body has precommitted. Local governments reserve fund balance for a variety of future spending including capital projects, inventory, and encumbrances, among others. There has been considerable debate on whether reserved fund balance ought to be considered a source of slack, mostly because reservations can be rescinded and fund balance resources reappropriated toward other purposes.

The jurisdiction's management identifies "designated" fund balance for some specific purpose during the next fiscal period. Because management makes the designation, and not the governing body, designations are technically nonbinding. Fund balance is often designated for provisional needs such as pending litigation or anticipated employee wage increases. Some consider these designations a source of financial slack because the designations themselves can be modified or even lifted without running afoul of GAAP. However, managers are often reticent to adjust fund balance designations because doing so can disrupt financial planning, capital acquisitions, and other purposes for the designations. For these and other reasons there is and will continue to be disagreement on whether designated fund balance is a source of financial slack.

The third classification is unreserved, undesignated fund balance (herein called "unreserved fund balance"). Unreserved fund balance carries no restrictions on its future use and is available for immediate appropriation in the next fiscal year. Most consider this category a source of slack financial resources.

It is important to note that fund balance is the cumulative difference between fund assets and liabilities. That is, it represents the sum of all the jurisdiction's annual differences between assets and liabilities. Intrayear differences between assets and liabilities—often called "ending balances" or "closing balances"—are a key driver of fund balance levels. Current assets in excess of current liabilities will increase fund balance, and current liabilities in excess of current assets will decrease it, but "fund balance" is the cumulative difference between assets and liabilities across all fiscal years.

Most analysis of local government fund balance focuses on the general fund. Nonetheless, large fund balances are common in other governmental funds such as special revenue funds, capital projects funds, and debt service funds.

Compared to the general fund, the timing of large resource inflows and outflows more directly affects fund balances in these other funds. For example, if a local government sells bonds to finance street repairs at the end of the fiscal year, most of the bond proceeds will not be applied to their intended use until the next fiscal year. In turn, those residual resources will be reported as fund balance in their relevant debt service and capital projects' funds at the end of the fiscal year, even though they will likely be spent soon after the start of the next fiscal year. Local governments that transfer these types of balances into the general fund can easily confound the relationship between slack resources and financial condition in the general fund. By contrast, a local government can also transfer fund balance out of the general fund into other governmental funds, in turn understating what most consider its pool of "general" slack resources. Usually state laws, not accounting standards, determine whether local governments have that latitude. Much of the variation in fund balance levels and management practices is attributable to variations in those state laws.

Enterprise funds such as public utilities and municipal golf courses also tend to have high levels of slack. That slack can take many forms, but the most often mentioned is the cumulative difference between revenues and expenses, also known as "retained earnings." If a local government controls an enterprise fund it can usually supplement its general fund balance with retained earnings and other forms of enterprise fund financial slack. Previous research shows cities and counties that operate their own utilities tend to have larger general fund balances for precisely this reason (Hembree and Shelton, 1999).

Net Assets

Net assets are the difference between assets and liabilities on the full accrual basis of accounting. This accounting treatment is different from the modified method. It highlights how transactions affect the organization's overall, long-term financial condition rather than its financial condition in the current fiscal period. In addition to changing when and how transactions are recognized, full accrual accounting also shifts the focal point of slack resource analysis away from individual governmental funds and toward a broader emphasis on "activities" in all the governmental funds. Most local governments account for revenues and expenses associated with basic public services—public safety, parks and recreation, public health, and so forth—in the "governmental activities" section of the Statement of Net Assets. Net assets in the governmental activities are a useful indicator of local government financial condition (Chaney, Mead, and Schermann, 2002).

Net assets are reported in three different categories, and most analysts consider only one of those categories a source of slack resources. First is net assets invested in capital assets. Because capital assets are illiquid—that is, a jurisdiction cannot easily sell them or convert them to cash—they are not considered a slack resource. The second is restricted net assets. This covers net assets in special revenue funds and other funds where resources must be applied to a specific purpose and are therefore not available for other purposes. The third category, unrestricted net assets, is the portion of net assets that carry no direct restrictions on their use. Unrestricted net assets of the governmental activities are, for the most part, an accrual-based equivalent of general fund unreserved fund balance.

That said, unlike unreserved general fund balance, not all unrestricted net assets are available for appropriation in the next fiscal year. To illustrate, consider the following figures from the City of Redmond, Washington (available at: http://www.redmond.gov/insidecityhall/finance/cafr/cafrindex09.asp). At the end of fiscal year 2009, Redmond's unreserved general fund balance was $6.5 million, but its governmental activities unrestricted net assets were $83.8 million. This could imply that Redmond had substantial slack available in governmental activities outside its general fund. However, much of this difference is because of unrestricted net assets in two types of funds that have only an indirect relationship to Redmond's core services. The first are "internal service funds" such as fleet maintenance, information technology, self-insurance funds, and other areas that contribute to core services but are not directly and exclusively related to core services. Because their relationship with governmental services is not exclusive, internal service fund resources are available to finance other areas of Redmond's operations. In such circumstances, unrestricted net assets can overstate the amount of slack actually available for governmental activities. The same is true for resources in Redmond's capital projects funds. Most of the resources in Redmond's capital project fund will be applied at some point to capital projects related to essential government services. But until those projects are carried out, funds in the capital projects fund are technically fungible. Redmond officials could apply capital projects' resources toward other purposes, but doing so would be quite disruptive to the City's capital budgeting and finance plan. So again, unrestricted net assets can overstate slack resources immediately available to finance core government services.

Net assets are nonetheless a key indicator of the slack-financial condition relationship. This is because unrestricted governmental activities' net assets increase when a jurisdiction's governmental activities generate enough revenues to cover expenses. In other words, if a jurisdiction collects more than enough resources from general revenues such as property taxes and general sales taxes to cover the costs of providing general services such as public safety and parks, it will increase its governmental activities' unrestricted net assets. By implication, changes in governmental activities' unrestricted net assets across multiple years provide a reasonable indicator of the slack resources generated by a jurisdiction's day-to-day management of its core services.

We can gain further insights into the slack inherent in daily operations by observing the portion of the annual change in unrestricted net assets attributable to changes in general revenue sources versus restricted revenue sources. For instance, if a local government's governmental activities' unrestricted net assets increase by 5% in a year, how much of that increase was due to higher than expected general sales tax collections and how much was because of higher than expected returns on an earmarked sales tax for transportation infrastructure? Growth in unrestricted net assets as a result of the former suggest a stronger general financial condition than growth in net assets as a result of the latter.

Budget-Based Measures

There are many alternatives to GAAP-based definitions of financial slack. Some of the most closely observed are artifacts of state laws that dictate local government budgeting procedures. Most of these measures equate budget revenues and expenditures with the accounting treatment of assets and liabilities. For instance, much of the discussion about slack resources for local governments in Massachusetts is focused on "free cash," a budget-based measure of the unrestricted funds carried over from the previous year's operations. Free cash is distinct from fund balance because it is reduced by unpaid property taxes and certain other cash flow adjustments. As it is a budget-based measure, free cash levels can deviate substantially from fund balance levels.

Local government "reserve funds" in Kansas are another useful illustration. State law prohibits Kansas municipalities from passing budgets where revenues exceed expenditures. In effect, this prohibits local governments from building slack resources by "budgeting a surplus." However, two other aspects of state law allow jurisdictions to budget for a surplus. First is a provision that allows end-of-year balances to be carried forward to the next fiscal year. Those resources are effectively the same as fund balance in GAAP treatment. Second is a provision that allows jurisdictions to budget for interfund transfers to the general fund. Many jurisdictions "create" slack by budgeting for a sizable annual transfer from certain special revenue funds such as local sales tax funds or fee-based funds into the general fund. These budget-based measures are more central to the discussion of slack among Kansas municipalities than GAAP measures, particularly among small municipalities that do not prepare GAAP financial statements.

Variation in slack resource definitions is closely related to variation in state laws governing slack resource creation and management. Vanyolos (2009a) reviewed state rules and limitations on local government fund balance and reached two main conclusions. First, more than half the states have no explicit laws in this area. Second, among states with laws, there are wide variations in the types of restrictions on how fund balance is created, maintained, and used. Some states prescribe a minimum unreserved balance, some mandate minimum fund balance levels in a formal reserve or budget stabilization fund (see later in this chapter), some set maximum amounts for unreserved balances and/or reserve funds, and still others identify a minimum level of slack that can be exempted from balanced budget requirements.

Slack Resource Levels

By any definition, local governments have accumulated large amounts of slack. **Figure 12.1** illustrates the buildup of local government surplus over time. It plots the total surplus of all U.S. local governments from 1960 through 2010 as measured in constant 2009 dollars by the National Income and Product Accounts (NIPA). The dashed line is the total surplus for individual years, and the solid line is the total accumulated surplus since 1960. This figure shows that total local government surpluses have grown steadily, from close to zero in 1960 to more than $250 billion through the mid-1990s. At that point, the annual rate of increase doubled, and the total surplus grew to nearly $850 billion by 2009. Assuming a current U.S. population of approximately 300 million, this total surplus is roughly $2,800 per capita.

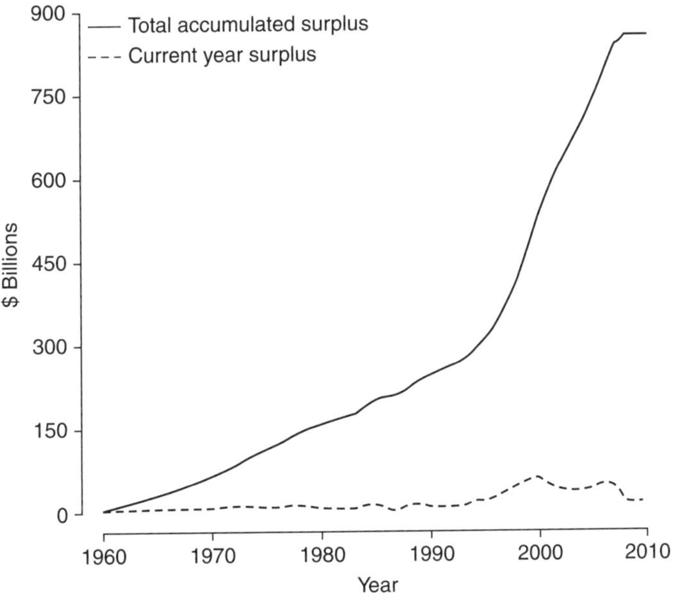

Figure 12.1 Total Surplus of All U.S. Local Governments, 1960–2010

Source: National Income and Product Accounts, U.S. Department of Commerce (in 2009 dollars)

A recent analysis of census data on local government "cash holdings" (Gore, 2009) corroborates this finding. That analysis showed the median level of cash holdings for individual municipalities–the census measure roughly akin to unreserved general fund balance–is between 80 and 100% of current annual expenditures. Also notable is that the standard deviations of those cash holdings were almost equal to the medians, which suggests wide variation across municipalities.

Other authors have studied fund balance levels and management practices within individual states, and all have reached similar conclusions about the proliferation of local government slack. Findings from those studies are summarized in **Table 12.1**. Vanyolos (2009a) reviewed fund balances in Florida counties from 1997 to 2008 and found the average balance was near 28% of total current expenditures. Hou and Wang (2009) showed the average fund balance level in North Carolina counties from 1990 to 2007 was 22% of current expenditures. Stewart (2009) found that from 1995 to 2004, more than half of all Mississippi counties had fund balance greater than 25% of total current expenditures, and more than a quarter had balances equal to or greater than half of total current expenditures. Gianakis and Snow (2007) analyzed "free cash" levels among Massachusetts municipalities from 1995to 2003 and found more than half kept free cash of at least 5-10% of current expenditures, and roughly 15% kept at least 20% or more. These free

TABLE 12.1 Summary of Findings on Local Government Slack Resource Levels

Author	Unit of Analysis	Period of Analysis	Median/Mean Level	Standard Deviation
Vanyolos (2009)	Florida counties	1997–2008	28%	20%
Stewart (2009)	Mississippi counties	1995–2004	10%	26%
Hou and Wang (2009)	North Carolina counties	1990–2007	22%	n/a
Gianakis and Snow (2007)	Massachusetts cities and towns	1995–2002	6%	5%
Hendrick (2006)	Suburban Chicago cities and villages	1997–2003	60%	80%
Marlowe (2005)	Minnesota cities	1990–2002	25%	42%
Hembree and Shelton (1999)	South Carolina cities	1997	45%*	n/a

Note: All slack levels are unreserved general fund balance/total general fund expenditures except Gianakis and Snow (2007), which is free cash/total current expenditures.

* Denotes an approximate figure determined from figures reported in the paper.

cash balances do not include balances in formal reserve funds that most Massachusetts municipalities maintain. Hendrick (2006) showed the average unreserved fund balance level for suburban Chicago municipalities from 1997 to 2003 was approximately 60% of current annual expenditures. Marlowe (2005) found the average fund balance among Minnesota cities from 1995 to 2004 was 25% of current annual expenditures. All in all, these results show most municipalities have slack resources equal to several months of current expenditures. This far exceeds the conventional wisdom of the "five percent rule" (Joyce 2001) and the 15–18% of current expenditures the Government Finance Officers Association (2002) recommends.

Also note that in almost every study, the standard deviation for slack exceeded the mean or median. This is consistent with Gore's findings on overall cash balances. These large deviations suggest that mean fund balance levels are not a particularly good indicator of "average" financial health because some jurisdictions keep almost no slack while others keep slack in excess of several years of current revenues.

Theory and Evidence on the Slack–Financial Condition Link

To this point, the focus has been on slack levels and their determinants. An equally or perhaps more important question is how slack resources affect local government financial condition. To address this question, we must reverse the direction of the analysis, in effect shifting financial slack from the dependent variable to an explanatory or independent variable. In this refocused analysis, the question becomes: do variations in slack resource levels and behaviors help to explain variation in local financial condition?

Financial management practitioners and state fiscal policymakers agree that slack is essential to local government financial condition. In fact, in states such as Michigan, North Carolina, and New Hampshire, failure to maintain adequate slack can trigger additional oversight or intervention by state authorities into local fiscal affairs. And yet, we know little about how the platitude that slack is good for financial condition actually shapes—or should shape—local financial management choices. For instance, what is the "optimal" level of local government slack? Is there a universal optimal level, or do certain factors dictate different levels for different types of jurisdictions? Do different definitions of financial condition dictate particular slack levels? Can financial managers leverage slack more effectively by deploying it at certain times or toward certain types of expenditures? Some of the empirical research on the slack resource-financial condition link has focused on these types of questions.

That research has followed from different assumptions about what aspect of financial condition slack is supposed to improve. Discussion in this section is organized around three of those aspects: expenditure stabilization, credit quality maintenance, and revenue volatility. The findings from this body of research suggest a simple conclusion: slack resources have little if any effect on financial condition, and the limited effect it has is contingent on the definition of financial condition.

Expenditure Stabilization

Much of the conventional wisdom about the slack-financial condition relationship follows from the recognition that local government financial condition has a cyclical component. That is, during the downturn years of the typical business cycle governments face the dual pressures of declining revenues and increased demand for social services. Many state governments have sought to address this problem with *countercyclical fiscal policy* tools such as *"rainy day" funds*. Under the rainy day fund model, a government deposits resources into a formal contingency fund during flush years and draws down those resources when revenues fall short of expectations. How and when fund resources are spent and replenished is typically predetermined at the fund's creation. Interestingly enough, states' use of these tools contradicts traditional public finance theory, which generally prescribes that only national governments should engage in countercyclical expenditure stabilization. Subnational attempts at stabilization, this theory suggests, are inefficient because most states and municipalities cannot leverage enough resources to truly affect their local economies. Moreover, the theory indicates, the differences in slack resource levels can exacerbate horizontal fiscal inequality (see, e.g., Gramlich 1987). Nevertheless, expenditure stabilization is clearly a central, if pragmatic, goal of contemporary state financial management. There is a large literature around the question of whether stabilization tools help to achieve that goal (see, e.g., Hou 2003 and Wagner 2003). To date, the findings on that question are mixed.

Many local governments also use these tools, but we know far less about how they use them or whether they actually stabilize expenditures. But to date, research in this area shows local government slack has little if any countercyclical effect on local government spending.

First, consider the evidence on local government rainy day funds. A formal rainy day fund or other explicit stabilization mechanism is perhaps the best indicator of a jurisdiction's intent to use slack to stabilize spending. Wolkoff (1987) published the first known analysis of local government practices in this area. His analysis was based on a survey of the largest (in terms of population) cities at that time. His results are presented in the "1987" column of **Table 12.2**. His main finding was that formal rainy day funds, or funds where city policy or statute clearly stated how and when stabilization funds would be used, were the exception. Only 7 of the 27 had such a fund. One of those 7—Los Angeles—operated something like a rainy day fund but without a formal expenditure stabilization policy or statute.

Wolkoff's findings were updated, and the new data are presented in the "2009" column of Table 12.2. These more recent data are from a review of the comprehensive annual financial reports and budget documents for these same cities for fiscal years 2008 and 2009 (where available). These new figures show Wolkoff's original conclusion holds today. In 2009, only 11 cities had a formal rainy day fund. Moreover, during this time, 3 created "stabilization-type" funds—similar to what Los Angeles had in 1987—that lack the strictures of a formal rainy day fund. Although interest in expenditure stabilization

TABLE 12.2 Formal Rainy Day Funds in U.S. Cities, 1987 and 2009

		1987	2009
Baltimore	MD	No	Yes
Boston	MA	No	No
Buffalo	NY	No	Yes
Cleveland	OH	No	Yes
Columbus	OH	No	No*
El Paso	TX	No	No
Honolulu	HI	No	Yes
Houston	TX	Yes	Yes
Indianapolis	IN	No	No
Long Beach	CA	No*	No*
Los Angeles	CA	Yes	Yes
Milwaukee	WI	Yes	Yes
New York City	NY	No	Yes
Norfolk	VA	No	Yes
Oakland	CA	No	No
Oklahoma City	OK	No	No
Omaha	NE	Yes	No*
Phoenix	AZ	No	No
Rochester	NY	No	No
Sacramento	CA	No	No*
St. Paul	MN	Yes	No*
San Antonio	TX	Yes	No
San Diego	CA	No	Yes
Tampa	FL	No	No*
Tucson	AZ	No	No
Virginia Beach	VA	Yes	No
Washington DC	DC	No	Yes

* Denotes other fund balance operates as a rainy day fund

has seemed to increase, most local governments seem to prefer information stabilization strategies.

This prevalence of informal rather than formal stabilization funds is especially evident among small- and mid-sized cities. A 2004 survey (Marlowe, 2006) of Michigan and Minnesota municipalities with populations of 500 to 50,000 showed less than half of those governments had a fund balance policy of any type, and less than 15% had a formal policy. If a fund balance policy is a necessary component of an explicit countercyclical stabilization strategy, then it seems most local governments do not have those strategies in place.

That most local governments lack formal rainy day funds does not necessarily mean slack does not stabilize expenditures. In fact, it is plausible that local governments prefer informal stabilization practices that employ slack resources other than formal reserve funds. The best possible test of this informal slack-expenditure stabilization relationship is whether slack resources broadly construed actually induce countercyclical patterns in expenditures.

Hou (2003) first tested this idea at the state level. His analysis followed the simple intuition that state spending follows a linear upward trend over time, so by implication, years where spending falls below the level that trend predicted can be called periods of economic downturn. The key empirical question in this type of analysis is whether the presence of slack resources reduces the rate at which state spending falls below predicted levels? Hou found that formal state budget stabilization funds have these types of countercyclical effects.

Marlowe (2005) used the Hou methodology to evaluate the slack-expenditure relationship for Minnesota cities from 1990 to 2000. That analysis showed formal rainy day funds had a marginal countercyclical effect; during periods of economic downturn, each additional one percent equivalent of annual revenues in a formal rainy day fund pushed annual expenditures one-tenth of one percent closer to their expected levels. Hou and Wang (2009) drew a similar conclusion from an analysis of North Carolina counties from 1990 to 2007. Such small stabilization effects are surprising given the high slack levels observed for most of the jurisdictions examined in these studies.

A potential drawback to these papers is that they may not be generalizable to the present. Both examined data from periods of overall economic growth when most local governments expanded current consumption in favor of saving for future consumption. Presumably, most have reversed course in the wake of the enormous revenue downturns brought about by the "Great Recession." If slack resources have noteworthy countercyclical effects, we would expect to see those effects in the recent data.

To test for those countercyclical effects some additional analysis was done based on a national sample of 600 municipalities and counties with populations greater than 35,000. Each jurisdiction in the sample reported slack resource levels and revenue collections each year from 2006 through 2009. **Figure 12.2** shows the median total general fund balance and unreserved general fund balance levels for four categories of cities (which includes towns,

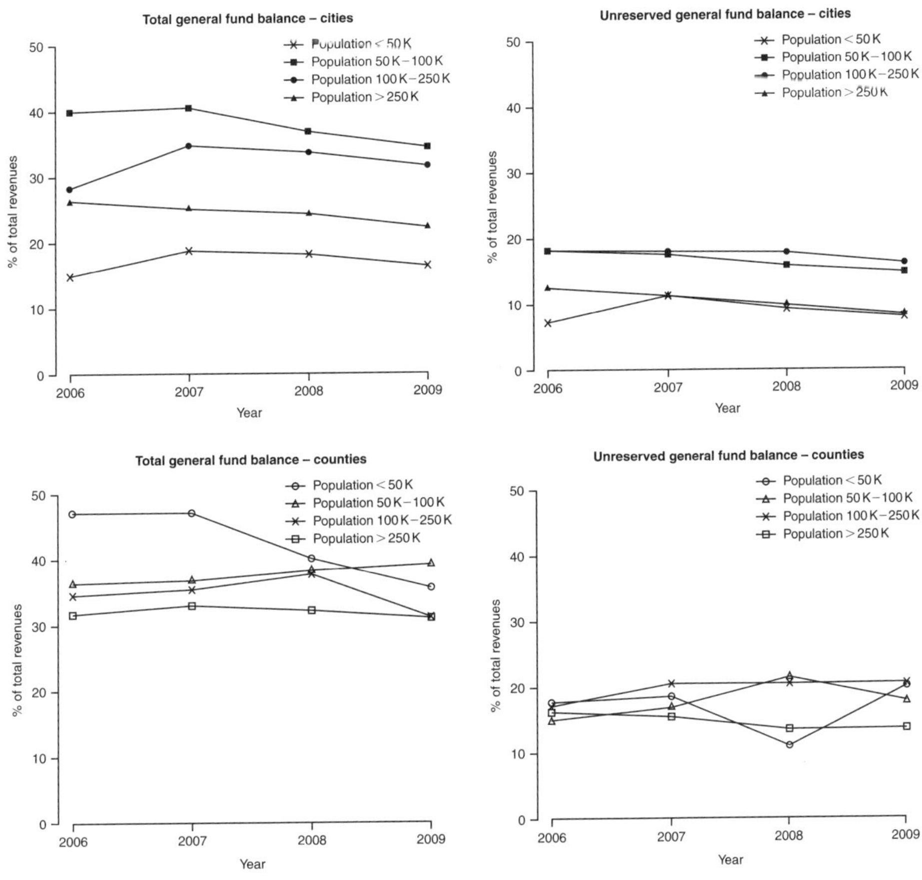

Figure 12.2 City and County Fund Balance Levels, 2006–2009

Source: Local government comprehensive annual financial reports (nominal dollars)

townships, boroughs, and villages) divided roughly into quartiles by population. Those categories are population less than 50,000; between 50,000 and 100,000; 100,000 to 250,000; and greater than 250,000. Fund balance levels are presented as a percentage of total revenues for all governmental activities (from each jurisdiction's Statement of Net Assets).

This figure shows that, as expected, fund balance levels decreased as the Recession took hold in fiscal years 2008 and 2009. However, those decreases are negligible. For most categories, the decrease in the median fund balance level from 2007 to 2009 was between 2% to 5% of total revenues. The exception was total general fund balance for the smallest population group of counties, where median levels fell from 48% of total revenues in 2007 to less than 37% in 2009.

A natural follow-up question is whether changes in fund balance correlate with changes in total revenues from governmental activities? If local governments backfilled lost revenues with fund balance, then fund balance levels should decrease following a drop in revenue collections. This claim was tested by calculating Pearson correlations between each jurisdiction's change in total governmental revenues and its change in total general fund balance for the next year. Those same correlations were also calculated in contemporaneous years. None of those correlations was greater than 0.15, and none was statistically significant at conventional levels. This suggests slack resources did not supplement lost revenue collections and, by implication, had little if any effect on spending patterns. That relationship might have changed for many jurisdictions in fiscal year 2010 and might continue to evolve if the current fiscal stress persists. But to date, the data are not consistent with the pattern we might expect if slack played a key role in expenditure stabilization.

Revenue Volatility

A separate line of research examines how governments use slack resources to buffer against potential revenue shortfalls. The intuition here is that slack is necessary to smooth revenue fluctuations across the business cycle, as opposed to stabilizing expenditures when revenues fall short of expectations. Much of this research follows from Joyce's (2001) often-cited paper on the determinants of state rainy day fund balances, and in particular the reasons why those balances are usually near 5% of annual revenues (the so-called five percent rule). Joyce tests the claim that states with more procyclical economies keep higher rainy day funds to compensate for the additional risk of revenue downturns during recessions. He found that, in fact, the structure of a state's economy had little bearing on its rainy day fund level.

A series of Pearson correlations were calculated to test the veracity of this claim at the local level. Specifically, two slack resource indicators—total general fund balance and unrestricted net assets in the governmental activities—were correlated with two economic condition indicators—a "revenue cyclicality" measure and an economic diversity measure—for a national sample of 242 local governments from 2005 to 2007. This analysis is based on the same data as Marlowe (2011). The revenue cyclicality measure is the standardized regression coefficient from a bivariate regression with each jurisdictions' total annual revenue collections as the dependent variable and its lagged annual value on the Philadelphia Federal Reserve's state coincident index—a measure that combines a variety of wage and employment data into a single indicator of statewide economic activity—as the independent variable. Those regressions were run each year from 1994 to 2006. A higher score on this cyclicality measure implies a more procyclical economy that is more vulnerable to revenue downturns during a recession. The economic diversity index is a Hirschman-Hirfindahl type indicator that combines into a single measure the percentages of the jurisdiction's residents that work in each of the five major employment categories identified by the U.S. Census. A higher score on this index indicates a more diversified economy that will dampen the effects of a recession on local government revenues.

These correlations showed jurisdictions with more procyclical revenues were no more likely to have higher fund balances or net assets than jurisdictions with less procyclical revenues. The same was true for the relationship between slack and economic diversity. Jurisdictions with more diversified economies were no more likely to have higher slack resource levels. Pearson correlations for these relationships were less than 0.25 and were not statistically significant. Consistent with Joyce's state level findings, the make-up of the local economy does not appear to correlate with slack resource levels.

Other authors have sought to better understand the revenue cyclicality–slack resources relationship by applying insights from the *Value-at-Risk* (VaR) framework. VaR is often used in corporate finance to determine the probability that a portfolio of investments will realize a particular gain or loss in the future. To answer this question, an analyst using the VaR framework fits a probability model to past fluctuations in a portfolio's returns and then extrapolates that model forward to estimate the probability of potential future gains and losses. Public financial management scholars have applied VaR to produce similar insights into the potential variability in government revenue collections. VaR is useful for thinking about the "optimal" level of slack resources because it identifies the level of slack a jurisdiction should keep to protect against revenue fluctuations at different levels of risk acceptance.

This type of work on revenue cyclicality provides some support for the high slack levels that many local governments keep. For instance, Kriz (2002) applied the VaR framework in an attempt to determine the optimal slack level for Minnesota cities. He found that if a typical jurisdiction "wished to sustain a three percent expenditure growth rate with a 75 percent confidence level, it would need savings equal to 91 percent of total revenues" (p. 5). When revenue volatility is measured this way, the need for high slack resource levels becomes more apparent. Thompson and Gates (2007) further explore the applicability to government revenue forecasting of VaR and other tools from corporate finance. They drew conclusions about the revenue volatility–slack resource link that closely followed Kriz.

Credit Quality

A subset of conventional wisdom about slack is focused on its implications for local government credit quality. This relationship is intuitive; slack resources can be invaluable if an unforeseen event threatens an issuer's ability to make timely debt service payments. Broadly speaking, credit ratings also provide a sort of index of financial condition. They incorporate multiple dimensions of financial stability and financial outlook into a single evaluation that investors can use to determine the financial risks inherent to a particular jurisdiction. The major credit rating agencies have endorsed the importance of slack resources in ratings criteria and other pronouncements that show the value to local governments of a healthy fund balance and, perhaps more important, of policies that dictate how slack resources will be maintained and used (http://www.nafoa.org/pdf/12Habits.pdf).

But like most platitudes about slack resources, this one begs several follow-up questions. Is the slack needed to protect a jurisdiction's credit quality contingent on that jurisdiction's economic and financial circumstances? Is there a point of "diminishing marginal returns" for the slack-credit quality relationship? What level of slack is necessary to preserve credit quality in the face of significant financial stress? It seems a simple heuristic ignores important variation in the slack-credit quality relationship across different types of jurisdictions.

A recent paper by Marlowe (2011) addresses some of these questions. This paper reports findings from an analysis of how slack resources affected bond ratings and borrowing costs on 250 new city and county bond issues from 2004 to 2007. Of all the research summarized so far, this analysis most directly models the slack-fiscal condition relationship. The results, which were adjusted with a multivariate model to account for other factors known to affect credit quality, suggested three main findings.

First, having some level of slack substantially improves a local government's credit quality. The difference between having no fund balance and some fund balance reduced the likelihood of receiving a lower credit rating by 3–5%. Second, this effect was especially strong for a lower population, less affluent (in terms of per capita income) jurisdiction. For them, having some fund balance compared to no fund balance reduced the likelihood of a lower credit rating by 8–11%.

The third finding was that local governments realize little credit quality benefit for keeping high levels of slack. According to estimates from that analysis, a typical issuer would need to maintain total general fund balance equivalent to 160% of current annual expenditures to reduce the likelihood of a comparatively low ("A") rating by 10–15%. Although much work remains to be done in this area, this initial evidence suggests the slack-credit quality relationship is not nearly as simple as conventional wisdom suggests.

GASB 54 and the Future of Financial Slack

As mentioned before, one of the main sources of variability in the slack-financial condition relationship is variability in the accounting treatment of fund balance. For instance, some jurisdictions treat fund balance designations as binding restrictions that preclude them from appropriating those resources in the next fiscal year. Under these circumstances, designated fund balance is not a source of financial slack. By contrast, other jurisdictions consider designations an advisory or suggested use that can be changed if those resources are needed for some other purpose in the next year. In this case, designated fund balance is a source of financial slack. These and other aspects of GAAP rules around fund balance were subject to different interpretations. By implication, the relationship between slack and financial condition was also not as clear as the accounting standards setters would have liked.

The GASB recognized these problems and attempted to correct them with *Statement 54 - Fund Balance Reporting and Governmental Fund Type Definitions*. The purpose of this standard was to improve the usefulness of fund balance information, namely to allow financial statement users to compare fund balance levels and management practices across jurisdictions. It will likely achieve that goal, and it will also affect the slack-financial condition relationship in three key ways.

First, many jurisdictions will report very different levels of uncommitted slack resources. This is because Statement 54 requires local governments to shift the focus of fund balance reporting from the intended use of fund balance in the next fiscal year, toward "restrictiveness" of fund balance commitments. Much of the fund balance that is restricted under current GAAP rules is not actually restricted in practice. For instance, designated fund balance is often used for purposes other than its original designation because management changed the designation. A related problem is that what some jurisdictions call reserved fund balance others call designated, and vice versa.

Statement 54 lays out a continuum of constraints within the unrestricted category. Under this new continuum, most or all of the "soft designations" under the current rules will be shifted into either a more or less restrictive category. Fund balance will be reported as "committed" if it is restricted for a specific use by the jurisdiction's governing body. "De-commitment" of those resources will require an equal and opposite action by that same governing body. "Assigned" fund balance is roughly equivalent to unreserved designated fund balance under the current GAAP standards. Assignments will be initiated by the governing body through an informal policy or action, or by an official(s) delegated by the governing body—such as the finance director or city manager—to make those assignments. Unassigned fund balance carries no restrictions on its future use. It is equivalent to unreserved fund balance under the current standard.

Under this new scheme, designated fund balance intended as financial slack will become "assigned" if the governing body is willing to assign it as "slack." But that assignment could carry important political consequences, particularly in the wake of the enormous fiscal stress many governments are now facing. If the governing body is not willing to make such an assignment those "soft designations" will become unrestricted fund balance. For this reason, many jurisdictions' unassigned fund balance will probably exceed their unreserved undesignated fund balance under the current standard.

A related issue is the specificity of fund balance assignments and restrictions in funds other than the general fund. The current standard allows local governments to transfer designated and unreserved fund balance resources out of the general fund and into a fund where resources have a more specific purpose, but without changing the classification. For this reason, it is not uncommon for local governments to have, for example, fund balance "designated for capital projects" in the capital projects fund. This treatment allowed some jurisdictions to understate the amount of unreserved undesignated fund balance in their governmental funds.

Statement 54 curtails this. It requires fund balance designations are made for a purpose more specific than the fund itself. For the previous example, this would suggest that "designated for capital projects" in the capital projects fund is not acceptable but "designated for street repairs" might be. For many jurisdictions, this will force much of what is now designated fund balance to be assigned by the governing body or to become unassigned and further increase the jurisdiction's total liquid fund balance.

The new rules also speak directly to stabilization funds. Under this new scheme, formal stabilization funds will be reported as committed fund balance because, in concept at least, they meet the GASB's criteria for a governing-body-imposed restriction on fund balance use. The new statement also recommends that jurisdictions that report a formal rainy day fund disclose key information about that fund—such as the authority that establishes the fund, when resources are added to the fund, and when fund resources can be used—in the notes to the financial statements. According to the survey research presented earlier, most jurisdictions that claim to keep fund balance for stabilization purposes lack a formal stabilization policy. Many jurisdictions will have to either create such a policy, or report fund balance currently reserved for stabilization as unassigned or assigned. Once again, this could greatly increase reported levels of highly liquid slack resources.

Finally, and perhaps most important, Statement 54 recommends that local governments establish comprehensive policies for all unrestricted fund balance. Those policies may speak to minimum levels of unrestricted fund balance, when unrestricted fund balance should be "spent down," and the conditions where low slack levels will be replenished. To create these policies local government financial managers will need their governing bodies to engage slack resource issues at a new, highly detailed level.

Conclusion

Empirical research on the relationship between slack and local government financial condition suggests a contradiction. On one hand, local governments tend to keep slack levels far in excess of what is presumably needed or recommended. Actual slack is routinely 25–30% of annual revenues, depending on the measure in question. On the other hand, there is no evidence that these high slack levels improve financial condition in any systematic way. They do not appear to boost spending during recessionary periods or to appreciably improve credit ratings. That said, it is premature to conclude slack has no bearing on financial condition. In fact, there is some initial evidence that slack may provide a hedge against revenue volatility, and it has been shown that keeping some slack improves credit quality relative to keeping no slack at all. Future work should continue to explore these dynamics, preferably by examining these relationships in municipalities that research has heretofore overlooked.

More than anything, these findings echo Gianakis and Snow's (2007) assertion that local governments' slack management is "highly contextualized" and related to political and institutional factors that have not been adequately incorporated into extant models. Many explanations have yet to be fully explored, even though almost all have important implications for the slack–financial condition link.

For example, Gore (2009) argues that excessive cash holdings might be related to traditional agency and oversight problems within local governments. Ironically, GASB 54 will likely help curb many of those problems because it requires governing bodies to engage fund balance policy decisions in new and intensive ways. A recent paper by Marlowe (2009) explores the claim that slack resources allow local governments to slow the rate of "tax ratcheting," or the tendency for tax rates to increase faster than the rate of inflation. This emerging line of research suggests slack affects tax rates and other fiscal policies more than it affects actual patterns of revenues or spending, a trend that demands future research.

Discussion Questions

1. What key factors should a local government consider when setting target slack resource levels? When setting policies about slack resources?
2. How have local governments used slack resources throughout the "Great Recession?" Has the Recession changed slack resource management going forward?
3. How will GASB Statement 54 affect fund balance reporting? How will it affect local government slack resource management practices and policies?

Glossary

Counter-cyclical fiscal policy: Policies designed to encourage governments to spend money during economic recessions and to save money during periods of strong economic growth. Cyclical in this case refers to the traditional business cycle.

Cyclical revenues: Revenue sources that yield more money during periods of economic growth than during recessions. Sales taxes and local income taxes tend to be more procyclical than property taxes.

Fiscal slack: Financial resources that have no immediate offsetting liability or obligation. Can include fund balance, net assets, free cash, rainy day funds, contingency funds, and others.

Fund balance: The difference between assets and liabilities in any governmental fund. A high fund balance suggests the entity has ample near-term resources to meet its near-term obligations.

GASB 54: A new accounting standard—formally known as "Fund Balance Reporting and Governmental Fund-Type Definitions"—designed to improve consistency in how state and local governments report different categories of fund balance.

Net assets: The difference between assets and liabilities on a governmentwide basis. The most often watched for governments is net assets of the governmental activities.

Rainy day fund: A formal policy for countercyclical expenditure stabilization. Most entities will spend their rainy day fund resources if revenue collections fall by a predetermined amount.

Value-at-Risk: A methodology, based on theories of probability and statistics, for determining potential financial losses. VaR can be used to consider an entity's appropriate fund balance by determining the range of revenue shortfalls a jurisdiction might experience over a given time period.

Recommended Resources

Gauthier, S. J. (2010). *An elected official's guide to fund balance and net assets: Using the GASB 34 model* (2nd ed.). Chicago: Government Finance Officers Association.

Government Finance Officers Association of the United States and Canada. (2009). Appropriate level of unrestricted fund balance in the general fund. Available at: http://www.gfoa.org/downloads/AppropriateLevelUnrestricted FundBalanceGeneralFund_BestPractice.pdf

Government Finance Officers Association of the United States and Canada. (2011). Replenishing fund balance in the general fund. Available at: http://www.gfoa.org/downloads/GFOA_BestPracticeReplenishingFundBalance.pdf

References

Chaney, B., Mead, D. M., and Schermann, K. R. (2002). The new government financial reporting model: What it means for analyzing government financial condition. *Journal of Government Financial Management, 51*(1): 26–32.

Gianakis, G. A., and Snow, D. (2007). The implementation and utilization of stabilization funds by local governments in Massachusetts. *Public Budgeting & Finance, 27*(1), 86–103.

Gore, A. K. (2009). Why do cities hoard cash? Determinants and implications of municipal cash holdings. *The Accounting Review, 84*(1), 183–207.

Government Finance Officers Association. (2002). Appropriate level of unreserved fund balance in the general Fund. Retrieved on November 12, 2010, from http://www.gfoa.org/downloads/budget-appropriate.pdf

Gramlich, E. M. (1987). Subnational fiscal policy. In J. M. Quigley (Ed.), *Perspectives on local public finance and public policy* (pp. 3–27). Greenwich, CT: JAI Press.

Helgeson, B., and Von Sternberg, B. (2009, December 8). Cities, counties survive aid cuts, for now. *Minneapolis Star-Tribune.*

Hembree, H., and Shelton, M. (1999). Benchmarking and local government reserve funds: Theory vs. practice. *Public Management, 81*(9), 16–22.

Hendrick, R. (2006). The role of slack in local government finances. *Public Budgeting & Finance, 26*(1), 14–46.

Hou, Y. (2003). What stabilizes state general fund expenditures in downturn years—budget stabilization fund or general fund unreserved undesignated fund balance? *Public Budgeting & Finance, 23*(3), 64–91.

Hou, Y. and Wang, W. (2009). "Do local governments save and spend across business cycles? Evidence from North Carolina." Working Paper, available at http://papers.ssrn.com/sol3/papers.cfm?abstract_id=1669799

Joyce, P. G. (2001). What's so magical about five percent? A nationwide look at factors that influence the optimal size of state rainy day funds. *Public Budgeting & Finance, 21*(2), 62–87.

Kriz, K. A. (2002). The optimal level of local government fund balances: A simulation approach. Proceedings of the 95th Annual Conference of the National Tax Association, 1–7.

Marlowe, J. (2005). Fiscal slack and countercyclical expenditure stabilization: A first look at the local level. *Public Budgeting & Finance, 25*(3), 48–72.

Marlowe, J. (2006). Fund balance, working capital, and net assets. In H. Frank (Ed.), *Public Financial Management* (pp. 357–381). New York: Taylor & Francis.

Marlowe, J. (2009). Budget variance, slack resources, and municipal expenditures. Paper presented at the Association for Budgeting and Financial Management Annual Conference.

Marlowe, J. (2011). Beyond 5 percent: Optimal municipal slack resources and credit ratings. *Public Budgeting & Finance, 31*(4), 93–108.

Schenk, T. (2009). Some cities warn of budget cuts while sitting on rainy day funds. Minnesota Public Radio Online. Retrieved on November 12, 2010, from http://minnesota.publicradio.org/display/web/2009/03/02/cityreserves/

Stewart, L. (2009). Examining factors that impact Mississippi counties' unreserved fund balance during relative resource abundance and relative resource scarcity. *Public Budgeting & Finance, 29*(4), 45–73.

Thompson, F., and Gates, B. L. (2007). Betting on the future with a cloudy crystal ball? How financial theory can improve revenue forecasting and budgets in the states. *Public Administration Review, 67*(5), 825–836.

Vanyolos, I. (2009a). The role of rainy day funds in local spending—evidence from Florida counties. Paper presented at the Association for Budgeting and Financial Management Annual Conference.

Vanyolos, I. (2009b). State regulations on local government fund balances: Survey and evidence. Working Paper. Florida Atlantic University.

Wagner, G. A. (2003). Are state budget stabilization funds only the illusion of savings? Evidence from stationary panel data. *Quarterly Review of Economics and Finance, 43*(2), 218–238.

Wolkoff, M. (1987). An evaluation of municipal rainy day funds. *Public Budgeting & Finance, 5*(2), 52–63.

Chapter 13

Managing Investments and Investment Risk

by William G. Albrecht

Introduction

Despite a somewhat intuitive and obvious connection, the investment management of idle public fund balances continues to lack consistent, substantive attention in 21st-century public administration literature concerning the fiscal health of local governments in the United States. Whereas the neglect may be regrettable, such an assertion will come as no surprise to those interested in the topic. A number of writers have lamented the inattention paid to this area of public policy. Commentators include scholars, practitioners, and students (e.g., Miller, 1998; Finkelstein, 2006; Nwagu, 1985). Even if nothing can be proven, there are at least three likely and interrelated reasons for why this is so.

First, investing funds is a revenue service activity in which money is used to make money (Reed and Swain, 1997). As a result, the ultimate goal is financial in nature. Local government management scholars and practitioners, however, remain fundamentally interested in the efficient, effective, and equitable provision of public goods and services whether or not investing occurs. Though few are likely to dispute the importance of investment outcomes, they are also diligent about not confusing means with ends.

Second, investment products and techniques have become complex. As ideas the approaches espoused have largely emerged from the deductive work and empirical observations of university style academics pursuing research agendas that are predominately focused on the perfection or imperfection of capital markets. The decision maker is rarely, if ever, assumed to be a local government investment manager and settings often ignore the influence of politics. Consequently, much of what is done arguably lacks relevance for practical public administration or even public financial management theory (Miller, 1991a).

Third, investment income is not a major source of local government revenue. According to U.S. Census Bureau statistics, interest income accounted for 3% of local government revenues in 2008. This summary measure coincides with the fact that despite perceptions emanating from highly publicized "bankruptcy" cases such as Orange County, California, in 1994, extremely large investment losses, leading to significant "revenue side" fiscal stress, are relatively rare events for local governments (Delisle, 2010). By comparison, intergovernmental aid and property taxes comprised 34% and 26%, respectively, for this same time period.

On the other hand, the absence of attention is odd as investment decisions are among the few administrative choices government officials have for exerting some amount of influence over fiscal situations that are often simultaneously shaped or caused by demographic, economic, and political factors (Honadle, Costa, and Cigler, 2003; Skidmore & Scorsone, 2010). Furthermore, in 2008, local government cash and security holdings totaled well in excess of $1.552 trillion; a substantive collective figure with the potential to maintain or improve the nation's overall financial health. Of course, capacity to act does not always guarantee good investment performance. And as history has shown, good investment performance does not always result from good practices.

This chapter briefly discusses the management of investments and investment risk across time. The central thesis is that prudent public sector practices should primarily focus on not detracting from a local government's fiscal capacity, which is defined as the ability to meet financial obligations as they come due on an ongoing basis (Government Accounting Standards Board, 2009). In this context, the pursuit of investment income is a secondary consideration even though the sole purpose for engaging in such activities is to earn a financial return.

The next section presents the economic rationale for investing idle public funds, in the form of cash, before delineating the concepts of financial and political risk. This discussion is followed by an overview of traditional investment risk assessment measures. Value-at-Risk is then presented as an emerging risk management tool that can support the public sector definition of liquidity while adjusting typical techniques to account for the onset or existence of fiscal stress. The chapter concludes with mentions of how Value-at-Risk can possibly remedy accounting requirements with investment oriented goals.

The Concept of Opportunity Loss

The primary justification for investing public funds is founded in the notion that even in a world of complete certainty an opportunity loss is imposed upon constituents when public money (e.g., cash), which is not immediately used to acquire or produce communal goods and services, is also allowed to remain unproductive or idle. Conceptually an opportunity loss is similar to the economic definition of opportunity cost whereby an action is judged according to what is given up, in the form of a best foregone alternative, as the course of action is pursued. The fundamental difference is that opportunity loss explicitly focuses on the economic gain that is not achieved by acting in the most efficient and effective manner possible (e.g., Orndorff and Syal, 1997).

Classical economic thinking posits that rational and purposive individuals or collections of individuals will not intentionally incur opportunity losses as doing so is counterproductive to maximizing their welfare. Instead, they are presumed to be willing to become investors by lending unproductive financial resources, in the form of principal, to borrowers in financial markets for a specified length of time. Accordingly, rational and purposive borrowers are assumed to be willing and able to compensate investors for the right to use the principal for the same duration. This may be accomplished by periodically remitting income payments (i.e., interest) and a final payment that may or may not include an increment above principal. The specifics of any transaction are secured through unambiguous and well-defined property rights that are binding on investors as well as borrowers.

With few exceptions, the view logically transfers to buying and selling activities. In either case, all forms of future remittance, including the giving back of principal, are generally referred to as cash flows. The sum of all cash flows in excess of principal is defined as the total monetary return on investment. Accordingly, excess cash flows as a percent of principal equates to a total rate of return on investment. Of course the value of either return measure would be zero if the principal amount were allowed to remain idle. In this case, the counterfactual value would amount to an opportunity loss.

Mathematically, the value of an opportunity loss can be assessed with a number of formulas that are capable of summarizing cash flows over time while accounting for compound interest. The most basic, shown in Equation 1 that follows, involves finding the future value of a present amount of money under the assumption that principal is invested for a period of time:

$$FV_n = PV_0 (1 + i)^n \qquad (1)$$

where

FV_n = Future value of principal at time n;
PV_0 = Present value of principal;
i = Interest rate (i.e., income as a proportion of PV_0);
n = Number of periods (e.g., years) that principal is invested.

Careful reflection reveals that the right and left hand sides will only remain equal to PV_0 if the value of i or n is zero. This, of course, would be the case if no investing activity took place. In any other instance, each side of the equation must increase.[1]

To illustrate, assume a borrower is willing and able to pay a lender 5% interest for the right to use \$100 of idle funds for one year. If the lender does not agree to the arrangement (or any other), then the lender will have \$100 at the end of one year as $\$100\ (1 + 0.00)^0$ equals \$100. However, if the lender accepts the offer, then the lender will have a positive \$105 cash flow at the end of the year as $\$100\ (1 + 0.05)^1$ equates to that amount. The \$5 increment above \$100 is the "potential" lender's opportunity loss from not lending. By implication, if the lender had accepted the borrower's offer of 5% when 10% was available on an otherwise identical investment, then the opportunity loss would also be \$5, which is the difference between \$10 and \$5 in interest.[2]

Empirical Evidence

Empirically the opportunity loss concept has guided the few known investigations of foregone investment returns at the state and local government level; most of which were conducted in the middle of the 20th century. For example, Blankenbeckler (1978) cites several examinations estimating losses of \$312 million in 1957; \$50–100 million in 1961;

TABLE 13.1 Local Government Holdings & Interest Earnings, 2007 (Millions, $)

	County	Municipal	Township	Special District	School District	Total
Cash & Securities	$390,105.46	$709,967.64	$32,997.11	$204,444.99	$218,499.63	$1,556,014.82
Interest Earnings	$10,947.26	$15,550.04	$1,148.23	$8,123.24	$9,276.66	$45,045.42
Interest per Day[a]	$29.99	$42.60	$3.15	$22.26	$25.42	$123.41

Source: U.S. Census Bureau

[a] Interest earnings divided by 365

$328 million in 1962; $453 million in 1967; and $667 million in 1972. These early works appear to have provided the foundation for an emerging "cash management" literature that, in summary, became concerned with all aspects surrounding idle funds as these monies constitute principal (Bland, 1986; Onwujuba and Lynch, 2002).[3]

Collectively, the body of knowledge is now a common feature in local government and finance textbooks or other training-oriented materials that are concerned with cash forecasting and budgeting, mobilization, and investment programs (e.g., Khan, 1996; Mikesell, 2007; Miller, 1991b; Reed and Swain, 1997). Though modern inquiries along similar lines are still difficult to acquire, a sense of potential 21st-century opportunity losses, by way of refraining from any investment activities, can be garnered by considering the information provided in **Table 13.1**. As shown, local governments reported more than $45 billion in interest earnings during 2007 while holding more than $1.556 trillion in cash and securities. Were such returns not earned an average opportunity loss of more than $123 million per day would have occurred.

Though such observations are essential for verification purposes, each has a counterfactual advantage as far as historical accounts are concerned. Methodologically, the hindsight is needed as total monetary return and total rate of return are artifacts of what is accomplished by investing. However, when taken at face value, retrospective evaluations such as those just mentioned are not sufficient for discussing the prospective investment of public funds. In reality, efforts to avoid publicly oriented opportunity losses involve investment and political risks.

Delineating Risk

The field of finance builds on classical economic thinking by adding the notion of investment risk, which in a broad sense, references the chance that the return on invested funds will be greater or less than what an investor expects. The foundation for inclusion is rooted in the Time Value of Money concept, which among other things, stipulates that a dollar in hand is worth more than one that is not because the chance of nonreceipt is eliminated. Nonreceipt can happen for any number of reasons. However, the public financial management literature tends to classify and summarize the probability for this type of occurrence as follows:

1. Default risk. The possibility a borrower will not be willing or able to fulfill obligations.
2. Interest rate risk. The possibility changes in interest rate will decrease an investment's value.
3. Market risk. The possibility an investment's return will decline because of market forces.

Writers have also not deviated from the private sector contention that investors (including the public) should expect to be compensated for incurring investment risk with a total rate of return that exceeds what would be earned in a risk-free environment. Furthermore, they assert that riskier investments ought to afford higher total rates of return than those that, all else constant, are less risky. Thus, one fundamental question is how much risk a particular public is willing and able to incur for the production of interest-oriented revenue.

Answers to this seminal query vary by jurisdiction and circumstances because few, if any, are likely to have identical levels of risk tolerance at a single moment in time much less across time. Even so, high levels of investment risk aversion have almost universally driven policies and administrative norms concerning the employment of idle money as constituents are understandably upset when nonreceipt happens. The implication is that politics influences current public investment practices and objectives, and investment managers are not free to act apart from political risk.

From a democratic theory perspective, political risk is not akin to invest risk. Rather political risk is an ex ante constraint-oriented tool that holds officials accountable for results that might occur from an investment decision.[4] Without political risk, the investment of public money is likely to reflect the preferences of those with administrative discretion or political power rather than the public whose money is to be invested. The prospect that constituents' preferences could be ignored is particularly important for local governments, which, in the context of American federalism, are presumed to be in the best position to respond to citizens' demands.[5]

Conversely, political risk poses a significant challenge for public fund administrators and politicians whose careers are often defined by investment performance. In recognition of this fact, most local governments have adopted prudent person investment policies, in concert with professional organizations such as the Government Finance Officers Association, which are subordinate to state laws. Though specific practices vary across governments, the following three objectives are a common theme as is their priority: Safety of principal, liquidity, and maximization of income.

TABLE 13.2 Correspondence of Public Fund Investment Objectives & Investment Risks

Objective: Definition	Risk
1. Safety of Principal: Safeguard principal amount invested.	Default
2. Liquidity: Ensure sufficient cash to meet obligations.	Interest
3. Maximization of Income: Earn a reasonable rate of return.	Market

Table 13.2 lists these objectives along with definitions and the investment risk each is presumed to address. Safety of principal, for example, is directed toward managing the possibility that principal can be reduced, in part or full, because of default. By comparison, maximization of income is meant to temper market risk, which cannot be avoided if investing activities are to occur, with a reasonableness standard that is incorporated into the definition. Although the intentional contradiction between the first and third objective is obvious, the most important point is whether or not the objective-risk correspondence actually affords the greatest opportunity for ensuring the prime objective (i.e., safety of principal).

According to Finkelstein (2006), the arrangement has had two major consequences. The first is that public fund managers are inclined to focus on default risk that poses a minor threat to the safety of principal given that many public funds are invested with high quality issuers such as the U.S. government. To the extent that it exists, default risk, which is an unsystematic risk, can be managed with diversification tactics that spread money and risk over multiple investments rather than concentrating in one.

The second consequence is related to the first in that interest rate risk, which is a systematic risk that cannot be controlled with diversification strategies, is given less attention even though changes in interest rates are far more likely to erode the monetary value of a local government's principal. As a result, Finklestein's (2006) conclusion is that liquidity should be the primary objective as the requisite is, in a de facto sense, more in line with the primary objective of principal preservation. Given that safety of principal is handled by attending to liquidity, Finkelstein goes on to suggest that income maximization and safety of principal should be ranked second and third, respectively, as far as investment plan priorities are concerned.

The argument is persuasive as interest rates are little more than the price of money. And interest rate changes reflect many economic factors such as the supply and demand relationship for idle funds, monetary policies, and investors' inflation expectations. But Finklestein's contention goes beyond this mundane mention when considering modern financial scandals. For example, when Orange County, California lost $2 billion dollars in 1994, much attention was given to the tactics employed by Robert Citron, then Orange County's treasurer, who was entrusted with a $7.5 billion local government investment pool. Citron's investment strategy involved a number of imprudent, speculative practices that were eventually condemned. Though the disapproval is appropriate, the case also serves as an example of illiquidity. Citron gambled on interest rates, put liquidity at risk, and after doing well for quite some time eventually lost an extremely large amount of principal (Jorion, 2007).

Infamous cases aside, the notion that liquidity should be ranked first among local government investment priorities is generally credible given that the investment of public funds is (or should remain) a support activity as far as American public administration is concerned. But the idea becomes even more convincing in the face of noninvestment related fiscal stress. During such periods, local governments can ill afford to lose public money, which is ultimately dedicated to covering communal obligations, as they attempt to avoid or minimize opportunity losses in financial markets. Hence a second fundamental (and interesting) question is how interest rate risk can be measured and managed under such circumstances.

Risk Measurement

To comprehend the measurement of risk in times of fiscal stress one must first understand the investments available for public funds to purchase (i.e., invest in) as well as how their prices and risk are determined under normal circumstances. Many public sector funds, for example, are invested in debt-oriented instruments such as bonds that have various par values, maturity dates, and coupon rates or nominal yields. Par value is the fixed amount that will be paid at the end of the investment, and maturity references the date that the payment will occur. Nominal yield is the stated rate of annual interest and is calculated as a percentage of a bond's par value.

Because these features are known at the time of purchase, bonds or bond-like investments are commonly known as fixed income investments.[6] To illustrate, a bond with a \$1,000 par value and a 6% nominal yield remits a positive \$60 cash flow to the investor at the end of each year for the entire life of the bond. This particular kind of constant cash flow is typically referred to as a coupon payment.

With such information in hand, the market price of a bond (or any investment resembling a bond) is then determined by discounting all cash flows by a required rate of return, which achieves an investor's revenue-oriented goal and then summing these values to get one monetary amount. Equation 2 summarizes the process as follows:

$$\mathrm{MP} = \sum_{t=1}^{n} \frac{1}{(1+r)^t} \times C_t + \frac{1}{(1+r)^n} \times P_n \qquad (2)$$

where

MP = Market price;
n = Maturity;
t = Time period;
C_t = Coupon payment;
P_n = Par value;
r = Required rate of return; and
Σ = Summation symbol.

Using the formula, the price of a 2-year bond with a \$1,000 par value and a 6% nominal yield, paid annually, will be worth \$982 if an investor's r is 7%.[7] Put another way, \$982 is the present value of all future cash flows that occur from investing in this particular bond. Likewise, the present value of the \$105 future value mentioned earlier is \$100 when the interest rate is 5%.[8]

Equation 2 also indicates that the price of a bond is a function of many things including the size and timing of P_n and C_t. However n and r, are what is most important for measuring risk as MP is particularly sensitive to these parameters that can and do change as the maturity date is approached.

The easiest way to see this is to note that the price of the bond mentioned would immediately increase from \$982 to \$1,038, a premium, if after being purchased interest rates suddenly dropped from 7% to 4%. Likewise, if interest rates instantly rose to 10%, the price of the bond would fall to \$931 if r was 7%. If the investor does not need to sell the bond, then the latter change will be of little consequence. But if the investor should need to sell the bond before the maturity date, to cover an urgent obligation, then the principal amount would be reduced by \$51 (\$982–931). The only way to avoid the loss is to not sell.

Though instantaneous shocks such as these are not likely to occur in practice, the possibility of such movements does increase with longer time periods and is reflected in upward sloping yield curves that plot various interest rates against different times to maturity. As a result, financial economists have developed measures of "duration" for estimating the effect that changes in interest rates can have on the prices of bonds and other fixed income investments. One measure, known as Macaulay Duration (MD) is given in Equation 3:

$$\text{MD} = \sum_{t=1}^{n} \frac{\text{PVCF}_t \times t}{\text{MP}} \qquad (3)$$

where

PVCF_t = Present value of cash flow at time period t (in years).

As shown, MD calculates the weighted average time to maturity where weights are determined by dividing the present value of a cash flow at time t by the market price. Accordingly, MD reveals how long an investor must wait until the principal amount is returned.

To illustrate, if an investor with a required annual rate of return of 7% purchases a two-year bond with a \$1,000 par value and a 0% nominal yield, then MD will be two years as that is how long the investor must wait to recover the principal when only one cash flow (i.e., par value payment) is involved. If, however, the nominal yield is positive, then MD will be less than two as a portion of the principal is returned to the investor, as coupon payments, before the maturity date is reached.

MD is frequently used by investment managers when decision makers wish to discuss duration in terms of time. But MD can also be adjusted to give another sensitivity measure known as modified duration. This is done in Equation 4:

$$MD^* = MD \div [1 + r^*] \tag{4}$$

where

MD^* = Modified duration;

r^* = Market interest rate (or Yield to maturity).

In terms of a definition, MD* typically references the percentage change in a bond's price for a 1% absolute change in interest rates (California Debt and Investment Advisory Commission, 2007). As such, MD^* is a semi-elastic measure of responsiveness.

The second and fourth columns of **Table 13.3**, Panel A present MD^* calculations for two hypothetical bonds, X and Y, with different maturities (1 year for X and 30 years for Y),

TABLE 13.3 Duration-Oriented Calculations for Hypothetical Bonds X & Y

Panel A: Modified Duration Metrics & Market Prices & for Bonds X & Y[a]

r^* [1]	MD^{*b}_X [2]	$MP_X{}^c$ [3]	MD^{*b}_Y [4]	$MP_Y{}^c$ [5]	Weighted Duration[d] [6]
0	1.00	$1,000	30.00	$1,000	15.50[e]
1%	0.99	$990	29.70	$742	15.35
2%	0.98	$980	29.41	$552	15.20
3%	0.97	$971	29.13	$412	15.05
4%	0.96	$962	28.85	$308	14.90
5%	0.95	$952	28.57	$231	14.76

Panel B: Changes in Market Price for Bond Y for Various Changes in r^*; MP_Y = $552

	MD^*_Y	MD^*_Y	MD^*_Y	MD^*_Y	MD^*_Y
Δr^*	28.57	28.85	29.13	29.41	29.70
±0.25%	$39.43	$39.81	$40.20	$40.59	$40.99
±0.50%	$78.85	$79.63	$80.40	$81.17	$81.97
±1.00%	$157.71	$159.25	$160.80	$162.34	$163.94
±1.50%	$236.56	$238.88	$241.20	$243.51	$245.92
±2.00%	$315.41	$318.50	$321.60	$324.69	$327.89

[a] Subscripts refer to bonds X and Y, respectively; [b] $MD \div (1 + r^*)$; [c] $\$1{,}000 \div (1 + r^*)^n$;. [d] $.50\,(MD^*_Y + MD^*_Y)$; [e] Average life of an equally weighted portfolio.

identical par values of \$1,000, and 0% nominal yields. To demonstrate, when r^* is 2%, MD^* for bond X is 0.98 and bond Y is 29.41. This suggests that a 1% increase (decrease) in r^* can be anticipated to decrease (increase) the price of bonds X and Y by 0.98% and 29.41%, respectively. In the same way, when r^* is 5% the price of bond X can be expected to increase (decrease) by 0.95% for a 1% decrease (increase) in r^* while the price of bond Y can be expected to change by 28.57% for the same kind of changes.

Panel B of Table 13.3 gives rough estimates of changes in MP for bond Y given possible changes in r^*. The figures are derived by inputting values into Equation 5:

$$\Delta MP \approx \Delta r^* \times MD^* \times MP \tag{5}$$

where

ΔMP = Change in market price (or market value);
Δr^* = Change in r^*; and
$\approx$ = Approximately equal to.

For example, the ΔMP_Y value of \$159.25 (row four, column three) is calculated by multiplying a 1% change in r^* by a MD^* value of 28.85 and a MP_Y equal to \$552 ($\$1{,}000 \div 1.02^{30}$). Consequently, the price of bond Y can be expected to decrease by approximately \$159.25 if Δr^* is equal to +1% and increase by approximately \$159.25 if Δr^* is equal to –1%.

A point worth emphasizing is that, as with Panel A the Δr^* figures presented in Panel B are absolute percent changes, not relative percent changes. To avoid confusion, investment professionals usually talk in terms of basis points where one basis point is an absolute increase or decrease of 1/100th of a percent. Thus the 0.25% figure given in the second row of Table 13.3, Panel B references a 25 basis point change while 2.00% is the same as 200 basis points. Accordingly, an Δr^* value of –1.00% equates to a 100 basis point decrease.

Either way, the fact that these figures are estimates can be confirmed by noting that the actual market price changes for the Δr^* scenarios just given is an increase of \$190 (\$742–\$552) when interest rates decrease from 2% to 1% and a decrease of \$140 (\$412–\$552) when interest rates increase from 2% to 3%. **Figure 13.1**, which extends the example in Table 13.3, Panel A demonstrates "why" by imposing a duration line that is tangent to bond Y's market price–interest rate curve at r^* equal to 2%.

As shown, the inverse relationship is nonlinear and convex toward the origin. Consequently duration metrics, which are linear, tend to overestimate reductions in MP when r^* increases and underestimate increases in MP when r^* decreases. This consequence is not strictly limited to MD or MD^* as the slope of the duration line, which measures the change in monetary value for a one unit change (percent difference) in interest rates, is another form of duration known as dollar duration.

Nonetheless, linear metrics such as MD^* are helpful for estimating differences such as the 0.25% change (or smaller) given in row two, column one of Table 13.3, Panel B. MD^* is also useful for approximating market price reductions for bonds with shorter maturities. This can be seen by noting that the market price–interest rate relationship for bond X, with

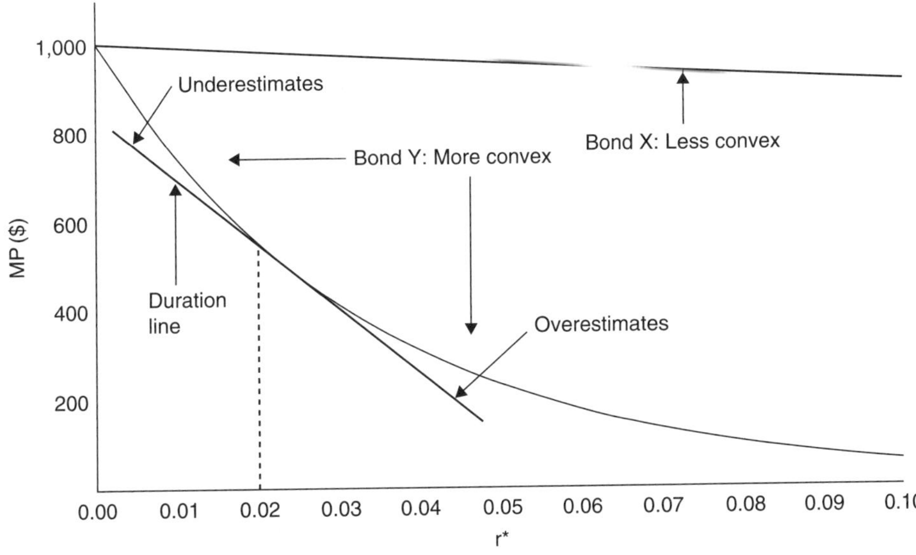

Figure 13.1 Market Prices, Returns, & Duration

a maturity of one year, is far less convex than that of bond Y. The overall conclusion is also reflected in the smaller MD* figures given in the second column of Table 13.3, Panel A.[9]

Managing Risk

Though no known academic studies exist, documenting how local government public fund administrators currently go about assessing interest rate risk, Finkelstein's (2006) work, which is rooted in practical experience, suggests that average life, a very simple measure of duration, is most often used. If so, then average life is also likely to be employed, quite frequently, when creating portfolios of bonds and other fixed income securities. Portfolio construction is the process of allocating portions of idle monies to various investments rather than concentrating in one. As such, portfolio-oriented investment strategies connect to the diversification issues mentioned earlier.

The problem with average life, as a measurement of risk, is that calculations simply weight times to maturity by the portions of funds invested in any security. All other factors (e.g., amounts and timing of cash flows) are ignored. For example, the average life of an equally weighted portfolio consisting of bonds X and Y in Table 13.3, Panel A equates to 15.50 (0.50 × 1 + 0.50 × 30). Consequently all cash flows are assumed to be equal. This is clearly not the case when r* is greater than zero. For this reason and other reasons, Finkelstein (2006, pp. 111) states that "one of the most egregious errors of public fund management is the continued reliance on average life as a measure of interest-rate risk."[10]

By comparison, the duration measures discussed earlier account for unequal cash flows as well as their timing. An example of possible results is given in the sixth column of Table 13.3, Panel A while continuing to assume that equal amounts of money are invested in bonds X and Y. The outcome is a weighted average of individual modified durations that are all significantly less than any value for MD^*_Y. However, they are also considerably more than any MD^*_X. Either way, the point is to show that public fund administrators can manage interest rate risk by including or eliminating bonds with different durations. Monetary changes can then be calculated for a portfolio to determine if a particular loss of principal, because of an increase in interest rates, will present a challenge to meeting obligations, planned or unplanned.

Aside from the convexity issue, a primary weakness underlying duration metrics, as presented earlier, is that in isolation managers must determine what the likelihood for a particular interest rate change will be as the technique does not provide such information. Practically expected values might be used. To illustrate, if a well-seasoned manager believes that there is a 60% chance of a two basis point (i.e., 0.02%) increase and a 40% chance of a one basis point (i.e., 0.01%) increase, then an average change, for a given time period, can be calculated by multiplying each interest rate change by the probability of occurrence to get .016%. However, this experience-based approach ignores modern portfolio techniques that are capable of summarizing investment-oriented risk in a manner that is statistically valid and managerially useful.

When employed, the most often used statistical measure of investment risk is the standard deviation of an investment's (or portfolio of investments') historical rates of return. To date, no other metric has had a bigger effect on the investment management literature, public or private, because assumptions underlying normal distributions have a number of useful properties. This includes the fact that for any normally distributed variable a particular observation is more likely than not to be closer to an average value. Furthermore, normal distributions tend to peak at an average value while gradually and evenly lowering as more extreme values, above and below the average, are accounted for. As a result, confidence intervals can be constructed to determine the probability that a particular return will lie above or below another so long as the future can be deemed to not be unlike the past.

Unfortunately, standard deviation is not a perfect technique for modeling the probabilistic aspects of investment risk because empirical observations confirm that investment data do not always conform to assumptions underlying normal distributions. Furthermore, the measure is of limited use when principal preservation is a primary concern because standard deviation includes upside risk in the form of gains as well as downside risk, in the form of losses. For better or worse, this particular measurement is completely connected to the definition of risk mentioned earlier: the chance that the return on invested funds will be greater or less than what an investor expects.

Whereas the first problem is beyond the scope of this chapter, the following section discusses how this customary view of risk can be amended and applied by local government investment managers to assess and manage interest rate risk during periods of fiscal health and stress. The adjustment is known as Value-at-Risk.

Value-at-Risk

Compared to duration, Value-at-Risk (VaR) is a recent addition to public sector literature that is financially oriented.[11] Albrecht, Shamsub, and Raga (2009), for example, use VaR to assess risk taking by state and local government public pension funds. In addition, Cornia and Nelson (2003) employ VaR when analyzing rainy day funds in the state of Utah. The latter researchers also use their case study to advocate support for VaR analytics in public management decisions that confront uncertainty. However, practitioners' and academics' willingness to accept their proposal is, as of yet, unclear.

By comparison, VaR is frequently used by commercial banks in meeting reserve requirements on invested assets. Furthermore, regulators have applied VaR analytics to assess compliance. Conceptually, these private sector notes resemble what public fund investment managers or kinds of trustees must do and consider if public money, in the form of principal, is to be subject to any level of liquidity risk.

In terms of a definition, VaR measures the worst expected loss that an investor might incur over a given time interval, under normal market conditions, at a given confidence level (Butler, 1999). Like duration, VaR is not a consistent measure of risk as a number of approaches are available for computing VaR metrics. Nonetheless, VaR is capable of incorporating duration metrics into base-line calculations. Equation 6, which is based on Jorion (2007), does this by adjusting Equation 5 as follows:

$$\Delta MP^*_{C.L.} \approx \Delta r^*_{C.L.} \times MD^* \times MP \tag{6}$$

where

$\Delta MP^*_{C.L.}$ = Worst dollar loss for a specified time period at a given confidence level;
$\Delta r^*_{C.L.}$ = Worst change in r^* for a specified time period at a given confidence level; and
C.L. = Confidence level.

Again, careful reflection reveals two important points. First, Equation 6 simply incorporates a specific Δr^* into the fifth equation. The particular value, however, is dependent on how confident a decision maker needs to be a certain loss will not occur during a specified period of time. Usually 95% or 99% confidence levels are chosen. Second, though Equation 6 culminates in a dollar-oriented figure, VaR can also be expressed as a proportion or percent as the product of the first two terms is measured in these kinds of units (i.e., change in basis points multiplied by modified duration). This is often what a commentator is referring to when discussing VaR results without qualification. However, some baseline types of analyses may not include MD^*.

Example.

Table 13.4, Panel A presents daily and annual VaR calculations for three hypothetical fixed income portfolios labeled X, Y, and Z under the assumption that $100,000 of idle funds is available to be invested for 1 year. As shown, portfolio X, which consists of a single bond, has a $\Delta r^*_{C.L.}$ value of 1.12% when a 95% confidence level is chosen. Multiplying

TABLE 13.4 Value at Risk Calculations for Three Hypothetical Portfolios (Principal, \$100,000)

Panel A: VaR for 95% Confidence Level; $\rho_{XY} = 0.50$ [a]

Portfolio (1)	$\Delta r^*_{95\%}$ (2)	MD* (3)	Daily VaR (2) × (3) = (4)	Worst Daily \$ Loss \$100,00 × (4) =(5)	Worst Annual \$ Loss[e] (5) × $\sqrt{T}$ = (6)
X[b]	1.12%	0.50	0.56%	\$560	\$8,854
Y[c]	1.02%	1.00	1.02%	\$1,020	\$16,128
Z[d]	0.92%	0.75	0.69%	\$690	\$10,910

Panel B: VaR for Portfolio Z; $\rho_{XY} = 1.00$[a]

Confidence (1)	$\Delta r^*_{C.L.}$ (2)	MD* (3)	Daily VaR (2) × (3) = (4)	Worst Daily \$ Loss \$100,00 × (4) = (5)	Worst Annual \$ Loss[e] (5) × $\sqrt{T}$ = (6)
95%	1.07%	0.75	0.80%	\$800	\$12,649
99%	1.50%	0.75	1.13%	\$1,130	\$17,867

[a] ρ_{XY} = Correlation coefficient; [b] \$100,000 invested in a single bond other than bond Y; [c] \$100,000 invested in a single bond other than bond X; [d] Equally weighted portfolio of bonds X and Y; [e] T = 250.

1.12% by 0.50, which is the modified duration metric for portfolio X, gives the daily VaR figure of 0.56%. This figure is then used to calculate the worst daily dollar loss, \$560, loss under the assumption that 100% of idle funds are invested in portfolio X. The fifth column uses the square root of time rule to scale the worst daily loss into an annual amount. The assumption is that 250 days of investment data were used to estimate daily VaR statistics. The Appendix to this chapter provides detailed information on $\Delta r^*_{C.L.}$ calculations and other adjustments.

To summarize the results, over the next 250 days, an investor planning on purchasing portfolio X can be 95% certain that no more than 0.56% of principal will be lost on any given day. Put another way, the worst expected loss that a local government might expect to incur, by selling bond X before the maturity date is reached, is \$560 if the data used to calculate the figures represent normal market conditions and a 95% confidence level is chosen. Likewise, the decision maker can be 95% confident that no more than \$8,854, which is approximately 9% of principal, will be lost in a year because of positive changes in market interest rates.

The calculations and interpretations for portfolios Y and Z in Table 13.4, Panel A are identical to that for portfolio X. However, Z is an equally weighted portfolio of X and Y. For this reason, all of the figures given in the fourth row fall between the values in rows two and three under the assumption that the interest rate changes for X and Y are moderately and positively correlated (i.e., $\rho_{XY} = 0.50$). Because of this assumption, the VaR figures, percents and dollars, are less than they would be if ρ_{XY} equaled 1.00. To see this note, that the VaR figures in the second row of Panel B are determined by assuming perfect positive correlation. The third row continues the illustration by increasing the confidence level to 99%. Thus an investor focusing on portfolio Z can be 99% certain that over the next 250 days no more than 1.13% of principal will be lost on any given day if ρ_{XY} is equal to 1.00.

VaR and Local Governments' Fiscal Health

Whereas the preceding discussion focused on the technical aspects of VaR, the point of this section is to indicate managerial implications if local governments employ VaR to ensure safety of principal by way of focusing on liquidity and interest rate risk. The most obvious way VaR accomplishes this objective is by implicitly suggesting that high confidence levels, such as 95% and 99%, should be chosen. This is so the probability of a worst loss can be used to determine whether such an event can be tolerated in light of upcoming obligations, certain or uncertain. Furthermore VaR, as a hyper expected value metric, can be used to assist public fund managers during various phases of a local government's fiscal health.

For example, in the absence of fiscal stress and immediate obligations, a public fund manager contemplating portfolio Z in Table 13.4 might prudently choose to proceed with the assumptions given in Panel A. If obligations were more near term, then he or she might choose to evaluate the decision at a 99% confidence level to determine whether the local government actually has the ability to withstand such an event.

If, however, fiscal stress is present or onsetting for whatever reason, then the administrator might opt to proceed with the assumptions underlying Table 13.4, Panel B even if historical data indicates that investments are not perfectly, positively correlated. In doing so, the administrator is essentially ignoring the benefits of diversification, and interjecting nonnormal market conditions, to determine maximum risk exposure in the form of lost principal. The final row of Table 13.4, Panel B indicates that the public, whose money is at stake, can be 99% confident that no more than $1,130 of principal value would be lost on any given day if portfolio Z should be sold prior to maturity, under nonnormal market conditions.

Finally, combinations are also possible. For example, if a local government knew that $60,000 of idle funds would be needed very near term while another $40,000 was not, then a manager might evaluate the investment of $60,000 under the assumption of perfect positive correlation, at a 99% confidence level, and the $40,000 under the assumption of normal market conditions at a 95% confidence level. The approach, if implemented, is very much in line with Finkelstein's (2006) argument that liquidity should be attended to first to ensure safety of principal and that maximizing income should come second as far as public sector investment priorities are concerned. Furthermore, this type of strategy allows for the reasonable pursuit of investment oriented income. If default risk is a concern then diversification tactics can be used to address these issues as well.

Conclusion

Normatively speaking, the opportunity loss concept provides the raison d'être for investing public funds as, all else constant, positive cash flows enhance constituents' overall ability to maintain or acquire additional levels of goods and services over time. In the absence of investment, the status quo can only be maintained or improved upon if other primary sources of revenue, particularly in the form of taxes, remain the same or are increased. Correspondingly, reductions must occur along with declines in primary revenue sources as is what often happens during periods of fiscal stress.

Philosophically, such decreases are not inherently undesirable. However, decisions should ideally be based on true social costs and benefits rather than an unnecessary constraint on constituents' ability to pay. If the definition of a relevant public extends to borrowers as well, then the argument becomes even more compelling as idle funds are not available to members who may wish to use them for current consumption or in productive processes that benefit the citizenry as a whole. Economic theory predicts and studies confirm that investment interaction is important for all forms of national and subnational governments in various phases of development (e.g., Soto, 2003).

Investing public funds in general, however, is not without political and financial risk. And neither form of risk is independent of each other or other factors including fiscal stress. Though some empirical evidence suggests that local government cash managers, themselves, are not risk seeking (e.g., McCue 2000; Miller, 1991a), other studies, focused on different levels of government and investment arenas, indicate that there may be a limit as far as fiscally induced risk taking is concerned .

Borick (1998), for example, found a positive and statistically significant correlation between the levels of investment risk allowed by state governments and their levels of fiscal stress. Furthermore, as the first decade of the 21st century ends public pension funds appear to be assuming unprecedented levels of risk in an attempt to improve funding levels that have eroded for a variety of reasons. Though the outcome of such decisions is not yet known, the fact that such actions are being pursued because of underfunding is by itself testimony to what can happen in the field of public administration when financial concerns usurp mission-based goals.

VaR, the analytic risk metric ultimately discussed here is, under certain assumptions, capable of addressing this kind of risk exposure. This statement is meant to underscore the view that in addition to being an administrative tool, VaR can extend into the sphere of regulation by requiring that VaR metrics be reported. Jorion (2007) notes that if VaR metrics had been applied and communicated to Orange County, California, officials in 1994, the disaster may well have been avoided.

Again, putting exceptional cases aside, VaR may also assist decision makers with mitigating more common things such as the unintended consequences associated with various policies and accounting rules. Finkelstein (2006), for example, suggests that the Government Accounting Standards Board Statement Number 31 (GASB 31) is a major problem for public fund investment practice. GASB 31 requires governments to report investments at fair value, which is defined as the amount at which a financial instrument could be exchanged in a current transaction between willing parties, other than in a forced or liquidation sale (Finkelstein, 2006, p. 54).

Finkelstein's contention is that public fund investment managers' decisions are ultimately shackled to the unavoidable systematic risk (i.e., ups and downs) of the market. Consequently, they focus more on meeting accounting requirements than on sound investment practices. Connecting Jorion, an academic, with Finkelstein, a practitioner, suggests that VaR might help remedy or at least mitigate this problem in a prudent manner that is fairly easy to understand by practitioners who are ultimately concerned with ensuring that sufficient cash is available to meet obligations during periods of fiscal health and fiscal stress.

Endnotes

1. Though the value of *n* can never be less than zero in these types of calculations, the value of *i* can be under certain assumptions. This special case is ignored here.
2. Identical conclusions can be reached with proportions by noting that Equation 1 can be rewritten as $r = \sqrt[n]{FV_n \div PV_0} - 1$. Multiplying this result by 100 gives a percent return.
3. An important point to note is that the research listed here typically referred to opportunity losses as opportunity costs. Furthermore, the investigations were often directed at assessing the consequences of leaving large cash balances in zero-interest demand deposit accounts. According to Onwujuba and Lynch (2002), in the 1950s, governments held approximately 40% of their financial assets in cash and checking accounts. This fell to 15% and 5% in the 1970s and 1980s, respectively.
4. This view is at odds with the private sector literature that adds political risk to the list of investment risks noted earlier.
5. Practically, political risk also involves decisions about what to invest in. Many local governments, for example, continue to permit or encourage social investments that purport to stimulate economic development. Cooper (1972) found that such tactics do not stimulate local economic activities.
6. Par values, maturity dates, and coupon rates are delineated in bond indentures (i.e., contracts). As such, bond indentures correspond to the unambiguous and well-defined property rights mentioned earlier. Some advanced indenture topics (e.g., call provisions) are not discussed here.
7. Although $1,000 is a typical bond par value, many bonds pay interest semiannually. In these cases, the number of periods doubles while interest rates are adjusted by dividing them in half. For simplicity, only annual periods are considered here.
8. In this instance, 5% is what the investor actually earns as only one time period is under consideration. For multiple time periods, the investor will need to reinvest intermittent cash flows at a rate equal to r, for the entire life of the bond, to achieve the required rate of return, which is also known as "Yield to Maturity."
9. In practice, convexity can be used with duration to improve on approximations that duration alone will give. However, the topic is outside the scope of this chapter.

10. Average life resembles the payback rule that is often discussed in capital budgeting and cost benefit literature. The payback rule simply looks at the amount of time needed to recover an initial investment while ignoring other monetary flows. For this reason alone, the technique is not considered a best practice.
11. Macaulay duration is named after Frederick Macaulay, an economist who developed the metric in 1938.

Glossary

Capital market: any market (or market mechanism) where a private sector entity or government can raise money to fund operations and other long-term investments.

Convex: If a curve is convex toward the origin, then an inverse relationship exists between variables such as market prices and yields. In general, the greater the convexity, the less sensitive a bond's price is to increases in interest rates.

Ex ante: a term referring to future events or forward thinking decisions.

Local Government Investment Pool: An investment arrangement where local governments are permitted to commingle and invest cash balances. Returns or losses are typically distributed according to the size of deposits.

Semi-elasticity: a percentage change in a function (e.g., MD*) with respect to an absolute change in a particular parameter (e.g., interest rates).

Speculative investment practices: generally refers to investing in high-risk investments or the use of tactics that rely on economic circumstances to produce a return.

Systematic risk: aggregate market-oriented risk that cannot be managed with diversification

Unsystematic risk: risk that is specifically related to a particular investment and can be managed with diversification.

Yield curve: a graph that plots various interest rates, at a set point in time, of bonds with similar levels of default risk against different maturity dates.

Discussion Questions

1. What is the purpose of investing public funds? Discuss why the concept of opportunity loss is important.
2. Does the purpose of investing idle monies vary with the definition of fiscal health? Why do you think researchers have not paid more attention to this area of public policy?
3. Public administrators are often encouraged to be more businesslike and entrepreneurial. Does entrepreneurship have a role in public investment decisions?

4. Should more resources be devoted to local economic development projects rather than market-oriented investment activities? Should economic considerations be given more weight than those that are political?
5. Why is liquidity important? Is there ever a time when maximizing income should be given priority?
6. What potential role does VaR have in assessing the risks associated with investing public funds? How do you interpret a VaR metric?

Recommended Resources

Albrecht, W. G. (2008). Public funds investment strategies. In J. Rabin and E. M. Berman (Eds.), *Encyclopedia of public administration and public policy* (2nd ed.) (pp. 1623–1627). London: Taylor and Francis.

Baldassare, M. (1998). *When government fails: The Orange County bankruptcy*. Los Angeles: University of California Press.

Das, S., and J. Marin (1997). Value at risk models. In S. Das (Ed.), *Risk management and financial derivatives* (pp. 547–684). New York: McGraw Hill.

Government Accounting Standards Board. (March, 1997). Summary of statement no. 31. Retrieved on January 10, 2011, from http://www.gasb.org/st/summary/gstsm31.html

Khan, A. (2003). Learning from experience: Cash management practices of a local government. In A. Khan and W. B. Hildreth (Eds.), *Case studies in public budgeting and financial management* (pp. 553–567). New York: Marcel Dekker, Inc.

Philippe, J. (2009). Philippe Jorion's Orange County case: Using value at risk to control financial risk. Retrieved March15, 2010, from http://merage.uci.edu/~jorion/oc/case.html

Wong, J. D. (2008). Time value of money. In J. Rabin & E. M. Berman (Eds.), *Encyclopedia of public administration and public policy* (2nd ed.) (pp. 1923–1930). London: Taylor and Francis.

References

Albrecht, W. G., Shamsub, H., and Raga, K. (2009). A value at risk analysis of state & local government pension funds. *National Social Science Journal, 32*, 1–11.

Bland, R. L. (1986). The effect of cash management innovations on the investment income of local governments. *State and Local Government Review, 18*, 20–25.

Blankenbeckler, G. M. (1978). Excess cash management at the state and local government levels. *State and Local Government Review, 10*, 2–7.

Borick, C. P. (1998). Going to the market: The relationship between fiscal constraints and state investment management policies. *State and Local Government Review, 30*, 190–193.

Butler, C. (1999). *Mastering value at risk: A step by step guide to understanding and applying VaR.* Trowbridge, Willshire, England: Pearson Education Limited.

California Debt and Investment Advisory Commission. (2007). *Duration basics.* Issue Brief CDIAC #60-10.

Cooper, S. K. (1972). The economics of idle public funds policies: A reconsideration. *National Tax Journal, 25,* 97–99.

Corina, G. C., and Nelson, R. D. (2003). Rainy day funds and value at risk. *State Tax Notes, 29,* 563–567.

Delisle, E. C. (2010). *Fiscal stress faced by local governments.* Washington, DC: Congressional Budget Office.

Finkelstein, B. (2006). *The politics of public fund investing.* New York: Simon & Schuster Touchstone.

Government Accounting Standards Board. (2009). *GASB adds project addressing fiscal sustainability to current technical agenda.* Retrieved March 10, 2010, from http://www.gasb.org/newsletter/fiscal_sustainability_dec2009.html

Honadle, B. W., Costa, J. M., and Cigler, B. A. (2003). *Fiscal health for local governments: An introduction to concepts, practical analysis, and strategies.* San Diego: Elsevier Academic Press.

Jorion, P. (2007). *Value at risk: The new benchmark for managing financial risk.* New York: McGraw-Hill Companies, Inc.

Khan, A. (1996). Cash management: Basic principles and guidelines. In J. Rabin, W. B. Hildreth, and G. J. Miller (Eds.), *Budgeting formulation and execution* (pp. 313–322). Athens, GA: Carl Vinson Institute of Government.

McCue, C. P. (2000). The risk-return paradox in local government investing. *Public Budgeting and Finance, 20,* 80–101.

Markowitz, H. M. (1952). Portfolio selection. *The Journal of Finance, 7,* 77–91.

Miller, G. J. (1991a). *Government financial management theory.* New York: Marcel Dekker, Inc.

Miller, G. (1991b). Cash management. In J. E. Petersen and D. R. Strachota (Eds.), *Local government finance: Concepts and practices* (pp. 241–262). Chicago: Government Finance Officers Association.

Miller, G. (1998). *Investing public funds* (2nd ed.). Chicago, IL: Government Finance Officers Association.

Mikesell, J. L. (2007). *Fiscal administration: Analysis and applications for the public sector* (7th ed.). Belmont, CA: Thompson-Wadsworth.

Nwagu, C. O. (1985). Cash management in local governments: An evaluation of local government money management policies and practices, and constrains on the maximization of investment returns. Doctoral dissertation, Virginia Polytechnic Institute and State University. Dissertation Abstracts International 47/02, 653.

Orndorff, C. N., and Syal, A. (1997). *Investing local government funds: A guide for municipal finance professionals, board members, and investment managers.* New York: McGraw-Hill.

Onwujuba, C. C., and Lynch, T. D. (2002). Cash management practices in Louisiana municipalities. *Journal of Public Budgeting, Accounting, and Financial Management, 14,* 95–116.

Reed, B. J., and Swain, J. W. (1997). *Public finance administration* (2nd ed.). Thousand Oaks, CA: Sage Publications, Inc.

Skidmore M., and Scorsone, E. (2010). Causes and consequences of fiscal stress in Michigan-municipal governments (Lincoln Institute Product Code: WP10MS1). Lincoln Institute of Land policy.

Soto, H. D. (2003). *The mystery of capital: Why capitalism triumphs in the west and fails everywhere else.* New York: Basic Books.

Appendix

The standard deviation for portfolios X, Y, and Z in Table 13.4 are determined by substituting ad hoc values into the following equation:

$$\sigma_P = \sqrt{W_X^2\sigma_X^2 + W_Y^2\sigma_Y^2 + 2W_XW_Y\sigma_X\sigma_Y\rho_{XY}}$$

σ_P = Portfolio standard deviation;
W_X = Proportion of idle funds invested in portfolio X;
σ_X = Standard deviation of daily interest rate changes for portfolio X;
W_Y = Proportion of idle funds invested in portfolio Y;
σ_Y = Standard deviation of daily interest rate changes for portfolio X; and
ρ_{XY} = Correlation coefficient.

As written, the equation demonstrates that σ_P is equal to the standard deviation of one investment if the portfolio consists of nothing else. This is the case with portfolios X and Y in Table 13.4, Panel A.

Values for $\Delta r^*_{C.L.}$ are found by multiplying σ_P by a Z score, which indicates how far a particular value of a normally distributed variable (e.g., a particular interest rate change) is above or below the mean (i.e., average). Most introductory textbooks on statistics include tables with these values.

Table 13.A1 illustrates the derivation of the $\Delta r^*_{C.L.}$ values given in Table 13.4, Panel A of the chapter. **Figure 13.A1** supports this information with a visual depiction of the $\Delta r^*_{95\%}$ value for portfolio X.

Markowitz (1952) is usually credited for suggesting standard deviation as a measure of risk. VaR analyses that follow the general procedure discussed here are typically called Variance-Covariance. Other approaches involve historical methods as well as Monte Carlo

TABLE 13.A1 Calculating $\Delta r^*_{C.L.}$ for 95% Level of Confidence

Portfolio (1)	Z Score (2)	σ (3)	$\Delta r^*_{95\%}$ (2) × (3) = (4)
X	1.65	0.68%	1.12%
Y	1.65	0.62%	1.02%
Z	1.65	0.56%	0.92%

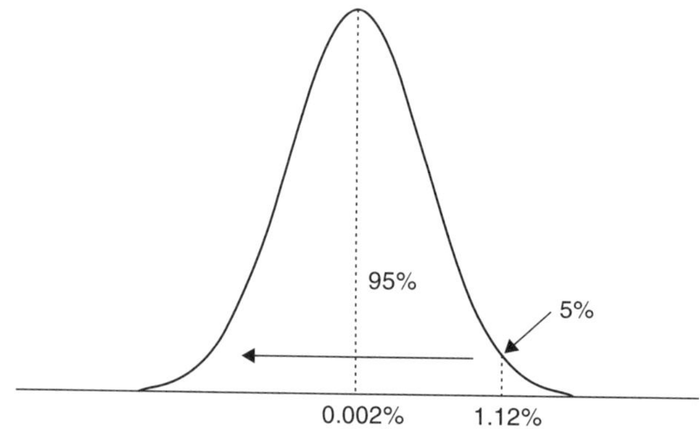

Figure 13.A1 VaR and Normal Distribution for Portfolio X

simulations (Butler, 1999). Whenever the square root of time is used, to convert daily values in to annual values, the following statistical result is used as justification:

$$\sigma_P = \sqrt{\frac{\sum_{i=1}^{T}(x_i - \bar{x})^2}{T}}$$

where

σ_P = Daily standard deviation;
x_i = Daily value;
$\bar{x}$ = Average daily value; and
T = Number of trading (i.e., business) days per year.

Note that taking the square root of squared daily differences returns the numerator back to ordinary daily differences. However T, which is not squared, is subsequently measured in square root days when the square root of the ratio is taken. Multiplying σ_P by $\sqrt{T}$ makes the adjustment. The 250 value for T is based on the typical number of business days in a year.

In practice, other distributional assumptions must also be met before complete conclusions can be reached about the results of such transformations. Readers may wish to refer to investment-oriented books that address this advanced topic and others underlying the brief presentation given here.

Part VI

Intergovernmental and Institutional Considerations

Chapter 14

Local Government Fiscal Health

An Intergovernmental Perspective

by Beth Walter Honadle

A Forest Metaphor

Metaphorically, taking an intergovernmental perspective helps the observer see the forest (a dense area that is home to a diversity of types of governments) and not just individual trees (single units of local government). Local governments are rooted in state constitutions and legislation, judicial decisions, history, and tradition. Their roots may wrap around the roots of other local governments and competitively take nutrients from their common soil. They may have symbiotic relations with each other as well, if the state allows. Their branches touch each other and are sometimes so intertwined and overlapping that, to the casual observer, it is hard to see where one ends and another begins. New units of local governments propagate and flourish in some fertile environments. Sometimes local governments die or are killed in a mass extinction ordered by the state. Sometimes parts of one local government are detached and grafted onto another one. There are different species of local governments, too—some for general purposes and some quite specialized. As haphazard as all this may seem, each state determines the morphology (form and structure) of the local governments within their borders. Viewed from above the forest, one sees that there are fifty tall (stately) "trees" of equal height; beneath and around these states are the types of local governments permitted by the state. Some local governments are offshoots envisioned as instruments of the state with relatively little autonomy, while others have decentralized or scattered patterns of seedlings that have grown up and clustered in places.

Source: Beth Walter Honadle

Introduction

This chapter presents a wide-angle view of the intersection of intergovernmental relations and the fiscal health of local governments. Its purpose is to complement other chapters in this volume by providing a larger context or conceptual framework for understanding fiscal health. Other chapters in the *Handbook of Local Government Fiscal Health* offer close-up shots focused on particular aspects of intergovernmental relations—fiscal federalism, state monitoring of local government finance, TABORs and TELs, consolidation of services, and state constraints on local government debt—that have clear and direct effects on local government finance. Indeed, these contributions are predominantly about policies and practices explicitly and purposefully designed to oversee, control, or support local government finances.

The thesis of this chapter is that it takes an intergovernmental perspective to understand the fiscal health of local governments. Local governments are not self-contained entities set off by themselves that have complete control over their structure, functions, and such fundamental aspects of finance as revenues, expenditures, and debt (Honadle, Costa, and Cigler, 2004, esp. pp. 10–12). According to Coe, "Each governmental level—federal, state, and local—affects the others. . . ." The linkages among them include grants and mandates, home-rule provisions of states, local government service contracts, transfer of functions, annexation, and other units of government (2007, p. 68)

Intergovernmental relations entail both vertical (federal-state-local) and horizontal (interlocal) relationships. On the vertical dimension, local governments' authority is subordinated to that of their state governments in almost every conceivable way. Federal government policies and practices also affect the fiscal condition of local governments through spending and by way of program guidelines that mandate certain expenditures.

Horizontal intergovernmental relationships—those between and among local governments—have consequences for the fiscal health, condition, and well-being of local governments. From state to state, the types, number, discretionary authority, assignment of functional responsibilities, fiscal oversight, and other characteristics of local government are distinct. The interconnectedness of local governments with other units of government presents both opportunities and challenges for local governments trying to maintain or improve their fiscal health.

The following section of the chapter presents the generic types of local governments in the United States, tracking numerical trends in these genres over the last half century. This "population" study of governments in the United States leads up to a conceptual framework for understanding how the intergovernmental system is an inescapable factor to understanding and shaping the fiscal health of local government in the United States. This overview draws attention to the variability of governmental structure among states and includes brief scenarios to illustrate how intergovernmental relations condition the fiscal health of the "creatures" of the states.

The Structure of Government in the United States

The definitive source of data on the number of units of government in the United States is the Census of Government, conducted by the U.S. Bureau of the Census every five years in years ending in "2" or "7"' (e.g., 1962, 1967, 1992, 1997). This section is based entirely on Census of Government data, using the Census definitions of different types of local government. The trends are presented using the Census classifications and data.

Most readers know that there is one national government and fifty state governments in the United States. Less commonly known and underappreciated is the fact that there are 89,476 units of local government, according to the most recent (2007) data by the Census of Governments.

Types of Local Government

When one talks about local government, it is important to understand that there are different types of local government. They serve different functions. Even though each state has its terminology for what it calls the units of government it allows, the Census has developed generic definitions so that it can collect comparable data for aggregation across states. This section starts by distinguishing between two broad categories of local government and then refines those categories further to identify more narrowly defined types.

General Purpose Local Governments

Some local governments are formed to provide general government functions rather than serve a particular functional purpose. There are three categories of general purpose local government, which, taken together, accounted for 39,011 of U.S. local governments in 2007.

Counties.

The Census defines counties as "organized local governments authorized in state constitutions and statutes and established to provide general government; includes those governments designated as counties, parishes in Louisiana, and boroughs in Alaska." Note that the Census definition is concerned with functional comparability, not what a county may be called in different states but mean essentially the same thing. According to the Census of Governments, there were 3,033 counties in 2007.

Municipal governments.

The Census defines municipal governments as "organized local governments authorized in state constitutions and statutes and established to provide government for a specific concentration of population in a defined area; includes those governments designated as cities, villages, boroughs (except in Alaska), and towns (except in the six New England states, Minnesota, New York, and Wisconsin)."

Once again, the Census definition provides a way of classifying like governments, regardless of what their states may call them or what they may choose to call themselves. In Ohio, the City of the Village of Indian Hill, says on its website, "With a population of around 5,900 people, [Indian Hill] is technically a city but its life style over the years has remained constant, that of a quiet residential community" (The Village of Indian Hill). This example helps readers understand that the technical definition does not alter a classification based on how a city wants to maintain its image. (A city by any other name is still a city to the Census, in other words.) According to the Census of Governments, there were 19,492 municipal governments in 2007.

Township governments.

The Census defines township governments as "organized local governments authorized in state constitutions and statutes and established to provide general government for areas defined without regard to population concentration; includes those governments designated as towns in Connecticut, Maine (including organized plantations), Massachusetts, Minnesota, New Hampshire (including organized locations), New York, Rhode Island, Vermont, and Wisconsin, and townships in other states." According to the Census of Governments, there were 16,519 township governments in 2007.

Non-general Purpose Local Governments

In addition to the three types of local government that states authorize to provide general government, other governments are formed for particular functional purposes. As a group, these non-general purpose local governmental units represented 50,432 (or greater than 56%) of all local governments in the United States in 2007.

School district governments.

The Census defines school district governments as "Organized local entities providing public elementary, secondary, and higher education, which, under state law, have sufficient administration and fiscal autonomy to qualify as separate governments. [This definition e]xcludes dependent public school systems of county, municipal, township, or state governments." According to the Census of Governments, there were 13,051 school district governments in the United States in 2007.

Special district governments.

The second non-general purpose type of local governments is special district governments, which the Census defines as "All organized local entities (other than counties, municipalities, townships, or school districts) authorized by state law to provide only one or a limited number of designated functions, and with sufficient administrative and fiscal autonomy to qualify as separate governments; known by a variety of titles, including districts, authorities, boards, and commissions." According to the Census of Governments, there were 37,381 special district governments (nearly double the frequency of municipal governments, the next largest category of local government) in the United States in 2007. This includes such governmental entities as port authorities, hospital districts, parks districts, library districts, parks boards, and other similarly specialized entities that have "*sufficient administrative and fiscal autonomy to qualify as separate governments.*" This point is reiterated with emphasis to make it clear that each of these special districts is a unit of government, not a department of another local government.

Numerical Trends in Types of Governments

Although the current distribution of each type of governmental unit is interesting and important to understanding the "subpopulations" among which intergovernmental relations happen, it is very revealing to review historical developments to show how the composition of the local government landscape has changed dramatically over the last several decades.

General Purpose Local Governments

The narrative regarding changes in numbers of general purpose local governments in the United States over the last half century is rather simple. As **Figure 14.1** shows, there has been a decline of well less than 1% in the number of counties (net loss of 19 over the period) since the middle of the last century. **Figures 14.2, 14.3**, and **14.4** show trends in numbers of municipalities (Figure 14.2) and townships (Figure 14.3) separately and then

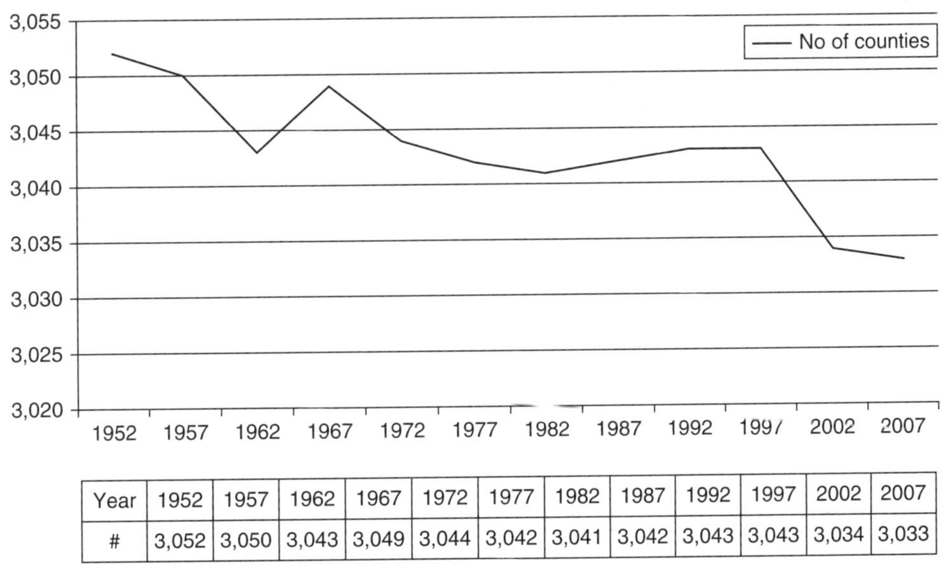

Year	1952	1957	1962	1967	1972	1977	1982	1987	1992	1997	2002	2007
#	3,052	3,050	3,043	3,049	3,044	3,042	3,041	3,042	3,043	3,043	3,034	3,033

Figure 14.1 County Government Trends, 1952–2007

Data from U.S. Census of Governments

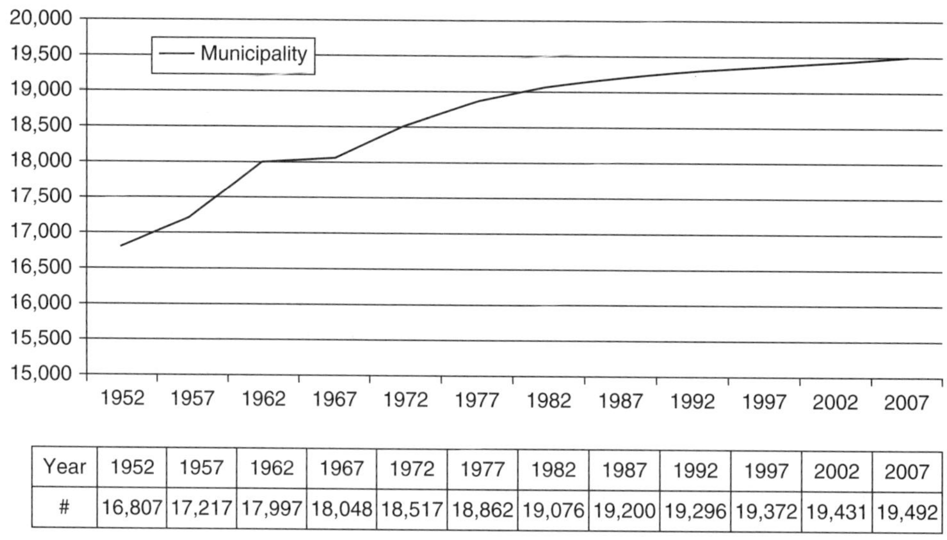

Year	1952	1957	1962	1967	1972	1977	1982	1987	1992	1997	2002	2007
#	16,807	17,217	17,997	18,048	18,517	18,862	19,076	19,200	19,296	19,372	19,431	19,492

Figure 14.2 Municipal Government Trends, 1952–2007

Data from U.S. Census of Governments

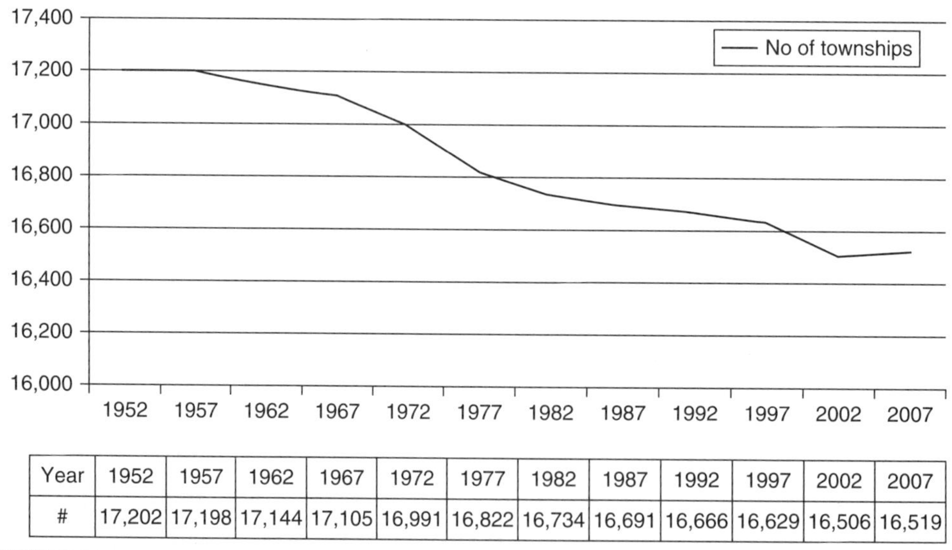

Year	1952	1957	1962	1967	1972	1977	1982	1987	1992	1997	2002	2007
#	17,202	17,198	17,144	17,105	16,991	16,822	16,734	16,691	16,666	16,629	16,506	16,519

Figure 14.3 Township Government Trends, 1952–2007

Data from U.S. Census of Governments

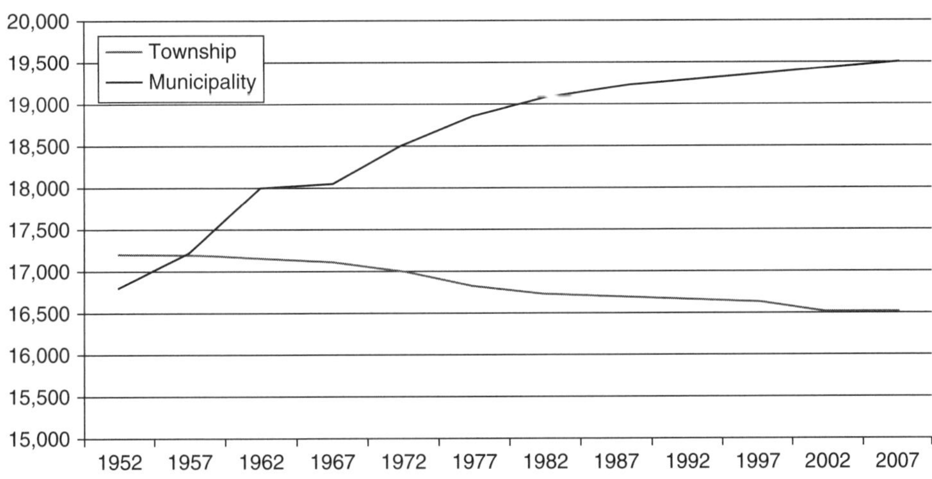

Figure 14.4 Township Governments Relative to Municipal Governments, 1952–2007

Data from U.S. Census of Governments

together (Figure 14.4) on one graph to show how their numbers have moved in relation to each other. The number of municipalities increased by nearly 16% (a net increase of 2,685 municipalities)—from 16,807 in 1952 to 19,492 in 2007. Over the same period, the number of townships dropped a net 683. Taken together, Figure 14.4 shows that by the 1962 Census, the number of cities had overtaken the number of townships and has continued to grow relative to the number of townships. There are a number of reasons for these trends. One is changes in the U.S. population. Some rural counties have lost population to the point that they are no longer able to perform basic county functions. There has been a spate of city-county consolidations (Leland and Thurmaier, 2004). Many townships have grown in population and demand for "city" services grew, so they transformed into the more urban type of municipal government. Through annexation of territory into cities, the remnants of some townships may not be viable or even allowable, depending on state laws or constitutions.

Non-general Purpose Local Governments

The trends for governments that do not serve general purposes are rather interesting. As **Figures 14.5** (school districts), **14.6** (special districts), and **14.7** (school districts and special districts shown on the same graph for comparison) show, their frequencies move in opposite directions. First, the number of school districts has decreased dramatically since 1952. Their numbers decreased by more than 80% from 67,355 in 1952 to 13,051 in 2007, with over three-quarters of the drop occurring between 1952 and 1972 as school districts consolidated for a variety of reasons, including the closure of nonfunctioning districts, integration of education that demanded the consolidation of racially imbalanced school

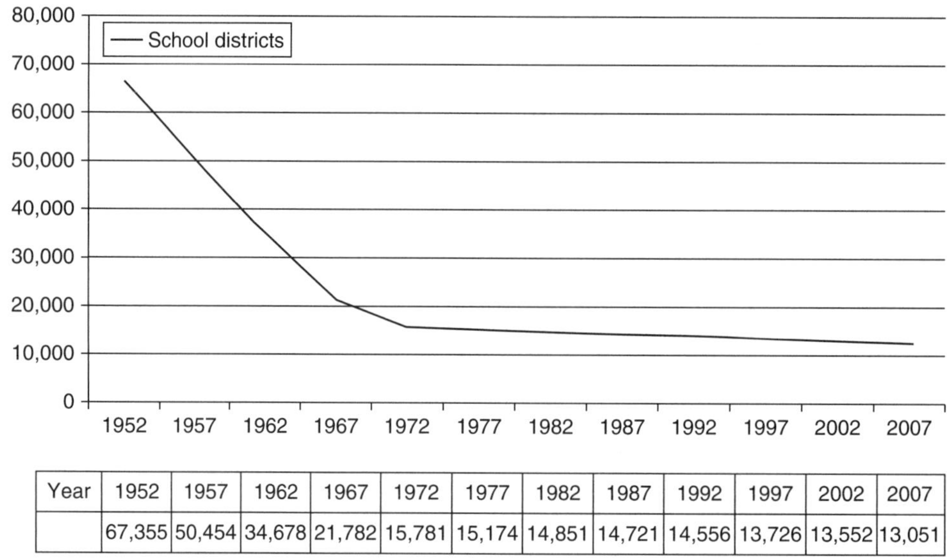

Year	1952	1957	1962	1967	1972	1977	1982	1987	1992	1997	2002	2007
	67,355	50,454	34,678	21,782	15,781	15,174	14,851	14,721	14,556	13,726	13,552	13,051

Figure 14.5 School District Trends, 1952–2007

Data from U.S. Census of Governments

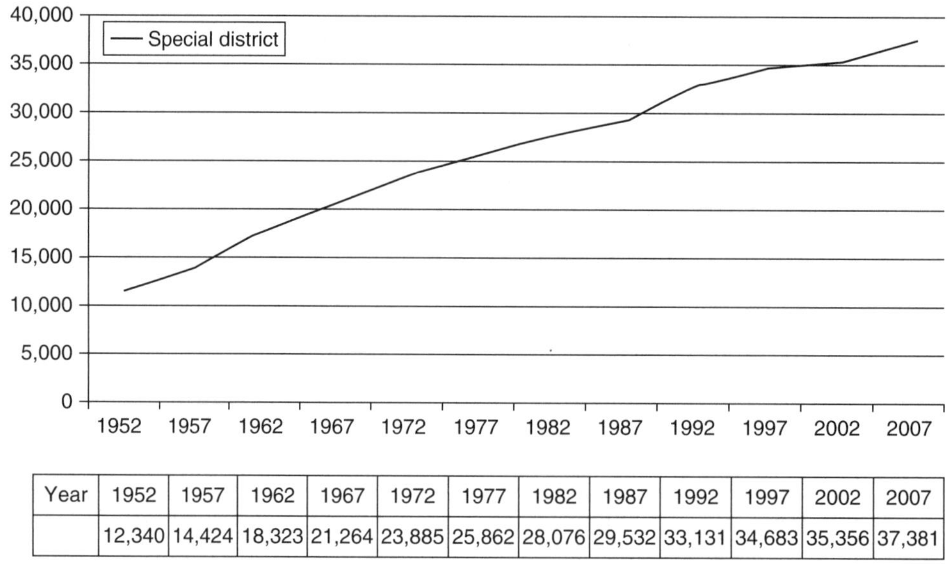

Year	1952	1957	1962	1967	1972	1977	1982	1987	1992	1997	2002	2007
	12,340	14,424	18,323	21,264	23,885	25,862	28,076	29,532	33,131	34,683	35,356	37,381

Figure 14.6 Special District Trends, 1952–2007

Data from U.S. Census of Governments

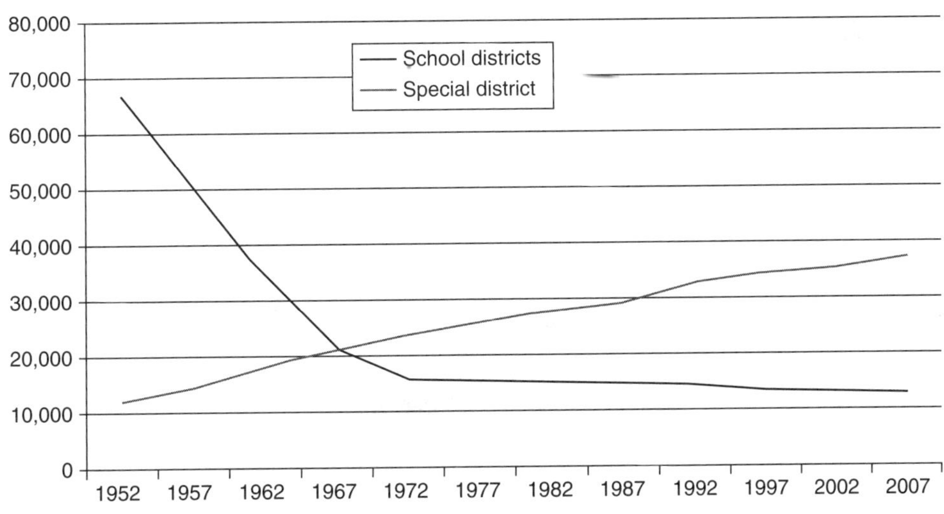

Figure 14.7 School Districts Relative to Special District Governments, 1952–2007

Data from U.S. Census of Governments

districts, and the dismantling of rural school districts that could not justify a school district for their small numbers of students.

By contrast, special district governments have mushroomed, more than tripling in number over this period, from 12,340 in 1952 to 37,381 in 2007. There are many reasons given for this sharp rise in special districts (see, e.g., Currie, Honadle, and DeBoer, 1999). Some reasons for their growth include liberalization of state policies that have allowed the creation of particular special districts, responses to state-imposed limits on revenues and expenditures by general-purpose local governments, attempts to garner political support for government expenditures by serving particular interests, efforts to de-politicize some functions by taking them out of general politics, endeavors to rationalize governmental boundaries with natural geographies (e.g., watersheds) or realize economies of scale, and the growth in public sector problems requiring specially trained technical staff, among others.

The trend in non-general purpose local governments reached a watershed after the 1967 Census when the number of special districts caught up with school districts and they were virtually tied in frequency. For the last four decades, special districts have been the most numerous and fastest-growing type of local government in the United States.

Variety Abounds

Although there are clear trends in the number of each type of local government in the United States, it must be emphasized that there is enormous variation from state to state

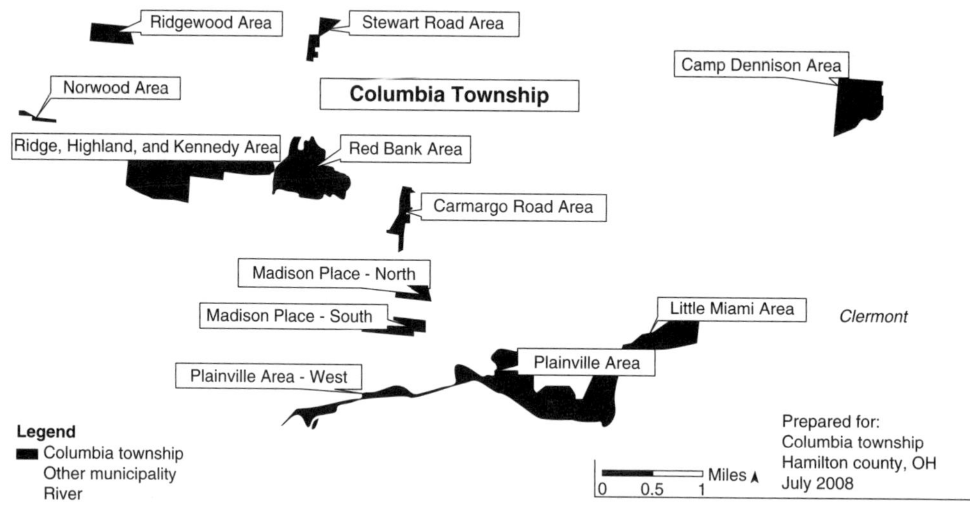

Figure 14.8 Map of Columbia Township

Modified from Hamilton County Department of Planning and Development

and within states. Thus, for example, the average state has 51 counties, but Texas has 254 counties while Delaware and Hawaii have but 3 apiece. Illinois has the most municipal governments of any state (1,299) compared to the average of 382 and Rhode Island with just 19. Minnesota has the largest number of townships (1,788), and many states have none. There are many anomalous cases such as Columbia Township in Ohio (see **Figure 14.8**, Map of Columbia Township), whose official website states that the township "is best described as an 'inland archipelago'—a group of nine 'islands' separated by a 'sea of municipalities.'"

Conceptual Framework

The foregoing section demonstrates how complex and complicated the structure of governance is in the United States. The states exhibit great variety in their stances toward local governments, and those approaches change over time. These intricacies allow for interesting experimentation and research. The objective of this section is to take a more conceptual look at the intergovernmental dimension of this structure with a focus on the fiscal health of local governments.

Local governments exist in a wide range of intergovernmental environments. A densely populated metropolitan region may have dozens of counties, hundreds of municipalities, numerous independent school districts, and a fragmented patchwork of overlapping special districts performing particular functions for defined areas. These "metro" areas may very well have the additional distinction of encompassing parts of different states (e.g., Ohio, Kentucky, and Indiana for Cincinnati and Minnesota and Wisconsin for Minneapolis-St. Paul). At the opposite end of the spectrum, a rural, sparsely populated county may have one relatively small city, the county seat; a few thinly populated townships; a school district or two wholly contained within the county's boundaries and maybe parts of other school districts that extend into the county; and perhaps a regional library or water district, all existing within one state's boundaries. Both of these scenarios entail intergovernmental relations that affect the fiscal health and condition of individual local governments within their respective areas. Thus, each situation must be understood in its unique context, taking into account the different states' constitutions and laws, history, local customs and practices, politics, differing demands for services, economic differences, varying opportunities, and other variables.

Because there is such diversity across places and evolution in policies over time, a simplified framework for putting the intergovernmental influence on fiscal health in perspective is in order. The framework presented in this chapter assumes the viewpoint of a local government to focus on some common influences by other governments on a local government's fiscal health.

Local Government Absent Intergovernmental Relations?

To understand how profoundly intergovernmental relations affect the fiscal health of local governments, start by imagining a hypothetical situation *without* intergovernmental relations at all. If an imaginary local government were a single, solitary public jurisdiction in a defined geographic area, it would have great discretion over and responsibility for its fiscal choices. To balance the budget and ensure fiscal health, the local government's managers would make decisions to increase or cut taxes, change the tax structure, borrow funds, assess fees for services, reduce expenditures, work to increase the local tax base, and so on, according to their sense of what is in the community's interests and based, of course, on politics and economic constraints.

To be sure, this local government would face important factors that are outside of its ability to control, such as the incidence of natural disasters, changing demographics, and business location decisions in a free-market economy. But, by and large, the local government would have absolute control over its financial management, setting its own limits, devising its own approach to providing for local services and financing them without external governmental influences. In theory, local actors would adjust their policies and practices based on their perceptions about opportunities, constraints, feasible alternatives, trade-offs among optional ways of doing things, and other considerations they deemed salient.

This hypothetical image of a local government absent intergovernmental relations is the antithesis of reality. Its purpose here is to lay the groundwork for showing how things really are and how the actual intergovernmental system is of paramount importance to local governments' fiscal health.

Enter Intergovernmental Relations

The insular local government just described is mythical. No such local government actually exists anywhere in the United States. In fact, a local government could not even come into being without the permission of a state. And, of course, all governments are subject to the Constitution of the United States and actions by the federal government.

State-local Dimension

State constitutions and legislation are the means by which local governments are formed. Each state determines what types of local government may exist, how they may be created and dissolved, how their boundaries may be changed, and whether local governments may enter into cooperative agreements with one another. The state may also institute measures that force local governments to consider the effects of their actions on the finances of other local governments and may use this information to decide whether to allow boundary adjustments to proceed. This list merely hints at some of the fundamentally important ways in which the states shape local governments.

With respect to revenues, the state can limit what types of taxes local governments may use, how they will administer those taxes, whether and how local governments can borrow funds, and other important considerations such as by how much a given revenue source may increase over a specified period of time.

The state may also impose financial reporting requirements, oversee local finances closely or scarcely at all, and even usurp local governmental authority to administer their own finances through state-appointed control boards (effectively a type of receivership). States may require local governments to hold public meetings to announce proposed changes in taxes or to present the state of the jurisdictions' finances publicly at prescribed intervals.

The state can mandate certain local government expenditures and forbid others. It may provide grants to subsidize local service provision. Likewise, it can unilaterally decide to cut or eliminate such funding, delay the disbursement of funds to help balance the state's budget or for other reasons, and attach strings to funds that local governments must accept as a condition of receiving state funding. The state may prescribe the allowable instruments for investment of local funds, and it may also require and/or limit local government fund balances from one fiscal year to the next. Also, states' funding responsibility for functions, such as K–12 education, vary across states and the differential impacts on equity and the ability of local governments to innovate are worthy of consideration (Wong and Shen, 2001).

Moreover, there are, in addition to state constitutions and statutes, voter-approved measures that tie the hands of local officials in terms of their fiscal actions.[1] The express purpose of these referenda is to do just that—to force local governments to behave in ways that they might not without the imposition of strict, explicit requirements that are increasingly incorporated into the state's constitution making them more difficult to undo than if they were created by statute.

There are at least two reasons for this. First, the state courts must abide by the constitution in their rulings, so these measures trump legislation. Second, the legal process for repealing state constitutional amendments presents formidable political obstacles, including a well-organized and well-financed campaign to undo these measures. The difficulty of repealing these kinds of constitutional limits on the fiscal discretion of local governments helps us understand why reformers choose this route in states where "going to the voters" is an option.

The authoritative reference work, *Home Rule in America: A Fifty-State Handbook*, defines home rule as "the ability of a local government to act and make policy in all areas that have not been designated to be of statewide interest through general law, state constitutional provisions, or initiatives and referenda" (Krane, Rigos, and Hill, 2001, p. 2). Much scholarly work and legal opinion have been written about the issue of "home rule." It is beyond the scope of this chapter to review this material (which is done very nicely in Krane et al's comprehensive treatment on the subject with a chapter devoted to each state's home rule provisions).

Federal-local Dimension

The Constitution of the United States does not reference local governments at all. It reserves certain powers to the states, leaving entirely up to each state any decisions about whether to create local governments and, if so, what powers they will have. But the federal government's actions do affect the fiscal health of local governments in many ways. One of these is intergovernmental grants-in-aid. In the 1970s and 1980s, General Revenue Sharing provided funds via formula to state and local governments. This program, begun during the Nixon presidency, was a way of helping local governments financially because the federal government had preempted some of the strongest forms of revenue raising. In some cases, small government officials did not know what to make of these unexpected disbursements. But, they came to depend on them. So, in the mid-1980s when the program was eliminated, local governments' fiscal health and condition were adversely affected. Another example of how the withdrawal of federal funding has, in effect, pulled the rug out from under local governments was the COPS FAST program of the 1990s. Always intended as a temporary program to fund 75% of the entry-level salary of newly hired police officers for community policing, local jurisdictions ultimately had to either foot the bill for the continuation of these officers or eliminate these positions once the funding ended.

There are many implications for local fiscal health of federal-local and state-local intergovernmental relations. Among the most important of these is the institutional framework each state develops for local government structure. It is important to understand the amount of discretion and what types of discretion each type of local government has. In addition, unfunded mandates, court decisions, and intergovernmental aids can affect the fiscal health of local governments. One issue from the local governmental view is the difficulty of planning for the long term because the state or federal government can offer funding (which might seem to help a local government's financial ability to meet local needs) and then withdraw those funds.

Interlocal dimension

Many aspects of interlocal governmental relations have implications for local governmental fiscal health. Once again, each state supplies the legal framework for what local governments may do relative to one another. For example, a state may allow local governments to enter into shared service agreements, contract with other local governments to provide services more economically to their residents, create multi-jurisdictional development districts, and so on. Although these seem like straightforward policies that enable local governments to pursue interlocal agreements that are in their mutual interests financially and otherwise, there are other interlocal issues that may arise unintentionally or as a side effect of each jurisdiction's acting in its own financial interests.

Three common scenarios illustrate this point:

- A school district issues bonds to finance the building of a new school and sports facilities. A city (i.e, a separate local governmental jurisdiction) with properties that overlap with the school district subsequently decides to finance capital projects with debt. The debt burden on properties that are simultaneously in both jurisdictions influences the city's capacity to support its debt. If the city's credit rating is thereby lowered, it will incur higher interest costs than it would have if the school district had not made its independent decision. In short, overlapping debt occurs when different political jurisdictions impose a debt burden on the same properties as other political jurisdictions; it occurs because properties are located within multiple jurisdictions (e.g., a city, a county, a school district, special districts, and a state) at the same time.
- A city lures a manufacturing company into an area with financial incentives. The county deems this to be advantageous because it will "create" jobs and generate revenues from property taxes paid by the workers. Meanwhile, a neighboring school district that had no voice in the city's economic development initiative has a surge in its student population as a result of the growth that puts pressure on its budget.
- A county is home to a popular tourist destination. This attraction enables the county to impose higher sales taxes to capture revenues from nonresidents who do not benefit from many of the services the county provides its residents. So, not only is the sales tax less of a benefit tax (a tax on the beneficiaries of particular services), but it also lessens the fiscal burden on the county relative to neighboring jurisdictions that lack the ability to export the tax. In general, tax competition among jurisdictions drives down revenues for local governments.

In other cases, the boundaries between jurisdictions and decisions regarding boundary adjustments can help or harm a given local government's financial situation. For example, before the cities of Branch and North Branch, Minnesota, were consolidated in 1994, the area's independent school district paid much more for its water service because of the location of its school buildings. Branch was a municipality that completely surrounded North Branch (the hole in the doughnut). North Branch had a water distribution system, and its policy was to charge nonresidential water customers double the rate of customers within its city limits. The North Branch Area School District's schools were on property just outside those limits. Thus, it was in the school district's interest to have the two cities merge because they would then be able to purchase water at a reduced rate (Honadle, 1998).

Sometimes state policymakers recognize that one local government's actions may have a negative impact on another jurisdiction's fiscal condition. The state of Ohio changed its annexation law in 2001 to require cities to pay "reparations" to compensate townships for lost tax revenues for a period of time after an annexation. In Minnesota, one of the criteria that must be considered in a municipal consolidation is the effect of the proposed boundary adjustment on neighboring jurisdictions.

It is important to note that the actual impact of interlocal governmental relations on any particular local government's fiscal health is largely situational. For instance, if a school had excess capacity and could accommodate additional students at little to no cost but would receive additional revenues from having new students, then a growth in population resulting from another jurisdiction's development policy could have a positive impact on its fiscal health. But, in other contexts, if a local government must increase its capacity to provide additional services due to population growth or industrial development but does not receive an adequate increase in revenues to cover the cost of this new demand on its services, then the local government's fiscal health would likely be harmed. The key point is that interlocal relations do have impacts on local governments' fiscal health. Unique factors related to local circumstances affect the form and extent of those impacts.

Implications for Fiscal Health of Local Governments

Depending on one's point of view, the intergovernmental perspective presented in this chapter has multiple applications. First, the intergovernmental way of thinking may help explain the fiscal health or condition of local governments; in other words, it may inform objective or so-called positive analysis. Second, this perspective can elucidate observation from a broader view, say of state or federal policy makers concerned with the overall effects of proposed or existing policies on local governments' fiscal health. A third application of the intergovernmental perspective on fiscal health is to help local government managers understand their jurisdiction's situation and suggest some clues to assist them in finding solutions that are more realistic by understanding their particular intergovernmental context. This final section of the chapter focuses on the implications at tree level (remember the forest-and-the-trees metaphor) or from an individual local government's point of vantage.

In an earlier work, the author (Honadle et al., 2004, 219–239) suggested that local officials consider choosing options from a comprehensive set of strategies that, taken together, could help address or avoid problems in a community's fiscal health. That 8-point approach consisted of the following strategies:

1. Be more efficient.
2. Expand the tax base.
3. Reduce the demand for services.
4. Shift costs to nonresidents.
5. Secure new sources of revenue.
6. Increase spending flexibility.
7. Improve management of existing resources.
8. Diversify revenue sources.

Aside from these options being subject to personal preferences, value judgments, political pressure, local strengths and opportunities, and other considerations, it is remarkable how most of them are explicitly intergovernmental in nature. A local government can explore and try to implement ways of being more efficient (#1). But, one way of providing services more efficiently might be to contract with other local governments at a favorable rate. This entails interlocal negotiations and entering into agreements that, as always, can only happen if their state allows them to do this. It is generally not permissible for a local government to contract with another government to provide a service that it is prohibited from providing on its own, for instance.

A local government might also try to figure out ways to reduce the demand for some services, such as through the institution of preventative measures (#3). Or, it could simply stop offering the service and force citizens to find other means for obtaining the service or go without. Alternatively, it could reduce effective demand by instituting a user fee for services that are nonrival in consumption, and it is possible to exclude consumers who do not pay to partake.

It might improve its management of the resources it currently has through maintenance and upkeep, conservation, or other means (#7). However, a local government will be constrained by the state in such areas as how it invests its cash even if local managers think they can manage things better another way.

A local government might want to expand its tax base (#2), but the state establishes the general guidelines to which that local government must conform. A locality cannot make items the state deems exempt from a sales tax part of its tax base nor change the property tax classification system its state might have devised. It could try to attract new business and help existing businesses expand, assuming it does so within state policies.

Shifting costs to nonresidents might be a feasible approach if the locality has something unique to offer so that nonresidents will be willing to pay for it. A "bed tax" (hotel tax), for example, might be one option, assuming the state allows it. In Ohio, some counties discovered that the state allows them to charge a small percentage of transfer tax and dedicate this resource to financing economic development activities. They convinced the public to accept this because most residents rarely sell their homes within the jurisdiction. But, every time a new business comes to town, there are large real estate transactions, so a small percentage tax yielded big returns—and shifted the cost of funding economic development activities pursued by the counties to businesses and outsiders. Therefore, individual governments might consider whether there are untapped opportunities in their state statutes that would allow them to capture revenues that they might be forgoing.

The options pertaining to securing new revenue sources and diversifying existing resources are all subject to what states permit. Moreover, the local government has to consider whether intergovernmental funds from the state or federal government support local purposes without costing too much in terms of compliance costs. They also need to consider the perceived likelihood that the funds will continue and, if not, whether they ought to have a plan for picking up the tab on what could become a popular program if and when intergovernmental aid is withdrawn.

Conclusion

In a handbook (an "instruction" or "operating" manual) about just about anything, there is usually a section that describes the parts of the device and describes how things go together to make it work. This chapter complements other chapters of this handbook of local fiscal health by delineating how a local government is a part of a bigger system. It has shown that the interactions between and among governments always have some potential to affect local fiscal health.

A state official wanting to make policy that avoids undue negative effects on local governments' fiscal health needs to take an intergovernmental perspective. This extends to a consideration of how state policies might create opportunities for some local governments to take advantage of state policies in ways that unintentionally affect the fiscal health of other local governments. Taking an intergovernmental perspective might help identify trade-offs in state policy, such as between mandating local expenditures that are deemed to be in the state' interest and adding to the fiscal burdens of local governments.

States have displayed great variation on their monitoring of the fiscal health of local governments (Hendrick, 2004; Honadle, 2003; Kleine, Kloha, and Weissert, 2003; Kloha, Weissert, and Kleine, 2005). Given the pivotal role of the states in their local governments, this intergovernmental oversight will continue to be an issue. States' fiscal conditions also impact local governments and should be considered in policymaking (Reschovsky, 2004). Likewise, the impact of federal policies is of ongoing importance and is a continuing source of concern for the Washington-based interest groups representing local governments (National League of Cities, 2003a and 2003b).

At the interlocal level, intergovernmental relations are both cause and effect of fiscal conditions of local governments. Local governments may pursue intergovernmental relationships with other local governments—within the confines of state policy—but, even without their doing anything, their fiscal health, to one degree or another, is affected by what other local governments do that is beyond their control.

At the conclusion of this chapter, a couple of points bear mentioning. One is that this chapter has not addressed the basic concept of fiscal health and what that really means. If it is just having a budget that is in balance and meeting financial obligations, there might be normative questions that should be answered. Consider a government with which this author worked as an advisor—in the midst of a process to assess the city's fiscal health and develop strategies for improving it, city officials decided that they no longer had a fiscal crisis when they laid off the entire police department. So, some solutions to problems of fiscal health might be like a person cutting off their arm to maintain a "healthy" weight. Thus, one's definition or concept of fiscal health bears on the assessment about how well off a local government is. The chapter has also not considered issues related to the economy or other factors on local government fiscal health. The focus has intentionally been on the intergovernmental dimensions of local fiscal health.

One thing is certain. If an analyst is studying a particular unit of government's fiscal health, inevitability they will need to examine how other units of government are involved in shaping that entity's financial condition. But, if one is interested in how entire classes of local governments are affected or in how higher levels of government directly or indirectly affect the fiscal health of local governments, then a broader, *intergovernmental*, perspective is in order.

Discussion Questions

1. How is your city's fiscal health affected by decisions made by other local governments in your region? How do your city's policies have fiscal impacts on other units of local government, such as the county, other cities, or school districts?
2. If you were the governor of a state, would you be concerned about how policies you advanced would affect local governments within your state? If so, what would you try to do about it?

Recommended Resources

Goodspeed, T. (1998). Tax competition, benefit taxes, and fiscal federalism. *National Tax Journal*, *51*(3), 579–586.

United States Advisory Commission on Intergovernmental Relations. (1985). *Bankruptcies, defaults, and other local government financial emergencies*. Retrieved from http://www.library.unt.edu/gpo/acir/Reports/policy/a-99.pdf. Accessed October 29, 2011.

United States Government, Accountability office, Report to the Ranking Member, Committee on the Budget, House of Representatives. (2010). *State and local governments: Fiscal pressures could have implications for future delivery of intergovernmental programs.* Washington, DC. GAO-10-899. Retrieved from http://www.gao.gov/new.items/d10899.pdf. Accessed October 29, 2011.

Keywords[2]

Intergovernmental relations, fiscal health, fiscal federalism, home rule, federalism, fiscal emergency, financial emergency

Acknowledgment

The author would like to thank Ramin Ahmadov, a doctoral student in political science at the University of Cincinnati, for research assistance in assembling the Census of Governments data.

Endnotes

1. As of 2006, "27 states ha[d] some form of TEL [tax or governmental expenditure limitation] in place." These could have been voter approved or passed by legislatures (Hill, Sattler, Jacob, O'Brien, and Robey, 2006).
2. This chapter has focused on the intersection of intergovernmental relations and fiscal health of local governments in the United States. A list of keywords for this chapter would be intergovernmental relations, fiscal health, fiscal federalism, home rule, federalism, fiscal emergency, and financial emergency. Readers wanting to know more about these topics will likely find these keywords useful as search terms for additional literature reviews. It is beyond the scope of this chapter to provide authoritative definitions of these terms. Comprehensive, precise definition of these terms would draw on law, politics, finance, public policy, and public administration in which the descriptors and emphasis or focus might vary. For present purposes, suffice it to say that the fiscal health or condition of local governments affects and is affected by intergovernmental relations. Those complex intergovernmental relations are both horizontal (between and among local governments) and vertical (between and among governments of different levels within the federal system of government.

References

Coe, Charles K. (2007). *Governmental and nonprofit financial management.* Vienna, VA: Management Concepts, Inc.

Columbia Township. (2010). General information about the township. Retrieved from http://www.columbiatwp.org/. Accessed October 29, 2011.

Currie, E. M., Honadle, B. W., and DeBoer, L. P. (1999). Exploring the growth of special district governments: Results of a Minnesota survey. *Hamline Journal of Public Law and Policy, 21*(1999), 67–93.

Hendrick, R. (2004). Assessing and measuring the fiscal health of local governments: Focus on Chicago suburban municipalities. *Urban Affairs Review, 40*(1), 78–114.

Hill, E., Sattler, M., Jacob, D., O'Brien, K., and Robey, C. (2006). *A review of tax expenditure limitations and their impact on state and local governments in Ohio.* Cleveland, OH: The Center for Public Management, Maxine Goodman Levin College of Urban Affairs, Cleveland State University. Retrieved from http://urban.csuohio.edu/publicmanagement/publications/tel31806.pdf. Accessed October 29, 2011.

Honadle, B. W. (1998) Projecting the public services and financial implications of municipal consolidation: Evidence from a small-city consolidation study. *The Regionalist, 2* (1/2), 41–53.

Honadle, B. W. (2003) The states' role in U.S. local government fiscal crises: A theoretical model and results of a national survey. *International Journal of Public Administration, 26*, (13), 1431–1472.

Honadle, B. W., Costa, J. M., and Cigler, B. A. (2004). *Fiscal health for local governments: An introduction to concepts, practical analysis, and strategies.* San Diego: Elsevier Academic Press.

Kleine, R., Kloha, P., and Weissert, C. S. (2003). Monitoring local government fiscal health: Michigan's new 10 point scale of fiscal distress. *Government Finance Review, 19*(3), 18–23.

Kloha, P., Weissert, C. S., and Kleine, R. (2005). Someone to watch over me: State monitoring of local fiscal conditions. *American Review of Public Administration, 35*(3), 236–255.

Krane, D., Rigos, P. N., and Hill, M. B., Jr. (2001). *Home rule in America: A fifty-state handbook.* Washington, DC: CQ Press.

Leland, S., and Thurmaier, K. (Eds.). (2004). *Case studies of city-county consolidation: Reshaping the local government landscape.* Armonk NY: M.E. Sharpe.

National League of Cities. (2003a). *The impact of federal fiscal policy on state and local fiscal crises: Roundtable proceedings.* National League of Cities. Washington, DC.

National League of Cities. (2003b). *Is the federal-state-local partnership being dismantled?: Roundtable proceedings.* National League of Cities. Washington, DC.

Reschovsky, A. (2004) The impact of state government fiscal crises on local governments and schools. *State & Local Government Review, 36*,(2), 86–102.

The Village of Indian Hill. (2010). Welcome to the Village of Indian Hill. Retrieved from http://www.ci.indian-hill.oh.us/index.aspx. Accessed October 29, 2011.

Wong, K. K., and Shen, F. X. (2001). Rethinking the Fiscal Role of the States in Public Education. *Government Finance Review, 17*(5), 8–13.

Chapter 15

Monitoring the Fiscal Health of America's Cities

by Lynne A. Weikart

Introduction

Who monitors the fiscal health of cities? What governmental agency alerts authorities that a city is on the edge of bankruptcy? Are there federal and state agencies empowered to deal with a city's fiscal stress? Our form of government does not allow an easy answer to these questions.

The U.S. Constitution does not mention cities; the founding fathers focused on the balance of political and economic power between the states and the federal government. Over the 220 years in the life of our nation, federal and state court decisions citing the Tenth Amendment have placed the municipal concerns squarely within the domain of the 50 states. "The powers not delegated to the United States by the Constitution, nor prohibited by it to the states, are reserved to the States respectively, or to the people."[1]

Court cases, such as *Clinton v. Cedar Rapids and the Missouri River Railroad* decided by Judge Dillon in 1868, let the states control their cities both politically and financially.[2] "Municipal corporations owe their origin to, and derive their powers and rights wholly from, the legislature. It breathes into them the breath of life, without which they cannot exist. As it creates, so may it destroy. If it may destroy, it may abridge and control" (*Clinton v. Cedar Rapids,* 1868). Judge Dillon was responding to the wave of municipal defaults in which municipalities lost their money while financing railroads. "He therefore advocated constitutional limitations and restriction of the franchise to taxpayers whenever any expenditure of money was at stake in order to prevent cities from engaging further in such transactions" (Frug, 1996, p. 1110). There was extensive rebuttal to Dillon. Eugene McQuillin in his multivolume treatise, *The Law of Municipal Corporations*, rose to the defense of cities. In an exhaustive survey, McQuillin traced the historical development of municipal corporations and found the essential theme to be a right to local self-government. He rejected the suggestion that cities were created by the state, arguing that "[s]uch [a] position ignores well-established, historical facts easily ascertainable. McQuillin strongly criticized courts that failed to uphold the right of local self-government" (Frug, 1996, p. 1110). However in most states, *Dillon's rule* prevailed, and now many states are Dillon states, and they tightly control city revenues. That control includes monitoring cities' fiscal health.

Fifty states created at least 50 different answers to the question of who monitors our cities' fiscal health and how. Some states responded to a municipal's fiscal crisis by creating a state financial board that takes over a city's finances for a limited period of time. A few states created ongoing state government agencies to monitor their cities' fiscal health; some of those states passed state laws to take over a city's finances. Cities also took action. Most medium or large size cities established a controller's office that at the least had the power to audit the finances of city agencies. City legislatures have created legislative fiscal offices with the mandate to examine a city's fiscal condition. The Office of the Independent Budget Analyst in San Diego is an example of that kind of legislative office. The only alternative institution independent of the executive and legislative branches that has a mandate to examine a city's fiscal condition is the Independent Budget Office in New York City. The federal government plays a very limited role. One of the few roles of the federal government in overseeing a city's fiscal health is found in the federal bankruptcy law.

Players other than government oversee some portion of the fiscal health of cities. *Bond rating agencies* play a role in monitoring cities' fiscal health. Bond rating agencies wield a great deal of power because these agencies rate municipal bonds. A less than stellar rating causes a city to pay greater interest rates, which can be quite costly over time. In some cities, interested citizens create nonprofits to analyze their cities' fiscal policies. There are also organizations that have helped create government capacity to monitor the fiscal health of cities including the Government Finance Officers Association and the International City/County Management Association (ICMA).

This chapter examines the structure and processes of these monitoring agencies and seeks to understand their strengths and weaknesses. Monitoring in this chapter is on a continuum that on one end can mean an institution has the power to examine a city's finances and let city officials know its conclusions and on the other end to a far greater power to take over a city's finances. The variety of monitoring agencies also has a variety of monitoring powers.

The Federal Role

Because of the Tenth Amendment, the federal government, whether executive, legislative, or judiciary, plays a small role in monitoring the fiscal health of cities. In 1884, the United States Supreme Court in *East St. Louis v. ex Rel. Zebley* held that "what expenditures are proper and necessary for the municipal administration, is not judicial; it is confided by law to the discretion of the municipal authorities. No court has the right to control that discretion much less to usurp and supersede it" (U.S. Supreme Court, 1884). It violated principles of federalism for federal courts to interfere with local democratic decision making about levels of spending. In *East St. Louis v. ex Rel. Zebley*, the Supreme Court gave current city expenditures absolute priority over payment of past obligations. In 1934, during the depths of the Great Depression, Congress passed a municipal bankruptcy law because municipalities across the country struggled to provide necessary services while facing a dramatic drop in tax revenues. This law permitted municipalities to restructure their debt and was an important tool given the inadequacy of traditional state remedies. However, the Municipal Bankruptcy Act was short lived. The Supreme Court in *Ashton v. Cameron Co. Water Improvement District* struck down the act as unconstitutional (by a 5 to 4 decision in 1935), finding the law violated state sovereignty under the Tenth Amendment. Michael McConnell (1993), Director of the Stanford Constitutional Law Center at Stanford University, explains the federal role when a city's fiscal condition turns decidedly red.

> Prior to 1933, there was neither state nor federal municipal bankruptcy legislation. Indeed, it appeared, for a time, that the Constitution prevented either level of government from touching the subject. For the federal government to do so would intrude into the internal governance of states and their political subdivisions and thus violate state sovereignty; for the state government to do so would impair the obligation of contracts [something the federal government may do but states may not]. Congress did not venture to pass a municipal bankruptcy law until the Great Depression, and the Supreme Court's first reaction was to strike it down. (McConnell 1993, p. 425).

Congress passed a second bankruptcy act requiring cities to get permission from their states if they sought federal bankruptcy. In 1938, in *United States v. Bekins*, the Supreme Court upheld Congress's second attempt to pass a municipal bankruptcy statute; and in 1942, in *Faitoute Iron and Steel Co. v. Asbury Park*, the Supreme Court upheld the states' authority to compel unwilling creditors to join in a plan of adjustment of municipal debts. Hence, because of the nature of our federal system, the federal law covers municipal bankruptcy with this caveat—state autonomy results in a narrow federal scope of municipal bankruptcy law as compared to private bankruptcy.

The federal government also played another role helping cities in fiscal stress—providing financial relief. In 1932, during the Great Depression, President Herbert Hoover signed the Federal Reconstruction Finance Act, which created a lending corporation to provide loans to small banks and private corporations. Later, President Harry Truman broadened the powers of the Federal Reconstruction Finance Corporation to provide loans to municipalities to avoid bankruptcy through guarantees (U.S. Secretary of the Treasury, 1959, p. 8).[3] It financed itself through the sale of capital stock and by borrowing from the Treasury. Certainly during President Lyndon Johnson's War on Poverty, the federal government provided many grants-in-aid to American cities. Federal help to support cities in fiscal crisis did not occur again until the 1970s.

During the 1970s recession, Congress sought to help one city in fiscal distress. "The 1975 New York City fiscal crisis occurred during the larger economic instability of the 1970s that was characterized by the globalization of American banking, the oil crisis, major inflation, and the collapse of real estate prices" (Weikart, 2009, p. 49). After much anxiety, Congress passed the New York City Seasonal Financing Act of 1975, permitting the City to borrow up to $2.3 billion a year for 3 years for short-term borrowing. Funds were repaid within the year, but the federal loan gave Congress carte blanche to hold hearings into the City's crisis and to closely study its cash flow problem. The federal government also demanded increased taxes of $200 million on personal income; increases in bank, estate, and cigarette taxes; an increase in the minimum corporate income tax; and an extension of the sales taxes to which the New York State Legislature agreed (Arthur Anderson Co., 1976). This marked the first time that the federal government sought such a direct role in the fiscal life of an American city. However, the role of the federal government in fiscally stabilizing the New York City fiscal crisis was small compared to the role New York State played.

The State Role in Monitoring the Cities' Fiscal Health

It was New York State that bailed out New York City. "Out of the total $14.4 billion of long-term financing for the city, the state, through *MAC* and the city, bore almost 89 percent, as compared to 10 percent contributed by the federal government" (Weikart, 2009, p. 47). Governor Hugh Carey sought and oversaw the creation and implementation of the Emergency Financial Control Board (EFCB) that took control of the city's spending. Thus, the state became responsible for the city's fiscal health.

American cities experienced their first fiscal crises in the 1880s. ACIR reported that 25% of local governments defaulted on their bonds in the 1880s fiscal crisis (U.S. ACIR, 1985). This was a wake-up call to many states, which then began asking about the fiscal health of their cities. In 1921, the basic form and structure of *financial control boards* (FCB) was established when the New Hampshire Legislature set up an FCB for Manchester (Missed Opportunity, 1997, p. 1).

The Great Depression saw another wave of massive bond defaults by cities. "At the outset of the Depression, municipal credit was again overextended and defaults began to occur. Nevertheless, a number of deficient units continued to borrow, prompting a number of states not only to tighten constitutional and statutory debt restrictions, but also to institute centralized supervision of certain aspects of municipal debt incurrence" (State Administrative, 1972, p. 488). Currently, 48 states impose debt ceilings on cities, including 41 states that place limits on the maximum duration of municipal bonds and 24 states that set interest ceilings for municipal debt (U.S. ACIR, 1993, p. 15). Additionally, 40 states have referendum requirements for municipal bond offerings. When municipalities face fiscal crisis or stress, state governments are faced with major decisions. The toughest response is to take over a city in the form of a receivership.

State Receiverships

During the late 1800s, a few states sought to take over revenue collection and then went a step further and created receiverships for cities in default, starting with Missouri in the mid-1870s. In Missouri, the State Legislature allowed bond owners, if municipalities defaulted, to collect payment through the collection of taxes (Hillhouse, 1935, p. 320).

In Texas, the State Legislature passed legislation that forced the Governor to hire a tax collector to collect taxes needed for repayment of bonds (Hillhouse, 1935, p. 324). During the Depression, some states required receiverships in municipal defaults. New Jersey passed a statute in 1933 that authorized a created agency, the Municipal Finance Commission, to impound taxes in excess of reasonable expenses, approve capital expenditures, and authorize the funding of indebtedness (Yale Law Journal, 1936, p. 703). It was not a total receivership since the Commission could not control expenditures or personnel.

The first formal municipal receivership was Memphis in the case of *Meriwether v. Garrett* in 1979. "The State Legislature literally dis-incorporated Memphis in 1879, transferring its territory and municipal functions to an entity called the "Taxing District of Shelby County," and the Governor appointed commissioners to put the financial affairs of the city into order" (McConnell, 1993, p. 460). The most famous *state receivership* was the Massachusetts takeover of the town of Chelsea. In 1991, the state refused to accept the city's budget, leaving the mayor unable to pay the city's bills. "Mayor John Brennan reacted by announcing that he would immediately ask the state to put Chelsea in receivership, a position he had publicly taken earlier in the year after citizens had turned down a tax increase. The state agreed to the receivership to save Chelsea from financial collapse and, it was hoped, to enable it to survive on its own" (Berman, 1995, p. 63). The Governor, William Weld, appointed a receiver to run the city, eliminated the mayor's position, and made advisors of Chelsea's elected officials. The receiver was empowered to cut spending and services, alter union contracts, and restructure government (Berman, 1995, p. 63). After three years of tough management decisions, Chelsea regained solvency. The State stripped Chelsea of democracy for those years, and in return, by 1995, Chelsea had a strong city council/city manager form of government and two years of budget surpluses. Today, a similar strategy has been adopted by the Michigan Governor who has suspended the powers of local officials in several cities.

State Financial Control Boards (FCBs)

The basic form and structure of State FCBs has not changed since the first full-fledged state *financial control board* was established for Manchester, New Hampshire, in 1921 (Missed Opportunity, 1997, p. 784). States have imposed FCBs several times since then. In the past 40 years, states have created FCBs to address fiscal crises in Chicago; Cleveland; Philadelphia; New York City; Yonkers; Washington, DC; and Bridgeport, Connecticut. These FCBs shared the common characteristic of being a state-created agency usually established by legislative statute to oversee the financial situation of a city because of a city's desperate fiscal condition. Board members were usually a mix of public managers and private citizens with expertise in finance and accounting.

The emphasis was upon debt restructuring to restore a city's creditworthiness and financial reform to reduce the risk of a reoccurrence of fiscal insolvency. FCBs often required cuts in services to balance the budget. Financial control boards have become an established tool to deal with cities in deep financial distress though most FCBs are time bound and not ongoing entities.

Table 15.1 The Composition of FCBs Was Similar Across the States

State*	# of Members	Appointment Characteristics
New York EFCB	7	Varied depending upon the city involved. Served at the pleasure of the governor.
MAC	9	Five appointed by governor; four by mayor. Served for four years.
Pennsylvania	5	Governor appointed executive & legislative officials.
Ohio	7	Not permitted to be an elected official within last five years. Served for life of Commission.

*New York State Governor Carey, in cooperation with banking officials, created two state entities: the Municipal Assistance Corporation (MAC) to sell bonds for NYC and the Emergency Financial Control Board (EFCB) to oversee NYC's finances. Pennsylvania and Ohio created FCBs for cities in general.

Cahill and James (1992) identify three levels of state power over their cities' finances. "The most extensive form of power would be control or oversight by the agency to supplant local decision making authority. . . . The [second and] most common form of authority and power gives a broad range of concerned parties important roles. . . . A third possible area of activity for oversight agencies is advisory in nature" (p. 91). There are 15 states with legislation that established ongoing entities to monitor in some degree their cities' fiscal health: Colorado, Florida, Illinois, Kentucky, Maine, Michigan, New Mexico, Nevada, New Jersey, Pennsylvania, North Carolina, Rhode Island, Ohio, Tennessee, and Wisconsin (Cahill et. al., 1994, p. 255). A few of these states with the strongest legislation are North Carolina, Ohio, Michigan, New Jersey, New Mexico, and Pennsylvania.

Individual States with Ongoing Legislation Monitoring Cities

North Carolina.

North Carolina has an extensive set of powers in a state monitoring system. At the height of the Great Depression in 1931, North Carolina established the Local Government Commission (LGC) to address the fiscal crises facing their cities. The LGC lives on today with a large staff to provide both technical expertise and regulatory oversight for cities in North Carolina that are in financial trouble. The LGC consists of a nine-member board: the State Treasurer, The State Auditor, Secretary of State, Secretary of Revenue (ex officio), three appointees by the Governor, one appointee by the President of the Senate, and one appointee by the Speaker of the House.

The LGC has enormous power because it controls the issuing of debt for all local governments in the state. "North Carolina is the only state legally responsible for the issuance of all local government debt" (Coe, 2007, p. 41) This includes GO bonds and notes, enterprise and utility bonds, public hospital bonds, and swap agreements. In addition, the LGC requires each local government to provide an independent financial audit in accordance with generally accepted auditing standards, to use of the state's standard audit contract, to seek approval of the chosen auditor, and permits payment to the auditor only after LGC has approved the audit report (42). The Commission has the statutory authority to impound the books and records of any unit of local government and to assume full control of all its financial affairs.

Ohio.

Ohio also has established an extensive level of financial authority over its cities. Ohio established the Ohio Fiscal Emergency Law in 1979 in response to Cleveland's financial crisis to help cities regain their fiscal health. In 1996, this "fiscal emergency protection" was enlarged to include counties and townships. In addition, a provision was added permitting the establishment of a "Fiscal Watch" status. The law allowed for the establishment of an Ohio Fiscal Watch Program overseen by the Ohio's Office of Auditor. The Fiscal Watch Program conducts reviews of city finances to determine whether a local government is nearing a fiscal emergency. This status provides early warnings to local governments that they are approaching emergency status. Depending on the severity of the problem, the Auditor of State may declare the government to be in "Fiscal Watch" or "Fiscal Emergency." If a government is placed in Fiscal Watch, the Auditor of State's Office provides free assistance to help the government regain its financial footing. If a Fiscal Emergency is declared, the State Auditor appoints a commission to oversee financial activity until the emergency is over and to develop long range plans to improve the financial outlook of the local government. At the current time, five local governments are under a state of "Fiscal Watch," ranging in time from 0.3 years to 7.5 years. In addition, 21 local governments are in a state of "Fiscal Emergency." A "Fiscal Emergency" can last for years; currently the time ranges from 0 to 12.6 years.

New Jersey.

New Jersey takes a very proactive approach in that it approves all local government budgets to make sure they are solvent and checks that revenues are not overestimated and that budgets meet statutory criteria. This state certifies local fiscal managers and stays involved in all aspects of the fiscal management of local governments. When a local government has a crisis, New Jersey can assume fiscal responsibility through intervention by the Local Finance Board. The Local Finance Board is the modern version of the Municipal Finance Commission of the 1930s.

If a locality is having problems, it is placed in the Distressed Cities Program, which provides discretionary state aid and technical assistance such as management, tax collection processes, and efficiencies. After a state takeover, New Jersey continues to monitor and provide unusual oversight under the Distressed Cities Program. When Camden became distressed, New Jersey passed special legislation providing for a state-appointed Chief Operating Officer with broad authority. In addition to providing economic development funds, the legislation also required a formal management study, the appointment of new directors, and the provision of economic development funds (Honadle, 2005, p. 10).

The Local Finance Board releases a municipality from control only after spending and personnel is under control. A typical example is East Orange, which had suffered from budget deficits for years. The Local Finance Board took over and made personnel cuts and improved the tax collection rate dramatically. By 2001, East Orange had a budget surplus and was released from control.

New Mexico.

Professor Beth Honadle, Director of the Institute for Policy Research and Professor of Political Science at the University of New Mexico, conducted a telephone survey consisting of 10 questions, which were administered to members of the National Association of State Auditors, Comptrollers and Treasurers in each of the 50 states between April and August, 2002 (Honadle, 2005, p. 3). The State of New Mexico's survey respondents identified two counties with fiscal problems that required state intervention. In both cases, the state had warned the counties from nine months to two years in advance of the crisis and repeatedly thereafter that there were problems. State officials appeared before the county commissioners when the counties did not take corrective action (as they normally do in this type of situation). Often, the media attention from these visits was reported to be enough to stimulate local action. The state also provided technical assistance to counties in crisis. In addition, the Board of Finance has an emergency fund to occasionally make loans (e.g., Grant County, so it could meet payroll). After a crisis is over, the state continues to monitor the county (Honadle, 2005, p. 3).

Pennsylvania.

Pennsylvania passed the Municipalities Financial Recovery Act of 1987 (47) applicable to all local governments. Under Act 47, municipalities annually report on 27 indicators related to their fiscal condition. The State Department of Community Affairs (DCA) "may declare a municipality officially distressed and appoint a state coordinator to develop and implement a plan to correct the problems" (Berman, 1995, p. 61). A municipality may reject this plan and develop its own, but the DCA has to approve the municipality's plan. Until it approves a plan, the DCA can withhold assistance provided by Act 47 and also withhold other revenues normally provided to the locality as regular state funding (Gannon, 1994, p. 283). Local governments classified as fiscally stressed qualify for state assistance in the form of technical assistance (up to $100,000) and qualify for grants and loans aimed at returning the community to a sound fiscal footing. Twenty-two boroughs and cities, including Pittsburgh, have been designated as fiscally stressed since 1987 (Washington State Office of Financial Management, 2006, p. 5).

Pittsburgh has had increasing fiscal troubles. The state crafted a five-year recovery plan in 2004 when it declared Pittsburgh a distressed municipality under Act 47. After five years, Pittsburgh was in the black, but the pension plan was in trouble. In 2009, the city council and mayor agreed to another five-year plan to address the pension fund and the continuing struggle to obtain sufficient revenues to pay for city services. The eroding tax base caused by residents moving to the suburbs and the growing expenditures because of an increased need for social services given the increasingly poor residential population in Pittsburgh as is common among older cities. In the West and South, there were thousands of annexations so that cities such as Houston, Phoenix, Charlotte, and Roanoke annexed their suburbs and consequently retained stronger tax bases.

Michigan.

Michigan established two laws, Public Act 70 of 1990 and Public Act 34 of 2001, intended to provide early warnings of a local government's fiscal distress by using 30 indicators. But state officials found the methodology cumbersome and ineffective. Then, state officials contracted with Michigan State University to identify new indicators. The Institute of Public Policy and Social Research created a 10-point scale to classify local governments into one of 4 categories: "fiscally healthy (0–4 points), fiscal watch (5 points), fiscal warning (6–7 points), and fiscal emergency (8–10 points)" (Kloha, 2003, p. 45). These indicators identified fiscal concerns such as long-term debt divided by population and total revenue divided by total expenditures. In addition, points were taken away if a local government's population declined or real taxable value growth was negative. The laws have real teeth.

Michigan has one of the most onerous state laws governing financial control of cities. In 2011 Governor Rich Snyder persuaded the state legislature to pass a new emergency financial control law building on the previous ones that allowed the emergency financial managers to cancel or amend union contracts and gave them full power over city operations. Local elected officials were no longer in charge. It was no longer a case of local officials negotiating with the state's representative; the state representative became the czar. Only four entities in Michigan, including Detroit's public school system, as of November 2011 are deemed distressed enough to require oversight by emergency managers but the number could rise.

Municipal Level

City Comptrollers

At the municipal level, a great deal of monitoring takes place through the offices of a city controller. Some municipalities require controllers to track expenditures and audit government agencies. Other municipalities give a great deal of power to the controller to take action if the municipality is in fiscal crisis. A good example is San Francisco where the Controller, in addition to being the chief accounting officer, is authorized to take the extraordinary step of rebalancing the budget if the city's budget is unbalanced and the mayor and city council do not act. Although the Controller has never implemented these steps, the fact remains that the Controller is in a position of great authority. Another example is the Comptroller of Milwaukee, Wisconsin, who in addition to auditing City agencies, also forecasts the revenue for the city budget.[4]

Alternative Institutions Building Capacity

Legislative Monitoring Offices

San Diego voters approved the Office of the Independent Budget Analyst (OIBA) in San Diego under Article XV of the City Charter. It established the Office of Independent Budget Analyst and gave the city council authority to determine its powers. Under the rules, the director serves at the pleasure of the city council. OIBA's duties are extensive providing that budget reports, forecasting, and special reports are all part of the office's mandate. The greatest responsibility of the IBA is to review the mayor's proposed budget and to publish their analysis of it within two weeks. Murtaza Baxamusa, Director of Research and Policy, Center on Policy Initiatives pointed out: "For a staff of 10, the sheer volume of output at the IBA is astounding: 700 docket items reviewed, 125 reports written, and 290 meetings staffed. This does not include the innumerable questions on services and budgets that the IBA staff has answered from the council and the public. In the transition to Strong Mayor-Strong Council, this office has emerged as one of the few winners for the public interest" (Baxamusa, 2009).

Independent Budget Offices

New York City's Independent Budget Office (IBO) is modeled after the Congressional Budget Office (CBO), which is modeled after California's Legislative Analyst's Office (LAO) that has been providing fiscal and policy advice to the State Legislature for more than 65 years. The Joint Legislative Budget Committee, a 16-member bipartisan committee, oversees the LAO. The office currently has a staff of 43 analysts and approximately 13 support staff.

But unlike the CBO or the LAO, New York's IBO serves more than the legislature. It is a publicly funded independent agency that provides nonpartisan information about the city's budget and financial condition to public officials, organizations, and private citizens. It was created in 1989 by a coalition of good government groups, such as the New York Public Interest Research Group and City Project, which lobbied to amend the City Charter to include an independent budget office, independent from the mayor and the city council. The New York City Charter Revision Commission, led by Frederick Schwarz, said that "There is a felt need that OMB [the Mayor's Office of Management and Budget] is overly dominant in the fiscal dialogue. There is a felt need for a balance to that" (Finder, 1989, p. 15).

IBO has been extraordinarily successful in providing objective reporting about the city's finances. Its independence is directly related to its funding. Under the City's Charter, the IBO must receive 10% of the budget of New York City's Office of Management and Budget for its own budget. Unlike the Office of the Independent Budget Analyst in San Diego, IBO is not dependent upon the city council or any politician for its funding or appointments.

New York City's mayors resisted the idea of an independent IBO. Mayor David Dinkins in 1992 refused to fund the office, as did Mayor Rudolph Giuliani, until forced to do so under court order in 1996. Once established, IBO had to sue Mayor Giuliani to get the data it requested even though the Charter explicitly provided that IBO was empowered to obtain data directly from government agencies. IBO has no oversight authority but has plenty of reporting authority. "The director shall be authorized to secure such information, data, estimates and statistics from the agencies of the city as the director determines to be necessary for the performance of the functions and duties of the office, and such agencies shall provide such information, to the extent that it is available, in a timely fashion" (NYC Charter, Chapter 11). It took two years of court battles for IBO to win that fight.

The City's Charter requires IBO to publish several reports. This has evolved into three reports: the Fiscal Outlook (a report about the future year's revenues and expenditures), Analysis of the Preliminary Budget, and an Analysis of the Executive Budget. IBO regularly produces many reports and news briefs about the city's revenues and expenditures for the city council and interested citizens, and its staff members testify before government agencies about the city's fiscal condition. IBO is governed by a four-member advisory board–the comptroller, the public advocate, one rotating member of the five borough presidents, and a council member the city council chooses. The board hires an executive director for a four-year term, and the executive director hires the staff. Doug Turetsky observed: "The trick is to create an organizational and funding structure that protects any IBO from political pressure, or even the appearance of pressure, to slant its findings. It means developing a 'good government' approach to picking a director and a means of funding the agency that doesn't force it to appeal to the executive or legislative branches for annual appropriations. That way public officials and the public at large can know that an independent budget office is giving them the best, unvarnished information it can" (2008). In addition, the comptroller and the public advocate appoint a 10-member advisory committee, that meets regularly with the executive director to discuss policy issues. Those 10 members have staggered five-year terms and must have extensive experience in the fields of finance, economics, accounting, public administration, and public policy analysis.

Bond Rating Agencies

Municipal bonds are loans to a city, state, or other state or local public institution that are repaid to investors. The issuer (government) borrows money from the buyers (investors) for a fixed number of years at a fixed interest rate. Bonds are used to raise money to help a city's cash flow and to raise capital for the city's infrastructure projects. In the early 1970s, the municipal bond market was small ($49 billion in 1975); now it is a $2.8 trillion market (Walter, 2009, p. 3). It is a significant part of the U.S. capital market and is exempted from the registration requirements of the Securities Act of 1933 and the system of periodic reporting under the Exchange Act of 1934 (Walter, 2009, p. 3). Congress established limited regulations for parts of municipal bond market, the brokers and dealers. Although Congress created the Municipal Securities Rulemaking Board (MSRB), the Board is prohibited from requiring any filings from the issuer (Walter, 2009, p. 4).

Eight private bond rating agencies in the United States have official designation to rate bonds. Three of the agencies dominate 90% of the municipal market: Moody's Investor Services, Fitch Ratings, and Standard & Poor's. The local government that wishes to receive a rating for a bond sale pays the rating agency. Often the municipality will go shopping to see which rating agency will give the best rating. The ratings range from AAA to BBB-. Ratings of municipal bonds that state and local governments issue are based upon the analysis of the primary factors relating to municipal finance: the economy, the issuer's finances, debt, governance/management strategies, and the bonds' structural features (Levenstein, 2009, p. 4). Because the cities are borrowing money, the cities must pay interest on that money. The ratings the bond rating agencies give will determine the amount of interest the cities pay based upon market forces. A high bond rating will come with a lower interest rate and still be marketable and a bond with a lower rating will require a higher interest rate to be attractive to investors.

Both the issuers (state and local governments) and the buyers (investors) are quite dissatisfied with bond rating agencies. Government officials complain that bond rating agencies charge too much, give too low a ratings to their bonds, and treat municipal bonds unfairly as compared to corporate bonds even though cities default far less than corporate entities (Fehr, 2009). Moody's senior bond manager commented that between 1970 and 2006, only 41 out of approximately 29,000 Moody's-rated municipal issuers defaulted. Twenty-two of these defaults occurred between 2001 and 2006. Tensions have risen since the 2009 fiscal crisis. U.S. Representative Barney Frank, chair of the House Financial Services Committee, sought to pass the Municipal Bond Fairness Act that will require credit rating agencies to provide the same credit rating standards for both municipal and corporate bonds. The three bond rating agencies are also moving in that direction. However, this bill has yet to pass.

However, the investors have a different concern; that is, that bond ratings agencies are not doing their job. The press has written about a wide range of disclosure violations by the municipalities, and the bond rating agencies have not challenged the silence of the municipalities (Walter, 2009, p. 4). The most significant violation was when the city of San Diego failed to inform investors of its unfunded pension requirements (United States of America before the Securities and Exchange Commission, 2006). Commissioner Elisse B. Walter of the U.S. Securities and Exchange Commission noted that "there have been numerous bid rigging, price fixing pay to play, and other scandals in this market." She concluded that "the credit rating agencies in particular . . . did not provide the necessary backstops for investors" (Walter, 2009, p. 5). In effect, the bond rating agencies that monitor the fiscal health of municipalities are limited in their effectiveness.

Nonprofits

A few cities have nonprofit organizations that were established during the Progressive Era of the early 20th century in large cities.

New York Citizens Budget Commission

There is another organization in New York City that has a mission to work for changes in the financial structure and processes of New York City and New York State governments and that is the NYC Citizens Budget Commission (CBC) formed during the Great Depression in 1932. CBC is an excellent example of the work of urban progressive reformers in the first part of the 20th century. CBC is funded primarily by contributions of investment bankers and major real estate developers. It does publish extensive critiques of the way the City finances and allocates its services; it does not have the objectivity of the IBO.

Chicago's Civic Federation

The Civic Federation is a nonpartisan research organization that examines Chicago's finances and suggests changes in both the revenue and expenditure side of the budget. Again it was established in 1894, at the beginning of the Progressive era. It has a more diverse contributors' list than the CBC. Recently, the Civic Federation has branched out and established the Institute for Illinois's Financial Sustainability with a similar mission to produce timely fiscal policy analyses about the state's budget.

These two organizations, CBC and Civic Federation, are examples of what a group of concerned citizens can do. It is often the case that business interests dominate such organizations; however, such organizations often present different points of view than the current elected officials and can have an effect upon public policymaking.

There are also organizations that have helped create governmental capacity to monitor the fiscal health of cities.

ICMA and GFOA

Two organizations have made an enormous difference in enlarging local governments' capacity to measure their fiscal health, although they do not have a monitoring role. One is the International City/County Management Association (ICMA) and the other is the Government Finance Officers Association (GFOA). Both have assisted local governments in creating financial performance measures (Mullins and Pagano, 2005). ICMA created a method of monitoring a local government's financial condition. GFOA also created financial management indicators for local governments. In the 1980s, GFOA recommend indicators to measure local financial conditions (Hughes and Lavediere, 1986, p 23).

The Center on Budget and Policy Priorities

The Center on Budget and Policy Priorities (CBPP), a Washington-based research organization and strategic policy institute, works on a range of federal and state issues. One of the most exciting initiatives in public finance is the State Fiscal Analysis Initiative by CBPP in which CBPP brings together nonpartisan, independent, nonprofit organizations in each of 31 states and the District of Columbia to conduct rigorous policy analysis and responsible budget and tax policies with a particular focus on the needs of low- and moderate-income families in each of their states. "The Council on Foundations presented its 2009 *Award for Distinguished Grantmaking through Collaboration* to the funders of the State Fiscal Analysis Initiative in recognition of what the network has accomplished–'to help broaden the debate around budget and tax policy through public education and the encouragement of civic engagement'" (SFAI). Funded principally by foundation money, these 31 nonprofits focus on financial issues and social welfare policy. A few of these nonprofits have extended their financial examination to their largest cities.

There are two nonprofits that have a focus on cities. New York's Fiscal Policy Institute (FPI), an independent, nonpartisan, nonprofit research and education organization, is committed to improving public policies and private practices to better the economic and social conditions of all New Yorkers. It created a New York City branch to study the effects of the recession on the City. The second city, Washington, DC, has the DC Fiscal Policy Institute that conducts research and public education on budget and tax issues in the District of Columbia, with a particular emphasis on issues that affect low- and moderate-income residents.

University Policy Centers

In recent years, several universities have helped create capacity by working closely with their state officials to design monitoring tools. Academics at the Institute of Public Policy and Social Research at Michigan State University created indicators of fiscal stress used to measure local governments' fiscal health. Professors in the School of Public and International Affairs at North Carolina University conducted similar work with North Carolina state officials. Universities can play a unique role in bringing their expertise to bear on creating financial performance measures that will enhance state efforts to install financial monitoring tools.

Conclusion

On the state level, Michigan, North Carolina, Ohio, and New Jersey have demonstrated methods to retain financial control of their cities. All have highly experienced staff empowered to take over a city's finances. North Carolina has the power to approve all local debt initiatives, and New Jersey approves all local budgets. These are powerful institutions that have demonstrated success.

There are two local initiatives in San Diego and New York City, which are models of what a city can do to control its finances. Both of these cities had citizens who took the initiative to change the city's charter or to encourage local legislation that permitted the establishment of these offices. Perhaps the IBO and the OIBA are the models for American cities. They are local; they understand local dynamics. They are not imposing solutions; rather, they point out the financial problems, and IBO does this without being influenced by politicians. City officials remain responsible to take action but city officials cannot claim ignorance to any fiscal problems when these independent budget offices are operating. The New York City model is especially robust because, unlike the San Diego model, the IBO is protected from council interference.

Clearly there are a variety of institutions monitoring our cities' fiscal health. These institutions sometimes offer one-time help through a financial control board and sometimes offer ongoing monitoring and support such as the states of Michigan, North Carolina, Ohio, or New Jersey. Cities are dependent upon the states except two cities, San Diego and New York City, which have taken the initiative to create independent monitoring institutions. And the Center for Budget and Policy Priorities can have an enormous influence upon municipalities' fiscal health if it were to extend the State Fiscal Analysis Initiative in its financial examination to cities other than New York City and Washington, DC. CBPP has become the leader in developing nongovernmental institutions that monitor the states' fiscal condition. It is a very impressive undertaking. Although most of the 31 nonprofits involved limit their attention to state issues, at least 2 of the nonprofits focus part of their attention on their cities. It will be interesting to see how the SFAI develops in the future. One possible path is for the 31 nonprofits to focus more analysis on the larger cities. If CBPP were to take this step, the effect would be significant because citizens and policymakers would be assured that independent watchdogs are tracking the fiscal health of America's largest cities.

Endnotes

1. Tenth Amendment to the U.S. Constitution.
2. Judge John Forrest Dillon, Chief Justice of the Iowa Supreme Court, authored the majority opinion that cities are creatures of the state and must be limited to those powers specifically granted to them by state laws or constitutions. Forty states have adopted some form of Dillon's Rule.
3. "Amendments to the RFC Act approved June 30, 1947, and May 25, 1948. . . . RFC was authorized, under section 4 (a) (8) of the amended Act, to purchase the securities of, or make loans to, municipalities, public agencies, and public corporations for the purpose of financing projects approved by law."
4. Controller and comptroller are similar positions.

Glossary

Bond rating agencies: Bond rating agencies are corporations registered with the Securities and Exchange Commission that assign credit ratings to issuers of debt, in this case, states and municipalities.

Dillon's Rule: This court decision, decided by Judge John Forest Dillon, has become the cornerstone of municipal law. Under Dillon's Rule, a municipality only has the power granted in the express words of the state statute, the power implied in the powers expressly granted, or the power otherwise implied as essential to the municipality.

Financial Control Board (FCB): As fiscal crises plagued American cities over the years, states established boards of prominent citizens who have control over the budget decision making of their cities.

Municipal Assistance Corporation (MAC): The state authorized MAC, a corporation New York State created during the 1975 fiscal crisis, to sell bonds for New York City to alleviate cash flow problems.

State receiverships: A state receivership occurs when a state takes over the finances of a local governmental unit, which can be a school district, municipality, etc. The degree to which the state controls the finances depends upon the laws of the individual states.

Discussion Questions

1. Why does the Tenth Amendment to the Constitution affect the governance of cities?
2. Who was Judge John Forrest Dillon and what effect did he have on the city governance?
3. What is the role of the federal government in monitoring the fiscal health of cities?
4. What did states impose on cities to limit their borrowing capacity?
5. What does a state receivership do to a city?
6. What is a state financial control board?
7. Describe North Carolina's state powers to monitor the fiscal health of cities.
8. Describe the role of the Independent Budget Office in New York City.
9. What is the role of bond rating agencies in monitoring the fiscal health of cities?
10. If you were a governor, what kind of monitoring capacity would you like your state to have to monitor the fiscal health of cities?

Recommended Resources

McConnell, M. W. (1993). When cities go broke: A conceptual introduction to municipal bankruptcy. *University of Chicago Law Review, 60*, 425.

Missed opportunity: Urban fiscal crises and financial control boards. (1997). *Harvard Law Review*, *110*, 733.

Mullins, D. R. and Pagano, M. A. (2005). Local budgeting and finance: 25 years of developments. *Public Budgeting and Finance* (Special Issue), 3–45.

O'Cleireacain, C. (1997). *Orphaned capital: Adopting the right revenues for the District of Columbia.* Washington, DC: Brookings Institute Press.

State administrative supervision of local government debt: The North Carolina model. (1972). *Duke Law Journal, 2*, 487–510.

U. S. Advisory Commission on Intergovernmental Relations (ACIR). (1985). Bankruptcies, defaults, and other local financial emergencies. Washington DC: Government Printing Office.

References

Arthur Anderson & Co. (1976). Report for the Secretary of Treasury regarding New York City financial planning & reporting under the New York City Seasonal Financing Act of 1975. Retrieved on February 5, 2011 from http://newman.baruch.cuny.edu/digital/2003/amfl/mac/pdf_files/Economic_Reports/ 06-23-76.pdf

Baxamusa, M. (2009, April 27). Quoted in "Pocket change: Analyzing San Diego's budget analyst" by Steven Bartholow. San Diego News Network. Retrieved on January 28, 2011 from http://www.sdnn.com/sandiego/2009-04-27/politics-city-county-government/pocket-change-lyzing-san-diegos-budget-analyst#ixzz0sXvwK7S5

Berman, D. R. (1995). Takeovers of local governments: An overview and evaluation of state policies. *Publius, 25*(3), 55–70.

Cahill, A. G., and James, J. A. (1992). Review: Responding to municipal fiscal distress: An emerging issue for state governments in the 1990s. *Public Administrative Review, 52*(1), 88–94.

Cahill, A. G., James, J. A., Lavigne, J. E., and Stacey, A. (1994). State government responses to municipal fiscal distress: A brave new world for state-local intergovernmental relations. *Public Productivity & Management Review, 17*(3), 253–264.

Clinton v Cedar Rapids and the Missouri River Railroad. 1868. 24 Iowa 455.

Coe, C. K. (2007). Preventing local government fiscal crises: The North Carolina approach. *Public Budgeting & Finance, Fall*, 39–49.

Fehr, S. C. (2009, March 31). States spar with credit rating agencies. Stateline.org. Retrieved on March 10 ,2011 from http://www.stateline.org/live/details/story?contentId=388447

Finder, A. (1989, June 23). Charter panel backs creating a budget office. *New York Times*. Retrieved on March 10, 2011 from http://www.nytimes.com/1989/06/23/nyregion/charter-panel-backs-creating-a-budget-office.html?scp=4&sq=%22independent+budget+office%22&st=nyt

Frug, G. E. (1996). The geography of community. *Stanford Law Review, 48*, 1047.

Gannon, D. P. (1994). Analysis of Pennsylvania's legislative program for financially distressed municipalities and the reaction of municipal labor unions. *Dickinson Law Review, 28*, 281–305.

Hillhouse, A. M. (1935). *Municipal bonds: A century of experience*. New York: Prentice-Hall.

Honalde, B. W. (2005). Incrementalism redux: State roles in local government fiscal crises. Paper presented at the 59th International Atlantic Economic Conference, London, England. Available at: http://www.ipr.uc.edu/documents/ACFE4D.pdf

Hughes, J. W. and Laverdiere, Raymond (1986. December). Comparative local government financial analysis. *Public Budgeting and Finance, 6*(4), 23–33.

Kloha, P. (2003, June 1). Monitoring local government fiscal health: Michigan's new ten point scale of fiscal distress. *Government Financial Review*. Retrieved on February 16, 2011 from http://www.allbusiness.com/government/580633-1.html

Levenstein, L. (2009, November 25). Statement before the Rating Agency Working Group. New York: Moody's. Retrieved on February 16, 2011 from http://www.naic.org/documents/committees_e_rating_agency_091118_moody.pdf

McConnell, M. W. (1993). When cities go broke: A conceptual introduction to municipal bankruptcy. *University of Chicago Law Review, 60*, 425. New York City Charter, Chapter 11(c). The Independent Budget Office. New York City, New York.

Missed opportunity: Urban fiscal crises and financial control boards. (1997). *Harvard Law Review, 110*, 733.

Mullins, D. R. and Pagano, M. A. (2005). Local budgeting and finance: 25 years of developments. *Public Budgeting and Finance* (Special Issue), 3–45.

SFAI (State Fiscal Analysis Initiative). Retrieved on February 23 ,2011 from http://www.statefiscal.org/

State Administrative Supervision of Local Government Debt: The North Carolina Model. (1972). *Duke Law Journal, 2*(2), 487–510.

Turetsky, D. (2008, October 13). An interview with Doug Turetsky, Independent Budget Office. Retrieved on February 26, 2011 from http://www.empirepage.com/2008/10/13/an-interview-with-doug-turetsky

U.S. ACIR, U.S. Advisory Commission on Intergovernmental Relations. (1993). Local government autonomy: Needs for state constitutional, statutory, and judicial clarification Washington DC: Government Printing Office.

U.S. ACIS, Advisory Commission on Intergovernmental Relations. (1985). Bankruptcies, defaults, and other local financial emergencies. Washington DC: Government Printing Office.

U.S. Secretary of the Treasury (1959). Final report of the Reconstruction Finance Corporation. Washington, DC: Government Printing Office. Retrieved on February 26, 2011 from http://fraser.stlouisfed.org/publications/rfc/issue/4976/download/80864/rfc_19590506_finalreport.pdf

United States of America Before the Securities and Exchange Commission in the matter of City of San Diego, California, Respondent. Order Instituting Cease and Desist Proceedings, Making Findings, and Imposing a Cease and Desist Order Pursuant to Section 8A of the Securities Exchange Act of 1944 and Section 21 C of the Securities Exchange Act of 1934. (2006). Retrieved on January 30, 2011 from http://www.sec.gov/litigation/admin/2006/33-8751.pdf

U.S. Supreme Court (1884). *East St. Louis v. United States ex Rel. Zebley*, 110 U.S. 324, http://supreme.justia.com/us/110/321/case.html

Walter, E. B. (2009, October 28). Speech by SEC Commissioner: Regulation of the municipal securities market: Investors are not second-class citizens. Retrieved on March 10, 2011 from http://www.sec.gov/news/speech/2009/spch102809ebw.htm

Washington State Office of Financial Management. (2006). Washington State local government fiscal stress analysis: A comparison to state assistance under Senate Bill 6050.

Weikart, L. A. (2009). *Follow the money: Who controls New York City mayors?* Albany, NY: State University of Albany Press.

Yale Law Journal Company. (1936). Comity by the federal courts to state statutory receiverships of defaulting municipalities *45*(4), 702–708. Retrieved from http://www.jstor.org/stable/pdfplus/791890.pdf. Accessed February 21, 2011.

Chapter 16

Measuring the Impacts of TELs on Municipal Financial Conditions

by Craig S. Maher and Steven C. Deller

Introduction

The study of government financial condition has taken on greater meaning as policymakers now struggle through one of the worst economic and financial crises in the past 50 years. To date, data availability, measurement inconsistencies, and limited generalizability have limited studies of local government financial condition. This chapter attempts to move the research forward by studying the determinants of municipal financial condition cross sectionally. We examine more than 1,000 municipalities in 47 states for fiscal year 2005. Recent work on qualifying local *tax and expenditure limitations* across the United States has greatly aided our research. Our findings reflect the importance of understanding municipal financial condition within the context of state-imposed limitations.

The fiscal pressure facing local governments today is more severe than has been experienced at any time in the past 50 years (Miller and Svara, 2009). Its severity is both deep and broad, affecting every state and local government in the United States. The hardest hit economic sectors, particularly the housing sector, have meant sizable reductions in the primary revenue sources of local governments; property and sales taxes (Miller and Svara, 2009; Hoene and Pagano, 2010). How local governments respond to the current fiscal crisis has been the focus of a number of recently released studies and website links provided by both professional organizations, including the International City/County Managers Association (2010), The Government Finance Officers Association (2010), the National League of Cities (2010), and academics groups (States as Facilitators or Obstructionists of Local Governments Conference, 2010). In helping communities cope with fiscal stress, much of the focus tends to be on overcoming short-term constraints through the drawing down of fund balances and long-term success through revenue growth and improved efficiencies. The challenges associated with growing the revenue base are exacerbated by the proliferation of tax and expenditure limitations (TELs) imposed on local governments. Today, local TELs exist in all U.S. states except for the northeastern states of Connecticut, Maine, New Hampshire, and Vermont. Unfortunately, there is little overlap between the fiscal health and TEL literatures.

From a practical standpoint, the biggest challenge in attempting to study local fiscal conditions is data uniformity. There exists a proliferation of studies since the 1970s attempting to measure *fiscal condition*; all of which are limited in their generalizability because of data constraints. As a result, we are left with a proliferation of empirical metrics specific to particular case studies (Hendrick, 2004 [also see Hendrick for a good summary of previous research]; Kloha, Weissert, and Kleine, 2005). This chapter adds to the existing research in two important ways; it examines the financial condition of a cross section of cities throughout the United States, and it explores the relationship between the fiscal condition of cities and state-imposed TELs. The remainder of the study proceeds as follows: literature review, description of TEL and financial condition measurement, methodology, results, and concluding comments.

Literature Review

Since the near fiscal meltdown of major U.S. cities such as New York in the 1970s, public finance scholars, government, and professional organizations have sought to provide analytical tools for the purpose of measuring fiscal condition in an attempt to prevent a repeat. One of the most commonly cited and influential bodies was the *Advisory Commission on Intergovernmental Relations* (ACIR), which produced a series of reports and studies throughout the 1970s and 1980s focusing on state and local government fiscal capacity issues (1971, 1979, 1981, 1988, 1989). Other federal reports tended to focus more on the effects of federal aid programs on local needs (Congressional Budget Office, 1978; U.S. Department of the Treasury, 1978).

Today, each of the three major local government organizations has tools for measuring fiscal condition. One of the more common of these is the International City/County Managers Association's *Measuring Fiscal Condition* (Nollenberger, 2004), which consists of 36 indicators for communities to track over time. The Government Finance Officers Association provides an award for fiscal stewardship (both budget and audit) and publishes a monthly magazine that included the popular "10-Point Test of Financial Condition" (Brown, 1989). This "10-Point Test" that Brown (1989) developed and Maher and Nollenberger (2009) updated is a set of indicators that can be easily calculated for smaller cities across the nation. The ratios are used by comparing an individual city to other similarly sized cities around the country. Since 2003, the National League of Cities has published an annual survey of city staff describing city fiscal conditions (the most recent, Hoene and Pagano, 2010).

Academics have also made contributions to both theoretical conceptualizations of fiscal condition as well as empirical measurements. Clark and Ferguson (1983) present one of the more comprehensive models of fiscal strain that captures relationships among political outcomes, the economic base, and fiscal policies. Ladd and Yinger (1989) developed a "need-capacity gap" framework that combines expenditure needs with revenue-raising capacity and applied it to the largest cities. Other important works during that era include Rubin's (1982) case study of a medium-sized Midwestern city and Levine and Rubin's (1980) edited work on cutback strategies. Hendrick (2004) as well as Honadle, Costa, and Cigler (2004) do commendable jobs of summarizing the range of such studies.

Building on Berne and Schramm (1986), Hendrick (2004) designed an "open system" theoretical framework for the study of fiscal health that captures three dimensions in local government: properties of the government's environment, balance of fiscal structure with environment, and properties of the government's fiscal structure. Studying communities in the Chicago area, Hendrick finds support for her more extensive theoretical framework of fiscal health and identifies *fiscal slack*, measured in terms of fund balance, degree of discretionary spending, level of off-budget fiscal activities, and size of the government to be particularly noteworthy and in need of further study. Seeking to predict fiscal condition, Kloha et al. (2005) developed a 10-point scale and applied it to communities in Michigan. Their scale includes population growth, real taxable value growth, large real taxable value decrease, general fund expenditures as a percentage of taxable value, general fund operating deficit, prior general fund operating deficits, size of general fund balance, fund deficits in the current or previous year, and general long-term debt as a percentage of taxable value.

Unfortunately, the generalizability of much of the research on fiscal condition is limited because of reliance on case studies or survey data (Downs and Rocke, 1984; Levine, 1980; Levine, Rubin, and Wolohojian, 1981). For instance, Pammer (1990) has conducted one of the few cross-sectional analyses of cities to study the degree to which 120 cities used a variety of retrenchment strategies in response to fiscal stress. Similarly, Ward (2001) surveyed local governments in Louisiana to gauge how they responded to fiscal stress. Unfortunately, in both cases there is little ability to generalize from the samples about the appropriate measures of fiscal condition to which the governments were responding. More recent research on the measurement of fiscal condition has also been confined to communities within a particular state; Hendrick (2004) studied communities in a Chicago suburb, and Kloha et al. (2005) focused on Michigan communities.

This lack of generalizability of fiscal condition research is particularly troublesome given that most of the policy efforts in the past 30 years to control local fiscal policies have been in the form of TELs. Dissatisfaction with taxation levels and perceived excessive government spending grew substantially over the latter half of the 20th century. As a result, the number of tax and expenditure limitations (TELs) efforts such as California's *Proposition 13*, Massachusetts's Proposition 2½, and Colorado's Taxpayers' Bill of Rights (TABOR) has grown. By 2006, 46 states had implemented state statutory or constitutional limits on local government tax revenue and expenditures, with 31 states placing limits on state taxes and/or expenditures (Deller and Stallmann, 2007; Mullins, 2004).

As Lowry and Alt (2001) reveal, any institutional structures, such as TELs, that limit fiscal flexibility can affect credit risk, which, by definition, is an assessment of financial condition. Though Wagner (2004) and Poterba and Rueben's (1999) research focused on the effect of TELs on credit ratings, the explanation of the relationship between the two is directly applicable to TELs and fiscal condition analysis. According to these scholars, TELs are intended to force fiscal discipline on state and local governments and introduce a certain degree of certainty into the taxing and budgeting process. As such, the level of risk associated with the presence of TELs should be reduced, hence improving their credit worthiness of those governments and in turn reducing the cost of borrowing. On the other hand, TELs can create barriers to fiscal flexibility and may inhibit the ability of state and local governments to raise sufficient revenues for future obligations, such as the repayment of credit or debt. If state and local governments are limited in their ability to raise revenues to repay credit or debt, the risk of default is higher, thus leading to lower creditworthiness. Lower credit ratings (weaker financial condition) in turn raise the cost of credit and debt.

But to our knowledge, no systematic analysis has examined the explicit relationship tax and expenditure limitations and notions of fiscal condition at the local level. Though many authors (e.g., Lowry and Alt, 2001; Poterba and Rueben, 1999; Wagner, 2004) have talked in vague terms about the affect of TELs on fiscal conditions, most studies (e.g., Abrams and Dougan, 1986; Bails, 1990; Joyce and Mullins, 1991; Lowery, 1983; Mullins and Joyce, 1996; Shadbegian, 1998, 1999; Skidmore, 1999) have focused on how affected governments alter revenue and/or expenditure policies. This study attempts to address this gap in the literature by explicitly examining the relationship between TELs and municipal fiscal conditions.

TEL Index

One of the primary difficulties for a systematic study of the influence tax and expenditure limitations have on fiscal policies and/or condition is the unique nature of each state's particular tax and expenditure limitation. As previously noted, 46 of the 50 states have some form of tax and expenditure limitation (TEL) in place on state or local governments, with the oldest being a 1875 limit on the growth in property tax rates in Missouri (Mullins and Wallin, 2004). But as Poterba and Rueben (1999) note, no two states are alike, and TELs range from limits on how fast specific taxes can increase for specific units of government to strict limits on how much government spending can increase from one year to the next.

Joyce and Mullins (1991) place tax and expenditure limitations into six broad classifications ranging from simple full disclosure—truth in taxation rules—to strict general revenue or expenditure increases. Full disclosure rules generally require some type of public discussions and a specific legislative vote prior to enactment of tax rate increases and require a majority vote of the legislative body to increase taxes and spending. These types of tax and expenditure limitations generally are not fiscally binding (i.e., it is usually possible to work around the limit). The most restrictive tax and expenditure limitations limit the amount or the percentage by which revenues and/or expenditures can increase from the previous year and are codified in the state constitution. Often tied to inflation rates, population growth rates, or growth in per capita income, these types of tax and expenditure limitations are the most binding for governments (Poulson, 2005).

Another complicating factor for research is the timeframe over which tax and expenditure limitations have been in place. West Virginia has had an overall local property tax rate limit in place since 1939 and Missouri placed its first focused property tax rate limit on local government in 1875 (Mullins and Wallin, 2004). Arkansas passed a supermajority requirement to raise taxes in 1934, Florida adopted limits on corporate income taxes in 1971, California's Proposition 13 was enacted in 1979, Colorado's Taxpayer's Bill of Rights (TABOR) in 1992, Massachusetts's Proposition 2½ in 1980, and Wisconsin's limit on the ability of local governments to raise property taxes in 1993 (Deller and Stallmann, 2007; Kornhauser, 2002; NCSL, 2005).

This significant heterogeneity across the states in terms of how the TELs are structured and the timeframe in which they were enacted create a significant problem in modeling the dynamics of the interplay between the tax and expenditure limitation and subsequent fiscal policies, government performance and fiscal condition. The heterogeneity has been addressed within the empirical literature by either studying individual states in isolation almost within a case-study approach or through the adoption of simplistic dummy variables in multivariate regression (e.g., Cutler et al., 1999; Deller and Stallmann, 2007; Mason, 2005; McGuire and Rueben, 2006; Stallmann and Deller, 2011). This almost default approach has severely limited the depth and generalizability of the TEL literature.

Modeled on the work of Poulson (2005), Amiel, Deller, and Stallmann (2009) (henceforth called ADS) construct a TEL Index that quantifies the severity or restrictiveness of the TEL of individual states on both state and local governments.[1] The work of ADS employs six characteristics, each of which affects how strict or binding a TEL is: (1) the type of TEL, (2) if the TEL is statutory or constitutional, (3) growth restrictions, (4) method of TEL approval, (5) override provisions, and (6) exemptions (see **Table 16.1**). Higher point values in each category correspond to stricter limitations, and lower point values correspond to more lenient limitations. The rankings in each category are ordinal and do not reflect magnitude. For example, in the ADS Index, a revenue and expenditure limit is worth six possible points and a tax revenue limit is worth two points. This does not mean that the former is three times more restrictive than the latter. Rather, it simply indicates that a TEL that restricts both revenue and expenditures is more severe than a TEL that limits only tax revenue. Although the ADS Index is annual from 1969 to 2005 and is constructed for both TELs imposed on state and local governments separately, for this research, we use the Local ADS Index for 2005, the most current year of the Index (see **Table 16.2**).

Fiscal Condition Measurement

There are as many empirical fiscal condition metrics available as there are studies, meaning no two are alike. That being said, fiscal condition seems to be generally accepted as the ability of a government to meet current and future obligations. This conceptual definition is consistent with Kloha et al. (2005), "fiscal stress . . . a failure to meet standards in the areas of operating position, debt, and community needs and resources over successive years" (p. 314); Hendrick (2004) "fiscal health . . . ability of government to meet its financial and service obligations" (p. 79); and Berne and Schramm (1986), "the probability that a government will meet its financial obligations" (p. 71).

The general empirical framework of fiscal condition measurement tends to incorporate measures of revenue and expenditure capacity, operating position, and fiscal flexibility

TABLE 16.1 Local TEL Index

Type of TEL	Points	Statutory/Constitutional	Points
Overall Property Tax Rate Limit	7	Full Disclosure	1
Limited to more than or equal to 2.5%	2		
Limited to more than 2.5%	1	**Scope**	
		Constitutional	1
Specific Property Tax Rate Limit	6	County	1
		Municipality	1
Property Tax Revenue (Levy) Limit	5	Special district	1
Limit less than or equal to inflation or 5%	3	Other	1
Limit less than or equal to 5%	2		
Limit more than 5%	1	**Overrides/Exemptions**	
		Sales Tax Option	
Assessment Increase	4	Other taxes	–1
No approved increases	4	Debt service	–1
Lower of 5%(or less) or CPI	3	Home rule	–1
Limit less than or equal to 5%	2	Special levies	–1
Limit more than 5%	1	Capital improvements	–1
		Emergency	–1
General Revenue Limit	3	Construction	–1
No new tax or rate increase	4	Other	–1
Limit equal to inflation and or population growth	3		
Limit is less than or equal to 5%	2	**Method of Override**	
Limit is between 5 and 10%	1	No approved overrides	4
		Super majority referendum	2
General Expenditure Limit	2	Majority vote by local representatives	1
Limit equal to inflation and or population growth	4	Simple majority referendum	1
Limit is equal to the change in per capita income	3	Appeal to courts	1
Limit is less than or equal to 5%	2	Appeal to state board	1
Limit is between 5 and 10%	1		

Source: Amiel, L., Deller. S. C., and Stallmann, J. (2009, May). The construction of a tax and expenditure limitation index for the US. Department of Agricultural and Applied Economics Staff Paper No. 536. University of Wisconsin-Madison. Retrieved on December 20, 2011, from http://www.aae.wisc.edu/pubs/sps/pdf/stpap536.pdf

TABLE 16.2 Local TEL Index 2005

AK	13	MT	20
AL	15	NC	7
AR	21	ND	16
AZ	32	NE	30
CA	36	NH	0
CO	38	NM	34
CT	0	NV	29
DE	9	NY	17
FL	22	OH	21
GA	11	OK	18
IA	19	OR	27
ID	16	PA	12
IL	20	RI	10
IN	9	SC	3
KS	8	SD	10
KY	26	TN	3
LA	19	TX	18
MA	14	UT	11
MD	11	VA	1
ME	0	VT	0
MI	37	WA	37
MN	8	WI	13
MO	20	WY	7
MS	7		

Source: Amiel, L., Deller. S. C., and Stallmann, J. (2009, May). The construction of a tax and expenditure limitation index for the US. Department of Agricultural and Applied Economics Staff Paper No. 536. University of Wisconsin-Madison. Retrieved on December 20, 2011, from http://www.aae.wisc.edu/pubs/sps/pdf/stpap536.pdf

(Berne and Schramm, 1986; Hendrick, 2004; Kloha, Weissert, and Kleine, 2005). The specific measures tend to be unique to each analysis. For instance, Ladd and Yinger (1984) combine revenue capacity and spending needs to create a "need-capacity gap" or "standardized fiscal health" approach. Hendrick (2004) measures revenue capacity in terms of own-source revenues relative to city wealth (tax base, personal income, and sales receipts). Clark and Ferguson (1983) measure fiscal strain by computing revenues per capita and dividing it by a city wealth index, population change, income, and a residual of revenues per capita.

Maher and Nolenberger (2009) computed general-fund revenues (excluding capital projects funds) per capita, intergovernmental revenues as a percentage of total general fund revenues, and own-source tax revenues as a percentage of general-fund revenues.

The diversity in spending measures is just as great. While excluding a revenue measure, Kloha et al. (2005) calculate general fund expenditures as a percentage of taxable value as one of their 10 measures of fiscal distress. Hendrick's (2004) measure of spending need consists of per capita expenditures relative to crime rates, housing age, population density, and whether a municipality was in a fire district. Clark and Ferguson's (1983) expenditure measure is calculated the same as their revenue measure. Berne and Schramm (1986) define spending within the context of current and future expenditure pressure. Maher and Nollenberger (2009) capture spending in terms of relative general fund spending per capita. Ladd and Yinger (1989) focused on costs and spending needs for only general government, police, and fire.

Fiscal flexibility captures the ability of governments to maneuver in both the short and long run. Hendrick (2004) uses the term "fiscal slack," which is meant to be more broadly defined than just unreserved fund balances. In fact, Hendrick defines fiscal slack in terms of four distinct measures; unreserved fund balance as a percentage of spending, capital expenditures as a percentage of total spending, enterprise income as a percentage of total own-source income (including enterprise), and debt service as a percentage of total spending. The importance of governments' ability to manage short-term fiscal shocks and provide fiscal flexibility through fund balances has been well documented (Holcombe and Sobel, 1997; Maher and Nollenberer, 2009; Pagano, 2002; Pagano and Johnston, 2000; Porterba, 1994). Hendrick's (2004) includes enterprise funds because they "provide opportunities for municipalities to share revenues and costs with a separate set of funds that are less visible to public scrutiny" (p. 98). Capital expenditures provide opportunities for municipalities to vary spending based on economic conditions (Hendrick, 2004; Levine, Rubin, and Wolohojian, 1981). Conversely, communities with sizable debt have less slack (Hendrick, 2004).

Measures of debt levels are found in nearly every study of financial condition. According to Kloha et al. (2005), "[l]arge levels of debt relative to the government's ability to generate revenue are a clear sign of fiscal distress" (p. 319). Similarly, Maher and Nollenberger (2009) state that debt is often limited by state governments and is an important indicator of credit worthiness (also see, e.g., Ammar et al., 2001; Benson and Marks, 2007; Johnson and Kriz, 2005). Clark and Ferguson (1983) measure debt per capita and divide it by a city wealth index, population change, and income. The purpose of measuring debt within the fiscal condition framework is, as previously mentioned, an attempt to capture current fiscal flexibility, but it also serves as a measure of future commitments (Berne and Schramm, 1986).

Another future commitment in need of consideration is pension obligations (Berne and Schramm, 1986; Maher and Nollenberger, 2009). In their update of Brown's "10-Point Test," Maher and Nollenberger (2009) measure unfunded pension liability as a ratio of the actuarial value of the plan's assets divided by the actuarial accrued liability. According to these authors, "[t]he level of funding differs significantly among cities, raising important concerns regarding the future financial condition of many jurisdictions" (p. 65). Another useful measure of future obligations, other postemployment benefits (OPEBs) such as retiree's insurance costs, is now required to be reported by the Government Accounting Standards Board (GASB), unfortunately it was not a requirement during our years under study.[2]

Finally, operating position is frequently included by public finance researchers to measure fiscal condition. Financial position is typically measured in terms of general fund operating revenues relative to general fund operating expenditures. According to Maher and Nollenberger (2009),

> This measure. . . is a financial indicator that the credit rating agencies review on a regular basis. Credit agencies are concerned when there are two consecutive years of deficits, a deficit in the current year that is larger than the deficit in the past year, a deficit in two or more of the past five years, or an abnormally large deficit—more than 5 to 10 percent. (63)

Kloha et al.'s (2005) 10-point "fiscal distress index" is composed of three different measures of operating position—current general expenditures relative to revenues, the existence of an operating deficit in the previous fiscal year, and whether the government had a fund deficit in both the current and previous year.

Another facet of fiscal condition measurement has to do with reliance on general fund data sources verses government fund sources made available by GASB 34 (Chaney, 2005; Wang, Dennis, and Tu, 2007). Most of the research to date has relied on general fund sources, yet as TELs have been adopted, communities are increasingly relying on funding services outside the general fund and through enterprise funds. This shift by municipalities suggests that fiscal condition, based solely on general fund statements, may no longer be adequate. The problem is that there is no consensus on the appropriate fiscal condition measures using governmentwide statements, for example, Wang et. al. (2007) use 11 indicators whereas Chaney (2005) uses 6. Furthermore, though there have been assertions made that the use of government-wide statements matters, there is currently no empirical evidence demonstrating that measured fiscal condition varies when comparing general fund-based analysis to governmentwide statements.

Once the measures have been defined, the next step in the financial condition analysis process has also been debated. The differences generally boil down to the extent to which it is appropriate to combine the indictors into one single measure of fiscal condition, or examine the components separately. For instance, Brown (1989) recommends a combined score based on a community's quartile ranking on each of the 10 indicators. If the individual elements or metrics are to be combined, how should they be combined, simple addition as suggested by Kloha et al. (2005), or perhaps through more rigorous statistical approaches such as factor analysis or principal component, or even cluster analysis? Should each individual metric have the same weight and if not how is the aggregation weighting scheme determined?

Others, such as Hendrick (2004, p. 85), assert that fiscal health is too complicated to combine into one single measure, "[t]he complexity and indirect nature of the relationships between dimensions make it difficult to construct one, comprehensive indicator of fiscal health or fiscal condition. Rather, measures of these dimensions should be constructed separately and assessed in relation to one another to produce a complete and more accurate picture of fiscal conditions."

As summarized by Honadle et. al (2004) and Hendrick (2004), there currently exist a number of studies attempting to measure fiscal conditions or health or stress. Despite the extent of the academic- and professional association-based literature and the increasingly widespread use of metrics of fiscal condition in modern management practices, the current state-of-the-art is lacking on several fronts. Whereas there is general widespread agreement on the theoretical characteristics of fiscal condition, a large breach exists between the theory and the empirics. Simply put, the empirical metrics that have been suggested in the literature appears to be all over the proverbial map. Indeed, Maher and Deller (2011) find evidence that "objective" metrics of fiscal health derived from secondary data are poor predictors of "subjective" metrics based on surveys of local officials' perceptions of fiscal health. Part of this divide between the theory and the empirical work is the lack of adequate secondary data sources. For example, reporting requirements, if any exist at all, vary significantly from state to state. Metrics that make good sense in one state may not be operational in another state. An additional problem is that all of the available studies on fiscal conditions that we are aware of ignore the presence of tax and expenditure limitations.

Methodology

The principle aim of this chapter is to measure the relationship between municipal fiscal conditions and TELs. This requires the operationalization of two complicated concepts (TEL and fiscal condition) as well as the creation of a dataset capable of measuring the relationship. Amiel, Deller, and Stallmann (2009) solved measurement of TELs, and we simply incorporated the 2005 local ADS Index values for each municipality. Because the ADS Index is constructed at the state level, each municipality within the same state is assigned the same Index value.

The Government Finance Officers Association (GFOA) initially collected the financial condition data. The GFOA requires that governments interested in receiving their Certificate of Achievement for Excellence in Financial Reporting award submit audit report information.[3] These GFOA data have been used in several studies of financial condition (Brown, 1989, 1993; Maher and Nollenberger, 2009). The only drawback of these data is that they are self-selected and, thus, do not constitute a true sample of U.S. cities. According to Maher and Nollenberger (2009), the "strength of the dataset is that it provides a consistent collection of audited financial data for municipalities throughout the country . . . one might think of the respondents as high-performing communities and thus providing a benchmark for all municipalities" (p. 62). In 2005, the GFOA collected audit report data on 1,746 municipalities from 47 states data (missing municipalities in Hawaii, New Jersey, and West Virginia). The number of municipalities in each state represented in the dataset range from 240 in California to 1 in Vermont. The average population size of municipalities is 67,748 and ranged from 33 (Indian Creek Village, Florida) to 8.1 million (New York City).

As the following details, our basic models can be expressed as:

$$\left.\begin{matrix} FC_j \\ \Delta FC_{j,t-1\rightarrow t} \end{matrix}\right\} = \alpha + \beta TEL + \sum_i \varphi_i Demograp_i + \sum_i \gamma_i Govtstruc_i + \varepsilon_j$$

Here FC_j is the jth fiscal condition metric and $\Delta FC_{j,t-1\rightarrow t}$ is the change in the jth metric over the time period t–1 to t. The variable *TEL* is the ADS Index for limits placed on local governments within the state, *Demograp* is a set of demographic variables describing the local community serviced by the municipality, and *Govtstruc* captures the characteristics of the structure of the municipality. Finally, the regression error term (ε) is assumed to be well behaved. Each are now discussed in turn.

Dependent Variables

Consistent with previous research, we measure municipal fiscal condition within the framework of current available resources (revenue and expenditure capacity, operating position, fiscal slack) and long-term commitments (debt and pension liabilities). Though the measurement of these concepts varies substantially across previous works, we have attempted to be as consistent with the field as possible. In addition to the measurement, there is also the issue of time frame. Researchers have examined fiscal condition from the perspective of a particular year (Brown, 1989; Clark and Ferguson, 1983; Hendrick, 2004; Ladd and Yinger, 1989; Maher and Nollenberger, 2009) whereas others make a compelling argument that change over time is appropriate (Kloha, Weissert, and Kleine, 2005). Because each captures a different dimension of fiscal condition and are, in most cases, dependent on one another, we have included both determinants of fiscal condition in 2005 and change in fiscal condition between 2003 and 2005. In our presentation of the basic model to be estimated, t-1 is 2003 and t is 2005 (see **Table 16.3**).

Own-source revenues.

The principle objective of this measure is to determine the ability of municipalities to manage fiscal stress (revenue capacity) through revenue growth. The specific measures of revenue capacity range from own-source taxes divided by personal income (ACIR, 1979) to revenues per capita divided by a city wealth index, population change, income (Clark and Ferguson, 1983) to own-source revenues relative to wealth (Hendrick, 2004). We measure revenue capacity as own-source revenues divided by taxable property. The expectation is that, all other things being equal, communities have more revenue capacity (less fiscal stress) the lower their own-source revenues relative to taxable property. It is suggested by

TABLE 16.3 Descriptive Statistics of Dependent Variables

	N	Minimum	Maximum	Mean	Std. Deviation
Revenues as pct. taxable property (2005)	1726	.00	18.88	1.0415	1.060
Pct. point change in revenues 2003–2005	1481	−13.83	6.29	−.0424	.7697
GF expends as pct taxable property (2005)	1726	.00	21.73	1.1822	1.224
Pct. point change in GF expends 2003–2005	1481	−19.98	9.04	−.0762	0.903
Unreserved fund balance as rct. GF revs (2005)	1738	−25.52	298.83	35.70	27.58
Pct. point chg. in fund balance 2003–2005	1492	−71.83	51.65	0.0869	12.34
Debt service as pct. expends (2005)	1739	.00	93.64	6.4796	8.21120
Change in debt service 2003–2005	1498	−1.20	1.58	−0.0074	0.135
GO debt as pct. taxable property (2005)	1728	.00	16.08	.7673	1.22343
Pct. point change in GO debt 2003–2005	1483	−14.27	12.38	−.0202	.85711
Pension assets to liabilities (2005)	1171	−69.87	389.22	80.357	30.16
Pct. point chg. pensionassets 2003–2005	979	−101.68	132.11	−5.81	16.84

the more practitioner-based studies of fiscal condition that just as, if not more important, than current revenue levels is the examination of trends over time (Brown, 1989; Maher and Nollenberger, 2009; Nollenberger, 2004). To accommodate this recommendation, change in own-source revenues (2003–2005) relative to taxable property has also been included. We expect an inverse relationship between these two measures; that is, municipalities with lower revenues per taxable property in 2003 would grow at a rate greater than municipalities that had higher revenues per taxable property.

General-fund expenditures.

Including spending as a measure of fiscal condition appears relatively straightforward. Communities spending more are, all other things held equal, in worse fiscal condition than those spending less (Brown, 1989). The reality is that this is too simplistic a view

(Hendrick, 2004). The more appropriate approach is to determine the extent to which expenditures are keeping pace with service demands and ability to meet those needs (Clark and Ferguson, 1983; Hendrick, 2004). Although conceptually appealing, practically capturing this concept is difficult. Hendrick (2004) measures spending relative to crime, housing age, density, and whether a community was in a fire district. Clark and Ferguson (1983) calculate per capita spending relative to a wealth index, population change, and income. Given data limitations and the inability to define a unifying measure, we use Khola et al.'s (2005) definition of general fund expenditures as a percentage of taxable property. Similar to the revenues measure, communities are considered to have more fiscal stress the greater their spending as a percentage of taxable property. Likewise, the greater the increase in municipal spending between 2003 and 2005, the more fiscally stressed the community.

Fiscal slack.

The most common measure of fiscal slack is the size of government's unreserved fund balances. We measure municipal fund balance as the sum of general-fund unreserved undesignated and unreserved designated funds divided by general-fund revenues.[4] A second measure of "slack" is debt service and was calculated as a percentage of general-fund expenditures. For measures of change, we subtracted the difference in ratios for 2003 from 2005. The expectation is that the growth/decline in these ratios will be a function of improving/declining financial condition. It should not be surprising to find communities with greater levels of slack in 2003 to grow less or decline between 2005 and 2003, compared to communities with less fiscal slack in 2003.

Future obligations.

The size of future obligations measured in terms of debt levels is frequently included in fiscal condition analyses (Berne and Schramm, 1986; Brown, 1989; Hendrick, 2004; Kloha, Weissert, and Kleine, 2005; Maher and Nollenberger, 2009; Nollenberger, 2004). More difficult to measure because of data availability is pension obligations (Berne and Schramm, 1986). In one of the few studies of fiscal condition where pension liabilities were computed, Maher and Nollenberger (2009) found that "The level of funding differs significantly among cities, raising important concerns regarding the future financial condition of many jurisdictions" (p. 65). We measured a municipality's future obligations with two ratios: general obligation debt as a percentage of taxable property and actuarial accrued assets in the government's pension fund as a percentage of its actuarial accrued liabilities. Change in future obligations was calculated as the difference between levels in 2003 from those in 2005.

Independent Variables

The key independent variable for this analysis is the severity of the tax/expenditure limit that states impose on municipalities. As discussed earlier, Amiel, Deller, and Stallmann

TABLE 16.4 Descriptive Statistics for Independent Variables

	N	Minimum	Maximum	Mean	Std. Deviation
Percent population less 18 yrs	1738	3.00	60.50	27.7510	7.60004
Per capita income	1738	60.50	137384	24708	11535
Per capita taxable property	1738	3086	20391767	107993	532508
Manager-council form of gov't	979	.00	1.00	.7763	.41693
Budget by chief admin. officer	1006	.00	1.00	.7664	.42333
Budget by chief financial officer	1006	.00	1.00	.0596	.23694
Population change 2003–2005	1499	−1.00	1028	.8687	26.61
Change taxable property 2003–2005	1489	−1.00	38357	48.21	1048

(2009) recently completed an analysis of TEL severity over time and across each of the 50 states. For 2005, the local TEL Index has a mean of about 15.9, standard deviation of 10.7, and a range of 0 to 38. Colorado has the most restrictive local TEL as measured by the ADS TEL Index with a value of 38, followed by Michigan and Washington with values of 37, then California with a value of 36. States with no TEL-type restrictions on local governments include Connecticut, Maine, New Hampshire, and Vermont. This is not to say that these latter states have "perfect flexibility" in generating revenues. For example, New Hampshire does not have a sales tax that can be a major source of revenues for many municipalities.

We hypothesize that the stricter the community's TEL, the worse its financial position. Specifically, TEL severity should be negatively related to fiscal slack (fund balance, change in fund balance) and positively related to operating position (debt service and change in debt service) and long-term commitments (debt as a percentage of taxable property and change in debt as a percentage of taxable property between 2003 and 2005). Popular studies of fiscal condition have typically measured revenue and expenditures on a per capita basis (Brown, 1989; Maher and Nollenberger, 2009; Nollenberger, 2004) or relative to tax base (Khola, Weissert, and Kleine, 2005). The expectation is that communities in stronger fiscal condition have lower relative revenues and expenditures. Whereas this may be appropriate for case studies of communities within states, it ignores differences in ability for communities to grow revenues and/or expenditures across states. This is why TEL severity needs consideration. We hypothesize that the stricter the community's TEL, the lower its general fund revenues and expenditures as a percentage of taxable property.

Demographic characteristics.

Determinants of community fiscal condition are typically associated with demographic attributes and internal management capacity (Berne and Schramm, 1986; Hendrick, 2004). For this analysis, five measures of community needs/capacity are included: the percentage of population age 18 or less, per capita income, taxable property per capita, population change between 2003 and 2005, and change in taxable property between 2003 and 2005[5] (see Table 16.4). Communities with greater resources, or wealth, are expected to be in stronger financial condition than those with less wealth. Similarly, the percentage of the population age 18 or less functions as a measure of service demand.

Government structure.

The ability of local governments to effectively manage finances is typically rooted in management structure. In fact, the financial management of a city plays an important role in determining bond ratings (Kammholz and Maher, 2008). It is expected that, all else being equal, local governments with a manager form of government, compared to a commission or mayor-council will perform better, including financially. To capture this relationship, we used ICMA's 2006 survey of governments. The survey provided response data on 1,006 of our available cases (58% of total). Of those communities, 75% represented council-manager forms of government. The ICMA dataset also enabled us to focus more closely on the financial management of the community. One of the questions asked respondents, "Who has the independent authority to develop and make recommendations for the budget submitted to the council?" The responses were: chief administrative officer (60%), chief financial officer (9%), chief elected officer (10%), a combination of chief elected and administrative officers (7%), and other (6%). Dichotomous variables were created to measure the impact of the chief administrative officer and the chief financial officer.

Results

Table 16.5 presents correlations among our dependent variables. In general, the relationships between the variables are generally weak, supporting the argument that the fiscal condition indices cannot be easily collapsed into a single measure. Aside from the strong relationship between revenues and expenses (0.951), no relationships are correlated above 0.40.

Except for FY 2005 operating position, all of the regression models are statistically significant[6] (see **Table 16.6**). The amount of variation in the dependent models explained by our independent variables varies from 2 to 30%. The models with the lowest r^2 were those attempting to explain variation in the 2003–2005 change in GO debt ($r^2 = 0.023$), fund balance ($r^2 = 0.039$), and municipal debt service ($r^2 = 0.05$). Models with the greatest predictive power were those explaining change in operating position ($r^2 = 0.301$), change in own-source revenues ($r^2 = 0.293$), and change in general fund expenditures ($r^2 = 0.212$). Regarding the latter models, the baseline values in FY 2003 were important determinants of the change variables, thus the change in own-source revenues between 2003 and 2005 was negatively associated with own-source revenues in 2003, and change in GF expenditures was negatively related to GF expenditures in 2003.

The findings generally support our primary research question in that the severity of state-imposed TELs on local governments affects most facets of local financial condition including revenues, expenditures, unreserved fund balances, debt service, general-obligation

TABLE 16.5 Pearson's Correlation Coefficients—Modeled Dependent Variables

	Fund Balance	Chg Fund Balance	Debt Service	Chg Debt Service	Revenues	Chg. Revenues	Expends	Change Expends	Debt	Chg Debt	Pension Liability	Chg Pension Liability
Fund balance		.085**	–.032	.008	–.165**	.043	–.193**	.041	–.139**	.019	–.005	.025
Chg fund balance	.085**		.007	–.067**	.015	.019	–.026	–.014	.021	–.017	–.010	.026
Debt service	–.032	.007		.297**	.004	.024	.005	.017	.390**	.006	.006	–.038
Chg debt service	.008	–.067**	.297**		–.028	–.045	–.009	–.023	–.060*	.080**	–.016	.023
Revenues	–.165**	.015	.004	–.028		.057*	.951**	.068**	.406**	.098**	.038	.013
Chg. revenues	.043	.019	.024	–.045	.057*		.062*	.926**	.125**	.359**	–.324**	–.024
Expends	–.193**	–.026	.005	–.009	.951**	.062*		.080**	.407**	.123**	.015	.014
Change expends	.041	–.014	.017	–.023	.068**	.926**	.080**		.130**	.379**	–.258**	–.022
Debt	–.139**	.021	.390**	–.060*	.406**	.125**	.407**	.130**		.323**	–.013	–.001
Chg debt	.019	–.017	.006	.080**	.098**	.359**	.123**	.379**	.323**		–.025	–.025
Pension liability	–.005	–.010	.006	–.016	.038	–.324**	.015	–.258**	–.013	–.025		–.009
Chg pension Liability	.025	.026	–.038	.023	.013	–.024	.014	–.022	–.001	–.025	–.009	

Note: * $p < .10$; ** $p < .05$; ** $p < .01$

TABLE 16.6 Relationship between Fiscal Condition and TELs, Demographics, and Management Form

	Own-Source Revs as Pct Property Value		Chg. Own-Source Revs 2003–2005		GF Expends as Pct Property Value		Chg. GF Expends 2003–2005	
TEL Index	–0.013	***	–0.0012		–0.016	***	0.0011	
Demographic Characteristics								
Pct. Population Less 18	–0.00011		–0.000067		–0.002		0.0011	
Per Capita Income	–0.0000079	*	–0.00000034		–0.000011	**	–0.00000067	
Per Capita Taxable Property	–0.00000248	***	–0.00000027		–0.0000030	***	–0.00000014	
Change in Population	0.00024		0.0058	***	–0.00048		0.00623	***
Change in Taxable Property	–0.00031		–0.00437	***	0.00044		–0.00423	***
Management Form								
Council-Manager	–0.035		–0.00052		–0.056		0.0079	
Budget-CAO	–0.00018		0.024		–0.057		0.008	
Budget-CFO	0.476	***	0.034		0.409	**	0.0.86	
Own-Source Revs 2003			–0.5611					
Expends as Pct Value 2003							–2.282	*
Fund Balance 2003								
Debt Service 2003								
GO Debt 2003								
Pension Funding 2003								
N	779		779		779		779	
Adj. R^2	0.102		0.293		0.125		0.212	

Note: * p < .10; ** p < .05; ** p < .01

debt, and unfunded pension liabilities. As hypothesized, the more severe the local TEL, the lower the level of the community's own-source revenues and general fund expenditures. Contrary to our hypothesis, TEL severity is positively associated with the size of a community's unreserved fund balance and the extent to which pension obligations are funded. The relationship between TELs and debt service and overall general-obligation debt is also contrary to our hypothesis. It appears that the stricter a municipality's TEL, the lower its GO debt and debt service. The existence of a statistical relationship between fiscal condition and TELs is much more consistent than that found between fiscal condition and either demographic characteristics or management form.

Management form was found to be related to several dimensions of municipal fiscal condition. Controlling for TELs and demographic composition, council-manager forms of government generally have less GO debt and pay less debt service than communities with other forms of government (principally mayor-council). From the perspective of financial condition analysis, it appears that who has authority over the budget process also matters. Communities with chief administrative officers (CAO) and chief financial officers (CFO) in charge of the budgeting process tend to have larger fund balances, and communities with CAOs grew their reserves at a higher rate between 2003 and 2005. In addition, communities where a CAO manages the budgeting process, GO debt grew at a higher rate between 2003 and 2005. Where a CFO manages the budgeting process, pensions were funded at a higher rate, and the level of pension funding grew at a higher rate between 2003 and 2005; furthermore, own-source revenues and spending were higher than other communities.

Our models also suggest that the demographic composition and change in its composition between 2003 and 2005 are related to fiscal condition. The community's wealth measured as per capita income was positively related to debt service and pension funding and negatively related to own-source revenues and GF expenditures. Community wealth measured as per capita taxable property was also negatively related to own-source revenues and GF expenditures, as well as debt service. The percent change in population and taxable property were positively related to changes in own-source revenues and changes in expenditures, and negatively related to change in GO debt. Change in population was also positively associated with change in debt service, whereas change in taxable property was positively related to change in fund balance.

Conclusion

This was an ambitious project in that we sought to examine the relationship between two complicated concepts in ways not previously done. Most research on both TELs and financial condition tend to be limited to case studies specific to a particular state. Though the case studies provide a rich theoretical base, they limit our ability to examine the effects of different policies across the states. This is particularly troublesome because state and local officials debate recovery strategies from the current economic crisis. Using the work by Amiel, Deller, and Stallmann (2009), we were able to quantify different TELs imposed on most communities throughout the United States. This was supplemented with audited financial data collected by the GFOA providing a unique dataset capable of measuring commonly identified measures of fiscal condition in a cross-sectional manner. The data are not perfect—the communities are self-selected and reflect more professional managed communities than a pure national sample. That being said, the positives of a large national sample of municipalities in nearly every state outweigh the negatives.

This study also revealed a flaw in some studies of financial condition. Several studies (Brown, 1989; Maher and Nollenberger, 2009) have suggested that relative revenues and/or expenditures by themselves reflect fiscal strength/weakness depending on whether a community was low (positive) or high (weak) compared to the comparison group. This, however, assumes that communities have the ability to grow equally while the reality is that TEL affect the extent to which can grow. Given the negative relationships between TEL strength and revenues/expenditures, the results suggest that such comparisons need to done within the context of TEL limits.

Our findings that TEL severity was positively associated with size of undesignated fund balance and the extent to which pension obligations are funded, while also being negatively associated with debt service and overall general-obligation debt challenge the notion that TELs inherently put communities in weaker financial position. It could be that TELs force communities to more effectively manage their resources by building reserves, funding future obligations better, and controlling debt. From the perspective of state policymakers, and perhaps taxpayers, TELs are having the desired effects (limiting spending and revenues) and forcing stronger fiscal management practices. On the other hand, the current economic downturn could very well alter these relationships. As tax bases decline and revenues drop, those communities under more strict TELs will have a more difficult time recovering, which may lead to more rapid drawing down of fund balances, incurring debt, and reducing pension funding. For example, we recently conducted a survey of municipal officials in Wisconsin, and when asked how they were responding to fiscal stress, one anonymous respondent wrote, "Levy limits and maintenance of effort requirements (state law limits municipal spending reductions on protective services) will ultimately deplete our reserves and force reduction/elimination of services." Another wrote, "It's a shame that a government that has been operating within its means for over 20 years is unable to increase property tax rates at times it may be needed" (Maher, Deller, and Kovari, 2011, p.8). Hoene and Pagano's (2010) recent survey of city officials found similar responses. They report:

> To cover budget shortfalls and balance annual budgets, cities are making a variety of personnel cuts, delaying or cancelling infrastructure projects, and cutting basic city services; and, ending balances, or "reserves," while still at high levels, decreased for the second year in a row as cities used these balances to weather the effects of the downturn.

The analysis also reveals that management form is related to local financial condition. Council-manager forms of government generally have less debt than communities with other forms of government, for example, mayor-council. Yet, from the perspective of financial condition analysis, it appears that who has authority over the budget process also matters. Communities with chief administrative officers and chief financial officers in charge of the budgeting process tended to have larger fund balances. Communities with chief financial officers running the budget process also tended to higher own-source revenues and general-fund expenditures and better funded pensions.

This analysis also confirmed the assertion by scholars such as Hendrick (2004) that a composite measure of financial condition is not possible given the different, unrelated dimensions. We found little relationship among each of our measures of financial condition, and those independent variables included in the models had varying effects, depending on the dependent variable.

A final observation about the models is their weak overall explanatory power. None of the models explained more than 20% of the variation in the dependent variable even when change was estimated and 2003 base values were included. This could be a function of two things, one being the self-selection bias associated with this dataset. It might be that there simply is not sufficient variation in the dependent variables to explain given that municipal officials choose to provide GFOA with their financial records to receive an award. Though we are not convinced this is the case (see **Table 16.3**), we cannot rule out the possibility. Another explanation is that over the past 25 years, most scholars have focused their attention on the definition and measurement of fiscal condition with little focus on its explanation. We assumed it could be explained by examining state fiscal limitations, management structure, and demographic attributes. Because of the weak findings, clearly more work needs to done on the development of models that more effectively explain variation in municipal financial condition.

Endnotes

1. For a detailed discussion of the indices used here, see Amiel, Deller and Stallmann (2009). The indices themselves and the data used to construct the indices can be downloaded at: http://www.aae.wisc.edu/pubs/sps/ under staff paper no. 536.
2. See Marlowe (2007) for a discussion of the anticipated size of OPEBs.
3. For additional information on the GFOA Certificate program see: http://www.gfoa.org/index.php?option=com_content&task=view&id=35&Itemid=58
4. Hendrick also argues that enterprise funds be included as a measure of fiscal slack. We analyzed enterprise income relative to general fund revenues per Hendrick (2004) and enterprise assets relative to liabilities per Maher and Nollenberger (2009). In both cases, the models were statistically insignificant.
5. These data were provided by the U.S. Bureau of Census.
6. The F Scores for the listed models had p values < 0.01.

Glossary

Tax and expenditure limitation (TEL): limitations on local spending and/or revenues imposed by state governments.

Advisory Commission on Intergovernmental Relations (ACIR): a national agency created to study federalism in the United States. This agency produced several important documents on government fiscal condition in the 1970s and 1980s.

Fiscal condition: the ability of an organization to meet its current and future fiscal obligations.

Proposition 13: Passed by initiative in 1978, this California law put strict limitations on local governments' abilities to increase property taxes. It is considered the first in a series of "tax revolt" actions aimed at controlling property tax increases.

Fiscal slack: the amount of budgeting "cushion," typically measured in terms of unreserved fund balance relative to general fund revenues.

Discussion Questions

1. What are some of the challenges associated with attempting to measure a government's fiscal condition?
2. How do tax and expenditure limitations (TELs) impact community's fiscal condition? Is it possible for TELs to have both positive and negative effects? Discuss.

Recommended Resources

Advisory Commission on Intergovernmental Relations. (1971). Measuring the fiscal capacity and effort of state and local areas. Washington DC: Government Printing Office.

Advisory Commission on Intergovernmental Relations. (1979). Measuring the fiscal blood pressure of the states: 1964–1975. Washington DC: Government Printing Office.

Advisory Commission on Intergovernmental Relations. (1981). Measuring local discretionary authority. Washington DC: Government Printing Office.

Amiel, L., Deller, S. C., and Stallmann, J. (2009). The construction of a tax and expenditure limitation index for the US. Department of Agricultural and Applied Economics Staff Paper No. 536. May. University of Wisconsin-Madison. Retrieved December 20, 2011from http://www.aae.wisc.edu/pubs/sps/pdf/stpap536.pdf

Brown, K. W. (1989). Ten-point test of financial condition: Toward an easy-to-use assessment tool for small cities. *Government Finance Review*, *9*(6), 21–26.

Clark, T. N., and Ferguson, L. C. (1983). *City money: Political processes, fiscal strain, and retrenchment*. New York: Columbia University Press.

Hendrick, R. (2004). Assessing and measuring the fiscal health of local governments: Focus on Chicago metropolitan suburbs. *Urban Affairs Review*, *40*(1), 78–114.

Hoene, C. W., and Pagano, M. A. (2010, October). City fiscal conditions in 2010. Research Brief on America's Cities. Washington, DC: National League of Cities.

Honadle, B. W., Costa, J., and Cigler, B. (2004). *Fiscal health for local governments: An introduction to concepts, practical analysis and strategies*. New York: Elsevier.

Ladd, H. F., and Yinger, J. (1989). *America's ailing cities: Fiscal health and the design of urban policy*. Baltimore: Johns Hopkins University Press.

Levine, C., and Rubin, I. (1980). *Fiscal stress and public policy*. Beverly Hills, CA: Sage Publications.

Maher, C., and Nollenberger, K. (2009). Revisiting Kenneth Brown's 10-point test. *Government Finance Review, 25*(5), 61–66.

Mullins, D. R. (2004). Tax and expenditure limitation and the fiscal response of local government: Asymmetric intra-local fiscal effects. *Public Budgeting and Finance, Winter*, 111–147.

References

Abrams, B., and Dougan, W. (1986). The effects of constitutional restraints on government spending. *Public Choice*, *49*(2), 101.

Advisory Commission on Intergovernmental Relations. (1971). Measuring the fiscal capacity and effort of state and local areas. Washington, DC: Government Printing Office.

Advisory Commission on Intergovernmental Relations. (1979). Measuring the fiscal blood pressure of the states: 1964–1975. Washington DC: Government Printing Office.

Advisory Commission on Intergovernmental Relations. (1981). Measuring local discretionary authority. Washington DC: Government Printing Office.

Advisory Commission on Intergovernmental Relations. (1988). State fiscal capacity and effort. Washington DC: Government Printing Office.

Advisory Commission on Intergovernmental Relations. (1989). Local revenue diversification: Local sales tax. Washington DC: Government Printing Office.

Amiel, L., Deller. S. C., and Stallmann, J. (2009, May). The construction of a tax and expenditure limitation index for the US. Department of Agricultural and Applied Economics Staff Paper No. 536. University of Wisconsin-Madison. Retrieved on December 20, 2011, from http://www.aae.wisc.edu/pubs/sps/pdf/stpap536.pdf

Ammar, S., Duncombe, W., Hou, Y., Jump, B., and Wright, R. (2001). Using fuzzy rule-based systems to evaluate overall financial performance of governments: An enhancement to the bond rating process. *Public Budgeting & Finance, Winter*, 91–110.

Bails, D. G. (1990). The effectiveness of tax-expenditure limitations: A re-evaluation. *American Journal of Economics and Sociology, 49*(2), 223–238.

Benson, E. D., and Marks, B. R. (2007). Structural deficits and state borrowing costs. *Public Budgeting & Finance, Fall*, 1–19.

Berne, R., and Schramm, R. (1986). *The financial analysis of governments*. Englewood Cliffs, New Jersey: Prentice Hall.

Brown, K. W. (1989). The 10-point test of financial condition: Toward an easy-to-use assessment tool for small cities. *Government Finance Review, 9*(6), 21–26.

Chaney, B. (2005). Analyzing the financial condition of the City of Corona, California: Using a case to teach the GASB 34 government-wide financial statements. *Public Budgeting, Accounting and Financial Management, 17*(2), 181–201.

Clark, T. N., and Ferguson, L. C. (1983). *City money: Political processes, fiscal strain, and retrenchment*. New York: Columbia University Press.

Congressional Budget Office. (1978). City need and the responsiveness of federal grants programs. Washington DC: Government Printing Office.

Cutler, D. M., et al. (1999). Restraining the leviathan: Property tax limitations in Massachusetts. *Journal of Public Economics, 71*,313–327.

Deller, S. C., and Stallmann, J. J. (2007). Tax expenditure limitations and economic growth. *Marquette Law Review, 90*(3), 497–554.

Downs, G. N., and Rocke, D. M. (1984). Theories of budgetary decision-making and revenue decline. *Policy Sciences, 16*, 329–347.

Government Finance Officers Association. Retrieved on February 1, 2010, from http://www.gfoa.org/index.php?option=com_content&task=view&id=937&Itemid=416

Hendrick, R. (2004). Assessing and measuring the fiscal health of local governments: Focus on Chicago metropolitan suburbs. *Urban Affairs Review, 40*(1), 78–114.

Hoene, C. W., and Pagano, M. A. (2010, October). City fiscal conditions in 2010. Research Brief on America's Cities. Washington, DC: National League of Cities.

Holcombe, R. G., and Sobel, R. A. (1997). *Growth and variability in state tax revenue: An anatomy of state fiscal crises*. Westport, CT: Greenwood.

Honadle, B. W., Costa, J., and Cigler, B. (2004). *Fiscal health for local governments: An introduction to concepts, practical analysis and strategies*. New York: Elsevier.

International City/County Managers Association. Retrieved on February 1, 2010, from http://icma.org/main/ns.asp?nsid=4316&hsid=1&ssid1=2505&ssid2=2506&ssid3=2506&scid=1

Johnson, C. L., and Kriz, K. A. (2005). Fiscal institutions, credit ratings, and borrowing costs. *Public Budgeting & Finance, 25*(1), 84–103.

Joyce, P. G., and Mullins, D. R. (1991). The changing fiscal structure of the state and local public. *Public Administration Review, 51*(3), 240–253

Kammholz, C. D., and Maher, C. S. (2008). Does revenue forecasting responsibility matter: The case of Milwaukee, WI. In J. Sun and T. D. Lynch (Eds.), *Government Budget Forecasting: Theory and Practice* (pp. 281–302). Boca Raton, FL: Taylor and Francis.

Kloha, K., Weissert, C. S., and Kleine, R. (2005). Developing and testing a composite model to predict local fiscal disparities. *Public Administration Review, 65*(3), 313–323.

Kornhauser, M. E. (2002). Legitimacy and the right of revolution: The role of tax protests and anti-tax rhetoric in America. *Buffalo Law Review, 50*(3) 819–930.

Ladd, H. F., and Yinger, J. (1989). *America's ailing cities: Fiscal health and the design of urban policy*. Baltimore, MD: Johns Hopkins University Press.

Levine, C. H. (1980). More on cutback management: Hard questions for hard times. In C. H. Levine (Ed.), *Managing fiscal stress: The crisis in the public sector* (pp.1–19). Chatham, NJ: Chatham House.

Levine, C., and Rubin, I. (1980). *Fiscal stress and public policy*. Beverly Hills, CA: Sage Publications.

Levine, C. H., Rubin, I. S., and Wolohojian, G. G. (1981). Resource scarcity and the reform model: The management retrenchment in Cincinnati and Oakland. *Public Administration Review, 41*(6): 619–628.

Lowery, D. (1983) . Limitations on taxing and spending powers: An assessment of their effectiveness. *Social Science Quarterly, 64*(2), 247–263.

Lowry, R. C., and Alt, J. E. (2001). A visible hand? Bond markets, political parties, balanced budget laws, and state government debt. *Economics and Politics, 13*(1), 49–72.

Maher, C., and Deller, S. (2011). Measuring municipal fiscal condition: Do objective measures of fiscal health relate to subjective measures? *Public Budgeting, Accounting and Financial Management, 23*(3) 427–451.

Maher, C., Deller, S., and Kovari, J. (2011). "How stressed are Wisconsin cities and villages?" Agriculture and Applied Economics Staff Paper No. 557. Madison, WI.

Maher, C., and Nollenberger, K. (2009). Revisiting Kenneth Brown's 10-point test. *Government Finance Review, 25*(5) 61–66.

Marlow, J., (2007). Much ado about nothing? The size and credit quality implications of municipal other postemployment benefit liabilities. *Public Budgeting and Finance, 27*(2) 104–131.

Mason, K. C. (2005). Panel's report: Tax limitations jeopardize state's economic future. *State Tax Notes*, Aug. 15, 487–488

McGuire, T. J., and Rueben, K. S. (2006). The Colorado revenue limit: The economic effects of TABOR. *State Tax Notes, 40*(May), 459–472.

Miller G. J., and Svara, J. H. (2009, January). Navigating the fiscal crisis: Testing strategies for local leaders. A White Paper from the Alliance for Innovation Commissioned by the International City/County Managers Association.

Mullins, D. R. (2004). Tax and expenditure limitation and the fiscal response of local government: Asymmetric intra-local fiscal effects. *Public Budgeting and Finance, Winter*, 111–147.

Mullins, D., and Joyce, P. (1996). Tax and expenditure limitations and state and local fiscal structure: An empirical assessment. *Public Budgeting and Finance, 16*(1), 75–101.

Mullins, D. R., and Wallin, B. A. (2004) Tax and expenditure ;imitations: Introduction and overview. *Public Budgeting and Finance, Winter*, 2–15.

National Conference of State Legislatures. (2005). Retrieved on December 20, 2011, from http://www.ncsl.org/programs/fiscal/tels2005.htm

National League of Cities. Retrieved February 1, 2010, fromhttp://www.nntp.nlc.org/about_cities/cities_101/149.aspx

Nollenberger, K. (2004). *Evaluating Financial Condition*. Washington, DC: International City/County Managers Association.

Pagano, M. A. (2002). Municipal capital spending during the boom, *Public Budgeting and Finance, 22*(2), 1–20.

Pagano, M. A., and Johnston, J. M. (2000). Life at the bottom of the fiscal food chain: Examining city and county revenue decision. *Publius: The Journal of Federalism, 30(Winter/Spring)*, 159–170.

Pammer, W. J. (1990). *Managing fiscal strain in major American cities: Understanding retrenchment in the public sector*. New York: Greenwood Press.

Poterba, J. M. (1994). State responses to fiscal crisis: The effects of budgetary institutions and politics. *Journal of Political Economy, 102*(4), 799–821.

Poterba, J. M., and Rueben, K. S. (1999). State fiscal institutions and the US municipal bond market. In J. Poterba and J. von Hagen (Eds.), *Fiscal institutions and fiscal performance* (pp. 181–207). Chicago: University of Chicago Press.

Poulson, B.. (2005, June). Grading the states' tax and expenditure limits: A fiscal discipline report card. Americans for Prosperity Foundation, p. 15. Retrieved on December 20, 2011, from http://www.americansforprosperity.org/includes/filemanager/files/pdf/afp_telrank_0705.pdf

Rubin, I. S. (1982). *Running in red: The political dynamics of urban fiscal stress*. Albany: State University of New York Press.

Shadbegian, R. J. (1998). Do tax and expenditure limitations affect local government budgets? Evidence from panel data. *Public Finance Review, 26*(2), 218–236.

Shadbegian, R. J. (1999). The effect of tax and expenditure limitations on the revenue structure of local governments, 1962–1987. *National Tax Journal, 52*(2), 221–237.

Skidmore, M. (1999). Tax and expenditure limitations and the fiscal relationships between state and local governments. *Public Choice, 99*(1–2), 77–102.

Stallmann, J. I., and Deller, S. C. (2010). Impact of tax and expenditure limitations on economic growth. *Applied Economic Letters, 17*(7), 645–648.

U.S. Department of Treasury, Office of State and Local Finance. (1978). Report on the fiscal impact of the economic stimulus package on 48 large urban governments. Washington DC: Government Printing Office.

Wagner, G. A. (2004). The bond market and fiscal institutions: Have budget stabilization funds reduced state borrowing costs? *National Tax Journal, 57*(4), 785–804.

Wang, X., Dennis, L., and Tu, Y. (2007). Measuring financial condition: A study of U.S. states. *Public Budgeting and Finance, Summer*, 1–21.

Ward, J. D. (2001). Responding to fiscal stress: A state-wide survey of local governments in Louisiana, a research note. *International Journal of Public Administration, 24*(6), 565–571.

Chapter 17

The Defragmentation of Authority

A Consolidation Approach to Public Service Delivery[1]

by Helisse Levine

Introduction

As an increasing number of local governments combat the fiscal challenges brought on by the economic and financial crisis of 2007–2008, consolidation of public services remains a highly debated solution to bring cost savings and efficiencies to both taxpayers and governments. Particularly, as local government fiscal health continues to decline and policymakers look for ways to cut costs and reduce financial stress, school consolidation is increasingly becoming a viable recourse to other measures, including increasing already soaring tax burdens, cutting vital teaching expenditures, drawing down fund balances to finance current spending, and/or deferring maintenance. Consolidation of government involves making government smaller by reducing the number of layers by sharing services such as highway departments, fire departments, school districts, sewer districts, and special districts; in other words, to reduce costs and promote efficiency in services through administrative efficacies achieved by eliminating waste and duplication. Proponents of consolidation (e.g., Hawkins, Ward, and Becker, 1991; Pierce, 1993; Rusk, 1993) argue that substantial economic benefits result from fewer, larger government entities, including economies of scale, economies of scope, greater government capacity and lower administrative costs that offset what others (e.g., Bish and Ostrom, 1973; Coulson, 2007; Fischel, 2001; Gramlich, 1993; Murray and Groen, 2004; Tiebout, 1956) believe are increased costs because of reduced competition by limiting choices.

Most recently, a longitudinal study of a consolidation effort in an urban school district in Tennessee by Cox and Cox (2010) found that "the district's expenditures increased substantially in every line item" (p. 89). Notably, several additional studies, including those by Scorsone (2010), Leland and Thurmaier (2005), Andrews, Duncombe, and Yinger (2002), caution that consolidation does not reduce cost savings across all jurisdictions and needs to be considered on a case-by-case basis. Notwithstanding that, cost savings as a result of economies of scale may result from consolidation across smaller-sized districts, Buchanan's (1971) seminal work reminds us that local control in the form of school board composition must also be weighed against the economic differences in citizen demand for and value placed on those "public" goods. Furthermore, attempts to maintain local control may also imply much more than loss of political influence and power on certain community members. As Ward and Risk (1992) explain: "Local control can also be a euphemistic stalling device to maintain and prolong exclusionary policies and discrimination against certain groups" (p. 18).

The purpose of this chapter is to examine school district consolidation as one area of the consolidation debate that has stimulated recent attention (Scorsone, 2010). Despite the "one shot" infusion of Recovery Act funding for education programs, currently, the sustained, statewide economic decline is directly linked to financial challenges being felt by local school districts across the state (Coulson, 2007; GAO, 2009). Using a simulation model, we ascertain whether the consolidation of Nassau County's 56 school districts will reduce administrative costs and, as a result, lower the property taxes of the homeowners residing in the County. Although simulation models have been used in pedagogy literature (Hildebrand, 2008; Milam, 2003; Proksch, Ross, and Estness, 2002), Frank, Christian, and Scutelnicu (2009) point out the lack of simulation and role-playing methods in informing the field of public administration.

Arguably, increased foreclosures and decreased home values continue to create cash flow problems for localities as property taxes go unpaid, creating a hardship for school districts that rely on those taxes to serve our children's educational needs. Also, budget problems at the state level have reduced state aid to schools at the same time that millage restrictions and assessment caps for some states have made it difficult for school districts to pick up the shortfall with their primary local revenue source, the property tax (Ulbrich, Saltzman, and Watt, 2009). For others, the increasing amount of property taxes and whether those taxes have become so high that the taxpayers can no longer afford to pay the school taxes the school district imposes have become a growing concern. Important consolidation literature by Duncombe and Yinger in 2001 and 2007 suggests that school district consolidation may lower the property tax burden by lowering costs per pupil and improving efficiency in the delivery of education services. It is hypothesized that eliminating excessive administrative staff and reintegrating school district student population into 10 districts will have a positive financial effect on the taxpayers of Nassau County, New York.

In the next section of this chapter, prior literature and models of school consolidation are discussed. Next, correlations that measure relationships between (1) the district school tax rate and district wealth and (2) average tax amount and district wealth are discussed. Then, using data retrieved from (1) The New York State Department of Education website, (2) Nassau County school district budgets, (3) Empire Center for New York Policy, and (4) FOIL requests from school district officials, a consolidation model is developed. A discussion of the simulation results and prospective areas for future study conclude.[2]

Background and Literature Review

School consolidation is the practice of combining two or more school districts for educational or economic benefits. The main argument for consolidation suggests that a company that achieves economies of scale lowers the average cost per unit through increased production because fixed costs are shared over an increased number of goods. Or in the present situation, as more school districts share the cost of the centralized administration, cost per household and/or school expenditures will decline. Therefore, consolidated school district can offer an expanded curriculum and a more prominent identity in the community while reducing costs through economies of scale. Benefits include additional state funding toward capital projects (Hu and Yinger, 2008), greater diversity in course offerings, increased variety in extracurricular activities, and reduced administrative and operations costs (Plucker, Spradlin, Magaro, Chien, and Zapf, 2007; Strange and Malhoit, 2005). On the other hand, consolidation can incur numerous liabilities, especially if the schools to be closed are the sole providers of community services. Although models of consolidation are based primarily on an economic model of efficiency in production, there is more to the consolidation issue than just finances. For example, a major force in the opposition to consolidation, as Ward and Rink (1992) identify, rests heavily on whether the local stakeholders (e.g., school board members) are willing to give up local control. Similarly, Hu and Yinger (2008) suggest that studies of consolidation must consider the values voters place on loss of control or on the extra time they and their children spend on getting to school. Buchanan (1971) argues that increasing the fiscal capacity of local governments through decentralization may result in more inefficiencies if "potentially—mobile central—city taxpayers who contribute to net fiscal surplus are not deliberately induced to remain in the sharing community by appropriate fiscal adjustments" (p. 1).

Between 1930 and 1970, 9 out of every 10 school districts in the United States were eliminated through consolidation (Berry, 2006/2007). Berry and West (2008) add that consolidation of schools was part of a larger effort to professionalize education that began in the late 19th century, characteristic of progressive reformers' principles to remove corruption and political machinery. "To the 'administrative progressives' of the day" they argue, "the concentration of authority over schools in the hands of professional educators seemed a cure for both the corruption of city school systems and the parochialism of rural ones" (p. 2). Strang (1987) adds that consolidation puts a formal organization in place that replaces local politics.

Although the rate of consolidation has slowed over the past decades, Duncombe and Yinger (2001) remind us that at least a few districts continue to consolidate every year in many states. For example, in a study of rural school districts in New York State, Duncombe and Yinger (2001) concluded that although instructional, operating, administrative, and transportation expenditures declined post consolidation, spending on capital actually increased. Also noted was the savings variance across district size; a 22% savings in smaller school districts versus only 8% in larger districts. Similarly, using New York State data, Duncombe and Yinger (2007) found that consolidation leads to large cost savings for small rural school districts. On the benefit side, school consolidation literature including Duncombe and Yinger (2001, 2010) identify indivisibilities, increased dimension, specialization, price benefits of scale, and learning and innovation as the five reasons supporting consolidation, whereas potential costs include higher transportation costs, labor relations effects, lower staff motivation and effort, and lower parental involvement.

The State of New Jersey Special Session Joint Legislative Committee on Government Consolidation and Shared Services issued a Final Report on December 1, 2006. One of those who gave testimony before the committee was the former Executive Director of the Center for Government Services at Rutgers University, Professor Ernest Reock, who proposed a plan for the consolidation of school districts. The proposal recommended that the high schools be converted into major regional high schools and to eliminate elementary districts. The proposal further recommended that there would be new school districts, even though the elementary schools would serve the same children and remain the same. Without providing any data, he stated that by reducing the current amount of school districts in half there would be "[a] savings of approximately $365 million per year, including administrative costs; the stabilization of district property tax bases; equalization in tax rates; and better integration of curriculum for students." Others who gave testimony argued against school consolidation, claiming that it would "diminish a parent's ability to affect educational decision-making at the local level." Still others who testified blamed the rising school taxes on the underfunding of districts by the state.

When it came time for the committee to make their recommendations, they compared data between the State of Maryland and the State of New Jersey. Maryland operated on a county-based school system while New Jersey has 616 individual school districts. The costs of the New Jersey education were higher. However, the commission noted that New Jersey ranks higher than Maryland, that New Jersey has smaller class sizes and is wealthier. The committee does not want to "disrupt the academic progress of New Jersey students." They recommended a pilot program of one county school board to administer a county school district. We have found no evidence that this pilot program was ever instituted. Finally, when it came to the high salaries of the superintendents of school systems, the recommended solution was to create a super superintendent on the county level to oversee all of the individual school superintendents. The governor would appoint this super administrator who would have broad authority to eliminate administrative waste and overhead, including direct authority over approval of local school budgets. There appears to be no indication that this recommendation was ever instituted.

According to the Citizens Research Council of Michigan's (CRCM) 1990 report, it appears that the State of Michigan does not have the same legal impediments to consolidation as the State of New York in the case of *East Jackson School v. State of Michigan* suggests:

> School districts and other municipal corporations are creations of the state. Except as provided by the state, they have no existence, no functions, no rights, no powers. They are given no power, nor can any be implied, to defy their creator over the terms of their existence. (133 Mich App at 139 as cited in CRCM, 1990)

The New York State Commission on Property Tax Relief issued a preliminary report on June 3, 2008. One of the report's proposals was to give the Commissioner of Education discretionary authority to order consolidation of school districts. The authority would be triggered by standards that include the size of the student population, declining enrollment, limited educational programs, ability to achieve fiscal savings, and high tax burden. For the consolidation to take place there would have to be approval of the Board of Regents and, of course, a public hearing in the affected school districts.

Another model of consolidation that was proposed and is currently implemented in the State of Maine during the 2008 school calendar consisted of reorganization regionalization and collaboration of the 290 Maine School districts into 26 school districts designated as Regional Learning Communities with 26 Superintendents and 26 Regional School Communities. The consolidation that the Maine School Superintendents Association supported believed that Maine schools must work together and use technology to provide a broad curriculum while maintaining efficient, cost effective operations. The school system should be reorganized into school administrative units to form more efficient and effective administrative organization and result in a decrease in the number of decision-making bodies.

Nassau County School Districts

A board controls each school district in New York. The rules and requirements of School Boards are set by Title 2 of the Education Law, Sections 1501 through 2613. Common School Districts are governed by Article 33, Union Free Districts are governed by Article 35, Central School Districts are governed by Article 37, and Central High School Districts are governed by Article 39. One of the most important duties of the board is to set the budget for the district. The board must reasonably estimate the expenditures necessary to run the school district (EDU§1608(1)). Then the Board of Education must present at public hearing a proposed budget. The law further provides that the budget must be in three separate parts, Programmatic, Capital Expenditures, and Administrative Expenses (EDU §(4)). The Board of Education must attach to the proposed budget the salaries, benefits, and any other compensation payable to any administrator who earns more than $85,000.00. However, the Commissioner of Education can increase that sum; and at the present time, the salary sunshine requirement has been raised from $85,000.00 to those administrators earning more than $97,000.00 (EDU §1608(5)). The board must also attach to the budget the New York State Board of Education Report Card (EDU §1608(5)). In addition, a public hearing must be held on the budget. The hearing must be no more than 14 days and no less than 7 days before the annual meeting. (EDU §1608(1)). The annual meeting and election must be held on the third Tuesday in May unless there is religious holiday that conflicts with that date. Notice of Date, Time, and Place of the public hearing and annual meeting must be published at least four times in the seven weeks prior to the hearing.

The Board of Education must make the proposed budget available for public review at least seven days prior to the budget hearing. After the date of the budget hearing and at least six days prior to the date of the budget vote, the school budget must be mailed to all qualified voters in the school district (EDU §(2)). The budget then must be presented to the voters for their approval.

A budget can only be voted on twice. Besides the recommended budget, the school board must also notify the community of the proposed contingency budget so that the community will be aware of what may occur if the school budget is voted down. If the voters do not approve a budget after two votes, the board must adopt a contingency budget. To pay for the budget, the school boards have the authority to levy taxes after the voters have approved the budget or the board adopted the contingency budget.[3] The budget is computed by the actual amount the school board requires, less expected state aid and miscellaneous revenues and balances. The balance is the amount that must be obtained by Real Property Taxes for Schools and Anticipated State School Tax Relief Program (STAR) Reimbursements.[4]

The property tax is the largest revenue source local governments use to finance education services. According to Thomas R. Suozzi (2008), former Nassau County Executive, approximately 64.2% of all property tax dollars in Nassau County in 2008 were spent on education. Given the national property tax median of $1,838 (U.S. Census Fast Facts, 2008), Nassau County has one of the highest property tax medians paid by residents in the country ($8,153), next only to Westchester County, New York ($8,422) and Hunterdon County in New Jersey ($8,244). In Nassau County, property taxes are distributed among different classes of property. In Nassau County, there are four classes of property, each with its own tax rate: Class 1 is for single-family homes; Class 2 is for apartments and condominiums; Class 3 is for utility company properties; and Class 4 is for commercial properties such as factories, offices, and stores. Each year, the county determines how much of the overall tax burden property owners in each of the four classes will pay. These tax burdens represent the proportion of the total *tax levy* property owners in each of the four classes paid.[5]

One of the reasons for disparity in the tax payments is because of the difference in assessments between properties in the wealthy and poorer areas. School taxes are not based on the income of its citizens but on the property values of the households within each school district. According the Office of Real Property Services of the State of New York (2008), the "real property tax is a tax based on the value of real property" (p. 2). All municipalities of the state raise the money that they need for police, fire protection, roads, and other municipal services via the property tax. The amount of the tax is based upon the *assessed value* of the property and the tax rate the municipal jurisdiction imposes. The tax assessor, who either the citizens or the governing board of the municipality elects, determines the assessment, and the assessment is based on the market value of the property. It must also be noted that although New York State law provides that all property in a municipality be assessed at the same uniform percentage of value, class assessing is authorized in Nassau County and NYC. On Election Day, 2008, the voters of Nassau County passed a referendum to make the assessor an appointed position rather than an elected position.

Assessed valuation is calculated by multiplying the stated market value of the property by the assessed valuation rate (which in 2006/2007 was ¼ of 1%, or .0025), multiplied by the tax rate per hundred. Taking the Baldwin district as an example, with a tax rate of 659.872%, the calculation of the school tax would be as follows:[6]

Market Value of Average House in Nassau	$458,500.00
	.0025
Assessed valuation rate of .0025	1,146.25
Baldwin rate 659.872%	6.59872
School tax	$7,563.78

As a result, wealthier, property-rich localities have the ability to collect more in property taxes. Having more resources to draw from enables the district to keep tax rates low while still providing adequate funding to their local school districts. However, poorer communities with less of a property tax base may have higher tax rates but still raise less funding to support the local school district. This can often mean that children that live in low-income communities with the highest needs go to schools with the least resources, the least qualified teachers, and substandard school facilities. A study by the Nelson A. Rockefeller Institute of Government reported that districts in New York State with higher incomes tended to have lower *effective tax rates* while those with higher poverty rates had higher tax burdens (Ward and Dadayan, 2009). The study concludes that according to the Census Bureau's American Community Survey (ACS) data, median property taxes as a proportion of household income were highest on Long Island, at 7.2% compared to a statewide average of 4.6%. The ACS data confirm the picture of a somewhat regressive property tax distribution, with lower income households paying a relatively higher level of income in property taxes than higher income households. Such is the case in Nassau County, where the four school districts that fall below the average district wealth have the highest school tax rates and pay the highest school taxes (Renwick, 2008).

According to the Nassau County Assessment Office, Real Property Class One assessments for tax year 2008/09 run from a low of 342.248% for the District of Lawrence to a high of 734.812% for the District of Levittown. Lawrence has the lowest tax rate yet it is one of the wealthiest school districts in Nassau County having a *Combined Wealth Ratio* (CWR)[7] of 3.093. In Nassau County, four school districts fall below the average district wealth—Hempstead, Roosevelt, Freeport, and Elmont. These same school districts have some of the highest school tax rates and pay some of the highest school taxes (BOCES, 2008).

Figures 17.1 and **17.2** show scatterplots of the correlations between (1) average tax dollars paid by residents in Nassau County by school district and Combined Wealth Ratio (CWR) and (2) average tax rates and CWR. The scatterplot indicates a high degree and negative correlation (-.73) between the two variables. Two things determine the amount of a particular property's tax bill: the property's taxable assessment and the tax rates of the taxing jurisdictions in which the property is located.

The scatterplot in Figure 17.2 shows a high degree of negative correlations between the CWR and Tax Rate Variables (-.63). The tax rates range from 327.188% (3.27188) for Valley Stream Central School District to 820.33% (8.20383) for Massapequa.

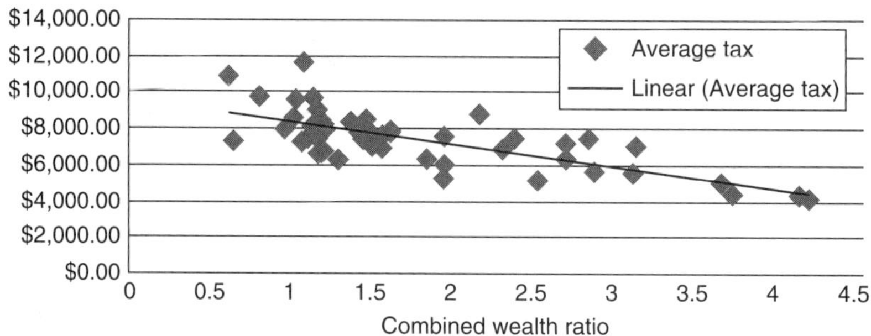

Figure 17.1 School District Average Tax Dollars and Combined Wealth Ratio.

Note: The mean tax dollars is on the y-axis, while the mean CWR score is on the x-axis. The line between the points is the regression of mean tax dollars and CWR variables.

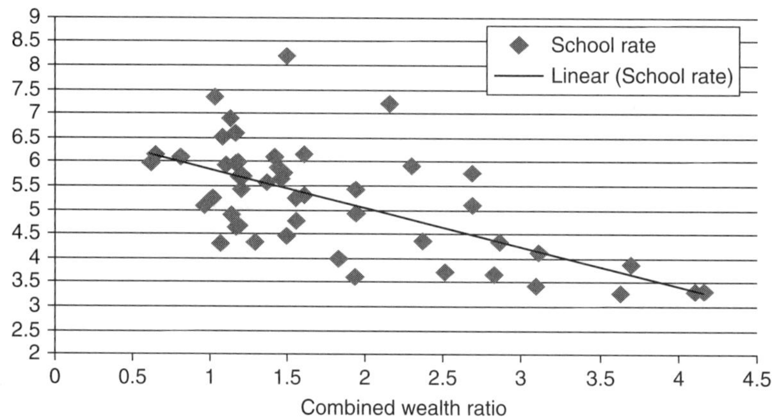

Figure 17.2 School District Average Tax Rate and Combined Wealth Ratio.

Note: The mean property tax rate (per thousand) is on the y-axis, while the CWR score is on the x-axis. The line between the points is the regression of property tax rate and CWR variables.

The charts show that that the percentage of the school tax and the amount of property taxes appear to have negative and strong correlations with the CWR of the school district. Houses valued for the same amount, here using the Nassau average of $458,500.00, pay a widely differing amount of school taxes. In fact, the richest school district, Oyster Bay East

Norwich, would pay school taxes of $4,196.27 for a house valued at $458,500.00 whereas the poorest school district, Hempstead, would pay school taxes of $10,926.06 for a house valued at $458,500.00 or 260% more in taxes.

A Consolidation Simulation Model

The simulated reorganization of the 56 Nassau School Districts that follows is based on a model similar to the one the State of Maine implemented, which reduced 290 school districts and 152 superintendents into 26 school districts to reduce the administrative personnel expenses. The New York State Department of Education provided the Comprehensive Information Report Card for each school district. We examined the school report cards to get the District Wide Total Expenditures per Pupil for the 2006/2007 school year. The Empire Center for New York Policy lists the projected enrollment, budgeted spending, School Property Tax Levy, Budgeting Spending per pupil, and Property Tax Levy per pupil for the 2008-2009 school years. Budgetary data were obtained from each of the 56 individual Nassau County School District websites, and FOIL requests to obtain Central Administrative staff salaries.

First, the total superintendents were reduced from 56 to 1 countywide elected or appointed superintendent, operating from a centralized county office. This office is assisted by (1) Curriculum, (2) Budget, (3) Human Resources, and (4) Community Services managers. The office also oversees 10 assistant superintendents who will each manage the newly formed school districts. The school districts are merged to average approximately 22,000 students per school district. The number of teachers and school facilities were not reduced nor were students relocated as a result of consolidation–only school administrative positions were eliminated. Within each town, we looked at the geographical proximately of neighboring school districts, the racial makeup percentage, and the student population within each district. Geography and racial population guided the consolidation of the 56 school districts into 10 new school districts as shown in **Figure 17.3**.[8]

Next, we developed an administrative tax savings formula by first calculating administrative costs of the 56 school districts before and after consolidation. Preconsolidation costs for the 56 districts including salaries of all Superintendents; Deputy Superintendents; Deputy Superintendents for Business, Curriculum, and Human Resources; Administrative Assistants; and Secretaries amounted to nearly $52.0 million in addition to $90.0 million in fringe benefits, for a total of $143.0 million. Additional fringe benefit costs were based on the average fringe benefit expense incurred in the East Williston (20.4%), Oceanside (16.9%), and East Rockaway (16.4%) school districts.[9] We assumed an average administrative fringe of 17.9% for the consolidation model.

Prior to consolidation, Nassau County administrative office salaries and fringe benefits total $142,889,399 of the aggregate $4,712,000,632 operating school budgets. If every single administrator and his or her staff were eliminated, the maximum savings that could be realized would be $142,899,319. All administrators cannot be eliminated because someone must be accountable for the duties. Therefore, the consolidation of the

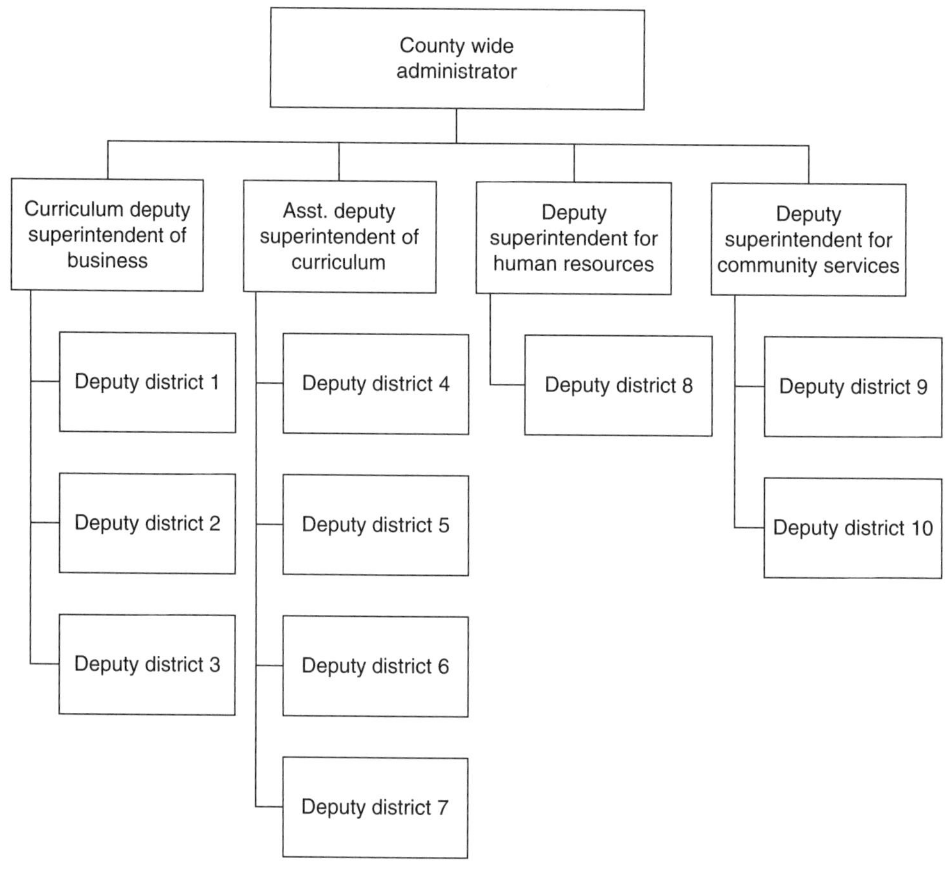

Figure 17.3 A Consolidation Model

56 school districts into 10 new school districts was based on geographic boundaries and the racial population of the students within the school. Adding the total administrative personnel and fringe benefits, we obtained the Old Administrative Costs for each of the 56 districts, which were distributed across the newly formed 10 consolidated districts. We then calculated the administrative costs for the newly formed consolidated districts. Because all districts would share equally in funding the Countywide Administrative Office, to arrive at the administrative savings per district, we subtracted the sum of (1) the New District Share of Countywide Office ($257,646) and (2) the New Administrative costs per District Consolidation from the Old Administrative Costs per new school district consolidation. The total savings for all the school districts, as illustrated in **Figure 17.4**, is $112,910,583. As shown in Appendix B, using the Nassau County Real Estate Tax average, there would be a Real Estate Tax Savings of 2.4% per homeowner.[10]

	Old Administrative Costs Per New School District Consolidation	New Administrative Costs Per New School District Consolidation	New District Share of Countywide Office	Savings Per District
District 1	$12,642,037	$1,806,005	$257,647	$10,578,385
District 2	9,476,082	1,895,216	257,647	5,685,649
District 3	13,274,197	2,654,839	257,647	10,361,711
District 4	18,556,519	3,092,753	257,647	15,206,119
District 5	13,630,115	2,271,686	257,647	11,100,782
District 6	13,337,158	2,222,860	257,647	10,856,651
District 7	18,143,531	2,591,933	257,647	15,293,951
District 8	13,654,252	3,413,563	257,647	9,983,042
District 9	14,047,286	3,511,821	257,647	10,277,817
District 10	16,128,144	2,304,021	257,647	13,566,476
Totals	$142,889,320	$25,764,698	$2,576,470	$112,910,583

New District Number	Number Students	Savings Per Student
1	17,745	$596.130
2	18,193	312.520
3	20,321	509.900
4	29,146	210.720
5	20,390	544.420
6	17,068	636.080
7	24,462	625.210
8	23,362	427.320
9	17,137	599.740
10	18,819	720.890

Figure 17.4 Savings from Consolidation

Conclusion

Local school districts across the country are feeling fiscal challenges because revenue streams that support our children's educational needs are decreasing as a result of the financial crisis of 2008. From the residents' side, in many localities, property taxes have increased to where it is becoming cost prohibitive to live. According to economist Charles Tiebout (1956), citizens look at the services that government offers and the taxes required to obtain those services and then move from one locale to the other based on the cost of the goods offered. In the situation of Nassau County, increasingly more citizens are finding the costs too high and are voting with their feet by moving off the island. It is hopeful that the legislators of Nassau County and the citizens of the various school districts will realize that there is an alternative to the skyrocketing real estate taxes that plague every homeowner in Nassau County.

The school tax problem affects each and every person who resides in the school district. The Nassau County homeowner is affected because their property taxes have increased to such an amount that it is impossible for a middle-income person to afford to pay their real estate taxes and utility costs. Once the cost of a mortgage is added, homeownership in Nassau County becomes the impossible dream. Those who bought their homes when prices were low and taxes were low now find themselves unable to afford the skyrocketing property taxes. The renter is also affected because the high cost of the real estate taxes is calculated in the cost of the rent, which makes affordable housing no longer an option. The school tax problem affects the business owner because the high cost of real estate taxes are factored into the rent or the monthly overhead expenses of the business, a cost that will ultimately be passed to the consumer.

Consolidation of public services has been offered as one solution to what has become a mounting and troublesome situation. The purpose of this chapter was to examine whether the consolidation of school districts in Nassau County would reduce administrative costs and lower the property taxes of the homeowners of Nassau County. A consolidation model of Nassau County's 56 school districts was developed, simulating the consolidation efforts the State of Maine implemented. Results illustrated that consolidating the 56 school districts into 10 school districts with one countywide administrator can save taxpayers nearly $113 million. It was also determined that a negative and strong correlation exists between both the district school tax rate and tax amount and the wealth of the district.

However, several limitations exist in this study. This simulation did not capture other than personal services (OTPS) costs of the central administration of the school districts such as transportation, supplies, equipment, and professional development. Nor did the simulation address academic performance although such an analysis would be a significant factor in a consolidation study going forward. An empirical design that considers generalizability to other jurisdictions would also add value to the school consolidation issue. It is important that future work in this area takes into account the implications of changes in managerial scope. In other words, framing the consolidation debate within a local control versus a consolidated political/management structure.

As public administrators, we must use methods that will lead us to manage agency programs wisely. As protectors of the public's funds, we must search for ways to alleviate the tax burden on citizens. This truly is a time where doing more with less is essential. By using consolidation models, the government will be able to assess whether centralization of school district operations will be beneficial during times of economic stress. Government administrators are in search of alternatives to resolve the economic crisis. Consolidation may be one consideration that is crucial to lowering property taxes and maintaining the stability and well-being of local governments and the residents who reside in them.

Endnotes

1. The author wishes to thank Jennifer Hernandez, Nathalie Montas-Pitts, and Wayne Miller for their contributions to this study.
2. For a comprehensive review of city-county literature, see Staley, S. R., Faulk, D., Leland, S. M., and Schansberg, D. E. (2005). The effects of city-county consolidation: A review of the recent academic literature. *Indiana Policy Review Foundation*, http://www.in.gov/legislative/interim/committee/2005/committees/prelim/MCCC02.pdf ; See also Leland, S., and Thurmaier, K. (2004). *Case studies in city-county consolidation: Reshaping the local government landscape.* New York: M.E. Sharpe Publishing. For an overview of school finance on Long Island, see Renwick, T. (2009). School finance on Long Island: An analysis of state and local funding patterns. *Long Island Index* (September 2008), http://longislandindex.org/fileadmin/pdf/2009_Index_Files/School_Finance_on_Long_Island_by_FPI.pdf
3. By law, the board cannot operate in a deficit. Education Law Section 1718 specifically states: "no board of education shall incur a district liability in excess of the amount appropriated by district meeting unless such board is specifically authorized to incur such liability."
4. STAR is the New York State School Tax Relief Program that grants an exemption from school property taxes for those residents who own and live in a one-, two- or three-family residence, mobile home, farm home, condominium, or cooperative apartment.
5. Base proportions play a major role in determining tax rates, though the school district has no role in calculating these proportions. Instead, the New York State Office of Real Property Tax Services and the Nassau County Assessor and Legislature determines them. For example, if Class 1 homeowners (who comprise the majority of property owners in most school districts) pay 75% of the total tax levy, the base proportion for Class 1 is .75. In that case, the tax rates in Class 1 will be 75% of the total tax levy, divided by the total assessed value of all properties in Class 1.
6. In other words, the tax rate for homeowners in Baldwin is $659.872 for each $100 of assessed value. So the school tax bill for the average homeowner is: $1,146.25 (assessed valuation) x $659.872 (tax rate)/100 = $7,563.78 (property tax). The effective tax rate is the tax levied as a proportion of property values). For a more in-depth discussion see http://www.orps.state.ny.us/pamphlet/taxworks.htm
7. The Combined Wealth Ratio, or CWR, is one measure of relative wealth, indexed against the statewide average (1.0) on property wealth per pupil and income wealth per pupil that the New York State Education Department (SED) uses to fund education
8. See Appendix A for Consolidated School Districts in Nassau County.

9. Fringe benefits include New York State Teachers Retirement, Social Security, Worker's Compensation, Life Insurance, Unemployment and Disability Insurance, Medical Insurance Opt Out, Health Insurance Administration/Dental, and Union Welfare Benefits.
10. See Appendix B for tax savings per "preconsolidation" school district

Glossary

Assessed value: taxable value of a property. In Nassau County, the assessed value of a home is 1/4 percent (.0025) of the market value, as determined by the county assessor's office, expressed as a dollar value.

Combined Wealth Ratio: measure of relative wealth, indexed against the statewide average (1.0) on property wealth per pupil and income wealth per pupil used by the New York State Education Department (SED) to fund education.

Economics to scale: the average cost of production decreases as output increases because fixed costs are shared over an increased number of goods.

Effective tax rate: used to calculate how much property owners pay in taxes.

Property class: different types of properties that are taxed at different rates. There are four property classes in Nassau County: Class 1 is for single-family homes; Class 2 is for apartments and condominiums; Class 3 is for utility company properties; and Class 4 is for commercial properties such as factories, offices, and stores.

Tax levy: the total amount of property taxes raised (or "levied") annually by the board of education.

Discussion Questions

1. Examine the structure of your City's public school system. To what degree has consolidation efforts been advanced? What are the greatest obstacles, if any, deterring these efforts?
2. What are the most significant benefits and costs of school district consolidation?
3. Most would agree that consolidation of government units is intended to improve the efficiency of providing governmental services to residents. However, not all would agree that consolidation actually produces efficient outcomes. Please discuss.

Recommended Resources

Buchanan, J. M. (1971). Principles of urban fiscal strategy. *Public Choice, 11*(Fall), 1–16.

Staley, S. R., Faulk, D., Leland, S. M., and Schansberg, D. E. (2005). The effects of city-county consolidation: A review of the recent academic literature.

Indiana Policy Review Foundation, http://www.in.gov/legislative/interim/committee/2005/committees/prelim/MCCC02.pdf

Leland, S., and Thurmaier, K. (2004). *Case studies in city-county consolidation: Reshaping the local government landscape*. New York: M.E. Sharpe Publishing.

References

Andrews, M., Duncombe, W., and Yinger, J. (2002). Revisiting economies of size in education: Are we any closer to a consensus? *Economics of Education Review*, *21*, 245–262.

Berry, C. (2006/2007). School consolidation and inequality, *Brookings Papers on Education Policy*, 49–75.

Berry, C., and West, M. R. (2010). Growing pains: The school consolidation movement and student outcomes. *Journal of Law, Economics, and Organization*, *26*(1): 1–29. [First published online August 28, 2008, at doi:10.1093/jleo/ewn015

Bish, R., and Ostrom, V. (1973). *Understanding urban government: Metropolitan reform reconsidered*. Washington DC: The American Enterprise Institute for Public Policy Research.

Buchanan, J. M. (1971). Principles of urban fiscal strategy. *Public Choice*, *11*(Fall), 1–16.

The Charter of Greater New York, 1897, New York State Laws of 1897, Chapter 378. Retrieved October 4, 2008, from http://www.mapsites.net/gotham01/webpages/gabbyl/consolidation.htm

CRCM, Citizens Research Council of Michigan. (1990, November). School district organization in Michigan. Report No. 298.Retrieved November 1, 2009 from http://www.crcmich.org/PUBLICAT/1990s/1990/rpt298.pdf

Coulson, A. (2007). School district consolidation, size and spending, *Mackinac Center for Public Policy*. Retrieved September 20, 2008, from http://www.mackinac.org/article.aspx?ID=8530

Cox, B., and Cox, B. (2010). A decade of results: A case for school district consolidation. *Education*, *131*(1), 83–92.

Duncombe, W., and Yinger J. (2001, January). Does school district consolidation cut costs? Center for Policy Research, Maxwell School of Citizenship and Public Affairs, Syracuse University.

Duncombe, W., & Yinger, J. (2007). Does school district consolidation cut costs? *Education Finance and Policy, 2*(4), 341–375.

Duncombe, W. and Yinger, J. (2010). School district consolidation: The benefits and costs. *School Administrator, 67*(5), 10–17.

Education Law, State of New York, Title 2, Sections 1501 to Section 2603.

Fischel, W. A. (2001). *The homevoter hypothesis*. Cambridge, MA: Harvard University Press.

Frank, H., Christian, P., and Scutelnicu, G. (2009). Generating the public financial management knowledge base: Analyzing method and direction as a sub-discipline of public administration. *Journal of Public Budgeting, Accounting & Financial Management*, *21*(2), 223–246.

Government Accountability Office (GAO). (2009). Testimony before the Committee on Oversight and Government Reform, House of Representatives. RECOVERY ACT. States' and localities' current and planned uses of funds while facing fiscal stresses. Retrieved on November 15, 2009 from http://www.gao.gov/new.items/d09831t.pdf

Gramlich, E. M. (1993). A policymaker's guide to fiscal decentralization. *National Tax Journal, 46*(2). ABI/INFORM Global, 229.

Hawkins, B., Ward, K., and Mary Becker, M. (1991). Governmental consolidation as a strategy for metropolitan development. *Public Administration Quarterly, 15*(2), 261.

Hildebrand, S. (2008). The effective use of simulation-based learning techniques in an undergraduate budgeting course. A Paper Presented to the 2008 Southern Political Science Association Conference, New Orleans, Louisiana, January 12, 2008.

Hu, Y. and Yinger, J. (2008). The impact of school district consolidation on housing prices. *National Tax Journal, 61*(4), Part 1.

Leland, S., and Thurmaier, K. (2004). *Case studies in city-county consolidation: Reshaping the local government landscape.* New York: M.E. Sharpe Publishing.

Milam, D. (2003). Practitioner in the classroom: Bringing local government experience into the public administration curriculum. *Public Administration Review, 63*(3), 364–369. Retrieved February 21, 2011, from ABI/INFORM Global. (Document ID: 335361911).

Murray, V., and Groen. R. (2004). Competition or consolidation? The school district consolidation debate revisited. Goldwater Institute No. 189 (January 12). Retrieved on September 15, 2009 from http://www.goldwaterinstitute.org/Common/Files/Multimedia/401.pdf

Nassau County Assessment Review Commission. (2008). Retrieved October 27, 2008, from http://www.nassaucountyny.gov/agencies/ARC/documents/SchoolRatesFinal2008-09ClassOne.pdf

Nassau County, Nassau School Districts & Nassau BOCES. (2008, September 22). In *School & municipal savings initiative: Opportunities for efficiencies though shared services.* Retrieved October 2, 2008, from http://www.nassaucountyny.gov/agencies/CountyExecutive/NewsRelease/2008/09-22-08.html

New Jersey Special Session Joint Legislative Committee. (2006, December 1). *Government consolidation and shared services, final report.* Retrieved September 23, 2008, from http://www.njleg.state.nj.us/PropertyTaxSession/jcgo.asp

New York City Board of Education. Retrieved October 28, 2008, from http://schools.nyc.gov/default.htm

Office of Real Property Services of the State of New York. Retrieved September 15, 2008, from http://www.orps.state.ny.us/pamphlet/taxworks.htm

Pierce, N. R. (1993). *Citistates: How urban America can prosper in a competitive world.* Washington DC: Steven-Locks Press.

Plucker, J. A., Spradlin, T. E., Magaro, M. M., Chien, R. W., and Zapf, J. (2007). Assessing the policy environment for school corporation collaboration, cooperation, and consolidation in Indiana. *Education Policy Brief, 5*(5), 1–16

Proksch, B., Ross, W., and Estness, T. (2002). Negotiation role-play exercise: Water, water, everywhere, but not a drop to drink: The Richland-River City dispute. *International Journal of Conflict Management, 13*(4), 355–380.

Renwick, T. (2008). School finance on Long Island: An analysis of state and local funding patterns fiscal policy institute (September 2009). *Long Island Index* 2009, School Finance on Long Island 3 Research conducted and report written by Trudi Renwick, Fiscal Policy Institute. Retrieved November 2, 2009 from http://longislandindex.org/fileadmin/pdf/2009_Index_Files/School_Finance_on_Long_Island_by_FPI.pdf, p. 2

Rusk, D. (1993). *Cities without suburbs.* New York: The Woodrow Wilson Center Press.

Scorsone, E. (2010). Local government consolidation: Assessing the evidence for cost savings and economic improvement. *State Notes Topics of Legislative Interest.* Retrieved September 2, 2010 from http://www.senate.michigan.gov/sfa/Publications/Notes/2010Notes/NotesSum10es.pdf

Staley, S. R., Faulk, D., Leland, S. M., and Schansberg, D. E. (2005). The effects of city-county consolidation: A review of the recent academic literature, Indiana Policy Review Foundation http://www.in.gov/legislative/interim/committee/2005/committees/prelim/MCCC02.pdf

Strang, D. (1987). The administrative transformation of American education: School district consolidation. *Administrative Science Quarterly*, *32*, 352–366. Retrieved September 30, 2008, from JSTOR.

Strange, M., and Malhoit, G. (2005, October). Bigger isn't always better: Why we should preserve small rural schools. *Leadership Insider: Practical Perspectives on School Law & Policy*. National School Boards Association. Retrieved February 21, 2009, from http://www.nsba.org/MainMenu/SchoolBoardPolicies/Newsletters/LeadershipInsiderOctober2005.aspx

Suozzi, T. (2008). Final report to Governor David A. Paterson. New York State Commission on Property Tax Relief. Retrieved December 12, 2009 from http://www.cptr.state.ny.us/reports/CPTRFinalReport_20081201.pdf

Tiebout, Charles. 1956. A Pure Theory of Local Expenditures. *Journal of Political Economy 64*, 416–424.

Ulbrich, H., Saltzman, E., and Watt, C. (2009). Options for Anderson County school districts. Prepared for the Anderson County Board of Education. Retrieved December 12, 2001 from http://www.boardofed.net/Anderson%206-24-09%20FINAL2.pdf

U.S. Census Fast Facts. Retrieved October 4, 2008, from http://www.fedstats.gov/qf/states/36000.html

Ward, R. B., and Dadayan, L. (2009). State and local finance: Increasing focus on fiscal sustainability. *Publius: The Journal of Federalism*, *39*(3), 455–475.

Ward, J. G., and Rink, F. J. (1992). Analysis of local stakeholder opposition to school district consolidation: An application of interpretive theory to public policy making. *Journal of Research in Rural Education, 8*(4), 11–19.

Appendix A: Consolidated School Districts in Nassau County

DISTRICT 1:	Malverne, Rockville Centre, Valley Stream 30, Valley Stream 13, West Hempstead, Franklin Square, Valley Stream Central
DISTRICT 2:	Elmont, Floral Park Bellerose, Garden City, Sewanka
DISTRICT 3:	Uniondale, East Meadow, Island Trees, North Merrick, North Bellmore
DISTRICT 4:	Hempstead, Roosevelt, Levittown, Wantagh, Seaford, Bellmore Merrick
DISTRICT 5:	Merrick, Freeport, Oceanside, Island Park, Long Beach, Bellmore
DISTRICT 6:	Baldwin, East Rockaway, Lynbrook, Lawrence, Hewlett-Woodmere, Valley Stream 24
DISTRICT 7:	North Shore, Syosset, Locust Valley, Plainview-Old Bethpage Bethpage, Glen Cove, Oyster Bay-East Norwich
DISTRICT 8:	Hicksville, Plainedge, Farmingdale, Massapequa
DISTRICT 9:	Great Neck, Port Washington, Manhasset, Jericho
DISTRICT 10:	Westbury, Roslyn, Herrick, Carle Place, New Hyde Park- Garden City, East Williston, Mineola

Appendix B: Average Tax and Savings by Nassau County School District

School District	Average Tax	Savings
Baldwin	$9,073.72	$217.77
Bellmore	$7,913.71	$189.93
Bethpage	$7,661.53	$183.88
East Meadow	$8,280.51	$198.73
East Rockaway	$8,413.48	$201.92
East Williston	$6,385.25	$153.25
Elmont	$8,021.37	$192.51
Farmingdale	$8,440.99	$202.58
Floral Park Bellerose	$6,343.10	$152.23
Franklin Square	$6,680.35	$160.33
Freeport	$9,798.15	$235.16
Garden City	$5,213.21	$125.12
Glen Cove	$6,295.20	$151.08
Great Neck	$5,060.65	$121.46
Hempstead	$10,926.06	$262.23
Herrick	$6,075.12	$145.80
Hewlett Woodmere	$8,842.42	$212.22
Hicksville	$6,377.73	$153.07
Island Park	$7,506.31	$180.15
Island Trees	$8,651.90	$207.65
Jericho	$7,092.99	$170.23
Lawrence	$5,602.85	$134.47
Levittown	$9,646.84	$231.52
Locust Valley	$4,461.20	$107.07
Long Beach	$5,309.43	$127.43
Lynbrook	$8,546.44	$205.11
Malverne	$7,831.18	$187.95
Manhasset	$4,387.85	$105.31
Massapequa	$6,978.37	$167.48
Merrick	$7,459.80	$179.04

(continued)

School District	Average Tax	Savings
Mineola	$7,510.23	$180.25
New Hyde Park Garden City	$7,088.41	$170.12
North Bellmore	$7,510.23	$180.25
North Merrick	$7,973.31	$191.36
North Shore	$5,309.43	$127.43
Oceanside	$7,689.05	$184.54
Oyster Bay East Norwich	$4,195.27	$100.69
Plainedge	$8,184.23	$196.42
Plainview Old Bethpage	$7,932.05	$190.37
Port Washington	$5,689.98	$136.56
Rockville Centre	$7,629.44	$183.11

Part VII

Debt Capacity, Management, and Policy

Chapter 18

Measuring and Monitoring Debt Capacity and Affordability

Market- and Nonmarket-based Models

by Kenneth A. Kriz and Qiushi Wang

Introduction

"How much debt can we afford?" often is the first question that should be answered when jurisdictions have to issue debt to finance capital projects. Assessing *debt capacity* and *debt affordability* plays an important role in state and local finance, particularly during financial crises, yet has scarcely been examined in the academic literature. Little specific guidance and empirically based research is available to subnational finance and debt managers to allow them to make informed decisions about affordability.

Debt affordability and capacity are key components of the fiscal health of a jurisdiction. In the extreme case where jurisdictions take on so much debt that they cannot afford to repay it, officials put the very independence of a jurisdiction at risk. Short of this situation, as debt burdens of a jurisdiction rise, borrowing costs for the jurisdiction may also rise, putting pressure on other parts of a government's budget. Also, credit ratings may fall, which increases borrowing costs and may also damage a community's reputation. A local government may also incur additional monitoring by their state as debt burdens rise. In essence, then, there are two ways to view debt affordability and capacity concerns. The first is through the lens of internal constituencies such as citizens or service recipients. The second is through the views of external agents such as bond raters or state agencies.

This topic is especially important given current economic and financial conditions. Debt of all sovereign entities, including national and state governments, is increasing dramatically. The median debt to personal income ratio for states during the period 1998–2009 has increased by almost one-third (**Figure 18.1**). This period was mostly before the economic downturn of 2007–2010. The combination of deteriorating financial position and economic weakness has caused several ratings downgrades during the most recent recession, and several jurisdictions are concerned over their ability to borrow to finance capital improvements.

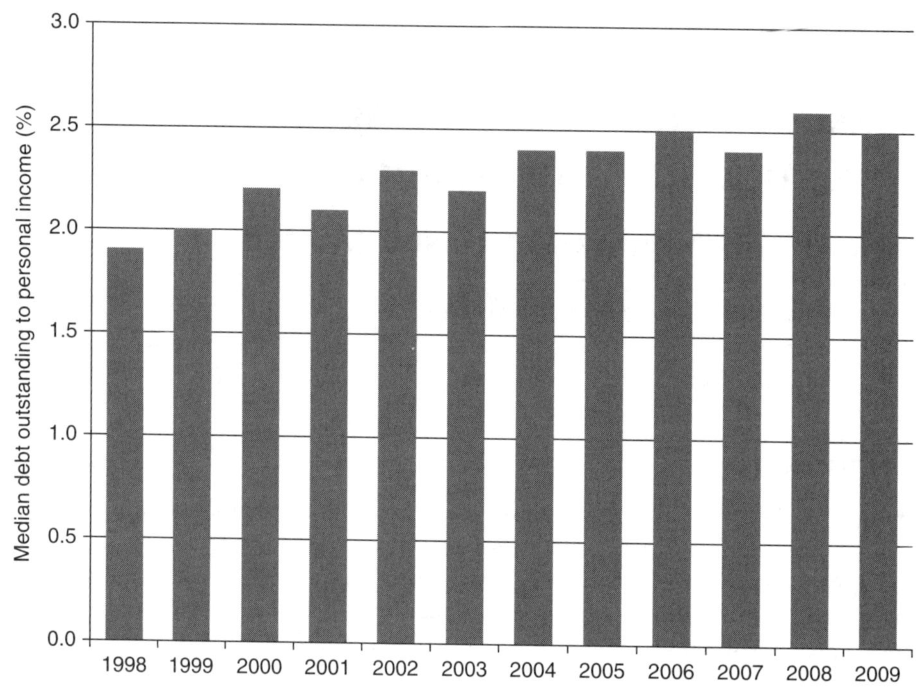

Figure 18.1 Median Debt Outstanding as a Percentage of Personal Income, 1998–2009

Data from: Lyons, K. (2009). 2009 Debt Medians Report: Based on 2008 Data. New York: Moody's Investors Service.

The purpose of this chapter is to survey and analyze the different ways that governments can measure how much debt they can afford. It first defines debt capacity and affordability and then provides some background knowledge on facts, concepts, and theories related to debt capacity and affordability. The chapter next discusses traditional models of measuring debt affordability, including debt ceiling, benchmarking, and linear regression. Then some major issues with traditional debt capacity models are explored, and three innovative models that attempt to address these problems are introduced. The chapter concludes by summarizing current progress on the research of debt capacity and debt affordability, giving a preview of future studies on this topic.

Background

In the private sector, debt capacity and debt affordability are virtually the same concept, referring to the amount of debt financing that an organization can acquire. Essentially, corporate debt capacity and affordability refer to the point that extra borrowing no longer increases corporate value. In the private sector, debt capacity analyses involve "the assessment of the amount of debt that the organization can repay in a timely manner without jeopardizing its financial viability," and it also refers to "total amount of debt a firm can incur, as restricted by covenant of a loan agreement, or by firm's articles of association."[1] In the public sector, debt capacity and debt affordability are two closely related concepts that measure the ability to borrow or "the ability to handle debt" (Hildreth and Miller, 2002, p.100), but at times they have a slightly different emphasis. Debt capacity focuses more on the total amount of outstanding debt relative to the total economic base from which jurisdictions can collect revenues to repay the debt. For example, Hildreth (2005) defines debt capacity as "the amount of financing that may be issued by the State within legal constraints without overextending the State's ability to repay its obligations... a measurement of the extent of additional debt that can be issued in the future given the State's existing debt level" (p. 17). Ramsey and Hackbart (1996) hold a similar view: "the level of debt and /or debt service relative to current revenues (or debt ceiling) that an issuing entity could support without creating undue budgetary constraints that might impair the ability of the issuer to repay bonds outstanding or make timely debt service payments." In contrast, debt affordability analyses emphasize "the burden associated with repaying debt. "To be affordable, the repayment of debt should not cause a jurisdiction's tax rate to increase to uncompetitive levels in order to cover the debt service, nor should the repayment of debt negatively impact the provision of ongoing public services" (Hildreth, 2005, p. 17). Despite the slight different emphasis of debt capacity and debt affordability, the key issue in both is how to measure them. Related to this issue are the determination of economic base, selection of appropriate indicators, and credit rating. The remainder of this chapter will use debt capacity and debt affordability interchangeably.

When state and local governments are facing capital and infrastructure needs that exceed the size of their current capital budget, most of them choose to meet those needs by borrowing. Most municipal debt takes the form of municipal bonds, although some may be in other forms, such as certificates of participation or lease-backed issues. Municipal bonds generally mature anywhere from 1 to 40 years from the issuance date. In recent decades, municipal borrowing has been growing rapidly and has become an important way for state and local governments to finance capital projects. By the end of 2005, there were $1.85 trillion in municipal bonds outstanding, representing 14.6% of GDP. Though it is commonly known that federal government debt is increasing dramatically, trends reveal that state and local governments are also issuing large amounts debt. From 2000 to 2005, total outstanding state and local debt soared from $1.19 trillion to $1.85 trillion,[2] an increase of 55%.[3]

Given the formidable size of the municipal securities market, even small changes in the interest rate can have a substantial financial effect on state and local finances. The potential financial effect on future generations is yet another important concern in making municipal borrowing decisions. Therefore, well-designed and carefully implemented *debt policies* that provide a set of guiding principles for finance managers are seen as the key to the success of capital planning and the long-term fiscal health of state and local governments. In this regard, the Government Finance Officers Association (GFOA) and other relevant agencies have promoted the use of formal debt policies as an important management tool for state and local finance managers. In general, debt policies are "written guidelines and restrictions affecting the amount, issuance process, and type debt issued by a government entity" and include such items as purpose of issuance, legal debt limitations, credit objectives, method of sales, and disclosure.[4] As of 1997, about 20% of GFOA municipalities have established debt policies, while other municipalities are content with using statutory guidelines as their debt policy. According to some researchers,[5] a reliable assessment of how much a government can afford to pay in debt service, as well as how much outstanding debt it can safely carry should be a starting point for government's debt policy because governments need to have a thorough understanding of debt affordability prior to making issuance decisions or forecasting future capital needs.

The existing literature on public debt addresses issues that fall into one of the three categories: descriptive, causal, and normative (Brecher, Richwerger, and Van Wagner, 2003). The descriptive literature has tracked the increase in state indebtedness, and identified a significant shift from issuing more full faith and credit general obligation (GO) bonds to issuing more nonguaranteed debt backed by specific revenue sources (Regens and Lauth, 1992). Causal studies (relying mainly on statistical methods) have sought to identify and interpret the factors that effect public debt levels and the variation in debt burden among states. Empirical models have found statistically significant relationships between debt levels and various economic, service demand, and political factors (Bahl, Duncombe, and Bunch, 1991). The normative literature recommends practices that should produce "good" debt policies. A survey of local debt issuers found some most important values advocated by these practitioners: (1) long-term debt should only be used to finance capital projects, (2) debt managers should retain responsibility to taxpayers to achieve the lowest possible interest rate on municipal bonds, and (3) bond maturities should be in line with the expected life of the project being financed (Simonsen, Robbins, and Kittredge, 2001). All of these studies have contributed to our understanding of public debt and laid a solid foundation for our inquiry into the debt capacity issue.

Traditional Debt Capacity Models

Although a significant body of literature on "how much debt is right" exists for private sector (Piper and Weinhold, 1982), much less literature is concerned with the measurement of optimal debt levels for state and local governments (Bernard, 1982). Debt affordability is typically estimated by one or more of the following three methods. The first method, the *debt ceiling approach*, compares a jurisdiction's debt level to a single value or multiple values of the measure itself. Often a debt ceiling is not an indicator but a specific goal—to maintain or achieve a target bond rating for a jurisdiction. This special case, referred to as *bond-rating oriented approach*, still consists of self-comparisons but is more complex than a simple debt ceiling. In contrast to the self-comparisons inherent in the debt ceiling approach, a *benchmarking approach* is used to compare a jurisdiction's own debt level to that of others. With this approach, agencies first select a "bench," such as national median or the median of a peer group, and then calculate and compare the selected debt capacity indicators ("marks") with those calculated from the "bench." The GFOA is currently recommending the benchmarking approach, and it is gaining popularity in state and local governments. The third method is to conduct regression analyses. A multiple linear regression is most commonly used with a debt capacity measure such as the "annual debt service on tax supported debt" as the dependent variable and a series of other important debt factors as independent variables. After formulating the best fitted regression model, the predicted values of each independent variable are then used to forecast the future debt level and then affordability or capacity is assessed.

In the remainder of this section, each of the three methods just mentioned will be discussed at length. It should be noted that a debt analyst can easily use more than one method or, in some cases, combine two or more of the three methods. For example, a debt ceiling can be compared with the average debt ceiling figure of a bench group; similarly, the debt level predicted by a linear regression model can also be compared with benchmarks. Using more than one method usually is more favorable because doing so can produce more accurate estimates of debt capacity.

Debt Ceiling

Simple and Complex Debt Ceiling

A simple debt ceiling, sometimes called the "rule of thumb" approach, is straightforward and relatively easy to implement. In this approach, a key variable that indicates debt capacity, usually debt outstanding or annual debt service, is contrasted against indicators such as revenue, personal income, population, property value, or historical debt (Ramsey, Gritz, and Hackbart, 1988, p. 231) A mandatory ceiling, usually based on experts' recommendation, "industrial standards," or policymakers' judgment, is then chosen to regulate borrowing. Representative rules of thumb include setting ceilings on debt service payments as a percentage of state and government expenditures, total debt per capita, or other level of debt capacity ratios. Many states currently use this approach to analyze and manage affordable state debt levels (Douglas, 2000). For instance, Connecticut's debt policy states: "Debt is limited to 4.5 percent of the previous year's tax receipts,"[6] and Tennessee's debt policy specifies: "Debt service must be less than 15 percent of general fund receipts."[7]

A more complex debt ceiling links debt level or debt service to multiple indicators. For example, the debt policy of Maryland limits debt service on general obligation debt to 8% of general fund and state property tax revenue and 3.2% of state personal income. In addition, Maryland's Capital Debt Affordability Committee recommends GO debt to personal income ratio targets based on continuing standards set in 1982 that are calculated to "strengthen" the states' AAA credit rating.[8]

Compared with a simple debt ceiling, the complex ceiling includes more debt considerations and leads to more balanced estimation of debt capacity. The weakness common to both types of debt ceiling, however, is that the "magic ratios" chosen to limit borrowing usually ignore many important determinants, are not statistically based, and do not change as the economic environment changes. Therefore the debt ceiling approach is largely incomplete, arbitrary, and static.

Bond-Rating Orientation

Debt affordability analysis is closely related to the municipal credit analysis conducted by the three major credit rating agencies: Standard & Poor's, Fitch, and Moody's. Discrepancy occurs when bond-rating agencies seek to determine the riskiness of the debt based upon a government's ability to repay the municipal bonds on schedule, while governments need to understand how much debt they can comfortably issue and carry "without creating undue budgetary constraints." It is imperative to distinguish these two overlapping, yet different perspectives to avoid confusion. In this chapter, bond-rating agencies' criteria is presented first, and the other models are discussed from a government perspective.

Debt affordability is generally understood by credit agencies in terms of tax-supported debt, such as general obligation bonds, lease bonds paid from general revenues, special assessment bonds, and tax-increment bonds. Each bond-rating agency uses a unique model (details of which are proprietary and hence unknown to the general public) to assess the credit quality of municipal tax-backed debt. It is generally agreed, however, that all three agencies routinely examine the following four factors:

1. *Economic factors*: Analysis of economic factors consists of an examination of the current and future economic health of a jurisdiction. These factors typically include unemployment rate; business diversification and industry concentration; mix of residential, commercial, and industrial property; demographic trends; personal income trends; property value per capita; poverty rate; and household income.
2. *Financial condition*: Financial condition measures the overall financial environment and flexibility of a jurisdiction. Included in this category typically are concerns about revenue limits, percent of mandatory expenditures, diversity of stability of revenue sources, operating surplus trends, and fund balance as a percent of revenues.
3. *Debt position*: Analysis of a jurisdiction's debt position concentrates on the attributes of the debt structure, monitoring future borrowing needs, resources available to pay the current and future debt services, and other features that might affect the structure and security of a bond issue.
4. *Administrative factors*: All three rating agencies place specific weight on management practice as a measure of the creditworthiness of a jurisdiction. Past history of management performance in balancing budget or managing capital needs, prudent investment policies, appropriate capital improvement programs, among others, are viewed as indicators of sound management practices.

For example, Standard & Poor's rating criteria for GO debt are as follows[9]:

- Economy,
- Financial performance and flexibility,
- Debt burden, and
- Management.

These four criteria are almost identical to the four categories mentioned earlier. The other two rating agencies, Fitch and Moody's use similar criteria.

A separate type of analytic framework usually is required for non tax-supported debt, including the large variety of revenue bonds. For an example, in addressing the risks of water and sewer revenue bond, each of the three credit agencies has developed a set of specific rating criteria, which are presented in Appendix A. Although each agency gives different names and definitions to them, these criteria are similar in content and can be roughly categorized and paralleled as in the three columns of Appendix A. At the heart of these analytical frameworks, despite a few discrepancies between one another, are the four most important considerations: economic, legal, operational, and fiscal. Higher-rated issuers will integrate these diverse considerations into a comprehensive multiyear management strategy. With regard to assessing debt capacity, the *Fitch Guidelines* state that "regulations, customer growth and capacity constraints . . . are each major determinants of a utility's capital improvement burden" (p. 5). In fact, Moody's and Standard & Poor's have adopted a similar view. As such, the criteria used in rating water and sewer revenue bonds and the debt capacity of the issuing entities seem to be highly correlated.

Perhaps in part because rating agencies have mature models to determine credit worthiness, state and local governments often attempt to imitate these models to estimate their debt capacity. However, they approach the problem from a government perspective and employ modifications to serve their own purposes, which usually are different from those of the rating agencies. In this regard, a large body of the existing debt affordability literature focuses on identifying income and wealth variables that are reasonable proxy measures of the fiscal capacity of a state and, consequently, can be used to predict debt capacity or debt affordability level for each state and local government. Hackbart and Ramsey (1990) pointed out that in some analyses, it is assumed that as a state's income and wealth increases, its capacity to meet debt service or its "debt affordability" proportionally increases. Therefore, as long as debt outstanding or debt service payment commitments expand in proportion to a state's economy and wealth, the rating agencies' concerns about the exhaustion or impending exhaustion of an issuing entities debt capacity should be mitigated and the state's debt rating should be maintained. Based on this belief, Ramsey, Gritz, and Hackbart (1988) related the level of debt an issuer could afford to the bond-rating process. They concluded that four variables–revenue, per capita income, population, and assessed value of real property–are both quantifiable and important to establish a credit rating for a state or local government and that if these four variables could be estimated for a future period, then the future debt capacity of a state could also be forecast. Ramsey, Gritz, and Hackbart (1988) attempted to employ this framework to estimate debt capacity, but the result was ambiguous.

Benchmarking

Simple Benchmarking

The GFOA recommends that issuers of municipal bonds undertake an analysis of their debt capacity prior to issuance because a comprehensive and routine analysis helps ensure that the issuing government will know all new debt issued is affordable and there is a balance between current and future capital needs. The two key components that comprise debt affordability analysis using benchmarking are ratio calculation and comparison to norms or standards. To this end, GFOA currently recommends an eight-step debt capacity analysis framework (Miranda and Picur, 2000). These eight steps are as follows:

1. Define study objective,
2. Collect data,
3. Construct indicators,
4. Define comparison groups for benchmarking,
5. Compare key indicators against peer group,
6. Establish debt issuance scenarios,
7. Use the "break-even year" methodology, and
8. Develop or revise formal debt policy. (Miranda and Picur, 2000, p. 11)

Indicator construction is critical to the success of benchmarking analysis. According to Miranda and Picur (2000), indicators should be valid: "an indicator is measuring what is supposed to measure" (p. 15). The GFOA suggests that a comprehensive debt analysis should take account of the following considerations (Simonsen and Brown, 2003):

- Debt service
- Direct debt
- Evaluation of economic trends that relates to government's finances, such as revenues, expenditures, and unreserved fund balance
- Measures of debt burden on the jurisdiction
- Statutory or constitutional limitations on debt issuance
- Market factors that impact the interest costs on municipal bonds issued by the jurisdiction (interest rate, market receptivity, and credit rating)
- Unfunded pension liabilities and capital leases

Debt service and direct debt are typical measures of debt affordability. Debt service consists of the principal and interest payment the state and local governments make every year; direct debt refers to a municipality's debt paid for by its general revenues including taxes, but excluding bonds that are self-supporting by means other than taxes (e.g., user fees or charges). Using these two measures, a variety of ratios can be constructed and some routinely used ratios are listed in Appendix B. In constructing these indicators, data source should be reliable. Miranda and Picur discussed the advantages and disadvantages of using comprehensive annual financial reports (CAFRs) for debt analysis and concluded that despite the disadvantages, CAFRs are more reliable than other data sources such as interviews or surveys.

The calculated indicators can only be meaningful when they are compared to norms or standards. Examples of these norms or standards include rules of thumb, medians, and benchmarks. Rules of thumb are simply some industry standards for certain ratios, which may be based on historical data, experts' opinions, or even arbitrary numbers. Medians are generally calculated by government type (state, local, school district, etc.) and population (e.g., median debt burden for municipalities with a population of 250,000 or more). Some rules of thumb standards and medians that Standard and Poor's[10] uses are shown in Appendices C and D. Although these rules of thumb and medians are self-explanatory and easy to use, they suffer from some serious problems that will be discussed at length in the following sections.

In benchmarking debt statistics, there are at least two intrinsic difficulties. First, the choice of comparable governments must be done with caution because no two communities are exactly the same. For instance, two jurisdictions may be similar in population and bond ratings but very different in terms of economic base and tax structure. Some important characteristics to consider when choosing comparison governments are population, revenue mix, service responsibilities, bond rating or credit quality, and whether the laws governing the use and issuance of debt are comparable (Simonsen and Brown, 2003). In a similar vein, Miranda and Picur (2000) select the comparison (peer) groups on the basis of the following two criteria: (1) city age, population, geographic region, and other characteristics; and (2) similarity of experience (p. 19).

A second difficulty with the benchmarking approach is that debt statistics may not be measured consistently across jurisdiction. Different governments may use different methods to calculate ratios. For example, some governments calculate debt ratios based only on general obligation bonds and ignore revenue bonds because state statutes or constitutions often define debt as general obligation debt for the purpose of state debt limits. Other self-supporting debt such as lease debt or certificates of participation may also be excluded in these calculations. This may be appropriate for deriving debt limits but may not be appropriate for conducting a debt affordability analysis.

After the eight steps are completed and the major problems are taken into account, benchmarking—comparing the target government against the peer group—can then be conducted. Basic techniques include comparing against the average of the peer group, calculating relative percentages or ratios of the peer group average, or ranking against the peer group. Debt burden statistics (direct debt, GO debt, bonded debt, etc.) are compared against its peer groups' burden ratios and a conclusion is formed.

To a great extent, using rules of thumb, medians, or benchmarking to determine debt affordability is an art rather than a science. Indicators can be constructed, ratios can be calculated, and benchmarks can be decided, but how to interpret them depends on human judgment. When there are multiple ratios for key debt statistics, it is possible that some ratios are low while others are high for the same jurisdiction. Furthermore, there is no way to completely solve the two major issues with the benchmarking approach: no two jurisdictions are as perfectly comparable (and in most cases, the confounding factors are not controllable), and the measurement problem can be mitigated but probably will not disappear completely. Lastly, ratios and benchmarks alone never tell the whole story. Other factors that may have not been included in the analysis, such as broadness of tax base, efficiency of management, and future economic growth potential, may distort results based on the calculated ratios and benchmarks.

Scenario Analysis and Break-even Year Method

GFOA recommends two other techniques that may improve the reliability of benchmarking analysis: scenario analysis and *break-even year method*. In scenario analysis, a simulated or pro forma set of multiyear operating results is developed to use as a basis for addressing the fundamental question of "How much debt can a government afford?" Debt issuance scenarios are then constructed to forecast values of specific indicators under different assumptions (e.g., no new debt, $10 million debt issuance per year, $20 million debt issuance per year). Based on this scenario analysis, a break-even year method addresses the question "How long will it take the government to reach the average for the comparison group?" assuming a specific scenario for a debt indicator (i.e., debt as a percentage of the operating budget). In essence, scenario analysis and break-even year method depend on the results from previous benchmarking steps, therefore they suffer from the same issues as benchmarking analysis itself.

Modified Benchmarking Approach

To address the deficiencies of typical benchmarking analysis, Hildreth and Miller (2002) argue that economic factors be more closely connected to debt factors in assessing debt affordability. Debt creation imposes an obligation to repay borrowed funds from a wealth base that is usually capitalized in property values. As a result, the ability to afford debt is tied to the local economy. Because diversity in the local economy is a factor in long-term economic health, it is very important in assessing relative debt levels, and the overlapping jurisdictions problem can aggravate the diversity problem through competition. Their key argument is that debt affordability studies should focus not only on debt levels but also on local economic concentration because the linkage between the two is important (Hildreth and Miller, 2002, p. 107). Hildreth and Miller's article provides a good complement to the benchmarking approach, but it does not (1) provide a new framework to analyze debt capacity, or (2) solve some of the serious conceptual and methodological problems that the benchmarking approach suffers.

Linear Regression Approach

Rating agencies and jurisdictions sometimes use a linear regression model to generate estimates of debt capacity. This is typically a two-step process: the first step is to select appropriate dependent and independent variables and to establish a good estimating equation to explain debt capacity; the next step is to substitute the predicted future values of the independent variables into the previous equation and calculate the future debt affordability.

In the first step, the basic linear regression model can be written as follows:

$$Y = a + b_1X_1 + b_2X_2 + b_3X_3 + \cdots + b_nX_n \tag{1}$$

where

Y = selected dependent variable indicating debt capacity

$X_1, X_2, ..., X_n$ = selected independent variables determining debt capacity

To operationalize equation (1) a dependent variable and a set of independent variables must be chosen. Ramsey, Gritz, and Hackbart (1988) conducted a survey of the states using the regression method to estimate their debt capacity. They found that the most frequently used dependent variables are "principal debt outstanding" and "annual debt service," and the most popular independent variables are "revenue," "personal income," "population or population growth," "assessed property value," and "historical debt." The null hypothesis being tested is that no statistically significant relationship can be found to exist between the set of independent variables and the dependent variable. If the null hypothesis can be soundly rejected, equation (1) would be appropriate to be used in the next step—predicting future debt capacity. Using a set of four independent variables, "assessed property value," "state revenues," "per capita income," and "population," Ramsey, Gritz, and Hackbart (1988) achieved a very successful model, with an R-squared value as high as 0.98.

In the second step, the values of $X_1, X_2, ..., X_n$ are predicted and then substituted into equation (1). A standard way to forecast future values is to use time series techniques such as ARIMA. The time series model to be estimated can be written as follows:

$$\begin{aligned} X_1 &= a + b_1 t \\ X_2 &= a + b_2 t \\ &\cdots \\ X_n &= a + b_n t \end{aligned} \tag{2}$$

Where

t = time

The underlying assumption of time series analysis is there is some kind of pattern that can be identified from the historical data and therefore the future values can be predicted with certain degrees of confidence. Other forecasting techniques, ranging from moving averages to regression estimation, can also be used if they can produce reliable estimates. Once the future value of each independent variable in equation (1) is predicted, the debt capacity—the dependent variable in equation (1) can be easily calculated.

So far, the linear regression approach has been the only empirically based method to estimate debt capacity that is currently in use. It has many advantages over debt ceiling and the benchmark method: it is backed by the rigidity of statistics and supported by historical data; it incorporates a large amount of information (reflected in the independent variables) into the estimation. However, the weaknesses of regression analysis are obvious too: it relies on the availability of quantitative data, and some important variables such as residents' willingness to use debt financing are hard to measure; it also relies on the forecast values of chosen independent variable, but no technique can guarantee their accuracy.

Bartle, Kriz, and Wang (2008) summarize current debt affordability models just discussed, accompanied by a brief description of each method, examples, states that have adopted the method, and a short discussion of the strengths and weaknesses for each method (**Table 18.1**). Some of the results are based on a survey of debt capacity measures in twelve states (Ramsey, Gritz, and Hackbart, 1988).

Assessment of Traditional Models[11]

There has obviously been much thought on the subject of debt affordability and capacity. Each of the models has its own strengths and weaknesses. However, to summarize the state of debt affordability research up to the early 2000s, the strengths and weaknesses of the traditional models are listed as follows.

Strengths

1. Good comparability: Benchmarking links target government to a peer group and allows for a horizontal comparison between the two. The regression approach seeks to achieve statistical comparability.
2. Comprehensibility: Debt ceiling and benchmarking results are easy to understand.

Weaknesses

1. Potentially misleading: Debt ceilings often have no analytical basis. Peer groups may or may not serve as good "benchmarks." Regression analysis may suffer from omitted variable bias.
2. Mostly static: Debt ceiling limits are typically not updated. Benchmarking looks at past and current situations and is not forward looking. Regression analysis approach involves projection and hence is dynamic only in name.
3. Incomplete: Many important financial, economic, and demographic realities of the jurisdiction are not taken into account.

TABLE 18.1 Summary of Existing Debt Affordability/Capacity Models

Main Methodology	Submethodology	Example	States
Debt Ceiling	Simple	"Debt service must be less than 15 percent of general fund receipts" (Connecticut)	CT, SC, TN
	Bond-rating oriented	"State policy has been to keep debt service at or below 5 percent of unrestricted revenues . . ." in order to "preserve the state's rating."	AL (MD*)
	Complex	Maryland limits debt service on General Obligation debt to 8% of general fund and state property tax revenue, and 3.2% of state personal income.	MD, WI, OR
Benchmarking (GFOA *Recommended)*	Typical	Virginia compares its Moody ratios to the national median.	VA, CA
	Modified	New York projects personal income, tax receipts, and population growth for five years and then compares predicted rations to national norms.	NY
Regression	Multivariate	Estimating equation to calculation debt capacity for Kentucky: $Y = a + b_1X_1 + b_2X_2 + b_3X_3 + b_4X_4$ (1) Y = Annual debt service on tax supported debt X_1 = Assessed value of real property X_2 = State revenue X_3 = Per capita income X_4 = Population	KY
	Time series		None

* Maryland uses both bond-rating oriented and complex methods. In fact, most states employ a combination of various methods to calculate debt capacity. For simplicity and clearness, this table categorizes them based on the most dominant method for each state.

New Approaches to Assessing Debt Capacity

To address the shortcomings of traditional models, researchers have created several innovative models each of which views debt affordability issue from a novel perspective and attempts to solve the issue with a distinctive design. Three of these innovative methods are introduced next.

Normal Curve Model

Brecher, Richwerger, and Van Wagner (2003) propose a three-step framework[12] to estimate debt affordability (pp. 68–69):

1. Identify and adjust the amount of relevant long-term debt, long-term debt including unfunded pension liabilities, resources available in the state of local economy to repay the debt and the resources available to account for the division of responsibilities between the state and its localities. The main purpose of this step is to filter out the amount of debt and resources that is irrelevant to debt capacity analysis for a particular jurisdiction. Examples of irrelevant debt and resources include short-term debt, long-term revenue bonds, and revenues that cannot be used to repay debt. In addition, if the analysis is conducted at the state (or local) level, only the debt and resources pertaining to that state (or local) government should be included;
2. Calculate the debt burden ratio of adjusted debt to adjusted resources. Higher ratios represent greater levels of indebtedness and less debt capacity. Assuming the square roots of the calculated ratios follow a normal curve, examine the distribution and identify a point that is sufficiently "out of line" (one standard deviation above the mean) with most jurisdictions' practices that it constitutes the beginning of a "danger zone."
3. Adjust the danger zone threshold to allow for the impact of the economic cycle. This step is needed because economic downturns are an important source of state and local fiscal stress and therefore states and localities should take account of the possibility of a decline in available resources for debt repayment due to recession. For instance, if a state's personal income (or other resource measures) falls X percent during a recession, a prudent debt policy of that state would keep debt X percent below the danger zone threshold calculated in previous two steps.

Although this normal curve approach to measuring debt capacity is still reliant on a comparison of debt ratio relative to other places at a certain point of time, it takes advantage of the normal distribution by setting the decision rule for danger zone at the point where the ratios are greater than one standard deviation above the mean. As a result, no arbitrary cutoff value or a rule of thumb is needed for making a judgment. Additionally, the calculations involved in this approach are not too complex and results are easy to interpreted and used in practice. The limitations of this model are that (1) it remains static—only data at one point in time are analyzed; (2) it is not a causal statistical model, implying that it cannot explain the growth or the variation in debt and debt burden among jurisdictions; and (3) more importantly, this model assumes that most states (the states with a debt burden ratio clustered around the middle line of the normal curve), no matter how much debt they have relative to resources, are borrowing at an appropriate level, leaving only those states with a significantly higher debt burden ratio in the danger zone. To some extent, the normal curve approach still reflects the spirit of benchmarking.

Stochastic Simulation Model

Kriz (2010) developed a simulation model of debt affordability that takes account of the stochastic nature of revenue growth. His model strongly refutes the notion that a single measure of debt affordability can in any way capture the likelihood that a jurisdiction will default on its debt. He concludes that simple benchmarking exercises are not worthwhile when seen in the context of the tremendous sensitivity of default likelihood to changes in variables such as tax base volatility. Even regression approaches taken in isolation can only tell us a limited amount about the likelihood of default. This is because regression results alone can only tell us about one variable such as the income elasticity of the tax base and little about other factors such as the willingness of the jurisdiction to forego current expenditures to sustain a capital investment program.

Kriz's (2010) approach is to dynamically model the budget constraint of a jurisdiction going forward. The fundamental equation in his model relates the maximum amount of borrowing as a percentage of the tax base as a function of the existing tax base and future tax base growth, the existing effective tax rate and future growth in this, the interest rate paid on the debt service, and the demand for expenditures on nondebt-related items. Kriz recognizes that this leads back to the regression (and projection) approach; instead he develops the model as a stochastic difference equation model to reflect the inherent uncertainty regarding the growth of the tax base. One of the key insights from this model is that part of what determines the likelihood of default for a jurisdiction is how willing the residents of the jurisdiction are to accept tax rate increases or expenditure cuts, so this variable is included in the stochastic simulation model. Kriz estimates a number of results and shows the relationship between each variable and the probability of default on a bond issue.

To use the Kriz model in practice, a finance officer would need information on current and past values of the variables in the model. To demonstrate, assume that a finance officer finds the following regarding his jurisdiction: average tax base growth of 5%, annual tax base volatility (the standard deviation of growth rates) of 2.5%, past growth rate of expenditures of 3%, initial effective tax rate of 5%, borrowing costs of 6%, average debt maturity of 30 years, debt as percent of tax base of 25%, and a willingness of the public to accept a 10% increase in taxes or cut in services. The model would predict an 8.18% chance of this jurisdiction defaulting on its debt over the 30-year period. If the same jurisdiction wanted a higher expenditure growth (averaging 4%), the probability of default would increase to 26.41%.

The structure of the Kriz model makes it very useful for a jurisdiction to get a ballpark estimate of the true default risk that it incurs by issuing debt and assessing their policy options going forward. The problems with the Kriz model in practice are (1) a need for much historical fiscal data, (2) the implicit assumption that past data are a good indicator of future patterns (although the Kriz model explicitly calculates the risk of bad data as compared to benchmarking models that cannot do this), (3) the subjectiveness of some of the "policy variables" such as the willingness of the public to accept a cut of a certain magnitude, and (4) the complexity of explaining the results.

Simultaneous Equation Model

Wang (2009) linked the question of debt capacity and affordability to the regional economy and argued that the optimal debt capacity or affordability point is where the debt maximizes regional economic growth. The theoretical framework to measure the debt capacity consists of constructing a simultaneous system of four endogenous variables including debt, borrowing cost, public investment, and regional economic growth. Empirical results from a simultaneous model reveal that public borrowing impacts state and local economy in a concave pattern, and the optimal level of borrowing is found to be in a range between $5,550 and $7,720 per capita for all states in the sample.

Wang's model should allow managers to calculate the optimal borrowing level through a series of statistical comparisons to the jurisdiction's peers in terms of their debt level, borrowing cost, public investment, and economic growth. Knowing these variables for the target jurisdiction and its peers, managers could estimate a "turning point" when additional debt goes from having a positive effect on its economy through the effects of infrastructure and service provision to a negative effect through increasing borrowing costs and the need to forego future projects.

Although the simultaneous model may not provide an immediate answer to the question "How much debt can we afford?" for individual government, it explains the causal relationship between several debt and economic factors, and gives a more accurate picture of debt capacity situation on the basis of rigorous data analysis and hypotheses testing. One major limitation of the Wang model is the need to use specialized statistical software to calculate the relationships among jurisdictions. Another issue with this analysis is that it requires a healthy amount of consistent historical data. Still, the model may provide state and local debt managers with a new perspective for measuring debt capacity in a more informed way.

Conclusion

This chapter discusses the importance of debt capacity and affordability issue in state and local public finance and covers a variety of methods of measuring and monitoring debt capacity and affordability. Accurately measuring debt capacity and debt affordability is vital for finance managers to make borrowing decisions and to assess the current fiscal health of their jurisdiction. Too much debt will do harm to the economy both in the short- and long-term as borrowing costs increase and credit ratings decrease. However, too little debt may harm a region in a social and economic sense if jurisdictions feel the need to bypass certain projects or programs based on a false sense of financial propriety generated through concern over debt levels. One area of concern emphasized in this chapter is that many of the current models of debt capacity and affordability suffer from being incomplete, static, and mechanical. Some innovative methods based on rigorous data analysis are emerging, but more and better models are needed to address the shortcomings of existing models and to provide a way for financial managers and the general public to get a sense of the fiscal health of a jurisdiction through measuring its debt load.

Endnotes

1. *Business Dictionary*. Retrieved March 22, 2010, from http·//www.businessdictionary.com/definition/debt-capacity.html
2. Federal Reserve data show that total "municipal" debt was $2.23 trillion in 2005, but this figure includes certain debt issued by nongovernment entities.
3. Data source: Thomson Financial Securities Data, BEA and Federal Reserve Board.
4. For details, see GFOA Recommended Practice "Development of a Debt Policy," GFOA 1995.
5. Larkin, R., and Joseph, J. C. (1996). "Developing Formal Debt Policies," in *Handbook of Debt Management*, G. J. Miller (ed.), New York: Marcel Dekker, pp. 277–282.
6. Municipal Finance Officers Association. (1983). *A review of debt capacity and debt management for the State of Alaska*, p. 148.
7. Ibid.
8. Maryland Debt Affordability Committee, *Report of the Capital Debt Affordability Committee On Recommended Debt Authorization for Fiscal Year 1988*, August 1, 1986, p. 21.
9. Standard & Poor's Public Finance Ratings Criteria for GO Debt. (2006). Retrieved March 28, 2010, from http://www.standardandpoors.com/prot/ratings/articles/en/us/?assetID=1245173095616
10. Standard & Poor's Criteria | Governments | *U.S. public finance: Key general obligation ratio credit ranges—analysis vs. reality*. Retrieved April 2, 2010, fromhttp://www.standardandpoors.com/prot/ratings/articles/en/us/?assetID=1245199733921
11. This section is based on Bartle, Kriz, and Wang, 2008.
12. There are six steps in their article, but the key steps are only three as summarized here.
13. Overlapping debt refers to the tax-supported principal owed by other governments that overlap the geography of the jurisdiction (city, county, school districts, and special districts) conducting the debt affordability analysis. Readers interested in the calculation of overlapping debt should see Simonsen and Brown (2003).

Glossary

Benchmarking approach: comparison of a jurisdiction's debt level to that of others, using national medians or peer groups.

Bond-rating oriented approach: use of measures to assess debt capacity and affordability that mirrors the approach taken by the major bond-rating agencies.

Break-even year method: based on a scenario analysis, this analysis answers the question, "How long will it take the government to reach the average for the comparison group?"

Debt affordability: calculations of the burden placed on a jurisdiction associated with repaying its debts.

Debt capacity: the amount of debt that can be issued without a jurisdiction overextending its ability to repay its obligations.

Debt ceiling approach: comparison of a jurisdiction's debt level to a single value or multiple values of an arbitrary measure.

Debt medians: measures of the typical value of debt for a jurisdiction of a specific type, size, geographic location, and other factors.

Debt policies: written guidelines issued by a jurisdiction regulating the amount, issuance process, and types of debt that may be issued.

Modified benchmarking approach: benchmarking approach that compares not only debt burdens but also measures of economic activity across jurisdictions.

Normal curve model: modified benchmarking approach that uses statistical properties of the normal distribution to assess relative debt burdens.

Discussion Questions

1. Debt affordability issues typically involve decisions and analysis that extend several years and decades into the future. What issues can you see with such an analysis? What methods should decision makers use to evaluate future forecasts of debt burdens?
2. The chapter discusses several approaches to assessing debt affordability. Which method do you think is the most complete in addressing the question of affordability? Which method would be easiest to implement? Discuss the trade-off in terms of the power of the models and the cost to implement them in terms of expertise, time, and other resources.
3. Typically, debt burdens are assessed in terms of some "base"—a measure that captures the ability of a jurisdiction to service its debts. Discuss the common bases used to assess debt burdens. Which is the most appropriate? Is there another way to capture the economic base of a jurisdiction that was not discussed in the chapter?
4. Municipal bond defaults are extremely rare. When in financial distress, issuers or other interested parties (such as state governments supporting local issuers) have shown a strong willingness to service debts. Given this, can an analyst be relatively liberal in assessing debt affordability? What values or principles are relevant for this discussion?
5. The chapter focuses on measuring subnational debt capacity. Do you think the same techniques can also be applied to measuring national debt capacity? If so, please discuss how a particular method can be implemented. If not, explain why.

Recommended Resources

Books

Feldstein, S. G., and Fabozzi, F. J. (Eds.). (2008). *The handbook of municipal bonds.* Hoboken, NJ: John Wiley & Sons.

Johnson, R. S. (2010). *Bond evaluation, selection, and management* (2nd ed.). Hoboken, NJ: John Wiley & Sons.

Mysak, J. (1998). *Handbook for muni-bond issuers.* Princeton, NJ: Bloomberg Press.

Software

Crystal Ball. Oracle. http://www.oracle.com/us/products/applications/crystalball/crystalball-066563.html

gretl. Allin Cottrell and Riccardo "Jack" Lucchetti. http://gretl.sourceforge.net/

SAS. SAS Institute Inc. http://www.sas.com/

STATA. StataCorp LP. http://www.stata.com/

Websites

Fitch U.S. Public Finance: http://www.fitchratings.com/jsp/sector/Sector.faces?selectedTab=Overview&Ne=4293330802%2b11&N=0

Improving Municipal Debt Efficiency: http://americancityandcounty.com/mag/government_financial_managementimproving_municipal/

Moody's U.S. Public Finance: http://www.moodys.com/researchandratings/market-segment/u.s.-public-finance/005003/4294966117/4294966623/0/0/-/0/rr

Standard & Poor's Governments: http://www.standardandpoors.com/ratings/govs-main/en/us

References

Bahl, R., Duncombe, W., and Bunch, B. (1991). The effect of constitutional debt limits on state governments' use of public authorities. *Public Choice, 68*(1-3), 57-69.

Bartle, J., Kriz, K. A., and Wang, Q. (2008). Assessing debt affordability for large capital projects: A case study. *Municipal Finance Journal, 29*(2), 1-20.

Bernard, J. (1982). Meeting state and local financing needs in the 1980s: Can the municipal debt market do its share? *Public Budgeting and Finance, Winter*, 59-70.

Brecher, C., Richwerger, K., and Van Wagner, M. (2003). An Approach to Measuring the Affordability of State Debt. *Public Budgeting & Finance, Winter,* 65-85.

Douglas, J. R. (2000). Best practice in debt management. *Government Finance Review, 16,* 2.

Hackbart, M., and Ramsey, J. (1990). State Debt Level Management: A Stable Credit Rating Model. *Municipal Finance Journal, Spring,* 79-96.

Hildreth, W. B. (1993). State and local governments as borrowers: Strategic choices. *Public Administration Review, 53,* 41-50.

Hildreth, W. B. (2005). *State of Kansas 2005 Debt Affordability Report.* Retrieved May 12, 2006, from http://hws.wichita.edu/index.php?option=com_remository&Itemid=109&func=fileinfo&parent=folder&filecatid=43.

Hildreth, W. B., and Miller, G. J. (2002). Debt and the local economy: Problems in benchmarking local government debt affordability. *Public Budgeting & Finance, Winter,* 99-113.

Kriz, K. A. (2010). *Debt Affordability: A Stochastic Model.* Paper presented at Association for Budgeting & Financial Management 22nd Annual Conference, Omaha, Nebraska, October 7, 2010.

Lyons, K. (2009). 2009 Debt Medians Report: Based on 2008 Data. New York: Moody's Investors Service.

Miranda, R. A., and Picur R. D. (2000). *Benchmarking and measuring debt capacity.* Chicago: Government Finance Officers Association.

Piper, T. R., and Weinhold, W. A. (1982). How much debt is right for your company? *Harvard Business Review, July/August,* 153-167.

Ramsey J. R., Gritz, T., and Hackbart, M. M. (1988). State approaches to debt capacity assessment: A further evaluation. *International Journal of Public Administration, 11,* 227–238.

Ramsey, J. R., and Hackbart, M. M. (1996). State and local debt policy and management. In G. Miller (Ed.), *Handbook of Debt Management* (pp. 255–276). New York: Marcel Dekker.

Regens, J. L., and Lauth, T. P. (1992). Buy now, pay later: Trends in state indebtedness, 1950–1989. *Public Administration Review, 52*(2), 157–161.

Simonsen, B., and Brown, R. (2003). Debt Affordability. In J. Rabin (Ed.), *Encyclopedia of Public Administration and Public Policy* (pp. 308–313). New York: Marcel Dekker.

Simonsen, B., Robbins, M. D., and Kittredge, B. (2001). Do debt policies make a difference in finance officers' perception of the importance of debt management factors? *Public Budgeting and Finance, 21*(1), 87–102.

Wang, Q. (2009). *The effect of public debt on state and local economic growth and its implication for measuring debt capacity: A simultaneous equations approach.* Paper resented at Association for Budgeting & Financial Management 20th Annual Conference, Chicago, October 25, 2008.

Appendix A: Water and Sewer Rating Criteria

Fitch (2007)	Moody's (1999)	Standard & Poor's (2007)
Community Characteristics	Local Economy and Customer Base	Economic Considerations
Customer Growth and Concentration	System Size and Assessment Base	Operational Characteristics
Capacity (Infrastructure)	System Demand and Capacity	
Compliance with Environmental Laws and Regulations	Regulation Risk, Regulatory Compliance	Legal Provisions
Capital Demands and Debt Policies	Maintenance of Assets, Strategic Focus	
Covenants	Rates, Rate Structures, and Rate-making Flexibility	Water and Sewer Rates
Charges and Rate Affordability		
Coverage and Financial Performance	Liquidity	Financial Data
Cash and Balance Sheet Considerations		
Crew (Management)	Governance and Management Quality	Management
	Construction Risk	
		Drainage Revenue Bonds
		Wholesale Systems' Legal Protections

Appendix B: Debt Affordability Indicators

Direct debt
Debt service
Debt margin
Debt per capita
Debt per capita including overlapping debt[13]
Debt as a percentage of real market value
Debt as a percentage of real market value including overlapping debt (also called debt burden)
Debt as a percentage of personal income
Debt as a percentage of personal income including overlapping debt
Debt service per capita
Debt service as a percentage of property tax revenue
Debt service per capita as a percentage of personal income per capita
Debt service as a percentage of general and debt service fund expenditures
Debt service as a percentage of operating expenditures
Impact of the debt on the tax rate
Impact of the debt on the average household
Accrued pension liability

Appendix C: Analytical Characterizations of Ratios

Analytical Characterization of Ratios	
Household/Per Capita Effective Buying Income As % of U.S. Level	
Low	Below 65%
Adequate	65%–90%
Good	90%–110%
Strong	110%–130%
Very strong	Above 130%
Market Value Per Capita	
Low	Below $35,000
Adequate	$35,000–$55,000
Strong	$55,000–$80,000
Very strong	$80,000–$100,000
Extremely strong	Above $100,000

Appendix D: Selected 2007 Medians for All Standard & Poor's Local Government General Obligation Ratings

Selected 2007 Medians for All Standard & Poor's Local Government GO Ratings	
Per capita EBI as % of U.S. level	95%
Household EBI as % of U.S. level	99%
Market value per capita	$73,960
Top 10 taxpayers as % of assessed valuation	8.10%
Total general fund balance as % of expenditures	21%
Debt service as % of expenditures	7%
Overall net debt per capita	$1,999
Overall net debt as % of market value	2.62%

Chapter 19

State Fiscal Constraints on Local Government Borrowing

Effects on Scale and Cost

by Juita-Elena (Wie) Yusuf, Jacob Fowles, Cleopatra Grizzle, and Gao Liu

Introduction

This chapter focuses on *fiscal institutions*, defined as those "institutions that set the background for fiscal decision making, analogous to the 'fundamental political, social, and legal ground rules' that structure economic and political activity" (Gordon, 2008, p. 274). Specifically, we look at fiscal institutions states impose on their localities and how these institutions constrain local government debt. This chapter examines how three types of fiscal institutions—*debt limits*, *bond referendum* requirements, and *tax and expenditure limits* (TELs)—affect the scale and cost of local government borrowing. Four broad questions are addressed:

1. What are the fiscal institutions through which states constrain local government debt?
2. To what extent have these state-imposed fiscal institutions been adopted by states to monitor and control their local governments?
3. How can these mechanisms constrain local borrowing and affect local governments' fiscal health?
4. Have these fiscal institutions had an effect on local government borrowing?

Statewide fiscal institutions can be traced back to the economic depression in the 1840s, although a second wave of institutions were spurred by California's passage of Proposition 13 in 1978, which placed severe restrictions on state and municipal governments' ability to generate revenue through taxation, including, most critically, strict controls on the property tax rates charged by counties. A rich literature exists that explores the rationale of voters and legislatures in adopting fiscal institutions. This literature broadly finds that adoption of fiscal institutions is prompted by public desire to limit taxation and introduce efficiency into governmental service provision (Mullins, 2003). The majority of empirical studies on the subject focus on state-level fiscal institutions, largely agreeing that these institutions have been at least somewhat effective in reducing public spending and containing government growth (Mullins and Joyce, 1996; Shadbegian, 1996; Skidmore, 1999).

However, researchers have also found that the effectiveness of these institutions widely varies across governments of various types, sizes, and purposes (Mullins, 2003).

Beyond revenues and expenditures, fiscal institutions also have important ramifications for other aspects of governments' fiscal health and well-being, particularly as they relate to borrowing. For example, the use of fiscal institutions may affect governments' performance on the capital market and thereby influence borrowing costs. In an efficient market, a municipal bond's expected default risk, a critical determinant of its yield, should incorporate the influences of fiscal institutions. Fiscal institutions may affect the default risk of government debts, thereby impacting the risk premium investors demand (Poterba and Rueben, 1997, 2001; Johnson and Kriz, 2005).

From the perspective of investors, some of these fiscal institutions lessen the flexibility of government finance and consequently increase the default risk of government full-faith indebtedness. For instance, "financial markets may view tax limitations as increasing the default risk of debt issues because of the constraints on the government's ability to raise revenues" (Johnson and Kriz, 2005, p. 85). Such limitations would increase the expected default risks of General Obligation (GO) bonds, which are pledged with governments' tax revenues. Limitations of other types, on the other hand, may be considered effective constraints on the arbitrary fiscal behaviors of governments and may be expected to lower the default risks of bonded indebtedness. Expenditure limitations fall in this category, because they reduce the possibility of unexpected government deficit and leave more resources to repay the outstanding debts. An institution subjecting all debt issues to popular vote, by providing the market with assurances that a majority of taxpayers support every issuance, may decrease the expected default risk and consequently bond yields, thereby reducing the municipality's capital costs. Similarly, debt limits, by imposing fiscal discipline and fiscal prudence, also should decrease the default risk and lower borrowing costs.

Fiscal institutions may also affect the size or scale of government borrowing. Debt limits impose caps on the government's debt level, thus restricting borrowing and lowering borrowing scale. Bond referenda, by requiring voters to approve the issuance of debt, may also restrict the use of debt financing and government borrowing. In contrast, TELs increase the government's reliance on debt, because tax limitations detract from the ability to raise taxes to finance government activities, while expenditure limitations reduce the ability to finance government using current revenues.

Figure 19.1 summarizes the potential effects of fiscal institutions on the scale and cost of government borrowing and subsequently the linkages to and implications for the government's fiscal health. Through their effects on borrowing scale and borrowing costs, fiscal institutions directly influence the government's debt service requirements. Smaller scale and lower cost borrowings result in lower debt service needs, in turn increasing the government's fiscal health because fewer resources are tied to debt service. Furthermore, lower levels of borrowing provide greater flexibility for the government to issue debt in the future, should the need arise, therefore positively affecting fiscal health. Note that these hypothesized relationships are theoretical, and that implementation issues may weaken or strengthen the linkages among fiscal institutions, government borrowing, and fiscal health.

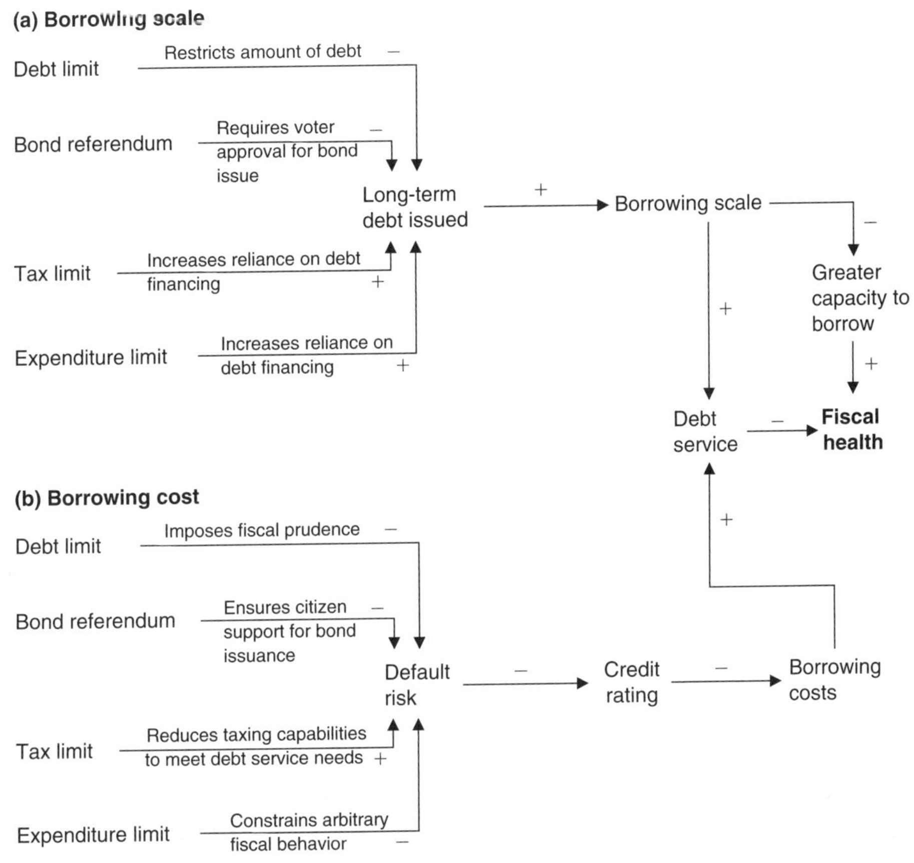

Figure 19.1 Theoretical Linkages Between Fiscal Institutions, Borrowing Scale and Cost, and Fiscal Health

This chapter reviews fiscal that institutions states impose on their local governments and discusses the effect of these fiscal institutions on local government borrowing. The next three sections provide an overview of three categories of state-imposed fiscal institutions: (1) debt limits, (2) bond referenda, and (3) TELs. The discussion focuses on fiscal institutions as mechanisms through which states can monitor and control local government borrowing behavior and constrain local debt. We provide the history and background of these fiscal institutions, review the extent to which these fiscal institutions are used across the states, and provide some examples of how they have been implemented across the various states. We then review the empirical literature to determine the effect that these fiscal institutions have had on local government borrowing scale and cost. Finally, we conclude by summarizing the state of the research on fiscal institutions states impose on their local governments and by suggesting a research agenda to further advance our knowledge.

Debt Limits and Debt Restrictions

Debt limits and debt restrictions were first introduced in state constitutions in response to the fiscal crisis in the 1840s created by failed investments in railroads and other types of infrastructure. The terms "debt limits" and "debt restrictions" are used widely in the literature; yet, the specific connotations of these terms are often ambiguous (Denison, Hackbart, and Moody, 2006). Debt limits are dollar limits on the maximum amount of debt that a government can issue. The limits are either specified as a maximum dollar value, a maximum amount of debt in relation to revenue or assessed property, or in terms of debt service payments as a percent of some measure of revenue (Denison et al., 2006; Nice, 1991).

Debt restrictions, on the other hand, come in many different forms and are not aimed at preventing borrowing per se but rather at specifying the procedures that state and local governments must abide by to authorize debt issuance. They regulate more than the amount of debt that a government can issue and frequently apply to the actual debt issuance process or characteristics of the actual bonds the state issues. For example, they may include a requirement that general obligation (GO) bonds be used only for specific purposes and issued only through a competitive bid process. In addition, many include provisions that allow a government to avoid the constraint of the limit and to authorize debt issuance if voter or legislative approval is obtained. Some states have both debt limits and debt restrictions. See **Figure 19.2** for different elements of debt limits and restrictions.

Although many states impose such constraints on themselves, virtually all states also impose debt limits on their local governments. One popular type of state-imposed debt limit is the debt ceiling, which is typically expressed as a percent of the property tax base of the local government. Some of these state-imposed debt limits also have provisions for exceeding the debt limit, such as subjecting all debt exceeding the debt limit to referendum approval.

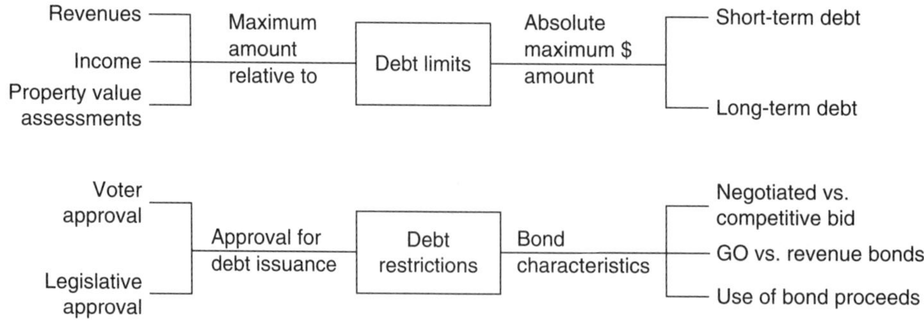

Figure 19.2 Different Elements of Debt Limits and Debt Restrictions

In New York State, for example,

> constitutional debt limits impose restrictions on the amount of debt that local governments can incur. Debt limits for counties, cities, towns, villages and school districts in cities (except for the Big 5 school districts) are percentages of the five-year average full valuation of taxable property within a municipality. The limit for school districts outside cities is a percentage of the current full valuation. Debt issued for the purpose of water supply and distribution and certain types of short term borrowings are excluded from the debt limit for counties, cities, towns and villages. In addition, a municipality can apply for exclusions from the limit for debt related to sewer projects and for certain types of self-liquidating debt.[1]

Pennsylvania statute sets limits differently on local government debt by using the concept of a borrowing base. A local government's borrowing base is defined by Pennsylvania statute as the local government's average annual revenue over the last three years. Under Pennsylvania's Local Government Unit Debt Act *(Title 53, Part VII, Subpart B, Chapter 80)*, the debt limit for townships and other local governments is 250% of their borrowing base, unless the voters approve additional debt through referenda.

Currently, only two states place no limits on debt issued by city and county governments. Eight restrict only debt issued by cities, while 40 states limit both city and county debt. **Figure 19.3** displays the distribution of debt limits across the United States.

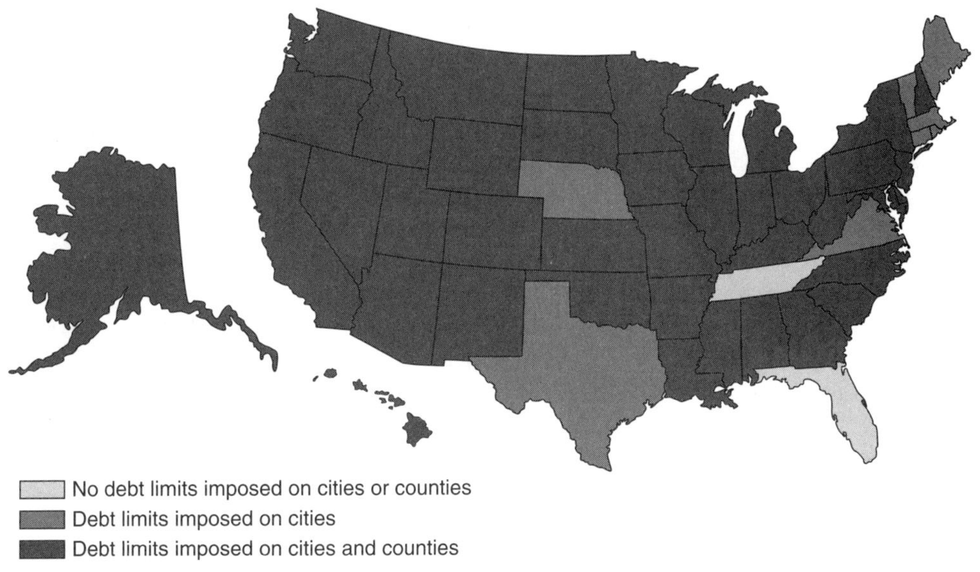

Figure 19.3 State-imposed Limits on Local Government Debt

Data from: U.S. Advisory Commission of Intergovernmental Relations (1993)

In theory, the effect of debt limits on borrowing costs can be explained from the credit rating perspective. A credit rating reflects the government's creditworthiness or likelihood of default, and historical research suggests that credit rating agencies take a government's debt capacity and debt management practices into consideration when rating a bond issue. The existence of debt limits suggest that state or local governments are fiscally prudent when it comes to debt financing and debt affordability and are viewed positively by credit rating agencies. This should translate into higher credit ratings and lower borrowing costs for issuers. Similar arguments apply to bond voting requirements.

Denison, Hackbart, and Moody (2009) suggest that formal debt limits are introduced in an effort to ease rating agency concerns or to avoid bond rating downgrades driven by excessive debt. They posit that as debt increases, credit rating agencies may question an issuing entity's capacity to fulfill its increasing debt service obligations and signal those concerns by lowering its credit rating, which ultimately increases borrowing costs.

Bond Referenda Requirements

Most states, in addition to using debt limits and restrictions as mechanisms to constrain local debt, also mandate that local debt issues be approved by public referendum. Unlike most other types of fiscal institutions, which function to explicitly limit the amount of debt issued, state referendum requirements simply stipulate that local governments secure the approval of voters before issuing debt while placing no explicit absolute or relative cap on actual debt levels.

Referendum requirements for local government issuance of debt have been widely adopted across the states. Of the 39 states that have adopted some form of referendum requirement, 12 require a referendum for only general obligation bond issues, and the other 27 require referendum for all issues, regardless of type (Advisory Commission on Intergovernmental Relations [ACIR], 1993). The distribution of referenda requirements is displayed in **Figure 19.4**.

States also differ in terms of the level of voter support they require to pass a local bond referendum. Although most states with a referendum requirement require a simple majority of voters to approve debt issues, some states require either a two-thirds or three-fifths supermajority for approval (ACIR, 1974). Finally, much variation exists across states in terms of both the specific purposes and types of local governments that are subject to the referendum requirement. In some states, debt issued by school districts, counties, or municipalities of certain classifications are exempt from seeking referendum approval to issue debt. Similarly, many states exempt debt issued to fund water and sewer capital projects from referendum (ACIR, 1961). In some states, referenda requirements are statutory, and in others these provisions are codified within the state constitution.

For example, Section 8 of Article 9 of the Constitution of Arizona states:

> No county, city, town, school district, or other municipal corporation shall for any purpose become indebted in any manner to an amount exceeding six per centum of the taxable property in such county, city, town, school district, or

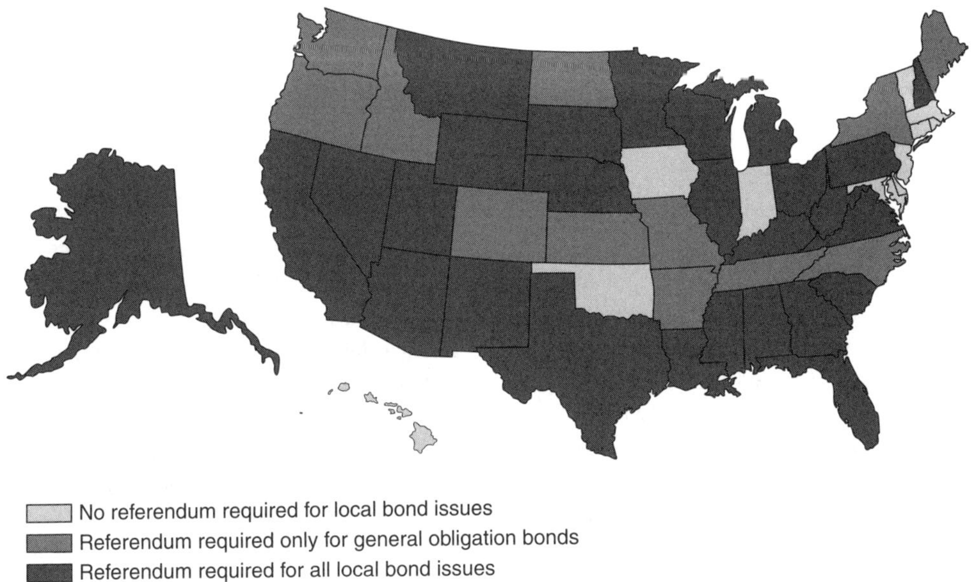

Figure 19.4 State-Imposed Referendum Requirements for Local Government Debt

Data from: U.S. Advisory Commission of Intergovernmental Relations (1993).

> other municipal corporation, without the assent of a majority of the property taxpayers, who must also in all respects be qualified electors, therein voting at an election provided by law to be held for that purpose[.]

Another example, using Section 18 of Article 16 of the California Constitution, states:

> No county, city, town, township, board of education, or school district, shall incur any indebtedness or liability in any manner or for any purpose exceeding in any year the income and revenue provided for such year, without the assent of two-thirds of the voters of the public entity voting at an election to be held for that purpose[.]

As these two examples reveal, the characteristics of referenda requirements as they exist across states are diverse. **Figure 19.5** summarizes the different elements that comprise bond referendum requirements.

There is much debate regarding both the effectiveness and impact of referendum requirements. From a theoretical perspective, several schools of thought emerge. As Farnham (1985) notes, these arguments generally begin with the theory of Ricardian Equivalence (Barro, 1974) that suggests that rational taxpayers should be indifferent to

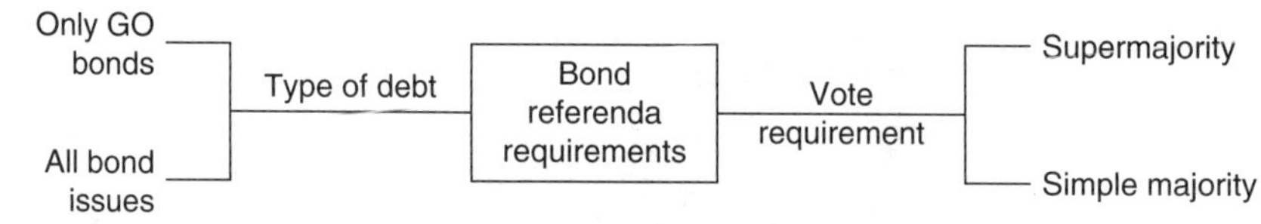

Figure 19.5 Different Elements of Bond Referenda Requirements

the issue of whether to fund government expenditures with debt or current revenues, implying that referenda are inherently unnecessary. However, others hold differing views. Buchanan (1958) argues that voters are biased toward debt financing because they enjoy the benefits provided by government services but dislike taxation, implying that referendum requirements are likely to be ineffective mechanisms for constraining local debt. He and others (see, e.g., McEachern, 1978) argue that this logic is particularly relevant in states that require only a simple majority for referendum approval. If we assume that elected officials align themselves with the preferences of the median voter, we would expect to observe equivalent debt levels, *ceteris paribus*, regardless of the existence of a simple majority referendum requirement because both the politician and referendum should directly reflect the median voter's preferences. As such, only in states that impose supermajority requirements would we expect to observe lower levels of local government debt. In these states, voters with preferences for less debt can capitalize on the supermajority requirement to impose their will on the median voter and restrain borrowing to a lower level than the median voter prefers.

Others, on the other hand, contend that the referendum—even in simple majority form—can indeed constitute a powerful mechanism through which local government borrowing can be constrained. Drawing on the classic principal-agent framework, scholars have argued that, under certain conditions, governments inherently prefer higher levels of debt than citizens, using expenditures funded by debt as a mechanism for restraining future government spending or as a way to increase contemporaneous political support. For example, Peltzman (1992), using federal and state data, finds evidence that voters are broadly more fiscally conservative than their governments. From this perspective, direct democracy is seen by many as the most effective and efficient way for the public to constrain government borrowing (Moak, 1982).

Tax and Expenditure Limits

TELs have been widely adopted throughout the United States. The most recent wave of TELs was spurred by the passage of California's Proposition 13 in 1978, a constitutional amendment approved by California voters that restricts the growth of both the assessment value and tax rate of real property. Proposition 13 heralded a wave of taxpayer revolt throughout the country. Within two years of the passage of the initiative, 43 states had adopted some kind of tax limitation (Mullins, 2004). To date, most states have imposed some type of TELs, either constitutionally or statutorily. These TELs are all intended to serve similar purposes: reduce tax burdens, constrain the size of government, and improve fiscal accountability (ACIR 1977, 1995; Ladd, 1978).

Table 19.1 provides an overview of the types and classifications of TELs. States impose many different types of TELs, including limits on property tax rates, limits on revenue, and limits on spending by local governments. As this table shows, TELs vary widely in their

TABLE 19.1 Types and Classifications of TELs

	Binding (Potentially)	Nonbinding
Overall property tax rate limitations	Rate ceiling is set that can only be exceeded by vote of the electorate, and applies to the aggregate tax rate of the local government	
	If coupled with a limit on assessment increases	Can be circumvented through alterations in assessment practices
Specific property tax rate limit	Same as overall property tax rate limit but applies to specific types of local governments or narrowly defined service areas	
	If coupled with a limit on assessment increases	Can be circumvented through alterations in assessment practices, or through interfund transfers
Property tax levy limit	Limits the total amount of revenue that can be raised through the property tax, independent of the property tax rate. Often enacted as an allowable annual percentage increase in the levy.	
	Are binding constraints, but can be minimized through diversification of revenue sources	
Limits on assessment increases	Controls the ability of local governments to raise revenue by reassessment of property or through escalation of property values	
	If coupled with an overall or specific property tax rate limit	Constraint can be avoided through increase in property tax rate
General revenue or general expenditure increases	Revenue limits cap the amount of revenue that can be collected. Expenditure limits cap spending during the fiscal year. Caps are often indexed to the rate of inflation.	
	Are binding constraints	
Full disclosure and truth in taxation	Generally require some type of public discussion and specific legislative vote prior to enacting tax rate or levy increase	
		Requires only formal vote of local legislative body

Adapted from: Joyce, P. G. and Mullins, D. R. (1991). The changing fiscal structure of the state and local public sector: The impact of tax and expenditure limitations. *Public Administration Review*, *51*(3), 240–253.

Adapted from: Mullins, D. R., and Joyce, P. G. (1996). Tax and expenditure limitations and state and local fiscal structure: An empirical assessment. *Public Budgeting & Finance*, *16*(1), 75–101.

implementation across states, both in terms of their scope and their stringency. Taxation limits in some states apply broadly, limiting the overall taxing power of local governments regardless of the underlying resource being taxed. Conversely, limits in other states apply only to taxes of certain types—the most common restriction being a limit on property taxes. However, even looking only at property tax limits reveals much diversity in terms of the specific characteristics of the limits as they have been implemented across states. Some states place explicit limits on the property tax rates that local governments can set. Others have chosen to set ceilings on overall property tax revenues, which constrain the total amount of property tax revenues that can be generated, independent of the tax rate. Finally, some other states have adopted assessment limits, which impose a maximum allowable increase in assessed values of the property tax. Assessment limits restrict local governments in their ability to generate increased revenues from rising property values or through reassessment of property values. Still other states have adopted hybrid limits, combining rate, revenue, and assessment limitations. California's Proposition 13 is one example of a hybrid limit as it combines both rate and assessment limits.

Expenditure limits, on the other hand, restrict the amount of money that local governments are authorized to spend. These limits are generally expressed as an annual percentage increase, constraining the future growth of government expenditures. Expenditure limits are typically applied only to own-source or general expenditures. Although expenditure limits in some states apply to all types of local governments, they are more commonly applied to school districts than to other types of local governments because many states use expenditure limits as a vehicle to promote equity across school districts with unequal local taxable resources. To date, eleven states impose expenditure limits on their school districts.

According to Joyce and Mullins (1991), state-imposed TELs on local governments can be categorized as "potentially binding" or "nonbinding" depending on how likely they are to successfully constrain a local government's ability to tax and spend. Spending and revenue limits are classified as potentially binding because they impose fixed ceilings that are difficult for local governments to circumvent. Conversely, limits on the property tax rate are classified as nonbinding because if local governments want to increase revenue from property tax rates, they can theoretically simply increase assessed property values to circumvent the state limit and generate additional revenue. Of course, this is predicated on the assumption that property values are currently assessed below full value (or the legal assessment limit); in times of stagnant or declining property values, reassessment could actually yield a decrease in revenue. This discussion notwithstanding, it is generally recommended that state officials seeking to create binding restraints to adopt property tax rate limits accompanied by an explicit provision that restrains the ability of local governments to increase assessed property values (Joyce and Mullins, 1991). Another institution considered to be binding is a limit on the property tax levy. This limitation generally pegs the growth rate of property tax with either the growth rate of inflation or the growth rate of residents' incomes. As such, it achieves a similar purpose to the hybrid limit previously proposed without specifically restricting rates or assessments. The survey by Mullins and

Joyce (1996) of TELs finds that 39 states impose either hybrid rate/assessment limits or limits on property tax levies, although 22 exclude debt service from being subjected to the TEL. Finally, on the expenditure side, expenditure limits that cap own-source spending are also considered binding.

TELs may affect the size of bonded debt of local governments, although the effect of debt-excluded TELs may differ from that of debt-included TELs. In some states, revenues and expenditures for debt service are exempt from the limitations. In this case, local governments may consider debt service as a way to circumvent the constraints of these fiscal institutions. Consequently, governments facing debt-excluded TELs may have larger levels of debt than those facing TELs that do not exclude debt service payments, all else constant. In other states, revenues and expenditures for debt service are subject to the constraint. This type of TEL is considered more binding than the former type and may limit governments' ability to raise revenue or service debt.

TELs can also influence the borrowing costs of local governments. On one hand, TELs promote fiscal responsibility among government administrators and residents, resulting in lower credit risks and capital costs. Expenditure limits are viewed positively in the financial market because they reflect prudent fiscal policy. Furthermore, the TELs can function to mitigate investor uncertainty regarding future government expenditures and revenues. Consequently, they may lead to lower credit risks and interest costs. On the other hand, TELs constrain the financial flexibility of governments, resulting in higher credit risks and higher capital costs. Revenue limits, for example, are seen as a limitation on taxing authority (Poterba and Rueben, 2001) and subsequently are thought to limit a government's ability to raise revenue or service debt. TELs may impair the future taxing capabilities of governments, resulting in lower credit ratings (Johnson and Kriz, 2005). Investors will, in turn, demand a higher return for the lower rating and increased risk of default due to its limitation on revenues, raising the cost of government borrowing.

TELs may be adopted by and affect different levels of governments. In some states, TELs universally affect all types of local governments, including counties, municipalities, and school districts. However, other states have chosen to exempt certain types of local governments from being subject to TELs. For example, the *property tax levy limit* that Rhode Island enacted in 1985 only applies to municipalities, exempting school districts and county governments. Conversely, the tax levy limit in Montana applies to both counties and municipalities but not to school districts. Even within the same state, some local governments may be exempted from certain TELs based on criteria such as location. For example, Pennsylvania exempts school districts in Pittsburgh and Philadelphia from the state-imposed property tax levy limit. Finally, in some states, local governments are empowered by statute or state constitution to adopt a local TEL that is more stringent than the state-imposed limit (Brooks and Phillips, 2009). **Table 19.2** summarizes the different state-imposed fiscal institutions that apply to local governments across the United States.

TABLE 19.2 State-Imposed TELs on Local Governments

State	Overall Property Tax Rate Limit	Specific Property Tax Rate Limit	Property Tax Revenue Limit	Assessment Increase Limit	General Revenue Limit	General Expenditure Limit	Full Disclosure
AK		M	M				
AL	C	C					
	M	M					
	SD	SD					
AR	C		C	C		C	
	M		M	M		M	
	SD			SD		SD	
AZ	C		C	C		C	
	M		M	M		M	
	SD			SD		SD	
CA	C	C		C	SD	C	
	M	M		M		M	
	SD	SD		SD		SD	
CO		C	C		C	C	C
		M	M		M	M	M
		SD	SD		SD	SD	SD
DE			C				C
FL		C		C			C
		M		M			M
		SD		SD			SD
GA		C					C
		SD					M
							SD

IA		C M SD		C M SD	SD	C
ID	C M SD	C M SD	C M SD			C M SD
IL		C M SD	C M SD			C M SD
IN			C M SD			
KS		C M SD		C M		SD
KY		C M	C M			C M
LA		C M SD	C M SD			
MA		M	M			
MD				C M SD		C M
MI	C SD	M SD	C M SD	C M SD		C M SD

(continued)

TABLE 19.2 State-Imposed TELs on Local Governments (cont.)

State	Overall Property Tax Rate Limit	Specific Property Tax Rate Limit	Property Tax Revenue Limit	Assessment Increase Limit	General Revenue Limit	General Expenditure Limit	Full Disclosure
MN		M			C M	SD	C M SD
MO		C M SD	C M SD				
MS			C M SD				
MT		C M SD	C M				C M SD
NC		C M					
ND		C M SD	C M				
NE		C M SD	C M			C M SD	C M
NJ			C			M SD	
NM	C M SD	C M SD	C M SD	C M SD			

NV	C M SD	M SD	C M		C M	C M SD
NY		C M SD		C M		
OH	C M SD		C M SD			
OK	C M SD			C M SD		
OR	C M SD	C M SD	C M SD	C M SD		
PA		C M SD	C			
PR			M			M
RI						C M SD
SC						C M SD
SD		C M SD				

(continued)

Table 19.2 State-Imposed TELs on Local Governments (cont.)

State	Overall Property Tax Rate Limit	Specific Property Tax Rate Limit	Property Tax Revenue Limit	Assessment Increase Limit	General Revenue Limit	General Expenditure Limit	Full Disclosure
TN							C M
TX		C M SD	C M SD				C M SD
UT		C M SD	C M SD				C M SD
VA							C M
WA	C M SD	C M	C M SD	C M SD			
WI		C			SD		
WV	C M SD	C M SD	C M SD				
WY		C M SD					

Notes: TELs are imposed by states on counties (C), municipalities (M), and/or school districts (SD).

Data from: Mullins, D. R. (2003). Popular processes and the transformation of state and local government finance. In D.L. Sjoquist (Ed.), State and local finances under pressure (pp. 95–162). Cheltenham, UK; Northampton, MA: Edward Elgar.

Empirical Findings

This section reviews and summarizes the empirical literature on the effect of fiscal institutions on government debt, in terms of both borrowing scale and borrowing costs. **Table 19.3** summarizes the extant empirical literature. To date, most studies have focused on the state level, with comparatively little empirical attention paid to the impact of state-imposed fiscal institutions on local governments. Earlier studies largely use samples from the Chubb Corporation survey on investors' estimations of 20-year state guaranteed bonds. More recent research has moved away from this reliance on survey data, instead using data from the bond issues themselves (see e.g., Johnson and Kriz, 2005; Liu et al., 2009; Rundle, 2009).

Although this literature to some degree can inform discussions of the effects of state fiscal institutions on local governments, it is important to note that critical differences between these two levels of government limit the usefulness of this exercise. First, though it can be argued that the adoption of a fiscal institution by a state reflects the preferences of citizens in that state, fiscal institutions imposed upon local governments imply a much weaker connection to voters, depending on the distribution of preferences across the municipalities in a state. Theoretically speaking, it is possible that a fiscal institution that all voters oppose in a municipality could nonetheless be imposed upon them by the state. Conversely, it is possible that a state-imposed institution could reflect the preference of all citizens in the affected municipality. While it is likely that the bulk of municipalities will fall somewhere between these two extremes, the connection between voters and the imposition of fiscal institutions by the state is weaker for municipalities than it is for states. In other words, there is an intrinsic (theoretical) exogeneity between the preferences of municipal residents and state-imposed fiscal institutions that does not exist at the state level.

Second, unlike the constraints imposed on state government revenues, expenditures, and debt, an analysis of the institutions states impose on local governments finds that they are generally defined more narrowly in scope. For example, tax limitations on local governments are typically imposed only on revenue generated from property taxes. Similarly, most state-imposed debt limits are typically linked to the property tax base of the local government and apply only to guaranteed debt. For these reasons, some researchers have argued that fiscal institutions may not have as strong an impact on local government fiscal behaviors because the inherent narrowness of these limits presents local governments with the opportunity to strategically circumvent them.

In contrast, Rundle (2009) suggests that there is "good reason to expect that fiscal rules may have even greater impact on interest rate costs at the municipal level" (p. 5). He argues that this may be due to differences in revenue diversity of local governments compared to states, where local government revenue sources are more concentrated because of the narrow taxing authority and less diverse economic base. Furthermore, financial information about local governments may be less readily accessible than those of state governments, and therefore fiscal institutions may signal information asymmetry between local

TABLE 19.3 Summary of Empirical Findings

Author(s)	Level of Government	Data	Fiscal Institutions	Effects
		Borrowing Size		
Clingermayer & Wood (1995)	State	State	TEL	+
			Debt limit	NS
Hur (2007)	State	State	Tax limit	+
			Revenue limit	+
			Debt limit	–
Bahl & Duncombe (1993)	State	State and local	GO debt limit	–
			Debt limit	–
			TEL	NS
Leigland (1994)	State	State	Debt limit	+
Ratchford (1941)	State	State	Debt limit	+
Heins (1963)	State	State	Debt limit	+
Nice (1991)	State	State	Debt limit	NS
Kiewiet & Szakaly (1996)	State	State	Debt limit	–
			Referendum	–
Farnham (1985)	Local	Local	Debt limit	–
			Referendum (simple majority and supermajority)	NS
McEachern (1978)	Local	Local	Referendum (simple majority)	NS
			Referendum (supermajority)	–
			Debt limits	–

Pogue (1970)	Local	State and local	Debt limit	–
			Referendum	N.S.
von Hagen (1991)	State	State	Debt limit	–
Feld and Kirchgässner (2001)	Swiss municipalities	Municipal	Referendum	–
		Borrowing Cost		
Rundle (2009)	Municipalities (cities, towns, villages, etc.)	Municipal bond new issue	Tax limit	+
			Spending limit	N.S.
			Debt limit	N.S.
Johnson & Kriz (2005)	State	GO new issue	Tax limit	+
			Spending limit	–
			Debt limit	+
			Referendum	N.S.
Wagner (2004)	State	Chubb Relative Survey	Tax limit	N.S.
			Spending limit	–
			Debt limit	–
			Debt limit	N.S.
			Spending limit	N.S.
			Tax limit	+
Poterba & Rueben (1997)	State	Chubb Relative Survey	Tax limit	+
			Expenditure limit	–
			Debt limit	NS
Bayoumi, Goldstein, & Woglom (1995)	State	Chubb Relative Survey	ACIR index (debt limit)	–

governments and their creditors. "This may cause the discount in interest rate for debt limits and expenditure limits (and premium for tax limits) to be of a greater magnitude than at the state level" (p. 6).

To date, studies have arrived at different and often contradictory conclusions regarding the effect of fiscal institutions on state and local governments. The next section reviews the empirical findings regarding the impact of fiscal institutions on government borrowing, focusing on costs and scale of borrowing.

Debt Limits

The empirical literature assessing the effect of debt limits on the capital costs borne by governments has been largely mixed and generally inconclusive. Bayoumi, Goldstein, and Woglom's (1995) study of states finds that debt limits reduce capital costs, as does Wagner (2004). However, Poterba and Reuben (1997) find no statistically significant relationship between debt limits and borrowing costs, while Johnson and Kriz (2005) find that debt limits increase borrowing costs, a finding that they attribute to the constraint that debt limits place on a state's future ability to generate revenue. Poterba and Reuben (2001) find that the existence of debt limits benefit states experiencing unexpected deficits by offsetting the negative impact of unexpected deficits on borrowing costs. Shifting the focus from state to local governments, Rundle (2009) finds no connection between debt limits and local government borrowing costs.

The literature assessing the effect of debt limits on the scale of government debt is somewhat more conclusive. Most studies have concluded that these limits appear to reduce overall debt burdens at both the state and local levels (Bahl and Duncombe 1993; Farnham 1985; McEachern 1978; von Hagen 1991). However, the results are not unanimous: Clingermayer and Wood (1995), in a study of the influence of politics on debt burdens, find that debt limits have no effect on aggregate long-term debt levels.

TELs

Empirical studies in both the political economy and public financial management literatures have largely agreed that TELs significantly affect the borrowing costs of state governments. Poterba and Reuben (1997) find that tax limits increase borrowing costs, while expenditure limits reduce borrowing costs. These findings are largely consistent with Johnson and Kriz (2005). Wagner (2004) observes a similar reduction in borrowing costs in states with expenditure limits across multiple model specifications but finds no consistently signed or statistically significant impact of tax limits. Rundle's (2009) study of municipal governments finds no effect for expenditure limits but finds that tax limits increase capital costs between 5 and 8 basis points.

Studies have also empirically examined the effects of TELs on the size and growth of government long-term debt. Most of these studies focus on state governments, with the only exception being Bahl and Duncombe (1993), who look at the aggregate debt burden of state and local governments. The findings regarding the effects of TELs on overall debt levels are mixed. Rueben (1995), relying on an instrumental variables approach to account for the potential endogeneity of TELs, finds that they reduce debt. Conversely, Hur (2007) finds that TELs increase the amount of total long-term debt, a finding mirrored by Clingermayer and Wood (1995). Finally, Bahl and Duncombe (1993) find no consistent statistically significant effect of TELs on total debt levels.

Referendum Requirements

Looking first at the state level, Kiewiet and Szakaly (1996) find the referendum requirement to be an effective constraint on overall debt levels and borrowing, as do Bohn and Inman (1996). However, the evidence on the impact of referendum requirements on local debt levels is much less conclusive. Pogue's (1970) study of the effect of multiple types of state-imposed debt constraints finds that referendum requirements are ineffective in constraining local government spending and overall debt levels. McEachern's (1978) cross-sectional analysis builds on Pogue's results but uses a more refined bond referendum variable that distinguishes between states with simple majority and supermajority referendum requirements. He finds that simple majority referendum requirements have no effect on local debt levels but does find that supermajority referendum requirements are associated with lower local government debt levels. Similarly, Feld and Kirchgässner's (2001) study of Swiss municipal governments finds that referendum requirements have a pronounced dampening effect on debt levels. On the other hand, Farnham (1985) reexamines the effectiveness of referendum requirements using a much larger sample of U.S. municipal governments than the earlier studies, concluding that neither simple nor supermajority referendum requirements are associated with lower debt levels.

To date, only a single study (Johnson and Kriz, 2005) assesses the impact of referendum requirements on state government capital costs, finding no connection between these requirements and credit rating or borrowing costs. No known literature exists that explores the relationship between referendum requirements and borrowing costs for municipal governments.

Conclusion

This chapter focuses on three types of state fiscal institutions and explores the ramifications of these institutions for local government fiscal health. From a purely theoretical perspective, one can argue that debt limits, bond referenda requirements, and TELs should have significant ramifications on not only the extent to which local governments can issue debt but also for capital market performance, thereby impacting local governments' borrowing costs and ultimately fiscal health. However, a review of the empirical literature finds surprisingly little research that directly speaks to these interrelationships, especially in terms of the impact of state-imposed fiscal institutions on costs of capital for local governments. Furthermore, the limited extant literature is largely inconclusive regarding these effects. Although some researchers have found that local governments in states with local taxation, expenditure and debt limitations seem to benefit from these institutions in terms of capital costs, it is less clear that these fiscal institutions are really enhancing fiscal prudence. This is evidenced in part by the decidedly mixed empirical findings regarding the relationship between fiscal institutions and overall levels of local government debt as discussed in the review of the empirical literature in this chapter.

Instead, the literature finds that state and local governments have been particularly clever in circumventing the spirit, if not the letter, of fiscal institutions. As von Hagen (2002) states, "the effectiveness of fiscal rules is limited at best because politicians are likely to find ways to circumvent them" (p. 266). For example, numerous scholars (Bennett and DiLorenzo, 1982, 1983; Bunch 1991; Sbragia 1996; Smith 1964, 1969) have documented the proliferation of public authorities, special districts, and other limited purpose governments in states with debt, revenue, and expenditure limits. Because these off-budget entities are typically not subject to state fiscal institutions, their use has permitted state and local governments to continue spending and borrowing outside the confines of state-imposed limitations—and largely outside the scrutiny of the public. Similarly, empirical evidence suggests that some state governments have responded to fiscal institutions by shifting service provision (and the accompanying expenditures and debt) to their constituent local governments, a phenomenon known as fiscal devolution (Heins 1963; Kiewiet and Szakaly 1996; Nice 1991; Stansel 1994). Finally, researchers have observed marked shifts in revenue structure in states with fiscal institutions. For example, empirical studies of governments in states with limits on guaranteed debt have generally found that these governments issue more revenue debt than their peers in states without similar institutions (Hur 2007; von Hagen 1991). Similarly, states with revenue or expenditure limits might turn to debt instruments as a way to circumvent these limits, actions that have serious potential consequences for inter-generational equity (Strauch 1998).

Although these efforts may have preserved (or at least prolonged) "business as usual" for many local governments in a broad sense, it is not unreasonable to argue that these extra steps have yielded an overall decline in local government efficiency and effectiveness by increasing governmental complexity and distancing government from citizens (Mullins, 2003). In times of fiscal prosperity, this disconnect may escape unnoticed. In times of fiscal decline, state and local governments can ill afford to continue to engage in inefficient practices and activities that may or may not be consistent with the preferences of the citizenry.

However, we should not dismiss the responsibility of the state to design and implement effective fiscal institutions. In crafting legislation that is designed to promote fiscal prudence and responsibility among local governments, policymakers must act carefully and deliberately to ensure that enacted legislation is consistent with both this goal as well as greater policy objectives. As this review of state fiscal institutions documents, many states seem to have been unsuccessful in this regard as *nonbinding constraints* allow local governments to continue unencumbered; worse, limits on local government's ability to tax and spend may inadvertently burden future generations with paying for current government goods and services. A more holistic approach to the creation and enactment of state fiscal institutions would prevent local governments from easily circumventing these restrictions. Additionally, states should recognize that fiscal institutions that appear on paper to apply uniformly to local governments might in fact have very differing effects on local governments of differing types and with differing constituencies. As many researchers have demonstrated, often it is the case that less prosperous local governments are disproportionately impacted by fiscal institutions as compared to their wealthier counterparts in terms of quality of local service provision, broadly defined (Downes and Figlio, 1999; Mullins, 2003; Mullins and Joyce, 1996). Despite these concerns, state fiscal institutions remain quite popular and will likely continue to be a reality for local government finance for the foreseeable future. Von Hagen (2002) suggests that subjecting local governments to fiscal institutions "seems the most straightforward approach to controlling their behavior and they seem attractive for simplicity and transparency" (p. 265). Yet, to what extent does this control come at the cost of local government's fiscal health?

On the whole, do local governments benefit from the imposition of fiscal institutions? Or are the external constraints imposed on them detracting from their overall financial condition? As this chapter reveals, this largely remains an unanswered question. Figure 19.1 summarized the theoretical linkages between fiscal institutions, local government borrowing, and fiscal health. The empirical literature examined and discussed in this chapter has focused on the relationship between fiscal institutions and government borrowing in terms of both borrowing costs and scale. However, capital costs and debt levels comprise only two of many aspects of fiscal health. Certainly, much work remains to be done. The current fiscal crisis has the potential to bring some of these issues to the forefront, although the extent to which this will occur remains to be seen. Regardless, the current economic contraction presents a unique opportunity for researchers to gauge the relative effectiveness (or ineffectiveness) of these fiscal institutions in promoting local fiscal health under conditions of duress.

The concept of debt capacity may offer a means of better understanding the linkages among fiscal institutions, borrowing costs and scale, and fiscal health. Debt capacity can be conceptualized as the level of debt and/or debt service relative to current revenues or debt ceiling that a government entity could support without creating undue budgetary constraints that might impair its ability to repay outstanding debt or make timely debt service payments (Hackbart and Ramsey, 1993; Ramsey and Hackbart, 1996). It reflects the amount of debt that a government entity can afford and/or the government's capacity to support greater levels of debt before there is an impact on the state's credit rating and borrowing costs (Denison et al., 2006). Debt capacity, therefore, has to do with a government's ability to sustain debt in the long run and should necessarily play a role in determining a government entity's fiscal health.

Denison et al. (2009) argue that a state's debt capacity is affected by the state's economy, its tax and revenue structure, and its willingness to incur debt obligations. For local governments, this debt capacity is further constrained by the fiscal institutions imposed by the state. TELs affect both the tax structure and the willingness to incur debt obligations. Bond referenda requirements ensure a stronger linkage between debt issuance and citizens' willingness for government to incur debt obligations. They note that there is no direct link between debt limits and debt capacity at the state level since debt limits may or may not be set at debt capacity. This is particularly true for debt limits states impose on their local governments. States with strong aversion to debt may set very low debt limits for their local governments to discourage borrowing. Other states may impose more generous debt limits that exceed the debt capacity of their local governments. The effectiveness of such debt limits as a control mechanism, then, comes into question, given the absence of this linkage between debt limits and debt capacity. In fact, Miranda and Picur (2000) suggest that factors such as debt ratios and debt burdens of similar governments should be criteria for determining local government debt capacity. These factors may have greater bearing on local government fiscal health than the state-imposed debt limit. Future research should focus on incorporating the fiscal institutions examined in this chapter, in addition to other types of institutions (e.g., balanced budget requirements or antideficit rules), into the discussion, especially at the local level. Future research should concentrate on more empirical analysis focusing on how the different fiscal institutions interact with each other to affect fiscal health. Researchers should work on separating the effects of the different types of institutions and take a more complementary approach to understanding not only the fiscal effects but why specific institutions were created and adopted by some localities and not others, as well as how these institutions have evolved over time.

Endnote

1. http://www.osc.state.ny.us/localgov/finreporting/cdl.htm

Glossary

Bond referendum: A bond referendum is a fiscal institution that stipulates that governments must secure the approval of voters before issuing debt.

Constitutional fiscal institution: This is a fiscal institution that is codified in the state constitution. Constitutional institutions are thought to be more binding than statutory institutions, all else equal, because of the relative procedural difficulty of amending constitutions in most states.

Debt limits: Debt limits are a fiscal institution that specifies the procedures that state and local governments must abide by to authorize debt issuance, either by establishing a fixed dollar amount to the total allowable debt burden or by creating a moving limit that is based on factors such as property values.

Fiscal institutions: Fiscal institutions are the official regulations and rules that impact governmental fiscal policymaking.

Nonbinding constraint: Nonbinding constraints are a category of fiscal institutions that are easily circumvented by local governments. For example, state adoption of a property tax rate limit in isolation represents a nonbinding constraint because local governments can circumvent it through a reassessment of property values.

Potentially binding constraint: Potentially binding constraints are a category of fiscal institutions that are not easily circumvented by local governments. For example, a state property tax levy limit is said to constitute a potentially binding constraint because of its fixed nature. Similarly, a hybrid limit that restricts both property tax rates and assessments is considered to be a potentially binding constraint.

Property tax assessment limit: A property tax assessment limit places restrictions on the ability of the local government to generate additional property tax revenue by reassessing property values.

Property tax levy limit: A property tax levy limit places restrictions on the total amount of revenue that can be generated through the property tax but places no specific restrictions on property tax rates or assessments.

Property tax rate limit: A property tax rate limit places restrictions on the revenue generated through the property tax by creating an upper limit on the rate at which local governments can tax property. Many states allow local governments to exceed the property tax rate limit only if specifically given the authority to do so through referendum.

Statutory fiscal institution: This is a fiscal institution that is created in state statute rather than in the state constitution. All else equal, statutory fiscal institutions are thought to be less binding than constitutional fiscal institutions because of the relative ease with which they can be amended by legislatures.

Tax and expenditure limits (TELs): Tax and expenditure limits are fiscal institutions designed to restrict the growth of governments by restricting either the ability of governments to generate additional revenue through taxation or through the restriction of governmental expenditures.

Discussion Questions

1. As described in this chapter, states impose different types of fiscal institutions onto their local governments. What are the advantages and disadvantages for the states of imposing these fiscal institutions? What are the advantages and disadvantages for local governments of being subjected to these institutions?
2. Many scholars argue that efficient capital markets impose more efficient and effective restraints on governmental behavior than fiscal institutions. What do you think? What are the pros and cons associated with relying on one approach or the other?
3. In this chapter, the authors suggest that fiscal institutions can be categorized as constitutional or statutory and binding or nonbinding. How do these differing taxonomies relate to each other, and what other approaches can you think of that

could be used to categorize fiscal institutions and to study their effects on local government fiscal health?

4. The focus of this chapter is on fiscal institutions adopted by the states and imposed on their respective local governments. In addition to those state-imposed fiscal institutions, local governments in many states are permitted to adopt their TELs, debt limits, and/or bond referendum requirements, provided that these institutions are at least as severe as those the state imposes. For example, Baltimore has a locally imposed annual limit on property assessment increases, and the city of Chicago has a local cap on property tax increases. Why would local governments adopt these fiscal institutions? What are the advantages and disadvantages?
5. Suppose that you are undertaking research on the impact of state-imposed fiscal institutions on local government finances. Beyond their possible effects on local government debt, what other effects on local government financial health would you expect? Why?
6. Numerous researchers have found that the adoption of fiscal institutions has had a negative impact on quality of local government service provision, especially in poorer areas (Downes and Figlio, 1999; Joyce and Mullins, 1991). However, most surveys on the subject find that citizens have trouble identifying the level of government responsible for the provision of specific goods and services. What are the implications of this finding for the overall expected impact of fiscal institutions on governmental fiscal well-being?
7. The economist Charles Tiebout, in a paper published in 1956, argued that a key advantage of providing public services at the local level is that it enables citizens to move to a locale where the local taxation and service levels match personal preferences. What are the implications of state-imposed fiscal institutions for the ability of citizens to "vote with their feet"?
8. Despite the mixed empirical support for the effectiveness of fiscal institutions, they remain quite popular across the United States. What do you think accounts for this popularity?

Recommended Resources

Dye, R. F., and McGuire, T. J. (1997). The effect of property tax limitation measures on local government fiscal behavior. *Journal of Public Economics, 66*, 469–487.

Dye, R., McGuire, T., and McMillen, D. (2005). Are property tax limitations more binding over time? *National Tax Journal, 58*(2), 215–225.

Elder, H. (1992). Exploring the tax revolt: An analysis of the effects of state tax and expenditure limitation laws. *Public Finance Quarterly, 20*(1), 47–63.

Howard, M. (1989). Tax and expenditure limitations: There is no story. *Public Budgeting and Finance, 83*(9). 83–90.

Kousser, T., McCubbins, M. D., and Moule, E. (2008). For whom the TEL tolls: Can state tax and expenditure limits effectively reduce spending? *State Politics and Policy Quarterly, 8*(4), 331–362.

Kousser, T., McCubbins, D. M., and Rozga, K. (2008). When does the ballot box limit the budget? Politics and spending limits in California, Colorado, Utah, and Washington. In E. Garret, E. A. Graddy, and H. E. Jackson (Eds.), *Fiscal challenges: An interdisciplinary approach to budget policy*. 290–321. New York: Cambridge University Press.

Liu, P., and Thakor, A. (1984). Interest yields, credit ratings, and economic characteristics of state bonds: An empirical analysis. *Journal of Money, Credit and Banking*, 344–351.

Matsusaka, J. (1995). Fiscal effects of the voter initiative: Evidence from the last 30 years. *Journal of Political Economy, 103*(3), 587–623.

Peterson, G., and Solomon, A. (1973). Property taxes and populist reform. *Public Interest, 30*, 60–75.

Raimondo, H. J. (2001). State Limitations on local taxing and spending: Theory and practice. *Public Budgeting & Finance, 3*(3), 33–42.

Shadbegian, R. J. (2003). Did the property tax revolt affect local public education? Evidence from panel data. *Public Finance Review, 31*(1), 91–121.

Shannon, J., Bell, M., and Fisher, R. (1976). Recent experience with local tax and expenditure controls. *National Tax Journal, 29*, 276–285.

Sokolow, A. D. (1998). The changing property tax and state-local relations. *Publius: The Journal of Federalism, 28*, 165–187.

Strauch, R. R. (1998). *Budget processes and fiscal discipline: Evidence from the US states.* Working Paper. Bonn: Center for European Integration Studies (ZEI).

Waisanen, B. (2008). *State tax and expenditure limits.* Washington, DC: National Council of State Legislatures.

Winkler, D. R. (1979). Fiscal limitations in the provision of local public services: The case of education. *National Tax Journal, 32*(2), 329–342.

References

Advisory Commission on Intergovernmental Relations. (1961). *State constitutional and statutory restrictions on local government debt.* Washington, DC: Advisory Commission on Intergovernmental Relations.

Advisory Commission on Intergovernmental Relations. (1974). *Federal-state-local finances: Significant features of fiscal federalism.* Washington, DC: Advisory Commission on Intergovernmental Relations.

Advisory Commission on Intergovernmental Relations. (1977). *Measuring the fiscal "blood pressure" of the states—1964–1975.* Washington, DC: Advisory Commission on Intergovernmental Relations.

Advisory Commission on Intergovernmental Relations. (1993). *State laws governing local government structure and administration.* Washington, DC: Advisory Commission on Intergovernmental Relations.

Advisory Commission on Intergovernmental Relations. (1995). *Tax and expenditure limits on local governments.* Washington, DC: Advisory Commission on Intergovernmental Relations.

Bahl, R., and Duncombe, W. (1993). State and local debt burdens in the 1980s: A study in contrast. *Public Administration Review, 53*(1), 31–40.

Barro, R. (1974). Are government bonds net wealth? *Journal of Political Economy, 82*(6), 1095–1117.

Bayoumi, T., Goldstein, M., and Woglom, G. (1995). Do credit markets discipline sovereign borrowers? Evidence from U.S. states. *Journal of Money, Credit and Banking, 27*(4), 1046–1059.

Bennett, J., and DiLorenzo, T. J. (1982). Off-budget activities of local government: The bane of the tax revolt. *Public Choice, 39*(3), 333–342.

Bennett, J.T. and DiLorenzo, T.J. (1983). Underground government: The off-budget public sector. Washington, DC: Cato Institute.

Bohn, H., and Inman, R. P. (1996). *Balanced budget rules and public deficits: Evidence from the U.S. states.* Cambridge, MA: National Bureau of Economic Research, Inc.

Brooks, L., and Phillips, J. (2009). *Constraining the local leviathan: The existence, origins, and effectiveness of municipally-imposed tax and expenditure limits.* University of Toronto Working Paper. Toronto, Canada: University of Toronto.

Buchanan, J. (1958). *Public principles of public debt.* Homewood, IL: Irwin.

Bunch, B. S. (1991). The effect of constitutional debt limits on state government use of public authorities. *Public Choice, 68*(1), 57–69.

Clingermayer, J. C., and Wood, B. D. (1995). Disentangling patterns of state debt financing. *American Political Science Review*, *89*(1), 108–120.

Denison, D. V., Hackbart, M. M., and Moody, M. J. (2009). Intrastate competition for debt resources. *Public Finance Review, 37*(3), 269–288.

Denison, D. V., Hackbart, M. M., and Moody, M. J. (2006). State debt limits: How many are enough? *Public Budgeting and Finance, 26*(4), 22–39.

Downes, T. A., and Figlio, D. (1999). Do tax and expenditure limits provide a free lunch? Evidence on the link between limits and public sector service quality. *National Tax Journal*, *52*(1), 113–128.

Farnham, P. G. (1985). Re-examining local debt limits: A disaggregated analysis. *Southern Economic Journal, 51*(4), 1186–1201.

Feld, L. P., and Kirchgässner, G. (2001). Does direct democracy reduce public debt evidence from Swiss municipalities. *Public Choice, 109*(3), 347–370.

Gordon, T. M. (2008). The calculus of constraint: A critical review of state fiscal institutions. In E. Garret, Graddy, E. A. and Jackson, H. E. (Eds.). *Fiscal challenges: An interdisciplinary approach to budget policy.* 271–289. New York: Cambridge University Press.

Hackbart, M., and Ramsey, J. R. (1993). Debt management and debt capacity. In R. Lamb, Leigland, R. J., and Rappaport, S. P. (Eds.). *The Handbook of Municipal Bonds and Public Finance.* New York: New York Institute of Finance, p. 316–348.

Heins, A. J. (1963). *Constitutional restrictions against state debt*: Madison: The University of Wisconsin Press.

Hur, M. (2007). Fiscal limits and state fiscal structure: An analysis of state revenue structure and indebtedness. *Municipal Finance Journal, 28*(3), 19–35.

Johnson, C. L., and Kriz, K. A. (2005). Fiscal institutions, credit ratings, and borrowing costs. *Public Budgeting & Finance, 25*(1), 84–103.

Joyce, P. G. and Mullins, D. R. (1991). The changing fiscal structure of the state and local public sector: The impact of tax and expenditure limitations. *Public Administration Review, 51*(3), 240–253.

Kiewiet, D. R., and Szakaly, K. (1996). Constitutional limitations on borrowing: An analysis of state bonded indebtedness. *Journal of Law, Economics, and Organizations, 12*(1), 62–97.

Ladd, H. F. (1978). An economic evaluation of state limitations on local taxing and spending powers. *National Tax Journal, 31*, 1–18

Leigland, J. (1994). Public authorities and the determinants of their use by state and local governments. *Journal of Public Administration Research and Theory, 4*, 521–544.

Liu, G., Fowles, J., and Yusuf, J. (2009). *New York State fiscal institutions and municipal borrowing: Do debt and taxation limits really impact capital costs?* Paper presented at the Association for Budgeting and Financial Management Annual Conference. Washington, D.C.

McEachern, W. A. (1978). Collective decision rules and local debt choice: A test of the median voter hypothesis. *National Tax Journal, 31*(2), 129–136.

Miranda, R., and Picur, R. (2000). *Benchmarking and Measuring Debt Capacity.* Chicago: Government Finance Officers Association.

Moak, L. (1982). *Municipal bonds: Planning, sale, and administration.* Chicago: Municipal Finance Officers Association.

Mullins, D. R. (2003). Popular processes and the transformation of state and local government finance. In D.L. Sjoquist (Ed.), *State and local finances under pressure* (pp. 95–162). Cheltenham, UK; Northampton, MA: Edward Elgar.

Mullins, D. R. (2004). Tax and expenditure limitations and the fiscal response of local government: Asymmetric intra-local fiscal effects. *Public Budgeting & Finance, 24*(1), 111–147.

Mullins, D. R., and Joyce, P. G. (1996). Tax and expenditure limitations and state and local fiscal structure: An empirical assessment. *Public Budgeting & Finance, 16*(1), 75–101.

Nice, D. C. (1991). The impact of state policies to limit debt financing. *Publius: The Journal of Federalism, 21*(1), 69–82.

Peltzman, S. (1992). Voters as fiscal conservatives. *The Quarterly Journal of Economics, 107*(2), 327–361.

Pogue, T. (1970). The effect of debt limits: Some new evidence. *National Tax Journal, 23*(1), 36–49.

Poterba, J. M., and Rueben, K. S. (1997). *State fiscal institutions and the U.S. municipal bond market.* NBER Working Paper No. 6237. Cambridge, MA: National Bureau of Economic Research.

Poterba, J. M., and Rueben, K. S. (2001). Fiscal news, state budget rules, and tax-exempt bond yields. *Journal of Urban Economics, 50*(3), 537–562.

Ramsey, J., and Hackbart, M. (1996). State and local debt policy and management. In G. Miller (Ed.), *Handbook of Debt Management.* New York: Marcel Dekker.

Ratchford, B. U. (1941). *American state debts.* Durham, NC: Duke University Press.

Rueben, K. S. (1995). Tax limitations and government growth: The effect of state tax and expenditure limits on state and local government. Mimeograph. Cambridge, MA: Massachusetts Institute of Technology.

Rundle, J. (2009). *Institutional aspects and fiscal outcomes of U.S. municipal governance.* Fairfax, VA: George Mason University.

Sbragia, A. M. (1996). *Debt wish: Entrepreneurial cities, U.S. federalism, and economic development.* Pittsburgh, PA: University of Pittsburgh Press.

Shadbegian, R. J. (1996). Do tax and expenditure limitations affect the size and growth of state government? *Contemporary Economic Policy 14*, 22–35.

Skidmore, M. (1999). Tax and expenditure limitations and the fiscal relationships between state and local governments. *Public Choice, 99*(1-2), 77–102.

Smith, R.G. (1969). Public authorities in urban areas. Washington, DC: National Association of Counties.

Smith, R.G. (1964). Public authorities, special districts, and local government. Washington, DC: National Association of Counties.

Stansel, D. (1994) *Taming leviathan: Are tax and expenditure limits the answer?* Cato Policy Analysis No. 213. Washington, D.C.: Cato Institute.

Strauch, R. R., (1998). *Budget processes and fiscal discipline: Evidence from the US states.* Working Paper. Bonn: Center for European Integration Studies (ZEI).

von Hagen, J. (1991). A note on the empirical effectiveness of formal fiscal restraints. *Journal of Public Economics, 44*, 199–221.

von Hagen, J. (2002). Fiscal rules, fiscal institutions, and fiscal performance. *The Economic and Social Review*, *33*(3), 263-284.

Wagner, R. (2004) The bond market and fiscal institutions: have budget stabilization funds reduced state borrowing costs? *National Tax Journal, 57*(4), 785–804.

Chapter 20

Good Debt, Gone Bad

The 2007–2009 Crisis in Municipal Debt Markets

by Gary R. Rassel and Robert S. Kravchuk

Introduction

The financial crisis that began in 2007 created insecurity regarding the status of the municipal bond market, the safety of municipal bonds as investments, and, in turn, the fiscal health of state and local governments. In 2008, many local governments suddenly found their bond ratings downgraded because of the shaky financial condition of the bond insurers. And because of the failure of the market for certain variable rate debt instruments, accompanied by a lack of liquidity from financial institutions, some governments were required to pay increased and accelerated amounts on their debt. The systemic factors causing the market crisis of 2007–2009 were largely beyond the control of individual municipal issuers. These factors were the source of previously unknown and unforeseen risks. They included the subprime mortgage crisis and the attendant use of *collateralized debt obligations* (CDOs) by key financial institutions and traditional providers of credit enhancement to municipal borrowers. Much of the explanation for the severely reduced market liquidity in 2009 and 2010, and the all but complete withdrawal of bond insurers, can be traced to the significant exposures to subprime mortgage-based instruments that these institutions held in their portfolios.

The municipal debt market, however, has been less affected than the market for corporate debt in this period of market turmoil. Municipal issues defaulted far less frequently than similarly rated corporate issues, and recovery rates remained much higher. With the subprime crisis in view, this chapter reviews the history of the municipal debt market, including the history of defaults, and the most prominent current market segments—fixed obligations and variable rate debt obligations—to trace the evolution of the market into its current state of crisis and the effect of that crisis on state and local governments. The critical observations that emerge from our review of both historical default rates and the most recent market turmoil are:

- Default patterns historically show a decided increase during recessions; that is also true of the 2007–2009 period.

- The municipal debt market has been historically susceptible to turmoil in the real estate markets. This was again the case in 2007–2009.
- Most defaults occur in issues of so-called conduit financing, whereby public monies are used to fund what are essentially private land and community development projects and healthcare facilities.[1]
- Unlike past waves of default, however, in 2007–2009, the failing fiscal position of institutions upon which issuers have come to rely for credit enhancement jeopardized what were otherwise good state and local government debts.
- The municipal bond market, along with other sectors of the economy, has been damaged by the subprime fiasco of 2007–2008, impacting the finances of state and local governments and their ability to borrow. An economic slowdown beginning in 2007 also affected the revenues of state and local governments and limited their ability to repay debt—although the declines in revenues were not large until 2008.

We then discuss the extent to which these market conditions have affected the fiscal health of governments and may do so in the future. This is followed by further discussion of factors that researchers, creditor institutions, and citizens may turn to for help in assessing fiscal health.

A Cautionary Tale

The financial crisis of 2007–2009 affected state and local borrowers in some ways very much like past economic crises and in other ways unlike them. Many, if not most, of the abuses in the previous crises derived from the employment of state and municipal bond funds in support of private enterprise—land development schemes and internal improvements such as canals and railroads (Hughes, 1977). Waves of municipal bond defaults accompanied the economic crises of 1837–1843, 1873–1879, 1893–1899, and 1929–1937, which were aggravated by policies of public support of private economic development that can only be described as "footloose" (Hempel, 1971). Such *conduit bonds* have always been problematic, insofar as they involve public guarantees for private risks. This pattern was repeated in the period leading up to 2007–2009 (Sigo, 2009). The 2007–2009 situation was aggravated by the failure of many special purpose governments to meet obligations on their bonded debt. When markets fluctuate in unfavorable ways—in this case, the bursting of the real estate bubble—the anticipated project cash flows needed to pay the debt fail to materialize, with deleterious effects on the municipal debt issued to finance these projects.

The use of public credit to finance projects whose material benefits would largely accrue to private developers also preceded the crises of the past. The vast proliferation of specialized units of local government, coupled with the aggressive use of variable rate debt obligations, certificates of participation, and other-than-general-obligation debt instruments, has circumvented the statutory limits that states have placed on municipal debt

(Bunche, 1991; Poterba, 1995; Poterba and Rueben, 1997, 1999, 2001; Strickland, 1969). Issuing bonds through special purpose governments often allows general purpose governments to avoid voter approval requirements as well (Ackerman, 2007; Bunche, 1991).

Turning to the new realities, for governments whose fiscal policies prevent community development projects from unduly compromising their finances, we find a different pattern, one whose root causes are also ultimately located in the real estate market but with different dynamics. The previous crises resulted in the promulgation of statutory debt limits, disclosure requirements, and associated regulations that were designed to prevent the past abuses. Adherence to state (and federal) regulations, as well as reasonable and prudent standards of modern public financial management, has become a hallmark of professionalism in governmental administration. The developing structure of municipal bond market regulation for the first 150 years of the republic has been one of overcoming and preventing the abuses that caused or worsened the prior wave of defaults. Strict state constitutional and statutory limits on the permissible size of municipal debt, requirements for the legal advice of competent bond counsel, fiscal disclosures, and use of third-party trustees have provided great security for investors' funds and promoted public confidence in municipal bonds. Both investors and municipal debt issuers have benefited from the regulatory structure that evolved. In the crisis of 2007–2009, however, even well-run, financially sound governments found themselves at risk, despite improved fiscal management practices. We therefore begin with a cautionary tale about one of them:[2]

> A local housing authority, having a AA ("double A") bond rating, was financed through bond issues each structured in the form of variable rate bonds, secured by letters of credit issued by foreign banks. The financing was used to construct mixed use residential-commercial housing units in an urban center. Under the terms of the letters of credit, the bank services the debt, with the authority reimbursing the bank from amounts it received through either a sales tax increment or property tax increment. The bonds are structured so as to be remarketed on a monthly basis. The holders of the bonds "surrender" the bonds monthly, to the remarketing agent, who resells the bonds at (usually) a different interest rate.[3]
>
> After these bonds were issued, the bank that had issued letters of credit was downgraded by Standard and Poor's and Moody's. As a consequence, many financial institutions and money market funds were not able to keep these bonds in their portfolios, so were required to sell them and not purchase these same bonds back as they had done in the past.[4]
>
> In the case of the housing authority, the bank downgrade "poisoned" the bonds so that the remarketing agent couldn't sell the bonds in the open market. According to the terms of the letter of credit, the bank was forced to take possession of the bonds. That is, they were converted to "bank bonds." When a bond is forced to be converted to a bank bond, the contract further calls for increasing the interest rate to a higher, predetermined rate.[5]

The remarketing agent continues to remarket the bonds on a monthly basis. Should the remarketing agent be unable to find a buyer (at any price), the bonds remain with the bank, which becomes the lender/investor.[6] If the remarketing agent is unsuccessful in remarketing the bank bonds within a certain predetermined period of time, then the bonds may be either converted to "term loans," or placed on an accelerated amortization schedule.[7] In the case at hand, the authority's problem was exacerbated when its revenues fell because developers were unable to attract sales tax producing commercial tenants, and property taxes languished due to sluggish residential unit sales.[8] The effect on the authority's budget is to divert a larger proportion of funds to debt service, reducing its ability to fulfill its stated public policy mission. The irony is that the issuer had done everything called for by both the law and prudent financial management.

Development of the U.S. Municipal Debt Market

The issuance of municipal debt in the United States predates the formation of the republic. The first recorded debt issue was on the part of the Massachusetts Bay Colony in 1751. In 1790, under Treasury Secretary Alexander Hamilton's plan, the federal government assumed all state debts to establish the credit worthiness of the United States. From 1790 to 1820, little state and local debt was issued, with the notable exception of New York. The first modern-style general obligation bond, backed by the taxing power of the issuer, took place in 1812, when New York City pledged its "full faith and credit" to repay the bond proceeds, with interest. In the early 19th century, both New York State and Indiana issued bonds to finance the Erie Canal and a series of locks along the Ohio River near what is now Louisville, Kentucky. New York's issue to finance construction of the Erie Canal was among the very first securities traded on the New York Stock Exchange. In another milestone, the Port of New Orleans in the early 1800s was the first independent government authority to finance development based on its own fiscal strength. Between 1825 and 1838 alone, state debt issuance grew ten-fold, from just under $14 million to over $140 million a year. A spike in borrowing occurred in the 1860s. State governments bore a large proportion of the cost of fighting the Civil War during that crisis. For instance, the Commonwealth of Pennsylvania issued some $3 million in bonds to build defenses to guard its territory against a Southern attack (Dwight, 2007). By and large, however, state and local debt issued remained relatively stable until the 1880s.

In the second half of the nineteenth century, and into the twentieth, municipal bonds provided a major source of financing for transportation and other infrastructure development projects (including water, sewer, ports, and mass transit) for major cities such as New York, Philadelphia, Chicago, and Houston. The first special *revenue bonds* were issued in 1885, by Wheeling, West Virginia, in order to finance construction of the city's water and gas works. All told, these and similar projects brought municipal debt outstanding, from 1900 to the onset of the Great Depression, from approximately $2.1 billion, to $14.9 billion, or from around $27 per capita to $125 per capita. The period of most rapid increase occurred after 1919. Hempel (1971) reports that records indicate the average annual debt issued never exceeded $500 million until 1919. But from 1921 through 1931, the yearly amount issued exceeded $1.1 billion each year, with an average amount of $1.4 billion, almost a three-fold increase in less than a decade.

In another milestone, the creation in 1921 of the Port Authority of New York and New Jersey empowered, for the first time, an interstate entity to issue debt in the form of revenue bonds on its own credit, requiring no prior voter referendum. It should be noted that, during this time, municipal issues became relatively more attractive than corporate bonds, owing to the exemption of interest payments from the federal income tax, enacted by the 16th Amendment in 1913. The Great Depression and the Second World War saw roughly a decade-and-a-half of neglect of state and local infrastructure. Combined with the forces of rapid urbanization—and suburbanization—the pent-up demand for infrastructure renewal and construction propelled states and localities to borrow at unprecedented levels. Municipal debt outstanding subsequently grew from around $66 billion in 1960 to more than $360 billion in 1980, a more than 600% increase.

By 1975, about $58 billion in municipal debt was being issued annually, almost the sum total of all municipal debt outstanding just 15 years earlier. Growth of the "muni market" has proceeded apace in the years since then, reaching $1.8 trillion by 2002 and $2.3 trillion by 2007. In that year, municipal bonds were sold by more than 60,000 issuers, up from 52,000 in 2002. In 2009, municipal debt outstanding had reached nearly $2.8 trillion. Municipal debt outstanding per capita increased from approximately $27 in 1900 to $5,167 in 2000.

Some 80,000 municipal issuers had outstanding debt in the municipal market in 2009. The most recent growth has been the most rapid. From 1988 to 2000, municipal debt outstanding grew at a constant rate. However, new issues rose sharply in 1996 and began to accelerate thereafter. Average annual issues were around $150 billion from 1996 through 2000. Between 2000 and 2005, issues of municipal bonds averaged over $230 billion annually. This increase is reflected in the growth of total debt outstanding (see **Figure 20.1**).

The all-time record year for new issues was 2007, when more than $429 billion was issued. Despite this rapid growth, municipal debt as a percentage of total bond issues remained fairly constant at around 7–9% since the late 1990s (see **Figure 20.2**).

Figure 20.2 shows the percent of total that different types of bond issues constituted for four dates from 1996 through 2008. Whereas the municipal portion of the total remained relatively constant, the total in others fluctuated. In particular, the mortgage-related and asset-backed categories increased substantially as a percent of total issues in 2005. This spike reflects the mid-decade pyramiding of debts based on the employment of mortgages as collateral to extend further credit. Asset-backed securities, as a category, also includes so-called second-order derivatives, which are bonds backed by the (first-order) bonds issued on the basis of the original mortgage-backed securities. Note, also, how rapidly the amount of these latter bonds fell by the end of 2008.

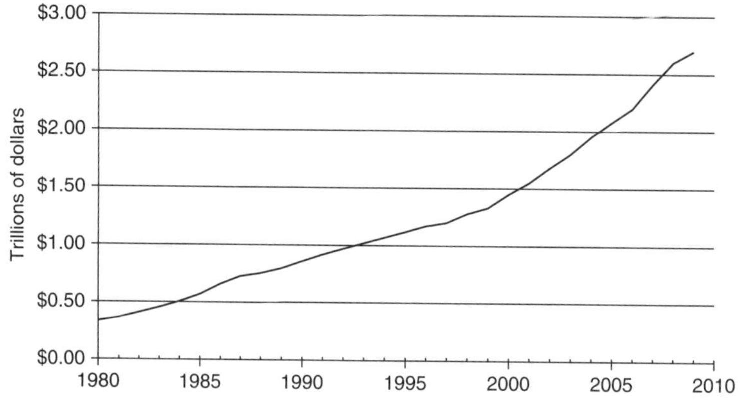

Figure 20.1 State and Local Debt Outstanding, 1980 to 2009

Data from: U.S. Bureau of the Census. Census of Governments, State and Local Government Finances by Level of Government, 1992–2009. Accessed at www.Census.gov/govs/;

U. S. Bureau of the Census. (1990). Historical Statistics of Government Finances and Employment. Compendium of Government Finances (U.S. Department of Commerce, U.S. Government Printing Office.); and

U.S. Bureau of the Census. (1997). Summary of State and Local Government Finances, 1972–1992. Compendium of Government Finances (U.S. Department of Commerce, U.S. Government Printing Office).

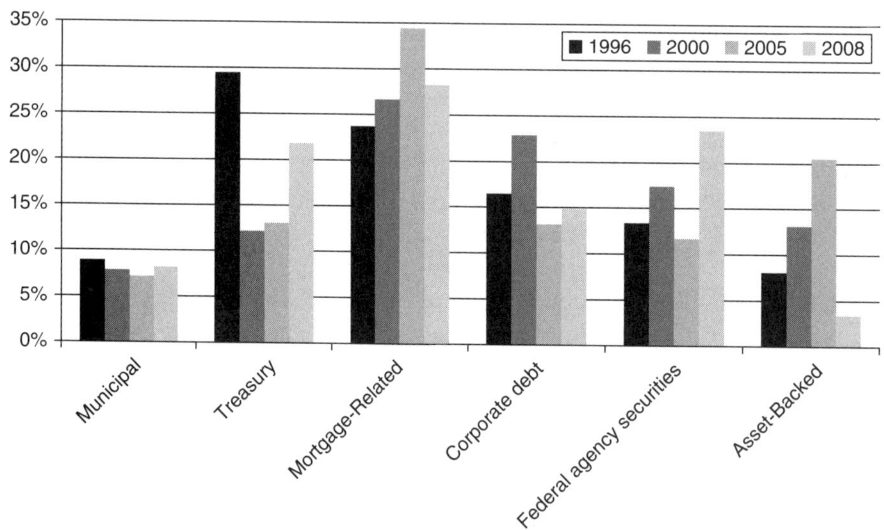

Figure 20.2 Bond Type as Percentage of Total Bonds Issued, 1996–2008

Source: Gorton, G. B. (2010). *Slapped by the invisible hand: The panic of 2007*. New York: Oxford University Press, p. 39.

The Recent Market Turmoil

The U.S. municipal securities market has become a much more complex market in the very recent past, one that requires dramatically higher levels of investor sophistication. The expanded use of new financial products and services—especially other than fixed-obligation bonds—has fueled tremendous growth in municipal borrowing, especially in the period 2007–2008. Such products include variable rate debt obligations (of various kinds), auction rated securities, *interest rate swaps*, and similar products—many of them so-called synthetic securities. Historically, municipal markets have been susceptible to the business cycle, with defaults tending to peak during periods of economic depression. Waves of municipal debt defaults have accompanied each of the four previous periods of economic distress.[9] These periods of default were preceded by rampant real estate speculation, fueled in part by local and state authorities lending public money directly to entrepreneurs, developers, and speculators, financed by municipal borrowing. The ensuing economic recession in each instance caused a failure of the anticipated cash flows to materialize, leading to defaults. It is important to understand that since the Great Depression of the 1930s, municipal default rates have been far less and recovery rates on defaulted municipal debts have been far greater than for corporate issues. Despite the vagaries of the business cycle and its effects on debt markets generally, municipal bonds have remained far safer investments than corporate bonds.

The most recent period of market turmoil differs from the past—including the sizable defaults of the Great Depression—in several marked ways. First, the federal promotion of mortgage lending to subprime customers exposed municipal property tax bases to greater delinquency rates, owing to the heightened risk of foreclosure that manifested itself in 2007–2009. This placed many governments' revenues in a "vise" at precisely the worst time. Nationwide, property tax revenues declined about 2% in late 2007 and early 2008; although property tax receipts increased from 2008 to 2009, the annual increase was the lowest since 1995 (Boyd, 2010; U.S. GAO, 2010). Sales and income tax revenues declined by a much greater amount. Local governments, relying more heavily on property taxes than other revenue sources experienced declines in revenues; however, they fared better than state governments that rely more heavily on income and sales taxes. In the second quarter of 2009, the states suffered a 17% year-on-year fall in revenues, and 10.7% in the third quarter. State government tax revenues for the first three quarters of 2009 were the worst in more than 50 years (Boyd, 2010; Dadayan and Boyd, 2009). In 2010, total state government budget deficits were projected to reach approximately $175 billion, or 26% of revenues. Year 2011 is expected to be even worse.

Second, severely reduced market liquidity resulted from the lack of trust among critical financial institutions, precipitating a "wholesale" banking crisis, different in critical ways from the retail crisis of the Great Depression era (Gorton, 2009). This has both raised borrowing costs and decreased the market's ability to accommodate municipal demands for credit. Third, ratings downgrades—and in some instances outright bankruptcy—of traditional institutions of credit enhancement (i.e., banks, municipal bond insurers) has exposed retail investors to new risks, as well as raised municipal borrowing costs. Defaults on municipal debt rose from $331 million in 2007 to $8.2 billion in 2008—an all-time high—before falling to $6.3 billion in 2009. The dollars are large, but the volume of default is miniscule by historical standards, currently just 0.54% of all outstanding municipal debt.

There were 183 defaults in 2009, the largest number since 1992, up from 162 in 2008. The total of $14.5 billion in municipal defaults for 2008 and 2009 exceeds the total amount of cumulative defaults in the preceding 8 years (Mysak, 2010). In the ten years from 1999–2008, inclusive, municipal bond defaults totaled $24.13 billion on a total of $3.4 trillion issued during the same period (Mysak, 2009a). The current wave of defaults set some records. The much publicized bankruptcy of Vallejo, California in 2008 was the largest municipal default in 14 years. It is instructive to note that the most significant defaults have been on special obligation bonds and variable rate debt, not on *general obligation bonds* paying fixed rates of interest. Many municipal authorities that have defaulted were involved in land development and health care facilities projects.

Examples of default can be found nationwide. For instance, across the country from California, Jefferson County, Alabama, from March 2008 to June 2009, was unable to pay even the interest cost on $ 3.7 billion of sewer bonds. For many other projects, investors failed to recover their investment, some settling for a mere fraction of their original investment. A $5.8 million Kansas Development Finance Authority issue, whose proceeds were used to build apartment buildings, recovered 87.5¢ on the dollar. In another instance, certificates of participation (COPs) that Arvin, California, sold to build a $7.8 million golf course recovered only 28¢. And the investors in a taxable $690 thousand Bell County, Texas, Health Facilities Development Corporation being used to construct a nursing home lost their entire investment (Mysak, 2010).

Major issuers, including governments once thought impervious to default, have taken strong steps to avoid it. In late 2008, for instance, to avoid loss of control of the finances (for failure to meet its contractual debt management benchmarks), the New Jersey Turnpike Authority proposed rather dramatic toll increases, averaging 60 cents per passenger car in 2009, plus an additional 90 cents in 2012 (NJTA, 2008). That would amount to an average increase of 5.2 cents per mile in 2009, and another 10.1¢ in 2012.[10] The capital city of Pennsylvania, Harrisburg, early in 2010 faced a $2 million debt payment on a new "trash-to-energy" incinerator owned and operated by an independent municipal authority, due March 1, and another $68 million in debt service due later in the year (McNichol, 2010). The city also guaranteed some $9 million in debt payments owed by the incinerator, which has been in default since 2009. Because Harrisburg has reached its general obligation (GO) debt limit, as of February 2010, the city was weighing a possible Chapter 9 bankruptcy filing. Finally, the State of California, facing a 2010 budget deficit of $20.7 billion and $83.5 billion in long-term debt ($64 billion in general obligation debt), will need to fund some $6 billion in 2010 debt service expenditures. Moody's and Standard & Poor's give the state single-A ratings; Fitch puts the state at BBB, just two grades above junk bond status.

TABLE 20.1 Growth of Special Municipal Districts, 1992–2007

No. Districts	National	California	Colorado	Illinois	Nevada	Florida
1992	31,555	2,797	1,252	2,920	156	462
1997	34,683	3,010	1,358	3,068	153	526
2002	35,052	2,830	1,414	3,145	158	626
2007	37,381	2,765	1,904	3,249	146	1,051
Percent Change from Previous Census of Governments						
1997	9.02%	7.08%	7.81%	4.82%	–1.96%	12.17%
2002	1.05%	–6.36%	3.96%	2.45%	3.16%	15.97%
2007	6.23%	–2.35%	25.74%	3.20%	–8.22%	40.44%

Source: U.S. Census Bureau. Government Organization. Various years. www.census.gov/prod/www/abs/govern.html

Like previous default waves, which exhibited regional patterns, the current wave also has a regional component. Of the 183 bond issues defaulting in 2009, 97 were Florida-based community development (CD) districts. Florida had 600 community development districts in 2009, and 105 of them had gone into default (Mysak, 2009a, 2009b). A little over one-quarter of the 162 issues that defaulted in 2008 were also Florida CD bonds. By and large, it has been the failure of the real estate market that doomed many of these schemes. For instance, the Pine Ridge Plantation Community Development District, charged with developing 736 acres near Jacksonville, Florida, drew down its reserves to repay its investors some $20.1 million in bonds it had sold as recently as 2006. The problem was that by January 2010, only 48 of the planned 736 single-family homes in the district had been sold (Mysak, 2010). Most special districts or special purpose governments rely on a revenue stream that is not secured by general tax revenues to pay bond debt. This makes their bonds more risky and in turn can contribute to the default rate of municipals bonds. **Table 20.1** summarizes the growth of special districts since 1992 nationally and in specific states, selected because of reported high foreclosure levels. It comes as no real surprise that the greatest growth in numbers of special districts has occurred in Florida, where a disproportionate share have been community development districts.

Historical Default Rates

The rapid expansion of municipal debt levels could not occur without at least some experience of overborrowing and the associated defaults. Prior to the Great Depression, there were three major periods of municipal default (Cohen, 1989; Hempel, 1971). Each one coincided with a more general economic downturn, revealing a historical relationship between economic cycles and waves of municipal defaults. A preceding period of unregulated, profligate issuance of municipal debt also aggravated each wave of default. In turn, each period was followed by waves of legal reform, and the imposition of new regulations. The first occurred during the Panic of 1837, and the ensuing economic depression of 1837–1843. During this period, around one-half of all municipal debt fell into default, involving 12 defaults by state and local units between 1839 and 1843 (Hempel, 1971, p. 17). Cohen (1989) further reports that some "nine states could not meet their payments and defaulted on $122 million" (p. 56). Of this amount, $13.8 million was repudiated and never repaid.

A large proportion of the defaulted debt had been used to finance internal improvements, such as canals and railroads, and to charter banks to finance private development projects (Hughes, 1977). Today these types of issues are referred to, politely, as "conduit" financing. Issuers appeared unwilling to satisfy the debt, preferring to have the bondholders bear the burden of default instead of the firms whose bankruptcies precipitated the losses (Hempel, 1971, p. 35). Consequently, this period of freewheeling public debt financing was reined in through the amendment of state constitutions to place strict upper limits on the amount of debt a municipal government was permitted to issue, to prohibit gifts or loans of state funds directly in support of private firms or individuals, and to place a ban on the holding of stock in private companies by state and local governments. Few defaults occurred between 1843 and 1860. But there were some 30 defaults reported during the Civil War (Hempel, 1971).

The second major period of municipal default began in the immediate post-Civil War period, during Reconstruction, and reached its peak in the depression of 1873–1879. Most of the defaults involved outright repudiations, mostly by Southern states. Approximately $150 million was never repaid (Hempel, 1971, p. 18). The focus of reform during that wave was squarely on the legal form of the bond deal, with a special emphasis on the need for competent bond counsel to draft the proper legal documents, not the least of which is the indenture, specifying the rights and obligations of all parties to the bond. As a consequence of this experience, statutes were enacted in every state to require the official opinion of an independent bond counsel.

The third major period of default before the Great Depression occurred during the depression of 1893–1899. Defaults rose quite rapidly in the mid-1890s, involving nearly 60 governments and $130 million, or 10% of debt outstanding. Governments in default remained large in number from 1895 through 1906, but the defaulted issues mainly consisted of relatively small amounts that had been loaned to finance local real estate booms or western irrigation projects gone bad (Hempel, 1971, p. 18). Defaults were highest in the central and western regions, those most susceptible to land speculation.

By far and away, the greatest number of municipal defaults occurred during the Great Depression years, 1929–1937. During this 8-year period, some 15.4% of all U.S. municipal debt was past due at some point or other, amounting to a total of $2.85 billion. Approximately 7% of all outstanding municipal debt was defaulted, involving 4,800 governments. In the decade preceding the stock market crash, municipal debt service expenditures rose more rapidly than revenues, seriously reducing the fiscal flexibility of many governments. With state and local revenue systems suffering the same fate as the declining national income, interest charges rose from 8.3 to 10.7% of revenues from 1922 to 1932; total debt service rose from 12.7 to 19.7% (Hempel, 1971, p. 38). In 1931, special assessment and revenue bonds accounted for the largest number of defaults, slightly over one-third, or in excess of 1,500 instances of default, despite accounting for only 2% of all outstanding debt. Clearly, revenue bonds were defaulting at rates exceeding the average.

Owing to their steady improvement in financial management capabilities and a widespread willingness to pay, municipal governments recovered more rapidly than in previous periods of default. So much so, that by 1939, there was barely $200 million in outstanding debt in default. By 1938, all 48 cities with populations exceeding 25,000 that were in default in 1929–1937 were out of default.

Recent Developments in Key Market Segments

Several related developments affected the municipal bond market situation; most involve the collapse of the mortgage-backed and asset-backed securities, either directly or indirectly. These developments include the demise of bond insurance and insurance providers, the decline of variable rate demand obligations, the inability or unwillingness of traditional financial institutions to provide credit enhancements, particularly letters of credit, and the failure of the auction rate securities market. These are discussed in the following paragraphs.

Bond Insurance

Until recently, bond insurance played a key role in the municipal market. Bond insurance provides additional guarantees to the investor that the interest and principal on the bond will be repaid even if the issuer defaults. A high bond rating indicates to investors that the issuer is a good credit risk and that principle and interest on the bond will be paid on schedule. If the rating is lower, the interest rate required to place the bond is higher. Bond insurance provides an extra measure of safety and can provide the assurance of a higher rating. With bond insurance, the insurer provides its rating—essentially the rating of the bond is tied to the credit rating of the insurer. To be effective, the insurer must have the highest possible rating. And therein lies a problem.

Originating in 1971, bond insurance gradually covered an increasing percent of issues over time. The municipal bond insurance business began with one company—Ambac Financial Group. Soon other companies joined the market, and in 2008, nine firms were actively writing bond insurance for municipalities (Parkinson, 2008). The business grew from 1.8% of issues insured in 1975 to a peak in 2005 when about 58% of new issues were insured. In 2007, more than 50% of outstanding issues were insured. Without insurance, bonds for many municipalities would have been more difficult to sell (Agriss, 2008; Lemov 2010).

In 2007, seven municipal bond insurers had triple-A ratings from the three major rating firms, Standard and Poor's, Moody's, and Fitch. When they insured a bond, the government that issued it got the benefit of those high ratings. As long as everybody who was insured had a triple-A rating, everything traded freely. Because municipal bond issuers rarely defaulted, insurers made good money on the premiums. Many issuers and insurers believed that issuers were able to borrow in the financial markets at lower rates than would have been possible otherwise.

The insurers got into trouble, however, when they expanded their business by insuring—and investing in—collateralized securities tied to subprime mortgages on individual homes (Lemov, 2010). To enhance earnings, most of the *monolines*, those companies specializing in bond insurance, had begun insuring these collateralized debt obligations (CDOs). The insurance companies collected fees to guarantee the mortgage debt against the possibility that borrowers could not meet their obligations. The insurers also invested heavily in these instruments with their own capital. But, unlike the municipal bond market with low default rates, the subprime market was hurt by numerous defaults—many homeowners could not pay their mortgages. Many issues based on the packages of these mortgages failed costing investors and insurers. The bond insurance companies lost in two ways—on their own investments and with insurance payouts. As these issues began to fail in 2007 and 2008, the rating agencies reviewed insurance companies' exposure to this market and began lowering the ratings of the bond insurance firms. By the end of November 2008, no municipal bond insurer was left with a triple-A rating from all three credit rating services. The monolines along with many others were victims of the subprime mortgage debacle.

Several bond insurance companies left the market altogether. When the insurers' ratings were downgraded, their issuer-clients' ratings fell with them. Others were left without insurance. Some creative but less costly bonds, such as the variable rate debt obligations discussed later, were no longer available to any issuer and some markets shut down almost completely. Because the ratings of municipal issues that these firms insured was tied to the firms' rating, the issues themselves were downgraded. The ratings of the insured bond issues suffered, in turn damaging the credit of the issuers and, in many cases, requiring higher interest payments and debt restructuring. Bond insurance became more difficult to obtain and many issuers found it difficult to place new issues. Eventually, some firms regained ratings but several went out of business altogether. By the end of 2009, only two bond insurance companies were writing policies—the Assured Guaranty Corporation, which acquired Financial Security Assurance Inc. on July 1, 2009, and Berkshire Hathaway Assurance Corporation.

Variable Rate Debt Instruments

Municipal bond issues expanded substantially in number, amount, and complexity over the last 35 years. As the municipal bond market grew and the number of issues and total number of issuers grew, so did the types of instruments created to issue the debt. Various variable rate debt instruments became more common. **Figure 20.3** illustrates the trend in variable rate debt financing from 1988 through 2007. Although the percent of total

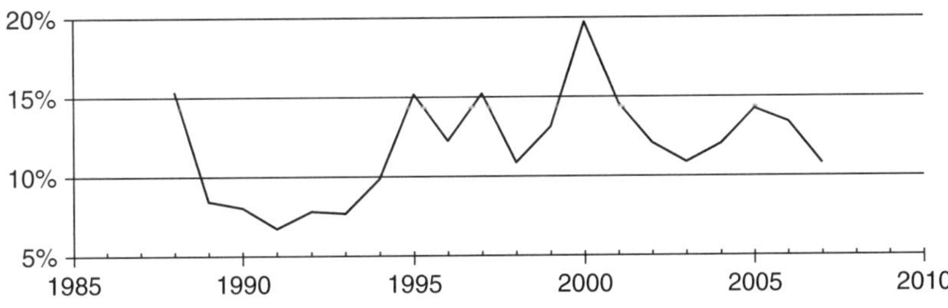

Figure 20.3 Variable Rate Debt as a Percent of Total, 1988–2007

Source: The Bond Buyer (online database).

debt issued as variable rate fluctuated considerably over time, varying from a low of 6% to a high of 20%, the long-term trend increased between the early 1990s and 2006. In 2006, this percent dropped and then decreased sharply again in 2007. Issuance of variable rate debt instruments continued to decline following 2007 (SIFMA, 2010).

Two of these instruments are *variable rate debt obligations* (VRDO) and a special form of VRDO, auction rate securities (ARS). VRDOs are issued as long-term bonds but have short-term interest rate reset periods. They permit owners—the investors—to "put" their bonds back to a remarketing agent appointed by the issuer. Holders who put their bonds back to the remarketing agent receive par value of the bonds in return. Hence, the terminology "demand obligations": the investor can demand to be repaid on short notice. In most cases, the reset period for VRDOs is one week. It can be as short as one day and as long as nine months. As added protection, VRDOs are backed by a letter of credit or a standby bond purchase agreement to ensure timely repayment of principal and interest and to ensure that all tendered bonds will be paid (Agriss, 2008.)

The letter of credit is usually supplied by a commercial bank, for a fee, to provide liquidity and as a guarantee of payment. Banks may also provide standby purchase agreements to ensure the bond can be paid on demand. The economic troubles of 2007–2009 impacted the banks' willingness and ability to provide such letters of credit and purchase agreements, further restricting the ability of state and local governments to issue debt. Letters of credit totaled $20.7 billion in 2007. They rose to a high of $71.5 billion in 2008 and covered almost 20% of the market. Then, following the recent economic troubles, through November of 2009 letters of credit enhancements fell to $18.7 billion or about 5% of the market (SIFMA, 2009).

Auction-Rate Securities

Auction-rate securities (ARS) are long-term variable-rate instruments with interest rates reset at periodic and frequent auctions. They are often marketed to issuers as an alternative

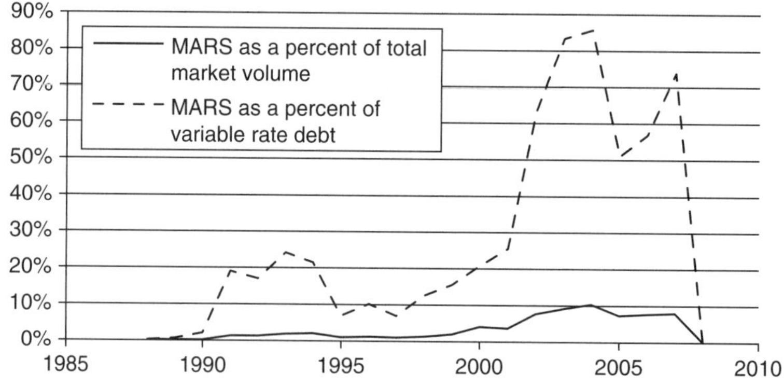

Figure 20.4 Municipal Auction Rate Securities as a Percent of Total, 1988–2008

Source: The Bond Buyer (online database).

variable-rate financing vehicle and to investors as an alternative to money market funds. This allows borrowers to treat long-term debt as short-term debt for interest rate purposes. Investors historically were able to liquidate ARS positions at face value at frequent auctions, leading many to consider them almost like cash. **Figure 20.4** shows the growth in ARS issues from 1988 to 2008 and the growth in variable rate debt for that time. Although the overall percent of total municipal debt that is variable rate is not large, that percent grew substantially in recent decades with especially large increases between about 1991 and 2006. Most of that growth was in ARS issues.

In early 2008, the auction-rate market was estimated to be about $330 billion outstanding. Long-term, often tax-exempt, debt instruments issued by municipalities or other entities comprise approximately 75% of the auction rated market. Although municipalities are major participants in the auction-rate market, these issues comprise a relatively small portion of municipal debt outstanding (Lee, 2008). For any particular municipal issuer, however, ARS may be a large share of its debt and failure of this market can have substantial impact.

For both issuer and investor to benefit from ARS, the auctions have to work. After more than two decades of stable auction-rate market conditions, this market experienced unusual and difficult conditions. These problems originated with the broader subprime and credit crisis. In 2007, a few auctions failed. By February 2008, due to the widening credit crisis and problems at the insurers, auction-rate demand dried up, leading to numerous auction failures. In only three days in February, more than 1,000 auctions failed. Some observers declared that the ARS market had "virtually collapsed" (Lee, 2008). **Figure 20.5** shows the percent of ARS auctions that failed in February 2008.

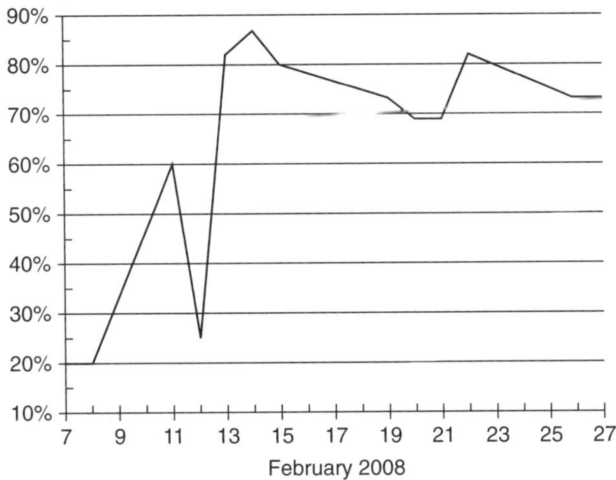

Figure 20.5 Auction Rate Failure

Source: Lee, S. (2008). "Auction Rate Securities: Bidder's Remorse?" NERA Economic Consulting. Accessed at www.nera.com.

The auction market collapsed just as investors began to worry about the financial health of the bond insurers who had guaranteed the debt. The collapse exposed governments to penalty rates of 12% or more—a huge increase in costs at the worst possible time. Aurora, Colorado, for example, faced an interest rate increase on some of its debt from 3.5% to 14%. As a result of the ARS market failure many governments scrambled to convert ARS debt to other variable rate debt including variable rate demand obligations (Cooke, 2008; Lee, 2008).

The Future

Two thousand eight was a tumultuous year for the municipal bond market (Resnick, 2009). Those events just discussed changed the landscape for municipal bonds dramatically, making it much harder for issuers, especially those with lower ratings, to sell bonds. The following sections address the current status and future of institutions whose actions affected the municipal bond market.

Credit Enhancement and the Future of Bond Insurance

The bond insurance business in 2010 is but a shadow of what it was 2 years earlier. From meager beginnings, in a span of less than 40 years, the municipal bond insurance business grew into a major industry. Then in 2010, the business was down to just two companies actively writing insurance and only around 9% of new issues being insured (Lemov, 2010; SIFMA, 2010). These "monolines" along with many others were victims of the subprime mortgage debacle. Because the ratings of municipal issues insured by these firms were tied to the firms' rating, the issues themselves were downgraded. The overall use of credit enhancement for municipal bonds has continued to decline. In the years 2001 through 2007, 63% of new issues received some kind of enhancement, either in the form of insurance, letters of credit or other coverage. The new issues supported by any type of credit enhancement dropped to 46% in 2008 and to 16% in 2009. In the first quarter 2010, 10.3% of the total municipal issue was enhanced compared to 20.9% in the first quarter 2009 and 59.1% enhanced for the five-year average of 2004 through 2008. In the first quarter of 2009, approximately 12% of new issues were covered with bond insurance; for all of 2009 the figure was only 9.5% and for the first quarter of 2010 that had dropped to 7% (SIFMA, 2010). Existing insurers predict that within five years they will cover about one-third of issues.

Although only two bond insurers were writing insurance at the end of 2009, other firms are working to enter the market and efforts are underway to rebuild bond insurance. The National League of Cities proposed creating a publicly owned insurance entity (Lambert, 2009; McGee, 2009). At the same time, however, many have questioned the value of bond insurance and whether insurance lowers borrowing costs; it might not. For issues rated triple B or lower, the desirability of insurance is clear. The issues most in need of insurance are those that have been shown to have higher risk: hospitals, nursing homes, private colleges, and senior living facilities. Small-scale, single-A issuers are also a target market for insurers. Large, highly rated issuers are less likely to see a benefit from bond insurance. The insured market is likely to continue shrinking as a percent of outstanding debt; investors will prefer to purchase bonds based primarily on the underlying credit of the issuer (American City and County, 2009; McGee, 2009). These factors will increase pressure for more transparency with regard to financial statements and disclosure by state and local issuers.

Uninsured bonds have been coming to the market at historically low yields. From March to the end of December of 2009, 15.8% of all new issues were *Build America Bonds* (BAB), authorized under the Economic Recovery and Reinvestment Act of 2009. These were largely sold without insurance. BAB have higher yields than other comparable municipal bonds because they are taxable and appeal to a broader base of investors–not just those individuals to whom the tax exemption is important. Most are of high grade; more than 65% are rated AA or higher (McGee, 2009).

Is There a Future for Variable Rate Debt?

In 2010, most municipal issuers who in past years would have used variable rate issues turned to fixed rate debt. The bond insurance meltdown affected state and local governments greatly. Many, having purchased what they thought was guaranteed insurance protection, went beyond the conventional form of borrowing by issuing auction rate and other variable rate debt. These instruments usually had rates well below long-term rates—making them attractive to state and local agencies. When the auction market collapsed, however, governments using auction rate securities (ARS) were exposed to penalty rates of 12% or more—a huge increase in costs. The ARS market collapse also exposed some issuers to demands that they repay the bonds sooner rather than later. In Texas, for example, a county faced balloon payments on $117 million in variable-rate debt stadium bonds. The public authority issuing the bonds found itself obliged to pay off the debt in 5 years instead of 23 (Lemov, 2010). Although some municipal issuers had entered into interest rate swaps to hedge their interest rate risk and make total interest payments more predictable, many had not, nor had they budgeted for higher interest costs. Municipalities, therefore, had strong incentives to restructure their auction-rate debt. Many local governments and state agencies converted variable to fixed rate debt or plan to do so. For example, Purdue University, a state funded institution, converted $81.75 million of variable rate bonds to fixed rate. A Mississippi county proposed converting variable to fixed-rate debt, thus changing variable rate debt outstanding from 69% of total debt to 25% (Austin, 2010; Moody's, 2009 Pierog, 2008; Seymour, 2010a).

The risks of variable rate debt have caused great concern among local and state finance officials and regulatory agencies. States differ in the extent to which state and local governments use variable rate debt, however. A Moody's study showed that two-thirds of variable rate debt had been issued in only four states: Tennessee, California, Texas, and Pennsylvania (Moody's, 2009). Cities in Tennessee have the highest amount of variable rate debt of cities in any state in the country (Schrade, 2010). Tennessee's State Comptroller proposed limiting local governments to a variable rate debt limit of no more than 25% of total debt. The proposal would also require more transparency from vendors offering variable rate debt instruments.

The ability to issue variable rate debt is further limited by a shortage of liquidity, at least for the near future (Seymour, 2010a). A large volume of municipal variable rate debt expires in 2010 and 2011. Banks might not have the liquidity to renew these instruments or may be unwilling to do so without charging a high fee. A viable alternative for state and local governments caught in this situation is to sell fixed rate bonds to redeem the VRDOs.

The Municipal Securities Rule Making Board has proposed to the U.S. Securities and Exchange Commission (SEC) that it impose several restrictions regarding variable rate debt. These would require that information be provided on: how and when interest rates are set, the types of bidders and number of orders to buy and sell auction rate securities, and who provides liquidity to the issuer (Preston, 2010). In a separate action, the SEC approved changes pertaining to municipal bond disclosure. These require additional disclosure of financial statements and notification of other events by the underlying borrower for VRDO's. Prior to these changes several disclosure requirements for other bonds did not apply to VRDOs (U.S. Securities and Exchange Commission Municipal Securities Fact Sheet, May 26, 2010).

The Future of the Municipal Bond Market: Buyers and Sellers

The bond buying market has changed significantly over the past two years (Guevara and Claytor, 2009; Miller, 2009). Until the 1980s, banks were the biggest buyers of municipal bonds. Because of changes in 1986 in the U. S. tax code, banks are no longer the primary buyers of tax-exempt bonds (Seymour, 2010b). After the mid-1980s, individuals and trusts accounted for more than 50% of the purchases of new issues. Following the recent turmoil, institutional investors who had previously comprised two-thirds of all buyers, largely abandoned the market to hoard cash, shore up financials, and "wait out the storm." This left issuers to court the only remaining buyers—retail investors that rarely looked past highly rated, short-term bonds. At the end of the first quarter of 2010, households held more than one-third of the approximately $2.8 trillion in municipal debt outstanding (Ellis, 2010). In contrast to institutional investors, individuals are more likely to depend upon official offerings statements as the primary source of information about bonds (Guevara and Claytor, 2009). Retail investors usually lack the research resources to evaluate individual issues and generally rely more on ratings. Bond insurance may also be more important to them.

The net result is that investors now find it more difficult to assess the quality of bond offerings. Many investors, feeling mislead by inflated ratings in the mortgage-backed securities market, naturally are wary about the quality of an issuer's credit worthiness. In past years, bond insurance would have assured investors of safety. That assurance is now hard to come by. Insured bonds previously often secured the highest ratings, eliminating the need for investor credit analysis. If bond insurance is not available, issuers must seek other ways to receive a superior credit rating. To improve ratings that are below "double A," they can improve performance, enhance reserves, and institute sound financial management practices and debt management policies. Knowledgeable investors, even less sophisticated ones, are likely to look more closely at the underlying credit quality of the issuer than in previous years. Credit rating agencies are also under pressure to recalibrate ratings and to begin using the same system as with corporate bond ratings. Research shows that corporate bonds have a higher default rate than comparably rated municipal bonds. It remains to be seen if changes in the scale for municipal bond ratings will impact the investing public's preference for either type of bonds (Guevara and Claytor, 2009).

Regarding local government's plans for using traditional instruments to issue debt, a May 2010 National League of Cities report concluded that the state of America's cities threatened to become worse in the near future (McFarland, 2010). In this report on the impact of the housing market on property tax revenues, 67% of city officials surveyed said that the commercial property market had declined over the past year. More than 50% said that business start-ups, retention, and growth declined in each of the past two years. Sixty-three percent indicated that poverty worsened from the previous year, the highest percent giving this answer since 1992 when the question was first asked. Perhaps most important to municipal bond issuance, 68% had delayed or were canceling capital projects.

Government budget shortfalls are likely to become more severe as tax collections respond to the worsened economic conditions. Reports in 2009 and 2010 were negative regarding the finances of the state and local government sector (Cooke, 2009; U.S. GAO, 2010). The revenue situation will severely limit state and local governments' ability to take on new debt in the near future. With the decline in tax receipts and other revenues and falling property values, state and local issuers are likely to take longer to come out of this recession even as the economy improves. These conditions also increase the pressure to obtain bond insurance, particularly for mid- to small-size issuers in the A-rated category.

Observers can find reasons for optimism even though the financial situation of state and local governments appears to be dire. The probability of default for general obligation bonds and traditional revenue bonds, those issued to provide important services directly to the public, is remote. And the amount of debt service in most municipal and state government budgets is reasonable (BlackRock, 2009). Unfunded pension and healthcare liabilities for employees and retirees as well as state Medicaid costs, however, will create additional problems. These liabilities will add to the burden of governments' operating budgets and further constrain their ability to issue new debt. In part, the unfunded pension amounts are because of investment losses brought about by the poor economy and may recover, at least partially, along with the economy. Given all this, some observers believe that state and local governments have numerous reasons to make timely and full payment on debts and will do so.

Considering all of the events of the past few years, the municipal bond market showed surprisingly robust activity in 2010. In 2009, approximately $331 billion in new, tax free municipal debt was issued, the lowest amount since 2002. This does not include the new, taxable, Build America Bonds (BAB) authorized in 2009 with a subsidy of 35% of the interest cost provided by the national government. BAB issues were about 26% of all issues in 2009 and these included more than $400 million of municipal bonds. Total issues for 2007 and 2008 were estimated at $420 billion and $390 billion, respectively (SIFMA, 2010). In the first quarter of 2010, municipal issuance totaled $103.7 billion, compared to $85.4 billion in the first quarter of 2009.

Investors seeking safety are choosing municipal bonds over other investments. This activity helps keep interest rates low and makes it easier for states and localities to issue debt. In particular, it helps issuers stuck with troubled variable rate bonds to refinance at fixed rates.

What will happen in the future? The Build American Bonds were intended to temporarily aid state and local governments and help stimulate the economy. Originally authorized for two years, they are not likely to be extended. In his FY 2011 budget, President Obama proposed to extend Build America Bonds for three years at a reduced subsidy. The United States House of Representatives passed a bill in March of 2010 to extend them for two years and gradually reduce the subsidy from 35% to 30% by 2012. A one-year extension was proposed following the November 2010 election. At the end of the year, however, BAB were not extended.

In the current economic climate, state and local governments are delaying capital investments when they can to avoid construction and financing costs. The BAB provided an additional incentive to avoid issuing traditional municipal bonds. At the same time, some investors are likely to anticipate increases in state and federal income taxes and so will have an additional incentive to buy tax free bonds. Infrastructure needs, expiration of BAB, and possibly increased income taxes present an interesting set of challenges for governments at all levels.

Conclusion

Despite the recent spate of defaults, the municipal debt market retains much of its luster. Liquidity problems, and not underlying credit quality issues, appear to be the main feature of the municipal market crisis that began in 2007. Aside from some real payment problems, primarily in Florida, the recent market crisis has been much less of a problem for municipal issuers than for those in the corporate sector. In general, these municipal defaults were not caused by weaknesses in the fiscal health of city, county, or state governments. Some of the well-publicized defaults were by jurisdictions struck by the combined problems of variable rate issues, auction rate securities, and bond insurance firms. Nor are the number of defaults in this recent period a good indicator of overall fiscal health of these governments. The stresses on fiscal health generally come from other factors.

To be sure, municipal issuers have had to make adjustments in the face of investors who have grown wary, including issuing more fixed rate, general obligation debt in 2009 and 2010 than recent trends would have predicted. The market, therefore, remains open to prudently managed issuers. Those jurisdictions having issued debt for public or private entities dependent on the real estate market are most at risk. And states and localities heavily dependent on housing, automobile, and financial services may have a higher risk profile. But in general the low default level of the traditional municipal bond market is likely to remain.

What does this portend for the fiscal health of local governments? What lessons can governments take from the history of defaults, the collapse of the variable rate bond market, and the exit of bond insurance to protect fiscal health in the future? The decline in revenues has limited state and local governments' ability to take on new debt and will continue to do so. These governments will have a more difficult time balancing the cost of ongoing operations, including service on existing debt, with the need for long-term capital financing. Issuers are likely to consider more carefully any decision to issue bonds and to focus more on general obligation bonds. As well, citizens may be much more critical of the borrowing their government's leaders proposed.

Our review suggests that in the absence of bond insurance, and possibly in the absence of reliable bond ratings, better assessment of the underlying credit quality and riskiness of loans is necessary. The underlying ability of the issuer to repay a proposed loan as well as the type of bond are important. Wise investors will want to consider answers to the following questions: What revenue source has been pledged for repayment? What has been pledged to secure repayment if this revenue source is not sufficient? What external conditions could cause interest rates to increase or repayment schedules to accelerate? All of these should be considered separately from any bond rating and in addition to commonly used fiscal indicators of credit quality.

As this chapter argues, state and local governments are advised to be much more careful about taking on new debt of any amount and about the type of debt they incur. Revenues declined for most state and local governments during 2007–2010; however, there is little reason to expect these governments not to pay existing debts. As noted, the defaults on debts during this recent period were mostly by special purpose governments that had essentially issued revenue bonds for private income earning projects.

Finding more adequate methods of evaluating credit worthiness at the investor level would be helpful and may be necessary. Researchers can serve various audiences by developing, identifying, and disseminating information on reliable indicators of fiscal health for use by a wider segment of the general public including average investors. Better information about the relationship between debt levels and other indicators of fiscal health and how to evaluate them would be helpful. Communicating this to retail investors and the general public will better equip them to assess the ability of governments to pay debt service on time and in full. Some observers have suggested making information in state and local government financial statements more transparent. The GASB—Government Accounting Standards Board—could be a vehicle for this.

State governments may need to review legislation authorizing local governments' ability to issue debt. Most states, by constitution or statute, limit the amount of outstanding debt, particularly general obligation debt, that local governments are allowed to have. Some also limit the amount of total debt. As noted earlier in the chapter, these limits can often be circumvented by issuing debt through special purpose governments. In addition to more fully addressing the ability of special purpose governments to issue debt, state legislatures may need to limit the amount and purpose of variable rate debt issued by municipal governments as well as the amount of debt issued through conduit bonds.

A lesson of this chapter is that variable rate debt, although advantageous if used wisely, carries risks that may be unknown, unforeseen, and outside the control of the issuing government. Variable rate debt exposes municipalities to greater risk of suddenly increased payment in case of liquidity shortages and market failures. In the longer term, if governments turn to using more general obligation bonds with fixed rates, the default rate is likely to be lower, and the risks of variable rate debt can be largely avoided. If revenues to repay revenue bonds are insufficient, the taxpayers may not be required to make up the difference. However, a default of these bonds is likely to lead to higher interest costs for new and existing debt and make it difficult to issue bonds at all. A government may then feel obliged to pay the revenue bond debt with resources originally intended for other purposes.

According to a Government Accountability Office (GAO, 2010) report, the state and local government sectors face near- and long-term fiscal challenges that will grow over time. Although the sector's operating balance is currently negative, increases in federal grants-in aid—largely from the Recovery Act—alleviated some near term pressure, and operating balances improved from early 2009 to March 2010. New Recovery Act money, however, was not available after 2010. In the near term, the factors contributing to the operating imbalance are steep revenue declines, increased service demands because of economic distress, and longer term pressures of rising health care costs and pensions. Existing debt is not likely to add unforeseen amounts to this gap. However, economic conditions and the factors listed earlier are likely to make it more difficult for many governments to issue new debt. Additionally, as reported by the Rockefeller Institute, this sector is not likely to pull out of the recession for several years because state and local governments take longer than other sectors of the economy to recover (Boyd, 2010). To meet existing debt payments, state and local governments will have to meet revenue shortfalls by reducing expenditures elsewhere, by raising taxes, or both. Until the housing and commercial real estate markets improve, many tax revenues will not show much recovery.

It is too soon to tell if the availability of bond insurance will affect the fiscal health of local governments. Most likely many governments will not purchase bond insurance although they may have done so in the past. The rating agencies have been criticized because of failures to accurately rate many subprime mortgage packages. They are also under pressure to use the same rating scale to assess municipal bonds as corporate bonds. In recalibrating their scales, the firms may improve the ratings for municipal bonds. However, as this chapter suggests, investors are advised to focus more on assessing the fiscal health of local governments and their credit worthiness with indicators of fiscal health and to rely less on bond ratings.

The GAO projects that the state and local government sector's long-term fiscal position will steadily decline for decades in the absence of significant policy changes. Because most state and local governments are required to balance their operating budgets, these governments must make substantial policy changes to avoid growing imbalances. If governments learn the lesson of the dangers of conduit bonds and the risks of variable rate financing, many debt problems encountered in the most recent economic downturn can be avoided in the future. This means that governments will of necessity rely more heavily on general obligation and traditional revenue bonds. It may also mean that citizens will have to decide between fewer or a lower level of services and higher property taxes. They may find that both are in store for them.

Endnotes

1. We make no judgment regarding the public need or desirability of these projects, only about the structure of their financing and their relative vulnerability to default. Such projects ought to be evaluated on the basis of their individual merits.
2. The authors wish to extend their sincere thanks to Christine Martell, University of Colorado-Denver, for furnishing this example.
3. The advantage to the issuer is that the interest cost is typically lower than equivalent long-term rates. The advantage to the investor is that the bonds may be sold prior to maturity, at the investor's convenience, with no reduction in yield.

4. Financial institutions and money market funds having strict requirements to invest in securities with third-party guarantees, such as letters of credit, form a large market for these bonds. Owing to the fiscal crisis, some financial institutions currently are unable to hold bonds for two reasons. First, the bonds need to meet certain quality rating requirements. Second, money market funds periodically need to sell bonds in anticipation of calls for cash, when they expect investors to draw down their accounts, typically when companies and individuals are preparing to pay federal and state income taxes.
5. The rate hike is typically either a set rate or some percentage over prime.
6. The bank, acting as the bond trustee, may have different terms for different issues, depending on its own policies and procedures or the attorney/law firm who drafted the documents.
7. As a term loan, the maturity can be accelerated from the original term of the bonds (typically 25–30 years) to as little as five years or may become immediately due and payable. Interest rates on the bonds would increase from the monthly rate to a bank rate, based on the prime rate or LIBOR (London Interbank Offer Rate), plus a premium. There typically is little interest on the part of other banks to provide letters of credit renewals or to lend the authority money directly. Banks typically do not like to tie up their funds for long periods of time. The contract will therefore usually call for conversion of the debt to a term loan, with a shorter maturity, and a balloon payment in the terminal year, which necessitates that the issuer incur higher debt service costs in the short run and perhaps seek refinancing of the debt sooner than originally anticipated.
8. In response, some municipalities will enter into "moral obligation agreements," whereby they agree to assist tax increment-financed urban renewal authorities service their debts or to replenish reserve funds if that should become necessary.
9. A default is a situation when a debt obligation is not met, that is, the principal or interest payments are not paid when they are due. A default does not mean the debt is not repaid although this could be the case.
10. These would be the first toll increases since 2000 on the New Jersey Turnpike and since 1989 on the Garden State Parkway. One may wonder whether the lack of gradual toll increases was not a portent of fiscal problems "down the road" (as it were), requiring an all-too-rapid toll increase when it finally became necessary.

Glossary

Auction-rate securities (ARS): long-term variable-rate debt instruments with interest rates reset at periodic and frequent auctions. They are often marketed to issuers as an alternative variable-rate financing vehicle and to investors as alternatives to money market funds. This allows borrowers to treat long-term debt as short-term debt for interest rate purposes. Investors historically were able to liquidate ARS positions at face value at frequent auctions, leading many to consider them almost like cash. If an auction fails, the interest rate for the issuer is likely to increase, and the bond holder does not have a liquid investment.

Build America Bonds (BAB): taxable municipal bonds with special tax credits and federal subsidies for either the bond issuer or the bondholder. They were created as part of the American Recovery and Reinvestment Act signed into law in February 2009. The purpose of BAB is to reduce borrowing costs for state and local governments.

Collateralized debt obligation (CDO): a type of structured asset backed security (ABS) whose value and payments are derived from a portfolio of fixed-income underlying assets such as bonds and loans. CDOs' securities are split into different risk classes. Some well-known analysts and investors have warned that CDOs and other derivatives spread risk and uncertainty about the value of the underlying assets more widely rather than reducing the risk through diversification. This view became more widely held after the 2007–2008 credit crisis. Prior to 2008, credit rating agencies failed to adequately account for large risks such as whole sale mortgage defaults or a nationwide collapse of housing values when rating CDOs and other ABSs.

Conduit bonds: These are bonds, usually tax exempt, issued by a government entity on behalf of another organization. In this case, the issuer of the bond is not the obligor of the debt; that is, the entity for whom the bond is issued is obligated to pay the debt. The Internal Revenue Code limits participation as an obligor in conduit municipal bond offerings to certain not-for-profit entities (e.g., hospitals, museums, libraries) and to for-profit entities where debt is being issued for a defined qualified purpose. Municipal entities issue these types of bonds to provide the obligors with alternative outlets to fund qualified projects.

Fixed obligation (FO) bonds: Return a fixed rate of interest to the investor for the length of the bond. These are in contrast to variable rate debt obligation (VRDO) bonds, whose rates of return may vary according to market conditions. Around 75% of long-term municipal bonds offer fixed rates of interest.

General obligation (GO) bonds: Pledge the full financial strength and full taxing power of the issuers. These usually require that citizens support them in a referendum. Once the preferred form of municipal debt, GO bonds today constitute about 39% of long-term municipal debt.

Interest rate swaps: These are derivatives used to hedge interest rate risk. The bond issuer sets a fixed interest rate when the bonds are initially offered and enters into an agreement with another party who agrees to pay the issuer an amount equal to what the interest would be based on a selected index in return for the fixed interest rate amounts. On each payment date, the interest payments will be netted against each other.

Monolines: Insurance firms specializing in writing only one kind of insurance—that covering bonds. Initially these companies provided insurance to issuers of municipal bonds and guaranteed payment, for a fee, of the principle and interest on the bond if the issuer was not able to do so.

Refunded debt: debt that effectively "rolls over" as it comes due, to be replaced with new debt. Refunding bonds are those issued to incur new debt, the proceeds of which are used to pay the previous debt.

Special revenue obligation (SO) bonds (also known as revenue bonds): These pledge only a specific revenue source for repayment—generally user fees and service charges—and are therefore considered riskier than GO debt. They can usually be issued without a referendum. Currently SO bonds constitute about 61% of total municipal debt.

Synthetic securities: any combination of financial instruments structured to produce a market instrument with different characteristics than could otherwise be achieved, for example, higher yield, better liquidity, or interest rate protection. These securities mimic conventional financial instruments that may or may not be available to investors.

Variable rate debt obligations (VRDO): long-term bonds with short-term interest rate reset periods. Governments use various instruments for long-term borrowing that allow them to obtain lower short-term interest rates. The lower rate is available because the borrower agrees to pay an interest rate that can vary based on some predetermined mechanism. Variable rate demand obligations are one of these instruments. VRDOs permit investors to "put" their bonds back to a remarketing agent appointed by the issuer. Investors who put their bonds back to the remarketing agent receive par value of the bonds in return. Hence, the terminology of "demand obligations": the investor can demand to be repaid on short notice. VRDOs are typically backed by a letter of credit or a standby bond purchase agreement.

Discussion Questions

1. What were the major factors causing or leading up to each of the major periods of municipal defaults in the United States?
2. Explain why the use of special obligation revenue bonds by special purpose districts has led to more defaults than the use of general obligation bonds by general purpose governments such as cities and counties?
3. Under what market conditions would it be most tempting for municipal issuers to use variable rate bonds rather than fixed rate bonds?
4. How do auction rate securities differ from variable rate demand obligations?
5. The history of the municipal debt market in the United States spans almost 200 years and yet a bond insurance industry developed only in the second half of the 20th century. Discuss the various reasons for the late appearance of a bond insurance industry.
6. Evaluate the advantages and disadvantages of a municipality issuing "conduit" bonds. Do so from the viewpoint of both the issuer and the organization for which the bonds are issued.
7. Why are municipal bonds attractive to high income individuals as investments?
8. How do Build America Bonds (BAB) differ from traditional general obligation and special obligation revenue bonds? Why might municipalities choose to issue BAB instead of tradition general obligation bonds?
9. Why have municipal bonds been so much safer than corporate bonds?

Recommended Resources

The Bond Buyer, The Daily Newspaper of Public Finance. www.bondbuyer.com. Although a subscription is required to access all of the information provided by the *Bond Buyer*, many articles are available online to the general public.

Cohen, N. R. (1989). Municipal default patterns: An historical study. *Public Budgeting & Finance, 9*(4), 55–65. Recommended for historical information on municipal defaults and comparison of those occurring in the United States.

Gorton, G. (2010). *Slapped By the invisible hand: The panic of 2007.* New York: Oxford University Press. This work is highly recommended for historical context and a broad view of the events and changes over time in the banking system that led to the economic failures of 2007–2009.

Hempel, G. H. (1971). *The postwar quality of state and local debt.* New York: Columbia University Press and the National Bureau of Economic Research. Recommended for information on the type of jurisdictions most likely to default and the nature of the instruments in default.

SIFMA—The Securities Industry and Financial Markets Association. www.sifma.org; www.sifma.net. The interested reader can gain access to numerous publications through this organization's web sites.

References

Ackerman, A. (2007, August 31). The default rate debate. *The Bond Buyer.*

Agriss, T. (2008). *Municipal bond market issues: Recent developments.* New York: Black and Veatch.

American City and County. (2009). A lack of bond insurance is stalling government projects. Published August 1. Retrieved March 4, 2010 , from www.americancityandcounty.com

Austin, J. (2010). Purdue converts debt on bonds to fixed rate for $4.6 million savings. *Lafayette Online.* Retrieved February 18, 2010,from www.lafayette-online.com

BlackRock. (2009). State of the state and local governments. *BlackRock Investments, LLC.* Retrieved May 20, 2010, from www.blackrock.com

Boyd, D. (2010). Recession, recovery, and state-local finances. *The Nelson A. Rockefeller Institute of Government.* Published January. Retrieved April 5, 2010, from www.rockinst.org/government_finance

Bunche, B. S. (1991). The effect of constitutional debt limits on state governments' use of public authorities. *Public Choice, 68*(1/3), 57–69.

Cohen, N. R. (1989). Municipal default patterns: An historical study. *Public Budgeting & Finance, 9*(4), 55–65.

Cooke, J. (2008). Auction rate market shrinks by $21 billion as borrowers escape, Bloomberg, Published March 21. Retrieved February 26, 2010, from Bloomberg.com

Cooke, J. (2009). Moody's assigns negative outlook to U.S. local government sector." Published April 7. Retrieved February 26, 2010, from Bloomberg.com.

Dadayan, L., and Boyd, D. T. (2009, October). State tax revenues show record drop for second consecutive quarter. *The Nelson A. Rockefeller Institute of Government.* Albany, NY.

Dwight Asset Management Company. (2007). *Fixed income primer: Municipal bond market.* Burlington, VT and Portland, OR:. Dwight Asset Management Company.

Ellis, D. (2010). Is there a muni bomb in your portfolio? Published June 16. Retrieved July 28, 2010, from CNNMoney.com

Gorton, G. B. (2009). Slapped in the face by the invisible hand: banking and the panic of 2007. Paper prepared for the Federal Reserve Bank of Atlanta's 2009 Financial Markets Conference: Financial Innovation and Crisis, May 11–13, 2009.

Gorton, G. B. (2010). *Slapped by the invisible hand: The panic of 2007.* New York: Oxford University Press.

Guevara, T., and Claytor, M. (2009). *Where have the municipal bond buyers gone?* Indianapolis: Crowe Horwath International.

Hempel, G. H. (1971). *The postwar quality of state and local debt.* New York: Columbia University Press and the National Bureau of Economic Research.

Hughes, J. R. T. (1977). *The governmental habit: Economic controls from colonial times to the present.* New York: Basic Books.

Lambert, L. (2009). U.S. states, cities insure own bonds in new plan. Published May 18. Retrieved June 8, 2010, from www.reuters.com

Lee, S. (2008). Auction rate securities: Bidder's remorse? NERA Economic Consulting. Published May 6. Retrieved February 26, 2010, from www.nera.com.

Lemov, P. (2010). Whatever happened to bond insurance? *Governing.* January.

McFarland, C. (2010). State of America's cities survey on jobs and the economy. Washington, DC: National League of Cities. Published May. Retrieved June 8, 2010, from www.nlc.org

McNichol, D. (2010). Harrisburg, Pennsylvania, plan is weak, Moody's says. Retrieved April 7, 2010, from *Bloomberg.com.* Published February 11.

McGee, P. (2009). Bond insurance. *The Bond Buyer.* December 31.

Miller, J. (2009). Municipal bond market review and outlook. Nuveen Investments. Retrieved June 11, 2010, from www.nuveen.com

Moody's. (2009). Potential risks of variable rate debt and interest rate swaps for U.S. state and local governments are heightened by economic and financial crisis. Retrieved March 20, 2010., from www.Moody's.com

Moody's Investors Service, Global Credit Research Division. (2007). *The U.S. municipal bond rating scale.* New York: March.

Mysak, J. (2009a). Municipal defaults don't reflect tough times. Retrieved April 25, 2010, from Bloomburg.com. Published May 28.

Mysak, J. (2009b). Florida's bust propels muni default spike. Retrieved April 25, 2010, from Bloomberg.com. Published September 1.

Mysak, J. (2010). Making money in default with munis means only GOs. Retrieved April 25, 2010, from Bloomberg.com. Published January 27.

New Jersey Turnpike Authority (NJTA). (2008). Letter to His Excellency John Corzine, Governor. September 4.

Parkinson, P. (2008). Testimony to subcommittee on capital markets, insurance, and government sponsored enterprises, U.S. House of Representatives, Published February 14. Retrieved March 1, 2010, from www.federalreserve.gov/newsevents/testimony/Parkinson200802140.htm

Pierog, K. (2008). Over $1 billion insured variable rate debt converted–MBIA. Reuters, Published April 8. Retrieved March 20, 2010, from www.uk.Reuters.com

Poterba, J. M. (1995). Balanced budget rules and fiscal policy: Evidence from the states. *National Tax Journal, 48*(3), 329–336.

Poterba, J. M., and Rueben, K. S. (1997, September). State fiscal institutions and the U.S. municipal bond market. San Francisco: Public Policy Institute of California.

Poterba, J. M., and Rueben, K. S. (1999). *Fiscal rules and state borrowing costs: Evidence from California and other states.* San Francisco: Public Policy Institute of California.

Poterba, J. M., and Rueben, K. S. (2001). Fiscal news, state budget rules, and tax-exempt bond yields. *Journal of Urban Economics, 50*, 537–562.

Preston, D. (2010). Municipal regulator seeking expanded floating rate disclosure. *Bloomburg Business Week*, Published March 8. Retrieved April 7, 2010 from www.businessweek.com

Resnick, A. (2009, January 5). Bond buyer recaps "tumultuous year" for municipal bond market. *The Bond Buyer*.

Schrade, B. (2010). Tennessee cities struggle with variable rate debt. *The Tennessean*. Published January 3. Retrieved June 14, 2010, from www.knoxnews.com/new/2010/jan/03

Seymour, D. (2009). Another insurer steps up. *The Bond Buyer*. Published October 26. Retrieved April 30, 2010, from www.bondbuyer.com

Seymour, D. (2010a, May 21). Floating rate debt faces a liquidity issue. *The Bond Buyer*.

Seymour, D. (2010b, September 27). Banks return to munis. *The Bond Buyer*.

SIFMA. (2009a). Municipal report, 2009. New York: Securities Industry and Financial Markets Association.

SIFMA. (2009b). Municipal bond summit. New York: Securities Industry and Financial Markets Association.

SIFMA (2010). Research report. New York: Securities Industry and Financial Markets Association.

Strickland, H. B. (1969). *Inside the Trojan Horse: Understanding the specialized units of local government—municipal authorities*. Clarks Summit, PA Logo Publishing and Research.

Sigo, S. (2009, November 12). Districts in distress: More Florida CDDs may be in default. *The Bond Buyer*.

U.S. Bureau of the Census. Census of Governments, State and Local Government Finances by Level of Government, 1992–2009. Accessed at www.Census.gov/govs/.

U. S. Bureau of the Census. (1990). Historical Statistics of Government Finances and Employment. Compendium of Government Finances (U.S. Department of Commerce, U.S. Government Printing Office.).

U.S. Bureau of the Census. (1997). Summary of State and Local Government Finances, 1972–1992. Compendium of Government Finances (U.S. Department of Commerce, U.S. Government Printing Office).

U.S. Government Accountability Office (GAO). (2010, March). State and local governments' fiscal outlook: March 2010 update. (GAO-10-358). Washington, DC: Government Accountability Office.

U. S. Securities and Exchange Commission. (2010). SEC approves rule changes to enhance municipal securities disclosure. Washington, DC. Published May 26. Retrieved August 30, 2010 from http://www.sec.gov

Appendix: The Municipal Debt Market

The U.S. municipal debt market generally comprises all subnational capital financing. By convention, all state and local debt is referred to as "municipal debt" and is traded in a common market. This encompasses bonds and other marketable debt obligations issued by states and local governments, their various agencies, special districts, school districts, and other quasi-public bodies. The municipal debt market is large; in 2009, total municipal debt outstanding had reached \$2.8 trillion, or 19.6% of gross domestic product.

Munis can be taxable or tax exempt. In practice, most munis are tax exempt. Around 80% of municipal debt is sold through negotiated transactions with underwriters who ultimately sell the debt to investors on a retail basis. The remainder are placed with underwriters through a process of competitive bidding. A very small percentage—less than 1%—is sold via private placements. Municipal bonds are considered second only to U.S. government securities in terms of safety. The data bear this out. A Moody's 10-year study of investment-grade muni defaults found that they were five times less likely to default than AAA-rated corporate bonds and that lower-rated BAA munis have a lower default rate than higher-rated corporate issues (Moody's, 2007).

Index

C

F

J

K

L

Q

R